TRADE PROSPECTS
FOR DEVELOPING COUNTRIES

PUBLICATIONS OF
THE ECONOMIC GROWTH CENTER

LLOYD G. REYNOLDS, *Director*

LAMFALUSSY *The United Kingdom and the Six: An Essay on Economic Growth in Western Europe*

FEI & RANIS *Development of the Labor Surplus Economy: Theory and Policy*

BALASSA *Trade Prospects for Developing Countries*

BAER & KERSTENETZKY *Inflation and Growth in Latin America*

REYNOLDS & GREGORY *Wages, Productivity, and Industrialization in Puerto Rico*

BAER *Industrialization and Economic Development in Brazil*

MAMALAKIS & REYNOLDS *Essays on the Chilean Economy*

MOORSTEEN & POWELL *The Soviet Capital Stock, 1928-1962*

SNODGRASS *Ceylon: An Export Economy in Transition*

HELLEINER *Peasant Agriculture, Government, and Economic Growth in Nigeria*

MEAD *Growth and Structural Change in the Egyptian Economy*

KLEIN & OHKAWA (Eds.) *Economic Growth: The Japanese Experience since the Meiji Era*

TRADE PROSPECTS
FOR
DEVELOPING COUNTRIES

By

BELA BALASSA, J.D., PH.D.

Professor of Political Economy
Johns Hopkins University

A Publication of
The Economic Growth Center
Yale University

RICHARD D. IRWIN, INC.
HOMEWOOD, ILLINOIS
1964

First Printing, May, 1964
Second Printing, May, 1968

382
B18t
67472
September, 1969

Library of Congress Catalog Card No. 64–17248

PRINTED IN THE UNITED STATES OF AMERICA

LENOIR RHYNE COLLEGE

FOREWORD

THIS VOLUME is one in a series of studies supported by the Economic Growth Center, an activity of the Yale Department of Economics since 1961. The Center's Research program is focused on the search for regularities in the process of growth and structural change by means of intercountry and intertemporal analyses. The emphasis is on measurable aspects of economic growth and on the development and testing of hypotheses about the growth process. To provide more reliable statistical tests of theoretical hypotheses, the Center is concerned with improving the techniques of economic measurement and with the refinement of national data systems. The Center provides a home for the International Association for Research in Income and Wealth, which moved its headquarters from Cambridge University, England in 1962. The Center library endeavors to achieve a complete intake of significant economic and statistical publications from about 80 of the larger countries of the world.

Book-length studies supported by the Center are printed and distributed by Richard D. Irwin, Inc. Reprints of journal articles are circulated as Center papers.

> LLOYD G. REYNOLDS, Ph.D., *Director*
> GUSTAV RANIS, Ph.D., *Associate Director*
> HUGH T. PATRICK, Ph.D., *Assistant Director*
> MIRIAM K. CHAMBERLAIN, Ph.D., *Executive Secretary*

IN MEMORY OF
Professor Stephen Varga
TEACHER AND FRIEND

PREFACE

THIS VOLUME presents the results of an inquiry into the trade prospects of the developing countries in the period up to 1975. The projections of the study are conditional forecasts, in the sense that they depend on a set of assumptions. Some of these assumptions relate to economic variables, others to policies followed by developed, and by developing, nations.

Forecasting is a dangerous business. There is no need to refer to the uncertainties associated with the estimation of changes in economic variables, and the relationships between these variables, or, for that matter, the fiasco of a number of forecasts prepared in the past, to indicate the error possibilities attendant upon making projections. At the same time, there is an increasing demand for long-term projections. Information on the trade prospects of the developing countries is needed to provide assistance for preparing long-term development plans and for making recommendations on policies of trade and aid to be followed by the developed countries. More recently, the inauguration of the UN Development Decade and proposals made in connection with the United Nations Conference on Trade and Development focused attention on these issues.

While realizing the error possibilities associated with long-term projections, the present book aims at reducing the area of our ignorance concerning prospective changes in the trade of the less developed countries through a detailed investigation of apparent trends in the production, consumption, and trade of individual commodities and commodity groups. In doing so, it also purports to provide an empirical investigation of the often-voiced thesis on the unfavorable prospects of the developing countries in expanding their exports. This assertion has received much attention in the literature but arguments pro and con have mostly been couched in general terms without much reliance on empirical evidence.

Since the findings of the study depend to a great extent on the underlying assumptions, I have endeavored to specify these—as far as limitations of space permit—so as to enable the reader to consider the implications for the projections of changing some of the assumptions. Assumptions relating to economic policies and prices are of especial importance. The exports of less developed areas are influenced in a considerable degree by production and trade policies followed by the developed nations, while imports into developing countries depend, in part, on their long-term plans.

Further, the experience of the postwar period suggests that fluctuations in supply may cause substantial variations in the prices of primary products. Inadequacies of supply and restrictions on exportable production have led to price increases in recent years, for example, and should shortages arise in the future, the prices of some primary products may exceed the long-term level postulated in the present study. On the other hand, after the stability of recent years, cost-inflationary pressures may again give rise to increases in the prices of manufactured goods, the main import products of the developing countries.

In preparing this volume, I have incurred manifold obligations. I wish first to express my gratitude to several collaborators who have done much of the research on, and have prepared the first draft of, various sections and chapters of the book. Mary Painter of the OECD examined the prospects of trade between developing countries and Soviet-type economies, while others took part in projection work on individual commodities. Leslie E. Grayson, a private consultant to the project, took primary responsibility for projections on fuels, James F. McDivitt and John J. Schanz, Jr. of the Mineral Economics Department, Pennsylvania State University on nonfuel minerals and metals, and David Kendrick of the Massachusetts Institute of Technology on manufactured goods. Leslie Grayson also participated in work on income projections, while DeVerle P. Harris carried out much of the statistical work on nonfuel minerals and metals. Finally, among the numerous research assistants who participated in the project at one time or another, Gerald Skutt should be singled out for his perseverance and inventiveness. John P. Burnham prepared the index.

I am further indebted to the officials of numerous governmental and international organizations as well as business firms who have graciously given their time to enlighten me about matters of their competence. Although I cannot list all who provided help at various stages of research and writing, I cannot forgo mentioning the Commonwealth Economic Committee, the Food and Agriculture Organization of the United Nations, the Organization for Economic Cooperation and Development, and the U.S. Department of Agriculture.

Work on the study was undertaken at the request of the U.S. Department of State, Agency for International Development, that financed much of the research. Further, the Institute of Business and Economic Research at the University of California (Berkeley) provided assistance at the time when delays with financing would have otherwise caused interruption in the project. The final revision of the text was carried out while I was a consultant to the Secretary General of the OECD, while expenses related to the preparation of the manuscript for the printer were borne by the Economic Growth Center of Yale University. To all of these organizations, I am under special obligation.

BELA BALASSA

List of Abbreviations

US	United States
CA	Canada
NA	North America
WE	Western Europe
EEC	European Economic Community
EFTA	European Free Trade Association
UK	United Kingdom
NE	Northern Europe
SE	Southern Europe
JA	Japan
OC	Australia, New Zealand, and South Africa
DC	Developed Countries
LA	Latin America
AF	Africa
ME	Middle East
AS	Asia
LDC	Less Developed Countries
SB	Sino-Soviet Area

For an explanation of the geographical classification used, see p. 11.

TABLE OF CONTENTS

PART I. TRADE PATTERNS IN LESS DEVELOPED AREAS

PART II. PROSPECTS FOR INDIVIDUAL COMMODITIES

PART I

Trade Patterns
in Less Developed Areas

CHAPTER 1

Introduction

1.1 EXPORTS AND ECONOMIC GROWTH IN DEVELOPING COUNTRIES

IN RECENT years, doubts have been expressed concerning the adequacy of the transmission of economic growth from industrial countries to less developed areas. Whereas, in the absence of agricultural protection and adequate domestic supplies of raw materials, Britain's economic growth was transmitted to her suppliers of food and raw materials during the nineteenth century, it is alleged that the transmission mechanism does not operate satisfactorily in our time. Various arguments have been marshaled to establish this proposition: the low elasticity of demand for foodstuffs, agricultural protection in the industrial countries, the increased share of services in the consumer's budget, the shift toward less material-intensive products in manufacturing, the substitution of synthetics for natural materials, and the reduction of input requirements in individual industries.[1]

It has been argued that, as a result of the operation of these factors, the imports of primary products have the tendency to rise at a rate lower than the gross national product of the industrial countries, and the relatively slow expansion of this trade hinders the growth of incomes in nonindustrial areas. In this connection, reference has been made to the dual role of exports in the process of economic growth. On the one hand, exports are related to incomes in a multiplier-type relationship; on the other hand, export earnings serve as a restraint to the expansion of imports. In regard to the latter, it has been suggested that while the income elasticity of demand for imports is less than unity in the industrial countries taken as a group, the rate of increase of imports exceeds the growth of incomes in primary producing areas. Correspondingly, identical growth rates in the two groups of countries would be accompanied by a payment imbalance in favor of the industrial economies and,

---

[1]For a detailed discussion, see the contributions of Ragnar Nurkse, Raul Prebisch, and Dudley Seers [4, 5, 6].

under this assumption that exportable supplies grow at the same rate as GNP, this imbalance would lead to a deterioration in the terms of trade of nonindustrial countries.

In fact, in the years 1928-1955, imports into industrial countries grew at a rate considerably lower than their gross national product. During this period, an 88 per cent increase in the industrial countries' GNP was accompanied by a 38 per cent rise in the volume of imports (Table 1.1.1). But, at the same time, the terms of trade of the primary producing countries improved, inasmuch as their ex-

TABLE 1.1.1

EXPORTS OF PRIMARY-PRODUCING COUNTRIES TO INDUSTRIAL ECONOMIES
(1928 = 100)

	Volume			Unit Value			Value		
	1928	1937-38	1955	1928	1937-38	1955	1928	1937-38	1955
Temperate zone and competing tropical food	100	102	86	100	66	177	100	67	151
Noncompeting tropical foods	100	116	135	100	53	253	100	61	341
Agricultural raw materials	100	116	140	100	64	174	100	74	244
Nonfuel minerals and metals	100	109	144	100	82	223	100	89	320
Exports to industrial countries, excluding fuels	100	108	117	100	66	196	100	72	229
Fuels	100	137	479	100	101	213	100	138	1020
Exports to industrial countries, total[a]	100	109	138	100	69	197	100	75	271
Gross national product in industrial countries[b]	100	113	188	n.a.	n.a.	n.a.	n.a.	n.a.	n.a.

Source: Exports--Trends in International Trade, Report by a Panel of Experts, Geneva, GATT, 1958.

Gross National Product--United States: Economic Report of the President, 1963, p. 174; J. W. Knowles, "The Potential Economic Growth in the United States," Employment, Growth and Price Levels, Study Paper No. 20, Joint Economic Committee, Congress of the United States, 1960, p. 37. Canada: Dominion Bureau of Statistics, Canadian Statistical Review, Historical Survey, 1963 ed., p. 13.

Western Europe: O.E.E.C., Statistics of National Product and Expenditure, 1957, p. 19; I. Svennilson, Growth and Stagnation in the European Economy, United Nations, 1954, pp. 104-5.

Japan: Ginkos Nihon, Historical Statistics of Japanese Economy, 1962, p. 7.

Notes: [a]Includes manufactured goods.
[b]Prior to 1938, GNP in Western Europe estimated on the basis of changes in manufacturing production.

port prices rose, on the average, by 97 per cent, while the increase in the unit value of the industrial countries' exports was 80 per cent [2, p. 20].[2] Correspondingly, the purchasing power of the exports of primary-producing countries increased by 51 per cent.

The observed changes in import volumes and the terms of trade appear to conflict with the theory formulated by Prebisch and

---

[2]The error possibilities associated with the estimation of price changes in international trade should be noted at this point. In the case of manufactured goods, trade statistics often provide unit values rather than prices and, since unit values are calculated by dividing the value of trade by volume, these are affected by changes in quality and commodity composition. On the other hand, the "genuine" price indices will be affected by the choice of weights.

others, according to which a slowing down in the exports of primary-producing countries would be accompanied by a deterioration in their terms-of-trade. The results have also puzzled the authors of *Trends in International Trade* who—although emphasizing the restrictive effects of agricultural protection on the imports of primary products into industrial countries—expressed the opinion that agricultural protectionism cannot bear all the blame for the fall in the food imports of the industrial countries since this would have lead to a deterioration of the terms of trade of primary-producing areas [2, pp. 45, 87].

The apparent contradiction can be resolved, however, if consideration is given to changes in the size and direction of net capital flows and service items as well as to changes in the supply of primary products in nonindustrial countries. For the period under consideration, there had been a shift in the net balance of the capital and service accounts; whereas in 1928 the primary producing countries, taken together, had a deficit of $1.7 billion on capital and service accounts, this deficit gave way to a surplus of $0.3 billion in 1955 [2, p. 28].[3] At the same time, the largest improvement in the terms of trade was experienced in the case of tropical beverages, where supply shortages were prevalent in 1955, while the terms of trade of the exporters of other foodstuffs and agricultural raw materials deteriorated.

As regards the divergent trend of imports and incomes in industrial areas, differences in the experience of the years 1928–1938 and 1938–1955 should be noted. While the rise in the volume of imports into the industrial countries fell only slightly behind the growth of incomes in the first ten years, a 68 per cent increase in GNP was accompanied by a 27 per cent rise in import volumes in the seventeen years following.[4] The question arises, then, what factors contributed to the slowing down in the expansion of imports after 1938.

A review of the experience of individual commodities suggests that policy measures introduced during and after the Second World War had a considerable effect on the pattern of trade. These measures not only created obstacles to imports but also contributed to

---

[3]These developments are largely explained by the decline in service payments to the United Kingdom during this period as well as the receipt of public grants and loans in the amount of $1.6 billion in 1955 [2, p. 30].

[4]On the other hand, prices of primary products fell in the first part of the period and rose afterwards. But prices in 1937–38 were affected to a considerable extent by the recession and it appears more appropriate to consider price changes for the period as a whole.

the development of industries producing import substitutes as well as to import-saving improvements in domestic manufacturing. The production of synthetic rubber and fibers and the reduction of material input requirements in various manufacturing industries are examples.

Whereas synthetic rubber production was nil in 1938, by 1955 the share of natural rubber in rubber consumption fell to 42 per cent in the United States and 85 per cent in Western Europe [3]. In the same period, the share of cotton and wool in the fiber consumption of the two areas declined from about nine-tenths to 72 per cent [1]. And although the combined consumption of tobacco, cotton, wool, oils and fats in Western Europe increased by 12 per cent in this period, net imports into the area remained at 1938 levels. Finally, given the expansion of U.S. exports of cotton and soybeans, the net imports of these commodities into the two areas, taken together, decreased by 11 per cent.

The effects of agricultural protection are also observable in regard to the importation of foodstuffs competing with domestic production (wheat, maize, rice, butter, sugar, meat) in Western Europe. The imports of these foodstuffs into Western Europe fell by 18 per cent between 1938 and 1956, compared to an increase of consumption by 14 per cent. In the same period, the combined net imports of North America and Western Europe declined by one-half [2, p. 88].[5]

Note further that in several European countries and Japan exchange restrictions retarded the growth of the imports of tropical beverages, while subsidies and preferential tax treatment accorded to domestic producers as well as reductions in input requirements limited the increase of import demand for nonfuel minerals and metals. On the other hand, in conjunction with the discovery of oil deposits in developing countries and the shift from coal to oil, fuel imports rose fivefold between 1928 and 1955, accounting for a little over one-half of the total increase in the exports of primary-producing countries during this period.

The substitution of synthetics for natural materials continued

---

[5] While agricultural protectionism appears to be the main factor accounting for increased self-sufficiency in Europe, a system of subsidies as well as the spectacular growth of agricultural productivity contributed to the expansion of U.S. exports. Still, in the absence of subsidies, U.S. exports would have been lower and other exporting countries would have gained through larger exports or higher prices. On the other hand, several developing countries benefited from the surplus disposal program of the United States which got under way in 1954.

after 1955. This explains the relatively slow increase of imports of agricultural raw materials into industrial countries in recent years. (Table 1.1.2).[6] At the same time, the increased protection of the domestic production of sugar, cereals, and meat in Western Europe apears to have been largely responsible for the low rate of growth of the imports of temperate zone and competing tropical food-stuffs.[7]

TABLE 1.1.2

EXPORTS OF DEVELOPING COUNTRIES TO INDUSTRIAL ECONOMIES
(1955 = 100)

	Volume			Unit Value			Value		
	1955	1960	1961	1955	1960	1961	1955	1960	1961
Temperate zone and competing tropical foods	100	114	108	100	104	103	100	119	111
Temperate zone foods	100	122	113	100	107	108	100	131	122
Competing tropical foods	100	107	105	100	101	96	100	109	101
Noncompeting tropical foods	100	125	130	100	69	65	100	86	84
Agricultural raw materials	100	106	115	100	92	83	100	97	95
Nonfuel minerals and metals	100	144	145	100	85	85	100	122	123
Primary products, excluding fuels	100	119	122	100	88	83	100	105	101
Fuels	100	154	170	100	97	95	100	150	161
Primary products, total	100	126	132	100	111	104	100	140	137
Manufactured goods	100	149	149	100	110	111	100	164	166
Exports to industrial countries, total	100	127	132	100	91	88	100	116	116
Gross national product in industrial countries	100	119	124	n.a.	n.a.	n.a.	n.a.	n.a.	n.a.

Sources: Value--U.N., Monthly Bulletin of Statistics and Commodity Trade Statistics, various issues.
Unit value--For primary products, the indices are weighted averages of price indices for 53 commodities when the weights represent the export values of individual products traded between countries and industrial economies in 1953. (The commodity price-indices have been provided by courtesy of the U.N. Statistical Office.) The indices have been adjusted so that 1955 equals 100. For manufactured goods the U.N. price-index weighted by the 1953 value of the exports of manufactured products originating in the largest exporting countries has been used.
Volume--The index of export value divided by the unit value index.
Gross national product--See Tables A2.3.1-2.5.1.

In volume terms, increases have been larger in the imports of noncompeting tropical foods and nonfuel minerals and metals. In the former case, European consumption has risen considerably from the low postwar level and the fall in prices after 1955 has also contributed to higher levels of consumption although it erased the gain made in quantity terms. And while imports of nonfuel minerals and metals have hardly changed in the United States where increased imports for consumption have been counterbalanced by a reduction in the amount added to stockpiles, the limitations of its

[6]In addition to the years 1955 and 1961, data for 1960 have also been included in the estimates in order to ensure comparability with the projections of Table 3.1.3.
[7]For the composition of the various commodity categories, see Table A1.2.1.

natural resources and the high rate of growth of output in material-intensive industries have contributed to a rapid increase of imports into Western Europe.

Finally, with the continuing shift from coal to oil, past rates of growth of fuel imports have been maintained and the rise in the imports of petroleum and petroleum products accounted for over 40 per cent of the total increase of imports from developing countries between 1955 and 1961. Imports of manufactured goods into industrial countries have also increased rapidly, but, in absolute terms, this trade has remained small.

Although the figures of Tables 1.1.1 and 1.1.2 are not strictly comparable,[8] there is little doubt that since 1955 imports into industrial areas in relation to their gross national product have risen faster than in the period spanning the immediate prewar and postwar years. Improvements are shown in all commodity groups and, in the years 1955–1961, the volume of imports from developing areas increased at rates exceeding the growth of incomes in industrial countries. But the terms-of-trade of developing countries deteriorated during this period; while their import prices rose, on the average, by 3 per cent, export prices fell by 12 per cent.[9] Correspondingly, the purchasing power of the exports of developing countries to industrial economies increased by 13 per cent between 1955 and 1961, as compared to a 24 per cent rise in the gross national product of the latter countries.

Should we combine the data for the periods 1928–1955 and 1955–1961, it would appear that a 139 per cent rise in the gross national product of the industrial countries was accompanied by an increase in the volume of imports by a little over four-fifths (the annual rates of growth are 3.3 and 2.3 per cent, respectively). The performance of the developing countries has been somewhat better, however, since data for the years 1928–1955 include imports from Australia and New Zealand, whose exports are concentrated in commodities which have shown an absolute loss or a slight gain.

---

[8]The export data published by GATT refer to all primary producing countries while our figures exclude Australia and New Zealand. (According to the scheme of classification used in the present study, among primary producing countries Australia, New Zealand, and South Africa come in the developed country group; however, for statistical reasons, the exports of South Africa have not been excluded from the figures of Table 1.1.2.) At the same time, in the GATT study, Finland, Spain, and Yugoslavia are listed among primary producing countries while we have included these with industrial Europe.

[9]Changes in average import prices have been calculated by appropriately weighting the UN unit value indices for individual commodity groups with the 1953 extra-area imports of Latin America, Africa, the Middle East, and Asia.

Similarly, although a "splicing" of the unit value indices for the period 1928–1955 and 1955–1961 would indicate a slight deterioration in the terms of trade of the countries exporting to industrial areas, it appears that much of this change can be accounted for by the adverse developments experienced in the export prices of Australia and New Zealand.

We have noted above that, in the period spanning the prewar and the immediate postwar years, the major changes in the imports of industrial countries occurred in the years following the Second World War. It is of interest, therefore, to examine changes in the postwar period taken by itself. To exclude the immediate postwar years, as well as the period of the Korean War, we have chosen to compare data for the years 1953–54 and 1960–61.

As information provided in Table 1.1.3 indicates, the gross national product of the industrial countries rose by 31 per cent between 1953–54 and 1960–61, while the volume of imports originating in developing countries grew by 48 per cent. In the same period, developing countries experienced an 8 per cent fall in their export prices as against a 2 per cent increase in import prices, so that the increase in the purchasing power of their exports was 33 per cent.[10]

The largest increases have again occurred in fuels that accounted for one-half of the total increase in the exports of less developed areas. But part of the rise in the value of fuel exports was returned to the developed countries in the form of oil company profits. In 1960–61 the profits of foreign oil companies operating in developing countries amounted to about 30 per cent of the value of fuel exports and, even if we assumed that this ratio was higher in the mid-fifties, oil profits might have risen by nearly $1.0 billion between 1953–54 and 1960–61.

Should we consider the export earnings of the developing countries *net* of oil profits, a 30 per cent increase is shown. In the same period, the value of exports of primary products excluding fuels increased by only 8 per cent whereas the exports of manufactured goods rose by about one-half. Still, the latter has hardly reached 7 per cent of the total exports of less developed areas.

---

[10]By comparison, a 7 per cent fall in export prices and no change in import prices is shown by the United Nations [7, p. 448]. The UN indices include trade among developing countries, however, and this appears to have imparted an upward bias to the export price index and a downward bias to the import price index.

Among primary products, noncompeting tropical foods showed the best performance in volume terms, but the fall in the prices of coffee and cocoa from the high level experienced in 1954 lead to a decline in the value of exports. At the same time, despite the effects of protectionist policies followed in Western Europe, the exports of temperate zone foods increased in volume as well as in value terms, largely as a result of increasing purchases of meat and fish by the United States. Further, the poor showing of competing tropical foods is explained by the protection of domestic sugar production in the developed countries and the increasing importance of Ameri-

TABLE 1.1.3

EXPORTS OF DEVELOPING COUNTRIES TO INDUSTRIAL ECONOMIES

	VOLUME			UNIT VALUE	VALUE		
	1953-54 $ Million	1955 Prices	1960-61 Index 1953-54 = 100	1960-61 Index 1953-54 = 100	1953-54 $ Million Current Prices	1960-61 Index 1953-54 = 100	
Temperate zone foods	1,541	1,954	126.8	98.0	1,691	2,100	124.3
Competing tropical foods	1,899	2,056	108.3	92.9	2,013	2,026	100.6
Noncompeting tropical foods	2,881	4,044	140.4	59.2	3,258	2,708	83.1
Agricultural raw materials	3,647	3,991	109.4	107.2	2,970	3,485	117.3
Nonfuel minerals and metals	2,076	2,799	134.8	98.3	1,796	2,379	132.5
Primary products, excluding fuels	12,044	14,844	123.2	87.9	11,728	12,698	108.3
Fuels	1,846	5,237	283.7	97.8	1,811	5,025	277.5
Primary products total	13,890	20,081	144.6	90.5	13,539	17,723	130.9
Manufactured goods	447	1,109	248.1	110.7	446	1,225	274.7
Exports to industrial countries, total	14,335	21,189	147.8	91.7	13,985	18,947	135.5
Gross national product in industrial countries, $ billion	700.7	920.5	131	n.a.	n.a.	n.a.	n.a.

Source: See Table 1.1.2.

can soybeans in world markets, while imports of agricultural raw materials were affected by the continuing shift toward synthetic materials. Finally, exports of nonfuel minerals and metals into Western Europe rose at a rapid rate but U.S. imports of these materials have hardly changed.

It appears, then, that—in contrast to the predictions made by various writers—the purchasing power of the exports of developing countries increased approximately in proportion with the gross national product of industrial economies during the fifties, although wide differences are observed among individual commodity groups. The question arises whether we can expect these tendencies to continue or what changes may occur in the future. We address ourselves to this question in the following.

1.2 THE SCOPE AND BASIC ASSUMPTIONS OF THE STUDY

In the present study, we set out to examine prospective trends in the exports and imports of developing countries, as well as future changes in the so-called invisibles (transportation costs, tourism, investment income, etc.), in order to arrive at an estimate of the current account balance of developing areas. Projections refer to the years 1970 and 1975, with 1960 taken as the base year.

For purposes of the investigation, countries have been classified in three groups: developed, less developed, and Soviet-type economies. The first category includes, in addition to the industrial areas—North America, Western Europe, and Japan—three primary-producing countries that are customarily regarded as developed (Australia, New Zealand, and South Africa). Within Western Europe, a further distinction has been made between the countries of the European Economic Community, the United Kingdom, Northern Europe, and Southern Europe. The countries participating in the European Economic Community (Common Market) are Belgium, France, the Federal Republic of Germany, Italy, Luxembourg, and the Netherlands. Northern Europe is defined as comprising Austria, Denmark, Finland, Iceland, Ireland, Norway, Sweden, and Switzerland, whereas Greece, Portugal, Spain, Turkey, and Yugoslavia have been included in the southern group.

According to the system of classification employed in this study, the countries of Latin America, Africa, the Middle East, and Asia are regarded as "developing" or "less developed." Latin America is defined to include all countries of South and Central America as well as Mexico and the West Indies. Africa is understood to refer to the African continent, with the exclusion of South Africa. The countries of the Near East in Asia, most of which derive the bulk of their export earnings from the sale of petroleum, come in the Middle East, while the noncommunist countries of Asia situated to the west of Iran—Japan excluded—and a few small islands in the Pacific are included under Asia.

With regard to the developing countries, the above-mentioned geographical regions have been taken as units in estimating future trade flows, that is, we have considered the external transactions of each region with the exclusion of intraregional trade. Prospective changes in the foreign trade of individual countries have not been dealt with, partly to ease computational work, and partly because the use of a more detailed country breakdown leads to larger forecasting error. Nevertheless, the estimates given for individual commodities can provide assistance in evaluating the trade prospects of particular countries.

In estimating the future export earnings of less developed areas, seven commodity categories have been distinguished. Foodstuffs are grouped according to the degree of competitiveness with the products of developed countries, and according to the climatic conditions under which they are produced in less developed areas (temperate zone, competing tropical, and noncompeting tropical foods). Raw materials are classified according to their origin as agricultural or nonagricultural, when the latter category includes all nonfuel minerals and metals. Finally, fuels and manufactured goods make up the remaining two groups.[11]

Developed countries loom large in the export trade of developing economies. In 1960, the imports of these countries from less developed areas amounted to $19.6 billion, accounting for 87.3 per cent of the total exports of the latter.[12] In the same year, the share of Soviet-type economies was 5.5 per cent ($1.2 billion) while trade among developing regions accounted for the remainder ($1.6 billion). Given the importance of developed countries as export markets for less developed areas, this trade has been estimated on a commodity-by-commodity basis. On the other hand, the limited availability of information and the important role played by noneconomic factors does not permit a detailed estimation of exports to the Sino-Soviet area and interregional trade among less developed regions.

Estimates on the future imports of developed countries from developing economies are given in two variants, reflecting different assumptions made as regards the growth of incomes in the former area. Variant I is based on our estimate of the "most likely" growth rate, while Variant II corresponds to the high income or target estimate. The income projections appear in Chapter 2.

The impact of income changes on imports has been estimated directly—imports expressed as a function of income—or indirectly, by estimating domestic demand and supply, with allowance made for trade among developed countries. Further adjustments have

---

[11]See Table A1.2.1

[12]All trade has been expressed in f.o.b. prices. In the case of Western Europe and Japan where imports are measured in c.i.f. prices, adjustments have been made on the basis of available information on the spread between the c.i.f. and f.o.b. prices of individual commodities (see table A1.2.2).

been made to take account of expected changes in prices, with consideration given to the interaction of demand and supply in the determination of equilibrium prices and quantities. The projections for individual commodities are given in Chapters 6–12. A detailed summary of the results is provided in Chapter 3 while the methodological problems of projections are examined in the Appendix to this chapter.

Chapter 4 contains projections on the future exports of developing countries to the Sino-Soviet area and on interregional trade among less developed regions. In the same chapter, estimates on the import requirements of developing regions have been derived from assumed relationships between incomes and imports. As in the case of developed countries, a "most likely" and a "target" income variant is used. In addition, alternative estimates of import requirements are given for each income variant, depending on the assumed values of the income elasticities of import demand.

The confrontation of export and import projections provides an estimate of the trade balance of the developing regions. In Chapter 5 prospective changes in service items are dealt with and estimates of the current account balance of less developed areas are presented. In the same chapter, a number of policy alternatives are examined which can be used to fill the "current account gap" that is expected to arise after consideration given to prospective changes in trade and nontrade items. These policy measures include accelerated growth in the developed economies, the reduction of trade barriers to the exports of developing countries, increased imports into the Sino-Soviet area, import substitution in the framework of regional integration projects, and capital inflow.

REFERENCES

[1.] FOOD AND AGRICULTURE ORGANIZATION. *Per Capita Fiber Consumption Levels*. Commodity Bulletin Series 31. Rome, 1963.

[2.] GENERAL AGREEMENT ON TARIFFS AND TRADE. *Trends in International Trade*. Report by a group of experts. Geneva, 1958.

[3.] INTERNATIONAL RUBBER STUDY GROUP. *Rubber Statistical Bulletin*.

[4.] NURKSE, RAGNAR. *Patterns of Trade and Development*. The Wicksell Lectures. Stockholm, 1959.

[5.] PREBISCH, RAUL, "Commercial Policy in the Underdeveloped Countries," *American Economic Review, Papers and Proceedings* (March, 1959), pp. 251–77.

[6.] SEERS, DUDLEY, "A Model of Comparative Rates of Growth in the World Economy," *Economic Journal* (March, 1962), pp. 45–78.

[7.] UNITED NATIONS. *Statistical Yearbook*, various issues.

CHAPTER 2

Economic Growth in Developed Countries

2.1. INTRODUCTION

LONG TERM income projections are designed to indicate the growth prospects of a national economy. Following Kuznets, we can distinguish between expectational and intentional projections; in the first instance the observer as "onlooker" considers developments that appear likely under certain assumptions, in the second the observer is also an active agent who formulates objectives and uses various instruments in order to implement these goals [18].

Needless to say, the distinction between the two forms of projections is not, and cannot be, clearcut. Economic plans, if not implemented, assume the character of expectational forecasts, while the "publication effect," i.e., reactions on the part of free economic agents to a published projection, can propel an expectational forecast toward its fulfillment. In fact, governments may use the publication effect as an instrument to induce certain behavioral patterns and thereby to implement a forecast.

The income projections of the present study do not reproduce targets set by governments, such as the Japanese income-doubling plan or the OECD target of a 50 per cent increase in the gross national product of the member countries over the sixties, but give expression to alternatives that are judged probable in the light of available information. To reduce computational work, we have restricted the number of alternatives to two:

(I) an estimate considered "most likely" on the basis of past experience and information on prospective changes during the period of projection;

(II) a high or optimistic estimate which is still within the range of possibilities, provided that appropriate economic policies are followed. This estimate can actually be considered a target since it presupposes the implementation of economic policies aimed at attaining a higher growth rate, although it is not necessarily identical

14

with a target set by a national government—e.g., if the latter is considered unrealistic.

As noted in the appendix on methodology, the GNP projections of the present study have been derived by estimating the growth of employment and productivity in the individual countries. In the case of the large industrial countries, separate estimates have been prepared for the main sectors of the economy in order to utilize information on sectoral productivity trends and to assess the contribution of the intersectoral movement of the labor force to economic growth. For purposes of projecting import demand, estimates on population, per capita GNP, per capita disposable income, and industrial production have also been given. Although the statistical tables include projections under the two income variants, in the textual discussion we concentrate on the most likely income alternative.

In Section 2 of this chapter future trends in population and employment are examined, while the subsequent sections provide estimates on gross national product in the industrial countries. These estimates are summarized in Section 6, which also contains projections on per capita incomes and industrial production. Finally, in Section 7 separate consideration is given to national income in those nonindustrial countries which have been included in the developed country group (Australia, New Zealand, and South Africa).

2.2. POPULATION AND EMPLOYMENT—1950–1975

The estimation of future population requires projecting birth rates, death rates, and migration; among these, uncertainties are associated primarily with the forecast of fertility rates and migration. In regard to the birth rate, it is difficult to foresee the number of children that girls presently of high-school age will have given birth to over the period under consideration, while migration is affected by discretionary measures on the part of governments as well as by changes in social and economic condition. Nevertheless, with some exceptions such as Ireland, Australia, and Canada, errors in the estimation of future migration do not significantly affect the population forecasts since, as a rule, the migrants compose only a small part of the population. At the same time, from the point of view of estimating the labor force, differences in the projected birth rates hardly matter, since members of the 1975 labor force were already born in 1961.

In the present study only one set of population projections has been provided. This solution has been chosen partly because for a large number of countries only a single estimate is available, and partly because the experience of recent years often permits a choice among alternative forecasts prepared a few years back. Estimates on the total population of developed countries for the years 1950–1960 and projections for 1970 and 1975 are given in Tables 2.2.1 and A2.2.1. Considering that some commodities are consumed exclusively or chiefly by persons over 15 years of age, estimates have been provided for this age group, too (Table A2.2.2).

While differences in the projected birth rates do not affect the labor force forecasts, the same cannot be said about migration. From the point of view of estimating the rate of growth of GNP, not the proportion of migrants in the total labor force, but rather its ratio

TABLE 2.2.1

TOTAL POPULATION OF DEVELOPED COUNTRIES ACCORDING TO
GEOGRAPHICAL GROUPINGS, 1950-1975

(Thousands)

	1950	1955	1960	1970	1975
United States	151,683	165,270	180,670	214,220	235,600
Canada	13,712	15,698	17,814	21,480	23,500
Western Europe	322,227	336,618	353,489	385,463	402,121
Common Market	155,236	161,442	169,128	182,055	187,925
West Berlin.............................	2,139	2,195	2,200	2,200	2,200
United Kingdom	50,363	51,221	52,539	55,930	57,480
Northern Europe.......................	33,321	34,402	35,558	37,277	38,261
Southern Europe.......................	81,168	87,358	94,064	108,001	116,255
Japan	82,900	89,000	93,419	101,937	106,200
Oceania and South Africa	24,195	27,114	30,372	37,987	42,721
Developed Countries, Total..............	594,717	633,700	675,764	761,087	810,142

Source: Table A2.1.1.

to the yearly increment of labor force is relevant, and this ratio has been high in some countries—especially in those with a low natural increase of the working population (e.g., Germany). Further uncertainties attach to changes in school attendance, female labor force participation rates, and the age of retirement.

The error possibilities related to the above factors explain the frequent revisions of labor force forecasts. Still, for reasons of statistical convenience, a single estimate of the labor force has been provided in the present study, with reliance placed on the most recent available national projections. Employment forecasts have been arrived at by deducting the estimated number of military and unemployed from the projected labor force. Data on employment for the years 1950, 1955, and 1960, and projections for 1970 and 1975 are given in the country tables of the following sections.

North America

In 1958, the U.S. Bureau of Census published four series of population projections for the United States, corresponding to alternative assumptions as to future fertility rates [*31*]. After the results of the 1960 Census became available, a revised series of projections was prepared, this time including the two new states, Alaska and Hawaii [*32*]. Under the assumption that current fertility rates will be maintained in the future, the U.S. population would reach 214 million in 1970 and exceed 235 million in 1975, corresponding to a 30 per cent increase over the entire period. A slightly lower rise is expected in population above the age of 15, with a total gain of 28 per cent.

On the basis of the 1958 Census forecast, the Bureau of Labor Statistics prepared labor force estimates up to 1975 [*33*]. These estimates were subsequently revised to take account of the new population forecasts and the observed lowering of labor force participation rates [*34*]. The revised projections of the Bureau of Labor Statistics are 85.7 million for 1970 and 93.0 million for 1975. Our estimates, prepared independently from the BLS, give identical figures for 1970 and show a labor force slightly larger for 1975.

In order to arrive at an estimate of the employed population, allowance need also be made for military service and unemployment. We have assumed that 3 per cent of the total labor force would belong to the armed forces in the period under consideration (as against 3.5 per cent in the late fifties) and have calculated with an unemployment rate of 4 per cent.

A number of population forecasts are available for Canada. In 1957, the Royal Commission on Canada's Economic Prospects prepared four series of estimates up to 1980 using alternative assumptions as to the rate of immigration [*12*, chap. 4], and, subsequently, R. E. Caves and R. H. Holton presented estimates for 1965 and 1970 [*3*, chap. 8]. In making projections, we have relied on the estimates of the Royal Commission while allowing for actual immigration in the years 1955–1960 and assuming a steady decline of immigration in the future. Although the resulting estimates are lower than the forecasts of the Royal Commission, they still exceed somewhat those of Caves and Holton. The projected increase for the total population is 32 per cent, and that of the over-15 age group, 31 per cent.

Accordingly, we have revised the Royal Commission's estimate for labor force and employment, with a further adjustment made by assuming a 4 per cent rather than a 3 per cent rate of unemployment for 1970 and 1975. Judging from the experience of the fifties, the latter does not appear to be a plausible figure.

Western Europe

For most Western European countries, the OEEC published population projections based on replies to a questionnaire by the individual member countries [20]. These forecasts assume unchanged, or moderately declining, fertility levels and small decreases in mortality rates. With the exception of Switzerland and Turkey, estimates on migration are given also.

In the present study, the OEEC forecasts have been accepted for the smaller countries of Western Europe[1] but these have been revised in the case of the Common Market countries and the United Kingdom. The revisions incorporate the results of more recent population censuses as well as new estimates on migration. In regard to Germany, actual figures have been substituted for the migration forecasts up to 1961 while an immigration of 100,000 persons per year has been assumed for later years. We have further assumed a yearly emigration of 150,000 persons for Italy, 15,000 for the Netherlands, and an immigration of 15,000 per year for Belgium, 120,000 for France, and 70,000 for the United Kingdom. In the case of France, an immigration of about 800 thousand people from Algeria has also been taken into account.

National sources and UN population projections have been consulted in regard to countries for which no information is given in the OEEC study. A Finnish source provides forecasts up to 1975 [11], while in the case of Yugoslavia national estimates are available for 1970 [2]. In the later instance, we have utilized the projections prepared by the UN in arriving at an estimate for 1975 [29]. The projections given in the same source have been accepted for Greece, Iceland, and Luxembourg. Finally, West Berlin's population has been assumed to remain unchanged.

The results indicate a rise in population during the period 1960–1975 in all countries of Western Europe, ranging from 0.5 per cent in Ireland to 45 per cent in Turkey. Larger than average increases are anticipated also in Yugoslavia (18 per cent), the Netherlands (17 per cent), Greece (16 per cent), and Finland (15 per cent), while in most other countries increases fall in the 5 to 10 per cent

---

[1]Adjustments have been made in the case of Ireland to allow for actual emigration up to 1961.

range. In Western Europe as a whole, population is expected to rise from 353 million to 402 million.

In most countries under consideration, expected changes in population over 15 differ little from changes in total population. Low birth rates during the Second World War will cause a relative decline of the over-15 age group in Austria and Germany, however, while a change in the opposite direction is expected to occur in the Netherlands, Portugal, and Yugoslavia.

The OEEC publication also contains labor force projections. These have been arrived at under the assumption of constant activity rates by age group and sex, with adjustments made for changes in school attendance, the age of retirement, migration, female employment, and other factors. In the case of the Common Market countries, we have corrected these estimates on the basis of more recent official projections [4], while for the United Kingdom female labor force participation rates have been revised upward. Finally, in regard to countries for which OEEC forecasts are not available, we have assumed activity rates to continue at levels experienced in the second half of the fifties.

In order to arrive at employment forecasts, allowance has also been made for military service and unemployment. We have surmised that countries participating in the North Atlantic Treaty Organization (with the exception of Turkey) would have 2 per cent of their active population in the armed forces. This proportion is lower than the 1960 ratio for countries that have had overseas obligations (Belgium, France, the Netherlands, and the United Kingdom), but it is somewhat higher for Western Germany, representing a more equitable distribution of the burden of defense. A 3 per cent ratio has been postulated for Turkey, while the armed forces are assumed to require about 1 per cent of the labor force in the neutral countries (Austria, Finland, Ireland, Sweden, and Switzerland).

Unemployment rates have been projected on the basis of past experience, and expected changes in the demand for and the supply of labor. A 1 per cent unemployment rate has been assumed for France, Germany, the Netherlands, the United Kingdom, the countries of Northern Europe (except for Ireland), and Yugoslavia, and a 2 per cent rate for Belgium, Ireland, and Italy. We have also surmised that in Greece, Portugal, Spain, and Turkey unemployment rates would fall to 5 per cent by 1970, and to 4 per cent by 1975.

Japan

The new *Ten-Year Plan* of Japan provides population projections for 1970 [14]. Estimates for 1975 have been derived from an earlier Japanese projection [15], with appropriate corrections made on the basis of the Plan's forecast for 1970. Japan's population is expected to reach 106 million by 1975, a 14 per cent increase over 1960. By reason of the projected fall in the birth rate, the anticipated increase in population over 15 is considerably larger (26 per cent).

The Japanese plan also contains estimates for labor force and employment up to 1970. Employment for 1975 has been forecast by assuming unchanged activity rates after 1970.

Oceania and South Africa

In the case of Australia, we have utilized the population projections prepared by Borrie and Rodgers [1] and assumed net immigration to fall from 90,000 in 1960 to 50,000 by 1965 and to remain at this level afterward. The estimates of the New Zealand Department of Statistics, corrected for net immigration of 7,500 a year, have been used in regard to New Zealand [19], while population projections prepared by the United Nations have been accepted in the case of South Africa [29]. Finally, with the exception of Australia where Borrie and Rodgers' projections have been used, we have estimated the future labor force by assuming labor force participation rates to remain approximately at levels experienced in the second half of the fifties.

2.3 INCOME PROJECTIONS FOR NORTH AMERICA

Over the period 1947–1960, the gross national product of the United States rose at an annual rate of 3.5 per cent. Higher growth rates were experienced in the first half of the period (3.8 per cent), and lower rates in the second half (3.2 per cent). But since *actual* rates of growth were greatly affected by the recession in 1960, it has been suggested that estimates should be prepared on the growth of *potential* output, corresponding to a level of reasonably full employment. Most observers agree that such a level is reached when the number of unemployed does not exceed 4 per cent of the labor force. Normal business conditions also mean a larger labor force in response to the greater availability of job opportunities, and a higher average number of working hours for those employed. In the 1947–1960 period, these factors, taken together, would have led to a yearly increase of man-hours approximately 0.2 per cent higher than the increase actually experienced, with a corresponding rise in the rate of growth of GNP.

It has also been suggested that recessions produce on-the-job unemployment and a higher ratio of nonproductive (clerical, sales personnel, etc.) to productive employment so that a fall in unemployment would further raise labor productivity. According to the Council of Economic Advisers, the productivity gain at higher employment levels would have raised the growth rate by 0.2 per cent over the 1947–1960 period [8, p. 113]. On the other hand, potential output, as estimated by Denison, corresponds to a 0.1 per cent gain in productivity [6, p. 258].

The discrepancy between the two estimates is due, in part, to the different reference years used. Whereas the CEA regards 1955 as a high-employment year and estimates potential output accordingly, Denison has assumed that actual GNP was equal to potential GNP in 1957. But beyond the choice of a reference year we face the problem as to what extent lower unemployment would have led to higher productivity levels in the year 1960.

To the extent that unemployment is caused by a decline in economic activity, there is a positive correlation between employment and productivity over the business cycle. Such a relationship does not hold in a situation where technological unemployment exists, however. In the opinion of the present writer the low level of employment in 1960 was not a purely cyclical phenomenon but was caused, in part, by the introduction of labor-saving devices. This would explain that while in the period 1954–1960 the annual rate of increase of productivity per man-hour in the economy as a whole was lower than in 1947–1954, in the same period manufacturing productivity grew considerably faster than in earlier years (3.3 per cent and 2.6 per cent, respectively). It is questionable whether productivity could have increased at a much higher rate if unemployment were at lower levels, although under full employment manufacturing employments would have gained at the expense of agricultural and, possibly, tertiary occupations.

These considerations indicate the need for separately estimating employment and productivity in the main sectors of the economy. Given the available breakdown of hours worked, we have prepared estimates for the following sectors: agriculture, manufacturing, and nonmanufacturing industries. In making projections, we have calculated with a slight slowing down in the movement of the labor force from agriculture to nonagricultural employments and have assumed that the tertiary sector would make further gains within the latter. Further, a slowing down in the growth of agricultural productivity has been assumed, with recent rates of productivity growth roughly maintained in the other two sectors (Table A2.3.1).

Our results indicate an average annual 2.6 per cent rise in private output per man-hour for the period 1960–1970 and 2.5 per cent in 1970-1975, as compared to 3.1 per cent in 1947–1960. This decline is explained by the assumed slower rate of productivity growth in agriculture, the decreasing rate of movement from agriculture to industrial employments and the relative increase of employment in the tertiary sector.

Correspondingly, GNP per man-hour would rise at a rate of 2.5 per cent a year in 1960–1970 and 2.4 per cent in 1970–1975, while employment is expected to increase at an annual rate of 1.8 per cent and 1.7 per cent in the two periods, respectively. Average annual man-hours per worker have been estimated by assuming that the yearly average 0.5 per cent decline in potential hours would continue. Thus, actual hours per worker would fall at an annual rate of 0.4 per cent between 1960 and 1970 and 0.5 per cent between 1970 and 1975 (Table A2.3.2).

Our projection indicates a growth rate higher than that experienced in the period 1947 to 1960, since the expected decline in the rate of increase of productivity would be more than offset by the faster rise in labor input. At the same time, the anticipated increase in GNP per worker is one-half larger than the approximately 1.5 per cent annual increase of productivity in the 1909–1957 period, and the projected growth rate of GNP would exceed the long term rate of increase of the gross national product by about one-fourth [*16, 6*].

A number of recent projections of the U.S. gross national product are given in Table 2.3.1. For purposes of comparison, we have also included the forecast prepared by the Paley Commission in 1952. The latter has apparently greatly underrated the growth potentialities of the United States economy; projected employment in 1975 was given at a level 12 per cent (i.e., by over 10 million) lower than in recent forecasts and the growth of productivity over the period 1950–1960 was also underestimated.

Substantial differences are found in more recent projections, too. For the period 1960–1970, estimates range from the Council of Economic Advisers' 4.9 per cent target rate to Denison's forecast of 3.7 per cent, corresponding to a gross national product of $814 and

TABLE 2.3.1

ALTERNATIVE PROJECTIONS OF UNITED STATES GROSS NATIONAL PRODUCT, 1960-1975 (1960 PRICES)

	(1) Civilian Employment	(2) Average Weekly Hours	(3) Total Working Hours	(4) Productivity (GNP per Man-Hour)	(5) Gross National Product	(6) Gross National Product	(7) Civilian Employment	(8) Average Weekly Hours	(9) Total Working Hours	(10) Productivity (GNP per Man-Hour)	(11) Gross National Product	(12) Gross National Product
	Percentage Change per Year 1 9 6 0 - 1 9 7 0				Billions of Dollars 1960 Prices 1970	1970	Percentage Change per Year 1 9 7 0 - 1 9 7 5				Billions of Dollars 1960 Prices	1975
1 Paley	0.9	-0.6	0.3	2.5	2.8	631	0.9	-0.6	0.3	2.5	2.8	725
2 CEA	1.9	-8.4	1.5	3.4	4.9	814	-	-	-	-	-	-
3 Knowles	1.8	-0.4	1.4	3.2	4.6	803	1.7	-0.5	1.2	2.8	4.0	977
4 NPA	1.9	-0.6	1.3	3.2	4.5	788	-	-	-	-	-	-
5 OECD	1.7	n.a.	n.a.	2.7	4.4	778	-	-	-	-	-	-
6 RFF	1.8	-0.3	1.5	2.5	4.0	746	1.7	-0.3	1.4	2.3	3.7	896
7 Denison	1.8	-0.4	1.4	2.3	3.7	718	1.7	-0.5	1.2	2.2	3.4	849
8 Our estimate	1.8	-0.4	1.4	2.5	3.9	740	1.7	-0.5	1.2	2.4	3.6	883

Sources: 1. The President's Materials Policy Commission, Resources for Freedom, Report, Vol. 2, Washington, 1952, pp. 111-12. Estimates refer to the period 1950-1957.
2. Council of Economic Advisers, Annual Report, Economic Report of the President, Washington, 1962, p. 115.
3. Knowles, J. W., "The Potential Economic Growth in the United States," Employment, Growth, and Price Levels, Study Paper No. 20, Joint Economic Committee, Congress of the United States, Washington, 1960, p. 40.
4. National Planning Association, The Economy of the American People, Washington, 1961, p. 196.
5. Organization for Economic Co-operation and Development, Policies for Economic Growth, Paris, 1962, p. 28.
6. Resources for the Future, Inc., Resources in America's Future, The Johns Hopkins Press, 1963, pp. 539-42, Medium Estimate.
7. Denison, E. F., The Sources of Economic Growth in the United States and the Alternatives Before Us, Washington, Committee for Economic Growth, 1962, p. 45, 259.
8. Table A2.3.1. Most likely estimate.

$718 billion in 1960 prices, respectively. On the other hand, projections for the period 1970–1975 show smaller discrepancies.

It appears that in the higher projections adequate consideration has not been given to sectoral changes in employment and productivity. However, the extrapolation of past productivity trends for the economy as a whole is of limited validity, since past over-all growth rates have been determined by sectoral productivity trends and by the intersectoral movement of the labor force.

If separate estimates are prepared for the major sectors, a rate of increase of GNP slightly below 4 per cent appears plausible, although under optimistic expectations as regards the results of an effective growth policy, the rate of growth could exceed 4 per cent. The attainment of a higher growth rate would require a more rapid movement of the labor force from agriculture to manufacturing, a slowing down of the movement to the tertiary occupations, and higher rates of productivity growth in the individual sectors.

Canada

The 3.8 per cent average annual rate of increase in the gross national product of Canada during the period 1947–1960 conceals different trends in employment and productivity. As shown in Table A2.3.3, during the second part of the period employment grew faster than beforehand, while there was a decline in the rate of growth of productivity.

For recent years, data on the net output of major sectors are available in current prices only and, in the absence of sectoral deflators, reliable estimates on productivity trends in the individual sectors could not be obtained. If the agricultural wholesale price index is used to deflate value added in agriculture, productivity in this sector appears to have grown at a rate of over 3 per cent a year during the base period, exceeding the long term rate of 1.5 per cent. We have calculated with a 2.0 per cent increase in our projections. This forecast is higher than the medium estimate given by Caves and Holton (1.5 per cent) [3, p. 296] and the 1.2 per cent assumed by the Royal Commission [12, p. 215].

During the period 1947–1960, labor productivity rose at an annual rate of about 2.5 per cent in industry and construction and 1.5 per cent in the tertiary sector. We have assumed that these rates will be maintained over the next 15 years. By comparison, according to Caves and Holton's medium estimate, GNP per worker in the nonagricultural sector would rise at a rate of 2 per cent a year between 1955 and 1970 [3, p. 298], while the low and the high estimates of the Royal Commission for the business sector are 1.7 per cent and 2.4 per cent, respectively [*12*, p. 218].

We have further assumed that past employment trends will continue in agriculture, while the rise in nonagricultural employment will be increasingly taken up by the tertiary sector. And since the tertiary sector exhibits a lower than average growth of productivity, its increased relative importance is expected to lead to a slight slowing down in the advance of productivity on the national economy level. Still, high rates of increase of employment may contribute to a 4.5 per cent rate of growth of GNP between 1960 and 1970, with a 4 per cent growth rate projected for 1970–1975.

The growth rate of the 1960–1975 period will be greatly affected by the anticipated absorption of unemployment existing in 1960. If comparison is made with 1955, a 4.1 per cent growth rate is obtained. For the same period, the Royal Commission estimated Canadian GNP to grow at an annual rate of 4.0 per cent or 4.6 per cent, depending on whether the lower or the higher alternative is chosen [*12*, p. 226], while the medium estimate given by Caves and Holton shows a growth rate of 4.0 per cent for 1955–1970 [*3*, p. 298]. Thus, our "most likely" estimate differs little from these projections, while our high alternative (4.4 per cent)—which assumes not only larger productivity gains in the individual sectors but also a faster pace of industrialization—approaches the higher variant of the Royal Commission's forecast.

2.4. INCOME PROJECTIONS FOR WESTERN EUROPE
European Economic Community

The gross national product of the European Common Market countries was increasing at a fast pace throughout the fifties. Increases were especially large in the period 1950–1955 when the postwar reconstruction and rehabilitation of these economies boosted the growth rate. And although the rate of expansion slackened somewhat in the second half of the decade, it still exceeded all forecasts.

The reduction of internal trade barriers, the high rate of investment, rapid technological change, and the availability of labor reserves in several of these countries have all contributed to economic growth in recent years. But rapid growth in these countries is not an unprecedented phenomenon. In the twenties, for example, comparable rates of productivity growth were experienced in Germany and in France [*24*]. In the past, however, a period of rapid expansion was soon followed by one of absolute or relative decline. In attempting to forecast future developments, the question needs to be answered as to whether the rate of expansion of recent years can be maintained.

Inasmuch as developments in the first half of the fifties were greatly influenced by nonrecurring factors, we have used—for the Common Market as well as for other countries of Western Europe —1955–1960 as the base period. It is suggested here that many of the underlying factors that determined the growth of productivity in this period will continue to act during the period of projection. The high ratio of productive investments to GNP is likely to be maintained, and the process of technological improvements is expected to continue. Also, the impact of the Common Market's establishment will be increasingly felt so as to make up for the expected slowing down in the expansion of exports to nonparticipating countries. Yet, given the anticipated reduction in working hours, the continuation of past trends in output per man-hour is not incompatible with a decline in the rate of growth of output per man. Finally, productivity trends on the national economy level will also be influenced by intersectoral shifts in employment.

The rural-urban movement of the labor force will continue in all countries under consideration. The decline of employment in agriculture is likely to be most pronounced in Germany and in Belgium, where agricultural production is expected to expand at a rate lower than the EEC average. On the other hand, in view of Common Market agricultural policy, a rapid expansion in farm output is anticipated in the other countries of the Common Market, especially in France and Italy, accompanied by a slower rate of contraction in agricultural employments (Table A2.4.1).

Hand-in-hand with the decline in agricultural employment, continuing increases in agricultural productivity are expected in the countries of the EEC. The expansion of large-scale farming at the expense of the peasant farming of marginal plots will raise productivity, particularly in France and Germany, and the future rate of increase of productivity is assumed to be only slightly lower in Belgium, Italy, and the Netherlands.

The decrease of employment in agriculture, as well as the absolute rise in total employment, will be taken up by industry and the tertiary sector. But given the rapid expansion of demand for services at higher income levels, the share of industry in the increment of the nonagricultural labor force is expected to decline—though in varying degrees—in all member countries.

We have noted above that, in projecting future levels of output per worker, prospective changes in hours worked should be taken into account. Past trends in productivity, too, have been affected by changes in working hours. In industry, the only sector where reasonably accurate information is available, we find that French data on value added per man-year overstate the increase of productivity per man-hour given that the length of the workweek (including overtime) increased during the fifties. On the other hand, hours worked have been falling in Germany, and some declines have taken place in other EEC countries, too [13].

The described changes have reduced intercountry differences in working hours so that the average workweek is now about 45 hours in all countries. It is assumed here that weekly hours will fall over the next 15 years as some of the increase in incomes will be taken out in the form of leisure. However, this decline will be restrained by the tightness of the labor market so that it may not exceed 0.4–0.5 per cent a year.

It should be added that the reduction of the workweek does not necessarily lead to a proportional decline of output per man. Rather, American experience indicates that the shortening of hours can be offset, wholly or in part, by increasing labor efficiency. Denison argues, for example, that in the United States a slight reduction in hours from a level of 49 hours a week was fully offset by an opposite change in output per man-hour, while at 40 hours a week a 1 per cent decrease in hours reduced output per man by only 0.6 per cent [6, p. 40]. We have assumed here that about one-half of the reduction in working hours in the Common Market—as well as in other European countries—would be compensated by increasing labor efficiency due to shorter working hours.

Taking into account the impact of the reduction of hours on productivity, as well as the possible effects of economic integration and other factors, we may expect some decline in the rate of growth of productivity in Common Market industries. The slowing down of productivity growth is likely to be more pronounced in Germany where the most rapid increases took place during the fifties, whereas a reduction of Italy's technological lag can accelerate the growth of productivity in her industry.

With some modifications, we have relied on past experience in projecting future increases of productivity in services. Here again an improvement in the Italian performance is expected while, despite a projected slowing down in her productivity growth, Germany would still show the highest rate of increase.

The resulting rates of growth of productivity on the national economy level are generally somewhat lower than the rates experienced in the years 1955–1960 (Table A2.4.1). This reduction follows chiefly from the relative increase of employment in the tertiary sector which generally exhibits lower productivity, and from the anticipated reduction in working hours. Still, output per man would rise at a rate of 3.3 per cent a year in the Common Market taken as a whole, exceeding the rate of increase experienced in the interwar period by a comfortable margin in all countries [24, p. 32].

Among the member countries of the Common Market, the projected increase in GNP per man is the largest in Italy, with France, Germany, Luxembourg, the Netherlands, and Belgium following. At the same time, in 1960–1970, employment is expected to grow at an annual rate of 1.4 per cent in the Netherlands, 0.8 per cent in France and Luxembourg, 0.7 per cent in Italy, 0.3 per cent in Belgium, and 0.1 per cent in Germany, while smaller differences are anticipated in the five years following. For the period 1960–1975, gross national product is estimated to rise at an annual rate of 4.1 per cent in the Common Market as a whole, with larger than average increases projected for France and Italy (Tables 2.6.1 and A2.4.2). The projected rates of growth would be 0.5 per cent higher under the high income alternative, however.

Table 2.4.1 compares some recent projections on economic growth in the Common Market countries for the period 1960–1970. With the exception of Italy, small differences are observed in the employment forecasts, while larger discrepancies are found with respect to the projection of productivity growth. But any of these estimates is higher than earlier forecasts. For the 1955–1975 period, the medium projection of GATT [10, p. 27] and that of Ingvar Svennilson [27] indicated a rate of growth of 3.3 and 2.6 per cent, respectively, while Dewhurst [7, p. 120] predicted Common Market GNP to grow at a rate of 3.2 per cent between 1955 and 1970. In these projections, a slower increase of employment *and* productivity was assumed as compared to later forecasts.

We have separately estimated the gross national product of West Berlin, assuming productivity to rise at the same rate as in the industrial sectors of Germany, with employment remaining constant. Accordingly, GNP expressed in 1960 prices would rise from 12,000 million marks in 1960 to 20,880 million marks in 1975.

United Kingdom

The United Kingdom did not present a distinguished economic record for the fifties. As industrial productivity was increasing at a

TABLE 2.4.1

ALTERNATIVE PROJECTIONS FOR THE GROSS NATIONAL PRODUCT OF THE EUROPEAN ECONOMIC COMMUNITY, 1960-1970

	Employment					Productivity							Gross National Product							
	(1)	(2)	(3)	(4)	(5)	(1A)	(1B)	(2)	(3)	(4)	(5A)	(5B)	(1A)	(1B)	(2)	(3A)	(3B)	(4)	(5A)	(5b)
Belgium	0.5	0.3	n.a.	n.a.	0.5	2.95	3.35	3.15	n.a.	n.a.	2.7	3.2	3.45	3.85	3.45	2.6	3.6	n.a.	3.2	3.7
France	0.7	0.6	n.a.	0.8	0.8	3.7	4.15	4.4	n.a.	4.1	3.6	4.1	4.5	4.95	5.0	4.4	5.2	5.0	4.5	5.0
Germany	0.35	n.a.	n.a.	0.3	0.3	3.5	3.9	n.a.	n.a.	3.7	3.5	4.0	3.9	4.2	(5.6)	4.9	5.7	4.1	3.8	4.3
Italy	0.9	1.1	n.a.	0.9	0.7	4.3	4.9	3.3	n.a.	4.1	3.7	5.2	5.25	5.85	4.4	5.0	5.9	5.0	4.4	4.9
Netherlands	1.35	1.5	n.a.	n.a.	1.4	2.8	3.35	3.3	n.a.	n.a.	2.8	3.3	4.15	4.6	4.8 (5.0-)	5.1	5.9	n.a.	4.2	4.7
Common Market	0.7	n.a.	n.a.	n.a.	0.8	3.6	4.05	n.a.	n.a.	n.a.	3.3	3.8	4.3	4.8	4.8 (5.3)	4.7	5.5	n.a.	4.1	4.6

Sources: (1) Communauté Économique Européenne, Rapport sur les perspectives de développement économique dans la C.E.E. de 1960 à 1970, Bruxelles, 1962. Variants A and B.

(2) Association Scientifique Européene pour la Prévision Economique à Moyen et à Long Terme, Europe's Future in Figures, ed. R. C. Geary, Amsterdam: North Holland Publishing Co., 1962.

(3) Food and Agriculture Organization, Agricultural Commodities--Projections for 1970, Rome, 1962, A: low estimate, B: high estimate.

(4) Organization for Economic Cooperation and Development, Policies for Economic Growth, Paris, 1962. This projection is conceptually comparable with our high (target) estimate.

(5) Our estimates, A: most likely, B: high estimate.

slow rate and no gains were forthcoming through the reallocation of the labor force from agriculture to industry, the growth of GNP did not exceed 2.5 per cent a year. We have projected an acceleration in the rate of growth of productivity in industry and in services, with some slowing down in the rise of productivity in agriculture (Table A2.4.3). Even considering reductions in working hours, GNP per man would thus rise faster than in the preceding period, chiefly as a result of increasing capital-labor ratios and anticipated improvements in technological methods.

With employment rising at approximately past rates, gross national product would increase at an annual rate of 2.9 per cent between 1960–1970 (Table 2.6.1). This estimate exceeds all earlier projections, which range between 2.05 and 2.75 per cent,[2] although it falls short of the 4 per cent official British target for 1961–1966 [28] and the 3.3 per cent growth rate proposed for the period 1960–1970 in the OECD report [21, p. 28]. The latter figure compares with our high estimate of 3.4 per cent.

Northern Europe

Among the countries of Northern Europe, economic growth during the fifties was especially rapid in Austria, Iceland, and Switzerland. Lower rates were experienced in the Scandinavian countries, while Ireland showed the smallest increase in the group. Information on the sectoral breakdown of employment and GNP is not available for most of these countries, hence only aggregate projections have been prepared, although we have attempted to take account of available information on sectoral trends. It has further been assumed that existing intercountry differences in hours worked will be reduced.

It is expected that improvements in low-productivity agriculture, the movement of labor force into industry, and increasing capital-labor ratios will continue to give Austria the highest rate of increase of productivity within the group. Still, given the assumed constancy of employment, Austria would experience a rise in GNP smaller than most other countries.

Some differences are foreseen in regard to the other countries of the group, too. We have assumed that, in the period 1960–1970, GNP per man-year would rise by 2.8 per cent a year in Denmark, Norway, and Switzerland, 2.6 per cent in Finland and Iceland, 2.4

---

[2]Deakin, 2.05–2.4 per cent [5, p. 211]; Dewhurst, 2.1 per cent [7, p. 120]; FAO, 2.4 per cent [9]; Saunders, 2.75 per cent [25, p. 216]; and Svennilson, 2.3 per cent [27].

per cent in Sweden, and 2.2 per cent in Ireland. Slightly lower increases have been assumed for 1970–1975, taking into account expected reductions in hours worked and the continuing movement of the labor force into the tertiary industries (Table A2.4.3).

For Northern Europe as a whole, a 3.2 per cent annual increase of the gross national product has been projected for the 1960–1970 period, and a 2.8 growth rate for 1970–1975. By comparison, Dewhurst calculated with a 3.0 per cent growth rate for 1955–1970 [7, p. 120] while Svennilson estimated the gross national product of the Scandinavian countries to grow at a rate of 2.9 per cent a year between 1955 and 1975 [27]. But even our high estimate, 3.7 per cent for the sixties, falls short of the 4.1 per cent target rate of the OECD.

Southern Europe

Compared to other Western European countries, the projection of GNP is considerably more difficult for the southern group, considering that here the success or failure of development policy has a decisive influence on economic growth. Correspondingly, in the case of these countries, the difference between our most likely and high estimates is greater than in the previous instances.

Among the countries of Southern Europe, the highest rate of productivity growth has been projected for Yugoslavia, although our estimate is still considerably lower than that given in the since discarded official plan which expected GNP to rise at a rate of 11.4 per cent a year between 1960 and 1965 [26, p. 58]. Our most likely estimate of the rate of growth of GNP in Yugoslavia is 5.4 per cent for the years 1960–1970, corresponding to a 4.0 per cent yearly increase in output per man. In the same period, productivity has been projected to rise at a rate of 3.5 per cent in Greece and Spain and 3.0 per cent in Portugal and Turkey (Table A2.4.4). These rates are slightly lower than those experienced in 1955–1960, but higher than the estimates given by Dewhurst [7, p. 120].

The projected rate of growth of GNP is highest in Turkey where employment may rise nearly 3 per cent a year. Our most likely estimate envisages a 6 per cent growth rate for 1960–1975, while our high estimate equals the 7 per cent official target for the 1961–1976 period [23, p. 13]. Given the high rate of growth of employment in Southern Europe as a whole, the gross national product of this group of countries has been projected to rise at a rate exceeding the European average. Our most likely estimate of the rate of growth of GNP is 4.9 per cent and the high estimate 5.9 per cent (Table 2.6.1).

2.5. INCOME PROJECTIONS FOR JAPAN

Output per man was increasing at an annual rate of 6.4 per cent in Japan during the fifties, while the gross national product was rising at an average rate of 8.8 per cent a year—exceeding the growth rates experienced in other industrial countries by a comfortable margin. About one-third of the increase in productivity can be attributed to the movement of the labor force from agriculture to nonagricultural occupations; the remaining two-thirds is explained by the high rate of productivity growth in the individual sectors.

We have accepted the estimate of the Japanese planning agency on the intersectoral allocation of the labor force in 1970, and the same estimate served as a starting point for the projection of employment in the major sectors of the economy for 1975. However, we have found the productivity estimate given in the Japanese plan overly high [*14*, pp. 16, 25], and have adjusted the rates of increase of output per man in the individual sectors by taking account of the probable slackening in the expansion of exports and the prospective decline in working hours (Table A2.5.1). The resulting rate of increase of output per man is 4.5 per cent between 1960 and 1970 and 4.1 per cent between 1970 and 1975. Intersectoral shifts of employment account for part of the decline as compared to the previous decade.

With account taken of the expected slowing down in the increase of employment, our most likely estimate of the rate of growth of Japanese GNP is 5.4 per cent for the period 1960–1970 and 5.0 per cent for 1970–1975, considerably below the 8.8 per cent growth rate observed during the fifties. Even our high estimate, 6.4 per cent for the period 1960–1970, is lower than the 7.2 per cent foreseen in the Japanese income-doubling plan.

2.6. A COMPARISON OF GROWTH RATES IN INDUSTRIAL COUNTRIES

In order to ensure the comparability of national GNP data, appropriate conversion ratios expressing the purchasing power of the various currencies need to be applied. Purchasing power parities are estimated as ratios between the values of a given bundle of commodities expressed in different national currencies. Purchasing power parities generally differ from exchange rates since the latter are determined by the demand for and the supply of internationally traded goods, by invisible transactions, and by capital movements.

As a rule, the exchange rate overvalues the purchasing power of the currency of a country with relatively higher incomes, since higher productivity in such a country is accompanied by higher relative prices of services which do not enter into the determination of exchange rates. For example, while the German exchange rate was 4.2 marks to a dollar in 1955, the purchasing power parity rate was 2.9 in the same year. Consequently, an international comparison of national incomes at exchange rates would overestimate income levels in the richer countries.

In the present study, purchasing power parities have been used as conversion ratios in regard to the gross national product and disposable income of industrial countries. In a comparison of the purchasing power of the two currencies, customarily two parity ratios are estimated, each based on the commodity composition of expenditure in one of the countries. Whenever available, U.S. and average European weights have been employed and a geometric average of the results has been taken. Further, in cases where the necessary information was available, separate conversion ratios were applied in regard to gross national product and disposable income (Table A2.6.1). The projections of gross national product for various groups of industrial countries, expressed in 1955 dollars by the use of purchasing power parities, are given in Table 2.6.1. For the period 1960–1970, our most likely estimate indicates a rate of growth of GNP of 3.9 per cent for the industrial countries taken together, and a slightly lower rate for the years 1970–1975. Compared to the postwar period, the projections entail an acceleration of the growth of GNP in North America and in the United Kingdom and some slowing-down in the other groups of countries. A large rise of employment in North America, an increase in the rate of productivity growth in the United Kingdom, and a slackening in the advance of productivity in other areas would account for the projected developments.

According to our most likely estimate, the European Economic Community would attain the 4.1 per cent growth rate envisaged by the OECD for 1960–1970. This rate would be surpassed in Southern Europe while lower rates have been projected for North America, Northern Europe, and the United Kingdom. For Western Europe, taken as a whole, the projected rate of growth of GNP is 3.9 per cent, lower than the OECD target rate of 4.1 per cent, but higher than some earlier estimates. In 1957, the UN Economic Commission for Europe calculated with a 2.4 per cent growth rate for the period 1955–1975 [*30*, V, p. 2], more recently Dewhurst estimated

TABLE 2.6.1

EMPLOYMENT AND PRODUCTIVITY OF INDUSTRIAL COUNTRIES ACCORDING TO GEOGRAPHICAL GROUPINGS: GROSS NATIONAL PRODUCT

(in 1955 U.S. dollars)

	1950	1955	1960	1970	1975	Percentage Change per Year 1950 to 1955	1955 to 1960	1950 to 1960	1960 to 1970	1970 to 1975
UNITED STATES										
Gross National Product (million $)	321,900	397,500	446,100	I 667,200 / II 700,100	804,500 / 865,400	4.3	2.4	3.3	3.9 / 4.4	3.6 / 4.1
Employment (1,000)	59,748	62,943	66,681	79,700	86,700	1.0	1.2	1.1	1.8	1.7
Gross National Product per Man ($)	5,388	6,315	6,690	I 8,371 / II 8,784	9,279 / 9,981	3.2	1.2	2.2	2.1 / 2.6	1.9 / 2.4
CANADA										
Gross National Product (million $)	21,943	26,999	31,530	I 49,190 / II 51,146	59,956 / 63,527	4.2	3.2	3.7	4.5 / 5.0	4.0 / 4.4
Employment (1,000)	4,976	5,364	5,955	7,547	8,370	1.5	2.1	1.8	2.4	2.1
Gross National Product per Man ($)	4,410	5,033	5,295	I 6,518 / II 6,777	7,163 / 7,590	2.7	1.0	1.8	2.1 / 2.5	1.9 / 2.3
WESTERN EUROPE[1],[3]										
Gross National Product (million $)	233,280	297,460	a 371,948 / b 394,659	I 576,377 / II 608,562	691,533 / 750,748	5.0	4.5	4.8	3.9 / 4.4	3.7 / 4.3
Employment (1,000)	123,317	131,482	a 139,018 / b 150,103	165,224	172,551	1.3	1.1	1.2	0.9	0.9
Gross National Product per Man ($)	1,892	2,262	a 2,676 / b 2,630	I 3,488 / II 3,683	4,008 / 4,351	3.7	3.3	3.5	2.9 / 3.4	2.8 / 3.4
COMMON MARKET[2]										
Gross National Product (million $)	123,783	167,719	a 215,057 / b 216,409	I 324,237 / II 340,216	394,223 / 423,810	6.3	5.1	5.7	4.1 / 4.6	4.0 / 4.5
Employment (1,000)	62,405	66,907	a 70,915 / b 71,315	76,968	79,454	1.4	1.2	1.3	0.8	0.6
Gross National Product per Man ($)	1,984	2,507	a 3,033 / b 3,035	I 4,213 / II 4,420	4,962 / 5,334	4.8	3.9	4.3	3.3 / 3.8	3.3 / 3.8

UNITED KINGDOM[1]

Indicator	(1)	(2)	(3)	(4) I / II	(5) I / II	r1	**r2**	**r3**	r4 I / II	r5 I / II
Gross National Product (million $)	63,161	71,674	80,906	I 107,490 / II 112,850	122,490 / 131,690	2.6	**2.4**	**2.5**	2.9 / 3.4	2.6 / 3.1
Employment (1,000)	22,539	**23,477**	24,173	I 25,570	26,120	0.8	**0.6**	**0.7**	0.6	0.4
Gross National Product per Man ($)	2,802	**3,053**	3,347	I 4,204 / II 4,413	4,690 / 5,042	1.7	**1.8**	**1.8**	2.3 / 2.8	2.2 / 2.7

NORTHERN EUROPE[2]

Indicator	(1)	(2)	(3)	(4) I / II	(5) I / II	r1	**r2**	**r3**	r4 I / II	r5 I / II
Gross National Product (million $)	32,620	40,023	48,791	I 66,645 / II 69,963	76,502 / 82,325	4.2	**4.0**	**4.1**	3.2 / 3.7	2.8 / 3.3
Employment (1,000)	14,984	15,406	15,898	I 16,612	16,856	0.6	**0.6**	**0.6**	0.4	0.3
Gross National Product per Man ($)	2,177	**2,598**	3,069	I 4,012 / II 4,212	4,539 / 4,884	3.6	**3.4**	**3.5**	2.7 / 3.2	2.5 / 3.0

SOUTHERN EUROPE[3]

Indicator	(1)	(2)	(3)	(4) I / II	(5) I / II	r1	**r2**	**r3**	r4 I / II	r5 I / II
Gross National Product (million $)	14,786	19,304	a 27,194 / b 44,494	I 72,111 / II 79,345	91,250 / 105,328	5.5	**7.1**	**6.3**	4.9 / 6.0	4.8 / 5.8
Employment (1,000)	23,389	25,692	a 28,032 / b 39,117	I 46,074	50,121	1.9	**1.8**	**1.8**	1.7	1.7
Gross National Product per Man ($)	632	751	a 970 / b 1,137	I 1,565 / II 1,722	1,821 / 2,101	3.6	**5.3**	**4.5**	3.2 / 4.3	3.1 / 4.1

JAPAN

Indicator	(1)	(2)	(3)	(4) I / II	(5) I / II	r1	**r2**	**r3**	r4 I / II	r5 I / II
Gross National Product (million $)	23,857	35,608	55,604	I 94,035 / II 103,410	119,930 / 138,350	8.3	**9.3**	**8.8**	5.4 / 6.4	5.0 / 6.0
Employment (1,000)	35,720	40,880	44,720	I 48,690	50,800	2.7	**1.8**	**2.3**	0.9	0.9
Gross National Product per Man ($)	668	871	1,243	I 1,931 / II 2,124	2,361 / 2,723	5.5	**7.4**	**6.4**	4.5 / 5.5	4.1 / 5.1

Sources: Tables A2.3.1, 2.5.1, and 2.6.1.

Notes: [1] 1950 to 1960a exclude the Saar and West Berlin.
1960b to 1975 include the Saar and West Berlin.
[2] 1950 to 1960a exclude the Saar.
1960 to 1975 include the Saar.
[3] 1950 to 1960a exclude Spain.
1960 to 1975 include Spain.

European GNP to grow at a rate of 2.9 per cent [7, p. 120], while Kristensen suggested limits of 1.75 to 3.25 per cent [17, p. 254].

The rate of increase of GNP is an imperfect indicator of economic performance, however, since it is also influenced by the growth of employment. If we compare rates of growth of output per man instead, the most rapid rate of advance is indicated for Japan, the Common Market, and Southern Europe, in that order. Northern Europe occupies a middle position, while the United States and the United Kingdom would experience the lowest rates of productivity growth according to our projections.

The future rise of per capita incomes is further influenced by changes in the employed-dependent ratio. With few exceptions, our projections envisage a lower rate of increase of GNP per head in the high income countries and a more pronounced rise in those with lower incomes. Correspondingly, relative—although not necessarily absolute—differences in living standards would be reduced. Also, by 1975, Canada and Germany are expected to reach the present level of per capita GNP in the United States (Table A2.6.2).

It has further been necessary to estimate per capita disposable income in the individual countries in order to derive income elasticities for the postwar period and to project future demand for consumer goods. In making projections, we have assumed that disposable income will increase at the same rate as gross national product. This hypothesis gives expression to the assumption that there will be no change in the combined share of government and undistributed profits in the gross national product. Actual and projected changes of per capita disposable income in the individual countries are shown in Tables 2.6.2. and A2.6.3.

Finally, Table 2.6.3. provides information on the growth of industrial production, actual and projected.[3] In the case of countries for which sectoral breakdowns are provided, the future increase of industrial production has been estimated on the basis of past relationships between industrial production and value added in industry, with consideration given to the secular increase in the share of value added in industrial output. Past evidence on the ratio of industrial production to gross national product, as well as international comparisons, have been relied upon in the case of countries for which only aggregate GNP estimates are given.

---

[3]Industrial production is defined to include mining, manufacturing, electricity, gas, and water.

TABLE 2.6.2

INDUSTRIAL COUNTRIES: DISPOSABLE INCOME PER CAPITA IN 1955 $

	1950	1951	1952	1953	1954	1955	1956	1957	1958	1959	1960	1970 I	1970 II	1975 I	1975 II
United States	1,525	1,521	1,534	1,584	1,579	1,660	1,716	1,718	1,694	1,751	1,762	2,190	2,300	2,383	2,564
Canada	1,058	1,092	1,121	1,159	1,124	1,175	1,250	1,238	1,264	1,292	1,296	1,675	1,742	1,867	1,981
Belgium	820	842	834	853	898	933	971	982	979	993	1,045	1,369	1,435	1,558	1,678
France	646	673	693	717	773	824	885	949	918	912	960	1,372	1,440	1,612	1,733
Germany	539	595	643	694	748	832	886	944	978	1,012	1,078	1,455	1,526	1,729	1,848
Italy	368	380	392	417	420	437	449	469	477	499	524	758	794	905	973
Luxembourg	740	785	839	890	910	957	1,013	1,046	1,078	1,083	1,109	1,449	1,521	1,653	1,778
Netherlands	555	552	564	610	668	745	772	762	775	793	852	1,159	1,216	1,309	1,408
United Kingdom	879	861	857	883	913	953	968	979	987	1,026	1,087	1,359	1,425	1,507	1,620
Austria	517	558	553	567	625	717	763	816	830	867	926	1,223	1,283	1,400	1,505
Denmark	932	891	899	938	947	912	916	943	966	1,033	1,097	1,421	1,492	1,582	1,701
Finland	485	541	557	531	568	630	635	613	591	612	660	837	879	931	1,001
Iceland	587	639	603	670	728	774	797	746	807	803	791	1,023	1,084	1,146	1,250
Ireland	532	534	533	559	568	582	572	574	557	593	627	807	856	888	970
Norway	883	870	868	869	894	925	970	971	916	941	1,002	1,257	1,318	1,406	1,512
Sweden	827	823	866	867	902	940	949	964	951	968	1,019	1,298	1,362	1,417	1,526
Switzerland	788	810	826	855	914	968	1,005	1,040	1,021	1,058	1,079	1,494	1,565	1,696	1,823
Greece	188	190	188	225	230	233	262	270	279	269	278	389	429	464	536
Portugal	222	243	244	247	254	269	279	282	276	277	276	383	422	452	522
Turkey	159	190	206	225	198	216	214	232	253	230	249	350	386	411	476
Yugoslavia	159	171	143	162	179	189	190	222	226	265	283	427	517	470	597
Japan	197	214	242	251	257	282	302	320	336	369	393	609	670	746	860

Sources: Tables A2.6.1 and 2.6.3.

2.7. GROWTH PROSPECTS IN OCEANIA AND SOUTH AFRICA

For industrial countries it is permissible to estimate the future growth of GNP independently of the prospects of trade in primary commodities. This cannot be said of Australia, New Zealand, and South Africa, however, since the rate of growth of GNP in the latter countries depends, to a large extent, on the future expansion of their exports of primary products. And, given the uncertainties associated with trade in temperate zone agricultural products that are the principal exports of these countries, projection of the gross national product involves a considerable margin of error. Nevertheless, the error introduced thereby into the estimates of the export earnings of developing countries will not be large since the countries of Oceania and South Africa, taken together, take less than 3 per cent of the exports of less developed areas.

The error possibilities of the estimation of future GNP in the three countries under consideration may be seen from a comparison of growth rates in the period 1950–1960 and 1951–1960. As a result of the decrease in the demand for wool and other temperate zone agricultural products after the temporary peak reached in the second half of 1950, and the decline in the prices of these commodities from the high levels reached during the first months of the Korean War, the gross national product of the three countries fell after 1950 and the 1950 level was reached again only in 1954 in Australia and New Zealand and in 1953 in South Africa. Correspondingly, the rate of growth of GNP in 1951–1960 was 3.7 per cent in Australia, 3.3 per cent in New Zealand, and 5.0 per cent in South Africa, as against annual rates of increase of 2.1, 2.1, and 3.3 per cent for the years 1950–1960.

In the period 1951–1960, output per man increased at an annual rate of 1.3 per cent in New Zealand, 1.9 per cent in Australia, and 2.8 per cent in South Africa. The differences in the rate of growth of productivity are largely explained by the unfavorable export pattern of New Zealand and her continuing reliance on agricultural pursuits as against the more favorable production and export pattern of Australia and the advances made in industrialization by South Africa.

We have assumed here that past differences in the rate of growth of productivity would continue, although at a reduced scale, and calculated with an annual rate of increase of productivity of 1.3 per cent for New Zealand, 1.6 per cent for Australia, and 1.9 per cent

TABLE 2.6.3

INDUSTRIAL COUNTRIES ACCORDING TO GEOGRAPHICAL GROUPINGS: INDICES OF INDUSTRIAL PRODUCTION

	1950	1951	1952	1953	1954	1955	1956	1957	1958	1959	1960	1970 I	1970 II	1975 I	1975 II
United States	82	89	92	100	94	106	109	110	102	116	119	176	187	209	227
Canada	83	90	94	100	100	110	120	120	120	129	130	204	214	252	270
Western Europe	86	94	94	100	109	119	126	131	134	143	157	241	257	296	324
Common Market	80	92	94	100	110	122	132	140	144	153	171	273	289	340	370
United Kingdom	94	98	95	100	108	114	114	116	114	122	130	176	187	203	221
Northern Europe	92	98	97	100	108	117	121	126	129	135	146	205	217	236	258
Southern Europe	86	88	90	100	114	128	138	155	168	183	205	381	438	555	634
Japan	57	77	83	100	108	117	144	167	168	208	262	525	587	706	835

Source: In all cases except those noted below, OEEC, General Statistics, January, 1962.
Finland; IMF, International Financial Statistics, February, 1962.
Japan; Japanese Economic Indicators, January, 1962.

Note: The following weights have been used in the calculations: Belgium 4.6, France 15.2, Germany 23.1, Italy 9.3, Luxembourg 0.2, Netherlands 3.8, Saar 0.5, United Kingdom 31.5, Austria 2.1, Denmark 1.5, Finland 0.8, Ireland 0.6, Norway 1.5, Sweden 4.4, Greece 0.7, Portugal, 0.6, Turkey 1.0, Yugoslavia 2.1. The weights refer to 1953 and have been derived from OEEC, Statistical Bulletins, Definitions and Methods I, Indices of Industrial Production, Third Edition, Paris, 1958, and U.N., Patterns of Industrial Growth, 1938-1958, New York, 1960, p. 460. The industrial production of the European OECD countries (excepting Portugal, Spain, and Switzerland) has been taken as 100, and that of Western Europe other than Spain and Switzerland as 103.5. Industrial production indices for Switzerland and Spain are not available.

for South Africa. At the same time, employment is expected to rise at a rate of 2.0 per cent a year in New Zealand, 1.9 per cent in Australia, and 2.3 per cent in South Africa, so that the growth rates of GNP would be 3.3, 3.4, and 4.1 per cent in the three countries, respectively. Higher rates could be achieved with an improvement in export prospects and an acceleration of the industrialization process, however (Table A2.7.1).

REFERENCES

[1.] BORRIE, W. D., AND RODGERS, RUTH. *Australian Population Projections, 1960–1975.* Canberra: Australian National University, 1961 (mimeo).

[2.] BREZNIK, DUSAN. "Zapazanja 1 prognoze nekih kategorija buduceg stanovnistva fnrj sa oscrtom na natalitet 1 mortalitet," *Statisticka Revija* (September, 1956), pp. 217–34.

[3.] CAVES, R. E., AND HOLTON, R. H. *The Canadian Economy—Prospect and Retrospect.* Cambridge, Mass.: Harvard University Press, 1959.

[4.] COMMUNAUTÉ ECONOMIQUE EUROPÉENNE. *Rapport sur les perspectives de développement économique dans la C.E.E. de 1960 à 1970.* Brussels, 1962.

[5.] DEAKIN, B. M. "Exercise in Forecasting the Gross Domestic Product of the United Kingdom to 1970," *Europe's Future in Figures,* (R. C. Geary, ed.) pp. 191–213. Amsterdam, North Holland, 1962.

[6.] DENISON, E. F. *The Sources of Economic Growth in the United States and the Alternatives Before Us.* New York: Committee for Economic Development, 1962.

[7.] DEWHURST, J. F., AND ASSOCIATES. *Europe's Needs and Resources.* New York: Twentieth Century Fund, 1961.

[8.] COUNCIL OF ECONOMIC ADVISERS. *Annual Report, Economic Report of the President.* Washington, D.C., 1962.

[9.] FOOD AND AGRICULTURE ORGANIZATION. *Agricultural Commodities—Projections for 1970.* Rome, 1962.

[10.] GENERAL AGREEMENT OF TARIFFS AND TRADE. *The Possible Impact of the European Economic Community, in Particular the Common Market, upon World Trade.* Geneva, 1957.

[11.] HARTMAN, TOR. "Vaestonkehityksen ennuste vuoteen 1975 saakka," *Tilastokateauksia,* No. 4 (1959), pp. 44–52.

[12.] HOOD, WM. C., AND SCOTT, A. *Output, Labour and Capital in the Canadian Economy.* Toronto: Royal Commission on Canada's Economic Prospects, 1957.

[13.] INTERNATIONAL LABOUR OFFICE. *International Labour Review* (June, 1962), Supplement.

[14.] JAPANESE ECONOMIC PLANNING AGENCY. *New Long-Range Economic Plan of Japan (1961–1970).* Tokyo: The Times of Japan, 1961.

[15.] JAPANESE WELFARE MINISTRY, INSTITUTE OF POPULATION PROBLEMS. "Estimate of Future Population (1955–65 with extension to 2015)," *Jinko-Mondai Kenkyu* (March, 1958), pp. 60–65.

[16.] KENDRICK, J. W. *Productivity Trends in the United States.* National Bureau of Economic Research, Princeton, N.J. Princeton University Press, 1961.

[17.] KRISTENSEN, THORKIL (ed.). *The Economic World Balance.* Copenhagen: Munksgaard, 1960.

[18.] KUZNETS, SIMON. "Concepts and Assumptions in Long-Term Projections of National Product," *Long-Range Economic Projection; Studies in Income and Wealth,* Vol. 16, pp. 9–38. Princeton: Princeton University Press, 1954.

[19.] NEW ZEALAND DEPARTMENT OF STATISTICS. *Monthly Abstract of Statistics,* August, 1962.

[20.] ORGANIZATION FOR EUROPEAN ECONOMIC COOPERATION. *Demographic Trends, 1956–1976, in Western Europe and in the United States.* Paris, 1961.

[21.] ORGANIZATION FOR ECONOMIC COOPERATION AND DEVELOPMENT. *Policies for Economic Growth.* Paris, 1962.

[22.] ORGANIZATION FOR EUROPEAN ECONOMIC COOPERATION. *Towards a New Energy Pattern in Europe.* Paris, 1961.

[23.] ORGANIZATION FOR ECONOMIC COOPERATION AND DEVELOPMENT. *Turkey.* Economic Surveys by the OECD, Paris, 1963.

[24.] PAIGE, D. C.; BLACKABY, F. T.; AND FREUND, S. "Economic Growth: The Last Hundred Years," *National Economic Institute Review* (July, 1961), pp. 24–50.

[25.] SAUNDERS, C. T. "Outline of a Possible Ten Year Projection for the British Economy, 1960 to 1970," *Europe's Future in Figures,* pp. 214–47.

[26.] SECRETARIAT FOR INFORMATION OF THE YUGOSIAV FEDERAL EXECUTIVE COUNCIL. *The Five-Year Plan of Economic Development of Yugoslavia, 1961–1965.* Belgrade, 1961.

[27.] SVENNILSON, INGVAR. *Prospects of Development in Western Europe, 1955–1975.* Stockholm, 1959.

[28.] UNITED KINGDOM NATIONAL DEVELOPMENT COUNCIL. *Growth in the United Kingdom Economy to 1966.* London: Her Majesty's Stationery Office, 1963.

[29.] UNITED NATIONS. *The Growth of World Population.* New York, 1958.

[30.] UNITED NATIONS ECONOMIC COMMISSION FOR EUROPE. *Economic Survey of Europe in 1957.* Geneva, 1958.

[31.] U.S. DEPARTMENT OF COMMERCE, BUREAU OF THE CENSUS. *Illustrative Projections of the Population of the United States, by Age and Sex: 1960 to 1980.* Current Population Reports, Series P-25, No. 187. Washington, D.C., 1958.

[32.] U.S. DEPARTMENT OF COMMERCE, BUREAU OF THE CENSUS. *Interim*

Revised Projections of the Population of the United States, by Age and Sex: 1965 and 1970. Current Population Reports, Series P-25, No. 241 and No. 251. Washington, D.C., 1962.

[33.]   U.S. DEPARTMENT OF LABOR, BUREAU OF LABOR STATISTICS. *Population and Labor Force Projections in the United States, 1960 to 1975.* Bulletin No. 1242. Washington, D.C., 1959.

[34.]   U.S. DEPARTMENT OF LABOR, BUREAU OF LABOR STATISTICS. *Interim Revised Projections of U.S. Labor Force, 1965–75.* Washington, D.C., 1962.

CHAPTER 3

The Future of Exports from Developing Countries

3.1 PROSPECTS FOR THE EXPORTS OF DEVELOPING COUNTRIES TO DEVELOPED ECONOMIES

IN 1960, the f.o.b. value of goods exported by developing countries to developed economies was $19.5 billion. Of this total, petroleum and petroleum products, the single largest commodity group, accounted for one-fourth, $5.1 billion. Next to it, the exports of non-competing tropical products, agricultural raw materials, and non-fuel minerals and metals amounted to $3 billion each, whereas export earnings derived form the sale of temperate zone foods and competing tropical foods were 2–2 billion. Finally, developed countries purchased one million dollar's worth of manufactured goods from less developed areas.

Over one-half of these exports went to Western Europe in 1960 ($10.8 billion), one-third to the United States and Canada ($6.6 billion), while the combined imports of Japan, Oceania, and South Africa hardly exceeded 10 per cent of the total. Fuels, noncompeting tropical foods (chiefly coffee), and minerals and metals (copper, iron ore) account for much of U.S. imports. In Western Europe, fuels and agricultural raw materials (largely rubber and cotton) are of major importance, followed by noncompeting tropical foods, temperate zone foods, and nonfuel minerals and metals. Fuels and agricultural raw materials are also the principal imports of Japan (cotton and rubber) as well as for Oceania and South Africa (rubber).

Among developing areas, Latin America leads with exports of $7.9 billion in 1960, of which fuels account for one-fourth and non-competing tropical foods (coffee and cocoa) for over one-fifth. In Asian exports of $4.4 billion, agricultural raw materials (rubber and jute) are of chief importance, in Africa ($4.0 billion) minerals and metals, whereas Middle Eastern exports of $3.1 billion consist almost entirely of oil.

43

According to our projections, the exports of developing countries to developed economies, measured in 1960 prices, would rise from $19.5 billion in 1960 to $29.1 billion in 1970 and $36.0 billion in 1975 under the most likely income assumption, and to $30.5 and $38.9 billion in the two years, respectively, under the target income alternative. For the period as a whole, the projected increase in the gross national product of the developed countries is 80 per cent under the first variant and 96 per cent under the second, indicating an income elasticity of import demand exceeding unity (Table 3.1.1). By comparison, imports valued at constant prices rose by 48 per cent between 1953–54 and 1960–61 as against a 31 per cent increase in GNP.

But objections can be raised against calculating income elasticities from data expressed in constant prices, considering that actual—

TABLE 3.1.1

EXPORTS OF DEVELOPING COUNTRIES TO DEVELOPED
ECONOMIES

	1960	1970I	1970II	1975I	1975II
Exports to developed countries in 1960 prices,					
$ million	19,496	29,097	30,479	36,010	38,915
index	100	149.2	156.3	184.7	199.6
Exports to developed countries in current prices,					
$ million	19,496	26,734	28,418	33,054	36,217
index	100	137.1	145.8	169.5	185.8
Implicit export price index	100	91.9	93.4	91.7	93.1
Gross national product in developed countries, in 1955 prices,					
$ billion	964.0	1,439.3	1,519.5	1,739.3	1,888.2
index	100	149.3	157.6	180.4	195.9

Sources: Trade--U.N., Commodity Trade Statistics, 1960; OECD, Trade by Commodities, Foreign Trade, Series C, 1960, national trade statistics, and Table A3.1.1; Gross national product--Tables 2.5.1 and A2.7.1.

and projected—quantities and prices are, in fact, mutually interdependent. Rather, income elasticities should be estimated with reference to changes in quantities that would take place if prices remained unchanged. Such calculations can be made for past periods if an import demand function is fitted to the observations with income and relative prices as the independent variables,[1] although the interdependence of prices and quantities would bias the estimated coefficients.

Further difficulties arise in estimating income elasticities under the assumption of unchanged prices in regard to future imports.

---

[1]For the period 1953–1961, the total income elasticity of import demand on the part of industrial countries has been estimated as 1.2.—The expression "total income elasticity of import demand" is used in the present study to refer to the relationship between total imports and the gross natural product, while "income elasticity of import demand" is calculated from per capita data.

In the case of agricultural raw materials, where the largest price changes are expected to take place, demand would fall to a considerable extent if prices remained at 1960 levels. It can be safely said, for example, that hardly any natural rubber would be consumed by 1975 if rubber prices failed to decline. Yet the usefulness of a hypothetical income elasticity calculated under this assumption is doubtful since the results will greatly depend on the choice of the base year.

Note further that, from the point of view of the transmission of economic growth from developed to less developed countries, export earnings estimated at current prices are relevant. On the one hand, changes in demand conditions accompanying economic growth in the developed countries affect imported quantities as well as prices;[2] on the other, foreign exchange earnings expressed in current rather than constant prices will indicate the purchasing power of the exports of developing countries.

In terms of current prices,[3] the exports of the developing countries to developed economies have been estimated to reach $26.7 or $28.4 billion in 1970 and $33.1 or $36.2 billion in 1975, depending on the income assumption chosen. Exports would thus rise at an average annual rate of 3.6 or 4.2 per cent, reaching 170 or 186 per cent of the 1960 level in 1975 under the two income variants, respectively. By comparison, the money value of exports grew at an annual rate of 4.4 per cent between 1953-54 and 1960-61.

Reference should further be made to differences shown in the projections for the period 1960-1970 and 1970-1975. As Table 3.1.1 indicates, the expected decline in the export prices of several primary products has been assumed to take place largely during the sixties. Correspondingly, changes in exports measured in 1960 prices and in current prices would be roughly parallel after 1970, and in the latter period the rate of increase in the value of exports would exceed the growth of GNP in the developed economies. Still, for purposes of evaluating the export prospects of the developing

---

[2]This is not to deny the relationship between supply conditions and prices. For a given rate of growth of demand in developed countries, the value of imports will depend on the rate of growth of supply in less developed areas and the elasticities of demand and supply. The reader should note that the expression "demand conditions" is used here to refer to demand on the part of developed countries which is affected by changes in incomes and the domestic supply of competing commodities.

[3]As noted in the Appendix to Chapter 1, primary product prices have been projected under the assumption that the prices of manufactured goods would remain at levels experienced in 1960.

economies in the fifteen-year period up to 1975, we can regard the entire period as a unit.

Turning to prospective developments in the main markets for the exports of developing countries, note that exports to Japan are expected to show the highest rate of expansion during the period of projection. Under the most likely income assumption, Japanese imports from less developed countries, expressed in current prices, have been projected to increase one and one-half times between 1960 and 1975. In the same period, imports into Oceania and South Africa would rise by 80 per cent, while the projected increases are 75 and 43 per cent for Western Europe and North America, respectively (Table 3.1.2).[4]

TABLE 3.1.2

DEVELOPED COUNTRIES: GROSS NATIONAL PRODUCT AND IMPORTS FROM LESS DEVELOPED COUNTRIES (current prices)

	1960	1970I	1970II	1975I	1975II
North America, imports from LDC, $ million	6,597	7,931	8,262	9,407	9,913
index	100	120.2	125.2	142.6	150.3
gross national product, index	100	150.0	157.3	181.0	194.5
Western Europe, imports from LDC, $ million	10,831	15,184	16,124	18,901	20,764
index	100	140.2	148.9	174.5	191.7
gross national product, index	100	146.1	153.9	175.0	189.3
Japan, imports from LDC, $ million	1,404	2,694	3,030	3,557	4,180
index	100	191.9	215.8	253.3	297.7
gross national product, index	100	169.1	186.0	215.7	248.8
Oceania and South Africa, imports from LDC, $ million	664	925	1,002	1,189	1,360
index	100	139.3	150.9	179.1	204.8
gross national product, index	100	145.4	155.7	175.4	194.4
Developed countries, total imports from LDC $ million	19,496	26,734	28,418	33,054	36,217
index	100	137.1	145.8	169.5	185.8
gross national product, index	100	149.3	157.6	180.4	195.9

Sources: Trade--Table A3.1.1.
Gross national product--Tables 2.5.1 and A2.7.1.

Various factors are expected to contribute to the rapid expansion of Japanese imports. To begin with, gross national product in Japan has been projected to more than double in the period 1960–1975, as against an increase by about four-fifths in North America, Western Europe, Oceania, and South Africa. Further, the Japanese economy is at an earlier stage of industrial development than are the United States and Western Europe, and hence the expansion in the material-intensive branches of industry will be more pronounced here. And, since Japan is poorly endowed with fuel and other mineral re-

---

[4]In the following discussion, all projections will be expressed in current prices, and will refer to the most likely income alternative. Information on imports under the high income variant is given in the statistical tables. Projected price changes are shown in Table A1.5.1 (cf. also the discussion of the prospects for individual commodities below).

sources, she will have to rely on imports for much of her increased raw material requirements. Finally, the transformation of the Japanese diet will benefit the less developed countries through larger imports of coarse grains, oilseeds, and tropical beverages (Table A3.1.1).

Differences in the projected rate of growth of imports into North America and Western Europe are largely explained by the disparate prospects for the imports of fuels and nonfuel minerals and metals in the two areas. Whereas, in terms of relative shares, the substitution of liquid fuels for coal has been by and large completed in the United States and Canada, the process of substitution has not yet run its course in Western Europe. With account taken also of prospective changes in relative prices, nearly the entire increase in European energy consumption can be expected to take the form of petroleum. At the same time, known oil reserves in Europe are small, so that the increase in oil consumption will have to be supplied by imports. The volume of fuel imports into Western Europe could thus triple between 1960 and 1975, while the rise in the imports of North America would hardly exceed two-thirds. Increases will be smaller in value terms, however, by reason of the expected decline in petroleum prices.

European imports of metals, too, are bound to rise at a rate considerably higher than U.S. imports. For one thing, the production of material-intensive commodities is likely to expand faster in the countries of Western Europe than in the United States and Canada. Moreover, Western Europe is less well endowed in metal-bearing ores than North America, and hence European countries will derive a larger proportion of the increase in metal consumption from imports. Finally, due to differences in business attitudes and government regulations, the shift toward importing nonferrous metals in the form of unwrought metal rather than ores and concentrates will be stronger in Europe than in the United States, augmenting thereby the increase in the value of imports of nonfuel minerals and metals.

Fuels and nonfuel minerals and metals would also account for the major part of the increase in the value of the exports of developing countries, taken as a whole. Out of a total increase of $13.6 billion, the rise in the exports of minerals and metals is projected to amount to $9.0 billion, as against an increase of $3.2 billion in the case of agricultural commodities, and $1.4 billion for manufactured goods (Table 3.1.3). These differences in prospective trends are especially noteworthy, partly because they provide a warning against oversimplification regarding the export prospects for primary products, and partly because of the uneven distribution of the exports of fuels and metals among less developed countries and regions.

In recent writings, much emphasis has been given to the low income elasticity of demand for primary commodities, the increased self-sufficiency of industrial countries in these products, and the substitution of synthetics for natural materials. These influences appear to be operating in the case of agricultural products where a 31 per cent increase in imports is foreseen as against an 80 per cent rise in the gross national product of the developed countries.

With respect to foodstuffs, the low income elasticity of demand should first be mentioned. If we exclude the southern countries of Western Europe, it appears that in developed economies the in-

TABLE 3.1.3

THE COMMODITY COMPOSITION OF THE EXPORTS OF DEVELOPING COUNTRIES TO
DEVELOPED ECONOMIES
(current prices)

	1960	1970I	1970II	1975I	1975II
Temperate zone foods, $ million	1,993	2,330	2,457	2,713	2,924
index	100	116.9	123.3	136.1	146.7
Competing tropical foods, $ million	2,127	2,113	2,172	2,284	2,372
index	100	99.3	102.1	107.4	111.5
Noncompeting tropical foods, $ million	3,095	3,955	4,027	4,469	4,573
index	100	127.8	130.1	144.4	147.8
Agricultural raw materials, $ million	3,146	3,608	3,819	4,106	4,457
index	100	114.7	121.4	130.5	141.7
Fuels, $ million	5,085	8,260	8,976	11,030	12,570
index	100	162.4	176.5	216.9	247.2
Nonfuel minerals and metals, $ million	2,975	4,656	5,069	6,073	6,809
index	100	156.5	170.4	204.1	228.9
Manufactured goods, $ million	1,075	1,812	1,898	2,379	2,512
index	100	168.6	176.6	221.3	233.7
Total exports, $ million	19,496	26,734	28,418	33,054	36,217
index	100	137.1	145.8	169.5	185.8

Sources: Trade--Table A3.1.1.
Gross national product--Tables 2.5.1 and A2.7.1.

come elasticity of demand for cereals and potatoes is negative, it is zero or slightly above zero for fish, oils and fats, sugar, and tea, and—with the exception of the United States—it is about 0.5-0.6 in regard to coffee, cocoa, fruits, meats, and tobacco.

In the case of temperate zone foods, the situation is further aggravated by reason of the protectionist policies followed by the countries of Western Europe, although developing countries will benefit from expected increases in the share of imports in the U.S. consumption of meat and fish. As a result of these influences, the exports of temperate zone foods from developing countries to developed areas would rise by 36 per cent, roughly 2 per cent a year, between 1960 and 1975.

Projected increases are considerably smaller for competing tropical foodstuffs (7 per cent). The low income elasticity of demand for oils and fats and the increasing share of the United States in the world market for oilseeds will unfavorably affect the prospects for the exporters of tropical oils, while the expected self-sufficiency of the Common Market countries in sugar, coupled with the decline in the share of imported sugar in U.S. consumption and the disappearance of the premium paid by the United States to Latin-American producers, are expected to lead to an absolute decline in the value of sugar exports to developed countries.

The prospects are more favorable with regard to noncompeting tropical foods where gains are foreseen especially in coffee, cocoa, and bananas. Per capita consumption will continue to rise, though at a decreasing rate, in Western Europe and Japan and some increases are anticipated in the United States too. All in all, the imports of these foods have been projected to increase by 44 per cent between 1960 and 1975.

Agricultural raw materials enter the production of clothing, automobile tires, lumber and paper products, and a variety of industrial products of lesser importance. While the income elasticity of demand for clothing is only slightly below unity, the demand for textile fibers is rising at a lower rate by reason of the shift toward high quality apparel. The expansion in the demand for natural fibers will be further mitigated by reason of the substitution of synthetic fibers for cotton and wool. Synthetic rubber will also continue to encroach upon the market for natural rubber so that the consumption of natural rubber in the developed countries is expected to increase by about 40 per cent as against a projected rise of over 70 per cent in the consumption of all rubber. Correspondingly, despite the favorable prospects for tropical timber, the increase in the exports of agricultural raw materials from developing countries, measured in 1960 prices, would not exceed 50 per cent in the period under consideration. At the same time, given the expected decline in the price of fibers and, more importantly, rubber, the value of exports expressed in current prices has been projected to rise by 30 per cent.

Different considerations apply to fuels and nonfuel minerals and metals. Although the income elasticity of demand for energy is below unity in countries that have reached a high level of industrialization, our previous considerations point to rapid increases in fuel imports. Thus, despite the projected decline in the price of petroleum and petroleum products, the value of the fuel exports of the developing countries may more than double in the period 1960–1975.

With the shift toward labor-intensive commodities in high income countries and reductions in per unit material requirements in some uses, the demand for nonfuel minerals and metals in these countries is expected to rise at a somewhat lower rate than their gross national product· But, given the limited availability of mineral resources in the main industrial countries, an increasing proportion of metal consumption will be satisfied by imports. This trend is especially strong in Western Europe, where the increase in the value of imports will be further accentuated by reason of the shift toward importation in metal form. In the period of projection, these influences are expected to lead to a doubling of the value of imports of nonfuel minerals and metals from developing countries.

Forecasting is more difficult in the case of manufactured goods where quantitative restrictions often limit imports originating in less developed areas. Information on possible changes in restrictions has been utilized here and separate projections have been prepared for commodities that are not subject to quotas. Taken together, we have projected the exports of manufactured goods from developing countries to rise by about 120 per cent between 1960 and 1975.

Differences in the export prospects for individual commodity groups will greatly affect the prospective export earnings of individual regions. Discoveries of new mineral resources in recent years, the "pull" of established markets growing at differential rates, and the impact of the European Common Market on trade are further important influences. Among the less developed regions, largest increases in exports are foreseen in Africa. African producers will benefit from the exportation of recently discovered oil and natural gas reserves, the rapid growth of demand in Western Europe for metals, as well as the preferential effect of the European Common Market.

While African exports are projected to rise by 116 per cent in the period 1960–1975, an 83 per cent increase is foreseen for the Middle East, where oil exports have been estimated to rise at a rate somewhat lower than the average by reason of the expected increase in the share of African oil in the world market. Still, her concentration in exports of oil place the Middle East in a favorable position as compared to Latin America and Asia, where agricultural products account for 56 and 66 per cent of total exports, respectively (Tables 3.1.4. and A3.1.2.).

Moreover, exports of fuels from Latin America to the slow-growing U.S. market are expected to rise at a relatively modest rate and the value of her sugar exports may actually decline. On the other hand, Asia is likely to derive considerable benefit from the projected expansion of imports of textiles into developed countries so that the rise in Asian exports may slightly exceed that of Latin America (48 and 47 per cent, respectively, in the period 1960–1975).

TABLE 3.1.4

EXPORTS OF DEVELOPED COUNTRIES BY REGIONS OF ORIGIN
(current prices)

		1960	1970I	1970II	1975I	1975II
Latin America,	$ million	7,931	9,872	10,479	11,662	12,630
	index	100	124.5	132.1	147.0	159.2
Africa,	$ million	4,038	6,747	7,163	9,167	9,871
	index	100	167.1	177.4	227.0	244.4
Middle East,	$ million	3,097	4,638	4,972	5,655	6,594
	index	100	149.8	160.5	182.6	212.9
Asia,	$ million	4,430	5,477	5,804	6,570	7,122
	index	100	123.6	131.0	148.3	160.8
Developed countries, total	$ million	19,496	26,734	28,418	33,054	36,217
	index	100	137.1	145.8	169.5	185.8

Source. Table A3.1.2.

3.2 TEMPERATE ZONE FOODS

In 1960, developed countries imported temperate zone foods from underdeveloped areas in the value of $2.0 billion, and these foods accounted for about one-tenth of the export earnings of the latter. Fruits and vegetables form the largest group, with sales of $560 million divided between oranges and tangerines, other fresh fruits, dried and preserved fruits, and vegetables. The corresponding figures for meat and eggs are $385 million; fish, $118 million; grains, $388 million; feeding-stuffs, $281 million; and beverages, $261 million (Table A3.1.1).

The countries of North America are large producers and exporters of cereals and several other foods included in this category. Correspondingly, U.S. and Canadian imports of temperate zone foods are relatively small ($370 million in 1960) and consist mainly of beef, fish, and a few fruits and vegetables. Beef imports originate in Argentina, Mexico, and Central America, fish comes chiefly from Mexico, fruits from India and the Philippines, and vegetables also from Mexico.

The largest food deficit area, Western Europe, takes over three-fourths of the exports of temperate zone foods from less developed areas. Argentina is a large supplier of beef, wheat, coarse grains, and feeding-stuffs to the European market, wine comes chiefly from Algeria, while fruits and vegetables are imported from Algeria,

Morocco, Israel, and a variety of sources in Latin America. Among Asian countries, India exports feeding-stuffs to Western Europe.

Japanese imports of temperate zone foods from less developed countries (maize from Argentina and Thailand, and rice from Burma) have been of little importance so far and amounted to $90 million in 1960. This circumstance is explained by the peculiarities of the Japanese diet and the reliance on imports from the United States. Finally, the countries of Oceania and South Africa, with their large surplus in meat, grains, and fruits, import negligible quantities of temperate zone foods.

The prospects for the exports of temperate zone foods from less developed areas are not too favorable. We have projected this trade to rise at an average annual rate of 2.1 per cent, reaching $2.7 billion in 1975.[5] In per capita terms, the rate of growth of imports would be 0.9 per cent, corresponding to an income elasticity of import demand of 0.3.[6] Among developed areas, the largest increases in imports are expected to take place in North America and Japan, with only a slight rise indicated in the case of Western Europe (Table A3.1.1). These discrepancies find their origin in the different "phasing" of the expansion of agricultural output in the United States and Western Europe and projected changes in the Japanese diet.

Improvements in productivity led to a decline in the importation of staples in the United States and the U.S. has emerged as a large exporter of cereals, feeding-stuffs, and oranges. The share of imports in the U.S. consumption of meat is on the increase, however, and imports are likely to supply much of the growth in fish consumption. On the other hand, Western Europe is a net importer of most temperate zone foods but shows an increasing degree of self-sufficiency in cereals and meat. Considering the possible effects of Common Market agricultural policy and improvements in agricultural productivity in Europe, a decline in cereal and meat imports appears likely and imports of wine from Algeria, too, are expected to fall. Finally, although rice imports into Japan are bound to disappear, the rise of meat consumption in Japan will necessitate increasing imports of coarse grains and feeding-stuffs.

In correspondence with expected developments in importing areas, differing trends are foreseen with regard to individual commodities. The United States looms large in the world market for

---

[5]No price changes have been assumed in regard to temperate zone foods.

[6]Under the most likely income assumption, per capita GNP in the developed countries has been estimated to rise at an average annual rate of 2.6 per cent.

fish, and will largely account for the expected doubling of fish imports from less developed areas in the period 1960–1975. She will also provide a market for prospective increases in the meat exports of developing countries, while the expansion of domestic meat production in other industrial areas is likely to be accompanied by rising purchases of feeding-stuffs. Despite the expected reduction in European coarse grain imports, the exports of coarse grains from developing countries may also increase as Japanese purchases of maize expand.

With increased demand for frozen and canned fruits, fruit juices, and early vegetables at higher income levels, an approximate doubling of the imports of preserved fruits and vegetables into developed countries is foreseen while increases in consumption—and imports—are likely to be somewhat smaller in the case of oranges and other fresh fruits. Taken together, the imports of fruits and vegetables from developing economies would rise by $380 million between 1960 and 1975, accounting for over one-half of the projected increase in the imports of temperate zone foods.

About 95 per cent of the imports of alcoholic beverages into developed countries goes to France. The bulk of these imports is low quality *vin ordinaire* imported from Algeria, in part as a result of the restriction of domestic wine production in France. Future developments will depend on economic policies followed in France and in Algeria but it can hardly be expected that imports would remain at the high level experienced in 1960.

Turning to the export prospects of individual regions, we find that increases in exports are expected to be largest (71 per cent) in the case of Asia, which is favored by the relative importance of fruits and vegetables in its exports of temperate zone foods as well as by the growth of Japanese purchases of maize. About average increases are expected in the exports of Latin America and the Middle East, whereas, despite the near-doubling of her exports of fruits and vegetables, the rise of African exports of temperate zone foods is unlikely to exceed 30 per cent by reason of the expected decline in Algerian exports of wine.

3.3 COMPETING TROPICAL FOODS

Oilseeds, sugar, and tobacco included in this category are produced in temperate as well as in tropical climate but developing countries produce these commodities mostly in the tropical zone. Imports of competing tropical foods into developed countries were valued at $2.1 billion in 1960, accounting for a little over one-tenth of imports from underdeveloped areas. The value of imports approached $1 billion in the case of sugar, as well as for oilseeds, oils, and fats, taken together, while tobacco imports amounted to $235 million.

The United States is a large exporter of oilseeds and tobacco and buys only small quantities of industrial oils from the Philippines and cigar tobacco from Latin America. On the other hand, about one-half of U.S. sugar consumption is supplied by producers in Latin America and the Philippines in the framework of the sugar quota system, and Canada buys much of her sugar from Commonwealth producers.

The countries of Western Europe take slightly over one-half of the exports of competing tropical goods originating in underdeveloped countries, and 80 per cent of the exports of oilseeds, oils and fats, and tobacco. The high level of imports of oils and oilseeds from Africa and Asia is explained by the unsuitability of European soil and climate for the production of oilseeds, while consumer preference for Virginia-type tobacco and low production costs in Rhodesia and Nyasaland benefit the tobacco producers of the latter. The tendency toward increased self-sufficiency in foods amenable to production in Europe has been evident in the case of sugar, however, and Western Europe's share in the world sugar market does not reach one-third.

On the other hand, Japan increasingly relies on imports from developing countries to satisfy her sugar requirements while purchasing oils and oilseeds mostly from the United States. Finally, the countries of Oceania and South Africa import tobacco from Rhodesia-Nyasaland but hardly anything else.

According to our projections, developed countries would increase their imports of competing tropical foods from less developed areas, expressed in 1960 prices, by about 18 per cent between 1960 and 1975, while in per capita terms a slight reduction is shown. The value of imports will be further reduced by reason of the disappearance of the premium paid by the United States to Latin-American producers and the expected decline in the prices of oils and fats. As of 1975, the discontinuation of the sugar premium will reduce the export earnings of Latin-American producers by $170 million, whereas the fall in the prices of oils and fats would cause a decline of $70 million. Correspondingly, the value of exports of competing tropical foods from developing to developed countries would not surpass $2.3 billion in 1975, exceeding the 1960 level by only 7 per cent.

Despite projected increases in the importation of oils, oilseeds, and tobacco, a decline in the value of U.S. imports of competing tropical foods is expected by reason of the disappearance of the sugar premium paid to Latin-American producers and the increased share of domestic producers in U.S. sugar consumption under the Sugar Act of 1962. While 49.5 per cent of sugar consumed in 1960 was supplied by foreign producers, import quotas were set at 46.5 per cent in 1961, with a further reduction to 40.0 per cent in the following year. And, although actual imports exceeded quotas in both years, domestic producers are apparently determined to increase output to levels specified in the Sugar Act.

At the same time, a fall in sugar imports into Western Europe is anticipated, in part because of the likely 100 per cent self-sufficiency in the Common Market and in part because of the expected decline in re-exports of sugar from Western Europe. Further, given the slow rate of growth of the consumption of oils and fats in Western Europe and increasing supplies made available by domestic production as well as by U.S. exports, an increase in imports of tropical oils and oilseeds does not appear likely. On the other hand, imports of fish oil from Peru will continue to rise and Rhodesia will be the chief beneficiary of the increase of tobacco consumption in Europe. Finally, Japanese imports may approximately double during the period of projection, reflecting large increases in the imports of oilseeds as well as sugar.

Among individual commodities, the largest increase in imports from developing countries is foreseen in the case of tobacco. Although, by reason of the discontinuation of imports from Cuba, U.S. purchases of cigar tobacco may change little, increased purchases by Western Europe would contribute to a 40 per cent rise in these imports. On the one hand, the share of imports in European consumption is expected to rise; on the other, low cost tobacco from Rhodesia-Nyasaland will continue to encroach upon the market for U.S. exports.

Different considerations apply to oilseeds, oils and fats. The most dynamic product within this category is fish oil; some increases are foreseen in regard to groundnuts, but imports of palm oil and palm kernel oil are likely to decline. Thus, despite increasing imports into Japan, oils and oilseeds originating in developing countries will hardly gain. Finally, increases in sales of sugar to Japan and Canada will not be sufficient to counterbalance the fall in the value of sugar exports to the United States and Western Europe.

Among developing areas, Latin America with her concentration on sugar imports is likely to experience a decline in export earnings derived from the sale of competing tropical products during the period under consideration, although without the discontinuation of the sugar premium exports an increase of 12 per cent would be shown. On the other hand, Africa and Asia expect gains of about 15–16 per cent; in addition to tobacco, African producers are likely to increase their exports of groundnuts, while the countries of Southeast Asia will benefit from their geographical proximity to Japan. Finally, the Middle East will remain an exporter of negligible importance of competing tropical products.

3.4 NONCOMPETING TROPICAL FOODS

Noncompeting tropical foods include bananas, coffee, cocoa, tea, and spices. Developed countries imported these foods in the value of $3.1 billion in 1960, representing 16 per cent of their imports from underdeveloped areas. Coffee imports, the second largest item among the exports of developing countries, amounted to $1785 million, with tea ($495), cocoa ($485), bananas ($246), and spices ($84) following.

The United States is the largest importer of coffee and spices and accounts for a substantial part of bananas and cocoa traded. But the United Kingdom is by far the largest tea importer, with the English-speaking member countries of the Commonwealth following. Western Europe also leads in imports of cocoa, while the higher price paid in European countries as compared to the United States augments the value of European banana imports. Finally, Japan imports negligible quantities of bananas and tropical beverages.

Whereas Latin America is the main supplier of noncompeting tropical foods to the United States, the countries of Western Europe rely to a considerable extent on African and Asian suppliers. U.S. imports of bananas originate exclusively in Central America and Ecuador, for example, while African bananas provide a large proportion of European consumption. With regard to coffee, we find that African producers have about 12 per cent of the U.S. market but account for one-third of European imports. Geographical factors, as well as the existence of preferential agreements between France, Italy, and the United Kingdom on the one hand, and their former colonies on the other, largely explain these differences in the origin of imports.

We have projected some decline in cocoa and tea prices while a slight rise in the price of robusta coffee has been assumed. Correspondingly, in 1975, the imports of noncompeting tropical foods into developed countries would amount to $4.5 billion measured in 1960 prices as well as in current prices. The 44 per cent increase of imports between 1960 and 1975 represents an annual rate of growth of 1.3 per cent in per capita imports, corresponding to an income elasticity of import demand of 0.5.

Among developed countries, Japan is likely to show the largest rise of imports from $22 million in 1960 to $189 million in 1975, as coffee and cocoa become more popular in Japan and restrictions on imports are removed. Increases will be more modest in North America and Western Europe. In the United States and Canada, the per capita consumption of bananas and tea will hardly change although some increases are expected in regard to coffee and cocoa. Increases in per capita consumption will be larger in Western Europe, but population growth will also be slower here so that the rise in the total imports of noncompeting tropical foodstuffs will be about 40 per cent in both areas. Finally, stagnating tea consumption will retard the growth of imports in Australia, New Zealand, and South Africa.

As regards individual commodities, imports of bananas, coffee, and cocoa are all expected to rise by about one-half between 1960 and 1975, but the increase in the value of cocoa imports will be reduced by reason of the assumed decline in cocoa prices. Smaller increases are likely to be forthcoming in the case of tea, since per capita consumption in the main tea consuming countries will hardly change and a fall in tea prices is also foreseen. Finally, only modest increases have been projected in the consumption and imports of spices.

By reason of the poor prospects for tea, Asian exports of noncompeting tropical products will rise relatively little. At the same time, the largest gains are likely to be derived by the exporters of Africa who are expected to increase their market share in all commodities. The Common Market preferential tariff will give advantage to the African producers of bananas, African exports will be benefited by the increased use of robusta coffee, and much of the gain in cocoa exports will also accrue to African countries since Latin-American producers are not likely to repeat their 1960 export performance for some time. Correspondingly, African exports of noncompeting tropical foods would rise by nearly four-fifths between 1960 and 1975, accounting for 30 per cent of the exports of noncompeting tropical foods from developing areas as compared to 25 per cent in 1960.

3.5 AGRICULTURAL RAW MATERIALS

Materials of animal[7] and vegetable[8] origin come in this category. Rubber is one of the most important foreign exchange-earning crops of the less developed countries with exports to developed areas amounting to $1,072 million in 1960. The corresponding figures for the other agricultural raw materials are: cotton, $727 million; wool and silk $281; forest products; $350; hides and skins, $219; jute, $139; hard fibers, $177; and animal and vegetable matter $181 million. All in all, exports of agricultural raw materials to developed countries amounted to $3.1 billion in 1960, accounting for 16 per cent of the export earnings of less developed areas.

Three-fifths of these exports go to Western Europe, one-fifth to North America, 15 per cent to Japan, and a little over 3 per cent to Oceania. The small share of the United States and Canada is explained by the self-sufficiency of this region in hides and skins, its export surplus in forest products and cotton, the high proportion of synthetics in its consumption of rubber, and the substantial degree of U.S. tariff protection on wool. By comparison, Western Europe is a large importer of all agricultural raw materials, and Japanese imports of cotton, forest products, and jute also exceed those of North America.[9] Finally, Australia, New Zealand, and South Africa import chiefly rubber and forest products from less developed areas.

Hides and skins originate in a variety of developing countries while rubber comes mostly from Malaya and Indonesia. Within the category of forest products, the United States purchases tropical timber chiefly in Latin America while Japan and Australia import from Southeast Asia, and the countries of Western Europe from Africa. Among developing countries, Argentina and Uruguay are exporters of wool, cotton comes from Egypt, Sudan, Syria, and Peru, jute from Pakistan, and hard fibers from the former British East Africa, the Philippines, and Brazil.

Prospective export earnings derived from the sale of rubber and textile fibers will be greatly affected by the competition of synthetics that bear influence on prices as well as on quantities consumed. The price of natural rubber would have to fall, for example, from 38.2 cents per pound in 1960[10] to possibly 22–23 cents in order

---

[7]Hides and skins, silk and wool.

[8]Rubber, forest products, cotton, jute, and other vegetable fibers.

[9]Note here that the United States imports mostly jute cloth rather than raw jute.

[10]Quotations refer to the New York price of No. 1. RSS II. rubber.

to clear the market, so that, despite the increasing volume of trade, a decline in the value of exports is expected. Similar conclusions apply to jute and gains shown in apparel fibers will be also mitigated by the expected weakening of prices.

Note further that, with the continuing shift toward the use of synthetic rubber, the increase in the demand for natural rubber in the period 1960–1975 is not likely to exceed 40 per cent as against the projected 72 per cent rise in the consumption of all rubber. Synthetics will also gain at the expense of natural fibers and fiber consumption is expected to expand at a slower rate than that of rubber. On the other hand, developing countries are likely to get a larger share in the market for cotton and wool so that their exports of apparel fibers may rise by about 40 per cent during the period of projection, against which an approximately 7 per cent decline in prices should be set. Exports of hard fibers may grow at about the same rate but trade in hides and skins and miscellaneous animal and vegetable materials will expand more slowly.

Within the agricultural exports of the developing countries, the prospects for forest products are the most favorable. With the growing demand for teak and rosewood furniture in the United States, the decline in the amount of quality wood available in Western Europe, and the increased reliance on imported timber in Japan, the volume of the exports of forest products from developing areas may surpass the 1960 level two-and-half times by 1975. Export earnings derived from the sale of tropical timber will be further augmented by the expected rise in prices amounting possibly to 15 per cent between 1960 and 1975.

With regard to agricultural raw materials taken as a whole, the projected fall in the prices of textile fibers and rubber is likely to predominate, however. Thus, while the volume of exports may reach 150 per cent of the 1960 level in 1975, the value of exports is estimated to rise only by 30 per cent, with forest products accounting for over two-thirds of an absolute increase of $1 billion.

By reason of the preponderance of rubber in U.S. imports, the value of imports of agricultural raw materials into North America will hardly change. At the same time, a 30 per cent increase is expected in imports into Western Europe, a 50 per cent rise in imports into Oceania and South Africa, and almost a doubling in Japan. In the latter case, the projected tripling in the imports of forest products would be the main contributing factor.

Differences in prospective trends for individual materials are responsible for the disparate prospects of the various exporting regions. Chiefly by reason of the rapid rise in the demand for tropical timber, the largest expansion would occur in the exports of Africa, while Latin-American producers would benefit from the expected increase in their market shares in wool and cotton. At the same time, the fall in rubber prices would lead to a decline in the value of exports of agricultural raw materials originating in Asia between 1960 and 1970, and, despite the projected trebling of timber exports from the Philippines and the islands of Greater Borneo, export earnings derived from the sale of agricultural raw materials in this area may rise by only 14 per cent during the period 1960–1975. The corresponding estimates are 53 per cent for Africa and 47 per cent for Latin America.

3.6 FUELS

Fuels—at the present almost exclusively crude petroleum and petroleum products—loom large in the exports of less developed countries. In 1960, the f.o.b. value of their fuel exports to developed economies was $5.1 billion—over 25 per cent of the value of total exports. But whereas, with a few exceptions, such as bananas, domestic enterprises predominate in the field of agriculture, the exploitation of oil takes place largely in the framework of foreign companies and a substantial part of the f.o.b. value of exports accrues to the latter. In 1960, for example, the repatriated profits of the oil companies amounted to $1.6 billion so that the foreign exchange earnings of less developed countries derived from the sale of fuels did not surpass $3.5 billion. However, following general usage, we deal with the f.o.b. value of exports under merchandise trade and will consider the profits of oil companies separately under service items.

The Middle East is the leading exporter of petroleum, with exports valued at $2.7 billion in 1960. Middle Eastern oil goes chiefly to Western Europe but increasing quantities are exported also to North America, Japan, and Oceania. Venezuela is the main supplier of the United States, although Venezuela, Trinidad, and the Netherlands Antilles sell petroleum and petroleum products to Western Europe, too. As yet, smaller quantities originate in Africa (Algeria, Libya, Nigeria) and Indonesian oil exports have risen little in recent years.

Although the income elasticity of demand for energy is below unity in highly industrialized countries, imports of fuels are expected to rise at a rate exceeding that of GNP by reason of the shift from coal to oil in Western Europe, Japan, and Oceania.

According to our projections, fuel imports measured in 1960 prices would increase at an average annual rate of 6.4 per cent in the period of projection, reaching $12.5 billion in 1975 (this figure includes $365 million worth of natural gas). But prices have fallen since 1960 and, in view of the pressure brought on prices as a result of the incentives provided for the expansion of oil production at present price and cost levels, a return to prices observed in 1960 is not anticipated. We have assumed a 15 per cent decline in the price of petroleum and petroleum products from the level experienced in 1960 so that the value of fuel imports from developing countries would be $11.1 billion in 1975. The largest increases are foreseen in Japan, followed by Western Europe and Oceania, while the rise of U.S. imports may not exceed 40 per cent.

In the United States and Canada, the shift from solid to liquid fuels has been largely accomplished by 1960 and hence the demand for petroleum is expected to grow at about the same rate as energy consumption as a whole. However, increases in import quotas may, to some extent, raise the share of imports in domestic consumption. At the same time, imports of natural gas from Mexico are likely to remain small.

On the other hand, given the relatively high production cost of European coal, a decline in coal production is expected in Western Europe and—despite larger coal purchases from the United States— a fall in the consumption of coal is foreseen. Also, nuclear energy is not likely to supply a substantial proportion of European energy consumption before 1980 and, with the exception of a few countries in Northern and Southern Europe, only a moderate expansion in the production of hydroelectricity is anticipated. Thus, the 70 per cent increase of energy consumption in Western Europe will necessitate an approximately threefold rise in the consumption of oil and natural gas between 1960 and 1975. Given the relatively small domestic production of petroleum, oil imports would rise *pari passu* with consumption, while an increasing proportion of natural gas consumption would be satisfied from Algeria.

Developments in Japan will follow a similar pattern, except that an absolute decline in coal consumption is not foreseen. But, with the rapid growth of GNP, energy consumption will rise at a more rapid rate than in Western Europe so that imports of petroleum may nearly quadruple during the period of projection. The shift from solid to liquid fuels will be less pronounced in Oceania and South Africa, although oil imports will rise to a considerable extent from the low level observed in 1960. Finally, by reason of the continuing tendency to locate refineries in consuming centers, the share of crude petroleum is expected to increase somewhat in the oil imports of all areas.

As to the origin of imports, the entry of Africa as a large producer and exporter of petroleum and natural gas should be noted. We have projected the value of African fuel exports to rise from $176 million in 1960 to $2,354 million in 1975, of which $337 million would be natural gas. At the same time, Indonesia will benefit from the growth of Japanese consumption while exports from the middle East and Latin America are projected to increase by 82 and 55 per cent, respectively. The relatively low rate of increase of Latin-American exports would be due to the slow growth of U.S. imports and the cost disadvantage of Venezuelan as compared to Middle Eastern oil.

3.7 NONFUEL MINERALS AND METALS

This category includes iron ore, nonferrous ores, concentrates, and unwrought metal, metal scrap, crude fertilizer, and a variety of miscellaneous minerals. Within a total of $3.0 billion, copper is of greatest importance for the less developed countries, with exports amounting to $1.2 billion in 1960. Iron ore occupies second place ($517 million), with tin ($248), bauxite and aluminum ($181), manganese ($125), lead ($90), and zinc ($70) following. In the same year, the exports of all other nonferrous metals taken together were valued at $216 million, those of metal scrap $89 million, and crude fertilizers, $248 million.

Western Europe is the largest importing area for all metals except bauxite and aluminum, while the countries of North America possess large deposits of several metals and provide a substantial proportion of their metal requirements from domestic sources. Canada is, in fact, a net exporter of all major metals excepting tin and imports bauxite for re-exportation in metal form. The countries of Oceania, too, are net exporters of metals; Japan, however, relies on imports for much of her needs.

Ownership relationships and propinquity are the principal factors determining the geographical distribution of trade in metals. With the exception of tin and manganese, the United States and Canada buy minerals and metals chiefly from Latin America. Africa provides, however, for over 40 per cent of U.S. imports of manganese while Malaya and Indonesia are the chief suppliers of tin. On the other hand, Latin America takes second place to African producers in European mineral and metal imports, and Japan purchases much of her iron ore, bauxite, manganese and copper from Asia.

With the exception of aluminum, the consumption of the various metals in the industrial countries is projected to expand at a rate lower than the growth of GNP; yet the imports of most of these metals are expected to rise more rapidly than the increase of aggregate output by reason of the reduced relative importance of domestic sources of supply in consuming countries and the increased share of developing countries in world trade. The shift from the exportation of lesser-valued ores and concentrates to higher-valued unwrought metals will further benefit the developing economies. Correspondingly, the value of exports of nonfuel minerals and metals from less developed areas would grow at an annual rate of 5 per cent to reach $6.2 billion at constant prices and $6.1 billion at current prices by 1975.[11] The difference between the two figures is explained by the projected decline in copper and aluminum prices as against increases in the price of tin.

Among importing areas, metal consumption in Japan is expected to rise more rapidly than in Western Europe and, with the sole exception of zinc where the Japanese resource endowment is more favorable, imports will also increase at a higher rate. Differences in the rate of growth of imports are reduced, however, if only purchases from less developed areas are considered since the latter are likely to gain in the European market at the expense of Canada and the United States, while a larger proportion of Japanese imports of iron ore and aluminum will come from Oceania. Finally, as far as prospective increases in the value of imports are concerned, the differences are minor; we have projected an increase of 138 per cent to take place during the period 1960–1975 in Japan as against 132 per cent in Western Europe. These results are explained by the more pronounced shift from the importation of ores and concentrates to unwrought metal in Western Europe as compared to Japan. This disparity is of especial importance in the case of aluminum where processing costs—and hence differences in the unit values of bauxite, alumina, and aluminum—are the largest.

By comparison, the increase in the value of exports of nonfuel

---

[11]Note that, similar to the case of fuels, a considerable portion of the value of ores, concentrates, and metals originating in developing countries accrues to foreign companies. Although information on the amount of repatriated earnings is limited, in 1960 these profits may have amounted to about $0.5 billion, 15–20 per cent of the value of exports.

minerals and metals from less developed areas to the countries of North America (chiefly the United States) may not exceed two-thirds during the period under consideration. On the one hand, metal consumption in North America is expected to rise at a lower rate than in Western Europe or Japan; on the other, a larger part of the increase in domestic requirements may be supplied from within the region. Finally, note that in view of the U.S. system of quota regulations on zinc and lead imports and the preponderant role of domestic aluminum production in satisfying the requirements of the area, the shift toward the importation of metals in processed form will be relatively slow.

Among individual metals, the consumption of aluminum is expected to rise at the highest rate in all industrial countries, while iron ore leads with respect to the projected rate of increase in the volume of imports from less developed areas by reason of the slow expansion of domestic production in the importing countries. Nevertheless, the shift from lower-valued ores and concentrates to higher-valued unwrought metals in the exports of developing countries will place aluminum and zinc ahead of iron ore as far as the value of trade is concerned. Our projections entail an over fivefold increase in the value of the exports of aluminum ore and metal from the less developed countries in the period 1960–1975, as against an approximately 150 per cent rise in the case of zinc and 140 per cent for iron ore.[12] At the same time, the value of the exports of copper may increase by about 80 per cent, that of manganese and lead 60 per cent, and tin 40 per cent, while a doubling of exports has been projected in regard to ferroalloys other than manganese. The supply of metal scrap available for export in the developing countries is likely to be reduced, however, and relatively modest changes are expected in regard to crude fertilizers.

Prospective increases in the importation of nonfuel minerals and metals will benefit chiefly the producers of Africa and Latin America. African producers are expected to increase their share in European imports of all metals, while much of the increase of imports into North America will come from Latin-American countries. But African producers will also export increasing quantities

---

[12] These differences are explained if we consider that in 1960 the average unit value of bauxite traded was $60–$70 per ton of the aluminum content as compared to $130–$140 for alumina, and $480–$490 for aluminum, while the corresponding figures for zinc concentrates and metal were $130 and $250, respectively. On the other hand, it has been assumed that iron would continue to be shipped in the form of ore.

of iron ore, copper, and aluminum to the United States, and Latin-American exports to Western Europe, too, will expand. All in all, the value of African exports has been estimated to increase one and one-half times between 1960 and 1975, with aluminum accounting for one-third of an absolute increase of $1.5 billion. A rise of 80 per cent is projected for Latin America, while smaller gains will be obtained by the countries of Asia by reason of the importance of tin in their exports.

3.8 MANUFACTURED GOODS

Manufactured products have only recently assumed importance in the exports of developing countries. While in 1953 these countries exported manufactured goods to developed economies in the value of $0.4 billion, exports surpassed one billion dollars in 1960 and accounted for about 5 per cent of the value of total exports. Slightly less than one-half of these exports went to North America and to Western Europe, respectively, 7 per cent to Oceania, and practically nothing to Japan.

Among the commodities included in this category, textile products lead with exports of $593 million in 1960, followed by chemicals ($119 million), silver, pearls, and precious metals ($94 million), leather and footwear ($81 million), veneer and plywood ($50 million), machinery and metal manufactures ($42 million), and other manufactured goods $96 million.

Within the textile group, cotton textiles ($316 million) and jute manufactures ($175 million) are the principal items. Trade in textile products is determined to a considerable extent by the existence of formal or informal quotas in many of the importing countries. The two largest importers of cotton textiles from developing areas, the United States and the United Kingdom, rely largely on an informal system of quotas, while quantitative restrictions are formal—and rather more severe—elsewhere. At the same time, the United States, Australia, and New Zealand freely admit jute manufactures, but imports are restricted in Western Europe.

In view of the limitation of textile imports by quotas, the play of competitive forces will have little impact on prospective changes in this trade. With regard to cotton textiles, we have assumed that the International Cotton Textiles Agreement would continue until 1975, while existing patterns of trade in jute manufactures, floor coverings, and other textile products have been assumed to be maintained through the period of projection.

Correspondingly, the imports of textiles would approximately double during the period 1960–1975, although increases would be considerably smaller in the case of jute manufactures. At the same time, given the high income elasticity of demand for luxury products, the imports of various goods such as perfume materials, hand-woven carpets, worked silver and precious metals, and pearls, may nearly triple. But the largest expansion is foreseen in the plywood and veneer exports of the developing countries, partly because of the rapid growth of the consumption of veneer products, and partly because of the shift toward the exportation of timber in processed form in Southeast Asia.

Taken together, the exports of manufactured goods from developing to developed countries have been projected to rise at an annual rate of 5.5 per cent, exceeding the increases estimated for fuels and for nonfuel minerals and metals. By reason of increased imports of cotton textiles into the countries of Continental Europe, the share of Western Europe would increase somewhat to reach 50 per cent of exports totaling $2.4 billion in 1975. At the same time, little change is expected in the export shares of the individual regions.

CHAPTER 4

Import Requirements of Less Developed Areas and the Trade Gap

4.1. ECONOMIC GROWTH IN DEVELOPING COUNTRIES

WHEREAS THE foreign exchange earnings developing countries derive from their exports to developed economies can be estimated with some degree of confidence, the error possibilities multiply as we get to the projection of import requirements. Imports into developing countries, as well as the geographical and the commodity composition of these imports, are greatly influenced by the rate of economic growth and structural changes in these economies, and past relationships between incomes and imports can be of only limited use in making projections. At the same time, a considerable degree of uncertainty surrounds the growth prospects of less developed areas.

Economic growth in developing countries is affected by a number of economic and noneconomic factors. Among the economic determinants of growth, we may single out the rate of saving, the expansion of exports, the process of import substitution, and the inflow of foreign capital. But available information concerning the effects of these variables on the growth rate and their interrelationship in the process of economic development is not sufficient to derive quantitative relationships in the form of an economic model that could be used for purposes of projection. At the same time, prospective changes in saving ratios can hardly be predicted and neither can the extent of import substitution nor the magnitude of the future capital inflow be foreseen with confidence. Moreover, a host of noneconomic variables (political and social structure, attitudes to work and risk taking, etc.) bear influence on the process of economic growth but these are not quantifiable and are likely to undergo changes over time.

Thus, any projection of future growth rates in developing countries will necessarily involve a large margin of error. In arriving at some tentative figures in the present study, consideration has been given to past trends, as well as to national plans, projections on export earnings, and information on prospective developments. But account had to be taken of the fact that national plans provide growth targets rather than projections and these targets often prove to be overly optimistic.

As in the case of developed economies, two income variants have been distinguished in regard to developing areas (Latin America, Africa, Middle East, Asia), a "most likely" and a "high" or target alternative. The two variants are related to the income alternatives postulated for developed countries since the expansion of the exports of less developed areas is dependent on the rate of growth realized in developed economies. Further, the attainment of the target rate of economic growth in the developing countries presupposes the successful implementation of growth-oriented economic policies and a substantial capital inflow.

The assumed growth rates as well as data for past periods are shown in Table 4.1.1 while a comparison with the estimates of other researchers are given in Table 4.1.2. As regards the years 1950–1960, differences in the results for the 1950–1955 and 1955–1960 subperiods should be noted. These differences are largely explained by favorable world market conditions for primary products during and immediately following the Korean War and a slackening in the growth of exports afterward.[1] For purposes of the subsequent discussion, the period 1950–1960 is considered as a unit, however.

Various factors would point to an acceleration of economic growth in the case of Latin America. Given the large differences shown in the growth rates of individual countries during the fifties and the increasing relative importance of countries with a better growth performance, a continuation of past rates of growth in all countries of the area would lead to higher growth rates for the entire region. Further, our projections indicate an improvement in the export prospects of Latin America, inasmuch as exports have been estimated to rise at an annual rate of 2.8 per cent in the period 1960–1975, as against 2.4 per cent in 1950–1960,[2] and the

---

[1]According to UN statistics, the f.o.b. value of exports of the developing countries rose by 24 per cent between 1950 and 1955 and 15 per cent between 1955 and 1960 [*19*].

[2]The projections refer to estimated changes in the value of exports to developed countries and the Soviet bloc under the assumption that the most likely income variant is realized in developed economies (Tables 3.5.1 and 4.3.2). Data on extraregional trade for the period 1950–1960 have been derived from [*19*].

TABLE 4.1.1

ECONOMIC GROWTH IN DEVELOPING AREAS[a]

	1950	1955	1960	1970	1975	Annual Rate of Growth				
						1950 to 1955	1955 to 1960	1950 to 1960	1960 to 1970	1970 to 1975
LATIN AMERICA										
Gross Domestic Product	40,650	51,140	61,750	I 94,100 / II 100,600	I 117,800 / II 130,900	4.7	3.8	4.0	4.3 / 5.0	4.6 / 5.4
Population	160.7	181.1	204.7	263	299	2.4	2.5	2.4	2.6	2.6
Gross Domestic Product per Capita	252.9	282.4	301.7	I 357 / II 382	I 394 / II 437	2.2	1.3	1.8	1.7 / 2.4	2.0 / 2.7
AFRICA										
Gross Domestic Product	14,750	18,160	21,720	I 32,500 / II 35,100	I 40,500 / II 45,600	4.3	3.6	3.9	4.1 / 4.9	4.4 / 5.4
Population	197.8	217.8	240.9	300	338	1.9	2.0	2.0	2.2	2.4
Gross Domestic Product per Capita	74.5	83.4	90.2	I 108 / II 117	I 119 / II 135	2.3	1.6	1.9	1.9 / 2.7	2.0 / 2.9
MIDDLE EAST										
Gross Domestic Product	4,340	5,750	7,300	I 11,000 / II 12,100	I 13,700 / II 15,800	5.8	4.9	5.3	4.2 / 5.2	4.4 / 5.5
Population	39.4	45.1	51.7	67	76	2.7	2.8	2.8	2.7	2.6
Gross Domestic Product per Capita	110.1	127.5	141.2	I 163 / II 181	I 178 / II 208	3.0	2.1	2.5	1.6 / 2.5	1.8 / 2.8
ASIA										
Gross Domestic Product	45,500	57,100	68,750	I 103,700 / II 109,900	I 129,300 / II 141,600	4.6	3.8	4.2	4.2 / 4.8	4.5 / 5.2
Population	651.0	716.1	797.1	1,010	1,140	1.9	2.2	2.1	2.4	2.5
Gross Domestic Product per Capita	69.9	79.7	86.2	I 103 / II 109	I 113 / II 124	2.6	1.5	2.1	1.8	2.0
DEVELOPING COUNTRIES, TOTAL										
Gross Domestic Product	105,240	132,150	159,520	I 241,300 / II 257,700	I 301,000 / II 333,900	4.7	3.8	4.3	4.2 / 4.9	4.5 / 5.3
Population	1,048.9	1,160.1	1,294.4	1,640	1,853	2.0	2.2	2.1	2.4	2.5
Gross National Product per Capita	100.3	113.9	123.2	I 147 / II 157	I 162 / II 180	2.6	1.6	2.1	1.8	2.0

Sources: U.N. Yearbook of National Accounts Statistics, Growth of the World Population, and Statistical Yearbook; paid other U.N. documents, IMF, International Financial Statistics.

Note: [a]Gross Domestic Product in millions at 1950 prices, population in millions, Gross Domestic Product per capita in 1950 dollars.

Alliance for Progress program is also expected to have beneficial effects on the region's growth.

On the other hand, the projected increase in exports, taken by itself, does not warrant a high rate of growth of GDP, while changes in the pattern of import substitution promise difficulties for future expansion. In the period 1950–1960, import substitution in consumer goods was an important factor contributing to economic growth but much of the possibilities for import substitution in these commodities have by now been exhausted. In the words of Raul Prebisch: "The stage of easy substitution is past. It was relatively easy to substitute imports of industrial items of current consumption and of some durable consumer goods, and there is little left to substitute in this field in Latin America [9, p. 105]."

TABLE 4.1.2

ESTIMATES OF GROWTH RATES OF GNP IN DEVELOPING COUNTRIES
(average annual rates)

	A Rosenstein-Rodan		B FAO		C Our Estimates			
			1958	1970	1960-70		1970-75	
	1961-71	1971-76	Low	High	I	II	I	II
Latin America								
Gross Domestic Product	4.1	4.6	4.4	5.2	4.3	5.0	4.6	5.4
Population	2.6	2.7	2.5	2.5	2.6	2.6	2.6	2.6
GDP per Capita	1.5	1.9	1.9	2.7	1.7	2.4	2.0	2.7
Africa								
Gross Domestic Product	3.0	3.5	3.8	5.2	4.1	4.9	4.4	5.4
Population	1.6	1.6	2.4	2.4	2.2	2.2	2.4	2.4
GDP per Capita	1.4	1.9	1.4	2.7	1.9	2.7	2.0	2.9
Middle East								
Gross Domestic Product	4.3	4.5	3.6	4.9	4.2	5.2	4.4	5.5
Population	2.1	1.9	2.3	2.3	2.7	2.7	2.6	2.6
GDP per Capita	2.2	2.6	1.3	2.5	1.6	2.5	1.8	2.8
Asia								
Gross Domestic Product	4.3	4.5	3.6	4.9	4.2	4.8	4.5	5.2
Population	2.1	1.9	2.3	2.3	2.4	2.4	2.5	2.5
GDP per Capita	2.2	2.6	1.3	2.5	1.8	2.4	2.0	2.7

Sources: A--Rosenstein-Rodan: "International Aid for Underdeveloped Countries," Review of Economic and Statistics, May, 1961, pp. 107-37.
B--FAO, Agricultural Commodities--Projections for 1970, pp. A 3-4.
C--Table 4.1.1.

Substitution in the case of capital goods is more difficult and it requires substantial investment. At the same time, the prospects for the inflow of foreign capital during the sixties are rather poor and much of domestic savings is still not channeled to productive occupations in the domestic economy. If we also consider the disruptive effects of political uncertainty in some of the larger Latin-American countries (Argentina, Brazil) during the early sixties, it appears questionable whether we can assume an acceleration of economic growth in the period 1960–1970 under the "most likely" income alternative.

Higher growth rates could be reached in the years following, however, and faster growth would correspond to our high (target) income variant (Table 4.1.1). Still, the latter (5.1 per cent for 1960–1970 and 5.4 per cent for 1970–1975) is lower than the target rates shown in national plans which range from 5.5 per cent in Chile to 8.0 per cent in Bolivia.[3] But an examination of these plans suggests that they are often based on overly optimistic assumptions as regards the prospects for exports and the possibilities of import substitution.

Among less developed areas, Africa is expected to show the highest rate of growth of exports during the period of projection (5.4 per cent), but the same rate of increase of exports was experienced during the fifties when the gross domestic product only grew at an annual rate of 3.9 per cent. Still, with a more rapid expansion in the production of commodities for domestic consumption in the newly independent countries, an improvement in the growth performance of this region is expected, although the transfer of political power may involve some dislocation of economic activity in a few countries.

For purposes of projection, we have calculated with a growth rate of 4.1 per cent for the period 1960–1970 and 4.5 per cent for 1970–1975 under the most likely income assumption, and 4.9 and 5.4 per cent for the two periods, respectively, under the target income alternative. Note further that relatively few African countries published economic plans and several of these plans do not include a growth target. In cases when growth targets are available, considerable intercountry differences are shown—reflecting perhaps more the optimism of the planners than a realistic appraisal of the possibilities for economic growth.[4]

Among developing areas, the Middle East experienced the highest rate of growth of GDP and exports during the fifties; 5.3 and 9.6 per cent respectively. Our projections indicate a slowing down in the expansion of exports, however, with an annual rate of increase of 4.1 per cent for 1960–1975. Correspondingly, the growth

[3]Representative target rates are: Bolivia, 8.0 percent for the period 1958–1971 [*10*]; Brazil, 7.0 per cent for 1962–1965 [*11*]; Chile, 5.5 per cent for 1961–1970 [*12*]; Colombia, 5.6 or 6.5 per cent for 1958–1970 [*13*]; Peru 5.9 per cent for 1960–1970 [*14*]; and Venezuela, 7 per cent for 1962–1975 [*15*].
[4]The relevant figures are: the United Arab Republic, 7.2 per cent for the period 1960–1970 [*17*]; Morocco, 6.1 per cent for 1958–1964 [*16*]; and Nigeria, 4.0 per cent for 1960–1968 [*2*].

of incomes is bound to slow down and it appears questionable whether the rate of increase of GDP would exceed that of exports by a substantial margin.[5]

As far as prospective changes in export performance are concerned, the situation in Asia is similar to that of Latin America inasmuch as a 2.8 per cent annual increase in exports has been projected for the period 1960–1975 as compared to 2.5 per cent in the fifties. But Asia, too, faces the problem that further possibilities for import substitution in consumer goods are limited [23, p. 59]. Taking account also of institutional rigidities observed in several of the Asian countries, an acceleration of economic growth for the sixties has not been projected under the most likely income assumption, although our high income alternative (4.8 per cent) roughly corresponds to planned targets in the larger countries of the area.[6] Higher rates of growth would be reached in the early seventies.

For the developing areas, taken together, our projections indicate a growth rate of 4.2 per cent for the period 1960–1970 and 4.5 per cent for 1970–1975 under the most likely income assumption, and 4.9 and 5.3 per cent in the two periods, respectively, for the high income variant. For the period of projection taken as a whole, the "most likely" growth rates approximately correspond to the rate of increase of GDP shown in the fifties, with improvements expected in the latter part of the period. At the same time, our high income variant is comparable to the 5 per cent target for the Development Decade announced by the United Nations, although here again differences are shown in regard to the two subperiods.

Note, however, that the prospects appear to be less favorable if calculation is made in per capita terms. Due to the expected upsurge of the population, a continuation of growth rates experienced during the fifties would lead to a decline in the rate of increase of per capita incomes, although an improvement would be shown as compared to the second half of the fifties. But even if the target income alternative were realized, the corresponding annual increase of 2.5 per cent in per capita incomes would entail a widening in the absolute gap between living standards in developed countries

---

[5]A more optimistic view is expressed in the economic plan for Iran where an annual growth rate of over 8 per cent has been assumed [8].

[6]Planned targets are: the Federation of Malaya, 4.4 per cent for 1961–1965; India, 5.0 per cent for 1961/62–1965/66; Pakistan, 4.8 per cent for 1960/61–1964/65; the Philippines, 6.0 per cent for 1963–1967; and Thailand, 5.0 per cent for 1961–1966. A higher rate of growth is planned in some of the smaller countries: Ceylond, 8.8 per cent; Taiwan 8.0 per cent; South Korea, 7.1 per cent; as well as Burma, 7.6 per cent [22, p. 3].

and in the less developed areas, given that per capita incomes have been projected to rise at a rate of 2.0 per cent in North America, 2.9 per cent in Western Europe, and 4.4 per cent in Japan under the most likely income assumption, and 2.5, 3.4, and 5.4 per cent under the high income variant (Tables 2.2.1 and 2.6.5).

4.2. IMPORT REQUIREMENTS IN DEVELOPING COUNTRIES

Given the assumed rate of growth of GDP in the developing regions, the next question concerns the relationship between incomes and imports. Estimation may proceed by utilizing information provided by cross-section data, time series observations, and national plans. The first method has been suggested by Hollis B. Chenery who claimed that the results of cross-section regressions calculated from data of 62 countries for the period 1952–1954 would indicate systematic changes in imports as development proceeds [1]. In Chenery's calculations, per capita imports have been taken to depend on per capita income and population:

(1)
$$M/N = A_0 Y/N^a N^\beta$$

When M = imports, Y = National income, N = population, and A_0 is a constant.

The results show α to be equal to 0.987 while β is -0.281. Thus, other things being equal, per capita imports would rise at a rate slightly lower than the growth of incomes per head, while a larger population would be associated with smaller per capita imports. According to Chenery, the negative coefficient of population indicates the decline of imports due to an increase in market size, since population is taken as a proxy for extent of the market, while "an increase in market size lowers costs and thus permits the substitution of domestic production for imports" [1, p. 645].

Should these results be applied in estimating future imports, the growth of population in the developing countries would be accompanied by declining imports per head. For example, if per capita incomes were to grow at an annual rate of 1.8 per cent and population at a rate of 2.4 per cent a year,[7] imports per head would rise at an annual rate of 1.1 per cent. Correspondingly, the increase in total imports would be 2.9 per cent a year as against a 4.2 per cent rise in the gross domestic product.

---

[7] The weighted average of our estimates for developing countries in the period 1960–1970 as shown in Table 4.1.1.

Doubts arise about the applicability of this method in forecasting, however. We have noted above that Chenery regards population as a proxy for market size. Yet the negative import coefficient of population gives expression not only to the "market effect," attributed to the exploitation of large scale economies in a wider market, but also to a "trading effect" which associates a larger number of domestic trading units[8] with a smaller volume of international trade. In other words, the greater the number of trading units in a country, the greater will be, *ceteris paribus,* the relative importance of internal trade, and the smaller the share of imports (exports) in the gross national product. For example, the low propensity to import in the United States as compared to Belgium is, in part, explained by the fact that a larger part of the world population lives in the United States than in Belgium.

But this relationship appears only in a cross-section of individual countries and it does not operate over time, since the growth of population in every country will not alter the relative proportions between domestic and foreign trading units. Thus, the application of the results derived from a cross-section study of country data will impart a downward bias to the projections, and hence this method has not been employed in the present investigation.

The time-series method has deficiencies of its own. With structural changes taking place in the developing economies, the ratio of imports to GDP changes, and shifts occur in the commodity composition of imports. Still a comparison of the experience of regions at different stages of economic development can provide an indication of possible future developments.

Over the period 1950–1961, the total imports of African and Asian countries increased at about the same rate as their gross domestic product, while the total income elasticity of import demand was 1.4 in the case of the Middle East and 0.6 in Latin America. Extra-area imports increased at a higher rate, however, partly because import substitution could be effected with greater ease against the less sophisticated commodities imported from neighboring countries, and partly because the process of industrialization required increasing imports of machinery which were available in industrial countries only. In the period 1955–1961, for which more detailed information is available, we find that the total income elasticity of import demand in Latin America was 0.4 in regard to all imports and 0.5 for extra-area imports, while the cor-

---

[8]For present purposes, the number of trading units has been taken to be identical to the population of particular countries.

TABLE 4.2.1

THE GROSS DOMESTIC PRODUCT AND EXTRA-AREA IMPORTS IN DEVELOPING AREAS[a]
($ million, constant prices)

	Latin America[b]		Africa[c]		Middle East[d]		Asia	
	1955-1956	1960-1961	1955-1956	1960-1961	1955-1956	1960-1961	1955-1956	1960-1961
Food (0,1)	577	731	761	1,180	451	760	818	1,372
Agricultural Raw Materials (SITC 2,4 less 28)	253	394	235	322	142	246	359	587
Fuels (3)	456	383	483	633	80	114	280	407
Minerals, and Metals (28, 67,68)	451	642	268	381	170	300	437	686
Chemicals (5)	641	907	369	584	173	319	547	841
Machinery and transport equipment (7) of which passenger cars and their parts	2,222 (247)	2,662 (294)	1,690 (116)	1,923 (151)	693 (88)	1,043 (128)	1,356 (143)	1,904 (217)
Nondurable manufactured products other than chemicals (6.8 less 67, 68)	1,369	1,182	1,854	1,866	695	796	1,339	1,025
Total (0, -8)	6,059	6,901	5,660	6,889	2,404	3,578	5,136	6,822
Gross National Product	46,100	61,700	21,200	27,600	4,800	7,500	56,200	69,800

Sources: Gross Domestic Product: U.N., Yearbook of National Accounts Statistics and Statistical Yearbook, IMF, International Financial Statistics, various issues.

Trade: U.N., Monthly Bulletin of Statistics, March, April, 1961 and 1963.

Notes: [a]Imports in 1953 prices, gross domestic product in 1950 prices. Data are yearly averages. In regard to various groups of manufactured goods for which U.N. price indices are not available, a weighted average of the export prices of the main industrial countries has been used (Cf. Bela Balassa, "Recent Developments in the Competitiveness of American Industries and Prospects for the Future," U.S. Congress Joint Economic Committee, Factors Affecting the United States Balance of Payments, Washington, 1962, p. 44.

[b]Excluding the Caribbean.

[c]Including South Africa.

[d]Including Egypt, Lybia, Sudan, Somaliland, and Ethiopia.

responding coefficients were 0.9 and 1.0 in Africa, 1.7 and 1.8 in the Middle East, and 1.2 and 1.5 in Asia.

Table 4.2.1 provides information on the gross domestic product and the extra-area imports of various regions in the years 1955–56 and 1960–61 for eight commodity groups in terms of constant prices, while Table 4.2.2 shows the composition of imports for the year 1960 expressed in current prices.[9] It appears that the ratio of extra-area imports to the gross domestic product is the smallest in Latin America and Asia, larger in Africa, and highest in the Middle East. At the same time, nearly one-half of Latin-American imports consist of chemicals, machinery, and transport equipment (other than passenger cars), while this proportion does not exceed one-third in the other areas.

The observed disparities in the time pattern and the composition of imports reflect interregional differences in the process of import substitution and the level of economic development. In Latin America, the industrially most developed region, the ratio of imports to GDP is the lowest and the proportion of capital goods in imports the highest. The large amount of intraregional trade reduces the extra-area import coefficient in Asia, but imports of machinery into this region are still relatively low. Finally, the process of import substitution has barely begun in Africa, while the countries of the Middle East import much of their needs in food, raw materials, and manufactured goods.

Between 1955–56 and 1960–61, the gross domestic product of the countries of Latin America rose by 22 per cent while the increase of extra-area imports was 12 per cent, indicating a total income elasticity of import demand slightly above 0.5. Import substitution in nondurable goods and increased self-sufficiency in petroleum appear to to be chiefly responsible for the observed lowering of the import/GDP ratio. Extra-area imports of nondurable goods (other than chemicals) and fuels declined by about 15 per cent in the above period, while increases have been experienced in all other commodity groups.

With oil exploration proceeding in some of the large fuel-importing countries, (Argentina, Brazil), an increase in the imports of fuels from outside the area may be avoided in the period of projection. On the other hand, many of the possibilities of import

---

[9]Note, however, that comparability is reduced by reason of the fact that, in the absence of information on individual countries, in Table 4.2.1 we had to use the geographical classification of the United Nations instead of the one employed in the present study.

TABLE 4.2.2

EXTRA-AREA IMPORTS OF DEVELOPING AREAS, 1960
($ million, current prices)

	Latin America $m	%	Africa $m	%	Middle East $m	%	Asia $m	%	Developing Areas $m	%
Food (0, 1)	895	10.9	938	15.4	507	18.8	1,241	17.5	3,582	14.9
Agricultural Raw Materials (2,4 less 2,8)	384	4.7	207	3.4	158	5.8	538	7.6	1,287	5.3
Fuels (3)	300	3.7	507	8.4	52	1.9	377	5.3	1,236	5.2
Minerals and Metals (28, 67, 68)	686	8.3	340	5.6	230	8.5	673	9.5	1,929	8.0
Chemicals (5)	898	10.9	427	7.0	194	7.1	655	9.3	2,174	9.0
Machinery and Transport Equipment (7) of	3,348	40.8	1,817	29.8	781	29.0	1,985	28.0	7,931	32.9
which passenger cars and their parts	(340)	(4.1)	(290)	(4.8)	(115)	(4.3)	(236)	(3.3)	(981)	(4.1)
Material intensive manufactures (6, 8 less 67, 68)	1,648	20.1	1,749	28.7	694	25.8	1,540	21.8	5,631	23.4
Miscellaneous (9)	49	0.6	107	1.7	77	3.1	74	1.0	307	1.3
TOTAL	8,209	100.0	6,092	100.0	2,693	100.0	7,083	100.0	24,077	100.0

Sources: U.N., Monthly Bulletin of Statistics, March and April, 1961.
U.N., Commodity Trade Statistics, 1960 and information received from the United Nations Statistical Office.

Note: aNumbers in parentheses refer to SITC categories.

substitution in consumer goods have been exhausted, and hence the importation of these commodities may increase *pari passu* with the growth of population in the future. Also, in conjunction with the expected acceleration in the process of industrialization, imports of machinery and chemicals may rise at a rate exceeding that for the gross domestic product in Latin America. Thus, even though the ratio of imports of foods and raw materials to the gross national product may fall somewhat, the rapid decline of the import/GDP ratio observed during the fifties is unlikely to be repeated. In the present study, we have assumed that a 1 per cent increase in GDP would be associated with a 0.7–0.8 per cent rise in extra-area imports in the years 1960–1975.

These figures can be compared to import targets contained in national plans. With the exception of Brazil, the total income elasticity of import demand derived from information provided in the plans is between 0.6 and 0.9 in the countries of Latin America with Bolivia and Chile at the lower and Venezuela and Peru at the higher end of the scale.[10] At the same time, a perusal of the plans suggests that these countries intend to restrain the increase of imports chiefly in the case of commodities (agricultural products, nondurable consumer goods) that are imported also from neighboring economies, so that the rise of extra-area imports would be greater than the average. In fact, in cases when an appropriate breakdown is given, the imports of capital goods are planned to increase approximately in proportion to the gross domestic product.

A rise in imports over the actual level observed in 1961 has not been envisaged in the plan of Brazil for the period 1963–1965 [11]. But the plan does not specify what instruments would be used to attain this objective. It has been noted, for example, that the planners gave no indication as to how the proposed reduction in machinery imports would be realized and the possible ways of providing for the machinery needs of domestic production of nondurable goods have not been explored. At the same time, a reduction in the import/GDP ratio from the low level attained in 1961 (9 per cent) to 5 per cent in 1965 does not appear plausible [7, p. 148].

Extra-area imports have been rising approximately in proportion to the growth of GDP in Africa. Increases have been experienced in all commodity groups with the exception of nondurable consumer goods. But the area is expected to provide a larger proportion of its fuel needs from domestic sources in the future. Moreover, with

---

[10]For references, see p. 71 above.

the expansion of the production of simple manufactures, extra-area imports of nondurable manufactured products (excluding chemicals), which accounted for 29 per cent of imports in 1960 as compared to 20 per cent in Latin America and 22 per cent in Asia, may decline during the period under consideration. On the other hand, imports of machinery and chemicals will rise at a rapid rate and several of the countries of Africa will have to rely on imports for increasing their consumption of temperate zone foods. Correspondingly, the total income elasticity of import demand is not likely to fall much below unity; in the present study, we have calculated with elasticities of 0.9–1.0.

By comparison, a unitary income elasticity of import demand has been assumed in the Nigerian plan [2] and 1.1 in the economic plan of Morocco [16]. Imports may increase at a lower rate in the United Arab Republic, however, although—for reasons mentioned in connection with the Brazilian plan—the absolute decline in imports envisaged in the Five-Year Plan of Egypt (1960–1965) will hardly be forthcoming. The inadequacies of the plan can be indicated by reference to the statement according to which domestic production would replace *all* mineral imports by 1965 [17, p. 85].

The Middle East, the main petroleum-producing area, has increased its imports at a rate considerably faster than the growth of GDP in the last decade. Given the natural limitations of food production and the lack of manufacturing industries in much of the region, the share of imports in domestic consumption is likely to further increase. In the present study, we have calculated with a total income elasticity of import demand of 1.2. This coefficient has also been used in the Third Plan of Iran [8].

U.S. shipments of food and agricultural raw materials under the P.L. 480 program accounted for much of the increase in Asian imports of foods and beverages in the second half of the fifties. By 1960, the annual value of shipments under P.L. 480 reached $1 million, about two-thirds of which went to Asia [26]. Future changes in these imports will greatly depend on the expansion of domestic production in Asia and the availability of surplus food and other agricultural products from the United States. Given the uncertainties surrounding the prospects of agricultural production in Asia and the P.L. 480 program in the United States, it is difficult to foresee prospective developments although further increases are likely to take place.

Note also that the possibilities for import substitution in nondurable consumer goods have been largely exhausted in Asia and, as in the case of Latin America, the imports of these commodities are likely to increase rather than decline in the future. At the same time, industrialization is expected to require imports of machinery and chemicals to rise at a rate exceeding the growth of GDP. Similar developments are foreseen in regard to fuels, given that most countries of Asia rely on imports for their petroleum needs.

Assuming that the rapid expansion of food imports observed in the second half of the fifties will not continue, the above considerations would indicate an income elasticity of import demand of around unity for Asia. Yet, with the exception of Malaya and Pakistan, the national plans of Asian countries envisage imports rising at a rate lower than the growth of GDP. Much of the import substitution envisaged would take place at the expense of neighboring countries, however, in foodstuffs, agricultural raw materials, and nondurable consumer goods. At the same time, rapid increases in imports of machinery are planned, that come largely from outside the region. Thus, the rate of increase of extra-area imports would exceed that for all imports by a considerable margin.

The perusal of the individual plans has led the UN Economic Commission for Asia and the Far East to conclude that, for the region as a whole, it would be necessary "to increase imports of capital goods and materials for capital goods by 10 per cent a year and total imports by 6 per cent, although the latter figure will be higher if there is insufficient restraint on inflation" [*21,* p. 96]. Given that planned increases in the gross national product average about 5–6 per cent, an income elasticity of import demand slightly exceeding unity is implied in the above statement. In the present study, we have assumed that this elasticity would be about 1.0–1.1.

The projections indicate an increase in the extraregional imports of developing countries from $24.1 billion in 1960 to $34.8–$36.2 billion in 1970 and $42.4–$45.1 billion in 1975 under the most likely income assumption and $37.1–$38.9 and $47.0–$50.5 billion if the target rate of income growth were reached. The largest increases are shown for the Middle East and Asia and a relatively smaller rise in Latin America and Africa (Table 4.2.3).

4.3 TRADE AMONG DEVELOPING REGIONS

Trade among developing regions amounted to $1.6 billion in 1960, accounting for 7 per cent of the combined extra-area exports of these areas. The biggest item was fuel ($589 million), followed by food ($373 million), manufactured goods ($323 million), and

TABLE 4.2.3

EXTRA-AREA IMPORTS INTO DEVELOPING AREAS[a]

	1960	1970I			1970II			1975I			1975II		
		a	b	c	a	b	c	a	b	c	a	b	c
Latin America	8,209	11,030	11,250	11,470	11,580	11,860	12,150	12,910	13,320	13,750	13,950	14,460	15,000
Africa	6,092	8,760	8,930	9,100	9,370	9,590	9,830	10,660	10,990	11,340	11,900	12,320	1,278
Middle East	2,693	4,330	4,400	4,490	4,820	4,930	5,060	5,550	5,700	5,870	6,540	6,790	7,060
Asia	7,083	10,690	10,890	11,100	11,320	11,590	11,870	13,320	13,700	14,100	14,590	15,100	15,660
Developing Countries, Total	24,077	34,810	35,470	36,160	37,090	37,970	38,910	42,440	43,710	45,060	46,980	48,670	50,500

Source: Table 4.2.2.

Note: The following income elasticities of import demand have been used in the calculations: Latin America, 0.7, 0.75, 0.8; Africa, 0.9, 0.95, 1.0; Middle East, 1.15, 1.2, 1.25; and Asia, 1.0, 1.05, 1.1.

agricultural raw materials ($274 million). The Middle East and Asia are the largest exporters; the former accounts for much of the fuels traded among developing regions while the latter exports chiefly textiles, rubber, and jute.

The countries of the Middle East import the largest amount of foodstuffs from other developing economies but, with the shift in purchases to developed countries, these imports have changed little during the fifties. In connection with the rising consumption of tropical foods, increases are expected to be forthcoming during the period of projection, however. Some rise in the exchange of food-stuffs between Africa and Asia is also anticipated and these areas may buy increasing quantities of temperate zone foods from Latin America. On the other hand, the food imports of Latin America from other developing countries are likely to remain small.

In regard to trade in agricultural raw materials among developing areas, shipments from Africa to Asia and from Asia to Latin America are of importance. African countries export mainly cotton and hard fibers, while Asia ships rubber and jute. African exports may continue to rise at the slow rate observed during the fifties, while the expansion of synthetic rubber production will restrict the growth of imports of natural rubber into Latin America. Substantial increases are not expected in regard to other agricultural raw materials either.

Fuel imports into Africa and Asia have been expanding rapidly during the last decade. In view of our previous discussion, Asian imports are likely to rise at a rate exceeding the growth of GDP during the period of projection, while increased self-sufficiency in petroleum will lead to a slowing down in the growth of fuel imports into Africa. At the same time, fuel imports into Latin America and the Middle East—the main exporting areas—will remain small.

There is little trade in minerals and metals among developing regions. Rhodesia exports some copper and Malaya ships tin, but otherwise the metal needs of developing countries are supplied by domestic production and by purchases from industrial countries. The pattern of trade is expected to change during the period of projection, yet the main shift is likely to take the form of substituting domestic production for imports within the individual areas, while trade among developing regions may not increase substantially.

The bulk of trade in manufactures among less developed areas takes the form of textile exports from India and Hong Kong to destinations in Africa, Latin America, and the Middle East. Except for shipments to the Middle East, increases in these exports have been small in recent years, chiefly by reason of the protection of the domestic textile industry in the countries of Latin America and Africa, and this tendency is expected to continue in the future. On the other hand, the exchange of chemicals, leather, rubber goods, and some other nondurable goods may increase further.

All in all, trade among less developed areas has been projected to rise from $1.6 billion in 1960 to $2.2 billion in 1970 and $2.6 billion in 1975 under the most likely income assumption and to $2.3 and $2.9 billion, respectively, if the target rate of income growth were reached (Table 4.3.1.). In the period 1960–1975, taken as a whole, the exports of Latin America, Africa, and the Middle East to other less developed regions would increase by over two-thirds, while Asian exports have been projected to rise by less than one-half. The relatively slow growth of exports from Asia is explained by the continuing process of import substitution against textiles in both Latin America and Africa.

TABLE 4.3.1

DEVELOPING COUNTRIES: EXPORTS TO OTHER LESS DEVEOPED COUNTRIES
($ million, current prices)

	1960	1970I	1970II	1975I	1957II
Latin America	174	250	260	310	320
Africa...........................	327	420	440	520	580
Middle East	570	800	850	990	1,130
Asia............................	539	680	720	790	850
	1,610	2,150	2,270	2,610	2,880

Source: Table A4.3.1.

4.4 EXPORTS OF DEVELOPING COUNTRIES TO THE SINO-SOVIET AREA[11]

Trade between developing countries and the Sino-Soviet area has expanded at a rapid rate in recent years. Exports from less developed areas to Eastern Europe increased from $225 million in 1953–1954 to $1,094 million in 1960–1961, while the corresponding figures for exports to Communist Asia are $174 and $262 million. At the same time the share of the centrally planned economies in

[11]The Sino-Soviet area comprises the centrally planned economies of Eastern Europe excluding Yugoslavia (for short, Eastern Europe) as well as Mainland China, Mongolia, North Korea, and North Vietnam (for short, Communist Asia).

the extra-area exports of developing areas increased from 2.4 per cent in 1953–54 to 5.5 per cent in 1960–61.

A few commodities dominate the imports of the Sino-Soviet area from developing countries. In 1960, the combined imports of cotton, rubber, and sugar into Eastern Europe amounted to $539 million out of total imports of $968 million, while the corresponding figures for Communist Asia were $188 and $275 million. Further commodities of importance are cocoa with imports into the Sino-Soviet area valued at $59 million in 1960; coffee, $42 million; textile yarns and fabrics, $37 million; and wool, $34 million (Table 4.3.1).

This trade has been influenced to a considerable extent by political considerations, as indicated by the expansion of cotton imports from the United Arab Republic after 1955 and the jump in imports of Cuban sugar from 300 thousand tons in 1957–1959 to 2.1 million tons in 1960 and 4.8 million tons in 1961. In fact, the rise in sugar imports between 1960 and 1961 equaled the total increase in the value of imports of the Sino-Soviet area from less developed regions. Given the importance of political factors, any projection of imports into the Sino-Soviet area is subject to a large degree of uncertainty. While available information concerning individual commodities can indicate possible trends in these imports, the magnitude of future changes is difficult to predict. Also, should another Latin-American or African country establish close relationships with the Soviet Union (or Mainland China), drastic changes in import policies may be forthcoming but cannot be foreseen.

Moreover, it is hardly possible to appraise the effects of a further cooling-off of Soviet-Chinese relations on trade with the developing countries although the Soviet Union may be inclined to buy some goods presently purchased from China in less developed areas and the latter might also supply Mainland China with raw materials that are now imported from the Soviet Union. Political considerations, too, may induce China to enlarge her trade with developing countries while economic difficulties may have the opposite effect.

In projecting the future imports of the main agricultural commodities into Eastern Europe, we have used the estimates prepared by the FAO as a point of departure. The FAO estimates have been based on information provided in national plans and official pronouncements in these countries and cover 70 per cent of the imports of Eastern Europe from developing countries [4]. With respect to some further commodities, information derived from the UN *Economic Survey for Europe in 1960* has been utilized, while other imports have been related to the expected increase in the national income of Soviet bloc countries. With consideration given to a possible slowing down in the economic growth of Soviet-type economies, we have projected the national income of the countries of Eastern Europe to increase by about 70 per cent between 1960 and 1970, and 30 per cent in the years 1970–1975.[12]

Information on the prospects for exports into Communist Asia is scarce and long term plans are not available for the countries of this area. Neither does a consideration of past trends provide a clue for future developments since—in response to crop conditions, foreign exchange availabilities, and political factors—imports from developing areas have fluctuated to a considerable extent. In the present study, some simple assumptions have been made in regard to the future course of this trade. In general, it has been assumed that foreign exchange difficulties will restrain the expansion of imports into Communist Asia and that much of the actual increase will take the form of machinery and transport equipment, rather than primary products and simple manufactures supplied by less developed countries.

As elsewhere in this study, 1960 has been taken as the base year for the projections. Trade matrices according to SITC commodity classes have been published by the United Nations [18], while national statistical publications and the FAO *Trade Yearbook* have been utilized in estimating trade flows for individual commodities. In cases where national publications provide information only on quantities traded, value data have been calculated by the use of average unit values in world trade [5].[13] Finally, in estimating the future value of exports to the centrally planned economics, account has been taken of prospective changes in the prices of individual commodities as indicated in Table A1.5.1.

Temperate Zone Foods

The centrally planned economics imported temperate zone foods from underdeveloped areas in the value of $67 million in 1960, hardly exceeding 5 per cent of their total imports from developing countries (Tables 4.4.1 and A4.4.1). Shipments of fruits—citrus fruits as well as dates—to Eastern Europe accounted for much of

---

[12]The assumed average annual rate of growth is 5.5 per cent as against a rate of growth of about 7 per cent indicated in the national plans of these countries for the first half of the sixties [24, III, p. 4].

[13]Sugar imports from Cuba provide an exception. In this case, unit values derived from the *Trade Yearbook* of the U.S.S.R. have been used in regard to those countries of the Sino-Soviet area that publish only quantity data.

TABLE 4.4.1

EXPORTS OF DEVELOPING COUNTRIES TO THE SINO-SOVIET AREA BY COMMODITY GROUP

	1960			1970			1975		
	Eastern Europe	Communist China	Sino-Soviet Area	Eastern Europe	Communist China	Sino-Soviet Area	Eastern Europe	Communist China	Sino-Soviet Area
Temperate Zone Foods	56	11	67	118	16	134	166	22	188
Competing Tropical Foods	146	36	182	334	95	429	355	96	451
Noncompeting Tropical Foods	126	1	127	329	1	330	492	1	493
Raw Materials Agriculture	553	191	744	613	189	802	679	209	888
Fuels	0	2	2	0	4	4	0	5	5
Ores and Base Metals	38	10	48	76	16	92	106	21	127
Manufactured Goods	48	23	71	96	37	133	136	48	184
Total	967	274	1,241	1,566	358	1,924	1,934	402	2,336

Sources: U.N., Monthly Bulletin of Statistics, March and April, 1963, FAO, Trade Yearbook, 1961, and national trade statistics.

these imports although the main suppliers of citrus fruits have been Greece and Spain. Imports of meats are negligible and, if the need for imports of cereals arises, purchases are made in developed countries.

In conformity with projections made by the FAO for citrus fruits [4, p. 29], we have assumed that exports of temperate zone foods from developing areas to Eastern Europe would double within a decade. Smaller increases have been projected for Communist Asia.

Competing Tropical Foods

Until recently, imports of competing tropical foods into centrally planned economics had been small and the area as a whole was a net exporter. This situation changed abruptly in 1960 when the establishment of Soviet political ties with Cuba was accompanied by large purchases of Cuban sugar. Sugar imports into Eastern Europe reached 1.7 million tons in 1960 and 3.8 million tons in 1961 as compared to an average of 0.3 million tons in the years 1957–59. Similar changes have taken place in Mainland China where imports of Cuban sugar rose from 17 thousand tons in 1957–59 to 450 thousand tons in 1960 and 1 million tons in 1961.

Although self-sufficiency in sugar could be insured in Eastern Europe, barring political changes imports from Cuba are expected to continue. The Soviet Union has undertaken a commitment to purchase 3 million tons of raw sugar annually in the period 1962–1965, and we have postulated that imports into Eastern Europe will equal this quantity in 1970 and 1975.[14] It has further been assumed that sugar imports into Mainland China would remain at the level observed in 1961.

The remaining imports of this category consist largely of tropical oils and oilseeds ($27 million in 1960). We have calculated with a doubling of these imports in the period 1960–1970 and a 40 per cent increase between 1970 and 1975. Correspondingly, the exports of competing tropical foods from developing areas to the Sino-Soviet area would rise from $182 million in 1960 to $429 million in 1970 and $451 million in 1975.

Noncompeting Tropical Foods

Foreign exchange considerations have restricted the consumption—and imports—of bananas, coffee, and cocoa in Soviet-type economies while the Soviet Union and China are large producers

---

[14]This estimate is approximately at the midpoint of the 1 to 4–5 million tons range suggested by the FAO [4, p. 40].

of tea. In 1960, imports of noncompeting tropical foods from developing countries amounted to $127 million, of which Communist Asia took $1 million. Chinese imports will hardly rise in the period under consideration, hence we can restrict our discussion to Eastern Europe.

Imports of coffee and cocoa were given low priority in the past but the policy makers announced their intention to permit an expansion of these imports in the future. Nevertheless, there are no firm indications as to the magnitude of this increase during the period under consideration and hence any estimate is necessarily of a tentative character.

In regard to coffee we have accepted the FAO projections which have been based on an analogy as to the pattern of consumption in tea-drinking Russia and in Japan, as well as in Czechoslovakia and Eastern Germany as compared to Italy. Taking the mid-point of the range given in the FAO estimates, we have calculated with per capita consumption of 2.7 kg for Czechoslovakia and Eastern Germany, and 0.5 kg for the Soviet Union and other countries of Eastern Europe in 1970 [4, p. 25]. Correspondingly, coffee consumption (imports) in the area would reach 245 thousand tons in 1970 as compared to about 53 thousand tons in 1960. A further 50 per cent rise in per capita consumption has been assumed for the period 1970–1975.

Czechoslovakia and Eastern Germany are also the largest consumers of cocoa in Eastern Europe. Available information indicates future increases in consumption and imports in these countries. In the present study, we have calculated with per capita consumption of 1.5 kg in 1970 and 1.6 kg in 1975 as compared to 0.9 kg in 1960. These estimates correspond to our projections for France[15] and are in conformity with the FAO forecasts. The latter appear to be on the low side, however, as far as cocoa consumption in the Soviet Union is concerned. With consideration given to trade agreements signed between the U.S.S.R. and several African and Latin-American countries and the announced intention of the Soviet government to raise levels of cocoa consumption, we have assumed that cocoa consumption per head in the Soviet Union, as well as in other countries of Eastern Europe excepting Czechoslovakia and Eastern Germany, would reach 0.4 kg in 1970 and 0.5 kg in 1975, i.e., the levels projected for Yugoslavia.[16] Correspondingly, cocoa

---

[15]Table A 8.2.1.

[16]By comparison the FAO projects per capita cocoa consumption of 0.25 kg in the Soviet Union and 0.45–0.6 kg in the other countries of the group for 1970 [4, p. 26].

imports into Eastern Europe would rise from 92 thousand tons in 1960 to 175 thousand tons in 1970 and 285 thousand tons in 1975.

Banana imports into Eastern Europe were negligible in 1960 but the policy of increasing trade relations with the less developed countries may lead to a considerable expansion of this trade. Nevertheless, given the substitutability of domestic fruits for bananas, it appears unlikely that Western European consumption levels would be approached in this area. We have assumed here that per capita banana consumption in Czechoslovakia and Eastern Germany would reach the level projected for Italy (3.5 kg in 1970 and 4.5 kg in 1975), and that the Yugosalv consumption level would apply to the other countries of Eastern Europe (0.8 kg in 1970 and 1.2 kg in 1975). Banana imports into Eastern Europe would thus reach 290 thousand tons in 1970 and 440 thousand tons in 1975 as compared to 17 thousand tons in 1960.

Finally, despite the expected increase in the degree of self-sufficiency in the Soviet Union, some rise in tea imports into Eastern Europe is likely to be forthcoming and imports of spices may also grow. Taken together, the exports of noncompeting tropical goods from developing areas to Eastern Europe would reach $329 million in 1970 and $492 million in 1975 as against $126 million in 1960.[17]

Agricultural Raw Materials

With a trade value of $744 million, agricultural raw materials accounted for 60 per cent of the total imports of the Sino-Soviet area from less developed countries. Within this category, special attention should be given to cotton and rubber, the imports of which were valued at $298 and $275 million, respectively.

The imports of natural rubber into the countries of Eastern Europe have been increasing rapidly in recent years but, according to the FAO, the expansion of the production of synthetic rubber may lead to a decline of imports in the future. At the midpoint of the range of estimates given by the FAO, natural rubber would account for 10 per cent of total rubber consumption in the Soviet Union and 35 per cent in the other countries of Eastern Europe [*4*, p. 12].

The FAO estimates may be on the low side, however. Although the goal of 95–96 per cent self-sufficiency in rubber has been announced in the U.S.S.R., various considerations suggest that this

---

[17]The maintenance of 1960 imports of $1 million have been projected for Communist Asia.

objective may not in fact be pursued in the foreseeable future. Rather, with the expected 40 per cent decline in the price of natural rubber as compared to 1960, and increased rationality in Soviet planning, it appears plausible that a lower degree of self-sufficiency will be aimed at. For purposes of projection, we have assumed that natural rubber imports would provide 18 per cent of Soviet rubber requirements in 1970 and 16 per cent in 1975, while the corresponding estimates for the other countries of Eastern Europe are 40 per cent in 1970 and 35 per cent in 1975.

The imports of natural rubber into Eastern Europe would thus surpass 1960 imports of 332 thousand tons by a considerable margin in 1970, while the 1961 imports of 493 thousand tons would be reached but not exceeded. However, the latter figure represents the combined effects of delays in the completion of synthetic rubber-producing facilities and stockpiling of natural rubber and can hardly be used as a basis for comparisons. Imports would further rise to possibly 600 thousand tons in 1975. At the same time, we have assumed that all imports would come directly from the producing countries rather than by way of London, augmenting thereby the increase in imports from less developed areas. Finally, a further expansion in the imports of natural rubber into Mainland China has been projected, although this increase may not be sufficient to counterbalance the reduction in the value of imports due to the expected decline in rubber prices, given that China is expected to embark on the production of natural rubber [*3*, p. 11. 84].

Cotton is the leading import of the countries of Eastern Europe from the developing areas, with an import value of $234 million in 1960. But, on the basis of indications given in national plans, the FAO reached the conclusion that prospective increases in the production of cotton and synthetic fibers in the Soviet Union would augment the Russian export surplus in cotton to such an extent as to cover the import needs of the other countries of Eastern Europe [*4*, pp. 16–17]. In the present study, we have assumed that although total imports of cotton into Eastern Europe might decline, purchases from developing countries would remain at levels observed in 1960, partly to fulfill the need for long-staple cotton and partly to maintain trade relations with certain cotton-producing countries (e.g., Egypt). Similar considerations apply to Mainland China.

The FAO also expects some decline in the imports of wool while we have assumed that imports from developing countries would be maintained also in this case. Still, the value of wool imports, as well as those of cotton, would fall somewhat by reason of the expected decline in the prices of these fibers.[18]

The U.S.S.R. has been reported to plan attaining self-sufficiency in jute by 1965 [25, V. p. 15]. Yet jute imports into the other countries of Eastern Europe are likely to rise and, on balance, imports into the entire area may increase somewhat from the level observed in 1960 ($21 million). Finally, imports of agricultural raw materials not included in the above categories, such as hides and skins, tropical timber, other vegetable fibers, animal and vegetable matter, taken together appear to account for $112 million in 1960. However, this figure has been derived as a residual and may hence represent an underestimation in other categories. For purposes of projection, we have calculated with an increase of these imports by one-half between 1960 and 1970 and one-fifth between 1970 and 1975.

Minerals and Metals

The countries of the Sino-Soviet area export oil and several metals and import small quantities of a few minerals, valued at $50 million in 1960, from the less developed areas. We have assumed here that imports would increase at a rate somewhat higher than the national income in these countries. Fuel imports into China would rise at a higher rate, however, if purchases from the Soviet Union were reduced.

Manufactured Goods

Developing countries exported manufactured goods, chiefly textiles, to the Sino-Soviet bloc in the value of $71 million in 1960. According to the UN *Economic Survey for Europe in 1960,* should Eastern European markets be opened to consumer goods manufactured in less developed areas, the imports of these commodities may reach $1.5–$2 billion by 1980 [25, V. p. 18]. But the fulfillment of this prediction would presuppose a major change in trading policies, as well as planning methods, in Eastern Europe and no such changes are contemplated in the countries in question. In the present study, we have assumed that imports would double within a decade, corresponding to a total income elasticity of about 1.3.

Taken together, the exports of developing countries to Eastern Europe have been projected to rise from $0.97 billion in 1960 to $1.57 billion in 1970 and $1.93 billion in 1975, while the correspond-

---

[18]Table A 1.5.1.

TABLE 4.4.2

EXPORTS OF DEVELOPING COUNTRIES TO THE SINO-SOVIET AREA BY THE REGION OF ORIGIN
(current prices)

	1960			1970			1975		
	Eastern Europe	Communist China	Sino-Soviet Bloc	Eastern Europe	Communist China	Sino-Soviet Bloc	Eastern Europe	Communist China	Sino-Soviet Bloc
Latin America	264	42	306	597	103	700	706	104	810
Africa	301	73	374	396	80	476	499	86	585
Middle East	67	7	74	100	6	106	125	6	131
Asia	335	152	487	473	169	642	604	206	810
Developing Countries, Total	967	274	1,241	1,566	358	1,924	1,934	402	2,336

Sources: U.N., Monthly Bulletin of Statistics, March and April, 1963, FAO, Trade Yearbook, 1961, and national trade statistics.

ing figures for Communist Asia are $0.27, $0.36, and $0.40 billion. The largest increases in exports are expected to take place in regard to some competing tropical products, while the prospects for agricultural raw materials are the least favorable. Correspondingly, Latin-American exporters of coffee, cocoa, and bananas would enjoy the greatest gains (Table 4.4.2).

4.5 THE TRADE BALANCE OF LESS DEVELOPED REGIONS

According to our projections, the exports of developing countries to the Sino-Soviet area would rise at a rate somewhat higher than their exports to developed economies.[19] Nevertheless, given the importance of the developed countries as export markets for less developed areas, the export prospects of the latter are little affected by the inclusion of exports to the Sino-Soviet area in the estimates. While exports to developed economies have been projected to increase by 69.5 per cent between 1960 and 1975 under the most likely income assumption and 85.8 per cent if the target rate of income growth is reached, the estimates are 70.7 and 85.9 per cent if trade with the centrally planned economies is included.[20]

In appraising the export prospects of individual areas, account has also been taken of trade among less developed regions. According to the estimates of Table 4.5.1, the extraregional exports of Latin America would rise by 51.7 or 63.2 per cent between 1960 and 1975, depending on the income assumption chosen. The corresponding figures are 114.3 or 130.1 per cent for Africa, 73.7 or 108.1 per cent for the Middle East, and 49.5 or 60.3 per cent for Asia.

The projections on the future exports and imports of less developed areas are summarized in Table 4.5.2. The estimates indicate an increase in the trade deficit of the less developed areas, taken together, throughout the period under consideration. Much of this increase would occur during the sixties, however, by reason of the assumed decline in the prices of several primary products between 1960 and 1970. Under the most likely income assumption, the trade deficit of the developing countries is estimated to rise from $1.3

---

[19]For the period 1960–1975, the projected annual rate of increase of the value of exports to the Sino-Soviet area is 4.3 per cent and to developed countries 3.6 and 4.2 per cent, under the most likely and the high income assumptions, respectively.

[20]The final estimates are further affected by the assumed constancy of special category exports.

TABLE 4.5.1

THE EXPORTS OF DEVELOPING COUNTRIES
($ million, current prices)

	1960				1970I				1970II				1975I				1975II			
	DCa	LDC	SSA	Totalb	DCa	LDC	SSA	Totalb	DCa	LDC	SSA	Totalb	DCa	LDC	SSA	Totalb	DCa	LDC	SSA	Totalb
Latin America	7,963	174	306	8,497	9,920	250	700	10,920	10,530	260	700	11,540	11,720	310	810	12,890	12,690	320	810	13,870
Africa	4,069	327	374	4,863	6,790	420	480	7,780	7,210	440	480	7,780	9,220	520	590	10,420	9,930	580	590	11,190
Middle East	3,100	570	74	3,811	4,640	800	110	5,620	4,980	850	110	6,010	5,660	990	130	6,850	6,600	1,130	130	7,930
Asia	4,471	539	487	5,566	5,540	680	640	6,930	5,860	720	640	7,290	6,640	790	810	8,320	7,190	850	810	8,220
Developing countries, total	19,603	1,610	1,241	22,737	26,890	2,150	1,930	31,250	28,580	2,270	1,930	33,060	33,240	2,610	2,340	38,480	36,410	2,880	2,340	41,910

Sources: Tables 3.1.4, 4.3.1, 4.4.2.

Notes: aExports to developed countries include, in addition to the estimates of Table 3.1.4 (SITC classes 1-8), miscellaneous items (SITC class 9) amounting to $107 million in 1960 (Latin America, $32 million; Africa, $31 million; Middle East, $3 million; Asia, $41 million). A 50 per cent increase has been assumed for 1960-1970, and 80 per cent between 1960 and 1975.

bThe total exports of developing countries also include so-called special-category items (chiefly items of a military interest), reported for 1960 as follows: Latin America, $54 million; Africa, $86 million; Middle East, $67 million; Asia, $69 million. These exports have been assumed to remain at 1960 levels throughout the period under consideration.

billion in 1960 to \$4.3 billion in 1970 and \$5.2 billion in 1975, if, for all regions, the medium estimate of the income elasticity of import demand is chosen.[21]

TABLE 4.5.2

TRADE BALANCE FOR DEVELOPING COUNTRIES
($ billion, current prices)

	1960			1970I			1970II		
	Exports	Imports	Balance	Exports	Imports	Balance	Exports	Imports	Balance
Latin America	8.49	8.21	+0.28	10.9	a 11.0	-0.1	11.5	11.6	-0.1
					b 11.3	-0.4		11.9	-0.4
					c 11.5	-0.6		12.1	-0.6
Africa	4.86	6.09	-1.23	7.8	a 8.8	-1.0	8.2	9.4	-1.2
					b 8.9	-1.1		9.6	-1.4
					c 9.1	-1.3		9.8	-1.6
Middle East	3.81	2.69	+1.12	5.6	a 4.3	+1.3	6.0	4.8	+1.2
					b 4.4	+1.2		4.9	+1.1
					c 4.5	+1.1		5.1	+0.9
Asia	5.57	7.08	-1.51	6.9	a 10.7	-3.8	7.3	11.3	-4.0
					b 10.9	-4.0		11.6	-4.3
					c 11.1	-4.2		11.9	-4.6
Developing Countries, total	22.73	24.07	-1.34	31.2	a 34.8	-3.6	33.0	37.1	-4.1
					b 35.5	-4.3		38.0	-5.0
					c 36.2	-5.0		38.9	-5.9

	1975I			1975II		
	Exports	Imports	Balance	Exports	Imports	Balance
Latin America	12.9	a 12.9	-0.0	13.9	14.0	-0.1
		b 13.3	-0.4		14.5	-0.6
		c 13.8	-0.9		15.0	-1.1
Africa	10.4	a 10.7	-0.3	11.2	11.9	-0.7
		b 11.0	-0.6		12.3	-1.1
		c 11.3	-0.9		12.8	-1.6
Middle East	6.9	a 5.5	+1.4	7.9	6.5	+1.4
		b 5.7	+1.2		6.8	+1.1
		c 5.9	+1.0		7.1	+0.8
Asia	8.3	a 13.3	-5.0	8.9	14.6	-5.7
		b 13.7	-5.4		15.1	-6.2
		c 14.1	-5.8		15.6	-6.7
Developing Countries, total	38.5	a 42.4	-3.9	41.9	47.0	-5.1
		b 43.7	-5.2		48.7	-6.8
		c 45.1	-6.6		50.5	-8.6

Source: Tables 4.3.2 and 4.5.1.
Note: (a) The trade deficit of the developing countries shown for 1960 is somewhat higher than the \$1.1 billion figure given in U.N. statistics (<u>Monthly Bulletin of Statistics</u>, March, 1963). The causes of the discrepancy appear to lie in the different procedures used in estimating the exports of developing countries to developed areas; while we have relied on the import statistics of developed countries, the United Nations accepted the export figures reported by the developing nations.

---

[21]To indicate the sensitiveness of the estimates to the values assumed for the income elasticity of import demand in the developing countries, three variants reflecting different assumptions with regard to this elasticity have been given for each income alternative. For 1975, for example, the trade deficit of the developing countries would be \$3.9 or \$6.6 billion under the most likely income assumption, if the extreme values of the import demand elasticity were chosen for all regions.

Substantial differences are indicated with respect to the trade prospects of individual areas, however. According to our estimates, practically the entire increase in the estimated trade deficit of the developing countries would take place in Asia, whose deficit would grow from $1.5 billion in 1960 to $5.2 billion in 1975. The large deterioration in Asia's projected trade balance reflects the slow growth of her exports as well as the rapid increase in import requirements.

By comparison, an improvement is foreseen in the case of Africa, no change in the Middle East, and some deterioration in Latin America. It appears that the expected rapid expansion in African exports of minerals and metals would contribute to a reduction in the deficit of this area, while, despite the relatively low income elasticity of import demand assumed for Latin America, the rate of increase of exports in the latter region would fall behind that of imports.

Compared to estimates made under the most likely income assumption, the trade deficit of the less developed regions would be larger if target rates of income growth were reached in developed as well as in developing countries. This result is largely explained by the assumed difference between most likely and target growth rates in developing as compared to developed economies. Should target rates be reached in all areas, the projections would entail a trade deficit of $5.0 billion for the developing countries in 1970, and $6.8 billion in 1975.[22]

The prospects for the balance of trade of developing countries would be even less auspicious if they were to attain target rates of income growth while the "most likely" income assumption applied to developed areas. Under these circumstances, a trade deficit of $6.8 billion would be shown for 1970 and $10.2 billion for 1975. Nevertheless, the results would still be more favorable than those arrived at by the United Nations Secretariat, which indicate a deficit of $12 billion for 1970 [*20,* p. 6]. But the United Nations estimate has been based on aggregate projections and hence it could not allow for structural changes, of which the most noteworthy is the projected decline in the self-sufficiency of the developed countries in nonfuel minerals and metals, accompanied by a shift towards importation in metal form. Correspondingly, the UN estimate of the export earnings of developing countries is lower than ours ($29 billion as compared to $31.2 billion), although

---

[22]Unless otherwise noted, the median income elasticity of import demand is applied in the projections.

the UN report has not taken account of prospective decreases in the prices of several primary products.[23] At the same time, the 1970 import requirements of the less developed areas are given as $41 billion in the UN report as against our estimate of $38.0 billion.[24]

Finally, comparison is more difficult with projections prepared by GATT. According to GATT, the trade deficit of the developing countries, other than the Middle East, would amount to $11–$15 billion in 1975 if their prospective exports of manufactured goods were not taken into account [6, pp. 15–19]. Using our projections for the exports of manufactures ($2.4 billion), a deficit of $8.5–$12.5 billion is shown. But this figure has been calculated at 1956–1960 prices, and a correction to the 1961 price level, approximately corresponding to our price assumptions, would increase the projected deficit by $2.5 billion.

Note further that the projections refer to individual regions and do not take account of intraregional differences. At the same time, in Latin America the largest increases in exports are expected to take place in countries producing nonfuel minerals and metals, while in Africa petroleum- and mineral-producing countries will share much of the increase. Intra-area trade in fuels will further contribute to a skewed distribution of export earnings and the trade balance. Further research would therefore be necessary to evaluate the trade prospects of individual countries in less developed areas.

REFERENCES

[1.] Chenery, H. B. "Patterns of Industrial Growth," *American Economic Review* (September, 1960), pp. 624–54.

[2.] Federation of Nigeria. *National Development Plan, 1962–1968.* Lagos, 1962.

[3.] Food and Agriculture Organization. *Agricultural Commodities—Projections for 1970.* Rome, 1962.

[4.] Food and Agriculture Organization. *Agricultural Commodities—the Outlook for 1970 in Eastern Europe,* Rome, 1963.

[5.] Food and Agriculture Organization. *Trade Yearbook 1961,* Rome, 1962.

[6.] General Agreement on Tariffs and Trade. *International Trade, 1961.* Geneva, 1962.

---

[23]In 1960 prices, our estimate of the export receipts of developing areas in 1970 would be $33.8 billion (a difference of $2.4 billion pertains to exports to developed countries and $0.2 billion to exports to the Sino-Soviet area).

[24]Note that the growth rates postulated in the UN paper correspond to our "most likely" estimate for the developed countries and the target rate of income growth for the less developed areas.

[7.] HUDDLE, D. L. "Plano Trienal: Critica de setor externo," *Revista Brasiliera de Economia,* December, 1962.

[8.] KINGDOM OF IRAN. *Outline of the Third Plan, 1962–1968.* Teheran, 1961.

[9.] PREBISCH, RAUL. *Towards a Dynamic Development Policy for Latin America.* New York; United Nations, 1963.

[10.] REPUBLICA DE BOLIVIA. *Plan nacional de desarrollo económico y social, 1962–1971.* La Paz, 1961.

[11.] REPUBLICA BRAZILIANA. *Plano trienal de desenvolvimento económico e social, 1963–1965,* Rio de Janeiro, 1963.

[12.] REPUBLICA DE CHILE. *Programa nacional de desarrollo económico, 1961–1970.* Santiago, 1961.

[13.] REPUBLICA DE COLOMBIA. *Plan general de desarrollo económico y social, 1960–1970.* Bogotá, 1962.

[14.] REPUBLICA DE PERU. *Plan nacional de desarrollo económico y social, 1962–1971.* Lima, 1962.

[15.] REPUBLICA DE VENEZUELA. *Plan de la nación, 1963–1966.* Caracas, 1962.

[16.] ROYAUME DU MAROC. *Plan quinquennal, 1960–1964,* Rabat, 1961.

[17.] UNITED ARAB REPUBLIC. *Cadre du plan quinquenal général, 1960–1965.* Cairo, 1960.

[18.] UNITED NATIONS. *Monthly Bulletin of Statistics,* March and April, 1963.

[19.] UNITED NATIONS. *Statistical Yearbook,* various issues.

[20.] UNITED NATIONS. *World Economic Survey, Part I, 1962.* New York, 1963.

[21.] UNITED NATIONS ECONOMIC COMMISSION FOR ASIA AND THE FAR EAST. *Economic Survey of Asia and the Far East, 1961.*

[22.] UNITED NATIONS ECONOMIC COMMISSION FOR ASIA AND THE FAR EAST. "Foreign Trade Aspect of the Economic Development Plans of ECAFE Countries," *Economic Bulletin for Asia and the Far East* (June, 1963), pp. 1–28.

[23.] UNITED NATIONS ECONOMIC COMMISSION FOR ASIA AND THE FAR EAST. "The Scope for Regional Economic Co-operation," *Economic Bulletin for Asia and the Far East* (December, 1961), pp. 52–75.

[24.] UNITED NATIONS ECONOMIC COMMISSION FOR EUROPE. *Economic Survey of Europe in 1959.* Geneva, 1960.

[25.] UNITED NATIONS ECONOMIC COMMISSION FOR EUROPE. *Economic Survey of Europe in 1960.* Geneva, 1961.

[26.] U.S. CONGRESS. *Seventh Semiannual Report on Activities Carried on under Public Law 480, 83rd Congress.* Washington, D.C., 1963.

CHAPTER 5

The Balance of Current Account Transactions and Policy Alternatives For a Balanced Expansion of World Trade

5.1 SERVICE ITEMS IN THE BALANCE OF PAYMENTS

IN THE preceding discussion of the trade prospects of developing countries, all exports and imports have been expressed in f.o.b. prices. To arrive at an estimate of the current balance, we have further to take account of transportation costs, investment income, travel expenditures, and other items that are classified as services (invisibles) in the balance of payments. Services are of considerable importance for the developing countries: receipts from services amounted to $6.0 billion in 1960 as against earnings on the merchandise account of $27.1 billion, while the corresponding figures on the payments side were $9.3 and $28.4 billion.[1] Expenditures by foreign governments in less developed areas loom large among receipts ($2.3 billion), with travel expenditures ($1.3 billion) following. On the payments side, freight and insurance ($2.2 billion) is, in fact, part of the cost of imports whereas the investment income for foreign companies ($3.4 billion) is largely a deduction from export earnings.

It appears, then, that much of the current account deficit of the developing countries takes the form of a deficit in services: $3.3 billion in 1960 as against an import surplus of $1.3 billion. But despite the importance of invisibles in the balance of payments of less developed areas, the reliability of statistics is generally low. While trade is documented with customs receipts, most countries

---

[1] The export and import data cited here include intra-area trade in each region in order to achieve comparability with the statistics on invisibles. Intra-area trade has been estimated on the basis of information derived from [12, 15]; with regard to payments and receipts on the service account, see Table A5.1.1.

99

rely on sampling to estimate travel expenditures and insurance, information on investment income is derived from the reports of private companies, and a mixture of the two procedures is used in estimating freight expenditures.

At the same time, a number of countries do not publish data on receipts and payments on the service account and statistical collections of such information are few and far between. In the present study, the balance of payments statistics of the International Monetary Fund have been utilized whenever available, and we have relied on national statistical sources in regard to countries not included in the IMF compilations. Finally, for countries that do not publish data on services, we have estimated freight expenditures from trade statistics, and investment income as well as spending by foreign governments on the basis of information given in the statistical publications of the developed countries.

Freight and insurance had to be estimated also in cases where imports are given in cif prices.[2] In such instances we have assumed that freight and insurance taken together amounted to 10 per cent of the cif value of imports,[3] except in the case of Mexico where the important role played by surface transportation warrants the use of a lower ratio. According to our estimates, the net payments of developing countries for freight and insurance were $1.8 billion in 1960.[4] These countries rely to a considerable extent on shipping by foreign companies and, in view of the large capital and foreign exchange outlay involved in setting up domestic shipping fleets, this situation is not likely to change materially during the period under consideration. In making projections, we have assumed that expenditures on freight and insurance will increase *pari passu* with the rise of imports into developing areas, except for some larger

---

[2]Apparently freight expenditures in such countries have been disregarded in a compilation of the United Nations [13], and this accounts for a substantial part of the difference between the relevant figures in the UN paper and those of the present study.

[3]The same assumption was made in [4].

[4]By comparison, the consolidation of the balance of payments of the developed countries shows a net balance of $0.6 billion on the freight and insurance account. The earnings of ships operating under the so-called "flags of convenience" and the underestimation of the earnings of ships flying the Greek flag account for much of the discrepancy between the two figures. In 1951, the unrecorded net receipts of the above companies, taken together, were estimated at $0.6 billion by H. F. Karreman [5, p. 37]. Although estimates for more recent years have not been prepared, available information on shipping fleets and freight rates [2, 16] suggests that these receipts might have increased by about one-half between 1951 and 1960.

countries in Latin America and Asia where domestic shipping facilities will be increasingly utilized·

The "other transportation" category includes the chartering of ships and airplanes, fees paid for the use of international waterways, and various other transactions. The largest item within this category is payment to Egypt for the use of the Suez Canal. Further increases are expected on this count while no change has been assumed elsewhere.

On the travel account, Latin America experienced a favorable balance in 1960, chiefly by reason of tourism from the United States. In other areas, however, fares paid to foreign airlines and shipping companies resulted in a deficit and, for the developing countries as a whole, only a small surplus is shown. But given the promotional activities underway in less developed areas, the establishment of national airlines in several of these countries, and the increasing radius of tourist travel, improvements are anticipated during the period of projection. We have projected the net balance of the developing countries in tourism and travel to reach $0.7 billion in 1970 and $1.0 billion in 1975. The largest increase in receipts has been assumed to take place in Latin America where proximity to the United States provides an advantage.

The payments of developing countries included under the heading "investment income" have been increasing at a rapid rate and approximately doubled during the fifties. Increases have been especially pronounced in interest paid to foreign governments and international organizations, given that the external public debt has nearly doubled between 1955 and 1960. Nevertheless, these payments have remained small in absolute amount and interest paid to foreign governments and the IBRD hardly surpassed 10 per cent of total foreign investment income in 1960.

Prospective changes in the interest burden of the external public debt will depend on the size and terms of future lending. The continuation of the expansion of guaranteed export credits will further augment the interest charges in the balance of payments of the developing countries, while changes in the earnings of foreign companies will be affected by the rate of increase of foreign private investment as well as by the export prospects of the industries where foreign companies are of greatest importance (oil and nonfuel minerals), and the tax treatment of these companies. We have assumed modest increases in the inflow of private capital, and a rise in the share of the producing countries in the profits of foreign companies.

Detailed estimates have been prepared for oil where a considerable amount of information is available (Table A5.1.2).

The investment income foreign companies are expected to derive from the production and refining of oil and prospective investment earnings in Israel have been included as a debit item in the balance of payments of the Middle East where foreign investment income may rise from $1.1 billion in 1960 to $1.5–$1.6 billion in 1970 and $1.7–$2.0 billion in 1975.

The expansion of oil production will account for much of the projected increase in the earnings of foreign companies in Africa. But, with the increasing mining activity and aluminum production, the profits of foreign companies engaged in mining and the processing of ores will also rise. Taken together, net payments to foreign companies and governments may reach $1.0 billion by 1975 as compared to $0.2 billion in 1960.

Smaller increases are foreseen in Latin America where the relatively slow expansion of oil exports and the cost *cum* tax squeeze on the oil companies are expected to restrain the rise of investment income, although the favorable prospects for nonferrous metals will benefit the foreign mining companies. Finally, the expected relatively moderate increase of foreign investment income in Asia would take the form of oil profits and interest payments on government debt. All in all, the net debit balance of the developing areas under the heading investment income has been projected to rise from $3.0 billion in 1960 to $4.4–$4.7 billion in 1970 and $5.2–$5.7 billion in 1975.

The next category in the service account includes expenditures by foreign governments, such as local purchases and wage payments by foreign military, diplomatic, and economic missions and contribution to specific defense expenditures. On the basis of information provided in national statistical publications and by the OECD, these expenditures of foreign governments in developing countries have been estimated at $2.35 billion in 1960. By comparison, expenditures by the governments of developing countries abroad—to a large extent contributions to international agencies—amounted to $640 million.

Future changes in expenditures by foreign governments are difficult to predict since much of this expenditure served military purposes in 1960 or was related to the administration of colonial territories and assistance given to the newly independent nations. It may be expected, however, that with the ending of the Algerian war and the independence of Algeria, the expenditures of the

French government in Africa will decline from the high level experienced in 1960. No change has been envisaged in other areas, so that the net receipts of the developing countries on the government account have been projected to fall from $1.7 billion in 1960 to $1.4 billion in 1975.

Finally, miscellaneous service transactions include, among other things, post and telegraphic services, royalties and patents, management fees, and rentals. Payments under this heading have become increasingly significant as many of the developing countries have come to hire foreign management services and use foreign patents in setting up domestic industries. These expenditures will ultimately decline, however, and no change has been assumed during the period under consideration.

TABLE 5.1.1

DEVELOPING COUNTRIES: SERVICE ITEMS IN THE BALANCE-OF-PAYMENTS (NET)
($ billion, current prices)

| | 1960 | | | | | 1970I | | | | |
	LA	AF	ME	AS	LDC	LA	AF	ME	AS	LDC
Freight and insurance	-0.7	-0.4	-0.2	-0.5	-1.8	-0.9	-0.6	-0.3	-0.7	-2.5
Other transport	-0.1	0.1	0	0	.0	-0.1	0.2	0	0	0.1
Travel	0.4	-0.2	0	-0.1	0.1	0.6	-0.1	0.1	0	0.6
Investment income	-1.4	-0.2	-1.1	-0.3	-3.0	-1.8	-0.7	-1.5	-0.4	-4.4
Government	0.1	1.0	0.1	0.5	1.7	0.1	0.7	0.1	0.5	1.4
Miscellaneous services	-0.1	-0.1	0	-0.1	-0.3	-0.1	-0.1	0	-0.1	-0.3
Services, total	-1.8	0.2	-1.2	-0.5	-3.3	-2.2	-0.6	-1.6	-0.7	-5.1

| | 1970II | | | | | 1975I | | | | |
	LA	AF	ME	AS	LDC	LA	AF	ME	AS	LDC
Freight and insurance	-0.9	-0.6	-0.3	-0.8	-2.6	-1.1	-0.7	-0.6	-0.9	-3.1
Other transport	-0.1	0.2	0	0	0.1	-0.1	-0.2	0	0	0.1
Travel	0.6	-0.1	0	0	0.6	0.8	0	0.1	0.1	1.0
Investment income	-1.9	-0.8	-1.6	-0.4	-4.7	-2.0	-1.0	-1.7	-0.5	-5.2
Government	0.1	0.7	0.1	0.5	1.4	0.1	0.7	0.1	0.5	1.4
Miscellaneous services	-0.1	-0.1	0	-0.1	-0.3	-0.1	-0.1	0	-0.1	-0.3
Services, total	-2.3	-0.7	-1.7	-0.8	-5.5	-2.4	-0.9	-1.9	-0.9	-6.1

| | 1975II | | | | |
	LA	AF	ME	AS	LDC
Freight and insurance	-1.2	-0.8	-0.4	-1.0	-3.4
Other transport	-0.1	0.2	0	0	0.1
Travel	0.8	0	0.1	0.1	1.0
Investment income	-2.1	-1.1	-2.0	-0.5	-5.7
Government	0.1	0.7	0.1	0.5	1.4
Miscellaneous services	-0.1	-0.1	0	-0.1	-0.3
Services, total	-2.6	-1.1	-2.2	-1.0	-6.9

Source: Table A5.1.1.

Our projections indicate an increase in the net deficit of the developing countries on the service account from $3.3 billion in 1960 to $5.1 or $5.5 billion in 1970 and $6.1 and $6.9 billion in 1975, depending on the income assumption chosen (Table 5.1.1.). The increase in the negative balance on invisibles is explained chiefly by the projected rise in the investment income of foreigners and in transportation costs, that will be hardly counterbalanced by the increase in receipts from tourism. The largest deterioration in the service accounts is foreseen in Africa where a positive balance of $0.2 billion in 1960 has been projected to give place to a $0.9 negative balance in 1975 as a result of the combined effects of the fall in the expenditures of the French government in Algeria and the increasing return flow of earnings on oil.

5.2 THE CURRENT ACCOUNT BALANCE OF DEVELOPING AREAS

Table 5.2.1 shows the current account balance of developing areas, actual and projected. The estimates provide evidence of the importance of the return flow of investment for the net export earnings of developing countries. In Africa, for example, the improvement in the trade balance has its counterpart in the increased earnings of foreign companies, while in the Middle East the rise in oil exports is accompanied by higher incomes for the oil companies.

TABLE 5.2.1

DEVELOPING COUNTRIES: CURRENT ACCOUNT BALANCE[a]
($ billion, current prices)

| | 1960 | | | 1970I | | | 1970II | | |
	Trade	Services	Current Account	Trade	Services	Current Account	Trade	Services	Current Account
LA	+0.28	-1.78	-1.50	-0.4	-2.2	-2.6	-0.4	-2.3	-2.7
AF	-1.23	+0.21	-1.02	-1.1	-0.6	-1.7	-1.4	-0.7	-2.1
ME	+1.12	-1.21	-0.09	+1.2	-1.6	-0.4	+1.1	-1.7	-0.6
AS	-1.51	-0.53	-2.04	-4.0	-0.7	-4.7	-4.3	-0.8	-5.1
	-1.34	-3.31	-4.65	-4.3	-5.1	-9.4	-5.0	-5.5	-10.5

| | 1975I | | | 1975II | | |
	Trade	Services	Current Account	Trade	Services	Current Account
LA	-0.4	-2.4	-2.8	-0.6	-2.6	-3.2
AF	-0.6	-0.9	-1.5	-1.1	-1.1	-2.2
ME	+1.2	-1.9	-0.7	+1.1	-2.2	-1.1
AS	-5.4	-0.9	-6.3	-6.2	-1.0	-7.2
	-5.2	-6.1	-11.3	-6.8	-6.9	-13.7

Sources: Tables 4.5.2 and 5.2.1.
Note: [a]The medium estimate of the income elasticity of import demand has been utilized in regard to all developing areas.

Under the most likely income assumption, the current account deficits of the developing countries, taken together, would rise from $4.6 billion in 1960 to $9.4 billion in 1970 and $11.3 billion in 1975 if the medium estimate of the income elasticity of import demand applied in all regions. The deficit would be greater, however, if target rates of income growth were realized in the world economy, partly because of the reasons explained in connection with the balance of merchandise trade in Chapter 4.5 and partly because higher exports from the developing countries are accompanied by larger foreign investment income, and higher imports by larger freight expenditures. The relevant estimates under the high (target) income assumption are $10.5 billion in 1970 and $13.7 billion in 1975.

Finally, should we assume that the developing countries reached target rates of growth while the gross national product of developed economies grew at "most likely" rates, the current account deficit of the less developed areas would amount to $12.0 billion in 1970, with a trade deficit of $6.8 billion and a service account deficit of $5.2 billion. The corresponding estimates for 1975 are $10.2 billion on the trade account and $6.4 billion on the service account, i.e., a current account deficit of $16.6 billion.

By comparison, the United Nations has estimated a trade gap of $12 billion and a service account deficit of $8 billion in 1970 [17, p. 6]. Our discussion in Chapter 4.5 indicates, however, that the UN trade gap projection is likely to be an overestimate, while the service account forecast is affected by the apparent overestimation of the deficit on invisibles in the base year ($4 billion in 1959).

Irrespective of the income variant chosen, a deterioration in the current account balance is indicated for all developing regions, although Africa would regain some of the loss suffered between 1960 and 1970 in the early seventies. Given the projected rise in its trade deficit, Asia is expected to show the most unfavorable picture and the current account deficit of Latin America and the Middle East will also increase.

In 1960, the deficit in the current account balance of the developing countries was financed by the inflow of foreign capital, official and private. According to data published by the OECD, the net flow of public capital from the member countries of the Development Assistance Committee (OECD countries and Japan) and international agencies to the less developed areas amounted to $4.0 billion in 1960 and net private investments to $2.5 billion (Table 5.2.2). In the same year, disbursements of grants and loans by the countries of the Sino-Soviet area were estimated at $186 million, and contributions by Australia and New Zealand at $72 million [6, p. 13], making up a total of $6.7 billion.

A lower figure (approximately $5.5–$6 billion) is indicated by the United Nations, chiefly because of differences in the estimates of private investment [14]. But, in any case, the recorded inflow of long term capital appears to exceed the current account deficit of the developing countries ($4.6 billion in 1960) by a considerable margin. Various reasons have been given to account for this discrepancy:

errors and omissions in current transactions, unrecorded repatriation of capital funds, unrecorded investment by nationals of developing countries abroad, and flight capital [*14*, p. 12]. Further
contributing factors are private transfers, short term capital movements, and increases in the gold and foreign exchange reserves of
developing countries, which items are not included either under
current transactions or under long term investments.

TABLE 5.2.2

THE BALANCE OF CURRENT TRANSACTIONS AND CAPITAL INFLOW IN
DEVELOPING COUNTRIES, 1960
($ billion)

| | Current Account Balance | Long-Term Capital Inflow (Net)[a] | | | | | |
| | | Overall Total | Total Bilateral | Official | Private | | |
					Net Lending	Export Credit	Multilateral Flow
Latin America	-1.50	1.49	1.48	0.32	0.91	0.25	0.01
Africa	-1.02	2.19	2.04	1.28	0.70	0.06	0.15
Middle East	-0.09	0.53	0.49	0.25	0.20[b]	0.04	0.04
Asia	-2.04	2.25	2.19	1.89	0.32[b]	-0.02	0.06
	-4.65	6.46	6.20	3.74	2.13	0.33	0.26

Sources: Current account balance--Table 5.2.1.
    Long-term capital inflow--OECD, The Flow of Financial Resources to Developing
    Countries in 1961, Paris, 1963, p. 74.
Notes: [a]The figures do not include aid by the countries of the Sino-Soviet area but, at any
    rate, trade between the developing countries and the centrally planned economies
    was approximately in balance in 1960 (U.N., Monthly Bulletin of Statistics, March,
    1963).
    [b]Our estimate.

A consideration of data for individual regions can be helpful in
explaining the causes of the observed discrepancies. According to
the estimates shown in Table 5.2.2, there is little difference between
the current account deficit and the imports of foreign capital in
Latin America and Asia, while large discrepancies are shown for
Africa and the Middle East. With regard to Africa, note that practically the entire $886 million errors and omissions indicated in
the balance of payment of France with the franc area [*3*, p. 5-
France] pertains to Africa. This item may be explained, in great
part, by the unrecorded repatriation of earnings by French nationals paid from French governmental funds abroad and the return flow of capital from Algeria.

The repatriation of capital from the former Belgian Congo and
some British colonies has further contributed to the difference between recorded current transactions and the inflow of foreign
capital in Africa. By comparison, unrecorded investments abroad
by the nationals of the oil-producing countries and increases in gold
and foreign exchange holdings account for much of the discrepancy
in the Middle East.

The next question concerns the measures to be used to fill the prospective "current account gap" of the less developed areas. Various alternatives will be discussed below: accelerated growth in developed economies, reduction of barriers to the exports of developing countries, increased trade with the Sino-Soviet area, regional integration in less developed areas, and capital inflow.

5.3 THE CONTRIBUTION OF ACCELERATED GROWTH IN THE DEVELOPED COUNTRIES TO THE EXPORT EARNINGS OF DEVELOPING ECONOMIES

Whereas the value of the exports of developing countries to developed economies has been estimated at $26.9 billion in 1970 and $33.2 billion in 1975 under the most likely income assumption, the attainment of the target rate of income growth in developed countries is expected to result in exports of $28.6 and $36.4 billion in the two years, respectively. Thus, the increase in the value of exports due to higher growth rates in developed areas would be $1.7 billion in 1970 and $3.2 billion in 1975 (Table 4.5.1).

But against these increases we should set the increment in the investment income of foreign companies associated with a larger amount of exports. According to information provided in Table 5.1.1, the increase in foreign investment income between the two variants would be $0.3 billion in 1970 and $0.5 billion in 1975, reducing the net gain developing countries obtain from an acceleration in the rate of growth of developed economies to $1.4 billion in 1970 and $2.7 billion in 1975. The net change in the balance of payments of the less developed regions will be further affected by reason of the fact that larger exports in these countries would also lead to higher imports through an increase in the rate of growth of incomes.

5.4 REDUCTION OF BARRIERS TO THE EXPORTS OF DEVELOPING ECONOMIES

Barriers to the expansion of imports from developing countries into developed economies take a variety of forms: discriminatory and nondiscriminatory tariffs, excise taxes, subsidies to domestic producers, embargoes, state trading, import licensing, and quantitative restrictions. The removal or reduction of tariffs and excise taxes would contribute to an expansion of imports but, in the absence of sufficient information on the responsiveness of domestic and foreign supply and demand to changes in price-relationships, the estimation of the probable effects of these measures on trade flows is subject to a considerable degree of uncertainty. Further difficulties are encountered in cases when quantitative restrictions, embargoes, state trading, and import licensing are applied.

In view of the difficulties of estimation, in the present study we aim at indicating possible developments under certain assumptions instead of attempting to provide numerical estimates in regard to the impact of lowering trade barriers on imports. An exception is the case of noncompeting tropical foodstuffs where, in the absence of domestic production, the error-possibilities of estimation are less pronounced.

Temperate Zone Foods

The evaluation of the effects of changes in domestic policies in the developed countries on imports of temperate zone foods from developing economies is especially difficult. To begin with, a variety of protective measures are employed in the importing countries which take the form of quantitative restrictions, import licensing, and tariffs, as well as subsidies. At the same time, developing countries account for a relatively small proportion of the quantities brought on the world market and their main competitors often apply policies aimed at supporting domestic incomes and prices. If we consider also the movement of temperate zone foods through noncommercial channels from the United States to some underdeveloped countries, it will be apparent that the effects of changes in production and trade policies on the pattern of trade are difficult to foresee. Still, we can indicate the possible impact of modifying various assumptions underlying the projections of the present study on the imports of temperate zone foods from less developed areas.

In estimating the future imports of meat, we have assumed that, except for purchases from Madagascar, the application of Common Market agricultural policy would lead to the disappearance of EEC beef imports, while in Britain the maintenance of the system of deficiency payments would be accompanied by stagnating imports of beef. The consequences of these policies are of considerable importance to suppliers in developing countries since the Common Market and the United Kingdom account for over nine-tenth of their meat exports to Western Europe, which consist almost entirely of beef. Should the regulations be amended so as to insure that developing economies maintained their share in the meat consumption of these countries as of 1960, their meat exports would exceed projected magnitudes by $88 million in 1970 and $103 million in 1975 (Table A5.4.1). Much of this gain would accrue to Argentina and Uruguay although there are possibilities for expanding exportable production in East Africa, too.

Similar considerations apply to cereals, given that Argentina, the largest exporter among developing countries, is a low cost producer of wheat, maize, and barley. There is no reason to assume that Argentina and other developing countries could not maintain their present share in European consumption, provided that agricultural policies in the Common Market and in the United Kingdom permitted imports to rise in proportion to domestic consumption. Under these assumptions, EEC and U.K. imports of wheat and coarse grains from developing countries would exceed projected magnitudes by $101 million in 1970 and $117 million in 1975 (Table A5.4.1). At the same time, the maintenance of Japanese imports of rice at 1960 levels would augment the projected export earnings of her Asian suppliers by $18 million.

With regard to oranges, the FAO estimated that imports into the European Common Market (excluding Italy), Sweden, and Norway would exceed projected levels in 1970 by $19 million if tariffs and internal duties in these countries were reduced by 50 per cent and by $39 million if tariffs and taxes were completely eliminated [*10*, p. 9]. Part of this gain would accrue to developed countries (United States, Spain, South Africa), however, whereas Algeria and Morocco may lose as a result of the elimination of preferential duties.

Trade in most other fruits takes place among the developed countries themselves, while noncompeting fruits other than bananas bear low duties in the industrial countries, and hence less developed areas could derive little gain from the elimination of tariffs. Similar considerations apply to vegetables and wine. Finally, feeding-stuffs enter duty-free in the main importing countries.

Competing Tropical Foods

The problems related to tropical oilseeds and oils, too, are rather complex. Although oilseeds of tropical origin pay no duty in Western Europe,[5] subsidies and compulsory mixing regulations have encouraged the expansion of rapeseed production in this area, and various measures have been taken, or are contemplated, with a view toward increasing the consumption of butter at the expense

---

[5]There is a preferential tariff of 10 per cent on the main tropical oilseeds in the United Kingdom, however, from which Commonwealth producers are exempt.

of margarine. Further, in the European Common Market, the domestic crushing industry is protected by tariffs on vegetable oils which hinder the shift from the importation of oilseeds to that of oils. Of greatest importance for the exporters of tropical oils and oilseeds is, however, the price-support system of the United States that has contributed to the rapid growth of U.S. soybean exports, reducing thereby the market opportunities for oilseeds of tropical origin.

But the increasing share of soybeans in European imports has been due, in part, to the increased demand for protein-rich oil and oilcake, and the expansion of soybean production in the United States has also made possible its distribution under the P.L. 480 program in several developing countries that have experienced supply deficiencies. Still, a reduction of subsidies in the industrial countries could lead to an improvement in the relative position of tropical oils through increasing the total imports of oils and fats into Western Europe and Japan and altering the price ratio between soybeans and oilseeds of tropical origin.

The removal of duties on vegetable oils would further benefit the developing countries. These duties have the double effect of providing protection to domestic crushers and raising the price of tropical oil on the domestic market. While the proximity of markets for oils and oilcake provides an advantage to the European crushing and refining industry, imports of oils (and oilcake) into the Common Market would be expected to rise after a removal of the tariff averaging around 10 per cent. And although substitution possibilities are limited in many uses, the ensuing fall in prices would improve the competitive position of tropical oils as against other oils and fats.

The probable effects of changes in production and import policies are difficult to assess. There are no reliable estimates available on the possible gain derived from the exportation of oils and oilcake as compared to oilseeds, and information on expansion possibilities in the production of the various tropical oils, too, is scarce. Nevertheless, it can be stated that inasmuch as the shift from the exportation of oilseeds to vegetable oils is restricted by the differential tariff of the Common Market, the immediate gain accruing to developing countries subsequent to the elimination of this duty would not exceed $20 million—10 per cent of the projected value of EEC imports of oilseeds from the nonassociated countries. Developing countries would derive a gain of a similar magnitude if their exports to the Common Market countries were to grow in proportion to the EEC's consumption of oils and fats other than butter.

The protection of domestic sugar production in the industrial countries takes a variety of forms. Quotas are used in the United States, in Japan, and in some smaller European countries, while a system of subsidies is applied in the Common Market and the United Kingdom. Despite improvements in the production of beet sugar, costs are generally lower in cane sugar producing areas and it has been suggested that, in the major industrial countries, the average unit cost of beet sugar exceeds the price that would develop in a free world market by a substantial margin. Although the marginal cost of sugar production will differ from the average cost at various levels of output, in the absence of protection sugar production in the industrial countries would fall to a considerable extent and the slack could be taken up by extending production in the main sugar-exporting countries [*8*, p. 67].

The possible effects of a liberalization of protective arrangements can be indicated if we consider that an increase in imports by an amount equal to 1 per cent of consumption in the industrial countries would amount to 285 thousand tons in 1975, i.e., $25 million at 1960 world market prices.[6] Should we assume for example, that the United States were to continue to import 46.5 per cent of her sugar needs instead of 40 per cent as envisaged, her sugar imports would exceed projected magnitudes by 750 thousand tons in 1975, valued at $54 million.

Next, we inquire into the effects of the removal of tariffs and excise taxes on sugar consumption under the assumption that domestic sugar production in the industrial countries would be maintained through a system of subsidies. According to estimates prepared by R. H. Snape, under these assumptions sugar consumption would have exceeded actual consumption by 7 per cent in North America, 9 per cent in Western Europe, and 50 per cent in Japan in 1959 [*8*, p. 65].[7] Although our calculations suggest that the price elasticities used by Snape are somewhat high, it would appear that, assuming the removal of all fiscal charges and the maintenance of domestic production through subsidies, sugar imports into the industrial areas would exceed the projected magnitudes by 1.8 million

---

[6]3.14 cents per pound, Cuban raw sugar, for destinations other than the United States.

[7]Snape calculates with average fiscal charges of 24 per cent in North America, 23 per cent in Western Europe, and 51 per cent in Japan, and with price elasticities of -0.28, -0.5, and -1.0 in the three areas, respectively.

tons in 1970 and 2.0 million tons in 1975, corresponding to an increase in the value of imports by $126 million and $137 million at world market prices (Table A5.4.1).[8]

Trade in tobacco would also expand if tariffs and excise taxes were reduced in the industrial countries but part of the gain would accrue to tobacco producers in the United States, Greece, and Turkey.

Noncompeting Tropical Foods

It has often been argued that a reduction or elimination of tariffs and excise taxes on tropical beverages and bananas would substantially increase the imports of these commodities. However, calculations made by the FAO suggest that the gain to developing countries would be rather small. According to the FAO, the imports of noncompeting tropical foods into the larger countries of Western Europe would exceed estimated levels for 1970 by $66 million at average prices of the years 1957–1959 if duties and excise taxes were halved and by $141 million if these charges were completely abolished. In current prices, the relevant figures are $53 and $112 million (Table A5.4.1).

About three-fourths of the total gain would be obtained in coffee —$81 million if all tariffs and taxes were abolished—followed by cocoa ($24 million), bananas ($5 million), and tea ($2 million).[9] In regard to coffee, estimates have been prepared in the present study, too, indicating an increase in the value of coffee imports over projected levels for the year 1970 by $34 or $77 million, depending on whether tariffs and excise taxes are reduced by 50 per cent or are completely abolished.

It appears then that the increase in the imports of noncompeting tropical foods into the larger countries of Western Europe following the abolition of tariffs and excise taxes would hardly exceed 7–8 per cent of projected imports. The results are explained by the low price elasticity of demand for noncompeting tropical products in Western Europe. Despite the existence of restrictive regulations, per capita consumption is approaching the saturation level

---

[8]By comparison, Snape's estimate was 2.2 million tons for 1959 and an estimate of 0.8 million tons has been arrived at by Tinbergen for the same year [*9*, p. 304]. In the latter case an overly low figure was used in regard to fiscal charges on sugar in the United States, however, and potential increases appear to have been underestimated in the case of several other countries, too.

[9]By comparison, Tinbergen gives estimates of $54 million for coffee, $8 million for bananas, and $1.5 million for tea for the year 1959 [*9*, p. 300].

in the high income countries of Europe, and by 1970 a fall in prices would not have a substantial effect on consumption.

Note further that the removal of tariffs on noncompeting tropical foodstuffs would result in a redistribution of export incomes among producing areas, since, in the absence of preferential tariffs in the European Common Market and the United Kingdom, nonparticipating countries would obtain a larger share in exports. This shift would thus favor low cost producers at the expense of high cost suppliers.

Agricultural Raw Materials

Most developed countries admit agricultural raw materials duty-free and although some countries (e.g., Japan) operate licensing systems, these are rarely restrictive. A major exception is the United States, where high duties are applied to wool and the importation of cotton is restricted by quotas.

In the United States, a specific duty (25.5 cents per pound) is levied on apparel wool, equivalent to an ad valorem tariff of about 25–35 per cent, depending on quality. In turn, the proceeds of this duty are used to subsidize the domestic production of wool. A reduction in tariffs would, then, have a double effect: it would lead to higher consumption as well as to lower domestic production of apparel wool. Should we assume that a fall in prices consequent upon the reduction of tariffs would contribute to an increase in per capita wool consumption by 0.1 kg a year, wool imports projected for the year 1975 would rise by 23 thousand tons, i.e., by about $35 million.[10] The same result would be attained if the share of imported wool in the consumption of apparel wool were to increase by about one-tenth. Much of this gain would accrue to Australia, New Zealand, and South Africa, however.

Cotton imports into the United States are regulated by quotas while cotton exporters receive a subsidy of 8.5 cents per pound. It is difficult to speculate on the probable effects of changes in the system of protection since the United States has been a residual supplier of cotton in the last decade. Thus, the U.S. supplied the difference between world import demand and the amount made available by other exporters in any crop year. Nevertheless, with the expansion of cotton production elsewhere, the United States would have to change this policy in order to maintain her share in

---

[10]Unless otherwise noted, average unit values of imports derived from trade statistics are used in the calculations.

the world market.[11] In such a situation, U.S. cotton exports would encroach upon the potential market of other producers. The effects of this policy can be indicated if we consider that a reduction in the share of the United States in the imports of other developed countries by one percentage point would correspond to an increase in the exports of other producers by 1.5 per cent, i.e., by nearly $15 million in 1975.

Note further that although some developed countries levy tariffs on imported hides and skins, in view of the small share of the producers of less developed areas in these exports, a reduction in tariffs would have little effect on the export earnings of developing countries. On the other hand, changes in Common Market policy as regards the importation of tropical timber would lead to an increase in the imports of sawn timber at the expense of round-wood.

Fuels

A variety of measures are used to protect the production of coal in Western Europe. However, in making projections, we have assumed a gradual liberalization of energy policies to take place with a concomitant increase in the share of oil in European energy consumption, and hence the effects of the removal of protective measures on imports are not separately considered.

The situation is different in the United States where the maintenance of the present quota system on petroleum and petroleum products is envisaged. Given observed differences in production costs, any increase in quotas would be accompanied by a corresponding rise in imports. Should we assume, for example, that the quotas were augmented by an amount equal to 1 per cent of U.S. oil consumption in 1975, and that the rise in imports took the form of crude petroleum, imports of crude oil would increase by 6.9 million tons. This increment in imports, if distributed among suppliers in developing areas in proportion to their projected exports to the United States, would represent a value of $91 million.

Nonfuel Minerals and Metals

Metal ores and concentrates as well as copper and tin metal are imported duty-free into Western Europe and Japan. The United Kingdom applies a small duty on aluminum, zinc, and lead imported from non-Commonwealth sources, however, while the ex-

---

[11]Cf. chap. 9.4.

ternal tariff of the EEC is 6 per cent for zinc, 7 per cent for lead, and 8.5 for aluminum. At the same time, in addition to tariffs, quotas restrict the importation of lead and zinc ores, concentrates, and metal into the United States.

Common Market duties on zinc, lead, and aluminum metal will hinder the shift from the exportation of ores to that of metal in the nonassociated countries. For the developing countries, however, this constraint is not likely to be of importance during the period under consideration in the case of aluminum; and, given the smallness of tariff and the relatively small value involved, it will have little effect on the value of lead and zinc traded.

By comparison, U.S. import quotas on lead and zinc ores, concentrates, and metal limit the total amount of imports as well as imports within each category. The removal of the quotas would, then, increase imports at the expense of domestic production and would raise the share of metal in these imports. Should we assume, for example, that quotas were liberalized so as to reduce projected levels of domestic production by one-fourth, and that the corresponding increment in imports would take the form of metal, lead imports would rise by about 60 thousand tons (approximately $12 million) and zinc imports by 105 thousand tons ($45 million). A large part of these imports would originate in Canada and Australia, however, and the share of the developing countries may not exceed one-third of the total.

Manufactured Goods

Several of the manufactured exports of the developing countries come under quantitative restrictions while others bear high duties. In practically all industrial countries, formal or informal quotas are applied on cotton textiles, which accounted for one-third of the imports of manufactures from less developed areas in 1960. France, Germany, the United Kingdom, Italy, and several smaller European countries use quantitative restrictions to protect their jute manufactures and, in some countries, imports of sewing machines, bicycles, and sports goods are also limited by quotas.

Whereas quotas limit the exports of manufactures from developing areas in absolute terms, the application of graduated tariffs discourage the exportation of commodities in processed form. Graduated tariffs—the progression of tariff rates according to the degree of fabrication—are applied in the major industrial countries with regard to hides and skins, rubber, timber, cotton, jute, metals, and several foodstuffs. In the European Common Market, for example, there is no duty on hides and skins, while a 10 per cent tariff is levied on leather, and 17–20 per cent on leather manufactures. Further, cocoa beans bear a 5.6 per cent duty, cocoa butter 22 per cent, cocoa paste 25 per cent, and cocoa powder 27 per cent. Similar examples can be given with regard to the United States and the United Kingdom.[12]

In this connection note that the disincentive effect of graduated tariffs is actually greater than the comparison of duties would suggest since the decision for exporting a commodity will not depend on differences in duties at different levels of processing but rather on the relationship between the increment in the duty and value added in the manufacturing process. The graduation of tariffs from raw materials to semiprocessed and processed goods does not continue as we move to more sophisticated products, however. While tariff rates rise from iron ore to pig iron and to steel ingots and finished articles of steel, duties again become lower on much of machinery and transport equipment.

Lower tariffs on highly sophisticated products as compared to the relatively simple manufactures exported by developing countries can be explained by reference to the process of negotiations on tariff reductions among industrial countries in the framework of GATT which takes the form of trading concessions for concessions. A continuation of this procedure is envisaged under the U.S. Trade Expansion Act, although tariff reductions will now apply to groups of commodities rather than to individual products. In this connection, it should be recalled that, under the Act, Congress has empowered the President to negotiate the elimination of tariffs in regard to commodities where 80 per cent of world exports originates in the United States and the European Common Market taken together and a reduction by one-half for other commodities.

A further consideration is that the application of restrictive measures on goods presently exported by developing countries is likely to affect the expansion of production in other manufacturing industries for exportation to industrial economies. Having experienced the imposition of restrictions on commodities that have come to be exported in recent years, entrepreneurs in less developed areas may feel obliged to make allowance for risk due to the possibility that restrictions would be applied to other goods as these come to be exported in larger quantities.

As to the effects of a reduction of restrictions on the manufac-

---

[12]For a commodity-by-commodity comparison, see [*17*, p. 79].

tured exports of developing areas, the possibilities of expansion can be indicated with regard to cotton textiles, for example. Even assuming the continuation of the International Cotton Textiles Agreement, the developing countries would supply only a small part of textiles consumed in developed areas, and further liberalization would bring increased imports.[13] Also, in view of the competitiveness of Asian jute manufacturing, the removal of quantitative restrictions in Western Europe would be accompanied by a shift in importation from raw jute to jute cloth and sacking.

Changes in the system of graduated tariffs would further contribute to increasing imports of foods and raw materials in processed form. Yet, given the error-possibilities associated with the measurement of substitution elasticities between the products of developed countries and developing economies, and the virtual absence of information on long term supply elasticities in the latter, we have not attempted to estimate the probable impact of a liberalization of import regimes on the manufactures of less developed areas. An indication of the relevant magnitudes can be given, however, if we consider that an increase in the imports of manufactured goods from developing economies by one-fourth over projected levels would amount to $0.6 billion in 1975—less than one-tenth of 1 per cent of the estimated increase in the gross national product of developed countries between 1960 and 1975.[14]

5.5 POSSIBILITIES FOR INCREASING EXPORTS FROM DEVELOPING COUNTRIES TO SOVIET-TYPE ECONOMIES

Although efforts have been made to increase the international division of labor within the Soviet bloc, the centrally planned economies apparently still maintain a policy of self-sufficiency vis-à-vis the developing countries. Comparative cost considerations play little part in this trade and imports are restricted to commodities that are not produced domestically, or are not available in sufficient quantities, excepting in cases when political expediency requires otherwise. At the same time, the system of priorities applied

---

[13]In 1960, the United States and the Common Market countries imported about 1 per cent of all domestically consumed cotton goods from developing countries [7, 11], and these proportions would reach 2 and 3 per cent, respectively, if the International Cotton Textiles Agreement were to be extended until 1975. But the proportion of cotton goods supplied by developing countries would not exceed 20 per cent in 1975 even in the United Kingdom where a more liberal import policy is applied (Cf. chap. 12.4).

[14]Note, however, that, in regard to most of these commodities, we should set the foreign exchange equivalent of the materials used in the manufacturing process against an increase in the exports of manufactures.

has led to limitations on the importation of consumer goods that are not available domestically, such as coffee and cocoa.

Announced plans in the countries of Eastern Europe indicate the continuation of the policy of self-sufficiency in the future. Self-sufficiency is a decisive factor in the planned increase of the production of synthetic materials, for example. As noted in Chapter 4.4, the Soviet Union aims at providing 97–98 per cent of domestic rubber consumption from home production, and the FAO estimated that by 1970 the degree of self-sufficiency in rubber would reach approximately 90 per cent in the Soviet Union and 65 per cent in the other countries of Eastern Europe.

By comparison, we have assumed that, in 1970, the Soviet Union would derive 18 per cent, and the other East European countries 40 per cent, of their rubber needs from imports of natural rubber. But these proportions are considerably lower than those projected for the United States (26 per cent) and Western Europe (47 per cent). Should the Soviet Union follow the American example and the other countries of Eastern Europe that of Western Europe, their combined rubber imports would exceed the amount projected by 162 thousand tons, i.e., $75 million at prices assumed to apply in 1970.[15] The corresponding figure would be nearly one-third larger in 1975.

Similar considerations apply to cotton and wool where we have assumed that imports from developing countries would remain at 1960 levels although national plans envisage a decrease of imports into the area. Should we assume instead that imports from less developed areas would rise at the same rate as imports into the industrial countries (1.2 per cent a year in the case of cotton and 2.0 per cent for wool), imports would exceed projected magnitudes by $58 million in 1975.

For further agricultural products, such as jute and, for a large part of the area, sugar, imports are likely to have a lower real cost than domestic production, although comparisons are made difficult by reason of the absence of scarcity prices in Soviet-type economies. Nevertheless, available information points to inefficiencies in the agriculture of these economies as compared to that of Western Europe. Thus, arguments for the opening of markets to imports of foodstuffs in Western Europe would apply a fortiori to the Soviet bloc.

---

[15]The midpoint of the FAO estimates of rubber consumption have been used in the calculations: 1550 thousand tons in the Soviet Union, and 540 thousand tons for the other countries of Western Europe [*1*, p. 13].

The possibilities of increased imports into Eastern Europe can be further indicated in regard to noncompeting tropical products. In the absence of limitations on imports, Soviet Russia could conceivably reach levels of per capita coffee consumption projected for Japan by 1975 (1.5 kg instead of 0.75 kg), while Czechoslovakia and Eastern Germany could attain the level assumed for Italy (4.6 instead of 4.0 kg), and the other countries of Eastern Europe that of Yugoslavia (1.9 instead of 0.75 kg). Correspondingly, an additional 196 thousand tons of coffee would be imported to Eastern Europe, valued at $137 million in 1960 prices. Further gains could be derived if imports of cocoa, tea, bananas, and spices were liberalized.

The Soviet Union and the more developed countries of Eastern Europe could also import labor-intensive manufactures from less developed areas. A comparison with the trade of industrial countries can be of interest here. Should we equate per capita incomes in Eastern Europe to that of Yugoslavia,[16] the gross national product of this area in the year 1960 would be estimated at 195 billion in terms of 1955 dollars—about one-fifth of a GNP of $964 billion in the developed countries.[17] But the latter countries imported manufactured goods in the value of $1,075 million from developing economies in 1960 as against Soviet bloc imports of $48 million. Had the countries of Eastern Europe attained the ratio between imports and GNP observed in the developed countries, they would have imported manufactures from less developed areas in the value of $215 million in 1960. And if gross national product in the Soviet bloc were to increase at an annual rate of 5.5 per cent,[18] these imports would have to reach $480 million by 1975, considerably higher than our estimate of $136 million for that year but lower than the $1.5–$2.0 billion projected by the UN Economic Commission for Europe for 1980 [*18*, V, p 18].

If we were to use the same analogy with regard to the total imports of the Soviet bloc from developing countries, it would appear that in 1960 the countries of Eastern Europe should have imported $4.0 billion worth of merchandise from less developed areas as compared to their actual imports of $1.0 billion. But one may argue that the Soviet Union is better endowed with natural resources than are Western Europe and Japan and hence we could not apply the import/GNP ratio calculated for the developed countries, taken

---

[16]Estimated at $625 for 1960 in terms of 1955 prices (Table A2.6.2).
[17]Table 3.1.1.
[18]Chapter 4.4.

together, to Eastern Europe. Should we use the ratio observed in regard to North America instead, the imports of the countries of the Soviet bloc from developing areas would have amounted to $2.7 billion in 1960. And, again assuming projected growth rates to be reached, these imports could surpass $6 billion in 1975 as compared to our projection of $1.9 bililon.

5.6 ECONOMIC INTEGRATION IN DEVELOPING REGIONS

Much has been said about economic integration in underdeveloped areas, but, so far, little has been accomplished. In Latin America, the establishment of the Free Trade Area has been followed by tariff reductions in a limited sphere and, in the absence of provisions for automatic reductions of duties, the momentum of integration appears to be slowing down as mutual concessions are more difficult to come by. In Africa, one can observe a process of disintegration rather than integration in recent years and, although several proposals for integration have been made, it is as yet uncertain which countries will eventually participate and in what kind of integration projects. Apart from the activities of the Organization of Petroleum Producing Countries, there is hardly any regional cooperation in the Middle East, and Malaysia is the only example of an economic (and political) union in Asia.

At the same time, intra-area trade in less developed areas has declined in importance over the last decade, in part because import substitution could be effected with greater ease against the less sophisticated products imported from neighboring countries. An extreme example is that of Asia where policies aiming at national self-sufficiency in agricultural products and simple manufactures have led to an absolute reduction of intra-area trade.

National plans do not envisage a greater degree of economic intercourse for the future, either. Import substitution continues to be directed to a considerable extent against commodities produced in other developing countries, and the long term plans give few indications of an increasing intraregional division of labor in manufactured goods.

Correspondingly, our projections on the future imports of less developed regions reflect the assumption that national commercial policies will be continued during the period under consideration. Yet, economic integration in developing regions would contribute to an improvement in the current account balance of these regions by reason of the large-scale economies obtainable in a wider market. On the one hand, the exploitation of economies of scale and external economies in a large market would further the expansion of manufacturing, thereby contributing to a reduction in import requirements and, possibly, to increases in the exports of manufactures; on the other, the cost of import substitution will be reduced as the size of the area increases.

These considerations point to the possibilities of improving the trade balance of developing regions through regional integration.[19] However, given the uncertainties related to future developments and the structural changes accompanying economic integration in less developed areas, no attempt has been made to estimate the probable effects of integration on international trade in the present study.[20] Still, the relative importance of reducing imports in the framework of regional integration projects can be indicated by reference to the fact that a fall in the income elasticity of import demand by one-twentieth would represent an improvement in the current balance of the developing countries by about $1.5 billion in 1975.

5.7 CAPITAL INFLOW

The flow of public capital to developing areas has risen to a considerable extent in recent years. According to the estimates published by the OECD, official contributions by the countries of the Development Assistance Committee increased from an average of $1.9 billion in 1950–1955 to $4.3 billion in 1959, $4.9 billion in 1960, and $6.1 billion in 1961 [6, p. 15].[21]

A number of assumptions can be made concerning future changes in the flow of public funds originating in developed countries. The continuation of the rate of increase of public assistance observed in recent years may be postulated, for example. Alternatively, we may assume that the proportion of the net flow of public capital in the gross national product of the developed countries will remain un-

---

[19]A detailed discussion on the impact of economic integration on resource allocation, trade, and growth in less developed areas has been given in my lectures on economic development and integration, at the Centro de Estudios Monetarios Latinoamericanos in Mexico City (to be published in book form).

[20]Several years ago, the UN Economic Commission for Latin America attempted to evaluate the impact of a Latin-American union on extra-area imports [19] but the reliability of the estimates is open to doubt.

[21]The figures include, in addition to bilateral assistance to countries in less developed areas ($3.7 billion in 1960), contributions to international organizations ($0.7 billion), grants and loans to Greece, Spain, and Turkey ($0.4 billion), and unallocated aid ($0.1 billion). On the composition of this assistance, see [6, pp. 4, 74].

changed or that the goal of 1 per cent of the combined national incomes of the capital-exporting countries stipulated in the UN General Assembly Resolution 1717 (XVI) will be reached.

It is suggested here that the first alternative has to be discarded since internal political considerations in the developed countries would hardly permit the continuation of the rapid rate of increase in the net amount of public assistance experienced in the recent past. Should we assume that increases in the net flow of public funds will proceed *pari passu* with the rise of GNP in the member countries of the Development Assistance Committee, the annual rate of increase of foreign aid would be 4.0 per cent or 4.6 per cent, depending on the income assumption chosen. A higher rate of increase would be indicated if the UN goal of 1 per cent of national incomes were reached since, according to an estimate of the United Nations, the relevant proportion was 0.7 in 1960 [*14*, p. 14].

Were we to calculate with a rate of growth of 4 per cent, taking the annual average of public assistance provided in the years 1959–61 as a basis, the net flow of public funds from the DAC countries would reach $7.6 billion in 1970 and $9.2 billion in 1975.[22] One may object that these estimates are on the low side since official contributions reached $6.1 billion already in 1961, but the reluctance of the U.S. Congress to increase foreign aid appropriations should temper an optimistic appraisal. Moreover, account had to be taken of the possibility that Greece, Spain, and Turkey would continue to share in the public assistance provided by the DAC group.

Some increases may be forthcoming in private capital flows, too, partly in the form of new investment, and partly through the reinvestment of the income of foreign companies at the place of operation. Private investment is subject to political uncertainty, however, and it is also affected by changes in tax laws and other factors that can hardly be foreseen. In the present study, we have assumed that, after a decline in the early sixties, net private investment (including guaranteed private export credit for more than one year) would reach $3.0 billion in 1970 and $3.3 billion in 1975 as compared to $2.5 billion in 1960. These increases would accompany the rise in world demand for raw materials and the process of industrialization in less developed areas.

Uncertainties relate to grants and loans originating in the Sino-

---

[22]Gross capital flows would have to increase at a higher rate, however, by reason of the increased burden of amortization associated with the anticipated shift from grants to loans.

Soviet area, too. While commitments of bilateral loans and grants to developing countries averaged $1.0 billion in 1959-61, actual disbursements reached only $186 million in 1960 and $294 million in 1961 [6, pp. 13-14]. We have assumed here that net disbursements would amount to $1.0 billion in 1970 and $1.2 billion in 1975, one-sixth of which would be supplied by Mainland China.[23]

Note, however, that the projected amount of loans and grants from the Sino-Soviet area would still be small as compared to capital flows originating in developed areas. If we assumed that the countries of Eastern Europe had one-fifth of the gross national product of the developed economies, they should have provided loans and grants in the amount of $0.9 billion in 1960 to match the public assistance supplied by the developed countries.[24] On the same basis, the net flow of foreign assistance from Eastern Europe would have to attain $1.5 billion in 1970 and $2.1 billion in 1975.[25]

According to the above projections, the net flow of public and private capital to developing countries would reach $11.6 billion in 1970 and $13.7 billion in 1975. These amounts would cover the projected balance of payments deficit of the developing areas, taken as a whole, irrespective of whether the most likely or the high (target) income alternative were realized in the world economy (Table 5.2.1). The flow of capital would, however, fall short of the current account deficit of $12.0 billion in 1970 and $16.6 billion in 1975, estimated under the assumption that developed countries attained "most likely" growth rates and developing economies target rates.

5.8 CONCLUSION

We have indicated alternative possibilities for filling the projected gap in the current account balance of the developing countries. It has been shown that the current account deficit of the developing countries, taken together, could be financed by the projected inflow of foreign capital, excepting the case that national income in these countries grew at target rates and developed economies attained "most likely" growth rates. Unrecorded reverse flows may continue to augment the current account deficit

---

[23]On commitments for financial assistance by China, see [14, p. 27].

[24]The relevant figure is $1.4 billion if the net transfer of economic resources is used as a criterion, since in the latter case private foreign investment should be included in the calculations. We have restricted the discussion to public assistance, however, by reason of the substantial return flow on private investments in the form of investment earnings.

[25]On assumptions regarding economic growth in Eastern Europe, see chap. 4.4.

of the less developed areas, however, although these flows are expected to decline to a considerable extent from the level experienced in 1960, when the decolonization of Africa gave rise to a capital flight.[26]

But even assuming that unrecorded reverse flows would be of negligible proportions, various considerations suggest that full reliance should not be based on foreign assistance. To begin with, an equality between the current account deficit and the inflow of foreign capital in the less developed areas, taken together, can conceal interregional and intraregional differences. Political considerations are likely to affect the distribution of public funds, and private investors will favor some areas as compared to others. The inflow of foreign capital may continue to exceed the current account deficit of the Middle East, for example, and private investment will also be directed to areas producing nonfuel minerals.

An additional consideration is that, in the absence of other measures, the inflow of foreign capital may not appropriately serve the objective of attaining high growth rates, since barriers to imports from developing countries and industrialization in the framework of narrow national markets will reduce the effectiveness of foreign investment. Moreover, the granting of foreign aid imposes a burden on the developed countries under conditions of full employment, while they would derive a long run gain from decreased protection by reason of the concomitant improvement in the allocation of economic resources.

The balance of payments effects of a liberalization of import restrictions on agricultural products in the developed countries should not be overrated, however. We have indicated above that the once-for-all gain developing economies would derive from the elimination of tariffs and excise taxes on bananas and tropical beverages in the main industrial countries would amount to relatively little. At the same time, given the small share of developing countries in

---

[26]The reader may also question the assumption of unchanged prices of manufactured exports from developed countries. Increases in these prices would augment the balance-of-payments deficit of the developing economies, although upward pressures on prices of primary products would also be generated. But export prices of manufactured goods hardly changed in the 1958–1962 period (using 1958 weights, the rise is 2 per cent, which is largely explained by the upward bias in the U.S. index), and while industrial countries may not be successful in restraining a rise in the consumer price index which is heavily weighted by services, the stability of export prices may well continue. At the same time, the increased demand for primary products, coupled with an insufficient rise in supplies, can raise the average price level of primary commodities, as shown by the experience of the year 1963.

world exports of temperate zone foods and the importation of such foods through noncommercial channels into several of these countries, it is difficult to evaluate the possible impact of a reduction of price support in the United States and a lowering of trade barriers in Europe on cereals, for example. These considerations apply to some extent also to oilseeds, while developing countries would decidedly benefit from a liberalization of policies concerning sugar, as well as from an increase in the imports of agricultural products into the Sino-Soviet area.

Further gains could be obtained from an increase in the U.S. quota on petroleum and, to a lesser extent, lead and zinc, although the benefits would accrue to countries that have favorable export prospects anyway. As a result, interregional and intraregional differences in export earnings would be further accentuated.

It appears, then, that countries producing minerals and metals not only have the most favorable export prospects among developing economies but these countries also attract foreign capital and are expected to benefit from a liberalization of trade policies in the developed countries. The disparities are likely to continue beyond 1975, inasmuch as the depletion of mineral resources in industrial economies will make them increasingly dependent on foreign sources of supply, while the growth of demand for foodstuffs will fall behind the increase in incomes.

If we also consider that, after the assumed adjustment in primary product prices during the sixties, exports originating in less developed areas have been projected to rise at a rate exceeding the growth of GNP in the developed countries (Table 3.1.1), it would appear that Prebisch and other writers have underrated the trade prospects of the developing countries. Should developed and less developed economies grow at identical rates, the main problem might lie not so much in the inadequate growth of the foreign exchange earnings of developing countries as in the uneven distribution of these earnings.[27]

Among the less developed areas, the prospects for the countries of Asia are the least favorable. In the period under consideration, these countries are expected to have over one half of the current account deficit of the developing regions, taken together. In the absence of substantial mineral resources, Asian economies would face increasing foreign exchange problems in the future if the produc-

---

[27]It is a different question that, under present arrangements, the current account deficit of the developing countries would be rising at an increasing rate if these countries attempted to grow at a rate faster than developed economies do.

tion and exports of manufactured goods failed to rise. India is a good example where the demand for the main agricultural export commodity, tea, will hardly increase at a rate exceeding the growth of population in the developed countries, while, in the absence of trade barriers, possibilities of expansion in the exportation of textiles exist.

In fact, the comparative advantage of countries that are poorly endowed with mineral resources will increasingly lie in labor-intensive manufactures and in industrial products that utilize domestic materials. It would be necessary, therefore, to encourage the exportation of manufactures from less developed areas. On the part of the developed countries, appropriate measures would include a liberalization of quotas and changes in the structure of tariffs.

The developing countries would derive further gains from an acceleration of economic growth in developed economies. In this connection, it should be recalled that the attainment of target levels of economic growth in developed countries would raise the net foreign exchange receipts of developing economies by $2.7 billion in 1975 over the level calculated under the "most likely" income assumption.

Potential gains derived from a liberalization of import-policies in Soviet-type economies, too, are substantial. We have seen, for example, that a modest increase in per capita coffee consumption in Eastern Europe promises greater benefit to the developing countries than the elimination of all taxes and tariffs on coffee in developed economies. Similar possibilities exist in regard to other tropical beverages, agricultural raw materials, and manufactured goods. In general, the estimates of the preceding section indicate that Soviet bloc countries play a considerably smaller role as importers and as sources of economic assistance to the developing countries than their relative income position would warrant.

But the application of the proposed measures in the importing countries does not guarantee that target rates of income growth would, in fact, be attained in less developed areas. Political uncertainty can give rise to a capital flight, monetary mismanagement may hinder the use of funds obtained abroad for productive purposes, inappropriate fiscal policies may lead to a misdirection of investment activity, and, last but not least, the existing social structure of a number of countries can obstruct the process of economic transformation.

Expressed differently, in order to attain target growth rates in less developed areas, it is necessary that developing countries successfully follow growth-oriented domestic policies. Should this not happen—and there are indications, especially in Latin America, that powerful obstacles stand in the way of an acceleration of economic growth—target rates would not be reached and the projected current account deficit of the developing countries would be correspondingly smaller. At the same time, policies aimed at regional integration can contribute to rapid growth *and* improve the current account balance of less developed areas.

Note finally that should target growth-rates be reached in developing countries, increases in income per head would still be relatively small if the rapid growth of population continued. Not only does per capita foreign assistance fall as population increases but a high rate of growth of population also leads to larger imports and smaller exports by reason of the pressure exerted on domestic resources. Correspondingly, appropriate policies designed to contribute to higher living standards in the developing countries should include a population policy.

These considerations indicate that, in furthering the objectives of the UN Developed Decade, sole reliance cannot be placed on measures taken by the developed countries. Rather, the successful implementation of the goal of steadily rising living standards during the Development Decade—and thereafter—requires the application of appropriate policies by developed countries, the Soviet bloc, as well as in less developed economies. Action in one field, such as trade policy or foreign aid, can have only a limited effect without measures taken in other areas.

REFERENCES

[1.] FOOD AND AGRICULTURE ORGANIZATION. *Agricultural Commodities— the Outlook for 1970 in Eastern Europe.* Rome, 1963.

[2.] FOOD AND AGRICULTURE ORGANIZATION. *Production Yearbook,* 1961.

[3.] INTERNATIONAL MONETARY FUND. *Balance of Payments,* Volume 13. Washington, D.C. 1962.

[4.] INTERNATIONAL MONETARY FUND. *Improvement of the Invisible Trade of Developing Countries.* United Nations Conference on Trade and Development, Preparatory Committee, E/CONF. 46/PC/33. New York, 1963.

[5.] KARREMAN, H. F., "World Transportation Account, 1950–1953." *Review of Economics and Statistics,* (February, 1958) Supplement, pp. 36–49.

[6.] ORGANIZATION FOR ECONOMIC COOPERATION AND DEVELOPMENT. The *Flow of Financial Resources to Developing Countries in 1961.* Paris, 1963.

[7.] "Per Capita Fiber Consumption," *Monthly Bulletin of Agricultural Economics and Statistics* (January, 1962), pp. 1–28.

[8.] SNAPE, R. H. "Some Effects of Protection in the World Sugar Industry," *Economica* (February, 1963), pp. 63–74.

[9.] TINBERGEN, JAN. *Shaping the World Economy.* New York: Twentieth Century Fund, 1961.

[10.] "Tropical Fruit and Beverages: Duties and Taxes in Western Europe," *Monthly Bulletin of Agricultural Economics and Statistics* (December, 1962), pp. 8–11.

[11.] UNITED NATIONS. *Commodity Trade Statistics, 1960.* New York, 1962.

[12.] UNITED NATIONS. *Direction of International Trade,* February–June, 1962.

[13.] UNITED NATIONS. *Improvement of the Invisible Trade of Developing Countries.* United Nations Conference on Trade and Development, Preparatory Committee, E/CONF.46/PC/21. New York, 1963.

[14.] UNITED NATIONS. *International Flow of Long-Term Capital and Official Donations, 1959–1961.* New York, 1963.

[15.] UNITED NATIONS. *Monthly Bulletin of Statistics,* March, 1963.

[16.] UNITED NATIONS. *Statistical Yearbook,* various issues.

[17.] UNITED NATIONS. *World Economic Survey, 1962, Part 1.* New York, 1963.

[18.] UNITED NATIONS ECONOMIC COMMISSION FOR EUROPE. *Economic Survey of Europe in 1960.* Geneva, 1961.

[19.] UNITED NATIONS ECONOMIC COMMISSION FOR LATIN AMERICA. *The Latin American Common Market.* New York, 1959.

PART II

Prospects for
Individual Commodities

CHAPTER 6

Trade Projections for Temperate Zone Foods

6.1 LIVESTOCK, MEAT, FISH, AND EGGS
(SITC 00, 01, 03,025)

Livestock, Meat, and Meat Preparations (SITC 00, 01)

Much of international trade in livestock and meat takes place among the developed countries themselves, and in less developed areas only Argentina, Mexico, and Uruguay export appreciable quantities of meat to high-income countries. Argentina derives 28 per cent of her export earnings from the sale of meat, Uruguay 19 per cent, and Mexico 6 per cent. Meat exports are assuming increased importance in Central America, too.

In 1960, developing countries exported meat to developed economies in the value of $365 million. Among the importing countries, the United States buys live animals and fresh and frozen meat from Mexico and Central America, but health regulations permit only the importation of canned meat from South America. The United Kingdom, the largest meat importer, purchases beef (and some mutton) from Argentina and Uruguay, and these countries also sell beef to the European Common Market. Greece and Switzerland also purchase some beef from Argentina and Uruguay. Meat imports into Japan are negligible, while Australia, New Zealand, and South Africa are net exporters of meat.

With few exceptions, per capita meat consumption has been rising in the industrial countries during the last decade, and pre-war consumption levels were surpassed in most of these countries around 1955 (Table A6.1.1). Consumption per head reached 84 kg in the United States in 1960, with Canada (80 kg) and France (73 kg) following, while the lowest consumption levels are observed in Japan (6 kg), Turkey (13 kg), Spain and Portugal (18 kg). Intercountry differences in meat consumption are explained, to a large extent, by differences in incomes and social customs, and by substitution possibilities between meat and fish. In Japan and, to a lesser extent, in Turkey, social habits account for the low level of meat consumption, for example, whereas in Portugal and in some other fish-exporting countries the availability of cheap fish has held back the growth of meat consumption.

In projecting the consumption of meat, we have relied on time-series estimates, budget data, and intercountry comparisons.[1] In the first step, the per capita consumption of all meats was forecast and, subsequently, the estimates have been broken down according to the main categories of meat. The following groupings have been used: beef and veal, pork, mutton and lamb, poultry, and other meat (offals, horse meat, game, etc.).[2] In estimating the shares of individual meats in consumption, we have utilized the results of budget estimates, international comparisons, and available information on prospective change in relative prices.

North America

The per capita consumption of meat exhibited an upward trend in the United States, and further increases are expected. In 1955, the income elasticity of demand for all meat derived from budget studies was 0.3, with higher values shown for beef and veal and a lower elasticity for poultry, while the consumption of pork does not seem to depend on the level of personal incomes.[3] In making projections, we have calculated with an income elasticity of demand of 0.3 for all meat and have assumed that larger than average increases would be forthcoming with regard to beef and veal, about average rise for poultry, and a decline or no change for pork, mutton and lamb, and other meat (Tables 6.1.1 and A6.1.1).

As regards U.S. trade in livestock and meat, differing trends are observed with respect to red meat as compared to poultry and offals. Imports of beef and veal, mutton and lamb, and pork have been rising over the last decade, with exports remaining approximately constant. Whereas, in the years 1950–52, 4.0 per cent of beef and veal, 0.9 per cent of mutton and lamb, and 0.5 per cent of pork consumed in the United States was imported, the corresponding

---

[1]Although the experience of the United States provides evidence on the effect of price changes on meat consumption, it has not been possible to include a price variable in the regressions, by reason of the insufficient information available in most countries for deriving a price index for meat and the difficulties encountered in international comparisons of meat prices. Consequently, in the regression equations given in Table A.6.1.3, per capita disposable income is used as the only independent variable.

[2]In the United Kingdom and Canada, meat products are also included in the latter category.

[3]Unless otherwise noted, budget elasticities have been taken from [6].

ratios were 5.7, 11.0, and 1.5 per cent in 1959–61, and, in the latter period, imports of red meat exceeded exports six times. On the other hand, imports of poultry and offals have remained small, while exports have been growing at a rapid rate.

TABLE 6.1.1

MEAT CONSUMPTION IN NORTH AMERICA AND WESTERN EUROPE
(thousand metric tons, dressed carcass weight)

	1960	1970I	1970II	1975I	1975II
United States					
Beef and veal	5,869	8,076	8,249	9,330	9,612
Pork	4,889	5,784	5,784	6,220	6,220
Mutton and lamb	344	364	364	401	401
Poultry	2,775	3,556	3,599	4,005	4,052
Other meat	1,038	1,307	1,328	1,484	1,508
Total meat	14,915	19,087	19,324	21,440	21,793
Canada					
Beef and veal	605	809	817	924	942
Pork	479	580	580	623	623
Mutton and lamb	25	30	30	33	33
Poultry	241	320	327	371	378
Other meat	101	125	129	143	146
Total meat	1,451	1,864	1,883	2,094	2,122
Common Market					
Beef and veal	3,447	4,648	4,743	5,200	5,383
Pork	3,335	3,890	3,942	4,175	4,276
Mutton and lamb	197	234	234	248	247
Poultry	870	1,579	1,686	1,991	2,138
Other meat	1,080	1,308	1,329	1,437	1,485
Total meat	8,929	11,659	11,934	13,051	13,529
United Kingdom					
Beef and veal	1,135	1,303	1,320	1,379	1,413
Pork	447	515	526	546	558
Mutton and lamb	610	688	699	736	753
Poultry	315	459	475	512	535
Other meat	1,045	1,146	1,158	1,201	1,219
Total meat	3,552	4,111	4,178	4,374	4,478
Northern Europe					
Beef and veal	616	770	791	842	877
Pork	912	988	995	1,026	1,036
Mutton and lamb	58	63	63	65	67
Poultry	101	204	224	254	282
Other meat	148	161	162	168	170
Total meat	1,835	2,186	2,235	2,355	2,432
Southern Europe					
Beef and veal	533	1,010	1,168	1,341	1,533
Pork	432	667	714	795	858
Mutton and lamb	424	625	665	758	813
Poultry	160	373	369	427	487
Other meat	227	338	356	397	443
Total meat	1,776	3,013	3,272	3,718	4,134

Source: OECD countries and Yugoslavia--OECD, Agricultural and Food Statistics, 1959 and 1962 and Food Balance Sheets. Finland--UN Statistical Yearbook.

The pattern of imports is greatly influenced by nontariff regulations. Embargoes are imposed on livestock and meat originating in countries in any part of which foot-and-mouth disease or rinderpest is known to exist. This regulation affects most severely Argentina and Uruguay, although imports from most European countries are prohibited, too. Correspondingly, the United States buys only canned beef from South America, while livestock is imported from Canada and Mexico, and fresh, chilled, and frozen beef from Australia, New Zealand, Ireland, Mexico, and Central America. Mutton and lamb, too, come from Australia and New Zealand, and pork and pork preparations from Western Europe and Poland.

The expansion of imports has been most pronounced in regard to boneless beef used in hamburgers and frankfurters. Given differences in production costs, we can expect further increases in these imports, and purchases of low-cost beef from Central America as well as livestock and beef imports from Mexico will also rise. Assuming present policies to continue, the proportion of imports in the U.S. consumption of beef and veal may reach 10 per cent by 1975, while the degree of self-sufficiency in pork and mutton and lamb may remain unchanged.

In conformity with forecasts prepared for the Royal Commission on Canada's Economic Prospects [*13*, p. 80], we have assumed that meat consumption in Canada would rise at a rate slightly higher than in the United States, while the pattern of consumption would approach that of the United States. With the exception of some processed meats originating in Argentina, Canada purchases meat from the United States, Australia, and New Zealand. This situation is not expected to change during the period of projection.

Western Europe

Among the Common Market countries, meat consumption per head approaches the U.S. level only in France (73 kg); it is 59 kg in Belgium, 56 kg in Germany, 46 kg in the Netherlands, and 28 kg in Italy. Information provided by time series, budget studies, and intercountry comparisons point to considerable increases in consumption during the period of projection. With the exception of Italy, income elasticities derived from these sources of information are between 0.4 and 0.7, with France at the lower and the Netherlands at the higher end of the scale. In the case of Germany and the Netherlands, we have also calculated with a trend factor of 0.1 kg a year per person.

Larger increases in consumption are expected in Italy, however, where all sources indicate income elasticities exceeding unity. Finally, prospective changes in incomes and relative prices are likely to contribute to shifts in the consumption of individual meats so that the composition of meat consumption in the Common Market would conform more closely to the U.S. consumption pattern. Poultry consumption is likely to grow at the highest rate in response to the expected lowering of prices due to greater efficiency in production, while the consumption of beef and veal may also rise at a rate exceeding that for all meats. Correspondingly, the relative share of pork, mutton and lamb, and other meats would decline in all EEC countries.

In 1960, Common Market imports of livestock and meat were valued at $410 million and accounted for 7 per cent of domestic consumption. The corresponding ratio is about 10 per cent for beef and veal, for poultry, and for offals; the EEC is self-sufficient in mutton and it is a net exporter of pork. Nearly one-half of Common Market imports originate in the EFTA countries, with Denmark as the most important supplier (livestock and poultry); about one-fifth come from the Soviet bloc (slaughter animals), one-tenth from the United States (poultry and offals), and one-eighth from Argentina and Uruguay (frozen beef).

The future prospects for the imports of livestock and meat will depend to a large extent on the application of the new agricultural policy of the Common Market. According to the regulations in effect, the fixed external tariff on pork and poultry is supplemented by variable levies, designed to counterbalance the difference in domestic and foreign prices and thereby to provide protection for home production. A combination of fixed and variable levies will be applied also to beef and veal. At the same time, quantitative restrictions on the importation of frozen and canned beef, sausages, and other meat preparations would be maintained.

These protective measures will provide an incentive for the expansion of livestock production in the Common Market, so that the degree of self-sufficiency in regard to beef and poultry is expected to rise, and export surpluses in pork meat may continue to grow. Of special significance is the impact of the common agricultural policy on beef, which accounted for about 60 per cent of Common Market livestock and meat imports and over 85 per cent of imports originating in the less developed countries.

According to the projection of the EEC Commission, in 1970 the production of beef in the Common Market would reach 4.7 million tons in carcass equivalent, compared to a consumption of 4.7 to 5.0 million tons [3, p. IV 20]. On the other hand, our consumption projection of about 4.7 million tons entails zero net imports for 1970, and home production has been assumed to fully provide for domestic needs in 1975, too. Still, assuming the continuation of exports to the African associated countries, the EEC will import small quantities of beef. At the same time, imports of meat preparations may rise somewhat, while a decline of poultry imports is foreseen.

The United Kingdom is the world's largest importer of livestock and meat, with imports accounting for 42 per cent of domestic consumption. In 1960, the f.o.b. value of these imports was $1020 million, half of which came from Western Europe (mainly livestock from Ireland and bacon from Denmark), one-fourth from Australia and New Zealand (mutton and beef), and nearly one-fifth from Argentina and Uruguay (frozen and canned beef, and some mutton).

British meat consumption increased considerably during the fifties, but comparisons with the period before 1954 are misleading by reason of the existence of rationing at that time. Since 1954, a 1 per cent rise in per capita disposable income has been accompanied by an approximately 0.5 per cent increase in meat consumption per head while an income elasticity of 0.2 has been derived from budget studies [*14*, p. 35]. Taking account of international comparisons of consumption levels, an elasticity of 0.4 has been assumed in the projections. The largest increases will take place in poultry, but—as distinct from the case of the Common Market—the relative share of beef, veal, and other meat may decline rather than increase, while that of pork and mutton is unlikely to fall [*10*, p. 123].

At the same time, domestic meat production will expand, especially in poultry and beef. Accordingly, the imports of the latter two meats will increase only if the target rate of income growth is reached. On the other hand, the imports of mutton and pork can rise *pari passu* with the growth of domestic consumption, and imports of canned meat may also increase somewhat.

In the countries of Northern Europe, the level of meat consumption is among the highest in Denmark and Ireland, the largest meat exporters in Europe. Less meat is consumed in the Scandinavian countries other than Denmark, while meat consumption in Austria and Switzerland is approximately at the German level. According to time-series estimates and the results of budget studies, the income elasticity of demand is between 0.4 and 0.6 in these countries, the exception being Finland, where we have calculated with an elasticity of 0.7. Much of the increase in consumption is expected to take the form of poultry and beef.

The situation is different in Southern Europe. In none of these countries has meat consumption per head surpassed 30 kg, and it is only 13 kg in Turkey. At the same time, the income elasticity of demand for meat appears to exceed unity in all countries of this group, so that substantial increases in consumption can take place during the period under consideration. The pattern of consumption is likely to conform, by and large, to the availability of various kinds of meat.

With the exception of Switzerland, the countries of Northern Europe are self-sufficient in meat, while, in Southern Europe, Greece, Portugal, and Spain import small quantities. In 1960, imports in the two areas taken together have not reached $150 million. Over one half of the imports originated in Western Europe and one-fourth in the Soviet bloc. Imports from developing countries have not surpassed $20 million, and consist mainly of beef purchased in Argentina. During the period of projection imports have been assumed to rise in proportion to domestic consumption in the net importing countries.

Japan

Per capita meat consumption in Japan fell from the prewar level of 4 kg to 2 kg after the war and has since reached 6 kg. Given the revolutionary changes in the pattern of consumption presently under way in Japan, any forecast of future meat consumption necessarily entails a large margin of error. We have assumed that the income elasticity of 1.2 derived from budget studies is applicable for the period of projection and have calculated with an additional trend of 0.2 kg per person a year.

Correspondingly, the total consumption of meat may more than double between 1960 and 1970 and increase one and one-half times between 1960 and 1975. Domestic production will also expand, although probably at a lower rate than consumption, so that imports may triple within a decade. Imports will continue to be concentrated in beef and veal, and in mutton.

Oceania and South Africa

Australia and New Zealand enjoy the highest levels of meat consumption in the world, with little change expected over the period of projection. At the same time, these countries will continue to increase their exportable production. Exports from South Africa may also rise.

The Price and Origin of Imports

As noted above, United States meat imports from developing countries consist almost entirely of livestock from Mexico, fresh and frozen beef from Mexico and Central America, and canned meat from Argentina and other meat-producing countries in South

America. Since feeding steers purchased from Mexico provide beef for a certain geographical area in the United States, these imports can be expected to rise in proportion to the growth of domestic consumption. At the same time, Mexico and the meat-producing countries of Central America may maintain their present share in U.S. imports of fresh and frozen beef, and canned beef imports originating in the Southern Hemisphere are also likely to increase from their low 1960 level.

Beef (fresh, frozen, and preserved) accounts for over 85 per cent of EEC's meat imports from the developing countries. Excepting small purchases from Madagascar, these imports originate in Argentina, and in other South American meat-producing countries. Given the prospective self-sufficiency of the Common Market countries in beef, imports from South America would largely disappear. Madagascar, however, could expand her exports to the EEC in the framework of the association agreements.

British meat imports from developing countries, too, consist almost entirely of beef. The United Kingdom purchases beef and veal from the meat-producing countries of South America and also from Kenya. Under the most likely income assumption, these suppliers are expected to maintain their present share in the unchanged U.K. imports, while sales would rise somewhat if the target rate of income growth were reached. Finally, increased sales of beef to Greece and Switzerland are also foreseen.

In view of trade agreements with Japan, Australia and New Zealand will maintain their place as the main supplier of meat to Japan during the period of projection. Thus, the present small imports from Argentina and India would hardly rise more than imports of all meat into Japan.

Beef prices have been fluctuating in recent years, but despite the fall in prices that took place in 1961, significant departures from the 1960 price level are not expected. Accordingly, under the most likely income assumption, the export receipts of the developing countries derived from the sale of meat would surpass the 1960 level by 10 per cent in 1970 and by 24 per cent in 1975, while the relevant figures are 20 and 43 per cent in the event that the target rate of income growth is reached (Table A6).

FISH AND FISH PREPARATIONS (SITC 03)

Imports of developed countries from less developed areas account for a negligible proportion of world trade in fish and fish preparations. In 1960, these imports amounted to $118 million, nearly half of which originated in Mexico and Morocco, where fish exports provide 6 to 7 per cent of export earnings. The largest importer is the United States (mostly shrimp, but also fresh fish from Mexico and several other Latin-American countries), with France following (sardines from Morocco).

International comparisons of consumption levels indicate large differences in fish consumption per head resulting from diversity in tastes and the price and availability of fish as compared to meat. While in the United States fish accounts for 5 per cent of the combined consumption of meat and fish, the corresponding ratio is 60 per cent in Portugal and Spain, and 48 per cent in Norway. At the same time, the projection of fish consumption involves a considerable margin of error, especially in countries with low consumption levels since changes in relative prices and promotional efforts may have a considerable effect on consumption per head.

North America

The per capita consumption of fish in the United States fluctuated between 4.6–5.0 kg over the last decade, and neither time-series data nor budget statistics give indication of an increase in consumption per head in the future. Correspondingly, we have assumed that the total consumption of fish would rise at the same rate as population.

The domestic production of fish has been approximately constant during the fifties, with small variations due to weather conditions and other causes. Within the rising imports, the share of the developing countries increased; in 1960, these countries supplied one-third of U.S. imports of fresh and frozen fish, as compared to 20 per cent a decade earlier, and have increased their share in the imports of preserved fish, too (9 per cent in 1960). Taken together, imports from less developed areas accounted for 30 per cent of U.S. imports of fish and fish preparations in 1960, with much of the remainder divided between Canada and Japan.

Although the prospective enlargement of domestic fishing fleets will lead to increases in U.S. production, the bulk of the growth of consumption is likely to be supplied by imports. Within the increased imports, the share of less developed countries is likely to rise further, and it may reach 35 per cent of the total imports of fresh and frozen fish. On the other hand, increases in the imports of Canada, the world's second largest exporter of fish, are not foreseen.

Western Europe

The countries of Western Europe, taken together, have an export surplus in fish, the largest exporters being Norway, Denmark, Iceland, Portugal, and the Netherlands. But domestic production does not fully satisfy consumption requirements in the Common Market countries other than the Netherlands, in the United Kingdom, and in Yugoslavia, whereas Austria and Switzerland import over 80 per cent of fish consumed domestically.

The deficit countries of Europe import most of their requirements from other countries of the area, from Japan, and from Canada, with developing countries supplying less than 10 per cent of gross imports. In 1960, French purchases from North Africa and Senegal accounted for about three-fourths of European fish imports originating in less developed areas, while much of the remainder went to Italy and Germany.

Fish consumption per head is generally high in the exporting countries (over 30 kg in Norway and Portugal, 25 kg in Spain, and between 15 and 20 kg in Sweden and Denmark); it is the lowest in Austria, Switzerland, Turkey (3–3.5 kg), and Yugoslavia (1.7 kg).[4] During the fifties, per capita consumption remained approximately constant in most countries under consideration, although some increases are shown in those with low consumption levels.

Prospective increases in consumption are likely to be small and there is no reason to assume that fish production in Western Europe could not keep up with the growth of consumption. Still, Common Market imports from areas that receive preferential treatment (Morocco, Tunisia, Senegal) will rise, possibly at the same rate as the increase in total consumption.

Japan

Japan is the largest fish exporter of the world, and imports only small quantities of fish from South Korea. We have assumed imports to remain unchanged during the period of projection.

Oceania and South Africa

New Zealand and South Africa are also fish exporters, while Australia is a net importer. Australian fish imports originate largely in South Africa and this situation is not likely to change in the future.

---

[4]Note that the consumption figures shown in Table A6.1.2 are not directly comparable, since in the individual countries these are expressed in terms of landed weight, product weight, and fillet weight, respectively.

The Price and Origin of Imports

Our projections indicate a substantial rise in United States purchases of fish and fish preparations from less developed areas, and little change elsewhere. Measured in 1960 prices, the exports of the developing countries would rise by 53 per cent between 1960 and 1970 and 97 per cent between 1960 and 1975. No change in f.o.b. prices has been assumed.

Eggs (SITC 025)

The United States and Canada are net exporters of eggs; they import negligible quantities, mainly from Australia. Western Europe is, however, a net importer and satisfies one-tenth of its consumption requirements by purchases from the countries of the Soviet bloc, Israel, Argentina, Australia, and South Africa. The largest importing countries of the area are Germany, Italy, the United Kingdom, Switzerland, and Austria. British imports have changed little in recent years, but imports into the other four countries have shown a steady increase. Among developing countries, Argentina and Israel export eggs in appreciable quantities to Germany and Italy, with exports valued at $20 million in 1960.

The per capita consumption of eggs is between 9 and 15 kg in the high income countries of Europe and 3 to 6 kg in countries with lower incomes. Budget estimates show income elasticities of 0.3 to 0.7 in the former group of countries and elasticities exceeding unity in the latter [6], indicating further possibilities for the expansion of consumption. The saturation level of egg consumption may be around 20–22 kg, if the experience of the United States can serve as a guide.

Eggs come under the same regulations as poultry in the EEC, and the expansion of production in France and the Netherlands is likely to cut into imports from Argentina and Israel. But this decline may be more than counterbalanced by increases in exports to other European markets, so that the exports of eggs from developing countries have been projected to reach $23 million in 1970 and $26 million in 1975 as compared to $20 million in 1960.

6.2 CEREALS AND FEEDSTUFF (SITC 04, 08)

Wheat and Coarse Grains (SITC 04, Except 042)

Wheat and coarse grains (for short, grains) are consumed directly, in the form of bread and flour, and indirectly, as animal feed and in industrial uses (e.g., beer). In 1957–59, in the developed countries, human consumption accounted for 74 per cent of wheat consumed, feed for 16 per cent, and seed and other uses for 10 per cent; the corresponding percentages for coarse grains were 6, 85, and 9 per cent [5, p. A51]. Coarse grains have been losing ground to wheat in human consumption, and, at the same time, direct uses have been declining in importance as compared to feed and industrial uses. On the one hand, the per capita human consumption of grains is declining as income increases; on the other, the rise in meat consumption at higher income levels is accompanied by an increase in feed uses.

These considerations indicate the need for separate considerations in regard to the direct and indirect consumption of grains. In forecasting human consumption, we have fitted a cross-section regression of the parabolic form for 1960 with disposable income per head as the independent variable and per capita grain consumption as the dependent variable, and this function has been used in making projections. Subsequently, the estimates have been adjusted by taking account of intercountry differences in the consumption of starchy foods as well as the substitution possibilities among these foods, such as grains, rice, and potatoes. The resulting estimates are shown in Table A6.2.1.

It has further been assumed that the share of wheat in the human consumption of grains will continue to rise, reaching 74 per cent in North America and 83 per cent in Western Europe in 1975 as compared to 72 and 81 per cent in 1957–59. Detailed projections for the feed and industrial uses of grains have not been prepared, however, and we have relied on the estimates of various experts instead. This solution has been chosen by reason of the uncertainties associated with the projection of the indirect consumption of grains. Future changes in feed uses are determined by the increase of meat production, as well as by changes in feeding techniques, and the substitution among various forms of animal feed, such as grains, oil cake, tallow, fishmeal, hay, and alfalfa.

Further uncertainties relate to the share of imports in domestic consumption and the contribution of the less developed countries to these imports. The developing countries supply about 14 per cent of the world exports of grains. Their share is 8 per cent in wheat, rye, and barley, 30 per cent in oats, and 35 per cent in maize. About two-thirds of these exports come from Argentina (mostly wheat and maize), accounting for nearly one-third of Argentina's export earnings. Much of the remainder originates in Mexico and Thailand.

North America

Both the United States and Canada are large exporters of grains, and import only small quantities of maize and cereal preparations from other countries. U.S. imports of maize from developing economies (chiefly the Dominican Republic) were valued at $1.7 million in 1960 and, given the possibilities of increased production in the United States, little change is expected in the future.

Western Europe

Future developments in Common Market imports of grains will be greatly affected by the application of the new agricultural policy of the EEC. According to this policy, variable levies are imposed on imports, corresponding to the difference between the domestic target price and the price of imports. Imports will thus be restricted to amounts that are not supplied by Common Market producers at the target price.

The protective effect of this policy will depend on the level at which domestic prices will be supported. This level has not yet been determined, and in the present study we have assumed that prices would be set at about the average of the relatively high German and lower French prices. An averaging of prices would have a stimulating effect on production in the Common Market, since the output of cereals could expand considerably in France while German production might fall little. An indication of the possibilities of expansion in France can be given if we consider that the French plan foresees a 30 per cent increase in agricultural production accompanied by an approximate doubling of exports between 1959 and 1965.[5]

The common agricultural policy is expected to reinforce apparent trends toward self-sufficiency. In regard to wheat, we find that over the last decade the human consumption of grains has remained approximately unchanged as the fall in per capita consumption was offset by the growth of population. At the same time, the use of wheat as feed increased from 1.1 million tons in 1950/51–1952/53 to 5.8 million tons in 1960–61. Still, the degree of self-sufficiency rose from 80 to 90 per cent by reason of a one-third increase in production.

Our projections envisage a decrease in the human consumption of wheat by about 5 per cent between 1960 and 1970, and 10 per cent between 1960 and 1975. A large part of this decline is ac-

---

[5]For a more detailed discussion, see [2].

counted for by the expected reduction of wheat consumption in France and Italy under the assumption that consumption patterns tend to become more homogeneous in the European Economic Community. On the other hand, the use of wheat for feed may increase so as to more than offset the fall in human consumption.

In 1958–60, Common Market imports of wheat and wheat flour in terms of wheat equivalent amounted to 3.7 million tons and exports to 2.3 million tons. With consumption increasing at a slow rate the expansion of domestic production is likely to lead to an export surplus in wheat by the late sixties.[6] Still, despite efforts made to expand the production of hard wheat in France and Italy, high quality Canadian hard wheat will continue to be imported, possibly at an annual rate of one million tons. Wheat imports from Morocco and Tunisia, too, may be maintained under the special agreement covering trade with France, but imports of soft wheat from the United States, Argentina, and the Soviet Union are bound to disappear.

Common Market imports of coarse grains amounted to nine million tons in 1958–60, corresponding to a degree of self-sufficiency of 78 per cent. Given the decreasing importance of coarse grains in human consumption, the decline in the direct consumption of coarse grains will be greater than in the case of wheat. On the other hand, with the projected expansion in meat production, the use of coarse grains as animal feed will rise rapidly, and increases are expected in industrial applications, too.

Nevertheless, indications point toward a rise in the degree of self-sufficiency. The mechanization of agriculture, the application of fertilizers, and the use of hybrid seed provide possibilities for increased yields, while the common agricultural policy is expected to give inducement to farmers to utilize these possibilities, and it may also lead to increases in the cultivated area. At the same time, improvements in feeding techniques, the increased use of soft wheat, potatoes, and oilcake as animal feed, as well as improved grassland management, may reduce the demands on coarse grains.

Under the assumption of constant prices in all producing countries, unchanged net imports of animal and vegetable products, and the absence of improvements in feeding techniques, a study prepared by the EEC Commission projected the degree of self-sufficiency in coarse grains to reach 80 per cent by 1970 in the Common Market, with the absolute amount of imports remaining approxi-

---

[6]By comparison, the EEC Commission forecasts zero net imports for 1970 [*3*, Table 24].

mately at 1958–60 levels. The commission notes, however, that a 20 per cent increase in the price of cereals in France, accompanying the equilization of prices in the EEC, could lower imports by 5.5 million tons, while improvements in feeding techniques would contribute to a fall by 2-3 million tons. On the other hand, a 5 per cent reduction in the average price of pork, poultry, and eggs is expected to contribute to an increase in grain requirements by 0.8 million tons [3, p. IV 63].

Considering that the expansionary effect of an equalization of prices on grain output in France is expected to outweigh its contractionary effect in Germany [9, 16], and taking account of possible improvements in feeding techniques as well as the projected fall of meat imports, we have projected imports of coarse grains into the Common Market to decline by three to four million tons under the most likely income assumption, and by one to two million tons under the high income assumption. No further changes have been envisaged between 1970 and 1975. A decline in coarse grain imports is also foreseen by the Economist Intelligence Unit [4, pp. 100–101] and by some individual experts [9, 12], while an increase is envisaged in the FAO projections [5, p. A51].

Developing countries account for one-third of EEC imports of coarse grains, of which about three-fourths is maize, imported chiefly from Argentina. The prospects for maize are better than for coarse grains as a whole, and although domestic maize production will expand especially in France and Italy, imports can be maintained at present levels or may even rise under the higher income assumption. On the other hand, barley imports are likely to disappear and that of oats decline, except for purchases from North Africa.

In 1958–60, the degree of self-sufficiency in the United Kingdom was 39 per cent in wheat and 67 per cent in coarse grains. Following the estimate of the Oxford University Institute for Research in Agricultural Economics [10], we have assumed that the increased use of wheat as animal feed will approximately offset the decline in human consumption. At the same time, in the absence of drastic changes in agricultural policies, domestic wheat production will continue to rise, so that imports may decline by about 10 per cent between 1960 and 1970, and 15 per cent between 1960 and 1975. Among less-developed countries, only Argentina exports wheat to the United Kingdom, accounting for 6 per cent of British imports in 1960.

An increase in the degree of self-sufficiency in coarse grains also is likely to be forthcoming in Britain, although imports may be maintained at approximately present levels.[7] Within these imports, purchases of maize, sorghum, and millet will continue to rise, while smaller quantities of rye and oats are likely to be imported. About one-tenth of British maize imports originate in Argentina, and smaller quantities of other cereals come from Morocco.

None of the countries of Northern Europe are self-sufficient in grains, and the possibilities for expanding production are also limited here. At the same time, the consumption of wheat is unlikely to rise above present levels, as increased utilization in animal feeding will hardly counterbalance the fall in human consumption. Wheat imports come chiefly from Canada, the United States, and the Soviet Union; less than 10 per cent originates in Argentina.

In view of the increased consumption of meat, larger quantities of coarse grains will be consumed, however, and imports of coarse grains into Northern Europe may double during the period of projection.[8] About 20 per cent of these imports originate in Argentina, with Canada, the United States, and the countries of Eastern Europe supplying much of the rest.

Imports and exports of grains approximately balance in Turkey and Yugoslavia, while Greece, Portugal, and Spain import about one-tenth of their requirement. Both human and nonhuman consumption is expected to rise in this area, but increases in production may lead to a higher degree of self-sufficiency. At any rate, imports of grains from the less developed countries are negligible.

Japan

Estimates by Yasunaga [15] as well as projections prepared by the Japanese Economic Planning Agency [11, p. 113] anticipate a fall in the human consumpiton of wheat and a small increase in total (human and nonhuman) consumption. Increases in imports do not affect the less developed countries, since Japan purchases wheat from Canada, the United States, and Australia.

In view of the projected expansion of meat production and the limited possibilities for increasing the domestic production of coarse grains, Japanese coarse grain imports (almost exclusively maize) will continue to rise at a rapid rate. On the basis of available infor-

---

[7]The FAO expects British imports of wheat as well as coarse grains to be maintained at 1957–59 levels [5, p. A51].

[8]The FAO envisages imports of coarse grains to rise from 2.3 million tons in 1957–59 to 5.6 or 6.6 million tons, depending on the income assumption chosen [5, p. A51].

mation, we have assumed a fourfold increase of imports within a decade. Japan imports maize from Argentina, Thailand, South Africa, and the United States.

Oceania and South Africa

Australia and South Africa are—and will remain—net exporters of grains. At the same time, New Zealand's import needs in wheat will continue to be supplied by Australia.

The Price and Origin of Imports

With regard to wheat, our conclusions suggest that Common Market imports from North Africa may be maintained, but that purchases from Argentina would cease. Argentina is also likely to lose markets in Britain, and although exports to Northern Europe are expected to continue, Argentine exports of wheat to Western Europe may fall by about one-half between 1960 and 1970 and decline further thereafter.

Among coarse grains, imports of maize from less developed countries are likely to rise during the period of projection, and some increases are expected in the importation of sorghum and millet, too. According to our projections, the United States and the Common Market countries would maintain, and the United Kingdom and Northern Europe would increase, their imports of maize from Argentina. Still, by reason of the expected decline of barley imports from Africa and imports of rye and oats from Argentina, Western Europe's imports of coarse grains from the developing countries would surpass 1960 levels only if the target rate of income growth were attained.

The rise in Japanese maize imports is expected to benefit chiefly the United States, whose maize exports to Japan increased nearly threefold between 1960 and 1961. Imports from South Africa may expand at approximately the same rate as the rise of total maize imports into Japan, while smaller gains are likely to be obtained by Argentina, Thailand, and Cambodia.

As to the future prices of wheat and coarse grains traded, forecasting is made difficult by the existence of government regulations on prices and production. Nearly all grain-producing countries rely on government support schemes so that prices become a policy variable. It is therefore a measure of ignorance, rather than an expression of confidence, that we assume average import prices of the years 1959–61 to apply during the period of projection. In this connection, the reader should note that the export shares of individual suppliers may also be profoundly effected by changes in U.S. agricultural policies.

RICE (SITC 042)

Mainland China, India, Japan, and Pakistan are the largest rice producers in the world, but domestic output generally serves the needs of home consumption in these countries, and rice exports originate chiefly in Burma, Thailand, and the United States. In 1959–61, Burma derived 67 per cent of her export earnings from the sale of rice, Thailand 34 per cent, and—among the smaller suppliers —Cambodia, 36 per cent.

Rice imports into developed countries account for a relatively small part of world trade (15 per cent in 1960), and have been declining over time by reason of the increased degree of self-sufficiency in Japan, the former largest importer. In 1960, the rice exports of developing countries to Japan were valued at $18 million; the corresponding figures are $1 million for North America, $27 million for Western Europe, and $3 million for South Africa.

North America

In recent decades, per capita rice consumption has been approximately constant in the United States and Canada, and it is expected to remain at present levels during the period of projection. On the other hand, exportable production in the United States may continue to rise. These exports are directed to Western Europe, Africa, Canada, and—mainly in the form of concessional sales—to various Asian countries.

Western Europe

Per capita rice consumption in Western Europe is below the pre-war level, although, in response to falling prices, some increases have been shown in recent years. We have accepted the FAO's estimate, according to which consumption per head would remain at levels experienced in 1960, so that consumption would rise at the same rate as population [7, p. 66].

In 1960, imports of rice into Western Europe amounted to 493 thousand tons, providing for about 20 per cent of total consumption. At the same time, 104 thousand tons of rice were exported. Imports came from the United States, Mainland China, Thailand, Madagascar, Burma, and Cambodia. The Common Market takes nearly two-thirds of the imports originating from outside Europe, while the remainder is approximately evenly divided between the

United Kingdom and the other countries of Western Europe. Some changes in the pattern of imports are expected, however.

Among the Common Market countries, Italy is a net exporter of rice, France produces about one-half of her requirements, while the other member countries do not produce rice. The rice producers of the Community will benefit from the protection provided by a system of variable levies to be applied in the framework of the common agricultural policy.

Still, we can expect trade diversion in rice to be limited. Considering the existence of consumer preference for long-grain rice in the importing countries of the Common Market, it may be expected that imports of long-grain rice from Thailand and the United States would be maintained at present levels. In addition, broken rice will continue to be purchased from Cambodia, Burma, Mainland China, and Vietnam, and imports from Madagascar may actually rise. Thus, although imports of round-grain rice from Egypt and the United States would suffer from Italian competition, the total imports of rice are likely to change little. Imports would fall, however, if the imposition of the variable levy led to a substantial increase in retail prices.

The United Kingdom and the countries of Northern Europe do not produce rice, and their consumption and imports have been projected to increase in proportion to the growth of population. At the same time, imports into Southern Europe (chiefly Yugoslavia) may expand at a somewhat higher rate.

Japan

Japan's dependence on rice imports has been progressively reduced in recent decades. By the early sixties, Japan is expected to become self-sufficient in rice; accordingly, we have assumed imports to be nil in 1970 and 1975.

Oceania and South Africa

Australia is a rice exporter, New Zealand imports small quantities of rice from Australia and the United States, whereas Thailand and Vietnam provide for most of the import needs of South Africa. Imports into South Africa have been assumed to rise somewhat over the period of projection.

The Price and Origin of Imports

In view of our discussion, Common Market rice imports from underdeveloped countries would continue at approximately present levels. Increases of imports into other areas of Europe will be modest in absolute terms, although developing countries will benefit from the shift of Italian exports toward the Common Market.[9] At the same time, Canadian imports from Latin America will be maintained, but Asian producers will not be able to find markets in Japan. Correspondingly, the rice imports of developed countries from underdeveloped areas would decline by about one third between 1960 and 1970, with some increases taking place afterward. No change in prices has been projected.

Feeding-Stuffs for Animals (SITC 08)

Imports of animal feeding-stuffs (oilcake, the by-products of grain milling, and fishmeal) into North America amounted to $13 million in 1960, the imports of Western Europe were valued at $377 million, and those of Japan at $15 million (Oceania and South Africa are exporters of feeding-stuffs and import negligible quantities). The United States purchases fishmeal from Peru and mixed feed from Mexico and Canada, while the latter buys feeding-stuffs almost exclusively from the U.S. The countries of Western Europe purchase oilcake from Argentina, the United States, India, the Soviet Union, and various African countries, and also import grain milling by-products from Argentina and fishmeal from Peru. Finally, much of the imports of feeding-stuffs into Japan originates in the United States and Argentina (oilcake and milling by-products).

As noted in connection with the projection of grain consumption, the demand for feeding-stuffs is affected by developments in meat production and feeding techniques as well as by the substitution among the various forms of animal feed. In regard to oilcake, the largest single product included in this category, mention should further be made of expected shifts toward the importation of oilseeds in Western Europe that would reduce the share of imports in the total consumption of oilcake.

North America

United States imports of feeding-stuffs have been rising in recent years, and further increases are expected. Purchases of fishmeal from Peru may more than double within a decade, while a smaller rise of imports of mixed feed from Mexico is envisaged.

---

[9]By comparison, the FAO expects rice imports into Western Europe to decline by about 10 per cent between 1957–1959 and 1970 [5, p. II, 10].

Western Europe

Imports of feeding-stuffs into Western Europe doubled between 1953–54 and 1959–60 but little increase has taken place between 1959 and 1961. Oilcake accounts for 70 per cent of these imports, fishmeal and the by-products of grain milling for about 15 per cent each. Approximately three-fourths of imports originate in the less developed countries; the remainder in the United States and the Soviet Union.

Given the shift from the importation of vegetable oils to that of oilseeds, the imports of oilcake will rise at a slower rate than the total use of oilcake as animal feed. On the other hand, the imports of the by-products of grain milling can increase in proportion to the growth of meat production (about 3–4 per cent a year), and fishmeal imports may rise at least double that rate.

Japan

Japanese imports of feeding-stuffs have shown considerable fluctuation over the last decade, but a definite upward trend has been observed in recent years. In 1961, imports more than doubled as compared to 1960, and were three times larger than in 1958. But imports in 1961 were greatly influenced by crop conditions in Japan, and further increases may not exceed that shown in the production of meat.

Oceania and South Africa

Australia, New Zealand, and South Africa will continue to export feeding-stuffs, and imports are unlikely to rise above the 1960 level.

The Price and Origin of Imports

The continuing rise of fishmeal imports will benefit Peru and, to a lesser extent, South Africa, while increases in the purchases of oilcake and grain-milling by-products may be divided approximately evenly among the main producing countries. Correspondingly, the export earnings less developed countries derive from the sale of feeding-stuffs would rise by about 40 per cent between 1960 and 1970, and 60 per cent between 1960 and 1975, the largest gains being made in Latin America (Table A6). No change in prices has been assumed.

6.3 FRUITS AND VEGETABLES (SITC 05)

FRESH FRUIT (SITC 051)

The consumption of fresh fruits has exhibited an upward trend in most countries of Western Europe, while decreases have been observed in the United States and Canada. In the United States, the increased consumption of processed fruits provides the main explanation for the fall in fresh fruit consumption. While the per capita consumption of fresh fruits fell from 60–65 kg in the interwar period to 45 kg during the fifties, that of all fruits, including juice and other fruit products, had been increasing until World War II, and has since fluctuated around 90 kg.

The experience of the United States cannot be immediately applied to the countries of Western Europe, however. Although in recent years the consumption of fruit juices and frozen fruits has increased substantially in Europe, it still accounts for only a small part of the total. And considering the important effect customs and tastes have on the consumption of processed fruit, it is difficult to foresee to what extent the U.S. pattern will be followed in Europe.

On the other hand, the possibility of a shift toward processed fruit reduces the applicability of information provided by budget studies which show the income elasticity of demand for fresh fruit to be about 0.6–0.8 in the high income countries of Western Europe [8, p. 7]. Furthermore, only limited validity can be attached to the extrapolation of past trends. By reason of the fluctuation of domestic supplies, year-to-year changes in consumption do not show sufficient regularity for deriving income elasticities with confidence and, also, shifts toward higher quality fruit reduce the reliability of measuring consumption by weight.

A comparison of consumption levels in various European countries does not give much help in forecasting consumption either, since no definite relationship can be discerned between per capita incomes and the consumption of fruit in the individual countries. As Table A6.3.1 indicates, Greece, with one of the lowest per capita incomes in Europe, has the highest level of fruit consumption, followed by Switzerland and Turkey. Although differences in the scope and reliability of statistics influence the results, disparities in tastes and in the availability of fruits appear as important determinants of the level of consumption.

These considerations indicate the difficulties encountered in estimating the future consumption of fresh fruits. In order to project import demand, we would further have to estimate the composition of consumption as well as the domestic supply of the various fruits. Given the error possibilities involved in forecasting demand and supply, the "residual method" of projection can be of little usefulness here. Instead, separate estimates have been prepared on the future imports of bananas, oranges, and all other fruits taken together. Bananas and oranges account for about two-thirds of all fruit traded between developed and less developed economies, and no other fruit accounts for more than 4 per cent of the total.

The import prospects of oranges and tangerines, and also of other fruits, are discussed in the present section, while banana imports are considered in Chapter 8. This arrangement has been chosen because bananas can be produced only in tropical climate and are an important source of export revenue for several underdeveloped countries situated in the tropical zone. For reasons of statistical convenience, tropical fruits other than bananas have been included in the "other fruit" category, however.

Oranges and Tangerines (SITC 051.1)

In most industrial countries, oranges and tangerines provide over 80 per cent of total citrus fruit consumed, the remainder being evenly divided between grapefruit and lemons. An important exception is the United States, the largest producer of grapefruit, where the consumption of grapefruit amounts to about one-third of the total. By reason of their importance, future demand for oranges and tangerines (hereafter referred to as "oranges") has been estimated separately, whereas grapefruit and lemons are included in the other fruit group.

North America

The United States is the largest exporter of oranges and imports a negligible quantity, chiefly from Mexico. Over the last decade, the per capita consumption of oranges, fresh and processed, has fluctuated around 28 kg. No increase is expected in the future, and despite the substantial frost damage of the winter of 1962, domestic consumption needs will be met from domestic supplies. In addition, U.S. production will provide for the import needs of Canada, and exports to western Europe are also likely to continue.

Western Europe

The budget statistics of European countries indicate that the income elasticity of demand for fresh oranges is somewhat higher than that for all fresh fruit. In the case of some larger countries for which estimates are available (France, Germany, the Netherlands, and the United Kingdom), budget elasticities range between 0.63 and 1.07 for oranges, as compared to 0.54 to 0.80 for total fresh fruit. The range becomes narrower if we exclude the German data which refer to 1950/ 51; the highest values are now shown for the United Kingdom: 0.76 for oranges and 0.67 for all fresh fruit. By comparison, in the United States the income elasticity of demand for citrus fruits was 0.35 in 1955.

But in projecting the future demand for oranges, it is not sufficient to consider only the consumption of fresh fruit. In recent years, an increasing proportion of consumption has taken the form of juices and other fruit products, hence the demand for oranges in all uses should be estimated. In this connection note that the demand for processed citrus fruit is more elastic than demand for fresh citrus. In the United States, for example, the income elasticity of demand for frozen citrus juice was around unity in 1955, while the corresponding value for the United Kingdom is 1.47 [*8*, p. 7 and *14*, p. 37].

Changes in the consumption of oranges (fresh and processed) can be indicated by data on the per capita availability of oranges, derived from production and trade statistics (Table A6.3.2). These estimates are subject to error in the case of the producing countries, since the crop year extends from one calendar year to the next, and, also, because of the exclusion of trade in processed fruit from the figures. In most of the countries under consideration (the main exception being Britain), the latter is relatively unimportant, however, so that the results are not greatly affected.

With the exception of the United Kingdom, prewar levels of orange consumption were exceeded in the early fifties in all countries of Western Europe. Consumption per head has since surpassed 10 kg in the countries of the Common Market, Greece, Norway, Portugal, Sweden, and Switzerland, while the lowest per capita consumption, 1.5 kg, is shown for Yugoslavia. Considering the large discrepancy between consumption levels in North America and in Western Europe, substantial increases may be forthcoming over the next decades.

Taking account of the results of budget studies and intercountry comparisons, we have assumed an income elasticity of 0.6 to apply to the Common Market countries with the exception of Italy, where a higher rate of increase of consumption appears likely.[10] Accord-

---

[10]Large increases are indicated by time-series data referring to the years 1950–60. But the increase of consumption in this period also reflects changes in tastes and eating habits.

ingly, under the most likely income assumption, the consumption (and imports) of oranges and tangerines in the Common Market countries other than Italy would reach 2105 thousand tons by 1970 and 2345 thousand tons by 1975, as compared to imports of 1630 thousand tons in 1960.[11] Still, the projected per capita consumption levels would fall short of the level reached in the United States by a considerable margin.

After a substantial decline in the immediate postwar years, the consumption of fresh oranges has shown considerable fluctuation in the United Kingdom, although an upward tendency has been apparent in recent years. But per capita consumption is still much below prewar levels, and it is among the lowest in Europe. This result has been explained by reference to the increased importation of processed fruit, restrictions on orange imports, and the rise in the relative price of oranges [1]. In projecting future imports, we have relied mainly on information provided by budget studies, and have assumed an income elasticity of demand of 0.7.

Among the countries of the Northern group, per capita orange consumption in Austria, Ireland, and Switzerland was rising more or less steadily throughout the fifties, whereas in Scandinavia the peak consumption levels of the years 1953–55 were generally not regained by 1960. But per capita consumption has risen in recent years in the latter countries, too, and further increases are expected. For purposes of projection, we have assumed an income elasticity of 0.6 to pertain to countries with higher consumption levels (Norway, Sweden, and Switzerland), and 0.8 to the remaining group of countries.

With the exception of Yugoslavia, the countries of Southern Europe are self-sufficient in oranges. Consumption in Yugoslavia is largely determined by government controls on imports. We have assumed that per capita consumption would at least double over a period of ten years.

Japan

During the period 1953–1960, a 1 per cent increase in per capita income was associated with a 1.5 per cent rise in the consumption of oranges in Japan. Lower income elasticities are likely to pertain to the 1960–1975 period, however, and domestic needs will continue to be supplied by home production.

---

[11]The corresponding estimate of the FAO is 2370 thousand tons for 1970 [5, p. II–59].

Oceania and South Africa

Australia and South Africa are orange exporters, while the value of New Zealand imports originating in less developed countries does not surpass $0.5 million. A substantial increase of the latter figure is not expected.

The Price and Origin of Imports

Should 1960 prices be maintained throughout the period of projection, imports of oranges into the nonproducing European countries would rise from 2430 thousand tons in 1960 to 3120 or 3190 thousand tons in 1970, and 3490 or 3620 thousand tons in 1975, depending on the income assumption chosen (Table 6.3.1).[12] Changes are expected in the origin of imports, however, chiefly by reason of the possible effects of the Common Market preference on imports.

TABLE 6.3.1

ORANGE CONSUMPTION (NET IMPORTS) IN THE IMPORTING COUNTRIES OF
WESTERN EUROPE
(thousand metric tons)

	1960	1970I	1970II	1975I	1975II
Common Market	1630	2106	2153	2345	2426
United Kingdom	426	515	526	558	581
Northern Europe	350	431	443	472	492
Yugoslavia	27	65	71	111	121
Western Europe, Total	2433	3117	3193	3490	3620

Source: Table A6.3.1.
Note: (c) without Italy.

The EEC Common Market tariff on oranges and tangerines will be 20 per cent between October 1 and March 15, and 15 per cent between March 15 and September 30. The total tariff charge on imports from third countries will increase thereby, since, prior to the establishment of the EEC, Germany levied a 10 per cent duty, the Benelux countries 13 per cent, while the 15.5–31.5 per cent French tariff applied to a relatively small quantity of imports. At the same time, oranges imported from Italy, Greece, and Algeria will pay no duty, and the produce of Morocco and Tunisia will continue to have free access to the French market.

In recent years, about 5 per cent of orange exports to the Common Market countries originated in Italy, and less than 1 per cent in Greece. Substantial increases are expected over the next decade

---

[12]The corresponding estimates of the FAO for 1970/71 are 3495 and 3895 thousand tons under the low and the high income assumptions, respectively. [5, p. II–59].

in Greece, but part of this expansion will be channeled into domestic consumption and into exports to the traditional East European markets for Greek oranges. In Italy, production may double over the period of projection, and exportable production may almost treble. At the same time, tariff preferences will provide an inducement to increase exports to the Common Market, but shifts in consumption will be restricted by reason of the unpopularity of Italian blood oranges outside southern Germany.

Preferential treatment accorded to Algeria is likely to lead to an increase in the cultivated area, but the results of expanded cultivation will not be forthcoming until the seventies and, in the meantime, the adverse effects of the political uncertainty of recent years will be felt. On the other hand, Morocco and Tunisia, who retain the privilege of duty-free entry to the French market, will continue to expand production so that the share of the producers of North Africa in EEC imports may rise somewhat during the sixties.

The privileged position of certain European and North African producers in the Common Market is expected to cause some reduction in the share of the competing suppliers of winter oranges (Spain, Israel, and, to a lesser extent, the United States), although the export possibilities of summer oranges from South Africa and Brazil will not be affected. On the other hand, Spain and Israel may increase their share in the markets of other nonproducing European countries.

It has been argued that by 1970 exportable supplies of oranges are likely to exceed import demand calculated at 1960 prices, and thus some fall in prices would be forthcoming [5, p. II-60]. The possible effects of eventual price changes have not been considered in the present study, however, partly because the increased home consumption of oranges in the producing countries could take up much of the surplus, and partly because price changes would not greatly affect export revenues. The latter conclusion follows from the observation that, by reason of the substitution relationships between oranges and home-produced fruit, the price elasticity of demand for oranges may be around unity.

FRESH FRUIT OTHER THAN ORANGES AND BANANAS
(SITC 051.2, 051.4–9)

This category includes fruits produced in temperate climate (apples, pears), the so-called Mediterranean climate (grapefruit, lemons, raisins, and dates), and the tropics (coconut, tropical nuts). With the exception of the countries of southern Europe and the

Southern states of the United States, imports of Mediterranean and tropical fruits from primary producing areas are not competing with home production in the industrial countries. At the same time, temperate zone fruits come in relatively small quantities from developing countries (chiefly from Argentina). Correspondingly, import demand for fruits other than oranges and bananas has been estimated directly, rather than as the difference between projected consumption and domestic supply.

In the countries of North America, the imports of these fruits from nonindustrial countries fluctuated around a constant level over the past decade and were valued at $86 million in 1960. For purposes of projection, we have assumed that imports would rise in proportion to the growth of population.

Western Europe's imports of fresh fruits other than oranges and bananas from developing countries reached $69 million in 1960. On the basis of available information past trends, we have assumed that a 1 per cent increase in per capita incomes would be associated with a 0.6 per cent rise in imports.

Japanese imports of this group of fruits originating in less developed areas increased by two-thirds between 1954 and 1960, but imports in absolute terms have not surpassed $2 million. A doubling over the next decade is projected. Finally, imports of fresh fruits other than bananas and oranges into Australia, New Zealand, and South Africa reached $4 million in 1960 and may show moderate increases during the period of projection.

All in all, our estimates indicate an increase of 24-25 per cent in imports of fresh fruits, other than bananas and oranges, from developing countries between 1960 and 1970, and a 38-40 per cent increase between 1960 and 1975. In the absence of evidence to the contrary, no change in price and origin of imports has been assumed.

DRIED AND PRESERVED FRUITS AND FRUIT PREPARATIONS
(SITC 052, 053)

Exports of dried fruits—mostly raisins, prunes, currants, figs, and dates—from developing countries to developed economies amounted to $25 million in 1960. Imports into North America have been stagnant in recent years, while a slight decline is shown in Western Europe. We have projected total imports to remain unchanged during the period of projection in all high income areas.

Frozen and canned fruits, jam, and marmalade, as well as fruit juice and fruit peels are included under preserved fruits and fruit preparations. Increasing quantities of these products have been exported by the less developed countries in recent years (exports to developed economies amounted to $90 million in 1960) and, in view of the determination of these countries to develop food-processing industries, this trend is expected to continue.

In the United States and Canada, imports of processed fruits have been rising at approximately the same rate as personal incomes. The continuation of this relationship has been projected for the period 1960–1975. About half of the imports come from developing countries.

European imports of fruit preparations and preserved fruits increased fourfold between 1951 and 1960, while the share of less developed areas in these imports remained at approximately 40 per cent throughout the period. Much of the remainder came from the United States and South Africa, and smaller quantities from Australia and Japan.

During the early part of the fifties, Western Europe's imports of processed fruits were restricted by quotas, hence the data referring to the years 1951–53 can hardly be used for prediction purposes. Between 1954 and 1960, per capita imports rose by 88 per cent, while disposable income per head increased by 26 per cent, corresponding to an import demand elasticity of 2.8. But the rate of increase of imports has been declining over time and a further slowing down is expected. In projecting future imports, we have calculated with an import demand elasticity of 2.0 and have further assumed that the share of developing countries in Western Europe's imports would remain unchanged.

Japanese imports of processed fruits, too, have been steadily increasing. Between 1953 and 1960, imports rose nearly fivefold, with nonindustrial countries providing 80 per cent of the increase. Despite this high rate of growth, Japanese imports of processed fruits, calculated on a per capita basis, barely surpassed one-fifth of imports into Western Europe, however. We have assumed that this discrepancy would diminish in the future, and calculated with an import demand elasticity of 2.5 for Japan.

Australia, New Zealand, and South Africa are exporters of processed fruit and fruit preparations and this situation is expected to continue during the period of projection. Finally, we have assumed that no change would take place in the price and the origin of imports in the developed areas. The combined projections for dried and processed fruit and fruit preparations are given in Table A6.

VEGETABLES (SITC 054,055)

The consumption of vegetables shows little regularity in the developing countries. As in the case of fruits, vegetable consumption appears to be determined to a large extent by availabilities and tastes, and no relationship is apparent between per capita incomes and vegetable consumption (Table A6.3.3). For developed countries, outside suppliers are of marginal importance, and chiefly, imports consist of early vegetables that are not competing with domestic production. A large proportion of these vegetables are food specialties, hence their consumption can be expected to increase at a faster rate than disposable incomes.

Vegetable imports into North America have approximately doubled over the last decade, with the less developed countries supplying over one-half of the total. But imports do not show much regularity; for example, the level reached in 1953 was surpassed again only in 1957. In the present projections, we have assumed a decline in the rate of growth of imports in the period 1960–1975, with per capita imports rising at a rate only slightly higher than that of income per head.

Western Europe's vegetable imports increased by about one half between 1954 and 1960, corresponding to an income elasticity of import demand of approximately 1.5. In projecting future imports, we have assumed an import demand elasticity of 1.3. Throughout the period of projection, the present two-thirds share of the developing countries is expected to be maintained.

Japanese imports of vegetables have shown large fluctuations during the period under review, and an upward trend is apparent only in the case of processed vegetables, which provide about one-fourth of the total. Future developments will greatly depend on the availability of fresh vegetables in Burma and Mainland China, who supply about three-fourths of Japanese imports. We have assumed that imports may double from their low level within a decade.

The vegetable imports of Australia, New Zealand, and South Africa from less developed countries have not reached $0.5 million by 1960, and no increase has been projected for the future. Finally, as in the case of processed fruits, we have assumed that the 1960 price level will pertain to the period of projection and that there will be little change in the origin of imports.

6.4 BEVERAGES (SITC 11)

Within this category, the imports of the nonalcoholic beverages (lemonades and other kinds of soft drinks) from less developed areas have not surpassed $0.5 million. No increase has been assumed for future years either, considering that the beverages in question are supplied almost exclusively from domestic bottling plants.

At the same time, the imports of alcoholic beverages (mostly wine) from developing countries were valued at $266 million in 1960, with Algeria supplying about 80 per cent of the total. In 1959-61, one-half of Algeria's export earnings were derived from the sale of wines directed almost entirely to France. Smaller quantities originated in Morocco, Tunisia, and various countries and territories in Latin America.

North America

United States imports of alcoholic beverages from less developed countries amount to a negligible proportion of domestic consumption. Nevertheless, imports have risen by nearly 50 per cent over the last decade, and this trend is expected to continue during the period of projection. Similar considerations apply to Canada.

Western Europe

About 95 per cent of Western Europe's imports of alcoholic beverages from developing countries goes to France. The bulk of these imports is low-quality *vin ordinaire,* produced mostly in Algeria. On the other hand, the net importing countries of Europe purchase wines of better quality, chiefly from France, Italy, Portugal, and Spain, and in 1960 only 5 per cent of their imports of alcoholic beverages originated in the less developed countries.

These disparities in trading patterns can be largely explained by differences in the pattern of consumption and in governmental policies. Whereas wine is regarded as a necessity in the main wine-producing countries of Europe, in most other countries it is a luxury item of consumption, and it rarely appears in the budget of low income households. The alcohol consumption of the low income groups is rather directed towards beer. (Data on wine consumption is given in Table A6.4.1.)

A further consideration is that imports into France are determined, to a considerable extent, by governmental policies. In the postwar period, a deliberate effort was made to limit wine production in Metropolitan France so as to make possible the importation of large quantities of wine from Algeria. In the late fifties, nearly 30 per cent of all wines consumed originated in North Africa, chiefly in Algeria.

Turning to projections, we note that the consumption of wine is approaching the saturation level in the main producing areas (France, Italy, and Portugal), so that consumption per head can hardly increase in these countries. On the other hand, wine consumption has been rising steadily in the net importing countries of Western Europe, and time-series data as well as the results of budget studies [6] indicate that in the latter countries the income elasticity of demand for wine exceeds unity.

Imports of wine into France will continue during the period under consideration but the quantity of imports will again depend on the governmental policies followed. In view of the political developments in Algeria, the French government may modify its policy regarding Algerian wine and, also, changes in ownership relations may have detrimental effects on wine production in Algeria. Given the expansion of the output of low quality wine in France and Italy, we have assumed that imports would not surpass one-half of the relatively high 1960 level in 1970. Some increases may be forthcoming in the seventies, however.

At the same time, much of the expected increase of wine consumption in the net importing countries of Western Europe is likely to be supplied chiefly by the Mediterranean countries of Europe. On the one hand, wines produced in this area appeal to the taste of consumers in the importing countries; on the other, production can easily keep up with increased demand. Still, some increase in imports from North Africa may be forthcoming.

Japan

Imports of alcoholic beverages are negligible in Japan and can be expected to remain so during the period under consideration.

Oceania and South Africa

The conclusion reached in regard to Japan is applicable also to Australia, New Zealand, and South Africa.

The Price and Origin of Imports

It can be concluded that, given the expected decline of French imports, the wine exports of the less developed countries would fall by over 40 per cent between 1960 and 1970, although some increases may be forthcoming in the 1970–1975 period. At the same time, it can be assumed that the wine prices of the years 1958–1960 will be maintained during the period of projection.

REFERENCES

[1.] BAIN, A. D., AND BROWN, J. A. C. "Trends in the Consumption of Citrus Fruit in the United Kingdom," *Journal of Agricultural Economics* (January, 1960), pp. 446–56.

[2.] BALASSA, BELA. "The Future of Common Market Imports," *Weltwirtschaftliches Archiv*, Band 90, Heft 2, 1963, pp. 292–316.

[3.] COMMUNAUTÉ ECONOMIQUE EUROPÉENE. *Le Marché commun des produits agricoles, Perspectives "1970"*. Etude No. 10. Brussels, 1962.

[4.] ECONOMIST INTELLIGENCE UNIT. *The Commonwealth and Europe.* London, 1960.

[5.] FOOD AND AGRICULTURE ORGANIZATION. *Agricultural Commodities—Projections for 1970*. Rome, 1962.

[6.] FOOD AND AGRICULTURE ORGANIZATION. *Income Elasticity of the Demand for Food*. Rome, 1959.

[7.] FOOD AND AGRICULTURE ORGANIZATION. *Trends Study on Rice: Consumption*. CCP/Rice/62/8. Rome, 1961.

[8.] GOREUX, L., AND WOLF, J. "Market Prospects for Citrus Fruit in Western Europe in 1965," *Monthly Bulletin of Agricultural Economics and Statistics* (November, 1959), pp. 1–11.

[9.] GRUPE, N. "Entwicklung und Möglichkeiten der Getreide-produktion in Frankreich," *Agrarwirthschaft*, October, 1961.

[10.] INSTITUTE FOR RESEARCH IN AGRICULTURAL ECONOMICS OF OXFORD UNIVERSITY. *United Kingdom: Projected Level of Demand, Supply and Imports of Farm Products in 1965 and 1975*. Washington, D.C.: U.S. Department of Agriculture, 1962.

[11.] JAPANESE ECONOMIC PLANNING AGENCY. *New Long-Range Economic Plan of Japan (1961–1970)*. Tokyo: The Times of Japan, 1961.

[12.] KRAUSE, L. B. "The European Economic Community and American Agriculture," *Factors Affecting the United States Balance of Payments*. U.S. Congress, Joint Economic Committee. Washington, 1962.

[13.] SLATER, D. W. *Consumption Expenditures in Canada*. Ottawa: Royal Commission on Canada's Economic Prospects, 1957.

[14.] UNITED KINGDOM MINISTRY OF AGRICULTURE, FISHERIES AND FOOD. *Domestic Food Consumption and Expenditure: 1958*. London, 1960.

[15.] YASUNAGA, TAKEMI. *A Study on Consumption and Forecast of Selected Agricultural Products in Japan*, 1960 (mimeo).

[16.] *Wirkungen einer Senkung der Agrarpreise im Rahmen einer gemeinsamen Agrarpolitik der Europäischen Wirtschafsgemeinschaft auf der Einkommensverhältnisse der Landwirtschaft in der Bundesrepulblik Deutschland*. Report by a group of Agricultural Experts. Brussels, 1962.

CHAPTER 7

Trade Projections for Competing Tropical Foods

7.1 OILSEEDS, OILS, AND FATS (SITC 023, 09, 4)

OILS AND fats are classified according to their origin as vegetable oils, animal fats, and marine oils. Vegetable oils include soft edible and inedible oils and hard oils; the main animal fats are butter, lard, and tallow, while whale oil, fish oil and seal oil come under the marine oil category.

Both vegetable and animal oils and fats find uses in human consumption and in industry. Butter, lard, and cooking and salad oils are consumed directly, while a variety of vegetable oils, fish oil, and whale oil are used in producing margarine and shortening. Finally, the industrial uses of vegetable oils, tallow, and fish and whale oil include soap manufacturing, paints and varnishes, floor coverings, synthetic materials, and animal feed.

Trade in butter takes place chiefly among the developed countries themselves, with New Zealand, Denmark, and Australia as the principal suppliers. Argentina, the only developing country exporting appreciable quantities of butter, supplies about 4 per cent of the amount traded. The United States is the largest exporter of lard and tallow, while—except for small quantities originating in Argentina—exports of developing countries are effectively nil. In the last decade, however, Peruvian exports of fishmeal have assumed increasing importance.

As a result of the spectacular expansion of her soybean production, the United States has become the main exporter of oils and oilseeds. Among less developed countries, Nigeria, the Philippines, Argentina, Senegal, and the former Belgian Congo are large exporters. In 1959–61, Senegal derived 76 per cent of her export earnings from the sale of oils and oilseeds, Nigeria, 44 per cent; the Philippines, 30 per cent; and Argentina and the Congo; about 10 per cent.

Considerable variations are observed in the human consumption of oils and fats among the developed countries. The per capita consumption of oils and fats in food products exceeds 25 kg in Denmark, Germany, and the Netherlands, for example, but it does not reach 21 kg in the United States. These differences are explained largely by customs and dietary habits, while consumption is correlated with the growth of incomes in the low income countries of Southern Europe. On the other hand, the industrial uses of oils and fats appear to increase with the rise of incomes.

In order to estimate the future imports of oils and fats originating in less developed areas, we have prepared separate projections in regard to the future demand for oils and fats in human consumption and in industrial uses, and have also considered the substitution possibilities within each category. The following breakdown has been used in making projections: butter (SITC 023), oilseeds (22), animal oils and fats (41), vegetable oils (42), and processed oils and fats (43).[1]

North America

In the United States, the per capita consumption of oils and fats has changed little during the last three decades. Present consumption levels in food products had been reached during the thirties, with a temporary lowering during the second world war and the immediate postwar years. Nonfood uses, too, are at levels attained in the years preceding World War II, although consumption was slightly higher during the forties. In recent years, the per capita consumption of oils and fats in food and nonfood products appears to have stabilized at around 20.5 kg and 10.5 kg, respectively.[2] But overall stability conceals important shifts within each of these groups.

Among food products, margarine has gained ground at the expense of butter, shortening has been substituted for lard, and the consumption of cooking and salad oils has steadily expanded. Within the combined consumption of the two main forms of table spreads (butter and margarine), the share of margarine increased from 12 per cent in 1930 to 55 per cent in 1960. During the same period, the share of shortening in cooking fats (lard and shorten-

---

[1]Imports of margarine and shortening (SITC 09) from the less developed countries have not reached $0.5 million in 1960 and are not expected to increase in the future. Similar conclusions apply to milk and cream (022) and cheese (024), which, together with butter, constitute the category of dairy products.

[2]Unless otherwise noted, quantities consumed and traded are expressed in terms of oil and fat content. Information for the United States has been taken from [*12*].

ing) rose from 44 to 62 per cent, although lard is also used indirectly in manufacturing shortening (Table A7.1.1).

The shift from butter to margarine can be attributed to changes in relative prices, the removal of restrictive regulations on the sale of margarine in states where such regulations were in effect, the standardization and quality improvement of margarine, and, more recently, the endeavor to reduce the cholesterol content of the food intake. It should be added that the substitution of margarine for butter in response to changes in relative prices may not be fully reversible, inasmuch as margarine appears to gain acceptance after price-induced increases in its consumption have taken place. Finally, the increase in the relative share of shortening is explained by quality improvements, the increased production of processed food, and the preference for shortening as against lard at higher income levels, whereas changes in tastes are chiefly responsible for the continuing rise in the consumption of cooking and salad oil.

On the basis of evidence from time-series and budget data, we have assumed that the per capita consumption of oils and fats in food products will remain at present levels in the United States. At the same time, as technological improvements take place in the manufacturing of margarine and shortening, these may gain further ground at the expense of butter and lard. Also, recent increases in the consumption of cooking and salad oils are expected to continue.

The nonfood uses of oils and fats, too, display conflicting trends. Declining soap sales due to the shift toward synthetic detergents in the postwar period have been accompanied by the reduced use of fats and oils per unit of product in soap making, while synthetic resins have been substituted for oils and fats in the manufacturing of surface coatings, and plastic materials have replaced vegetable oils in floor coverings. On the other hand, the use of fats in animal feeds, chemicals, and other industrial products has shown an upward trend.

Synthetic detergents will continue to displace soap, and synthetic resins are expected to make further gains in the manufacturing of drying oil products, although the per capita consumption of oils and fats in these uses may not decline substantially below present levels (2.2 kg in soaps and 2.1 kg in drying oil products in 1960, as compared to 5.4 and 3.6 kg in 1950). At the same time, the use of oils and fats in other industrial products—the per capita use of which increased from 3.5 kg in 1950 to 6.5 kg in 1960—is likely to rise further as larger amounts are used in animal foods and in the production of a variety of synthetic materials. On balance, present levels of consumption per person in all nonfood uses may be maintained in the future.

Turning to international trade, we note that while the United States had been a net importer of oils and fats before World War II, in 1960 exports exceeded imports six times, and imports did not surpass one-half of the prewar level. Still, after postwar readjustments had been made, imports of edible as well as industrial oils have again increased.

Imports of edible oils (mainly olive oil) rose steadily during the fifties and, given the increasing demand for high quality cooking and salad oil, further increases are expected. But olive oil is imported almost exclusively from the Mediterranean countries of Western Europe, while, for the purposes of the present study, imports of industrial oils[3] originating in less developed countries are of interest. These imports have risen little over the last decade, but there are indications for future increases during the period of projection (especially in special purpose oils), so that the imports may rise *pari passu* with domestic consumption.

The per capita consumption of oils and fats in Canada is approximately at the same level as in the United States, although Canadians eat considerably more butter. Consumption patterns are not expected to change significantly in the future. The larger part of Canada's $70 million imports of oils and fats came from the United States in 1960, and only a little over $14 million (mostly coconut oil and palm oils) from less developed countries. Imports from the latter group of countries have hardly risen during the last decade, and future increases are unlikely to exceed the growth of population.

Western Europe

In Western Europe, taken as a whole, the per capita use of oils and fats in food products surpassed the prewar level by 1953, and has shown moderate increases since. The nonfood uses of oils and fats were slower in catching up with prewar consumption but have recently exhibited a more rapid rate of increase. In 1960, food uses of oils and fats amounted to 19.4 kg, and nonfood uses to 5.3 kg per head.

As regards the food uses of oils and fats, differing trends have been observed in the countries of the Mediterranean and in other parts of Western Europe. In the former group of countries, per

---

[3]Mostly copra, coconut oil, castor oil, palm kernel oil, and palm oil. Copra and coconut oil are also used in producing margarine.

capita consumption has increased steadily, while in the latter it more or less leveled off after 1955. Different developments are expected in the two groups of countries during the period of projection, too.

Among the non-Mediterranean countries of Western Europe, the most recent budget surveys are available for the United Kingdom. According to these, the income elasticity of demand for fats and oils was around 0.05 in 1955 and also in 1958 [*11*, p. 36]. Budget statistics for other countries (Austria, France, Germany, and the Netherlands) refer to the early fifties, and show elasticities of 0 to 0.1 for fats and oils other than butter, while higher figures apply to butter [*5*]. Considering recent changes in consumption and the shift away from fatty foods due to dietary considerations, the per capita consumption of oils and fats in food products is unlikely to rise in the more developed countries of Europe, except in cases when consumption per head is below 20 kg. At the same time, in countries with higher consumption levels some decreases are foreseen.

Further increases in the food use of oils and fats will be forthcoming in the countries of the Mediterranean, however. In this area, consumption levels are substantially below the European average, and information provided by time-series and budget statistics points in the direction of increasing consumption.[4] If account is taken of comparative consumption levels, we can assume the income elasticity of demand for oils and fats in food uses to be 0.2–0.3 in Greece, Italy, Portugal, and Spain, 0.5 in Yugoslavia, and 0.6 in Turkey (actual and projected per capita consumption levels are given in Table A7.1.2).

The choice among the various forms of oils and fats in individual countries is determined by availabilities, relative prices, incomes, and tastes. Olive oil is preferred for cooking in the Mediterranean, for example, while lard, margarine, or butter serve the same purpose elsewhere in Europe. With some exceptions, butter consumption is higher in countries where livestock raising is of importance, and margarine is a more widely used table spread in others. In order to estimate future changes in butter consumption, past trends in the use of butter and margarine need to be reviewed.

In terms of product weight, the consumption of butter was 66 per cent of the combined consumption of butter and margarine in the European OECD countries before World War II and declined

---

[4]For example, in the mid-fifties, budget elasticities were 0.4 for Greece and 0.6 for Italy [*5*].

to 51 per cent after the war (Table 7.1.1). Further decreases had taken place in subsequent years until low butter prices induced consumers to switch back to butter. The consumption of butter declined again as prices rose in 1959, only to stage a comeback in 1960 when lower prices prevailed. Fluctuations in consumption levels have been especially pronounced in countries such as the United Kingdom, Denmark, and Sweden, where the largest price changes have taken place.

For the postwar period, the impact of price changes on butter consumption can be indicated for several countries if the ratio of butter to margarine prices is used as an independent variable (Table A7.1.4). But no association is apparent between relative

TABLE 7.1.1

PER CAPITA CONSUMPTION OF BUTTER AND MARGARINE
IN THE OECD COUNTRIES OF WESTERN EUROPE
(kg, product weight)

	Butter	Margarine	Butter and Margarine	Butter as a Percentage of the Combined Consumption of Butter and Margarine
1934-38	6.3	3.2	9.5	66.3
1950-51	5.3	5.1	10.4	51.0
1951-52	5.1	5.4	10.5	48.6
1952-53	4.9	5.8	10.7	45.8
1953-54	5.3	5.9	11.2	47.3
1954-55	5.4	6.1	11.5	47.0
1955-56	5.5	6.1	11.6	47.4
1956-57	5.5	6.2	11.7	47.0
1957-58	5.9	6.0	11.9	49.6
1958-59	6.3	5.9	12.2	51.6
1959-60	6.1	6.2	12.3	49.6
1960-61	6.4	6.0	12.4	51.6

Source: OEEC, Agricultural and Food Statistics, 1955 and 1962.

prices and the relative consumption of butter and margarine in intercountry relationships (Graph 7.1.1). Price differences have little to do with the use of butter in French cuisine, and statistically significant results cannot be derived even if the French data are left out of consideration.

Intercountry comparisons do not indicate any relationship between incomes and butter consumption either, irrespective of whether the United States, with one of the lowest consumption levels, is included in the sample. At the same time, butter consumption per head appears to have increased with incomes during the postwar period in Germany, the Netherlands, and the United Kingdom, while the opposite result is shown for Belgium, Sweden, and the United States. In the latter cases, the trend away from butter appears to be responsible for the results, although—because of the intercorrelation between income and time—the presence of the trend factor cannot be statistically established.

The income elasticity of demand for butter is uniformly positive in all countries if the results of budget surveys are considered, while that for margarine is negative in most instances. In the United Kingdom, for example, the corresponding elasticities are 0.3 and

FIGURE 7.1.1

RELATIVE CONSUMPTION AND PRICES OF BUTTER AND MARGARINE
SELECTED COUNTRIES, 1960

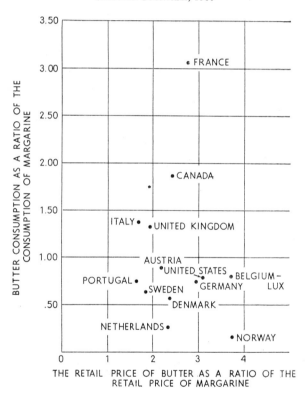

−0.3 [*11*, p. 36]. Thus, under *ceteris paribus* assumption, one would expect a shift toward butter as per capita incomes rise. However, improvements in technology are expected to lead to better quality—and possibly also to lower prices—of margarine, counteracting thereby the impact of higher incomes on consumption.

Among the countries of Western Europe who buy—or sell—butter on the world market, butter prices are the lowest in the United Kingdom, Denmark, Ireland, and Sweden. Since world market prices are not likely to decline much below present levels, substantial increases in butter consumption have not been projected in any of these countries, while a fall in consumption has been assumed for Ireland where consumption per head is about three times the European average.

The possibilities of increasing butter consumption are greater in the Common Market, where—with the exception of the Netherlands—in 1960 the retail price of butter was 60–70 per cent higher than in countries that trade on the world market. The increasing surplus in milk products points toward a rise in the consumption of butter, but, given the endeavor to maintain present prices paid to domestic producers, the subsidization of butter or the raising of taxes on margarine would be necessary to induce higher consumption. Since the possibilities of expanding exports are severely limited, we have assumed that some kind of a subsidy scheme will be applied either at the producer or the consumer level in order to clear the market in milk products, with a corresponding rise of butter consumption.

Increases in butter consumption are expected in Austria, Norway, and Switzerland, too. In all high income countries of Europe we have further assumed that "equilibrium" levels of consumption would be reached by 1970, and technological improvements favoring the consumption of margarine would counterbalance the impact of increasing incomes 1970 and 1975. Still, given the positive income elasticity of demand for butter, we have projected higher butter consumption levels to pertain to our high income alternative as compared to the most likely income assumption in 1970 as well as in 1975 (Table A7.1.2). Finally, a steady increase in the consumption of butter is foreseen in the countries of the Southern group, where the total intake of fats and oils will also rise.

Having estimated the future consumption of butter, the food use of other oils and fats is given as the difference between the projected consumption of oils and fats in food products and that of butter. Our next problem, then, concerns the future use of oils and fats in industrial products.

We have noted above that, following a temporary decline after the war, prewar consumption levels in the nonfood uses of oils and fats have been attained, and also surpassed, in most countries of Western Europe. Conflicting trends are responsible for these developments. On the one hand, the production of soap declined as compared to 1950 or the prewar period; on the other, oils and fats have come to be used in increasing quantities in the chemical industry.

Despite recent decreases in the production of soap, the relative importance of synthetic detergents is still much smaller in Europe than in the United States. For example, in 1960, over three times as much detergent as soap was used in the United States, whereas in the United Kingdom more soap was used than synthetic detergents [1, pp. 204–5]. We can expect, therefore, that the use of oils and fats in soap manufacturing will continue to decline in Western Europe. At the same time, the consumption of oils and fats in drying oils may change little, while significant increases are foreseen in other industrial uses, especially in the production of synthetic materials. Given the expected expansion in the chemical industry, the net result of these conflicting tendencies is likely to represent an absolute increase in the use of oils and fats in nonfood products and, in the more developed countries of Western Europe, American consumption levels may be approached by 1975 (Table A7.1.3).

Having surveyed possible changes in the use of oils and fats in food and nonfood products, we have next to consider the prospective contribution of domestic production and imports to European consumption. Separate consideration is given here to butter and to all other fats and oils taken together.

In recent years, the degree of self-sufficiency in butter was 98–99 per cent in the European Economic Community. The price support policy of the Common Market and other measures designed to stimulate livestock production in the EEC are expected to lead to the disappearance of butter imports, however. On the other hand, 90 per cent of butter consumed in the United Kingdom is imported, and 60 per cent of these imports come from outside Western Europe (mostly from Australia and New Zealand and, to a lesser extent, Argentina and South Africa). In the absence of changes in commercial policies, these relationships are likely to continue in the future. Finally, in all other countries of Western Europe, butter imports are negligible, and a rise during the period of projection is not foreseen.

Different considerations apply to oils and fats other than butter. The degree of self-sufficiency in these commodities, expressed in oil and fat equivalent, was about 50 per cent in Western Europe in the late fifties, although large differences are observed in regard to individual regions. The degree of self-sufficiency is about 20 per cent in the United Kingdom, 40 per cent in the Common Market, 80 per cent in Northern Europe, and 95 per cent in Southern Europe.

In the Common Market countries, the total consumption of oils and fats other than butter is expected to rise by about 10 per cent within a decade (Table 7.1.2). Increases in domestic production may be somewhat larger, however, since government policies are ex-pected to further the cultivation of rapeseed, while the rise in meat output will be accompanied by increased output of lard and tallow.

Consumption will grow at a lower rate in the United Kingdom, but, given the expected small expansion of production, a rise in the degree of self-sufficiency is not envisaged. Increases in produc-tion will be concentrated in lard and tallow, while the output of linseed and other vegetable oils is likely to decline.

The growth of the consumption and production of oils and fats other than butter in the countries of Northern Europe will approxi-mately equal that in the United Kingdom. On the other hand, sub-

TABLE 7.1.2

CONSUMPTION OF OILS AND FATS (OTHER THAN BUTTER) IN WESTERN EUROPE
(thousand metric tons of oils and fats equivalents)

	1960	1970I	1970II	1975I	1975II
Common Market	3666	4072	4090	4354	4373
United Kingdom	1303	1370	1365	1403	1397
Northern Europe	646	683	697	708	708
Southern Europe	1175	1690	1733	1919	2012
Western Europe, Total	6790	7815	7885	8384	8490

Source: Tables A7.1.2 and 7.1.3.

stantial increases in consumption are expected in Southern Europe and, although domestic production will continue to expand, im-ports are likely to rise at a higher rate than consumption.

Japan

The consumption of oils and fats has been increasing at a rapid rate over the last decades in Japan as the Japanese diet has be-come more diversified. In 1959, the per capita consumption of oils and fats in food end-products was 3.8 kg, compared to 1.6 kg in 1951 and 0.6 kg in 1934–36.[5] On the basis of time-series data, house-hold surveys, and cross-section data, Takemi Yasunaga derived an income elasticity of demand for oils and fats of 0.87 for urban households and 1.23 for the rural population. We have accepted these figures in our projections and have estimated per capita con-

---

[5]All Japanese data on domestic consumption and production are taken from [*14*].

sumption to reach 6.0 (6.5) kg in 1970 and 7.3 (8.3) kg in 1975 under the most likely (high) income assumption.

Although this increase represents a considerably higher rate of growth of consumption than in any other country under consideration, the estimated level of consumption would be still greatly below present levels in North America and in Western Europe. This discrepancy could be explained by differences in eating habits, but these habits might undergo changes within a short time, so that our projection should be regarded as a conservative estimate. Still, it roughly corresponds to present expectations as shown by the forecast of the Japanese Economic Planning Agency, which foresees the per capita fat content of all food to rise by 123 per cent between 1956–58 and 1970 [*8*, p. 113].[6]

In 1960, the total consumption of oils and fats in food products was 356 thousand tons, of which 142 thousand tons were manufactured from domestic materials. The combined production of rapeseed and soybeans, which gave 95 per cent of domestic supply in 1958–60, is not likely to rise however, and thus the brunt of increased consumption would fall on imports. Increased imports of soybeans and tallow will also be necessary for industrial purposes and as animal feed.

Oceania and South Africa

The per capita consumption of oils and fats in 1960 was 16 kg in Australia and 20 kg in New Zealand. Further increases are not expected in New Zealand, but higher consumption levels could be reached in Australia if the domestic price of butter were to fall. Still, increases in consumption can be provided from sources within the area, and imports will continue to be restricted to special kinds of oils and oilseeds (e.g., industrial oils). At the same time, a further expansion in the production and consumption of oils and fats is foreseen in South Africa, with imports rising somewhat from present low levels.

The Price and Origin of Imports

Butter. With the disappearance of Common Market butter imports, the only developed country importing butter from less developed areas will be the United Kingdom. Britain is expected to

---

[6]In 1956–58, consumption per head was 3.2 kg. Note also that the Japanese Ten-Year Plan calculates with a higher rate of increase of incomes than our target estimate.

continue to buy butter from Argentina in quantities purchased in 1961.

Vegetable Oils and Oilseeds. According to our projections, the imports of oils and oilseeds into North America originating in less developed countries would increase at the same rate as population (about 18.5 per cent between 1960 and 1970 and 30.4 per cent between 1960 and 1975). No change is assumed in the composition of these imports.

In regard to Western Europe, allowance should be made for stockpiling in 1960 which was largely responsible for the 6 per cent decline in European imports of oils and fats between 1960 and 1961. Correspondingly, while imports for consumption are projected to rise by 8 to 10 per cent between 1960 and 1970, and 15 to 18 per cent between 1960 and 1975, the increase in actual imports may not exceed 3 to 5 per cent and 9 to 12 per cent in the two periods, respectively.

In terms of oil and fat content, oilseeds and vegetable oils accounted for three-fourths of the net imports of oils and fats into Western Europe in 1960, the remainder being approximately evenly divided between animal fats and marine oils. As a result of compensating changes in regard to animal fats and marine oils, the share of oilseeds and vegetable oils is not likely to change much during the period of projection. Changes are expected in regard to the origin of imports, however.

The fifties have seen a rapid expansion in American exports of oleogenous materials and oils to Western Europe. In terms of value, the share of U.S. exports has risen from less than 10 per cent to 30 per cent in the case of oilseeds and to 20 per cent in regard to vegetable oils, with a corresponding decline in the share of Asian and Latin-American producers. Production policies followed in the United States will largely determine the future expansion of these exports. Available information indicates that U.S. exports of soybeans will make further inroads in the European market and may provide two-thirds of the increase in the imports of oilseeds and oils. On the other hand, the expected decline of imports from the Soviet bloc will benefit the underdeveloped areas.

Among the export products of the developing countries, the prospects for groundnuts appear to be good. Groundnut oil is used in cooking as well as in margarine, and the increase in demand will be satisfied by larger imports from Argentina, Brazil, and Nigeria. Given the expected fall in the production of soap in Western Europe, a decline in the imports of palm oil and palm kernel oil is likely to be forthcoming, however. At the same time, higher domestic consumption may contribute to a decrease of exports from the Continental countries of Asia, although the Philippines can supply larger quantities of copra and coconut oil.

These projections on the origin of imports should be regarded as highly tentative. Not only is the expansion of exportable production of soybeans in the United States influenced by governmental policies, but trade patterns are also affected by the amount of soybean oil made available through the P.L. 480 program for purposes of the deficit countries in various areas. Finally, the projections will change substantially if Mainland China re-enters the world market with large quantities of soybeans and groundnuts.

As regards the share of vegetable oils in the combined imports of oils and oilseeds, we note that the developing countries endeavor to establish domestic oil-crushing facilities, and some countries (Argentina and Senegal) even restrict or discourage the exportation of oilseeds. But powerful pressures act in the opposite direction. The user companies wish to utilize their crushing facilities, and technological improvements in oil crushing as well as the increased utilization of oilcake as animal feed in Western Europe bolsters the demand for oilseeds. Also, the 10–15 per cent tariff on vegetable oils in the Common Market, as against zero duty on oilseeds, favors the importation of the latter. Thus, although oil processing may expand in the African countries and territories associated with the Common Market, the relative shares of oils and oilseeds in Europe's imports from less developed areas are not likely to change much.

Imports into Japan almost exclusively take the form of oilseeds, and the by-product of oil processing is used as animal feed. A steadily increasing portion of imports (mostly soybeans) has originated in the United States. We have assumed this trend to continue so that the present share of the less developed countries in these imports (about one-fifth in 1960) would decline to approximately 15 per cent.

Finally, oilseeds imported by Australia and New Zealand will continue to come from the Pacific Islands, and the present geographical composition of vegetable oil imports into South Africa is also likely to be maintained.

Fats and Processed Oils and Fats

Western Europe and Japan are the main importers of animal fats other than butter. About two-thirds of Western Europe's imports consist of tallow and one-third of lard, both originating almost exclusively in the United States. Given the expansion of livestock raising in Europe, lard imports are expected to decline, although the new uses found for tallow in animal feeding and in the chemical industry may cause imports to return to the relatively high 1960 level by 1970. At the same time, a rise in tallow imports into Japan is expected.

In the marine oil category, whale oil accounts for two-thirds of Europe's imports, and fish oil for one-third. Natural limitations will restrict the expansion of whale oil production, and imports may remain at the 1960 level. On the other hand, although the continuation of the spectacular growth of fish oil imports experienced during the fifties cannot be expected, imports of fish oil may treble within a decade. Finally, imports of processed oils and fats from developing countries are not likely to rise much from their present low level.

Price of oils and fats have shown less variability than primary product prices in general. In the late fifties, prices of oils and oilseeds were only slightly lower than during the Korean War period, but the FAO price index showed a decline to 92 in 1960 and 91 in 1961 (1952–54 = 100). With increased competition from lard, tallow, and fish oil, some further weakening of oil prices can be expected. In fact, our import projections are based on the assumption that prices of vegetable oils and oilseeds would fall by 5–6 per cent, since, in the absence of a decrease in prices, animal fats would get a larger share of the market.

7.2 SUGAR, SUGAR PRODUCTS, AND HONEY (SITC 06)

Sugar is produced both in temperate and in tropical climate (beet sugar and cane sugar), production costs being generally lower in the latter case. Still, protectionist policies, coupled with improved beet-growing practices have lead to an increasing degree of self-sufficiency in the industrial countries. While sugar consumption in these countries rose by about 40 per cent during the fifties, the increase in imports was only 20 per cent.

A large part of world trade in sugar takes place in sheltered channels. Imports into the United States are regulated under the Sugar Act, and much of Commonwealth trade comes under the Commonwealth Sugar Agreement, whereas France and Portugal import sugar from their respective overseas territories. Cuba used to be the main supplier of the United States, but since 1960 the United

States has shifted purchases to other, mainly Latin-American, producers. Meanwhile, the Soviet Union has assumed importance as a market for Cuban sugar.

Aside from Cuba, the largest sugar exporters are the Philippines, the Dominican Republic, Australia, Taiwan, and Brazil. But sugar exports are of greatest importance for some small tropical islands; Mauritius derives 99 per cent of her export earnings from the sale of sugar; Réunion, 81 per cent; Barbados, 77 per cent; Fiji, 70 per cent, and Guadeloupe, 56 per cent. The corresponding proportions are 48 and 37 per cent, respectively, for the Dominican Republic and Taiwan.

Although sugar consumption has been growing in most industrial countries, increases have been generally smaller in recent years (Table A7.2.1). The slowing down in the growth of consumption at higher income levels indicates that sugar consumption has a saturation level at around 50 kg per head (in raw sugar equivalent), depending on customs, tastes, and other special circumstances.[7]

TABLE 7.2.1

SUGAR CONSUMPTION IN INDUSTRIAL COUNTRIES
(thousand metric tons)

	1950	1955	1960	1970I	1970II	1975I	1975II
North America........	8,170	8,352	9,670	11,482	11,482	12,623	12,623
Common Market.......	3,587	4,282	4,988	6,204	6,285	6,711	6,845
United Kingdom	1,968	2,733	2,900	3,087	3,087	3,173	3,173
Northern Europe	1,333	1,458	1,634	1,757	1,763	1,819	1,829
Southern Europe.......	689	1,047	1,121	1,550	1,656	1,755	1,918
Japan	398	1,090	1,336	1,937	2,049	2,273	2,443
Industrial Countries, Total	16,145	18,962	21,649	26,017	26,322	28,354	28,831

Source: Table A7.2.1.

Economic variables explain a large part of intercountry differences in consumption levels. Applying a multicountry function to observations for the years 1950–1960 in 18 industrial countries, we have found that about 80 per cent of the variation in consumption can be attributed to differences in incomes and relative prices (Table A7.2.2). Considering that income and price elasticities are generally lower in high income countries than in those with low income levels, we have used the semilogarithmic form of this function in deriving the elasticities used in the projections

---

[7]In comparing per capita consumption figures of individual countries, note should be taken of the error possibilities due to the sugar content of trade in food products. Adjustment for this trade has been made in the case of the Netherlands and Austria, but in the absence of such an adjustment, consumption figures in the United Kingdom and Denmark appear to be slightly overstated, and consumption in countries importing sugar products understated.

and have further taken account of information derived from budget studies and time-series data for individual countries.

Estimates on the future imports of sugar have also been corrected for trade in sugar products. Finally, trade in honey, included in this category, is relatively unimportant, and has not received detailed consideration.

North America

In the United States, per capita sugar consumption surpassed 50 kg of raw sugar equivalent during the twenties. This level has not been reached in any peacetime year since, and sugar consumption per head has fluctuated between 48 and 49 kg during the last decade. On the basis of prewar and postwar observations, and introducing a trend factor, the FAO has estimated income and price elasticities to be around 0.2–0.3 [6, p. 41]. But over the past two decades a negative trend factor has completely counterbalanced the possible impact of the growth of incomes on consumption, and the consideration of regional changes as well as the results of budget studies do not warrant a projection of rising consumption per head.

In the postwar period, per capita sugar consumption has declined in regions with higher than average income levels (New England and the western states), while increases have taken place in the South where sugar consumption was considerably below the national average. Also, the results of the 1955 budget survey indicate that whereas sugar consumption increases with income in the lower income groups, it is stable afterward, and it declines in the higher income groups. For the population as a whole, the budget elasticity has been calculated as −0.08 [6, pp. 33, 42].[8]

Approaching the problem in a different way, we note that over the last decade the decline in the direct consumption of sugar has been counterbalanced by an increase in indirect consumption (soft drinks, confectionery, bakery products, etc.). The shift from direct to indirect consumption will continue to take place in the future, but given the preoccupation with obesity in much of American society, it appears questionable that a net increase would be forthcoming. Correspondingly, we have assumed total sugar consumption to rise at the same rate as population (Table 7.2.1).

Sugar imports into the United States are regulated by quotas. In 1960, 49.5 per cent of sugar consumed in the United States was imported from foreign countries (trade with Puerto Rico is re-

---

[8]Both time-series and budget data include sugar consumption in sugar products.

garded as internal trade). Import quotas were set at 46.5 per cent in 1961 and were reduced to 40.0 per cent in the following year. Although actual imports exceeded the quota in both years, we have assumed the latter figure to apply to the period of projection. This assumption is in line with the observed tendency that domestic producers endeavor to fill their quotas.[9]

Given the reduction of the share of foreign suppliers in U.S. sugar consumption, imports are not likely to surpass the relatively high 1960 level before 1970. At the same time, the share of imports in domestic consumption is expected to be maintained throughout the period under consideration in Canada, where we have also assumed unchanged consumption per head.

Western Europe

Among Common Market countries, sugar consumption in Belgium, France, and Germany is about 30–35 kg per head as compared to 25–29 kg before the war. The results of budget surveys are available for France and Germany, and show income elasticities of about 0.3, while somewhat lower values are indicated by time series combining prewar and postwar observations [6, p. 36]. With consideration given to intercountry differences in per capita sugar consumption, we have used an elasticity of 0.3 in making projections for these countries.

In the Netherlands, sugar consumption has shown substantial increases over the last decade. While per capita consumption was 28 kg in the prewar period, it reached 46 kg in 1960. On the basis of recent experience, a slowing down in the growth of consumption is expected, however. This is also indicated by the low values of income elasticities derived from budget studies and long-term time series.[10] In projecting future consumption, an income elasticity of 0.1 has been assumed.

In Italy, sugar consumption per head more than doubled since the thirties, but at 22 kg it is still considerably below the European average. An income elasticity of 0.6 has been derived from budget studies [6, p. 36], while postwar time-series data indicate an elasticity of 0.75 for 1960 if a semilogarithmic function is used. In forecasting consumption, we have calculated with an income elasticity of 0.65.

---

[9]Note also that while small nonquota purchases abroad are envisaged, according to a provision of the Sugar Act only 35 per cent of purchases above the basic quota would be supplied by foreign producers.

[10]0.05 and 0.11, respectively.

By reason of fluctuations in measured consumption due to stock changes, these estimates have further been adjusted to take account of consumption data available for 1961. Correspondingly, sugar consumption in the Common Market as a whole would rise from 4.99 million tons in 1960 to 6.20–6.29 million tons in 1970 and 6.71–6.85 million tons in 1975, depending on the income assumption chosen. These projections compare with a consumption of 6.23–6.40 and 6.48–6.64 million tons, estimated by the FAO and the European Economic Community, respectively, for 1970 [*4*, p. A53, *2* p. IV.31].

In 1957–1959, the countries of the European Economic Community produced 96 per cent of their sugar requirements, and by 1961 the Common Market had become a net exporter of sugar. The EEC study cited above expects production to rise at a somewhat lower rate than consumption, so that the degree of self-sufficiency would fall below 95 per cent by 1970 [2, p. IV.3]. This result is based on the assumption that in 1970 the area under sugar beet would be the same as in the crop year 1961/62. But in 1961/62 the area under sugar was reduced by 8 per cent as compared to 1960/61 when large surpluses had been experienced and, given the agricultural policy of the Common Market, the depletion of inventories is likely to be followed by an increase in the cultivated area. Considering also the difference between our estimate of sugar consumption and that of the EEC, it appears questionable that an import surplus would be generated by 1970. Rather, we have assumed 100 per cent self-sufficiency under the most likely income alternative and small net imports in the event that the target rate of income growth is reached.

In estimating gross imports, account should further be taken of the exportation of sugar. Belgium, France, and the Netherlands have been importing raw sugar for refining and re-export, mainly to the former overseas territories. In 1960, re-exports amounted to 750 thousand tons of raw sugar equivalent, to which about 150 thousand tons exported by the Netherlands in the form of sugar products should be added. Inasmuch as African countries tend to develop refining facilities, the amount imported for refining is likely to decline, and in 1970 and 1975 direct and indirect exports of sugar may not exceed 600 thousand tons. Correspondingly, gross imports would amount to 600–700 thousand tons, as compared to 1150 thousand tons in 1960. Imports of honey may continue to rise, however.

Sugar consumption in the United Kingdom is among the highest in the industrial countries, which is explained, in part, by the relatively high consumption of confectionery and marmalade. Per capita consumption surpassed 55 kg in 1956 but has not shown any definite trend since. Considering also that the budget elasticity of demand for sugar and preserves was 0.06 in 1958 [*11*, p. 36], it appears appropriate to assume that per capita sugar consumption would remain at present levels throughout the period of projection.

Accordingly, the consumption of sugar in the United Kingdom is projected to rise from 2.90 million tons in 1960 to 3.09 million tons in 1970 and 3.17 million tons in 1975, as compared to 3.10–3.20 million tons estimated by the FAO for 1970 [*4*, p. A53]. The home production of sugar has been increasing in the United Kingdom, and has supplied one-third of its domestic requirements in 1960. On the basis of information provided in a study prepared by the Institute for Research in Agricultural Economics at Oxford University, we have applied the same ratio in the period of projection [*7*, p. 128].

To arrive at an estimate of gross imports, we have also to consider the re-export of refined sugar from the United Kingdom, destined chiefly for the members of the Commonwealth. Re-exports amounted to 600 thousand tons of raw sugar equivalent in 1960. With the construction of refineries in the importing countries, we have assumed this quantity to decline by about one-third during the period of projection, reducing thereby the rise in gross imports.

Sugar consumption per head is about 40–45 kg in the countries of the northern group, with the exception being Denmark where it approaches 60 kg. Considering the similarity in consumption patterns, we have assumed that the relationships observed in regard to the Netherlands pertain to this group of countries too, although in the case of Denmark further increases in per capita sugar consumption are not likely to be forthcoming.

With the exception of Austria and Denmark, the countries of the northern group are net importers of sugar, although substantial quantities are produced in Ireland and Sweden. We have assumed here that the proportion supplied by domestic producers would remain unchanged during the period of projection, so that imports would rise at the same rate as domestic consumption.

Per capita sugar consumption has not exceeded 18 kg in the countries of Southern Europe. The results of budget studies are available for Greece where an income elasticity of 0.7 is shown [*6*, p. 36], while time-series regressions of the semilogarithmic form indicate income elasticities ranging between 0.5 and 1.0 (Table A1.3.1). Taking account of intercountry comparisons of consumption levels, elasticities of 0.65–0.75 have been employed in the projections, the exception being Turkey, where a 1 per cent change in per capita disposable income may be accompanied by a 1 per cent rise in sugar consumption per head.

Among the countries of Southern Europe, Greece and Portugal, and, to a lesser extent, Yugoslavia and Spain, rely on sugar imports, while Turkey exports over 200 thousand tons a year. Greece and Portugal will continue to derive their sugar requirements from imports but, given the expected rapid increase in domestic production, Yugoslav and Spanish imports may remain at levels observed in 1960.

Japan

Sugar consumption in Japan has shown a rising trend over the last decade, although prewar consumption levels have been surpassed only in 1956. After the shortages of the early postwar period disappeared, per capita consumption has been increasing at a rate slightly lower than the growth of income per person. With consideration given to information provided by the Ten-Year Plan, an income elasticity of 0.7 has been used in making projections. At the same time, the Plan assumes a fourfold increase in domestic sugar production over the sixties [8, p. 95], with a corresponding fall in the share of imports which provided for about nine-tenths of Japan's sugar consumption in 1960.

Oceania and South Africa

Considering that Australia and New Zealand, taken together, are expected to remain net exporters of sugar, detailed projections have not been prepared for these countries. Gross imports from the less-developed countries were valued at $2 million in 1960 and may increase slightly over the next decade. Finally, South Africa is a larger exporter of sugar and will remain so in the foreseeable future.

The Price and Origin of Imports

Assuming 1960 prices to be maintained during the period of projection, sugar imports into industrial areas would rise by about 2–3 per cent between 1960 and 1970, and 10–12 per cent between 1960 and 1975.[10] Among developed countries, Australia and South Africa are large exporters, supplying over 20 per cent of British and Canadian requirements and less than 10 per cent of Japanese imports in 1960. In addition, in the year 1962, both of these coun-

---

[10]By comparison, the FAO expects an 8 per cent increase in imports between 1969–1971. [4, II p. 36]. The difference between the two estimates is explained by the higher share of imports in U.S. consumption assumed by the FAO.

tries received small allotments of the U.S. quota. We have assumed that Australia and South Africa will maintain their 1960 share in the imports of the United Kingdom and Canada, and will receive quotas comparable to those of 1962 in the United States. On the other hand, they may decline in importance as suppliers to the Japanese market. The remainder of the imports of industrial areas will be supplied by underdeveloped countries, except for small quantities originating in the Soviet bloc.

Among developing countries, the Philippines is expected to get a larger share of the U.S. market, and India and Taiwan will also have a small U.S. quota, although the bulk of imports will come from Latin America. The Commonwealth countries will continue to provide much of Canadian and British sugar requirements, while Common Market imports are likely to come exclusively from the French overseas departments (Reunion, Martinique, and Guadeloupe). Finally, no changes are projected to take place as regards the origin of sugar imported by other European countries, but imports from Latin America are likely to assume greater importance in Japan.

Turning to prices, we note that, in 1960, sugar prices differed considerably, depending on the coverage of market agreements. Whereas the world reference price (the f.o.b. price of 96° raw sugar in Cuba for destinations other than the United States) averaged 3.14 cents per pound, the U.S. c.i.f. premium price was 5.80 cents. After discounting for import duty and other costs, the United States paid a premium of 2.21 cents per pound above the world market price. In the same year, the United Kingdom paid a price nearly 60 per cent higher under the Commonwealth Sugar Agreement than for purchases made outside the Agreement.

Under the new U.S. sugar legislation, premiums paid on sugar originating in Latin America will disappear over a period of ten years, although the Philippines will continue to receive a premium. On the other hand, under the assumption that the Comonwealth preferential system will be maintained during the period under consideration, Commonwealth producers would continue to enjoy the present price differential in their sales to Britain. The question is, then, what prices will prevail on the world market.

By reason of the narrowness of the world market and the shifts in production and demand that have taken place in recent years, sugar prices have shown substantial fluctuation. In late 1961, prices dropped to about two-thirds of the 1960 level, but subsequently skyrocketed to an all-time high. Future developments will greatly depend on the production and trade of Cuba and cannot be foreseen with any degree of confidence. We have chosen here to calculate with 1960 prices by assuming that in the early seventies an equilibrium may develop at or around this price. Hence, forecasts prepared at 1960 prices have been corrected only in the case of the United States, where the premium paid on Latin-American sugar will be progressively eliminated.[11] It goes without saying that policy changes in the United States, Western Europe, the Soviet Union, or Cuba may invalidate this projection.

7.3 TOBACCO (SITC 12)

The United States is the largest producer and exporter of tobacco and, among the countries of Western Europe, Greece and Turkey also bring substantial quantities on the world market. The less developed countries, taken together, account for about 35 per cent of unmanufactured tobacco entering world trade. In 1959–61, 40 per cent of the tobacco exports of developing areas came from Rhodesia and Nyasaland, who derive one-fifth of their export earnings from the sale of tobacco. Much of the remainder originated in India, Brazil, Cuba, and Indonesia.

The United States has the highest consumption levels of tobacco; in terms of processing weight, consumption per head of population 15 years and over is around 5 kg. This consumption level is approached only by Canada (4.8 kg), while in western Europe tobacco consumption is the highest in the Netherlands (4.3 kg), Belgium (3.4 kg), and the United Kingdom (3.3 kg). The countries of Oceania also consume over 3 kg of tobacco per head.

North America

In the United States, the number of cigarettes consumed per capita of population over 15 was 3,888 in 1960, corresponding to 4.1 kg of tobacco, as compared to the tobacco content of all tobacco products estimated at 5.0 kg. Between 1950–52 and 1959–61, per capita cigarette consumption increased 11.3 per cent, while in the same period tobacco consumption per head in cigarettes declined 4.3 per cent, and in all tobacco products, 8.1 per cent [*13*, p. 12].

---

[11]The premium paid to Latin-American suppliers amounted to $160 million in 1960. By 1970, eight-tenths of the premiums that would have been paid on quantities purchased in that year will be lost, and in 1975 no premium will be paid. The loss of premium will reduce the export earnings of Latin-American sugar producers calculated at full premium rates by $124 million in the former year and $170 million in the latter.

Technological factors as well as changes in tastes are responsible for the observed fall in the per capita consumption of tobacco in the form of cigarettes as against the rise in cigarette consumption. The development of sheet tobacco which enables manufacturers to utilize the hitherto unused stems and small tobacco particles, improvements in the manufacturing process, and the smaller tobacco column in most brands of filter cigarettes have all contributed to this result. Finally, the decline in the consumption of pipe, chewing, and snuff tobacco explains the relatively larger fall in the consumption of tobacco in all tobacco products taken together.

As regards prospective increases in tobacco consumption, we note that time-series studies encompassing the period 1926-58 indicate an income elasticity of demand of 0.5-0.6 for cigarettes [10]. But cigarette consumption has been increasing at a slower rate in recent years, and a budget study for the year 1955 showed an income elasticity of only 0.12 [9]. Health considerations are likely to limit future increases in the smoking of cigarettes, and the continuing shift toward filter cigarettes, as well as technological improvements in tobacco manufacturing, can erase all gains made in cigarette consumption per head. Correspondingly, we have assumed that per capita tobacco consumption in the United States would remain unchanged during the period of projection.

The United States is a net tobacco exporter and imports only certain types of tobacco: oriental leaf from Greece and Turkey for blending with home-produced tobacco, and cigar leaf. With exports approximately unchanged, tobacco imports have risen by about one-half over the past decade and now amount to three-tenths of exports and one-tenth of domestic consumption.

Tobacco imports originating in less developed countries (almost exclusively cigar tobacco) amounted to 18 thousand tons in 1960, two thirds of which came from Cuba. The embargo on Cuban tobacco put into effect in early 1962 has halted imports from Cuba, however, and the Philippines, Columbia, and the Dominican Republic have become the largest suppliers of cigar tobacco to the United States. Cigar consumption will continue to rise in the United States, but the increased reliance on domestic tobacco (including Puerto Rican) and the boost given to imports by stockpiling in 1960 indicate that the 1960 import level may not be reached before 1965. This conclusion is not materially affected by the possible increase of Cuban cigar leaf exports to Canada. (By comparison, present Canadian imports do not exceed 2 per cent of those to the United States.)

Western Europe

During most of the fifties, the net imports of tobacco into Western Europe amounted to 35 per cent of consumption, but this ratio surpassed 40 per cent in 1960 as a result of the devastating effects of the blue mold disease. Greece and Turkey are the largest tobacco exporters, while smaller quantities originate in Italy and Yugoslavia. With the exception of France and Spain, all other countries imported most or all of their requirements. Over half of the 370 thousand tons of tobacco imported from outside Western Europe in 1960 came from the United States, the remainder from the developing countries—primarily Africa, and to a lesser extent in Asia and Latin America—and a small quantity from the Soviet bloc. Only 3 per cent of all imports is manufactured tobacco, for the most part American cigarettes.

Consumption forecasts made on the basis of income elasticities derived from budget studies postulate a large increase in demand. In the Dewhurst study it has been assumed, for example, that the income elasticity of demand for tobacco would be 1.0 for Greece, Portugal, and Spain, 0.8 for Finland, Ireland, and Italy, and 0.6 for the other countries of Western Europe (Turkey and Yugoslavia excluded) [*3*, p. 211]. These projections appear to overestimate future increases in the consumption of tobacco, however, chiefly because the budget estimates used in forecasting refer to expenditure on tobacco products rather than to the quantity of tobacco consumed. With regard to the latter, a consideration of past trends can be of interest.

The per capita consumption of tobacco exhibited a rising trend in the countries of Western Europe during the past decades, and prewar consumption levels were by and large surpassed in the mid-fifties. Still, U.S. consumption levels have been approached only in a few European countries, while consumption per head of population over 15 has not reached one-half of the U.S. level in others. At the same time, in most countries of Europe, per capita tobacco consumption has changed little in recent years (Table A7.3.1).

The question arises whether U.S. consumption levels would be reached—or approached—in the countries of Western Europe during the period under consideration. In this connection, note that international disparities in tobacco consumption are explained, in part, by differences in social habits and customs. Although the latter are related to the general level of well-being, the relationship between incomes and tobacco consumption is often tenuous. One may argue that urbanization and the increased participation of women in the labor force will lead to higher per capita cigarette consumption, but account should also be taken of the effects of the increased attention given to the link between smoking and cancer. On balance, it appears likely that increases in the per capita consumption of cigarettes will be modest in most of Western Europe.

The rise in tobacco consumption will be further reduced by the shift toward filter cigarettes and improvements in the manufacturing process. Among the Common Market countries, the per capita consumption of tobacco may change little in Belgium and the Netherlands, while a 10 per cent rise in incomes may be accompanied by a 3–4 per cent increase in tobacco consumption per head in France and Germany, and a 6 per cent increase in Italy.

In the second half of the fifties about 45–50 per cent of Common Market consumption was provided from domestic sources, but the degree of self-sufficiency fell to 42 per cent in 1960 as production declined from 164 to 140 thousand metric tons. The spreading of the blue mold disease led to further decreases in production in 1961. In Italy, 70 per cent of the crop was destroyed, and production in the EEC as a whole did not surpass one-half of the 1960 output.

However, as a result of disease control measures taken in 1961, production again increased, and it may equal the 1960 level in the mid-sixties. Taking account of the protective effect of the EEC tariff, tobacco production in Italy and France is likely to increase further so that domestic sources could provide for 45 per cent of consumption by 1975. Correspondingly, the gross imports of tobacco into the Common Market would rise from 184 thousand tons in 1960 to 230 thousand tons in 1970 and 250 thousand tons in 1975.

In the United Kingdom, per capita tobacco consumption had been increasing during the fifties. But the antismoking campaign has affected consumption already in 1961, and it is expected to have further repercussions in years to come. Thus, the increase in per capita tobacco consumption will be small, if any. All tobacco consumed in Britain is imported, but, in projecting future imports, account has also been taken of the large amount of stockpiling in 1960. In view of this, the imports of unmanufactured tobacco may not reach the 1960 level before 1970.

In Northern Europe, tobacco production is insignificant, and little change is expected in the future. Consumption per head increased slightly during the fifties and some further increases may be forthcoming. Consumption will expand faster in the southern group of countries, but here—with the exception of Portugal—the expansion of domestic production can provide for all foreseeable increases in consumption.

Japan

Per capita tobacco consumption has increased slightly in recent years in Japan and, with changes in social customs, further increases are expected. Imports amounted to 3–5 per cent of consumption in 1960; 90 per cent of imports came from the United States, the remainder from Western Europe, and only a small fraction from Asia and Africa. No change in imports from developing countries has been assumed.

Oceania and South Africa

Tobacco consumption has been rising in Australia and New Zealand, but the growth of domestic production greatly outweighed that of consumption. Correspondingly, imports declined steadily and despite expected increases in consumption, further declines are expected during the period of projection. Finally, exports and imports are in balance in South Africa, and this situation is likely to be maintained during the period of projection.

The Price and Origin of Imports

Whereas the tobacco exports of the developing countries to North America, Japan, Oceania, and South Africa may change little, exports to Western Europe will continue to expand. According to our projections, the net importing countries of Western Europe will import about 500 thousand tons of tobacco in 1970 and 550 thousand tons in 1975, as compared to imports of 450 thousand tons in 1960, and the share of the developing countries in these imports is likely to rise.

Approximately 30 per cent of Common Market imports comes from the United States, one fourth from Greece and Turkey, 40 per cent from the less developed countries, and a small quantity from Eastern Europe. The composition of imports will undergo changes, however, as a result of the 28 per cent common tariff on tobacco, with a minimum rate of 13.2 cents and a maximum rate of 17.2 cents a pound. This tariff is higher than the average of duties charged by the individual Common Market countries, and it represents a partial changeover from specific duties to an ad valorem tariff. Consequently, it benefits not only producers who receive preferential treatment but also the suppliers of low cost tobacco (e.g., Rhodesia and Nyasaland).

The preferential treatment accorded to Greek and Turkish tobacco will contribute to further changes toward the use of the so-called American-type blend which includes 10 per cent, or more, oriental tobacco. In addition, Greece is now growing some flue-cured tobacco and is experimenting with the burley type, both of which directly compete with U.S. tobacco.

A substantial increase of imports from Africa is also likely to be forthcoming, partly in the form of dark tobacco produced by the overseas associated countries, and partly as a result of the continuing expansion in the production of low cost Virginia-type tobacco in Rhodesia and Nyasaland. Larger imports from Rhodesia and Nyasaland will take place at the expense of imports from the United States, representing a continuation of the shift from American to Rhodesian flue-cured tobacco.

Until February, 1960, United Kingdom tobacco manufacturers were obliged to limit the use of tobacco imported from the dollar area to 61 per cent of total requirements. The lifting of restrictions has not led to larger imports from the United States, however, and the importation of U.S. tobacco declined in absolute as well as in relative terms. These developments are explained by the low cost of tobacco imported from Rhodesia-Nyasaland, and India. Assuming present policies to continue, it does not appear likely that the United States would recapture her former share in the British market.

The countries of Northern Europe and Portugal cover over one-half of their needs by imports from the United States. However, the share of the less developed countries in these imports has increased over the past decade, and further increases are expected in future years. On the other hand, tobacco imports from developing countries are not likely to change in Japan. Finally, we have assumed that tobacco prices observed in the years 1959–61 would pertain to the period of projection. Correspondingly, tobacco imports from less developed countries would rise by about 30 per cent between 1960 and 1970, and 40 per cent between 1960 and 1975.

REFERENCES

[1.] COMMONWEALTH ECONOMIC COMMITTEE. *Vegetable Oils and Oilseeds.* London, 1962.

[2.] COMMUNAUTÉ ECONOMIQUE EUROPÉENE COMMISSION. *Le Marché commun des produits agricoles, Perspectives, "1970",* Etude, No. 10. Brussels, 1962.

[3.] DEWHURST, J. F., AND ASSOCIATES. *Europe's Needs and Resources.* New York: Twentieth Century Fund, 1961.

[4.] FOOD AND AGRICULTURE ORGANIZATION. *Agricultural Commodities—Projections for 1970.* Rome, 1962.

[5.] FOOD AND AGRICULTURE ORGANIZATION. *Income Elasticity of the Demand for Food.* Rome, 1959.

[6.] FOOD AND AGRICULTURE ORGANIZATION. *Trends and Forces in World Sugar Consumption.* Commodity Bulletin Series, No. 32, Rome, 1961.

[7.] INSTITUTE FOR RESEARCH IN AGRICULTURAL ECONOMICS OF OXFORD UNIVERSITY. *United Kingdom: Projected Level of Demand, Supply and Imports of Farm Products in 1965 and 1975.* Washington, D.C.: U.S. Department of Agriculture, 1962.

[8.] JAPANESE ECONOMIC PLANNING AGENCY. *New Long-Range Economic Plan of Japan (1961–1970).* Tokyo: The Times of Japan, 1961.

[9.] SACKRIN, S. M., AND CONOVER, A. G. *Tobacco Smoking in the United States in Relation to Income.* U.S. Department of Agriculture, Market Research Reports No. 189, Washington, D.C. 1957.

[10.] SACKRIN, S. M. "Factors Affecting the Demand for Cigarettes", *Agricultural Economic Research* (July, 1962), pp. 81–88.

[11.] UNITED KINGDOM MINISTRY OF AGRICULTURE, FISHERIES AND FOOD. *Domestic Food Consumption and Expenditure: 1958.* London, 1960.

[12.] U. S. DEPARTMENT OF AGRICULTURE. *The Fats and Oils Situation.* March, 1962.

[13.] U. S. DEPARTMENT OF AGRICULTURE. Economic Research Service, *Tobacco Situation.* March, 1963.

[14.] YASUNAGA, TAKEMI. *A Study on Consumption and Forecast of Selected Agricultural Products in Japan,* 1960 (mimeo).

CHAPTER 8

Trade Projections for
Noncompeting Tropical Foods

8.1 BANANAS (SITC 051-03)

BANANAS are the most important tropical fruit traded and account for a substantial part of the foreign exchange receipts of the main producing countries. Over four-fifths of all bananas entering world trade come from Latin America; the largest exporters are Ecuador, Honduras, Panama, and Costa Rica, in this order. Bananas provided 71 per cent of the export earnings of Panama and 63 per cent of the foreign exchange receipts of Ecuador in 1959–61, while the corresponding ratios were 50 per cent for Honduras and 24 per cent for Costa Rica. Latin-American producers are the exclusive suppliers of bananas to the United States, but an increasing proportion of European imports comes from the Canary Islands and Central Africa—chiefly the Ivory Coast, Nigeria, Guinea, and Somalia. Smaller quantities of bananas originate also in Taiwan and in Western Samoa.

Nearly half of all exports go to the United States, where banana consumption per head is about 10.5 kg a year. Despite substantial increases that have taken place in recent years in Europe, this level has been approached only in a few European countries. An overall relationship between incomes and banana consumption is apparent from Figure 8.1.1. Countries with annual per capita incomes of $200–$400 consume less than 1.0 kg of bananas per head; consumption rises to 1.5–2 kg at income levels of $400–$600; it amounts to 5.0–8.0 kg in countries with per capita incomes of around $1,000, while the United States and Canada, with the highest income levels, consume the most bananas. Spain does not fit the pattern, however, inasmuch as the availability of bananas in the Canary Islands has contributed to relatively high consumption levels in this country.

North America

The per capita consumption of bananas reached 10 kg in the United States before World War I, and—with the exception of the two wars and the depression of the thirties—there has been little change in consumption levels since. During the fifties, per capita consumption was around 9 kg, and it again surpassed the 10 kg mark in 1959. Budget studies indicate that further increases could conceivably take place, since, according to the 1955 budget survey, the income elasticity of demand for bananas is about 0.25 [6]. However, given the shift of consumption toward processed fruit and the search for variety in the diet, future increases in consumption per head do not appear likely. We have therefore assumed banana imports to the United States to rise in proportion with the growth of population.

In the postwar period, per capita banana consumption more than doubled in Canada, surpassing 9 kg per head in 1960. For purposes of projection, we have assumed that by 1975 Canada will approach present U.S. consumption levels.

Western Europe

Banana consumption in Western Europe has followed a different pattern from that observed in the United States. Before World War II, consumption per head surpassed 3 kg only in the United Kingdom and the Netherlands, but it has been increasing rapidly since the war. In 1960, the per capita consumption of bananas exceeded the prewar level threefold in most of the Common Market countries, and substantial increases have taken place in Northern Europe and in the United Kingdom, too. On the other hand, despite the high rate of growth of consumption experienced in recent years, negligible quantities are consumed in the countries of the Mediterranean other than Spain, where the availability of cheap domestic fruits has checked the spread of banana consumption (Table A8.1.1).

Time-series data on per capita consumption in European countries suggest a high income elasticity of demand for bananas, although in the presence of declining prices we would overstate the effect of increases in incomes on consumption by excluding the price variable from the calculations. And even if allowance were made for the impact of the decrease in prices on consumption, the estimated statistical relationship would offer little help in forecasting imports, since the growth of consumption has been greatly influenced by changing tastes and eating habits. Actually, the rise in banana consumption has been part of the general increase of demand for tropical and citrus fruit.

The experience of the United States and the recent slowing down in the rate of increase of banana consumption in European countries with higher consumption levels indicate that the rapid expansion of imports to Europe cannot continue indefinitely. A consideration of budget data point to the same conclusion. In the

FIGURE 8.1.1

Incomes and Banana Consumption in Indurtrial Countries

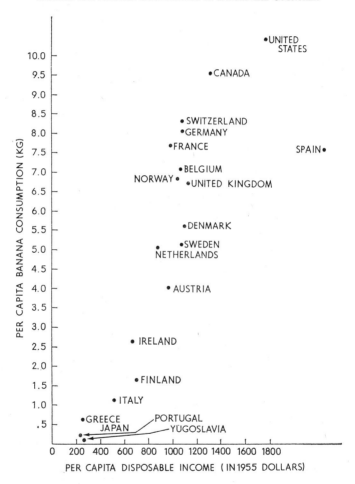

United Kingdom, where the results of more recent budget surveys are available, the income elasticity of demand for bananas derived from budget statistics was 0.66 in 1958, as compared to 0.77 in 1955, and 0.95 in 1937–39 [*15*, p. 37].

In the European Economic Community, per capita banana consumption in 1960 was 8.1 kg in Germany, 7.7 kg in France, 7.0 kg in Belgium and Luxembourg, 5.2 kg in the Netherlands and 1.8 kg in Italy. In recent years a slowing down in the rate of growth of consumption has been experienced in these countries, with the exception of Italy where an acceleration is shown. Taking account of intercountry differences in banana consumption, we have assumed an income elasticity of 0.35 to apply to Belgium, France, and Germany and 0.55 to the Netherlands, while in Italy the growth of banana consumption may exceed the rise in personal incomes. Further adjustments have been made to take account of future price changes resulting from the application of the common EEC tariff and expected reductions in the retail price of bananas in Italy.[1]

Banana consumption surpassed the prewar level in the United Kingdom only in 1960. In forecasting consumption, we have calculated with an income elasticity of 0.5 for that year. With consideration given to the shift away from fresh fruit, this elasticity has been set lower than the values derived from budget studies.

Moderate increases in consumption per head are expected in the countries of Scandinavia other than Finland, while in Finland the removal of restrictions on banana imports can lead to a substantial rise in consumption. Above average increases are likely to be forthcoming also in Austria and Ireland, where per capita consumption levels are relatively low. Finally, the high rate of growth of banana consumption experienced in recent years is bound to continue in the countries of the southern group, with the largest expansion foreseen in Yugoslavia where imports have been severely restricted by quotas.

Japan

A sharp reduction in trade with Taiwan after the war and exchange restrictions on banana imports are responsible for the low level of banana consumption in Japan. With the removal of restrictions, prewar consumption levels may soon be surpassed, and by 1975 per capita consumption can reach twice the prewar level.

Oceania and South Africa

Australia does not import bananas, while New Zealand satisfies her needs with imports from the Pacific Islands, and South Africa

---

[1] In Italy the banana market is regulated by a state monopoly, and retail prices averaged at 64 cents per kg in 1960 as compared to 36 cents in Germany. Prices were lowered to 56 cents in August, 1962 [*10*, p. 74].

buys bananas in Central Africa. Further increases in imports are expected in the latter two cases.

The Price and Origin of Imports

Estimates on banana consumption (imports) of developed areas are shown in Table 8.1.1, indicating an approximate 30 per cent increase between 1960 and 1970, and a 45 per cent rise between 1960 and 1975.[2] In order to arrive at estimates of import values, assumptions with regard to price changes also need to be made. In this connection, note should be taken of differences in unit values according to destination. Prices substantially above world market levels are paid by France and Italy to their former overseas territories, and by the United Kingdom to Commonwealth suppliers, while U.S. companies that own plantations in Latin America use a low accounting price for customs purposes. We have assumed present arrangements to be maintained during the period of projection and have calculated with unchanged prices, so that the value of imports into individual areas would rise in approximately the same proportion as the quantity of imports.

As regards the origin of imports, past relationships are likely to continue, the exception being the European Common Market and Japan. After the end of the transitional period, there will be a tariff of 20 per cent on bananas imported from nonparticipating countries into the EEC, while bananas originating in the overseas member countries will enter duty-free. The preferential duty would adversely affect the suppliers of Gros Michel bananas imported by the Benelux countries and Germany, provided that consumers were willing to shift to the Cavendish banana produced in the associated countries.

Recent changes in British consumption in favor of the Pojo variety of the Cavendish banana indicates the possibility of a shift away from the Gros Michel variety. And, although the traditional suppliers of the German-marked banana will have the benefit of a duty-free quota, at the end of the transitional period this quota will not exceed 75 per cent of the 1956 exports to Germany plus 50 per cent of the increase of imports since 1956. Consequently, we can expect that the share of nonassociated African producers and of Latin America will be reduced in the imports of the Common Market. Nevertheless, in view of the expected expansion of con-

---

[2]Spain is not included in the table, since Spanish purchase of bananas from the Canary Islands is regarded as internal trade.

sumption and the role played by quality differences, an absolute reduction of imports from Latin America does not appear likely.

Prospective shifts in the origin of imports into Japan are related to exchange regulations. Whereas during the fifties Japanese banana imports originated almost exclusively in Taiwan, after the freeing of restrictions an increasing proportion of imports will come from Latin America. (For estimates on the value of imports into developed countries according to areas of origin, see Table A8.)

TABLE 8.1.1

BANANA CONSUMPTION (NET IMPORTS) IN DEVELOPED COUNTRIES
(thousand tons)

	1950	1955	1960	1970I	1970II	1975I	1975II
North America	1217	1555	2072	2531	2531	2784	2787
Common Market	351	611	1018	1279	1303	1426	1459
United Kingdom	140	311	350	414	425	448	460
Northern Europe	51	129	177	217	222	237	246
Southern Europe[a]	0	0	21	30	33	43	49
Japan	10	27	40	255	275	361	404
Oceania and South Africa[b]	18	34	46	64	69	73	75
Developed Countries, Total	1787	2667	3724	4790	4858	5372	5480

Source: See Table A8.1.1.
Notes: [a]Excluding Spain.
[b]Excluding Australia.

8.2 COFFEE (SITC 071)

Next to petroleum, coffee is the most important export product of the developing countries, accounting for nearly one-tenth of their combined export income. Coffee has been traditionally the main export crop of Brazil and several other Latin-American countries. Receipts from the sale of coffee exceed 50 per cent of total export earnings in Brazil and Costa Rica, and 60 per cent in Colombia, Guatemala, and El Salvador. In the postwar period, coffee exports have assumed increased importance also in Africa. African producers increased their share in the world coffee market from 7-8 per cent in the thirties to 25 per cent in 1960, chiefly at the expense of Brazil, whose export share fell from 54 to 39 per cent in the same period. In the years 1959–61, coffee exports accounted for over 50 per cent of export earnings in Ethiopia and the Ivory Coast, and about 35 per cent in Angola, Kenya, and Uganda. Smaller quantities originate in some Asian countries (Indonesia, Malaya, and India).

In Latin America, and on higher altitudes in Africa (Ethiopia, Kenya, and Tanganyika), the more flavorful arabica is produced, while robusta is grown in other parts of Africa and Asia. The consumption of the latter variety has expanded rapidly in recent years, largely because of its use in soluble (instant) coffee. Also, robustas account for three-fourths of the coffee imports of France, in whose market the robusta-producing former associated territories receive preferential treatment.

Per capita coffee consumption exhibited a rising trend in all industrial countries up to World War II. In the United States, the growth of consumption accelerated during the forties, and, after a decline in the mid-fifties, consumption per head of population over 15 fluctuated around 10.5 kg.[3] On the other hand, imports into Continental Europe largely disappeared during the war, and consumption recovered to the prewar level only around 1955. American consumption levels are surpassed in Scandinavia, but have not been reached in any of the Common Market countries. Finally, per capita consumption hardly exceeds 1 kg in tea-drinking Britain and in Southern Europe (Table A8.2.1).

A possible way of explaining variations in coffee consumption is to take account of substitution possibilities between coffee and tea. Introducing the price of tea as a variable affecting the consumption of coffee has not given statistically significant results in regard to individual countries, however. On the other hand, in a sample of 16 industrial countries, with observations relating to 1960, a 1 per cent difference in the relative price of coffee as compared to tea appears to be associated with a 5 per cent difference in the ratio of coffee consumption to that of tea. Similar results have been obtained in a multicountry function where the United Kingdom and Ireland with their singular consumption pattern have been excluded from the calculations (Table A8.2.3).

These results are not applicable for purposes of forecasting, however. For one thing, the line of causation in the relationship between relative prices and consumption is not clear, since the choice between coffee and tea is often historically determined and governments in Europe endeavor to keep down the price of a beverage that is regarded as a necessity. Furthermore, the observed pattern of consumption in individual countries indicates that in the absence of substantial changes in the price ratio between coffee and tea, the likelihood for price-induced substitution is small.

North America

In the United States, coffee consumption per head reached 9 kg immediately before World War II and surpassed 11 kg during the

---

[3]Coffee and tea are drunk chiefly by adults; hence, per capita figures have been calculated per head of population over 15.

early postwar years. A sharp increase in coffee prices led to a fall of consumption in 1954, and, despite later decreases in prices, consumption per capita has not since recovered to the level attained in the late forties.

Rex F. Daly has estimated the effects of changes in incomes and coffee prices on consumption for the period 1922–1941 and found that over 77 per cent of the variation in coffee consumption can be explained by changes in incomes and prices. According to Daly's results, a 10 per cent rise in disposable income was accompanied by a 2.3 per cent increase in coffee consumption, and a 10 per cent fall in the price of coffee raised consumption by 2.6 per cent [1, p. 2].[4] An income elasticity of 0.22 has further been derived from U.S. budget data pertaining to 1955 [9, p. 32].

Changes in incomes and prices do not provide a satisfactory explanation for variations in coffee consumption if we consider data for the postwar period only.[5] It has become necessary, therefore, to introduce further explanatory variables: the number of cups of coffee drunk, changes in cup-yield ratios, and the shift toward soluble coffee. According to a winter market survey of the Pan-American Coffee Bureau, the average number of cups of coffee drunk per person 15 years of age and over increased steadily from 2.60 cups per day in 1950 to 3.34 cups in 1959, and reached, after a temporary fall to 3.17 cups in 1960, 3.39 in 1961. At the same time, the average number of cups of coffee obtained from a pound of green beans was 46 cups in 1949; it increased—in response to the rise in coffee prices after 1949—to 64 cups in 1957, and declined to 62 cups by 1959 (Table A8.2.2). The rise in the number of cups of coffee drunk and in cup-yield ratios between 1950 and 1959 imply an 8 per cent increase in the demand for green coffee on a per capita basis.

The demand for green coffee is further affected by changes in the share of soluble (instant) coffee. While the consumption of soluble coffee was negligible during the forties, its share in terms

---

[4]A considerably higher income elasticity (0.52) is obtained if observations relating to the interwar and postwar period are combined [9, p. 31]. But, in the presence of the upward shift in consumption during the forties, combining the data of the two periods introduces a bias in the estimates. Should we include a trend variable in the regression, the income elasticity is reduced again to 0.22 [16, p. 16].

[5]In the years 1947–1960, the income elasticity of demand for coffee appears to be negative, although this coefficient is not statistically significant (Table A1.3.1). Introducing a time trend as an explanatory variable does not improve the results either, by reason of the observed intercorrelation between income and time.

of cups drunk increased to 11.5 per cent by 1953 and to 21.5 per cent by 1960 [*11*, p. 28]. At the same time, by the late fifties, the cup-yield ratio for instant coffee was about one-fourth higher than for regular coffee. If account is taken of past improvements in the extraction rates of soluble coffee, [*12*, p. 26], the shift from regular to soluble coffee may have reduced the demand for coffee beans by about 3-4 per cent.

Changes in the number of cups of coffee drunk and in cup-yield ratios, as well as the shift toward soluble coffee, would thus indicate a 4 to 5 per cent rise in the consumption of green coffee on a per capita basis between 1950 and 1959. Actually, coffee consumption per head, expressed in green beans equivalent, rose by 4 per cent in the same period. But given the error possibilities associated with these estimates, we should not expect an exact correspondence between the results.

Several projections have been prepared in recent years concerning the future demand for coffee in the United States. Under the assumption that the 1947-49 price level would prevail in 1975 and the share of soluble coffee would reach 25 per cent, Daly estimated per capita coffee consumption to rise by 18 per cent between 1957 and 1975. In arriving at this forecast, Daly calculated with a 40 per cent increase in per capita disposable income between 1957 and 1975, and applied the elasticities derived in his paper [*1*]. An income elasticity of 0.22 has been used in the projection of the U.S. Department of Commerce, Business and Defense Services Administration, but in this case allowance has also been made for the continuation of the rising trend of consumption in terms of cups of coffee drunk at a rate of 0.8 per cent a year and for a lowering of cup-yield ratios to 58 cups per pound by 1965 [*16*, pp. 26-28]. Finally, the Pan-American Coffee Bureau has assumed the average number of cups of coffee per person to rise at an annual rate of 1.0 per cent and the cup-yield ratio to fall to 50 cups per pound by 1970, irrespective of changes in incomes [*13*, pp. 12-18].

In the present study, we have calculated with an income elasticity of 0.2 and have made allowance for the continuation of past trends in coffee drinking, although at a decreasing rate. This trend indicates the increased popularity of the institution of coffee breaks, the availability of coffee-vending machines, and the results of promotional efforts. The contribution of the trend factor to per capita consumption has been assumed to be 0.5 kg between 1960 and 1975.

Decreases in cup-yield ratios can further contribute to higher coffee consumption in terms of green beans. In this connection the question arises to what extent past increases in cup-yield ratios are reversible. As noted above, high coffee prices in the early fifties had induced consumers to "stretch" the use of coffee by making more cups per pound, but the subsequent fall in prices has led only to a small decrease in the cup-yield ratio. This result implies an element of irreversibility in consumer behavior. Still, there are indications for future decreases in cup-yield ratios. Consumers may react with a time lag and only after lower prices have prevailed over several years; also, future developments are likely to be influenced by the efforts of coffee producers to popularize stronger coffee. As a result, cup-yield ratios can be expected to fall, perhaps to 58 cups per pound by 1975. But the demand for coffee beans is not likely to rise proportionately, since fewer cups of the stronger coffee may be drunk. Correspondingly, we have assumed changes in cup-yield ratios to contribute to a 4 per cent increase in the per capita consumption of green coffee over the 1950–1975 period.

Finally, possible shifts in consumption from regular to instant coffee should be considered. In view of the slowing down in the growth of the consumption of soluble coffee in recent years, the share of the latter in total coffee consumption may not exceed 24 per cent by 1975, as compared to 21.5 per cent in 1960. Taking into account expected improvements in the extraction rates of soluble coffee, the increase in the share of soluble coffee would still reduce green coffee requirements by 1 to 1.5 per cent over the period of projection.

All things considered, per capita coffee consumption in green beans equivalent is estimated to reach 11.4 kg by 1970 and 11.8 kg by 1975 under the most likely income assumption, as compared to 10.5 kg in 1960. The corresponding total consumption (imports) would be 1.67 and 1.88 million tons as against 1.32 million tons in 1960. Imports would be slightly larger if the target rate of income growth were reached.

In Canada, per capita coffee consumption has been increasing steadily during the postwar period and has more than doubled since before the war. Most of this increase has taken place at the expense of tea. Still, coffee consumption per head barely exceeds one-half of the U.S. level. Utilizing data for the period 1921–1935 and 1949–1958, the FAO has derived an income elasticity of 0.56 for Canada [9, p. 31]. A similar result pertains to the postwar period taken by itself; hence we have applied this elasticity in making projections.

Western Europe

Coffee consumption in Western Europe had been sluggish in reaching the prewar level, but it continued to rise after the prewar figures were surpassed in the mid-fifties. In 1960, per capita consumption amounted to 11–12 kg in Scandinavia, and 4 to 8 kg in the Common Market countries excepting Italy, while it remained at low levels in the other countries of Western Europe.

Among the Common Market countries, coffee consumption is at the highest level in Belgium (8.4 kg per head), followed by the Netherlands (6.5 kg), France (5.9 kg), Germany (4.5 kg), and Italy (2.7 kg). In Germany and in Italy, consumption has been rising at a high but decreasing rate over the last decade, and a large part of the variation in consumption is explained by changes in incomes and prices.[6] Still, in making projections, we had to take account of the fact that part of the apparent income effect had been due to trend factors such as the catching up with prewar consumption levels and the increased popularity of coffee.

In forecasting consumption, we have assumed an income elasticity of 0.8 to pertain to Italy and 0.6 to Germany, and have calculated with an additional yearly 1 per cent growth in consumption to give expression to the rising popularity of coffee. Consumption will increase at a slower rate in response to the growth of incomes in Belgium, France, and the Netherlands, where income elasticities of 0.4–0.5 have been applied in making projections.

The EEC tariff on coffee has been set at 9.6 per cent. This represents a reduction from the higher French, German, and Italian tariffs, and an increase as compared to the zero duty prevailing in Belgium and the Netherlands. But given the small share of the duty in the retail price and the low price elasticities pertaining to 1970 and 1975, changes in tariffs will have little effect on consumption.

In the United Kingdom, tea has maintained its position as a staple beverage, and the per capita consumption of coffee has barely surpassed 1 kg per head. But coffee consumption has been increasing rapidly in recent years, and budget studies indicate a high income elasticity of demand for coffee [15, p. 39]. We have calculated with a unitary income elasticity for 1960, and have assumed that a trend factor expressing the increasing popularity of

---

[6]The application of the semilogarithmic functional form gives income elasticities of 1.3 for Italy, 1.1 for Germany, and 0.5 for France for the year 1960 (Table A3.1), while the budget elasticity was 0.8 in Italy in 1953 [9, p. 32].

coffee would further contribute to a 1 per cent yearly increase in consumption. Similar considerations apply to Ireland.

The countries of Scandinavia enjoy the highest level of coffee consumption in the world: 11–12 kg per person 15 years of age and over. Consumption has been rising steadily over the last decade, but only a limited expansion can be expected from present high levels. In making projections, we have calculated with an income elasticity of 0.2.

Among the other countries of the northern group, per capita coffee consumption is about 6.5 kg in Switzerland, and a little over 2 kg in Austria. We have projected consumption in Switzerland to rise at approximately the same rate as in France, while future changes in Austria have been assumed to correspond to those in Italy.

Coffee consumption has expanded during the last decade in Greece, Portugal, and Spain, but per capita consumption has not reached 2 kg in any of these countries. Future developments will greatly depend on government policies and changes in tastes. We have arbitrarily assumed an income elasticity of 1.5 to apply to these countries. Finally, import quotas have reduced imports to nearly zero in Turkey, and restricted the expansion of coffee consumption in Yugoslavia. With regard to Turkey, we have assumed that the 1950 consumption level will be reached by 1970, while in Yugoslavia consumption per head may double within a decade.

Japan

Per capita imports of coffee have been rising in recent years in Japan and reached 0.14 kg in 1960 and 0.25 kg in 1961. Coffee consumption is still confined to certain classes of city dwellers, however, and imports have been restricted by quantitative regulations. From available information on the possibilities of future increases, it appears that, following the removal of quotas, the rise of imports would accelerate and per capita coffee consumption may surpass 1 kg by 1970.

Oceania and South Africa

Coffee consumption per head has not yet reached 2 kg in Australia and New Zealand, although rapid increases have been experienced in recent years. The relative increase of population of non-British origin will further contribute to the popularity of coffee. In making projections, we have calculated with an income elasticity of 1.0 and have assumed an additional yearly 2 per cent trend in consumption. Smaller increases are expected in South Africa, however, where per capita coffee consumption changed little in recent years.

The Price and Origin of Imports

According to our projections, the coffee imports of the developed countries would rise by 34.1 or 36.8 per cent between 1960 and 1970 and by 53.3 or 57.6 per cent between 1960 and 1975, depending on the income assumption chosen (Table 8.2.1).[7] In the United States the increase in population, while in Western Europe, the projected rise in per capita consumption, would account for much of the increased imports. Despite large relative increases in consumption, imports to Japan and Oceania will remain small in absolute terms, however.

TABLE 8.2.1

COFFEE CONSUMPTION (NET IMPORTS) IN DEVELOPED COUNTRIES
(thousand tons)

	1950	1955	1960	1970I	1970II	1975I	1975II
North America	1145	1211	1380	1756	1772	1982	2002
Common Market	303	452	605	843	859	959	988
United Kingdom	39	31	54	73	73	79	88
Northern Europe	111	158	217	253	256	269	273
Southern Europe	26	34	44	89	100	118	130
Japan	0	4	10	79	94	123	148
Oceania and South Africa	21	16	25	39	40	50	51
Developed Countries, Total	1643	1905	2335	3132	3194	3580	3680

Source: Table A8.2.1.

Future changes in prices and in the composition of imports will depend to a large extent on the success—or failure—of coffee producers and consumers to reach an agreement on export quotas. In the absence of an international agreement, coffee prices and export earnings derived from the sale of coffee could fall substantially. The decline in prices would be due to the excess of exportable production over import demand (approximately 20 per cent in the 1960/61 and 1961/62 crop year), which is expected to continue throughout the sixties by reason of the large-scale plantings undertaken during the last decade.[8] At the same time, given the low price elasticity of demand for coffee, a fall in prices would lead to a substantial decline in export earnings.

---

[7] By comparison, the FAO expects exports to these countries to rise by 32 or 39 per cent between 1958–60 and 1970–72 at the low income and the high income assumption, respectively [2, pp. II 44–46].

[8] Mention should also be made of the large stocks accumulated by Brazil which were equal to approximately 80 per cent of the annual world production of coffee in 1961.

But a large decrease in export earnings does not appear to be politically acceptable. Hence, we have postulated that export quotas will continue to be regulated in the framework of the International Coffee Agreement, so as to forestall a fall in coffee prices by restricting the quantities brought on the world market. We have assumed that, as a result of the operation of the agreement, prices of arabica will be maintained at average levels experienced in the years 1959–61, while a 5 per cent rise in robusta prices will reduce the gap between the prices of the two main varieties of coffee.

Prospective changes after 1970 will also be influenced by new plantings during the sixties. On the basis of past experience one would expect the present coffee cycle to come to an end around 1970, implying a rise in coffee prices in the early seventies. But such an outcome would presuppose an absolute decline—or at least a slowing down—in new plantings. However, as long as an international agreement prevents prices from falling, the appropriate adjustments in plantings may not take place. Correspondingly, the growth of exportable coffee production is not likely to fall short of the increase in the demand for coffee, and a rise in prices is not anticipated.

A further question relates to the origin of imports. The export quotas envisaged in the International Coffee Agreement for the 1962–63 crop year would involve little change in the market shares of different areas as compared to 1960, the exception being that of Asia, where a higher quota has been allotted. These shares will not necessarily be maintained in future years, however, since the determination of quotas will be influenced by pressures coming from the side of the consuming and the producing countries.

The increased consumption of robusta-using solubles in many of the developed countries, quality improvements in robusta, and the increased plantings of arabica in the former British East Africa are expected to lead to a further rise in the share of African producers. In the European Common Market, these developments will be reinforced by the preferential treatment accorded to associated overseas countries. On the other hand, the strong preference for arabica in Germany will restrict the shift towards robusta, and the share of the associated countries in French imports may decline rather than increase since, under the EEC tariff, these producers will enjoy smaller preferential advantages than beforehand.

8.3 COCOA (SITC 072,073)

The period of rapid expansion in cocoa production, which established the pre-eminence of African producers in the world market, ended in 1939, and unfavorable sales prospects reduced production as well as new plantings during the war. As a result, shortages developed in the postwar years, and the price of cocoa greatly increased. Production caught up with demand in the late fifties, however, and a decline of prices set in after 1958.

After a temporary fall following the war, African exporters again regained their prewar share in world markets in the last decade. In 1960, Ghana and Nigeria, taken together, accounted for 50 per cent of world exports, while other African producers (chiefly the Ivory Coast and the Cameroons) supplied another 20 per cent. Much of the remainder came from Latin America, with Brazil providing nearly 15 per cent of world exports.

Cocoa is of especial importance for Ghana, who derives about 65 per cent of her export earnings from the sale of cocoa beans. In 1959–61, the corresponding proportion was 33 per cent for the Cameroons, 23 per cent for the Ivory Coast, 22 per cent for Nigeria, and 6 per cent for Brazil. Although the Cameroons, the Ivory Coast, and Brazil also export cocoa products, the transformation of cocoa beans into cocoa powder and cocoa butter usually takes place in the importing countries. Cocoa powder is used in making drinking chocolate and as a flavoring agent; both cocoa powder and cocoa butter are used in chocolate bars and other chocolate products and in cosmetics.

An intercountry comparison of cocoa consumption indicates higher consumption levels for the more developed countries of North America and Western Europe, and lower per capita consumption in the Mediterranean countries, Finland, and Ireland (Table A8.3.1). But within the former group of countries no relationship is apparent between per capita incomes and cocoa consumption per head. Consumption, measured as net imports of cocoa beans and cocoa products in terms of beans, is high in the countries traditionally exporting cocoa powder and chocolate (Switzerland and the Netherlands) and U.S. consumption levels are surpassed also in Belgium, Germany, the United Kingdom, and Austria. The explanatory value of economic variables does not increase if price comparisons are made; among countries with high consumption levels, the retail price of cocoa is one of the highest in Germany while it is around the European average in the Netherlands (no price quotations are available for Switzerland).

North America

In the United States, the rise in prices led to a fall in the consumption of cocoa during the fifties. Manufacturers reacted to the price increase by reducing the percentage of cocoa in chocolate bars and other cocoa products through the greater use of milk products and nuts and the development of cocoa substitutes. The substitution of other ingredients for cocoa was further stimulated by the steep price rise in 1954 when the deflated price of cocoa was four times the prewar average. The subsequent fall in prices has not brought about a reversal of this process, however. Although cocoa prices fell by one-half between 1954 and 1960, a significant expansion in consumption did not take place, and present consumption levels are still below prewar standards.

Assuming the level of prices experienced in 1960 to be maintained, future consumption patterns will be determined chiefly by changes in incomes and in the quality of cocoa products. In the absence of quality changes, per capita consumption can rise at rates indicated by time-series and budget statistics. Data for the period 1926–1939 and 1948–1954 show an income elasticity of 0.3, while the results of the 1955 survey indicate a budget elasticity of 0.4 [*3*, p. 61 and *8*, p. 32]. In projecting consumption, we have calculated with an elasticity of 0.35. Correspondingly, per capita cocoa consumption would increase from 1.6 kg in 1960 to 1.8 kg in 1970 and 1.9 in 1975. By reason of the similarity in consumption patterns, identical projections have been made for Canada.

Western Europe

Although inventory fluctuations cause considerable year-to-year changes in the reported consumption figures, an upward trend in per capita cocoa consumption is apparent in most Common Market countries and, with the exception of the Netherlands, present consumption levels exceed the prewar figures. But given the large fluctuations in prices, it would be hazardous to base projections on average trends shown over the last decade. At the same time, data on wholesale and retail prices of cocoa and cocoa products are not available for most countries.

Hence, in making projections, we had to rely on the fragmentary evidence provided in the case of countries where price statistics and the results of budget surveys are available. For the Netherlands, time-series data show an income elasticity of demand of 0.6 in regard to chocolate and chocolate products, while the budget elasticity of demand for cocoa and drinking chocolate is given as 0.3 [*4*, p. 26 and *8*, p. 32]. Considering that in developed countries the income elasticity of demand for chocolate and chocolate products is generally higher than that for cocoa powder and drinking chocolate, an elasticity of 0.4 has been used in making projections. The same value has been applied in the case of Belgium, Germany, and Britain, where the per capita consumption of cocoa is at approximately the Dutch level. Consumption is likely to increase at a more rapid rate in France, however, and a one-to-one relationship between per capita incomes and cocoa consumption may hold for Italy, where per capita cocoa consumption is among the lowest in Europe.

Cocoa consumption has had a checkered course in the countries of the Northern group, too. The results of budget studies and time-series regressions are available only for Austria, indicating a budget elasticity of 0.4 for cocoa and drinking chocolate in 1954–55, and an income elasticity of 0.8 for chocolate and chocolate products in 1958 [*8*, p. 32 and *4*, p. 26]. In making projections, we have assumed an income elasticity of 0.5 to apply in the case of Austria, Denmark, Norway, and Sweden, and a unitary elasticity for Finland where cocoa consumption is below 0.5 kg per head. On the other hand, the observed stability of per capita consumption at a level of 3.0 kg implies that an appreciable increase in cocoa consumption cannot be expected in Switzerland.

Greece, Portugal, Turkey, and Yugoslavia appear to be below the "cocoa line" at which the consumption of cocoa products is said to start increasing in response to rising incomes [*3*, pp. 56 ff]. For these countires, per capita cocoa consumption can be assumed to rise at rates exceeding the growth of income. Consumption levels are higher in Spain, however, and correspondingly the growth of consumption will proceed at a slower rate in this country.

Japan

The consumption of cocoa has made little headway in Japan and hardly surpassed 0.1 kg per head in 1960. There are indications for a rapid increase of consumption in future years, however, and we have assumed that per capita cocoa consumption would reach 1 kg by 1975.

Oceania and South Africa

The consumption of cocoa products has been rising steadily in recent years in Australia and New Zealand, and further increases are expected. We have assumed that a 1 per cent increase in disposable income would be associated with a 0.5 per cent increase in cocoa consumption per head in these countries, while a one-to-one relationship may hold for South Africa.

The Price and Origin of Imports

Should the 1960 price level pertain to the period of projection, our projections would indicate a 28.5 per cent increase in cocoa exports to the developed countries between 1960 and 1970, and a 46.5 per cent rise between 1960 and 1975, under the most likely income assumption. The corresponding figures are 30.6 and 49.8 per cent if the target rate of incomes is reached.[9] Considering also consumption prospects in other countries as well as prospective increases in production, the 1960 price of 28.4 cents per pound[10] appears to be on the high side, however.

Production will continue to expand in Africa where the new plantings undertaken in recent years as well as improvements in cultivation methods and advances in antidisease protection promise a steady increase in the cocoa crop. Better yields from recent plantings of improved hybrid stock point in the same direction. On the other hand, with the exception of Brazil, high costs will restrict the expansion of production in most of Latin America.

Although price fluctuations would be reduced through the operation of the proposed International Cocoa Agreement, the agreement will not affect cocoa prices as long as these remain within certain limits yet to be determined. We have assumed here the market clearing price in 1970 and 1975 would be at approximately the midpoint between the 1960 and 1961 level, i.e., about 25–26 cents per pound, and have adjusted the consumption projections accordingly.

In the case of coffee, substitution relationships are of little importance, and the price elasticity of demand at the retail level may be taken as approximately equivalent to the income elasticity. But this assumption cannot find application in regard to cocoa where substitution can take place at both the consumer and the producer level. First, consumers substitute sugar products for chocolate in response to price changes; second, changes in relative prices influence the manufacturer's choice among the various ingredients of cocoa products. These factors are reflected in the price elasticity for cocoa grindings. The FAO has calculated the latter for 12 industrial countries, and these results, as well as available information on income elasticity, internal taxes, marketing margins, and substi-

---

[9]The FAO estimates cocoa grindings to increase by 38–40 per cent between 1957–59 and 1970 if the price of cocoa is 24.0 cents per pound in the target year, and by 29–31 per cent if the price is 30.0 cents [2, II. p. 39]. Grindings increased by 4 per cent between 1957–59 and 1960.

[10]New York spot price for Ghana cocoa.

tution relationships [5], have been utilized in arriving at the elasticity coefficients used in the projections for 1970 and 1975.[11]

Further adjustments have been necessary in connection with changes in tariffs in the Common Market countries. While duties will not be paid on imports originating in the associated countries and territories, the envisaged 5.6 per cent EEC tariff on cocoa beans is higher than the average of duties actually applied in the member countries before the Treaty came into effect.[12] The common tariff will give a preferential advantage to the associated producers who presently account for about 30 per cent of the imports of the six countries. On the one hand, the exports of these territories will be, in part, reallocated from third countries toward the EEC; on the other, the expansion of the area under cocoa will be stimulated. More importantly, the 22 per cent preferential duty on cocoa butter, 25 per cent on cocoa mass, and 27 per cent on cocoa powder can lead to the establishment of cocoa-processing industries in the EEC associates.

TABLE 8.3.1

COCOA CONSUMPTION (NET IMPORTS) IN DEVELOPED COUNTRIES
(thousand metric tons)

	1960	1970I	1970II	1975I	1975II
North America.................	316	415	420	467	474
Common Market................	229	297	305	328	338
United Kingdom	95	113	115	120	123
Northern Europe...............	63	66	67	70	72
Southern Europe[a]	9	18	19	26	28
Japan.......................	13	61	61	96	96
Oceania and South Africa	23	33	35	39	41
Developed Countries, Total........	748	1003	1022	1146	1172

Source: Table A8.3.1.
Note: (a) excluding Spain.

The expected lowering of prices as compared to 1960 will reduce the increment of export earnings for all producing countries, so that export receipts from the sale of cocoa are projected to rise by about 20 per cent between 1960 and 1970, and 35 per cent between 1960 and 1975. This increase will be shared by the cocoa producers of Africa, Asia, and Oceania, while it may take a decade until Latin-American exporters regain the losses in export markets they

[11]The price elasticities employed in the estimation are: United States and Canada, −0.25; Belgium, Germany, and the Netherlands, −0.3; France, −0.4; Italy, −0.8; United Kingdom, −0.3; Switzerland, −0.2; Austria, Denmark, Ireland, Norway, and Sweden, −0.4; Finland, −0.8; Spain, −0.7; Greece, Portugal, Turkey, and Yugoslavia, −1.2; Japan, −1.0; Australia and New Zealand, −0.5. and South Africa, −1.2.

[12]Among the EEC countries only Germany levied a tariff on cocoa beans in 1957 (10 per cent ad valorem).

suffered in 1961. Correspondingly, a decline in the value of cocoa exports originating in Latin America is anticipated. (Estimates on cocoa consumption are given in Table 8.3.1., while changes in the value of cocoa imports according to the area of origin are shown in Table A8.)[13]

8.4 TEA (SITC 074)

Tea exports are of great importance for Ceylon and India; export earnings from the sale of tea account for three-fifths of total receipts in the former and one-fifth in the latter. These two countries provide about 70 per cent of world exports, with Indonesia and China supplying another 15 per cent. In recent years there has been a considerable expansion in exports from Africa, but the share of African tea in world markets has not yet surpassed 8 per cent. Finally, although tea production has increased in Latin America, this has been taken up mostly by domestic consumption.

Differences in customs and eating habits originating in historical accidents and trade connections account for much of the disparity in the level of tea consumption among industrial countries. This explains that while the annual consumption of tea per head of population over 15 reaches 5 kg in the United Kingdom and Ireland, most other European countries do not consume more than 0.1 kg per person. The British consumption level is approached in Australia and New Zealand, but tea consumption hardly exceeds 1.5 kg per head in Canada, and it is 0.4 kg in the United States (Table A8.4.1).[14]

North America

In the United States, per capita tea consumption has been hovering around 0.4 kg over the past decade, and it barely surpassed the prewar level in 1960. Conflicting trends are responsible for this outcome; while the consumption of iced tea has risen in recent years, this has been counterbalanced by the increased use of tea bags that require less tea per cup.[15] Future developments will greatly depend on the success of instant tea, the popularization of iced tea, and improvements in the quality of tea contained in the tea bags. But, in the absence of substantial quality improvements, an increase

---

[13]The figures exclude Spain since Spanish imports from overseas departments are regarded as internal trade.

[14]All per capita data refer to population of 15 years of age and over.

[15]Tea bags yield about 320 cups per pound as compared to 260 cups per pound of ordinary tea.

in per capita consumption does not appear likely, and we have assumed no change during the period of forecast. This projection is supported by the results of budget surveys which show a slightly negative income elasticity of demand for tea [8, p. 32].

Per capita tea consumption has been declining over the last decades in Canada, and it fell to three fourths of the prewar level in 1960. This decrease can be attributed to the influence of the U.S. consumption pattern, the increased use of tea bags, and the decline in the proportion of the population of British origin. It is expected that these factors will continue to act in the future and the lower consumption of tea in the younger age groups gives indication of prospective developments. In conformity with the projections prepared for the Royal Commission for Canada's Economic Prospects, we have assumed per capita tea consumption to fall to 1.4 kg by 1970 and 1.3 kg by 1975 [14, p. 101].

Western Europe

Among the Common Market countries, tea consumption per head exceeds 1 kg in the Netherlands; it is about 0.15 kg in Germany, but it does not reach 0.05 kg in Belgium, France, or Italy. The relatively high consumption levels in the Netherlands can be attributed to past Dutch-Indonesian relations. Per capita tea consumption in Holland declined from the prewar level, however, and neither the experience of recent years nor the 0.2 budget elasticity calculated for 1951 give promise for marked increases in the future. On the other hand, a high rate of growth of tea consumption is indicated in the other countries of the Common Market, especially in Germany and Italy, where per capita consumption doubled between 1952 and 1960. Yet the assumed doubling of consumption per head over the next decade would still mean little in absolute terms.

About 85 per cent of European tea imports go to the United Kingdom, while Ireland takes a further 4 per cent. Annual consumption per head increased steadily during the first half of the century in both countries and surpassed the prewar level during the fifties. It is highly questionable, however, whether consumption could continue to rise in the future. The income elasticity of demand for tea, derived from budget studies, appears to be 0.06 in the United Kingdom [15, p. 39], and the present rate of drinking of about 6–6½ cups a day per person aged ten years and over can hardly increase. Moreover, the rising trend of coffee consumption can be eventually damaging to the prospects of tea. We have postulated tea consumption per head to remain unchanged during the period of projection in both the United Kingdom and Ireland.

After a temporary increase in tea consumption due to the rationing of coffee, some declines have been experienced in the Scandinavian countries. Still, per capita consumption exceeds the prewar level by a large margin, and, judging from developments in recent years, further increases are expected. Similar considerations apply to Austria and Switzerland. Finally, prewar consumption levels have not been reached in the countries of the southern group, with the exception of Turkey. Future increases in consumption have been projected here, too.

Japan

Japan is a net exporter of tea and will continue to supply her domestic needs from home production with a small volume of high quality tea imported from Ceylon and plain tea from China.

Oceania

Per capita tea consumption has been declining in Australia, although a decrease is not shown for New Zealand. We have assumed here that, in conjunction with the increased consumption of coffee, a decline in tea consumption per head will be experienced in these countries. On the other hand, tea consumption may continue to rise in South Africa.

The Price and Origin of Imports

Our projections indicate that the tea imports of the developed countries would hardly rise at an annual rate exceeding 1 per cent (Table 8.4.1).[16] At the same time, the Third Five-Year Plan foresees a rise in tea production by over one-fourth between 1959 and 1965 in India, and an annual increase of about 2 per cent is expected in Ceylon. The tea producers of British East Africa and Nyasaland, too, have excellent possibilities for expanding production.

The prospects for a rapid rise in production accompanied by a slow increase of tea imports into the developed countries would precipitate a fall in prices unless domestic consumption in the producing countries or in other less developed areas rose sufficiently.

---

[16]Similar results have been reached by the FAO, although the FAO assumed that higher incomes would contribute to a rise of tea consumption in the United Kingdom [2, p. 50, II].

The experience of recent years shows potentialities for higher consumption, especially in India, the Middle East, and North Africa, but it is questionable whether the entire surplus would thereby be absorbed.

It appears likely that while African producers will expand their sales to the Common Market and the United Kingdom, the main Asian producers will have to restrict their exports to avoid a fall in prices. We have assumed here that prices would be stabilized at around the 1961 level, i.e., about 6–7 per cent below prices prevailing in 1960. Given the low price elasticity of demand for tea and the large marketing margin in the developed countries, the rise in consumption associated with the assumed decrease in prices

TABLE 8.4.1

TEA CONSUMPTION (NET IMPORTS) IN DEVELOPED COUNTRIES
(thousand tons)

	1950	1955	1960	1970I	1970II	1975I	1975II
North America	76	57	72	79	79	85	85
Common Market	12	15	20	31	33	39	43
United Kingdom.	161	212	226	235	235	240	240
Northern Europe.	17	16	15	17	17	17	18
Southern Europe	2	3	5	7	7	9	9
Oceania and South Africa	42	41	50	61	61	67	67
Developed Countries, Total	311	344	388	430	432	457	462

Source: Table A8.4.1.
Note: Excluding domestically produced teas.

would be small. Correspondingly, the increase in the value of tea exports to developed countries is unlikely to exceed 5 per cent between 1960 and 1970, or 13 per cent between 1960 and 1975 (Table A8).

8.5 SPICES (SITC 075)

The Standard International Trade Classification includes tropical spices as well as aromatic seeds and herbs in this category. In value terms, over four-fifths of imports are tropical spices, which are regarded as the only genuine spices by the trade. The most important among these is pepper, accounting for about one fourth of total imports, with cloves, nutmeg, and cardamon following. Aromatic seeds include mustard seed, caraway seed, celery seed, anise seed, and paprika.

Trade in spices, once the main form of exchange between Europe and the Far East, has declined in importance and accounts for less than 0.1 per cent of the export earnings of the less developed countries. Still, spices are of importance for the economies of some tropical islands. Zanzibar derives 74 per cent of her export income from the sale of cloves and clove oil; Grenada, 54 per cent from nutmeg and mace, while spice exports provide 10 to 20 per cent of export earnings for the Seychelle Islands, French Oceania, and Madagascar. However, the largest quantities of spices originate in India and Indonesia, where these account for about 3 per cent of export revenue.

A study of nine tropical spices (pepper, cloves, cardamon, cinnamon, nutmeg, mace, cassia, ginger, and pimento) has shown that, in most developed countries, per capita consumption declined after the war, and, despite later increases, it has not yet regained the prewar level [7]. The largest decline has taken place in the consumption of pepper, while increases are shown only in ginger. The fall in supply due to war destruction and the subsequent increase in prices is given as the main reason for the drop of consumption in the immediate postwar years, while the slow increase of consumption during the fifties is attributed to the shift away from highly seasoned food and to the increased popularity of processed food.

North America

The per capita consumption of the main tropical spices increased little in the United States and Canada during the fifties and has not surpassed three-fourths of the prewar level in 1960. The largest decline occurred in the consumption of pepper, which hardly exceeds one-half of the prewar figure. On the other hand, the consumption of aromatic seeds and herbs increased as compared to prewar, so that the per capita consumption of all spices stayed approximately constant.

Future developments will be determined chiefly by cooking and eating habits; given the small importance of spices in the family budget, it is questionable whether price changes would have much effect on consumption. The greater use of processed food will continue to cut into the market for spices, while increased sophistication in cooking will have the opposite effect. We have assumed per capita imports to remain unchanged during the period of projection.

Western Europe

Per capita consumption of spices in Western Europe is at a lower level than in North America, but there is no indication for an increase during the period of projection. Thus, on the basis of the experience of recent years, we have assumed that spice imports would rise *pari passu* with the growth of population.

Japan

Japan is an exporter of red pepper, and imports increasing quantities of a wide variety of spices. Imports have doubled between 1955 and 1960 and, in view of their present low level, may double again over the next decade.

Oceania and South Africa

Spice imports have been increased somewhat in recent years in Australia and New Zealand, but any future increase will be small in absolute terms. Similar considerations apply to South Africa.

The Price and Origin of Imports

According to our projections, the spice imports of developed countries would rise at a rate approximately equal to the growth of population in these countries. On the other hand, there are possibilities for a substantial expansion in the consumption of spices in the Middle East and Southeast Asia, where spices enjoy great popularity and their consumption is highly income-elastic.

Available information indicates an expansion of production, especially in India and Indonesia, but a large part of the higher output will be taken up by increased domestic consumption. It is difficult to judge, therefore, the possible increase in exportable output and future changes in prices. Prices have been subject to violent fluctuations in recent years, chiefly in response to short-term fluctuations in production. For purposes of projection, we have assumed that the prices observed in the period 1958–60 would pertain to 1970 and 1975. This assumption reflects the view that much of the increase in production will be taken up by higher consumption in the less developed countries and also in the Soviet bloc, which has recently become a large importer of spices.

REFERENCES

[1.] DALY, R. F. "Coffee Consumption and Prices in the United States," *Agricultural Economic Research* (July, 1958), pp. 1–11.

[2.] FOOD AND AGRICULTURE ORGANIZATION *Agricultural Commodities—Projections for 1970*. Rome, 1962.

[3.] FOOD AND AGRICULTURE ORGANIZATION. *Cacao*. Commodity Series Bulletin No. 27. Rome, 1955.

[4.] FOOD AND AGRICULTURE ORGANIZATION. *CCP/Cocoa/61/7*. Rome, 1961.

[5.] FOOD AND AGRICULTURE ORGANIZATION. *Europe's Demand for Tropical Agricultural Products*. ERC/62 (6) . Rome, 1962.

[6.] FOOD AND AGRICULTURE ORGANIZATION. *Income Elasticity of the Demand for Food.* Rome, 1959.

[7.] FOOD AND AGRICULTURE ORGANIZATION. *Spices—Trends in World Markets.* Commodity Bulletin Series, No. 34. Rome, 1962.

[8.] FOOD AND AGRICULTURE ORGANIZATION. *Tea—Trends and Prospects.* Commodity Bulletin Series, No. 30. Rome, 1960.

[9.] FOOD AND AGRICULTURE ORGANIZATION. *The World Coffee Economy.* Commodity Bulletin Series, No. 33. Rome, 1961.

[10.] GENERAL AGREEMENT ON TARIFFS AND TRADE. *Report of the Special Group on Trade in Tropical Products.* Geneva, 1963.

[11.] PAN-AMERICAN COFFEE BUREAU. *Annual Coffee Statistics,* 1960.

[12.] PAN-AMERICAN COFFEE BUREAU. *Annual Coffee Statistics,* 1962.

[13.] PAN-AMERICAN COFFEE BUREAU. *Prospects for United States Coffee Consumption in the Next 20 Years.* New York, 1959.

[14.] SLATER, D. W. *Canada's Imports.* Toronto: Royal Commission for Canada's Economic Prospects, 1957.

[15.] UNITED KINGDOM MINISTRY OF AGRICULTURE, FISHERIES AND FOOD. *Domestic Food Consumption and Expenditure: 1958.* London, 1960.

[16.] U.S. DEPARTMENT OF COMMERCE, BUSINESS AND DEFENSE SERVICES ADMINISTRATION. *Coffee Consumption in the United States, 1920–1965.* Washington, D.C., 1960.

CHAPTER 9

Trade Projections for Agricultural Raw Materials

9.1 HIDES AND SKINS (SITC 21)

RAW HIDES and skins other than furskins are the by-products of animal husbandry and provide the basic raw material for the tanning industry. The demand for hides and skins is determined by the consumption of footwear, industrial leather, and leather piecegoods, as well as by the availability and cost of substitute materials, while their supply depends on the demand for meat, milk, and wool that provide the major part of the proceeds of animal husbandry. Heavy leather made of cattle hides is employed as sole leather, harness leather, and for industrial purposes, while cattle hides, calfskins, and sheepskins supply most of the material for light leather used in shoe uppers, luggage, and other consumer goods.

Hides and skins other than furskins originate in countries with large livestock populations—the United States, Australia, New Zealand, Argentina, and South Africa—whereas the largest net importers are Western Europe and Japan. Imports into Western Europe have risen somewhat over the last decade and amounted to $248 million in 1960, one-half of which came from developing countries. Japanese imports expanded at a more rapid rate, but imports from less developed areas have remained small. Finally, exports and imports approximately balance in the United States with imports of $26 million originating in developing countries.

Western Europe is also the largest importer of furskins ($139 million in 1960), with North America following ($87 million). The Soviet Union, Afghanistan, South Africa, the United States, and Canada are large exporters. The amount of furskins traded changed little during the fifties, and imports from less developed countries were valued at $55 million in 1960.

North America

The United States and Canada export cattle hides and import mostly sheep- and goatskins and specialty skins (reptiles, buffalo, etc.). Imports have not shown any definite trend over the last decade and have been assumed to remain at the levels experienced in the years 1959–61 throughout the period of projection. It is expected that an increasing export surplus will be generated, however, since the domestic production of hides and skins will rise *pari passu* with the expansion of livestock raising whereas the substitution of synthetic materials and rubber for leather is likely to limit the increase in home consumption.

Western Europe

In projecting the demand for leather in Western Europe, one should first inquire into the prospects of the footwear industry, since this industry uses about 80 per cent of all leather produced. It has been suggested that in the countries of Western Europe the consumption of footwear increases at a rate exceeding the growth of disposable income. In the postwar period, for example, the income elasticity of demand for shoes in the European OECD countries was estimated to be 1.3 [*25*, p. 25].

While the demand for light leather in making shoe uppers has been increasing approximately in proportion with the growth of the consumption of footwear, light leather has lost ground to plastic materials in the making of fancy goods and luggage. At the same time, the consumption of heavy leather fell as rubber and synthetic materials increasingly replaced leather in soling, and the use of leather in military and farm equipment also declined.

Past relationships between shoe production and the use of light leather in uppers are not likely to undergo substantial changes during the period of projection, although plastic materials may encroach upon the market for leather. At the same time, plastics will increasingly replace light leather in the manufacturing of luggage and fancy goods, since plastic materials are more amenable to mass production. Finally, heavy leather will lose further ground to substitute materials, especially rubber and plastics, and its use in resoling and for industrial and other purposes, too, is expected to fall.

Nevertheless, we can assume some slowing down in the decline of the consumption of heavy leather, inasmuch as at higher income levels shoes with leather soles are in greater demand. Correspondingly, the rate of increase of leather consumption may exceed the approximately 1 per cent growth rate observed in the fifties. On the other hand, in view of the projected expansion of livestock raising, domestic supply is likely to rise faster than consumption, and thus imports may not increase more than 10–12 per cent in a decade. Imports will take the form of hides and skins as well as leather, with leather imports growing at a higher rate.

Japan

In the period 1950–60, the rise in the per capita consumption of leather exceeded the increase of income per head in Japan, but the increased use of rubber and plastic materials may slow down the growth of consumption during the period under consideration. The growth in consumption will be supplied almost entirely by imports.

Oceania and South Africa

Australia, New Zealand, and South Africa are net exporters of hides and skins, and imports from developing countries are unlikely to rise above their present low level.

The Price and Origin of Imports

Imports of hides and skins other than furskins into North America are expected to show approximately the same geographical composition in 1970 and 1975 as in 1960. Changes in the origin of imports are likely to be forthcoming in Western Europe, however. Imports from North and South America and Oceania will rise more than the average, while domestic output in India and in some African countries will be increasingly needed for the home industry. In this connection, note that the establishment of the Common Market will not affect trade patterns in hides and skins, since the associated countries do not receive preferential treatment in the EEC. Finally, developing countries may maintain their present share in imports into Japan, with shipments from Thailand rising at higher than average rates.

According to our projections, the increase in the imports of hides and skins other than furskins from developing countries would not exceed 10 per cent between 1960 and 1970 and 20 per cent between 1960 and 1975. At the same time, the differential rates of growth of the demand for, and the supply of, hides and skins is bound to bring down prices, so that the value of imports would rise only if the target rate of income growth were reached (Table A9).

*   *   *   *   *

As regards furskins, note that while the exports of developing countries to developed economies changed little during the fifties, some increases may be forthcoming during the period of projection.

Within the increased imports, a rise in the share of Latin-American producers is indicated, possibly at the expense of Afghanistan. No change in prices has been assumed.

9.2 RUBBER (SITC 23)

Natural rubber originated in Brazil, but Asian producers soon attained pre-eminence in its production. Malaya and Indonesia each account for one-third of the world output of natural rubber; Cambodia, Ceylon, and South Vietnam are also producers of some importance. Rubber plays an important role in the international trade of these countries. Malaya and South Vietnam derive nearly two-thirds of their export earnings from the sale of rubber, Indonesia 45 per cent, Cambodia 30 per cent, and Ceylon about one-fifth. Smaller quantities originate in Africa (Nigeria and Liberia) and Latin America (Brazil).

Rubber, natural and synthetic, finds its main uses in tires and tire products. In 1960, 63 per cent of the new rubber used in the United States and Canada served the purposes of the transportation industry, while the corresponding proportion was 55 per cent in the larger European countries. Further important uses are mechanical goods (belts, hoses, tubes), footwear, sportswear, latex foam products, and electrical installations.

The consumption of natural rubber had been rising rapidly until the early fifties and has been growing at a slower rate since. As a result of the substitution of synthetic for natural rubber, an absolute decline in the use of natural rubber is shown in the United States, and the share of synthetic rubber in total consumption rose everywhere. By 1960, synthetic rubber provided for about one-half of world rubber consumption; its share reached 69 per cent in the United States, 61 per cent in Canada, 38 per cent in Western Europe, 27 per cent in Japan, and 36 per cent in Oceania and South Africa.

Synthetic rubber (SBR) was first produced as a wartime emergency measure, but technological advances in the manufacturing process have saved it from abandonment after the war. Further improvements have helped to overcome some of the deficiencies of SBR (wear, groove cracking, and chipping resistance) so that, at least in the United States, it has captured much of the market for passenger car tires and has assumed increasing importance in other industrial applications, too. Natural rubber is still predominantly used in truck tires, however, where its heat-resisting qualities are of importance. But the development of stereo rubber, possessing qualities similar and, in some respects, superior, to natural rubber, threatens some of the remaining uses of the latter.

The projection of the demand for rubber can proceed in two alternative ways. One may relate rubber consumption to some aggregate variable (GNP or industrial production) or forecast activity levels in the rubber-using industries with the projection of input coefficients in specific uses. The combined use of the two methods has appeared desirable in the present investigation, although statistical difficulties have restricted the applicability of the second method. In this connection, mention should be made of the unavailability of time-series data on rubber consumption according to final uses in many of the countries under consideration, the difficulties of projecting original equipment, replacement, and export demand in the case of automobile tires, and the error possibilities associated with the forecasting of activity levels in other rubber-using industries.

Note further that data on the consumption of reclaimed rubber are not available for most countries under consideration; hence the projections refer to new rubber. At any rate, in the case of countries where information on the use of reclaimed rubber is available, its inclusion in the calculations has not improved the statistical relationships derived from time-series data.

North America

In the period 1950–1960, a 1 per cent increase in industrial production in the United States was accompanied by a 0.8 per cent rise in rubber consumption (Table A9.2.2). If this relationship were accepted for purposes of forecasting, the consumption of new rubber would be projected to rise from 1.58 million tons in 1960 to 2.23 or 2.34 million tons in 1970 and 2.59 or 2.78 million tons in 1975, depending on the income assumption chosen. These projections compare with 2.15–2.53 million tons estimated by the FAO for 1970 by the use of a similar method [*10*, p. II. 82].

The estimates need to be modified, however, by reason of the changes expected to take place in the various end uses. In the case of passenger cars we find that, in the period 1950–1960, a 1 per cent increase in per capita disposable income was associated with a 1.3 per cent rise in cars per capita.[1] But this relationship cannot be applied in making projections, since we have to take account of

---

[1]By comparison, Chow calculated an income-stock elasticity of 1.73 for the interwar period [*4*, p. 34]. Information on the number of registered passenger cars is given in [*35*].

the saturation level in the ownership of cars. Rather, with consideration given to trends in ownership and information provided by cross-section data, we have assumed that the income-stock elasticity would be slightly below unity in the period 1960–1970 and would fall further in subsequent years. Correspondingly, the number of cars per 1000 inhabitants 15 years and over would rise from 493 in 1960 to 601 in 1970, and 644 in 1975 under the most likely income assumption, and to 619 and 673 in the two years, respectively, if the target rate of income growth were reached.

Our projections entail an increase in the stock of passenger automobiles from 61.4 million in 1960 to 88–90 million in 1970 and 103–107 million in 1975. If we assume, on the basis of historical experience, an average life of about 11 years for automobiles and allow for international trade in cars, the number of automobiles produced would be 9.1–9.5 million in 1970 and 10.5–11.0 million in 1975, as compared to 6.7 million in 1960. Calculating with 5.3 tires of new equipment demand and 1.1 tires of replacement demand per automobile, the amount of automobile tires shipped can then be estimated as 145–148 million in 1970 and 169–176 million in 1975.

A similar method has been employed in regard to trucks and buses, excepting that, in the latter case, past relationships between industrial production and the number of trucks and buses in operation have been assumed to continue in the future. Subsequently, we have estimated the amount of rubber used in automobile tires by employing conversion ratios of 4.9 kg for passenger car tires and 18.1 kg for truck and bus tires. Finally, we have assumed that the other uses of rubber in the tire and tire-products category, such as tractor and implement tires, retreads, and repair materials, would maintain their present share in the total (24 per cent in 1960). Correspondingly, new rubber consumption in tire and tire products would rise from 1.01 million tons in 1960 to 1.37–1.42 million tons in 1970, and 1.55–1.64 million tons in 1975.

The consumption of new rubber in nontire products amounted to 0.57 million tons in 1960—approximately equal to the amount consumed in 1955, and nearly one-third larger than in 1950. Disparate changes in the various end uses accounted for these developments. The use of rubber in foam products increased to a considerable extent in the first half of the fifties but fell afterwards. At the same time, there has been a steady decline in the use of rubber in wires and cables, while increases are shown in most other applications.

Conflicting trends are expected to apply to the period of projection, too. The use of rubber in mechanical and athletic goods and toys may rise at about the same rate as industrial production; some other uses may increase at a slower rate, while the consumption of rubber in foam products is expected to decline further. Taken together, new rubber consumption in nontire products may reach 0.70–0.74 million tons in 1970 and 0.80–0.86 million tons in 1975.

The projections arrived at by employing the end-use method indicate new rubber consumption of 2.07–2.16 million tons in 1970 and 2.35–2.50 million tons in 1975, corresponding to an approximately 0.7 per cent increase in consumption for a 1 per cent rise in industrial production.[2] These estimates give expression to prospective changes in rubber-using industries and have therefore been accepted in the present study in preference to the higher aggregate projection.

In several respects, the situation in Canada is different from that of the United States. Whereas a 1 per cent rise in industrial production was accompanied by a 0.85 per cent increase in rubber consumption in Canada during the fifties, this elasticity is expected to rise rather than decline during the period of projection. These developments will follow from the expansion of domestic automobile production in Canada, abetted by various forms of protective measures. For purposes of projection, we have assumed rubber consumption to increase in proportion to industrial production.

Western Europe

In forecasting rubber consumption in Western Europe, distinction should be made between the producers and nonproducers of automobiles. In 1960, the major automobile-producing countries—France, Germany, Italy, the United Kingdom, and Sweden—accounted for 85 per cent of the consumption of new rubber in Western Europe. In the same year, per capita rubber consumption was between 4.4 and 5.7 kg in these countries, with the exception of Italy (2.1 kg), as compared to 2–3 kg in the high income car-importing countries of Europe and an average of 0.6 kg in Southern Europe. By comparison, rubber consumption per head is 8.8 kg in the United States and 5.2 kg in Canada.

Over the last decade, rubber consumption has been rising at approximately the same rate as industrial production in the major car-producing countries of Western Europe, the exception being

---

[2]By comparison, the medium projection of the Resources for the Future Study envisages that 1.36 million tons of new rubber will be used in tires and tire products, and 0.81 million tons in other rubber-consuming activities in 1970 [*23*, p. 957].

Sweden, where the high rate of increase of automobile exports contributed to a more rapid growth of the demand for rubber. Prospective changes in rubber consumption will again largely depend on future trends in the production of automobiles. But whereas in the United States trade in cars is of relatively little importance, this will greatly influence results in the individual countries of Western Europe, although not necessarily for Europe as a whole.

The income-stock elasticity for automobiles exceeded 2.5 during the fifties in all countries of Western Europe, with the exception of Turkey. In a report prepared by the National Institute of Economic and Social Research, it has been assumed that relationships observed in the years 1954–1959 would also pertain to the period 1959–1970. In the projections, an income-stock elasticity of 2.4 has been used in regard to Britain, and an elasticity of 2.5—together with a time trend of 5 per cent a year—for the other countries of Western Europe [*28*]. On the other hand, with reference to the experience of the United States, in the Dewhurst study it was assumed that income-stock elasticities of 1.6 and 2.0 would apply to the individual countries of Europe in the period 1955–1970 [*7,* p. 1007]. Thus, while the former report envisages the number of automobiles in the EEC and EFTA countries taken together to rise from 21.7 million in 1960 to 65.5 million in 1970, the latter calculates with a car stock of 35.2 million in the same terminal year. The corresponding estimates for the number of cars per 1000 population over 15 are 310 in the first case and 167 in the second, as compared to 112 in 1960.

It is suggested here that the forecast of the National Institute errs on the high side, while that of Dewhurst is an underestimate. On the one hand, we cannot expect the income-stock elasticities observed during the fifties to pertain to the period of projection; on the other, the experience of the United States is not directly applicable to Western Europe. Rather, we may assume that income-stock elasticities in the high income countries of Europe would decline from recent levels so as to approach elasticities shown for the United States around 1975. Larger relative increases are expected in the southern group of countries, however, where car ownership levels are very low.

In making projections for individual countries in Western Europe, we have further taken account of intercountry differences in levels of car ownership and population density.[3] The resulting

---

[3]For an international comparison of per capita car ownership, see Figure 9.2.1.

estimates show 224 or 257 cars per 1000 population over 15 in 1970 for the EEC and EFTA countries, depending on the income assumption chosen. For Western Europe as a whole, the relevant ratios are 93 for 1960, 185 or 213 for 1970, and 229 or 271 for 1975.

In order to arrive at estimates of annual additions to stock, we have further assumed that the life span of cars will be shortened to 11 years from the present 12 years. With regard to trade in passenger cars, we have relied on the forecasts of the National Institute [28] and the Economist Intelligence Unit [9]. Finally, some increase in the useful life of tires has been assumed.

FIGURE 9.2.1

PERSONAL INCOME AND PASSENGER AUTOMOBILES PER CAPITA OF 1000 POPULATION OVER 15 IN INDUSTRIAL COUNTRIES

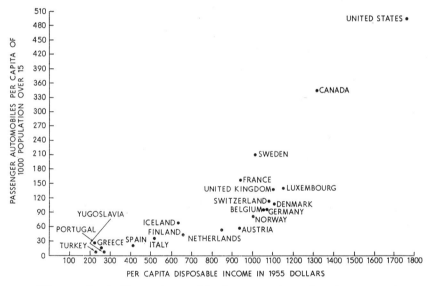

The results indicate that, with the exception of Italy, past relationships between industrial production and rubber consumption will not be maintained in the car-producing countries of Europe. Correspondingly, we have adjusted the elasticities derived for past periods (Table A9.2.2) downward, except in the case of Italy where rubber consumption is likely to increase at a rate exceeding that experienced during the fifties.[4] Further, we have calculated with a

---

[4]The elasticities used in estimating the future consumption of new rubber in the periods 1960–1970 and 1970–1975 are 1.0 and 0.95 for France, 1.1 and 1.05 for Germany, 1.2 and 1.2 for Italy, 0.85 and 0.8 for the United Kingdom, and 1.0 and 0.95 for Sweden.

one-to-one relationship between rubber consumption and industrial production in the case of Belgium, the Netherlands, and the car-importing countries of Northern Europe. Finally, an acceleration in the rate of growth of rubber consumption has been assumed in the case of Southern Europe, where an elasticity of 1.4 has been applied. Still, in the latter area rubber consumption per head would hardly surpass 1.0 kg in 1970 and 1.5 kg in 1975.

The resulting estimates show rubber consumption in Western Europe to rise from 1.09 million tons in 1960 to 1.71 or 1.82 million tons by 1970 and 2.10 or 2.32 million tons by 1975, depending on the income assumption chosen.[5] These results correspond to an approximately 1 per cent increase in rubber consumption for a 1 per cent rise in industrial production.

Japan

In the period 1950–1960, the income-stock elasticity for automobiles was 3.0 in Japan, while rubber consumption increased at a rate slightly lower than industrial production. In 1960, the number of passenger cars owned per 1000 population over 15 was only six, and per capita rubber consumption 2.5 kg. Considering the expected expansion of automobile production in Japan, past relationships can continue during the period of projection so that rubber consumption may approximately double between 1960 and 1975.

Oceania and South Africa

In Oceania and South Africa, little regularity is shown in the growth of rubber consumption, although an upward trend is apparent from the figures. In 1960, rubber consumption per head reached 6.0 kg in Australia, 2.4 in New Zealand, and 1.9 in South Africa. Given the expected increase in the domestic production and assembly of automobiles, it may not be unrealistic to assume that rubber consumption may rise at approximately the same rate as the gross national product in these countries.[6]

The Price and Origin of Imports

The future price of natural rubber is intimately related to competition between natural and synthetic rubber. Developments in the

---

[5] The relevant estimates for the Common Market and the United Kingdom are 1.06–1.13 and 0.39–0.41 million tons for 1970, as compared to the FAO forecasts of 1.05–1.17 and 0.36–0.41 million tons [*10*, p. II. 82].

[6] Data on industrial production are not available.

manufacturing of polyisoprene, polybutadiene, and ethylene-propylene rubber threaten the remaining uses of natural rubber—such as truck tires—where SBR was uncompetitive. Yet natural rubber could regain some uses lost to synthetics if improvements in productivity were translated into lower prices.

As a result of replanting larger areas with high-yielding material, the application of yield stimulants and high stem tapping, as well as advances in planting and processing techniques, yields per acre have been increasing over the last decade in most rubber-producing areas. The largest increases have taken place in Malayan estates where yields may rise by another 40 per cent during the sixties [20, p. 43]. Correspondingly, a steady expansion in the production of natural rubber is expected, and production costs may fall below present levels estimated at 10–12 cents per pound [20, p. 588]. Improvements are underway in small holdings and in other producing areas as well, although production costs are higher here.

The potentialities for expanding production are indicated by the available forecasts. For 1970, the FAO estimated the output of natural rubber to amount to 2.25–2.51 million tons [10, p. II. 82], while the estimate presented at a symposium organized by the International Rubber Study Group was 2.70 million tons for the same year [20, p. 56]. Available information indicates that the FAO estimate is on the low side, and we have accepted the forecast of the Rubber Study Group symposium instead. A further increase of 0.3 million tons has been envisaged for the period 1970–1975. During the sixties, the largest increases in production will be forthcoming in Malaya, with little change in Indonesia, while the smaller producers may maintain their present shares. Recent plantings in Indonesia indicate an expansion of production after 1970, however.

With consideration given to the substitutability of natural and synthetic rubber in various uses as well as the flexibility of mixing ratios, it can be assumed that the price of natural rubber will move so as to equate demand with prospective supply. At the same time, plans for the expansion of synthetic rubber-producing capacity will depend on the relative prices of natural and synthetic rubber. On the basis of a consideration of present plans, an oversupply in rubber is likely to develop in the mid-sixties, but the ensuing fall in prices is bound to lead to modifications in the construction of synthetic rubber-producing facilities. An equilibrium in the rubber market may be reached around 1970, with the price of natural rubber substantially below 1960–1961 levels.

In arriving at the final estimates, we have also considered the consumption and imports of natural rubber into the countries of the Sino-Soviet bloc and the developing areas. In 1960, the consumption of natural rubber in the former group of countries amounted to over one-fifth of world consumption and imports, while developing countries accounted for one-eighth of consumption and one-tenth of world imports. Consumption increases at a rapid rate in the Sino-Soviet area, but given the determination of these countries to raise the degree of self-sufficiency through expanding the production of synthetic rubber, the increase of imports from the 1960 level of 0.45 million tons will be relatively modest.[7]

Taking account of the interaction of prices and quantities, we have derived estimates for the consumption of natural rubber in the developed countries (Table 9.2.1) that are approximately in

TABLE 9.2.1

THE CONSUMPTION OF NATURAL RUBBER
(In thousand tons, and as a percentage of the total consumption of new rubber)

	1950		1955		1960		1970I		1975I	
	1,000 Tons	Per-cent	1,000 Tons	Per-cent	1,000 Tons	Per-cent	1,000 Tons	Per-cent	1,000 Tons	Per-cent
United States	732	57	645	42	487	31	542	26	559	24
Canada	47	67	45	48	36	39	44	30	50	28
North America	779	58	690	42	523	31	586	26	609	24
Belgium-Lux.[a]	12	94	22	82	15	56	18	45	20	42
France	104	93	136	87	129	58	164	45	188	42
Germany	90	95	150	85	148	58	184	45	215	42
Italy[a]	37	93	57	77	69	67	100	50	122	45
Netherlands	14	98	20	87	21	64	24	48	28	45
United Kingdom	223	99	252	92	183	61	186	48	196	45
Northern Europe[a]	45	99	54	81	62	63	67	48	72	45
Southern Europe[a]	15	100	27	na	49	82	67	60	88	55
Western Europe	512	91	721	87	676	62	810	47	929	44
Japan	61	100	89	95	168	73	236	55	272	50
Oceania and South Africa	57	100	86	90	67	64	71	48	77	45
Developed Countries	1409	69	1586	59	1434	46	1703	37	1887	35

Source: International Rubber Study Group, Rubber Statistical Bulletin, various issues.
Note: [a]Net imports.

line with the production forecasts. The estimates indicate a slowing down in the rise of the share of synthetic rubber during the period of projection. Nevertheless, given the relative inflexibility of the production of natural rubber, the increase of rubber consumption under the higher income alternative would be reflected primarily in larger purchases of synthetic rubber.

We have estimated the consumption of natural rubber in the developed countries to rise by 18.7 per cent between 1960 and 1970 and 31.6 per cent between 1960 and 1975 under the most likely income assumption, and slightly higher if the target rate of income

[7]Cf. chap. 4.4.

growth were reached. Increases in imports will, however, be larger, since in 1960 about one-fifth of U.S. and U.K. consumption came from stockpiles. Assuming re-exports of 0.1 million tons, imports of natural rubber into developed countries would reach 1.80 million tons in 1970 and 1.99 million tons in 1975. By comparison, the developed countries imported 1.43 milion tons of natural rubber in 1960.[8]

But the projected increase in the quantity of imports will not be reflected in import values, since equilibrium in the world rubber market would require the price of natural rubber to fall to a considerable extent as compared to prices prevailing in 1960. Once stereo elastomers are available in substantial quantities, the price of natural rubber would have to decline below that of stereo if natural rubber were to compete with the latter. It has been argued that, given the tread wear of a truck tire with different blends of rubber, natural rubber may have to sell at 20 cents a pound to preclude the use of cis-polybutadiene priced at $27\frac{1}{2}$ cents a pound [20, p. 23]. In some other applications, however, a smaller price differential will be sufficient to maintain the competitive position of natural rubber. Correspondingly, we have calculated with a market-clearing price of 22–23 cents per pound for natural rubber, as compared to 38.2 cents in 1960 and 29.5 cents in 1961.[9] Prices may decline even further, however, and it has been suggested that the natural rubber industry should plan to produce profitably at a price of 18 cents a pound [20, p. 61].

With the expected decline in rubber prices, export earnings derived from the sale of rubber would be about 20 per cent below the 1960 level in 1970, and would approximately equal the value of 1961 exports. The export earnings of the year 1960 would not be reached even in 1975 (Table A9).

9.3 FOREST PRODUCTS (SITC 24,25)

Forest products as defined here include all forms of unprocessed and processed timber. The developed countries taken together show a small import balance in forest products, amounting to about 2 per cent of their total consumption expressed in roundwood equivalent in 1960 (Table 9.3.1). This figure conceals substantial intercountry differences, however. In North America, the United States imports slightly over 10 per cent of her timber requirements, while more

---

[8]Re-exports amounted to 114 thousand tons in 1960 while inventories in consuming countries fell by 117 thousand tons.

[9]The price quotations refer to No. 1, RSS II.

than half of the output of Canadian timber is destined to be exported. In Western Europe, the Common Market countries and the United Kingdom are net importers; the import balance of the former amounts to one-third of its domestic requirements, while imports into Britain provide 90 per cent of home consumption. On the other hand, several Northern European countries export a large proportion of their output, with exports exceeding 50 per cent of domestic production in the case of Austria, Finland, Norway, and Sweden. Finally, a net import balance is shown in the countries of the southern group, excepting Yugoslavia, as well as in Japan, Oceania, and South Africa.

TABLE 9.3.1

ANNUAL NET TRADE OF INDUSTRIAL COUNTRIES IN FOREST PRODUCTS
(millions of cubic meters of roundwood)

Year	United States	Canada	North America	Common Market	United Kingdom	Other Western Europe	Total	Western Europe Net Exporters	Western Europe Net Importers	Japan	Oceania
1951	-35.7	45.2	9.5	-13.1	-28.3	43.3	+ 1.9	47.9	-46.0	-1.2	-4.1
1952	-34.0	43.8	9.8	-17.9	-21.5	36.3	- 3.1	41.5	-44.6	-0.5	-4.0
1953	-36.0	41.5	5.5	-18.6	-24.1	43.3	+ 0.6	48.5	-47.9	-1.7	-2.4
1954	-34.5	45.3	10.8	-24.2	-26.8	47.0	- 4.0	53.3	-57.3	-1.3	-3.8
1955	-36.6	48.9	12.3	-26.6	-31.2	51.7	- 6.1	58.3	-64.4	-1.0	-5.1
1956	-38.6	46.1	7.5	-28.0	-30.1	52.8	- 5.2	58.8	-64.0	-2.1	-4.0
1957	-33.7	44.2	10.5	-33.1	-29.1	55.4	- 6.8	61.0	-67.8	-2.1	-3.7
1958	-34.3	42.9	8.6	-32.4	-27.1	52.0	- 7.5	58.0	-65.5	-2.4	-3.7
1959	-39.0	44.6	5.6	-35.3	-29.0	55.6	- 8.7	61.8	-70.5	-3.9	-3.4
1960	-35.0	48.0	13.0	-41.2	-35.4	58.3	-18.3	66.9	-85.2	-5.0	-4.6

Source: FAO, *Yearbook of Forest Products Statistics*, various issues.

Over the last decade, little change has taken place in the United States' net trade position in forest products, with net imports amounting to about 35 million cubic meters of roundwood equivalent. This situation is the result of developments occurring during the first half of the century, which have transformed the United States from a net exporting country to the largest importer of forest products. Over 90 per cent of U.S. imports are supplied from Canada, and Canadian exports to Europe make North America a net exporter of timber.

Net imports of forest products into Western Europe, expressed in roundwood equivalent, amounted to 18.3 million cubic meters in 1960, while Western Europe had a positive export balance in 1951. But 1951 can hardly serve as a standard of comparison, since low levels of industrial production, foreign exchange difficulties, and the almost complete lack of imports from the Soviet Union greatly affected the pattern of trade after the war. If comparison is made with prewar years, the degree of self-sufficiency appears to have risen, and an increase in net imports is not indicated [*13, 38*]. On the one hand, in response to the reduced availability of imports from the Soviet Union, the northern countries of Europe expanded their timber production; on the other hand, the increase in the imports of the traditional importing countries was moderated by a rise in domestic production accompanying a relatively slow expansion of consumption.

With increasing demand for forest products, timber imports into Japan have risen considerably in recent years. But while the bulk of the timber imports of Western Europe come from North America and the Soviet Union, Japan's main sources of supply are the countries of the Far East. Finally much of Australian and South African imports come from North America, with smaller quantities originating in Asia and in Africa.

Reference has been made here to changes in the import balance of various regions, expressed in terms of roundwood equivalent. But an appraisal of prospective changes in trade patterns cannot proceed in aggregate terms. Forest products have manifold uses as fuelwood, roundwood, sawnwood, wood-based sheet material, paper and paperboard, all of which follow different trends and respond to changes in different economic variables.

While the less developed regions are net exporters of unprocessed wood, they rely largely on imports of woodpulp, paper, and paper manufactures from industrial countries. Correspondingly, although in terms of roundwood equivalent the less developed areas taken as a whole appear to be self-sufficient in forest products,[10] they have an adverse balance in value terms. Still, exports of roundwood and sawnwood loom large in the trade of several of the less developed countries. In 1959–61 these exports accounted for 60 per cent of export earnings in the case of the former French Congo, 55 per cent for Gabon, 40 per cent for North Borneo, and 20 per cent for the Philippines, Ivory Coast, and Honduras.[11]

Since there is little international trade in fuelwood, we deal exclusively with industrial wood in the present study.[12] Within the industrial wood category, five groups of forest products are distinguished in trade statistics: (1) roundwood (SITC 242), (2) sawnwood, including railway sleepers (243), (3) pulpwood (25), (4) plywood, veneer, and other wood manufacturers (63), (5) paper and

---

[10]The export surplus of Asia and Africa is counterbalanced by the deficit of Latin America and the Middle East.

[11]In the case of the Philippines, the figures include exports of plywood.

[12]Imports of cork from developing countries ($8 million in 1960) will also be added to the total imports of forest products.

paperboard (64). Among manufactured products, paper and paper board will be dealt with in connection with woodpulp, while trade in plywood, veneer, and other wood manufacturers will be taken up in more detail in Chapter 12.[13]

TABLE 9.3.2

AVAILABILITY OF FOREST PRODUCTS IN 1960
(millions of cubic meters of roundwood)

	Removals	Exports	Imports	Trade Balance	New Supply
North America	405.3	63.6	50.6	+13.0	392.8
United States	308.9	12.3	47.3	-35.0	343.9
Canada	96.4	51.3	3.3	+48.0	48.4
Western Europe	258.5	82.3	100.6	-18.3	276.8
Common Market	87.1	10.2	51.4	-41.2	128.3
United Kingdom	3.3	0.6	36.0	-35.4	38.7
Other W. Europe	168.1	71.5	13.2	+58.3	109.8
Japan	69.4	2.3	7.3	- 5.0	74.4
Oceania and South Africa	25.5	1.6	6.2	- 4.6	30.1
Developed Countries	758.7	149.8	164.7	-14.9	773.6

Source: FAO, *Yearbook of Forest Products Statistics*, 1962.

ROUNDWOOD AND SAWNWOOD (SITC 243, 244)
North America

A report prepared by the U.S. Department of Agriculture Forest Service examines past developments in the consumption of forest products in the United States and gives projections for 1975 [*29*]. It is shown that, in the period 1925–1952, the relative consumption of lumber declined by 38 per cent as compared to all other physical structure materials, while per capita lumber consumption decreased 20 per cent. The report attributes this decline to the rise in lumber prices, although more recent evidence indicates that technological trends have had much to do with these developments. Despite the fall of lumber prices relative to the prices of other structural materials in recent years, per capita lumber consumption decreased a further 20 per cent between 1952 and 1960 [*39*, pp. 39–41].

In projecting the future consumption of lumber, the end-use method has been employed in the report, and the consumption of lumber in various areas of construction, manufacturing, and shipping has been estimated. Projections for 1975 have been made under two alternative assumptions. Under both alternatives, the gross national product is assumed to rise by 78 per cent between 1952 and 1975; in addition, the higher alternative postulates unchanged relative prices and no further substitution against lumber, while

---

[13]Unless otherwise noted, information on the consumption and trade of forest products has been derived from [*13*].

the lower one assumes a relative increase in lumber prices and subsequent substitution of other physical structure materials for lumber.

According to the estimates of the Forest Service, the consumption of saw logs for lumber, expressed in roundwood equivalent, would increase from 182 million cubic meters in 1952 to 202 million and 237 million cubic meters under the two alternatives, respectively [*29*, p. 465]. The projection of the Resources for the Future Study falls between these figures [*23*, p. 812], while an earlier forecast of the Stanford Research Institute envisaged lumber consumption to amount to 195 million cubic meters in 1975 [*32*, p. 321]. The latter study estimated imports to reach 19 million cubic meters of roundwood equivalent in that year, while the figure given in the Forest Service Report for net imports is 13 million, corresponding to gross imports of approximately 16 million cubic meters. The discrepancy between the two estimates reflects different assumptions made with regard to the possible expansion of domestic production.

A study prepared by the Royal Commission on Canada's Economic Prospects expressed the opinion that Canada can easily supply the import needs of the United States in softwood. It was estimated that Canada might be called upon to export about 19 to 21 million cubic meters of lumber (in roundwood equivalent) to the United States in the late seventies, and would also be able to supply double this quantity, although at increasing costs [*6*, pp. 56–70]. A more recent estimate calculates exports to the U.S. at slightly over 20 billion cubic meters [*42*, p. 638]. Correspondingly, there is little expectation that the small quantity of softwood presently imported from Mexico would appreciably increase in the future. Actually, softwood imports from Mexico have been declining in recent years, and in 1960 these amounted to only about 2 per cent of the total quantity imported.

Different is the situation with regard to nonconiferous timber. About 90 per cent of U.S. imports of hardwood logs (mostly veneer logs) and 60 per cent of sawn hardwood imports are of tropical origin. At the same time, tropical timber accounts for nine-tenths of U.S. plywood imports and one-third of the imports of veneer.[14] In all instances, much of the remainder originates in Canada.

Over the last decade the rise of the imports of plywood and veneer has been accompanied by a decline in the purchases of veneer

---

[14]Note, however, that substantial quantities of sawnwood and plywood of tropical origin are imported after processing in Japan (Chapter 12.4).

logs in the United States, and by 1960 about 60 per cent of tropical timber imports took the form of plywood and veneer, with sawnwood accounting for two-thirds and logs for one-third of the remainder In the same year, imports of tropical hardwood amounted to 2.4 million cubic meters in terms of roundwood equivalent.

Given that the Philippines, the largest U.S. supplier, has been setting up timber-processing facilities, imports of hardwood logs are expected to decline further. On the other hand, larger quantities of tropical sawnwood are likely to be imported. Although, in a number of uses, teak, mahogany, rosewood, and other tropical timber are competing with domestic and Canadian maple, birch, and beech, the increased popularity of teak and rosewood furniture is expected to contribute to a rise in imports. Similar conclusions apply to Canadian tropical hardwood imports which amounted to less than 10 per cent of U.S. imports in 1960.

Western Europe

Lumber consumption in Western Europe has also lagged behind general economic activity. In the European OECD countries, for example, the consumption of sawnwood surpassed the 1935–38 level only in 1960, although industrial production more than doubled during the same period [26]. Disparate price movements and technological changes are responsible for this outcome. On the one hand, cement and steel have been substituted for lumber as lumber prices rose by approximately twice as much as the prices of competing materials; on the other hand, technological innovations have permitted a decrease in the use of lumber per unit of output in various fields of economic activity. Fiberboard and blockboard have come into use in the place of solid wood in woodwork, and metal scaffolding, prestressed concrete sleepers, while metal and concrete props have been substituted for lumber in construction.

By reason of the importance of technological change in the determination of the future demand for lumber, it is difficult to make forecasts even for relatively short periods. In the Dewhurst study, the consumption of sawmill products has been estimated to rise by 6 per cent between 1955 and 1970 [7, pp. 542–44], for example, but the consumption level assumed for 1970 has actually been exceeded by 1960. Moderate increases in per capita consumption may also be forthcoming between 1960 and 1975. The consumption of wood-based sheet material (plywood, fiberboard, and particle board) will increase at a much higher rate, however.

Western Europe imports about 4 per cent of her softwood requirements. Imports originate chiefly in the Soviet Union and Canada, with smaller quantities of sawnwood imported from Brazil. The Soviet Union and Canada can also provide for prospective increases of European imports of softwood.

On the other hand, hardwood imports amount to about 15 per cent of European consumption and come largely from tropical areas (Nigeria, Ghana, Sarawak, and Malaya). Imports have been rising rapidly during the fifties, especially in the Common Market countries where imports of tropical timber, expressed in roundwood equivalent, reached 3.5 million cubic meters in 1960 as compared to 0.7 million in the early fifties. Smaller increases have taken place in the United Kingdom where imports amounted to 1.7 million cubic meters in 1960, as against 1.0 million cubic meters a decade earlier. In the other countries of Western Europe, taken together, imports have not surpassed 0.5 million cubic meters.

Various factors have contributed to these developments. On the one hand, there has been a decline in the amount of quality wood available in Western Europe; on the other, with rising incomes, demand for high quality furniture and for plywood has risen. In addition to plywood and furniture making, tropical hardwood has also been used in shipbuilding and general construction (hydraulic installations, for example).

Imports of tropical timber into the United Kingdom have increasingly taken the form of sawnwood and plywood, while all other European countries purchase tropical hardwood chiefly in unprocessed form. Thus, although sawnwood and plywood account for three-fourths of U.K. imports, in Continental Europe the imports of plywood of tropical origin are negligible, and the share of sawnwood has not surpassed 15 per cent. In fact, over the past decade, imports of unprocessed timber rose faster than total imports.

Demand for hardwood in Western Europe will continue to rise during the period of projection, although possibly at a rate lower than that experienced over the last decade. We have assumed here that imports of tropical timber into the Common Market and other continental countries would double within a decade rather than in five years as in the period 1955–1960. Smaller increases are foreseen in the United Kingdom, where a slowing down in the growth of imports was experienced already in the late fifties.

Much of the imports of tropical wood into Continental Europe will continue to take the form of roundwood, while the share of sawnwood and plywood is expected to increase further in the imports of the United Kingdom. These differences are explained by the respective tariff structures of the consuming areas. Whereas processed timber from the Commonwealth countries enter the United Kingdom duty-free, the Common Market timber-processing industries are protected by a 10 per cent tariff on sawn hardwood and a 12.5 per cent duty on plywood and veneer. Nevertheless, in the framework of the association agreement, Gabon will export some processed wood to the Common Market countries.

Japan

In view of the limited possibilities for expanding the exploitation of forests in Japan, the Japanese deficit in timber will continue to grow. A joint report of FAO and the UN Economic Commission for Asia and the Far East estimated Japanese net imports of timber to rise from 1 million to at least 7 million cubic meters of round-wood equivalent between 1955 and 1975 [37, pp. 85–86]. Actually, net imports reached 5.0 million cubic meters in 1960, and 8.5 million cubic meters in 1961. On the basis of available evidence on future trends in consumption and domestic output, it may not be unreasonable to assume that timber imports into Japan would reach 20 million cubic meters of roundwood equivalent by 1970, and 32 million by 1975.

About two-thirds of Japan's imports come in the form of unprocessed tropical hardwood from Southeast Asia, while coniferous roundwood and sawnwood imported from North America and the Soviet Union account for much of the remainder. Given the pattern of timber consumption and the projected slowing down of exports of processed lumber, imports of softwood into Japan are expected to rise at a faster rate than those of tropical hardwood, although the latter may still triple during the sixties.

Oceania and South Africa

New Zealand is a net exporter of forest products, but Australia's deficit makes the entire region a net importer. Much of their round-wood imports originate in North America, while processed wood comes chiefly from Sarawak, Borneo, and the Philippines. Considering the continuing expansion in the output of timber in New Zealand, only a limited increase of imports is anticipated.

South Africa imports about 40 per cent of her timber requirements from Central Africa and Southeast Asia. But South African timber consumption is at low levels, indicating potentialities for future increases. Given the poor forest endowment of South Africa, much of the increase in consumption will have to be imported.

WOODPULP (SITC 251)
North America

The consumption of paper and paperboard in the United States increased from 4.9 million tons in 1914 to 31.4 million tons in 1955 and 35.5 million tons in 1960. Assuming a linear relationship between population and GNP on the one hand, and the consumption of paper and paperboard on the other, the USDA Forest Service estimated paper and paperboard consumption to reach 54.4 million tons by 1975 [*29*, pp. 426–38]. An identical forecast is given in a FAO study which uses, with certain adjustments, a lognormal function fitted to data of all regions of the world, although the latter estimate excludes fiberboard (about 5 per cent of the total) [*14*, p. 92]. Finally, interpolation of the RFF medium estimates for 1970 and 1980 gives 58.6 million tons for 1975 [*23*, p. 70].

Taking into account expected increases in the quantity of new woodpulp required per ton of paper and paperboard, the consumption of woodpulp in the manufacturing of paper and paper products would rise from 23.3 million tons in 1960 to approximately 43 million tons in 1975 if the forecasts of the Forest Service and the FAO were accepted, to which about 1.8 million tons of woodpulp destined to be used in nonpaper products should be added. The Resources for the Future study uses a lower pulp-to-paper ratio and arrives at an estimate of 41 million tons [*23*, p. 703]. Given the expected expansion of domestic production, an increase in the degree of self-sufficiency is anticipated [*29*, p. 464]. Imports will continue to be supplied chiefly from Canada, with smaller quantities originating in Scandinavia.

Western Europe

Per capita paper and paperboard consumption in Western Europe surpassed the 1938 level only in 1954 and reached 55 kg in 1960, as compared to U.S. consumption of 189 kg in the same year. The FAO study expects total consumption in Western Europe to exceed 30 million tons by 1975, corresponding to per capita consumption of approximately 90 kg. This level of consumption would require 24–25 million tons of woodpulp [*14*, pp. 34–53].

On the basis of available estimates on fellings, it appears that the 1965 target (17.2 million tons of woodpulp) could be met from European supplies. A deficit in woodpulp is likely to arise by 1970, however, and it may increase further in subsequent years [*14*, pp. 67–68, 127]. It is expected that prospective import needs will be supplied from North America and the Soviet Union.

Japan

Among industrial countries, Japan's consumption of paper and paperboard has shown the highest rate of growth in recent years and reached 4.4 million tons (47 kg per capita) in 1960. According to the FAO, per capita consumption would surpass the 100 kg mark by 1975, with total consumption amounting to 10.4 million tons. The pulp required for this expansion, 8.2 million tons, will be supplied predominantly from domestic sources, although some of the projected roundwood imports may also be used for pulping [*14*, pp. 40–41, 69].

Oceania and South Africa

Australia and New Zealand show one of the highest per capita paper consumption levels, and further increases are expected. The FAO foresees paper consumption in this area to reach 1.8 million tons in 1975, as compared to 0.8 million tons in 1955. Increased consumption will necessitate higher imports, but these will continue to come from Canada and Western Europe [*14*, pp. 51, 156]. South Africa, however, may remain a net exporter.

The Price and Origin of Imports

According to our projections, the volume of imports of forest products from the less developed countries would approximately double within a decade. At the same time, the pressing demand on supplies, as well as the need for exploiting forest areas at greater distances from the shores in Africa and Asia, is expected to lead to price increases. Correspondingly, we have assumed prices to rise about 10–12 per cent between 1960 and 1970, and 15–17 per cent between 1970 and 1975.

The increase in the imports of tropical timber will benefit especially the countries of Southeast Asia and Africa. Producers in Central Africa are the main suppliers of the European market, while the Philippines and North Borneo export to Japan. More modest increases are expected in Latin America, which accounts for much of U.S. imports of roundwood and sawnwood of tropical origin. At the same time, the exports of woodpulp from developing areas to developed countries are likely to remain nil.

9.4 TEXTILE FIBERS (SITC 26)

Textile fibers may be classified according to their origin (animal, vegetable, man-made) or their final uses (apparel, industrial). Animal fibers include wool, mohair, and other fine hair, and silk; cotton, jute flax, soft hemp, and hard fibers (abaca, sisal, henequen) are of vegetable origin, while man-made fibers comprise cellulosic (rayon and acetate) and noncellulosic (nylon, acrylic, and polyester) fibers.

Final uses serve as a basis for the classification employed in the present study. We first consider fibers that find their main uses in clothing, and second, fibers that are used chiefly for industrial purposes. The so-called apparel fibers: silk, wool, cotton, and man-made fibers come into the first category, while the second includes jute and other vegetable fibers.

APPAREL FIBERS (261–264)

Among natural fibers, cotton is of greatest importance for the developing countries, followed by wool.[15] In 1960, the cotton exports of these countries to developed areas were valued at $727 million, and wool exports at $278 million.[16] The less developed countries account for 55 per cent of world cotton exports, the United States supplies about one-third of the total, and the Soviet Union a further 10 per cent. Mexico, Brazil, and Peru account for much of the cotton exports of Latin America, while—in Africa and the Middle East—Egypt, Sudan, Syria, and Uganda are large exporters. In 1959–61 Egypt derived 70 per cent of her export earnings from the sale of cotton; Sudan, 57 per cent; Syria, 53 per cent; Uganda, 43 per cent, and Mexico and Peru about 20 per cent.

The leading wool exporters are Australia and New Zealand, followed by Argentina, South Africa, and Uruguay. Wool provides about one-third of the export earnings of Uruguay and 15 per cent for Argentina. These two countries, taken together, supply about 15 per cent of world wool exports, with Australia and New Zealand accounting for nearly two-thirds.

Natural and man-made fibers are good substitutes in a number of uses, and the choice among them is determined by relative prices as well as by various nonprice factors, such as availability, quality, and the development of new blends and properties of fibers. Given the importance of nonprice factors, economic variables explain a relatively small part of the variation in the consumption of each fiber taken separately. Although the introduction of a trend vari-

---

[15]By reason of its relative unimportance in consumption and trade, silk is not given separate consideration here. In 1960, silk supplied only 0.2 per cent of total fiber consumption, and imports of silk from developing countries did not surpass $3 million. We have assumed imports to be maintained at present levels during the period of projection.

[16]Including mohair and other animal hair.

able would improve the explanatory value of the regressions, a mechanical extrapolation of past trends cannot provide reliable forecasts. We have therefore chosen to estimate the future consumption of apparel fibers taken together, with a breakdown into the component fibers as a second step.

In the process of estimation, an effort has been made to prepare projections according to main uses. These include clothing, consumer-type products, home furnishings, and industrial uses. Consumer-type products (apparel linings, yardages sold in retail stores, narrow fabrics, shoes, travel ware, umbrella, medical and surgical uses, etc.) are often lumped together with clothing, since about three-fourths of these have clothing uses. Home furnishings include linens, towels, carpets, and draperies, while tires, transportation upholstery, tents, electrical appliances, yarns and thread, reinforced plastics, bags, and belting are the main industrial uses.

In regard to clothing, a direct and an indirect method of projection may be applied. According to the first alternative, future fiber consumption is estimated on the basis of past relationships between per capita disposable income and per capita fiber consumption, while the second method involves ascertaining the relationship between per capita disposable income and per capita clothing expenditure, with the separate estimation of changes in fiber consumption per constant dollar of clothing expenditure. The unavailability of data do not permit the application of the indirect method with respect to other final uses of apparel fibers, however. In the latter instances, estimation can proceed by relating fiber consumption to disposable incomes.

North America

For the United States, statistical information is available on the main uses of apparel fibers measured at the cutting or, in some non-apparel uses, at the weaving (finishing) level.[17] Estimation at the cutting or equivalent level is superior to measuring fiber use at the mills, since mill consumption conceals inventory changes that take place at the yarn-spinning, weaving, knitting, converting, and garment-fabricating levels. Also, there is a time lag between mill consumption and end use, and cyclical fluctuations, too, have a greater effect on the former. Finally, mill consumption data do not allow for trade in yarns and fabrics, while this trade is accounted for in end-use statistics.

---

[17]Unless otherwise indicated, all information on fiber consumption in the United States has been taken from [*33*] and on trade statistics from [*40*].

End-use statistics have some deficiencies of their own, however. The survey's coverage of military uses is incomplete, and a number of smaller uses, which are poorly documented statistically, have not been included. At the same time, there is some degree of double counting, inasmuch as the full processing waste is attributed to each individual end-use, although some of the waste is rerun, the latter operation being separately accounted for. Finally, end-use statistics do not allow for trade in finished textile products. We have attempted to remedy these deficiences by making appropriate corrections in estimating import requirements, and have adjusted the consumption figures for the fiber content of trade in finished products.

A further problem concerns the measurement of fiber consumption in quantitative terms. Fiber consumption figures are unweighted in the sense that the amounts of different fibers consumed are added, ton by ton. However, the "utility" of a pound of cotton or nylon is not identical, partly because processing losses incurred in spinning and weaving are higher for natural fibers than for manmade fibers, and partly because the same service may be performed by a lower weight synthetic or a higher weight natural fiber. In the present study, we have used the conversion ratios accepted by the U.S. Department of Agriculture to recalculate the fiber consumption figures published in the *Textile Organon* (Table A9.4.1).[18]

In projecting the demand for textile fibers in clothing uses, a direct and an indirect method of estimation have been applied. In both cases, consumption has been calculated per consuming unit rather than per person, since changes in the age distribution of the population have greatly affected the demand for clothing in the postwar period. Following the Textile Organon, we have assumed that per capita textile consumption in the 15–64 age group is double the per capita consumption under the age of 15 and above 65. In the final analysis, the data have been reconverted on a per capita basis.

Over the period 1949–1960, the income elasticity of demand for clothing appears to be 0.67[19] while that for textile fibers used in

---

[18]The following conversion ratios have been used: rayon and acetate—staple and tow, 1.10; filament yarn, high tenacity, 1.80; regular and intermediate tenacity, 1.51; noncellulosic fibers—staple, 1.37; filament yarn, tire yarn, 2.73; other, 1.74; glass, 1.70; cotton, 1.00; wool, 0.55 [*24*, p. 41].

[19]By comparison, an elasticity of 0.73 was derived for the years 1931–1940 and 1946–1955 [*8*].

clothing is 0.53 (Table A9.4.5). This discrepancy is explained by changes in the quantity of fiber consumed per constant dollar of clothing expenditure. As Figure 9.4.1 indicates, this ratio has been falling since 1950, although it has recovered somewhat since 1958. Various factors have contributed to this outcome. First, demand for heavy outerwear and underwear declined as a result of changes

FIGURE 9.4.1

THE CONSUMPTION OF APPAREL FIBERS IN RELATION TO CLOTHING EXPENDITURE IN
THE UNITED STATES

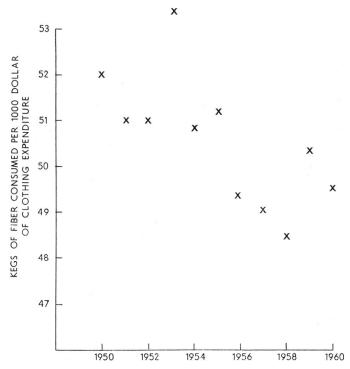

in clothing habits. Better heating of homes, offices, and factories, style changes, and the decreasing importance of manual labor have also been instrumental in the shift toward lighter-weight clothing. Last but not least, the quantity of fiber consumed per constant dollar of clothing expenditure declines as better quality clothing is purchased at higher income levels.

But changes in styles may have the opposite effect during the period of projection. Fabric weight increases as outdoor clothing is purchased and bulky sweaters and heavy woolen fabrics become more popular, for example. Still, some further reduction in the quantity of fibers per unit of clothing expenditure is expected as the demand for better quality clothing grows at higher income levels.

Applying the income elasticity of demand for clothing derived from the data of the period 1949–1960, and assuming a decline in fiber consumption per $1,000 of clothing expenditure from 50 kg in 1960 to 48 kg in 1970 and 47 kg in 1975, per capita fiber consumption expressed in cotton equivalent has been projected to rise from 7.9 kg in 1960 to 8.7 kg by 1970 and 9.0 kg by 1975 under the most likely income assumption, and to 9.0 and 9.4 kg if the target growth rate were reached. The corresponding estimates derived by the use of the direct method are approximately identical. These estimates have subsequently been adjusted downward to allow for possible declines in the income elasticity of demand for clothing at higher income levels (Table A9.4.1).

Per capita fiber consumption in other consumer-type products has fluctuated around a constant level during the fifties. While the use of fibers in medical, surgical, and sanitary equipment has been increasing, this has been counterbalanced by a decline in other applications. We have assumed per capita fiber consumption in these uses, taken together, to remain at the 1960 level.

On the other hand, fiber consumption in home furnishings rises with the growth of incomes; over the period 1949–1960, a 1 per cent increase in per capita disposable income was associated with an approximately 1 per cent rise in fiber consumption. This relationship reflects the high elasticity of demand for carpets and draperies and the lower elasticity for bedding. In making projections, we have assumed this elasticity to fall to 0.8.

Finally, a substantial fall in the industrial uses of fibers is indicated if calculation is made from unweighted data. Much of this decline can be explained by the growing use of stronger—and lighter—fibers. The latter factor has been especially important in regard to fiber used in automobile tires, which account for over one-third of all industrial uses.[20] But some decrease of per capita fiber consumption in industrial uses is shown also in terms of cotton equivalent. This decline can be attributed to the displacement of textile fibers by paper bags and bulk shipping in packag-

---

[20]As a result of the substitution of rayon and, subsequently, nylon for cotton in tirecords, a 58 per cent increase in tires shipped has been accompanied by a 7 per cent reduction in the quantity of fiber consumed in tire manufacturing during the period 1949–1960 [*1, 33*].

ing, and the substitution of plastics for fibers in automobile upholstery and slipcovers. These factors will continue to act in the
future, while fiber consumption in automobile tires and in some
other applications may increase somewhat. On balance, a small decline in the per capita industrial use of fibers is expected.

Given the projected changes in per capita fiber consumption, the
relative shares of individual fibers need to be estimated. Changes
in relative prices as well as nonprice factors are of importance here.
Price differentials between cotton and rayon staple influence, for
example, the cotton spinner's decision in choosing the appropriate
blend of fibers, and the decline of cotton prices is said to have
contributed to recent increases in the consumption of cotton in
clothing uses. It appears, however, that over the past decade the
effects of price changes on consumption have been overshadowed
by nonprice factors, such as the marketing of new fibers and blends
of fibers, and the development of new properties of individual
fibers.

A considerable degree of uncertainty surrounds prospective
changes in the prices of the main fibers as well as the possible
effects of nonprice factors on the consumption of individual fibers.
A comparison of some estimates on the consumption of natural
fibers indicate possible pitfalls in forecasting. In the case of cotton,
for example, Rex F. Daly expects a rise in per capita consumption
to 14.5 kg in 1975 [5], and an even higher rate of increase is foreseen by Keyserling [22, p. 29]. At the same time, Robson estimates
cotton consumption to fall to 8.1 kg by 1975 [30, p. 108] and a
decrease has been projected also by Black and Bonnen [2, p. 25].
Similar differences pertain to forecasts of wool consumption.

In the present study, the future consumption of natural fibers
has been estimated according to their main uses. In making projections, we have assumed that the approximate parity between cotton
and rayon prices will be maintained in the future—although probably at a level lower than that experienced in 1960. Wool prices,
too, may fall somewhat, and technological advances are likely to
lead to a decline in the price of most noncellulosic fibers, but not
necessarily of protein fibers. Further, we have utilized available information on prospective technological developments.

In clothing, cotton staged a comeback during the fifties, and the
share of cotton in the weighted consumption of textile fibers in
clothing uses increased from 57 per cent in 1949 to 62 per cent in
1960. Various influences contributed to this outcome. The decrease
in the relative price of cotton led to a rise in the cotton content of

blends in spinning. Greater use of shrinkage control and special finishes restored some of the previous uses of cotton, and the appeal of cotton as a quality fiber also increased.

But the gains made by cotton are likely to prove temporary, inasmuch as technological changes appear to favor man-made fibers through quality improvements and the development of new properties of these fibers. It can be expected, therefore, that the share of cotton in clothing uses will again decline, and increases in per capita cotton consumption will be small, if any.

Cotton consumption in other consumer-type products has been declining in recent years. In medical applications, for example, the share of cotton in fiber consumption fell from 100 per cent in 1949 to 65 per cent in 1960. The process of substitution is expected to continue in the future, and, given the increasing relative importance of medical uses in this category, per capita cotton consumption in consumer-type products may decline further.

Cotton has lost ground in home furnishings, too, especially in draperies and carpets. In drapery and upholstery fabrics, ease of care and fireproofness favor man-made fibers, while the resiliency and soil resistance of rayon make it superior to cotton in carpet yarns. Despite the projected large increases in these uses, the per capita consumption of cotton in draperies and carpets will continue to fall, and this decline is not likely to be counterbalanced by the increased consumption of bedding and towels, where cotton is used almost exclusively.

Finally, the near disappearance of cotton in tire cords has greatly reduced the absolute and relative share of cotton in industrial uses over the last decade. Some further declines are expected as a result of the substitution of man-made fibers for cotton in electrical installations and belting.

Our projections indicate a fall in the per capita consumption of cotton from 10.1 kg in 1960 to 9.5 kg in 1970, and 9.3 kg in 1975 under the most likely income assumption, and a somewhat smaller decline if the target rate of income growth were reached (Table A9.4.1). But the use of cotton in domestic manufacturing is further reduced by the expected increase in the importation of cotton goods.

Measured in the terms of raw cotton, the United States showed an export surplus of 100 thousand tons in cotton manufactures in 1950, but this surplus gave place to a small deficit in the late fifties. Given the weak competitive position of the U.S. cotton industry and the increase in the quotas accorded to the less developed countries and Japan, further increases in imports are expected, and the net import balance may rise from 10 thousand tons in 1960 to 100 thousand tons by 1970 and 150 thousand tons by 1975. Correspondingly, the use of cotton in U.S. manufacturing would amount to about 1.95 million tons in 1970 and 2.05 million tons in 1975, as compared to 1.81 million tons in 1960.

The United States is the world's largest cotton exporter, and imports chiefly long-staple cotton from Egypt. Imports are regulated by quotas, and it appears unlikely that the present share of cotton imports in domestic consumption would undergo substantial changes during the period of projection.

The per capita consumption of wool in clothing declined somewhat in the last decade; it amounted to 0.94 kg in 1960 as compared to 1.07 kg in 1949. This decline can be explained by the increased popularity of single-breasted suits, the reduction in fabric weight, and the substitution of man-made fibers for wool. The advantages of blends made with synthetic fibers (wool-polyester, wool-acrylic) would promise a further reduction in the amount of wool used in clothing, but various factors act in the opposite direction. Wool has a large share in the rapidly expanding knit outwear market, while advances made in the processing of wool (moth-proofing) and the strong appeal of wool as a quality fiber are expected to restrain future declines in other clothing uses. With consideration given to these influences, we have assumed that the per capita consumption of wool in clothing uses will stabilize around 0.95 kg.

In home furnishings, wool is used in carpets and blankets, and has incurred considerable losses in both. Man-made fibers have well-nigh replaced wool in blankets, while, in, terms of actual weight, wool's share in U.S. carpet manufacturing declined from two-thirds in 1949 to one-third in 1958. And although wool staged a comeback in 1959 and 1960 as its use in tufted carpets increased, it has again lost ground to man-made fibers. Nylon and acrylic fibers are expected to make further gains during the period under consideration. Thus, despite the projected large increase in the consumption of carpets, the per capita consumption of carpet wool is likely to decline from its high 1960 level. Some decreases in the use of wool in other consumer-type products and in industrial applications may also be forthcoming.

According to our projections, wool consumption per head, calculated on a scoured basis, would fall from 1.54 kg in 1960 to 1.48 kg in 1970 and 1.45 kg in 1975 under the most likely income assumption, while a somewhat larger consumption would be associated with the higher income variant. Since the decrease in per capita consumption would be concentrated in home furnishings and industrial uses, the total consumption of apparel wool would rise at about the same rate as population, while smaller increases would take place in the consumption of carpet wool. If adjustment is made for the double counting of reused and reprocessed wool, the consumption of apparel wool is estimated to increase from 157 thousand tons in 1960 to 186–191 thousand tons in 1970 and 205–210 thousand tons in 1975. The corresponding figures for carpet wool are 89 thousand tons in 1960, and 96–100 and 101–106 thousand tons in 1970 and in 1975, respectively.

The mill consumption of wool will further depend on the importation of wool manufactures. In 1960 imported wool goods accounted for 29 per cent of U.S. apparel wool consumption as against 12 per cent in the early fifties, whereas the share of carpet imports in the domestic consumption of carpet wool rose from 6 to 16 per cent in the same period [*41*, p. 63]. Subsequently, the raising of tariffs has led to decreases in the imports of wool fabrics and carpets, however, and future changes will also greatly depend on the trade policies followed by the United States. We have assumed here that, in the framework of the GATT negotiations, tariffs will again be reduced, and the proportion of the imports of wool manufactures in domestic consumption will be re-established at approximately the 1960 level.

Imports of apparel wool account for one-third of mill consumption in the United States, while all carpet wool is imported. Should the present system of subsidies be maintained, increases in the domestic production of wool may be small, so that almost the entire increase in mill consumption would be supplied by imports. Taking account of the temporary fall in stocks in 1960, the imports of apparel wool are estimated to rise by about one-third between 1960 and 1970, and two-thirds between 1960 and 1975. On the other hand, increases in carpet wool imports may not exceed 20 per cent over the entire period (Table A9.4.2).

Time-series data on fiber consumption at the fabrication level are not available for Canada, and consumption is measured as mill consumption plus net imports. Per capita consumption of textile fibers calculated on a ton-by-ton basis has declined since the end of the Korean War, but a slight increase is shown if weight differences among the individual fibers are taken into account. At the same time, there has been a decrease in the per capita consumption of cotton and wool. By 1960, wool consumption was at the U.S. level, but cotton consumption was one-third lower [27].

In 1953, clothing uses accounted for about 55 per cent of the consumption of apparel fibers in Canada, while one-third of the remainder went into household furnishings and two-thirds into industrial uses [3, p. 16]. According to the Royal Commission Report, the income elasticity of demand for textiles is 0.9 in Canada [31, p. 99], while an elasticity of 0.34 has been derived for the period 1950–1960 (Table A9.3.5). The latter value needs to be adjusted upward, however, by reason of the relative increases in the young and old age groups during this period. For purposes of projection, the income elasticity used for the United States has been employed also in the case of Canada. Fiber consumption will, however, rise at a lower rate as lighter weight fabrics come into use.

Within the increased consumption of fibers, wool may maintain its present share in clothing manufacturing, but it is likely to lose ground in home furnishings. At the same time, a decline in the per capita consumption of cotton is anticipated. Canada imports her entire cotton needs, while imports of wool provide over 80 per cent of her mill consumption. Cotton imports originate almost exclusively in the United States, and wool is imported mostly from the United Kingdom and Oceania.

Western Europe

Time-series data on fiber consumption according to end uses are not available for the countries of Western Europe; the statistics published by FAO refer to mill consumption corrected for the fiber content of yarns, tissues, and other fiber products traded (Table A9.4.1).[21] But fiber consumption measured at the mill level is affected by changes in inventories at various levels of fabrication, and inventory changes reduce the statistically observable relationship between per capita disposable income and fiber consumption per head. Stockpiling during the Korean War period and the decumulation of inventories following the war emergency have especially distorted data on mill consumption, and hence we have included only observations for the period 1953–1960 in the present investigation. 1950–1960 has been used as the base period in regard to expenditure on clothing, however.

---

[21]If not otherwise noted, all consumption figures have been taken from [12, 27]. The data are unweighted in the sense that the consumption of the various fibers is added, ton by ton.

As regards the final use of apparel fibers, information is available for the Common Market countries, the United Kingdom, and Sweden for the years 1954–1957. The results show an average of 56 per cent of apparel fibers used in clothing and other consumer-type products, 24 per cent in household furnishings, and 20 per cent in industrial uses [*19*, p. 35]. These figures compare with the corresponding breakdown for the United States (56:25:19), although the interpretation of the comparisons is hampered by differences in classification. In estimating prospective changes in fiber consumption, we have first calculated cross-section regressions, using the arithmetical average of observations relating to the years 1959 and 1960 for the industrial countries of North America and Western

TABLE 9.4.1

CONSUMPTION OF NATURAL FIBERS IN WESTERN EUROPE AND JAPAN
(thousand tons)

	1950	1955	1960	1970I	1970II	1975I	1975II
Cotton (lint)							
Common Market	705	718	892	1050	1068	1105	1141
United Kingdom.	359	304	312	367	373	362	368
Northern Europe	152	157	181	209	213	226	234
Southern Europe	180	272	311	421	472	487	510
Japan	124	286	404	460	470	500	510
Wool (clean basis)							
Common Market	251	230	286	313	332	323	342
United Kingdom.	134	128	124	123	129	126	136
Northern Europe	80	63	70	71	75	73	77
Southern Europe	57	63	75	106	110	124	132
Japan	18	52	100	132	143	138	149

Source: FAO, Per Capita Fiber Consumption Levels, 1948-1958, Commodity Bulletin series 31, Rome, 1960, and Monthly Bulletin of Agricultural Economics and Statistics, January, 1962.

Europe, in order to establish a relationship (1) between per capita disposable income and per capita clothing expenditure, and (2) between per capita disposable income and fiber consumption per head. In both instances about 80 per cent of the variation in consumption can be explained by intercountry differences in incomes. An income elasticity of 0.72 is shown in the former case and 0.55 in the latter (Table A9.4.5).[22] The discrepancy between the results is explained by the reduction of fiber weight per unit of clothing expenditure due to the increased use of light weight fibers in high income countries and the purchase of better quality clothing at higher income levels.

---

[22]By comparison, Milton Gilbert derived an income elasticity of demand for clothing of 0.84 for 1950 in a cross-section study of eight European countries and the United States [*16*, p. 66], while time-series and cross-section data on fiber consumption in the OEEC countries gave elasticities of 0.5–0.7 for the fifties [*18*, pp. 81–82].

Using time-series data, the income elasticity of demand for clothing has been calculated as 0.78 in the case of the Common Market countries, 1.21 for the United Kingdom, and 0.81 for other European countries. It should be added that in the United Kingdom the postwar rationing influenced the results, and for this country it is more appropriate to use a coefficient derived from the cross-section regression or to accept the elasticities estimated in the case of the Common Market or other European countries.[23]

On the basis of evidence provided by time-series and cross-section functions for the postwar period, an income elasticity of 0.7–0.8 appears to be appropriate with regard to clothing expenditure in the more developed countries of Western Europe, while somewhat higher values may apply to Southern Europe. At the same time, available information indicates that the income elasticity of demand for textile fibers in clothing uses is lower than that for clothing expenditure, and the difference between the two figures might be about 0.1–0.2.

Fiber consumption in household furnishings and industrial uses is likely to be more sensitive to increases in incomes, however. The income elasticity of demand for household furnishings in Western Europe is certainly higher than the U.S. figure, although the effects of increased demand for automobile tires on fiber consumption in industrial uses will be moderated by the shift to the use of nylon.

These considerations suggest that the income elasticity of demand for fibers may be around 0.6–0.7 in the more developed countries of Western Europe and 0.8 in the countries of the Southern group. The evidence provided by postwar data on fiber consumption appears to bear out these conclusions. For the period 1953–1960, the income elasticity of demand for fibers was calculated as 0.73 in the Common Market, 0.52 in the United Kingdom, 0.80 in Northern Europe, and 0.78 in Southern Europe (Table A9.4.5). Taking account of intercountry differences in per capita fiber consumption levels, the following elasticities have been applied in the projections: 0.7 for the Common Market, 0.6 for the United Kingdom, 0.75 for Northern Europe, and 0.8 for Southern Europe.

A further adjustment has been necessary, however, by reason of the increased use of lower weight noncellulosic fibers in the future.

---

[23]Higher elasticities have been derived from time-series data combining interwar and early postwar observations and from budget studies [*8, 11*]. But an upward bias is apparent in both instances. In the first case the postwar refurbishing of wardrobes influenced the results; in the second, an application of Friedman's permanent income hypothesis would suggest that part of clothing expenditure is financed from the transitory component of income.

Since the "utility" of noncellulosic fibers of equal weight is greater than that of natural fibers (and rayon), future fiber needs will be correspondingly reduced. This shift is indicated by technological trends as well as by the experience of the United States and Canada. While noncellulosic fibers account for over 10 per cent of fiber consumption in North America, the corresponding figure is 7 per cent for the more developed countries of Europe and only 2 per cent for the countries of the southern group.[24]

To allow for the shift toward lighter-weight fibers, we have calculated with a negative trend factor of 0.5 per cent of the 1960 consumption in the more developed countries of Europe, and slightly higher for the southern group. Correspondingly, under the most likely income assumption, fiber consumption per head would reach 12.0 kg by 1970 and 13.1 kg by 1975 in the European Common Market, 13.6 and 14.0 kg in the United Kingdom, 11.5 and 12.3 kg in Northern Europe, and 6.4 and 7.2 kg in the countries of the southern group (Table A9.4.3). These estimates compare with fiber consumption of 15.7 kg per head in the United States in 1960.

As regards the relative importance of individual fibers, note that the share of cotton and noncellulosic fibers in fiber consumption is smaller in Western Europe than in the United States and that of wool and rayon is correspondingly greater.[25] Climatic conditions, customs, the level of technological development, and relative prices largely account for these differences. The hot and humid summer favors cotton in the United States and, at the same time, technological advances have led to the use of noncellulosic fiber in a wide range of applications here. On the other hand, the high tariff restricts the consumption of wool in the United States, while in Northern Europe and, especially, the United Kingdom the cold climate and custom favor wool.

Technological advances as well as plans for the expansion of capacity indicate a rapid increase in the future consumption of noncellulosic fibers in Western Europe. Noncellulosic fibers will

---

[24]In order to achieve comparability, the unweighted figures published by the FAO have been used here in the case of the United States, too.

[25]For 1960, the respective relative shares are:

	United States %	Western Europe %
Cotton	66.5	52.7
Wool	7.7	17.2
Rayon	16.2	23.2
Noncellulosic	9.6	6.9
	100.0	100.0

gain at the expense of cotton (clothing, home furnishings), wool (suitings, carpets), and rayon (clothing, tires). Correspondingly, the share of cotton is expected to decline below 50 per cent by 1975 as against 53 per cent in 1960, although cotton would still benefit from the advance of fiber consumption, and the per capita consumption of cotton is expected to rise throughout Western Europe. We have projected cotton consumption in Western Europe to increase from 1.70 million tons in 1960 to 2.05 or 2.09 million tons in 1970, and to 2.18 or 2.25 million tons in 1975, depending on the income assumption chosen.

In 1960, wool consumption per head calculated on a clean basis was 1.6 kg in Western Europe and 1.2 kg in the United States. We have noted above that the difference in consumption levels is, in part, attributable to the higher relative price of wool in the United States, while in the United Kingdom and Northern Europe, where per capita wool consumption is the highest, climatic conditions and custom favor wool. Nevertheless, there is evidence that the substitution of man-made fibers for wool that has taken place in the United States is under way also in Europe. With the exception of the Southern European countries, the relative share of wool in fiber consumption is bound to fall as blends of noncellulosic fibers and wool become more popular in suitings and women's dresses, and nylon gains ground in carpet manufacturing. At the same time, present intra-European differences in per capita consumption levels are likely to be reduced. Taken together, wool consumption in Western Europe would increase at a rate but slightly higher than the growth of population.

In projecting the demand for cotton and wool in Western Europe, we also have to consider trade in textile manufactures. Net exports of cotton products (including yarn) declined by two-thirds during the fifties and amounted to 98 thousand tons of cotton equivalent in 1960. With increased imports from developing countries and Japan under the International Cotton Textiles Agreement, this surplus is likely to disappear by 1970, and it may give place to a net import balance in 1975.

Different is the situation with regard to wool. Given the expansion of Italian exports of woolen goods, the net exports of wool manufactures from Western Europe have not declined but rather increased during the past decade. Despite increasing competition from Japan, the present level of net exports (about 100 thousand tons of wool on a clean basis) may be maintained in the period under consideration.

In regard to future import demand, note that cotton production in Western Europe takes place almost exclusively in Turkey, Spain, and Greece. Domestic production nearly doubled over the past decade, and it reached 314 thousand tons in 1960. Production will expand further, so that the countries of the southern group, taken as a whole, will remain self-sufficient. The high income countries of Western Europe will continue to rely on imports, however. Still, taking account of changes in stocks in 1960, and assuming unchanged extra-area exports of cotton, the rise in cotton imports into Western Europe may not exceed 5 per cent in the period 1960–1975 by reason of the increasing net imports of cotton manufactures into the area (Table A9.4.4).

Wool production in Europe has been expanding at a slower rate; it increased by about one-fourth during the fifties. In 1960, production amounted to 128 thousand tons on a clean basis, one-half of which originated in the United Kingdom and Turkey. We have calculated with a yearly rate of increase of 1.5 per cent over the period of projection and assumed that the export of wool (in part, re-exports) would remain unchanged. Allowing for changes in stocks in 1960, imports would then rise by 15 or 21 per cent between 1960 and 1970 and 19 or 27 per cent between 1960 and 1975, depending on the income assumption chosen.

Japan

The consumption of the main apparel fibers in Japan has shown large, although somewhat erratic, increases over the last decade. Per capita fiber consumption surpassed 9 kg in 1960, approaching the level experienced in the more developed European countries, although living standards in Japan are substantially lower than in Western Europe.

In projecting the future consumption of textile fibers, we have calculated with an income elasticity of demand of 0.6 derived from observations referring to the period 1953–1960, and have further assumed a negative trend factor of 0.8 per cent a year, representing the reduction in fiber weight due to the increased use of noncellulosic fibers. Among the individual fibers, government support to production and plans for increases in capacity indicate the continuation of the recent high growth rate of the consumption of noncellulosic fibers. Yet, despite the expected reduction in the share of natural fibers, a rise in the per capita consumption of cotton and wool is foreseen.

Japanese exports of textile manufactures have also risen during the last decade. The net exports of cotton goods, expressed in cotton equivalent, have reached 226 million tons in 1960, while net imports have given place to an export surplus of 23 million tons in the case of wool manufactures [*18*, p. 115]. The Planning Agency foresees textile exports to double over the next decade [*20*, p. 76], but given the expected growth of textile manufacturing in the less developed countries, and the reluctance of American and European governments to admit Japanese textiles in large quantities, this estimate may be on the high side. We have accepted the Planning Agency's forecast for wool manufactures, but assumed a slowing down in the rate of growth of the exports of cotton goods.

Cotton is not produced in Japan, and the re-exports of cotton are negligible. With allowance made for the exports of cotton manufactures, cotton imports would reach 760 million tons in 1970 and 840 million tons in 1975 under the most likely income assumption, while the corresponding figures are 780 and 860 million tons under the higher income alternative. In 1960, cotton imports amounted to 701 million tons.

TABLE 9.4.2

IMPORTS OF NATURAL FIBERS INTO DEVELOPED COUNTRIES
(thousand tons)

	North America	Western Europe	Japan	Oceania & So. Africa	Developed Countries
Cotton					
1960	33	1622	701	36	2392
1970I	37	1670	760	70	2537
1970II	38	1700	780	75	2593
1975I	40	1680	840	85	2645
1975II	41	1740	860	90	2731
Wool					
1960	109	503	115	5	732
1970I	133	580	172	5	890
1970II	139	611	189	5	944
1975I	149	601	192	5	947
1975II	156	639	214	5	1014

Source: FAO, Trade Yearbook; U.N., Commodity Trade Statistics.

Domestic production of wool is small in Japan, and it is approximately balanced by re-exports. Thus, except for changes in inventories, wool imports into Japan will rise at about the same rate as mill consumption. According to our projections, the import level of the year 1960 would be exceeded by 60–70 per cent in 1970 and 70–80 per cent in 1975 (Table A9.4.4).

Oceania and South Africa

Per capita fiber consumption in Australia and New Zealand is slightly above 10 kg and has shown little change during the last decade. The two countries are the largest exporters of wool and satisfy much of their need for cotton textiles by the importation of cotton manufactures. Considering the availability of cheap cotton goods from Japan and elsewhere, this pattern is likely to be maintained in the future, and only a modest rise of cotton imports is expected from the present level of 19 thousand tons.

Consumption levels are considerably lower in South Africa, and the possibilities of expansion are also larger here. At the same time, the growing cotton textile industry will require imports of increasing quantities of cotton in this country.

The Price and Origin of Imports

Cotton. According to our projections, cotton imports into developed countries other than North America would amount to 2.5–2.6 million tons in 1970 and 2.6–2.7 million tons in 1975, as compared to 2.4 million tons in 1960.[26] At the same time, prospective changes in the relative shares of the producing countries in these imports will greatly depend on the policy followed by the United States.

Over the last decade the United States has been a residual supplier in the sense that the U.S. provided the difference between the world demand for cotton and the quantities supplied by other producers, since the latter could undercut the United States and sell practically all their produce. Correspondingly, the share of the United States in the world cotton market has shown large fluctuations; it averaged at about one-third over the last decade, but it was one-fourth in 1958 and 45 per cent in 1960.

But the United States could not in the future maintain its "traditional" share in world markets under the present policy, since relatively small increases in world demand are expected to be accompanied by a substantial rise of exportable output in several cotton-producing countries, and the latter can continue to undersell the United States. There are some indications, however, that a change in U.S. policy is forthcoming, and varying subsidies will replace the present flat subsidy of 8.5 cents a pound on cotton exports.

We have assumed that such a policy would indeed be followed, and that the United States government would endeavor to ensure about one-third of world exports of cotton to domestic growers. Still, the U.S. share in the world market would have to fall as compared to 1960. We have assumed that the United States would supply about 40 per cent of cotton imports into Western Europe

---

[26]The FAO estimate is 2.1–2.4 million tons for 1970 [*10*, p. II. 73].

and Japan during the period of projection, while in 1960 she accounted for 50 per cent of imports into the two areas. Thus, despite the relatively small increase expected in European and Japanese imports of cotton, the developing countries are likely to show substantial gains.

In less developed areas, exportable production is expected to rise, especially in Brazil, Central America, Syria, and the Sudan, while smaller increases are anticipated in Egypt and in Asia. At the same time, some decline in cotton prices is foreseen, since, without some easing in prices, the share of cotton in fiber consumption would be further reduced.

Wool. Increases in wool imports will be larger than in the case of cotton. We have projected imports into industrial countries to rise from 727 thousand tons in 1960 to 885–939 thousand tons in 1970 and 942–1009 thousand tons in 1975, depending on the income assumption chosen.[27] Within the rising imports, the share of Latin-American producers is bound to increase, since in 1960 the exports of these countries were at unusually low levels. Argentina and Uruguay may thus supply one-sixth of European imports as compared to 14 per cent in 1960, and Japanese imports from Latin America will also rise.

But similar to the case of cotton, a fall in wool prices is anticipated. Given the competition of synthetic fibers, the price increases of the 1961/62 crop year are expected to remain temporary, and wool prices may decline in the second half of the sixties. In the absence of a fall in prices, the consumption and imports of wool would not reach the projected level.

JUTE (SITC 264)

International trade in jute takes the form of raw jute, jute yarn, cloth, and bags. Raw jute accounts for the bulk of imports into Western Europe, Japan, and South Africa; the United States and Canada import chiefly jute cloth, while Australia and New Zealand are the main purchasers of jute bags.

Imports of raw jute into developed countries amounted to $139 million in 1960, over 80 per cent of which was destined for Western Europe. In the same year, developed countries imported jute cloth from underdeveloped areas in the value of $132 million and jute bags in the value of $43 million.[28]

---

[27] By comparison, the FAO estimate is 740–915 thousand tons for 1970 [*10*, II. 73].

[28] Trade in jute yarn takes place almost exclusively among the developed countries themselves.

Raw jute comes chiefly from Pakistan, while India is the main exporter of jute manufactures. Jute is the main foreign exchange earner of the Pakistan economy; raw jute accounts for 45 per cent of export earnings, and jute manufactures for another 15 per cent. At the same time, India derives one-fifth of her foreign exchange income from the sale of jute manufactures. Smaller but increasing quantities of raw jute are exported also from Thailand.

North America

In the United States, the apparent consumption of jute was 375 thousand tons in 1960, 85 per cent of which was imported in the form of jute cloth (burlap). As a result of the decrease in the demand for jute in packaging and in making rope and twine, jute consumption is about one-fifth below the prewar level, although its use as carpet backing material and in various industrial applications (automobile felts, upholstery, etc.) has risen. By the late fifties, floor coverings accounted for about 15 per cent of U.S. jute consumption; other industrial uses for 25 per cent, while packaging uses took the remainder [34].

The substitution of multiwall paper sacks for jute sacks, the development of bulk handling methods, and the trend toward pre-packaging for retailing in factories, or at the wholesale stage, account for the decrease of jute consumption in packaging uses, while synthetic materials have been substituted for jute in the making of rope and twine. These influences will continue to act during the period of projection, although the scope for further substitution appears to be limited. If we assume that the consumption of packageable goods will rise at about the same rate as population, the use of jute for packaging may not decline any further.

At the same time, the consumption of jute in floor coverings is expected to rise at rates exceeding those observed in the past by reason of the use of a second or double backing in tufted carpets. Increases are likely to be forthcoming in other industrial uses, too, so that in 1975 jute consumption (net imports) in the United States may exceed the 1960 level by 12–15 per cent. Increases are foreseen also in Canada, where the packaging uses of jute are of importance. In both cases, the entire increase in jute imports is expected to take the form of jute manufactures.

Western Europe

About 85 per cent of the jute needs of Western Europe are met by imports of raw jute. Consumption, measured as net imports, had been rising during the fifties, but it reached the prewar level only in 1960, when 575 thousand tons of jute were consumed. Increases in the use of jute as carpet backing material and reductions in packaging account for the observed charges. In the late fifties, one-fourth of European consumption was in carpeting, one-half in packaging, and one-fourth in other industrial uses.

As to prospective changes in jute consumption, substantial increases are expected in the use of jute in floor coverings. On the one hand, the income elasticity of demand for carpets is considerably higher in Western Europe than in the United States; on the other, the shift toward tufted carpets in Europe has yet to come. The consumption of jute in packaging is bound to decline, however, since the possibilities of substitution of paper sacks for jute bags are largely unexploited in Continental Europe, and developments in bulk handling methods as well as prepackaging in factories will further reduce the demand for jute.

Still, considering the relatively low share of packaging in jute consumption, and potential increases in carpeting and other industrial uses, a net increase in the consumption of jute is expected, possibly at about the same rate as in the United States.[29] But, in distinction from the case of the United States, raw jute will retain its place in European imports by reason of the protective measures applied to jute manufactures in much of Western Europe.

Japan

Japanese imports of raw jute doubled between 1955 and 1960, although a projection prepared in 1958 expected imports to reach only 115 per cent of the 1954–56 level in 1975 [*36*, p. 90]. Part of this increase served the expansion of exports of jute manufactures, however, which will face severe competition on the part of India and Pakistan in years to come. Thus, the rate of increase in raw jute imports is likely to slow down in the future.

Oceania and South Africa

Australia and New Zealand import chiefly jute bags for packaging bulk commodities. Imports have been increasing at a slow rate during the fifties, and, given the possibilities of substitution against

---

[29]Our projections for Western Europe correspond to the higher limit of the FAO forecast and exceed this limit in the case of the United States [*10*, p. II. 76]. The differences in the estimates are explained by the consideration given to the double backing of tufted carpets in our forecast and by different assumptions made with regard to the future possibilities for substitution against jute in packaging in the United States.

jute, the rise in imports is likely to fall behind the growth of output of these commodities. In the present study, we have assumed that in 1975 imports will exceed the 1960 level by about one-third.

By comparison, South Africa imports raw jute and exports small quantities of jute manufactures. On the basis of available information, imports have been projected to rise by about one-half in the period of projection.

The Price and Origin of Imports

According to our projections, raw jute imports into developed countries would exceed the 1960 level by 14–15 per cent in 1970 and 20–24 per cent in 1975. But prices will hardly remain at the high level reached in the 1960–61 marketing year when Pakistan had an exceptionally poor harvest, and the expected fall in prices will reduce export earnings. We have assumed here that, in the period under consideration, prices of raw jute would be about 15 per cent below the 1960 level.

OTHER VEGETABLE FIBERS (SITC 265)

This group of fibers includes soft (flax, soft, or true hemp) and hard (abaca, sisal, henequen) fibers. Flax has its uses in household linen and in sailcloth, while hemp is used in soft twines and cords. Both of these fibers are produced in temperate climate, and imports from less-developed areas are negligible. Consequently, a discussion of future changes in the consumption and trade of soft fibers falls outside the scope of this study.

Hard fibers are produced exclusively in less developed areas. The main producers and exporters of sisal are Tanganyika, Brazil, Kenya, and Angola, while abaca originates in the Philippines and henequen in Mexico.[30] Hard fibers are of greatest importance for the export trade of Tanganyika, where 27 per cent of export earnings are derived from the sale of sisal.

The chief outlet for sisal and henequen is in agriculture as binder and baler twine, and in industry as wrapping twine, although large quantities are used also in automobile and furniture upholstery. The switch from reaper-binders to combine-harvesters has led to a reduction in the use of binder twine, but this has been more than counterbalanced by the rise in the demand for baler twine. Increases are shown also in industrial uses, although the introduction

---

[30] In 1960, sisal accounted for 81 per cent of world exports of hard fibers, abaca 16 per cent, and henequen 3 per cent.

of adhesive tape has reduced the use of packing and tying twines.

The main outlet for abaca is marine cordage, such as ships' ropes and fishing nets. The demand for this fiber has been declining over the last decade by reason of the substitution of synthetic fibers in its various uses. Abaca is displaced by synthetic fibers in fishing nets, while nylon and polyester fibers that are more durable and resistant to water and chemicals encroach upon its market in ships' ropes. Finally, low grades of abaca are competing with sisal in agricultural uses.

North America

With the exception of the recession years, the consumption of hard fibers, taken as a group, has been growing steadily in the United States and Canada since World War II. But imports of unmanufactured fibers have fallen, as there has been an increase in the imports of twine and cordage from Mexico and Western Europe.

During the period of projection, some further increases in the use of hard fibers are expected, but these increases are likely to take the form of finished goods, while fiber imports may not surpass the level reached in 1959. Still, fiber imports would rise as compared to 1960, when the decline in the activity of the automobile and furniture industries, and delays in shipments of henequen from Mexico, reduced imports.

Western Europe

Imports of hard fibers into Western Europe approximately doubled during the fifties. This increase reflects a fourfold rise in the exports of twine and cordage to the United States, and an increase of domestic consumption by over two-thirds. The expansion of domestic consumption of hard fibers, in turn, can be attributed to the mechanization of hay and straw cutting and stacking, and to the growth of production in the automobile and furniture industries.

Some further increases in twine and cordage exports to the United States are expected, and Western Europe's own consumption of hard fibers will also rise. The experience of the United States indicates that the mechanization of harvesting is accompanied by the use of large quantities of baler twine more than counterbalancing the fall in the consumption of binding twine. The consumption of hard fibers in automobile and furniture upholstery may also increase, while the growing use of adhesive tape and the spreading of mechanical handling methods will have some adverse effects on imports.

Correspondingly, sisal imports will continue to rise, although probably at rates lower than those experienced during the last decade. The slackening in the expansion of imports is indicated by the relatively slow increase in the second half of the fifties. At the same time, there is little expectation that abaca would be used in increasing quantities for marine cordage. Still, the combined imports of sisal and abaca may increase by about 35–40 per cent within a decade.

Japan

Japanese imports of hard fibers doubled over the last decade. Much of this increase has taken the form of sisal for use in twine. A slowing down in the rate of growth of imports has been experienced in recent years, however, and it appears questionable whether imports would rise at an annual rate exceeding 3 per cent during the period of projection. As a result of the increased use of synthetic fibers, imports of abaca may actually fall.

Oceania and South Africa

The agricultural uses of hard fibers predominate also in Australia, New Zealand, and South Africa. Imports have been rising steadily over the last decade, and, with the expansion of agricultural production, further increases are expected.

The Price and Origin of Imports

Our projections would entail an increase of approximately 35–40 per cent in the imports of hard fibers by developed countries between 1960 and 1970, and a rise of over 50 per cent between 1960 and 1975. At the same time, substantial changes are foreseen in the geographical composition of these imports. Since trade in abaca is not likely to rise, exports from Asia (chiefly the Philippines) are expected to remain approximately at 1960 levels. But although the area under sisal may not increase in East Africa by reason of the shortage of suitable land, the introduction of higher-yielding varieties would allow for an expansion of African exports of sisal. The largest increases in production and exports are foreseen in Mexico (henequen) and Brazil (sisal), however, where government policies favor the expansion of cultivation.

Hard fiber prices were at a high level in 1960 following a period of intensive buying in 1959. Prices have weakened in 1961 and, given prospective developments in supply and demand, a return to the 1960 level does not appear likely. In making projections, we have calculated with prices 7-8 per cent lower than those prevailing in 1960.

9.5 CRUDE ANIMAL AND VEGETABLE MATERIALS (SITC 29)

CRUDE ANIMAL MATERIALS, N.E.S. (SITC 291)

This category includes a variety of materials of animal origin, such as bones, ivory, horns, hoofs, claws, and similar products, as well as human hair, bristles, guts, bladder, and stomachs of animals, fish waste, waste of raw hides and skins, birds' feathers, and natural sponges. Imports from less developed countries amounted to $46 million in 1960, with Western Europe taking two-thirds and North America nearly one-third. The countries of Southeast Asia accounted for one-half of this trade, the rest being divided between Latin America, Africa, and the Middle East.

The United States imported chiefly fish waste from Peru and Chile, bristles and brush-making hair from India, and birds' feathers from Taiwan. Imports from less developed countries fluctuated around $13 million over the last decade, and given the availability of many of the materials included in this group in North America, no future increases are expected.

Different is the situation in Western Europe. The countries of Western Europe purchased increasing quantities of animal materials from a variety of underdeveloped countries in the last decade. Imports include bones and horns from India, Pakistan, and Argentina, guts, bladder, and stomachs of animals from Iran, Argentina, and Morocco, and corals and shells from the Pacific Islands, with a total value of $30 milion in 1960. Further increases are indicated during the period of projection, and imports from less developed areas may rise by one-half within a decade. Imports into Japan may also increase.

Taken together, imports from developing countries are projected to reach $64-66 million in 1970 and $76-82 million in 1975, as compared to $46 million in 1960. Much of this increase will be shared by India, Pakistan, and Iran. No change in prices has been assumed.

CRUDE VEGETABLE MATERIALS, N.E.S. (SITC 292)

Included in this group are plants, seeds, bulbs, flowers, and parts of plants, kapok and bamboo, as well as natural gums, resins, balsam, and other vegetable extracts. Imports from underdeveloped countries were valued at $135 million in 1960, over half of which went to Western Europe. The largest exporters are India ($25 million), Sudan ($12 million), Morocco ($11 million), and Mexico ($9 million).

U.S. imports of vegetable materials from less developed countries —natural gums and other vegetable extracts from Sudan, India, Mexico, and Argentina, pyrethrum from Central Africa, and opium from India—have been fluctuating around $40–50 million during the last decade, with some slight increases shown in recent years. We have assumed here that imports would rise at about the same rate as population in the period of projection.

The countries of Western Europe imported natural gums, resins, and other vegetable extracts from India, Sudan, and Iran; bamboo and other materials used in baskets and rugs from Madagascar, Hong Kong, and Singapore; kapok from Morocco, and vegetable materials used in brushes and brooms from Mexico. Imports have increased little in the last decade and are assumed to rise at the same rate as population in the future. Similar considerations apply to Japan, Oceania, and South Africa.

REFERENCES

[1.] AUTOMOBILE MANUFACTURERS' ASSOCIATION. *Automobile Facts and Figures.*

[2.] BLACK, J. D., AND BONNEN, J. T. *A Balanced United States Agriculture in 1965.* Washington, D.C. National Planning Association, 1956.

[3.] CANADIAN NATIONAL INDUSTRIAL CONFERENCE BOARD. *The Canadian Primary Textile Industry.* Ottawa, 1956.

[4.] CHOW, G. *Demand for Automobiles in the United States.* Amsterdam: North Holland, 1957.

[5.] DALY, REX F. "The Long-Run Demand for Farm Products," *Agricultural Economic Review* (July, 1956), pp. 73–91.

[6.] DAVIS, JOHN, ET AL. *The Outlook for the Canadian Forest Industries.* Toronto, 1957.

[7.] DEWHURST, J. F., AND ASSOCIATES *Europe's Needs and Resources.* New York: Twentieth Century Fund, 1961.

[8.] EKSTROM. *Textile Consumption.* Stockholm, 1958.

[9.] THE ECONOMIST INTELLIGENCE UNIT. *Rubber Trends.* December, 1962.

[10.] FOOD AND AGRICULTURE ORGANIZATION. *Agricultural Commodities— Projections for 1970.* Rome, 1962.

[11.] FOOD AND AGRICULTURE ORGANIZATION. *Income Elasticity of Demand for Food.* Rome, 1959.

[12.] FOOD AND AGRICULTURE ORGANIZATION. *Per Capita Fiber Consumption Levels, 1948–1958.* Commodity Bulletin Series 31, Rome, 1960.

[13.] FOOD AND AGRICULTURE ORGANIZATION. *Yearbook of Forest Products Statistics,* various issues.

[14.] FOOD AND AGRICULTURE ORGANIZATION. *World Demand for Paper to 1975.* Rome, 1960.

[15.] GENERAL AGREEMENT ON TARIFFS AND TRADE. *International Trade, 1956.* Geneva, 1957.

[16.] GILBERT, MILTON, AND ASSOCIATES. *Comparative National Products and Price Levels.* Paris: OEEC, 1958.

[17.] HUNT, STANLEY. "The Concept of Utility Poundage," *Textile Organon.* March, 1954.

[18.] INTERNATIONAL COTTON ADVISORY COMMITTEE. *Prospective Trends in Consumption of Textile Fibers.* Washington, D.C., 1962.

[19.] INTERNATIONAL COTTON ADVISORY COMMITTEE. *Studies of Factors Affecting the Consumption of Textile Fibers.* Washington, D.C., 1960.

[20.] INTERNATIONAL RUBBER STUDY GROUP. *The Future of Natural and Synthetic Rubbers.* Proceedings of a Symposium organized by the International Rubber Study Group. London, 1962.

[21.] JAPANESE ECONOMIC PLANNING AGENCY. *New Long-Range Economic Plan of Japan (1961–1970).* Tokyo: The Times of Japan, 1961.

[22.] KEYSERLING, LEON. *Food and Freedom.* Washington, D.C. Conference on Economic Progress, 1961.

[23.] LANDSBERG, HANS H., ET AL. *Resources in America's Future.* Published for Resources for the Future, Inc. Baltimore: Johns Hopkins Press, 1963.

[24.] LOWENSTEIN, FRANK, AND SIMON, MARTIN S. "Textile Fiber Consumption in Cotton Equivalent Pounds," *Cotton Situation,* November, 1957.

[25.] ORGANIZATION FOR EUROPEAN ECONOMIC COOPERATION. *The Hides and Skins Industry in Europe, 1959,* Paris, 1961.

[26.] ORGANIZATION FOR EUROPEAN ECONOMIC COOPERATION. *Timber Statistics, 1960.* Paris, 1961.

[27.] "Per Capita Fiber Consumption Levels." *Monthly Bulletin of Agricultural Economics and Statistics* (January, 1962), pp. 1–29.

[28.] "Prospects for the British Car Industry." *National Institute Economic Review,* September, 1961.

[29.] RETTIE, J. C., AND HAIR, DWIGHT. "The Future Demand for Timber," *Timber Resources for America's Future.* Forest Resource Report No. 14. Washington, D.C., 1958.

[30.] ROBSON, R. *The Man-made Fibres Industry.* London: Macmillan, 1958.

[31.] SLATER, D. W. *Consumption Expenditures in Canada.* Ottawa: Royal Commission on Canada's Economic Prospects, 1956.

[32.] STANDARD RESEARCH INSTITUTE. *America's Demand for Wood, 1929–1975.* Tacoma, Washington: Weyershauser Timber Co., 1954.

[33.] *Textile Organon,* November, 1961.

[34.] "Trends in World Demand for Jute Manufactures." *Monthly Bulletin of Agricultural Economics and Statistics* (December, 1960), pp. 1–11, and (January, 1961), pp. 1–10.

[35.] UNITED NATIONS *Statistical Yearbook, 1961.* New York, 1962.

[36.] UNITED NATIONS ECONOMIC COMMISSION FOR ASIA. *Economic Survey for Asia and the Far East, 1959,* Bangkok, 1960.

[37.] UNITED NATIONS ECONOMIC COMMISSION FOR ASIA AND THE FAR EAST, AND FOOD AND AGRICULTURE ORGANIZATION. *Timber Trends and Prospects in the Asia-Pacific Region.* Geneva, 1961.

[38.] UNITED NATIONS ECONOMIC COMMISSION FOR EUROPE, AND FOOD AND AGRICULTURE ORGANIZATION. *European Timber Statistics, 1913-1950.* Geneva, 1953.

[39.] U.S. DEPARTMENT OF AGRICULTURE, FOREST SERVICE AND AGRICULTURAL STABILIZATION AND CONSERVATION SERVICE. *The Demand and Price Situation for Forest Products.* Washington, D.C., 1961.

[40.] U.S. DEPARTMENT OF AGRICULTURE, ECONOMIC RESEARCH SERVICE. *Statistics on Cotton and Related Data.* Statistical Bulletin No. 99, Supplement. October, 1961.

[41.] U.S. DEPARTMENT OF AGRICULTURE, ECONOMIC RESEARCH SERVICE. *Wool Situation.* May, 1961.

[42.] WILSON, D. A. "Demand Prospects for Forest Products," *Resources for Tommorow.* Conference Background Papers, Vol. 2, pp. 627–40.

CHAPTER 10

Trade Projections for
Fuels

10.1 ENERGY CONSUMPTION IN DEVELOPED COUNTRIES

MAJOR ENERGY supplies include coal, crude oil and oil products, natural gas, hydroelectricity, and nuclear power. For purposes of projecting the export earnings of the less developed countries, however, we need to deal only with trade in crude oil, oil products, and natural gas.

While there is substantial trade in coal, practically all of this takes place among developed countries, and the coal exports of developing nations are likely to remain negligible during the period under consideration.[1] Similar conclusions apply to hydroelectricity and nuclear power. Any trade that exists or will develop in these forms of energy is restricted to industrial areas.

On the other hand, crude oil and oil products are the most important sources of foreign exchange for the developing countries. The share of petroleum and petroleum products in the value of exports from less developed areas has been increasing over time and surpassed 25 per cent in the late fifties. The less developed countries provide nearly one-half of world petroleum and supply over nine-tenths of crude oil entering world trade.[2] The refining of petroleum takes place chiefly in the developed countries, however, and in 1960 less than 20 per cent of the petroleum exports of developing countries took the form of products.

Over one-half of petroleum traded originates in the Middle East, with the countries of the Caribbean supplying one-fourth. Most

---

[1] In 1960, France imported coal from Morocco in the value of $1 million, while Japanese imports from Taiwan and Korea amounted to $3 million. With industrial development in Morocco, her exports of coal may cease, while imports into Japan are likely to increase further.

[2] Petroleum production for domestic use in the United States and the Soviet Union largely accounts for the difference between these figures.

Middle Eastern producers (Kuwait, Saudi Arabia, Iraq, and Qatar) rely almost exclusively on the sale of petroleum, and petroleum exports provide nine-tenths of the foreign exchange receipts of Iran and the Middle East taken as a whole. In Latin America, Venezuela is the main producer and exporter of crude petroleum, while the Netherlands Antilles and Trinidad export chiefly petroleum originating in Venezuela in refined form. Petroleum and its products account for about nine-tenths of the export value of these countries and for one-fourth of the export receipts of all of Latin America.

Petroleum exports are of lesser importance in Asia, accounting for 5 per cent of the value of exports. Yet the exportation of crude oil and petroleum products is the main source of foreign exchange for Brunei and Sarawak, and Indonesia also derives one-third of her export earnings from the sale of petroleum. Finally, while in 1960 the share of petroleum in the export receipts of Africa did not exceed 5 per cent, recent finds are expected to make Algeria, Libya, and Nigeria large petroleum exporters in the next decade. Algeria will also export substantial quantities of natural gas.

Although only trade in crude oil, oil products, and natural gas needs to be estimated, the substitutability of the various energy sources necessitates a forecast of energy consumption taken as a whole. While some uses of energy are not interchangeable (e.g., gasoline is generally used to power an automobile, and coal in iron and steelmaking), in many applications coal, oil, gas, and nuclear energy are close substitutes. In the latter instances, a choice among the various sources of energy will be determined by relative prices, the cost of equipment, and convenience in use.

Energy sources are measured in different units—coal in tons, oil in barrels, electricity in kilowatt-hours, and gas in cubic meters. In order to achieve comparability, it is necessary to convert the statistics referring to individual energy sources into some common unit. A widely used method of conversion is to express all energy in terms of metric tons of coal-equivalent. This practice has also been followed in the present study.

In regard to the conversion ratios used, it should be noted that a single coefficient necessarily summarizes various applications of an energy source, and, depending on the application, this ratio can vary greatly. Further, as a result of technological improvements, the calorie equivalent of individual energy sources changes over time. Nevertheless, with one exception, identical conversion ratios are

used in the energy statistics published by international organizations. The exception is that of hydroelectricity.

There are essentially two ways of dealing with the problem of
hydroelectricity. One can calculate either the "true" value of a kilo-
watt-hour at the place of consumption, or its thermal power-station
equivalent. The former procedure has been adopted by the United
Nations, while the latter—which yields results three to five times
larger—is used in the statistical publications of the OECD and the
European Common Market.

For purposes of international comparisons, the conversion ratio
applied should express the calorific value of the energy source at
the place of consumption. This purpose is served by the conversion
ratio employed by the United Nations. On the other hand, the use
of the thermal power-station equivalent would lead to an overestimation of energy consumption in countries such as Norway that
rely heavily on hydroelectricity. Note further that while a common
conversion ratio should be used for every country, the thermal
power-station equivalent of hydroelectricity varies from country to
country and from year to year. For these reasons, we have adopted
the conversion ratios used by the United Nations (Table A10.1.1).
Also, unless otherwise indicated, all data on energy consumption
have been taken from UN sources [19].

Fuels have numerous intermediate and final uses; hence projections on energy consumption can be made in aggregate terms or
by the end-use (sectoral) method. In the former case, energy consumption is related to gross national product or industrial production; in the latter, separate estimates are given for the individual
energy-using sectors. The sectoral method has been employed in the
two OEEC reports on energy [12, 13], in the ECSC study on prospective needs and supplies of energy in the Common Market [4], as
well as in the study on energy consumption in the United States
prepared by Schurr and Netschert [16]. The application of the end-
use method did not appear practicable in the present study, however, although in making projections we have utilized available information on prospective developments in the main energy-con-
suming sectors, as well as the results of detailed investigations by the
OEEC and the European Coal and Steel Community.

Considering that energy is used at all stages of economic activity,
we have related total energy consumption to gross national product
for the individual countries (Table A10.1.2 shows the results of the
regression analysis for the period 1950–1960). Subsequently, a com-

parison has been made between energy consumption per head and per capita GNP in the industrial countries (see Figure 10.1.1).[3] The results of these comparisons, as well as information on prospective technological changes and sectoral trends, and the estimates

FIGURE 10.1.1

PER CAPITA ENERGY CONSUMPTION AND GROSS NATIONAL PRODUCT IN
INDUSTRIAL COUNTRIES, 1960

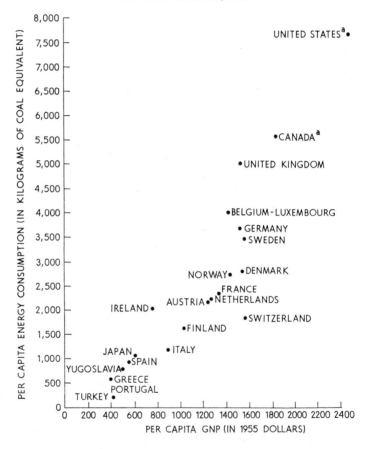

SOURCE: Table 2.6.1, United Nations *World Energy Supplies, 1957–1960*.
NOTE: 1957 data used for the United States and Canada, because in these countries
1960 was a recession year.

---

[a]Cross-section analysis was used earlier by Mason and by Robinson and Daniel [*11, 15*]. Particularly relevant is the latter attempt where the relationship between changes in manufacturing output and changes in energy consumption has been investigated in the major industrial countries.

of other researchers, have been utilized in adjusting these coefficients for purposes of projection.

North America

In the period 1950–1960, a 1 per cent rise in the United States gross national product was associated with a 0.84 per cent increase in energy consumption. Changes in the composition of output, as well as improvements in the efficiency of electricity generation, have contributed to a more or less steady decline in energy use per unit of GNP since World War I, however [16]. Further improvements in efficiency are expected, and the shift toward services will also contribute to a reduction of energy requirements in relation to output. Correspondingly, we have assumed that during the period of projection a 1 per cent rise in GNP would be accompanied by a 0.75 per cent increase in energy consumption, i.e., the total income elasticity of demand for energy has been taken as 0.75.[4] Energy consumption would thus rise from 1.45 billion tons of coal-equivalent in 1960 to 1.93–1.97 billion tons in 1970 and 2.20–2.27 million tons in 1975, depending on the income assumption used. In per capita terms, the relevant figures are 8.0 tons for 1960, 9.0–9.2 tons for 1970, and 9.3–9.6 tons for 1975.

In Canada, the rate of growth of energy consumption was identical to the rate of growth of GNP in the period 1950–1960. For reasons similar to those mentioned in connection with the United States, a downward adjustment in the income elasticity has been made. Still, Canadian energy consumption would increase by about one-half between 1960 and 1970 and 70–80 per cent between 1960 and 1975. At the same time, differences in U.S. and Canadian per capita energy consumption would be reduced.

Western Europe

Energy consumption in Western Europe is substantially below the U.S. level. In 1960, the per capita consumption of energy was 2.4 tons in Europe as compared to 8.0 tons in the United States. The highest consumption levels are shown in the United Kingdom (5.0 tons), followed by Belgium (4.0), Germany (3.7), and Sweden (3.5), while energy consumption per head has not reached 1 ton in any of the countries of the southern group.

---

[4]By comparison, an elasticity of 0.8 is implicit in the projections of Schurr and Netschert for the period 1955–1975 [16], and an elasticity of 0.73 for the years 1960–1970 in a later Resources for the Future Study [9, p. 292.]

Despite the observed differences in energy consumption per head, the income elasticity of demand for energy in Belgium, France, Germany, and the United Kingdom appears to have been lower than in the United States during the fifties (Table 10.1.2). These differences can be largely explained by consideration given to technological trends and the substitution of oil for coal. In the period 1950–1960, the more developed European countries adopted improvements in the field of electricity generation that had been introduced in the United States in earlier periods, reducing thereby the need for primary energy. More importantly, the share of liquid fuels nearly trebled in the Common Market and the United Kingdom between 1950 and 1960, as against a rise by one-fifth in the United States; and the higher efficiency attained in the utilization of liquid fuels has further reduced primary energy requirements per unit of output.[5]

These influences will continue to act in the future, although at a reduced rate. On the one hand, the share of liquid fuels in energy consumption, having reached 25–30 per cent in 1960, cannot continue to increase at rates experienced in the last decade; on the other hand, it is questionable whether past rates of improvements in the utilization of energy sources in specific uses can be maintained. Thus, although the increased use of secondary energy (electricity, gas) and the shift toward services will tend to reduce energy consumption per unit of output, in the major industrial countries of Western Europe the increase in energy consumption associated with a 1 per cent rise of GNP may be larger during the period of projection than in the fifties.

A comparison of the structure of energy consumption in Western Europe and the United States appears to strengthen these conclusions. As Table 10.1.1 indicates the U.S. per capita consumption of energy in final uses is at least twice that of the European OECD countries, and the largest differences are shown in "other transportation" (chiefly automobile) and in household uses. Given the projected rise in the stock of automobiles in Western Europe (Chapter 9.2) and expected increases in the use of domestic appliances at higher income levels, energy consumption in these applications is likely to expand at a rapid rate, although the overcrowding of

---

[5]These comments indicate that the conversion ratios used by international organizations in regard to liquid fuels may be on the low side. In fact, in some uses, this ratio appears to be 3 or 4 rather than 1.3–1.5, and the U.K. Ministry of Power has adopted a coefficient of 1.7.

roads may have a restrictive influence on the growth of the consumption of gasoline.

On the basis of these considerations, the elasticity coefficients derived from the data of the 1950–1960 period have been adjusted upward in the case of Belgium, France, Germany, and the United Kingdom. On the other hand, the high rate of increase of energy consumption in Italy and the Netherlands experienced during the fifties is not likely to continue.[6]

Our projections for the Common Market countries indicate an increase in energy consumption from 441 million tons of coal-equivalent to 630–657 and 750–800 million tons in 1970 and in 1975, depending on the income assumption chosen. The higher variant of

TABLE 10.1.1

FINAL ENERGY DEMAND BY END-USE SECTORS[a]

	United States, 1955			European OECD Countries (excluding Spain) 1960		
	Total	Per Capita	Per cent	Total	Per Capita	Per cent
Industry						
Steel	116.3	0.70	10.9	81.9	0.27	13.8
Other	205.9	1.25	19.2	171.2	0.57	28.9
Transportation						
Rail	36.6	0.22	3.4	32.9	0.11	5.5
Other	239.0	1.45	22.3	69.9	0.23	11.8
Domestic	472.2	2.86	44.1	237.2	0.79	40.0
All Sectors	1070.0	6.48	100.0	593.2	1.97	100.0

Source: Special communication from the OECD.
Note: [a]Energy consumption in million tons, per capita consumption in tons of coal equivalent.

the estimates is in conformity with the projections prepared by the European Coal and Steel Community in collaboration with the European Economic Community and Euratom. The projection of the European countries assumes a rate of growth of GNP approximately equal to our target estimate, and foresees energy consumption to rise to 662 million tons by 1970 and 803 million tons by 1975 [6, pp. 161–162].[7]

---

[6]The elasticities used in the projections are the following: United States, 0.75; Canada, 0.85; Belgium-Luxembourg, 0.7; France, 0.9; Germany, 0.75; Italy, 1.3; Netherlands, 0.9; United Kingdom, 0.65; Austria, 1.0; Denmark, 1.0; Finland, 1.3; Ireland, 1.1; Norway, 1.2; Sweden, 1.2; Switzerland, 1.2; Greece, 1.4; Portugal, 1.4; Spain, 1.4; Turkey, 1.4; Yugoslavia, 1.3; Japan, 1.1; Australia, 1.3; New Zealand, 1.3; South Africa, 1.3.

[7]For purposes of comparison, the ECSC projections of hydroelectricity have been adjusted for differences in the conversion ratios used.

Despite the relatively slow increase experienced in the last decade, the per capita consumption of energy in the United Kingdom is by far the highest in Western Europe. Correspondingly, future increases will be modest, although the 0.65 income elasticity used in the projections is still higher than that derived for the years 1950–1960 (0.43). By comparison, an elasticity of 0.7 has been assumed by the U.K. National Economic Development Council for the period 1961–1966 [*17*, p. 67].

With the exception of Ireland, a 1 per cent increase in gross national product was accompanied by an over 1 per cent rise in energy consumption in the countries of northern Europe during the fifties. In making projections, some downward adjustments in the coefficients have been made to give expression to expected shifts from solid to liquid fuels and changes in the industrial structure of these economies.

Finally, forecasting is especially difficult in regard to Southern Europe, because rapid structural changes can profoundly affect the pattern of energy consumption in the countries of this area. In making projections, we have calculated with an income elasticity of demand for energy of 1.4 in these countries, with the exception of Yugoslavia, where relatively high consumption levels suggest a lower rate of increase in the future.

For Western Europe as a whole, our projections indicate an increase of energy consumption from 842 million tons of coal equivalent to 1176 million tons by 1970 and 1389 million tons in 1975 under the most likely income assumption, and to 1236 and 1502 million tons if the target rate of income growth is reached. At the same time, per capita energy consumption would rise from 238 tons to 305–321 and 345–373 tons in the two years, respectively.

In regard to the European OECD countries, a comparison can be made with the estimate given in the Robinson report. According to the medium projection of the report, during the period 1955–1975 the gross national product of the former OEEC countries[8] would rise at an annual rate of 3.2 per cent and energy consumption at a rate of 2.75 per cent, corresponding to an implicit income elasticity of 0.85 [*13* pp. 25–31]. A more rapid increase of the gross national product (3.7 per cent a year) and a somewhat lower elasticity has been envisaged in the present study, and we have projected energy consumption in the former OEEC countries to rise at an annual rate of 3.0 per cent.

---

[8]The European member countries of the OECD except Spain.

Japan

In Japan, energy consumption increased at a rate slightly lower than the rate of growth of GNP during the fifties. But per capita energy consumption barely exceeded 1 ton in 1960, and, with rising incomes, a rapid increase of fuel consumption in household uses and passenger automobiles is expected. Taking account also of the shift to liquid fuels, which will tend to reduce this coefficient, we have calculated with an elasticity of 1.1 for the period 1960–1975. By comparison, energy consumption has been assumed to expand at the same rate as GNP in the Japanese Ten-Year Plan, but the latter still arrives at a higher consumption estimate, since it calculates with a rate of growth of 7.8 per cent as compared to our target estimate of 6.4 per cent [*8*, pp. 11, 90].

Oceania and South Africa

Energy consumption has been rising rapidly in Australia, New Zealand, and South Africa, and, with the development of manufacturing industries, further increases are expected. In making projections, we have assumed that a 1 per cent rise in the gross national product would be accompanied by a 1.3 per cent increase in the energy consumption of these countries.

10.2 ENERGY BALANCE SHEETS

North America

In regard to the United States, we have assumed that the share of the main energy sources would be stabilized at approximately 1960 levels (Table 10.2.1). A similar view has been expressed by Schurr and Netschert, whose conclusions also form the basis of the Report of the U.S. Senate Interior Committee's National Fuels and Energy Study Group [*16, 20*]. This result follows from the increasing importance of electricity—an area where coal is competitive with oil and gas—in U.S. energy markets, productivity improvements in coal mining, and developments in the transportation of coal.

Improvements in coal mining are related to the introduction of strip or open-cast mining, which contributed to a doubling of output per man between 1952 and 1961. In the field of coal transportation, the use of the so-called integral train should be mentioned, while prospective developments include the transportation of coal in liquified form. As a result of these improvements, the delivered price of coal fell, and reductions in transportation costs may lead to a further decline in prices.

TABLE 10.2.1

ENERGY CONSUMPTION IN DEVELOPED COUNTRIES
(million tons of coal equivalent)

	1950		1955		1960		1970I		1970II		1975I		1975II	
	Million Tons	Per-cent	Million Tons	Per-cent	Million Tons	Per-cent	Million Tons	Per-cent	Million Tons	Per-cent	Million Tons	Per-cent	Million Tons	Per-cent
United States														
Solid Fuels	451	41	404	32	357	25	450	23	458	23	490	22	505	22
Liquid Fuels	382	35	515	40	590	41	780	41	796	41	895	40	925	40
Natural Gas	248	23	351	27	482	33	650	33	662	33	725	33	740	33
Hydroelectricity	12	1	15	1	19	1	28	2	29	2	36	2	39	2
Atomic Power	-	-	-	-	-	-	19	1	20	1	55	3	58	3
Total Energy	1093	100	1285	100	1448	100	1927	100	1965	100	2201	100	2267	100
Canada														
Solid Fuels	37	55	29	35	20	20	25	17	26	17	28	16	29	16
Liquid Fuels	21	32	39	47	53	52	74	51	76	51	88	51	92	51
Natural Gas	3	4	6	7	16	16	31	21	32	21	38	22	40	22
Hydroelectricity	7	9	9	11	12	12	15	10	15	10	16	9	16	9
Atomic Power	-	-	-	-	-	-	2	1	2	1	4	2	4	2
Total Energy	68	100	83	100	101	100	147	100	151	100	174	100	181	100
European Common Market														
Solid Fuels	233	86	294	79	285	65	255	41	260	40	240	32	250	31
Liquid Fuels	29	11	61	17	129	29	307	48	324	49	404	54	436	55
Natural Gas	1	1	6	2	14	3	46	7	48	7	71	10	75	9
Hydroelectricity	6	2	8	2	13	3	16	3	17	3	18	2	19	2
Atomic Power	-	-	-	-	-	-	6	1	8	1	17	2	20	3
Total Energy	269	100	369	100	441	100	630	100	657	100	750	100	800	100
United Kingdom														
Solid Fuels	202	91	220	86	197	76	185	59	188	58	180	52	184	50
Liquid Fuels	21	9	35	14	61	24	112	35	116	36	139	40	150	41
Natural Gas	-	-	0	-	0	0	3	1	4	1	5	2	6	2
Hydroelectricity	0	0	0	-	0	0	-	-	-	-	-	-	-	-
Atomic Power	-	-	-	-	-	-	16	5	18	5	21	6	24	7
Total Energy	223	100	255	100	258	100	316	100	326	100	345	100	364	100

Northern Europe														
Solid Fuels	31	61	30	44	28	32	19	15	20	15	18	12	19	12
Liquid Fuels	13	26	29	42	46	52	83	67	88	67	99	68	108	69
Natural Gas	0	0	1	1	2	2	3	3	3	3	5	4	5	3
Hydroelectricity	7	13	9	13	12	14	19	15	20	15	23	16	25	16
Atomic Power	-	-	-	-	-	-	-	-	-	-	-	-	-	-
Total Energy	51	100	69	100	88	100	124	100	131	100	145	100	157	100
Southern Europe														
Solid Fuels	21	77	28	73	36	64	52	49	55	45	57	39	60	33
Liquid Fuels	6	20	9	22	17	30	43	40	54	45	75	51	102	57
Natural Gas	0	-	0	0	0	0	4	4	4	3	5	3	6	3
Hydroelectricity	1	3	2	5	3	6	7	7	8	7	11	7	13	7
Atomic Power	-	-	-	-	-	-	-	-	-	-	-	-	-	-
Total Energy	28	100	39	100	56	100	106	100	121	100	148	100	181	100
Japan														
Solid Fuels	39	84	46	70	62	57	77	39	80	37	85	33	90	31
Liquid Fuels	2	6	14	21	38	35	103	53	120	56	150	59	187	63
Natural Gas	0	0	0	0	1	1	3	2	3	1	4	2	3	1
Hydroelectricity	5	10	6	9	7	7	11	6	12	6	14	6	16	5
Atomic Power	-	-	-	-	-	-	-	-	-	-	-	-	-	-
Total Energy	46	100	66	100	108	100	194	100	215	100	253	100	296	100
Oceania and South Africa														
Solid Fuels	44	81	56	76	65	74	96	67	103	66	117	63	129	61
Liquid Fuels	10	18	17	23	21	24	42	29	47	30	60	33	73	35
Natural Gas	-	-	0	-	0	-	1	1	1	1	1	1	1	1
Hydroelectricity	0	1	1	1	1	2	4	3	4	3	6	3	7	3
Atomic Energy	-	-	-	-	-	-	-	-	-	-	-	-	-	-
Total Energy	54	100	74	100	87	100	143	100	155	100	184	100	210	100

Source: United Nations, World Energy Supplies, 1958–1961.

Compared to some earlier estimates, our projections indicate a smaller share for atomic power in total energy consumption. It appears that, despite some promising developments, the production of nuclear energy has not yet scored the necessary technological breakthrough to make it competitive with other fuels, whereas the decline in the price of traditional fuels has improved the competitive position of the latter.

In Canada, too, the share of solid and liquid fuels is expected to remain approximately unchanged during the period of projection, while the consumption of natural gas is likely to gain ground, mainly at the expense of hydroelectricity. In spite of the existence of substantial reserves, the potential for natural gas consumption is not yet fully utilized in Canada, and the share of natural gas in energy consumption is only one-half that in the United States.

Western Europe

The relative contribution of the individual fuels to Common Market energy consumption will greatly depend on the energy policy followed by the EEC. Present policies differ to a considerable extent among the participating countries, and future changes are subject to uncertainty, especially in view of the Council of Ministers' refusal to accept the proposal presented by the Common Market Commission. Our projections are based on the reported objective of the EEC to insure low cost energy from secure sources of supply [3, 7].

This objective would entail a reduction in the production of coal in the Common Market. Given the high—and rising—wage costs and the difficulties encountered in the mechanization of several of the coal mines of the EEC, coal production could be hardly maintained above a level of 100–120 million tons without the payment of subsidies. The projections of the European Coal and Steel Community, prepared jointly with the EEC and Euratom, indicate a range of possible outcomes depending on the assumptions made in regard to subsidies. According to the report of the three Communities, the production of coal in the Common Market area would be between 125 and 225 million tons in 1970 and between 125 and 200 million tons in 1975, to which about 30 million tons of lignite (expressed in terms of coal-equivalent) should be added.

In view of our expectations for a fall in fuel oil prices as compared to their 1960 level,[9] we have assumed that coal output would

[9]See pp. 286–87.

be in the lower range of the ECSC estimates, amounting to about 150 million tons in 1970, with some further lowering between 1970 and 1975. At the same time, 70–80 million tons of coal may be imported, chiefly from the United States. With consideration given to the domestic production of 30 million tons of lignite, the share of coal in the energy consumption of the Common Market would fall from 65 per cent in 1960 to 41 per cent in 1970 and 32 per cent in 1975, as compared to 25 per cent in the United States in 1960.

Petroleum will account for much of the increase in Common Market energy consumption, but in relative terms the rise in the consumption of natural gas may be even larger. On the one hand, in view of the recent discoveries of natural gas in the Netherlands and continuing increases in German output, the production of natural gas in the EEC may reach 24–25 million cubic meters in 1970 and one-third higher in 1975; on the other hand, increasing purchases from Algeria may lead to imports of 10–12 million cubic meters in 1970 and double this quantity in 1975. In projecting the imports of natural gas, we have assumed that a pipeline will be available to carry natural gas across the Mediterranean by 1970.

A comparison of our estimates with those of the three European Communities is given in Table 10.2.2. The largest differences between the two projections pertain to coal and nuclear energy. The report of the three Communities envisages a somewhat smaller decline in Common Market coal production, a greater increase in coal imports, and a more pronounced rise in the production of atomic energy after 1970. Correspondingly, estimates for oil and natural gas are slightly below those of the present study. Differences shown in regard to coal depend on the assumptions made about policies and prices, while the three Communities appear to be more optimistic in regard to the prospects of nuclear energy for the near future. By comparison, an earlier ECSC projection [5] envisaged oil consumption to surpass our higher estimate in 1975, while a considerably smaller share for oil was assumed by Paretti and Bloch [14].

In Western Europe, the United Kingdom is the only country which is expected to continue to rely on coal as its major energy source. British mines are more amenable to mechanization than their continental counterparts, and the heavy tax on fuel oil, as well as prohibitive restrictions on American coal and preferential treatment given to coal by nationalized undertakings in transportation and the utility field, have bolstered the share of domestically produced coal in British energy consumption (76 per cent in 1960). Nevertheless, liquid fuels have assumed increasing importance in

TABLE 10.2.2

ALTERNATIVE PROJECTIONS OF ENERGY CONSUMPTION IN THE EUROPEAN COMMON MARKET
(million metric tons of coal equivalent)

	Solid Fuels	Liquid Fuels	Natural Gas	Hydroelectricity	Atomic Power	Total Energy
1970						
European Communities	267-287	330-306	41-45	16	8	662
Percent	40-43	50-46	6-7	3	1	
Our Estimate	255-260	307-324	46-48	16-17	6-8	630-657
Percent	40-41	48-49	7	3	1	
1975						
European Communities	259-274	438-389	64-82	18	24-40	803
Percent	32-34	55-49	8-10	2	3-5	
Our Estimate	240-250	404-436	71-75	18-19	17-20	750-800
Percent	32-31	54-55	9	2	2-3	

Source: European Coal and Steel Community in collaboration with the Commission of the European Economic Community and Euratom, Etude sur les perspectives énergetiques à long terme de la Communauté Européene, Luxemburg, 1962, pp. 160-61, and Table 11.2.1.

Note: In order to facilitate comparison, the ECSC estimates for hydroelectricity have been recalculated by the use of the U.N. conversion ratios.

British consumption, and given the expected fall in fuel-oil prices and recent declines in British coal output (production fell below 195 million tons in 1961), it appears questionable whether the output target of the coal industry set for 200 million tons in 1966 [*17*, p. 70] would in fact be attained.

In the present study, we have assumed that coal production would decline below 190 million tons by 1970 and have calculated with zero net trade. Thus, much of the increase in British energy consumption would be supplied by petroleum, although imports of natural gas and the production of nuclear energy are also expected to rise. In fact, Britain is ahead of the Continental countries in the development of nuclear–energy generating capacity.

In drawing up energy balance sheets for Northern and Southern Europe, particular attention has been paid to hydroelectricity. In several of these countries (e.g., Norway, Yugoslavia), plans have been made for increasing energy output derived from hydroelectric installations. The share of oil and natural gas in energy consumption will also rise, while the consumption of coal is expected to decline in relative, although not in absolute, terms.

Japan

In Japan future developments are likely to conform to the pattern projected for Western Europe. In estimating the share of individual fuels in total energy consumption, we have relied on the forecasts contained in the Ten-Year Plan of Japan. A downward adjustment has been made in regard to coal, however, to take account of the relatively poor quality of Japanese coal and the abandonment of the "coal before oil" policy in 1962. In fact, the entire increase in coal consumption is likely to take the form of larger imports chiefly from the United States and Australia. Finally, the contribution of the various energy sources to consumption in 1975 has been derived by extrapolating the trend in shares projected for the period 1960–1970.

Oceania and South Africa

The projections for Australia and New Zealand reflect the expectations for the increased production of hydroelectricity. In Australia, much of the increase will come from the Snowy Mountain project, while in New Zealand geothermal energy (included with hydroelectricity) will assume importance. Moreover, by the mid-sixties, natural gas will become available from the recently discovered

Kapuni field in New Zealand, while the exploitation of petroleum will begin in Australia.

10.3 IMPORTS OF CRUDE OIL AND PETROLEUM PRODUCTS

The course of future trade policies will affect the imports of crude oil and petroleum products especially in the United States where imports provide a relatively small proportion of domestic consumption. Until 1963, U.S. imports of crude oil and petroleum products, excepting fuel oils, were limited to 9 per cent of consumption in the area east of the Rocky Mountains, and quotas applied also to imports into the West Coast area. These limitations did not pertain to oil originating in Canada and Mexico, however. As of January 1, 1963, the quota has been set at 12.2 per cent of the domestic output of crude oil and petroleum products other than fuel oil in the region east of the Rockies—this time without exception given to Mexican and Canadian oil. No change has taken place in the determination of quotas on imports into the West Coast area.

The size of future quotas will depend on government policy, the rate of growth of demand, and the pace of domestic oil exploration. Available information indicates that the latter factors are likely to lead to an increase in the share of imports in domestic consumption during the period of projection. We have assumed here that imports of crude oil would account for 15 per cent of consumption in 1970 and 17.5 per cent in 1975, while petroleum product imports would rise *pari passu* with the growth of oil consumption.

Canada will continue to import petroleum and petroleum products from Venezuela and the Middle East and export crude oil to the United States. At the same time, indigenous production is expected to increase by about 50 per cent between 1960 and 1970, and a further 20 per cent between 1970 and 1975. Correspondingly, for North America as a whole, the degree of self-sufficiency in oil would show a moderate decline throughout the period under consideration.

In order to determine the gross imports of petroleum into North America, exports of petroleum products also need to be estimated. Various influences will be operative here. On the one hand, given the high price of petroleum products in the United States, foreign countries are likely to take smaller quantities in the future; on the other hand, as trade in petroleum rises, more will be sold for ships. We have assumed that the latter influence will predominate, and hence exports of petroleum products will increase somewhat. The gross imports of petroleum and petroleum products into North

America, expressed in terms of coal-equivalent, would then rise from 151 million tons in 1960 to about 210 million tons in 1970 and 260 million tons in 1975. Within the rising imports, an increase in the share of crude petroleum is foreseen (Table A10.3.1).

Domestic production provides less than 10 per cent of oil consumed in Western Europe, and, despite the projected fivefold increase of domestic output in Yugoslavia and the assumed doubling of production in the European OECD countries during the sixties, the degree of self-sufficiency will not surpass 10 per cent in the period under consideration. At the same time, exports of petroleum products (chiefly for ships) can be expected to rise approximately at the same rate as domestic consumption, so that the gross imports of petroleum and petroleum products would reach 542 million tons of coal-equivalent in 1970 and 718 million tons in 1975 under the most likely income assumption, as compared to 264 million tons in 1960. The corresponding figures are 580 and 799 million tons under the higher income variant.

Within the increased oil imports, we expect the share of crude petroleum to rise from 82 per cent in 1960 to about 87 per cent by 1970 and to a slightly higher level in 1975. The projected change in the composition of imports represents a continuation of past trends, and it is largely explained by economic incentives that favor market-oriented refineries.

Finally, possibilities for the expansion of domestic oil production are limited in Japan, Australia, New Zealand, and South Africa, and hence increased imports will provide much of the increase in oil consumption here. Taking account of the rise of exports of petroleum products (for ships), gross imports into these countries may more than double within a decade. At the same time, the construction of new refineries will contribute to an increase of the share of crude petroleum in the rising imports.

Turning to the geographical composition of imports, we note that the supply pattern of oil is influenced by various economic and noneconomic considerations. These are: the competitive position of the oil-producing areas, the attitude of the governments of oil-producing countries toward exploration and extraction, the size of reserves, transportation costs, ownership relations, preferential tradingagreements, the diversification of supplies, and the quest for "safe suppliers" on the part of the importing countries. The latter argument is of special importance in regard to the importation of oil from the Soviet Union.

The last decade has seen a substantial expansion in the output and exports of Soviet oil. Output increased fourfold during the fifties, approaching one-half of U.S. production in 1961. At the same time, exports to Western Europe rose sevenfold. Further increases are planned for the sixties, and the expansion of Soviet oil exports into Western Europe is likely to be limited mainly by the reluctance of European governments to increase their reliance on Soviet oil. Although the energy policy of the Euorpean Economic Community has not yet been decided upon, and there are uncertainties regarding the policies to be followed by other governments, it may be realistic to assume that the share of crude oil and oil products purchased from Soviet bloc countries will not surpass 9–10 per cent of Western European imports, as against 7 per cent in 1960. A more rapid rise in oil consumption and imports is indicated under the higher income variant, however. Soviet oil exports to Japan may also increase to a considerable extent, while we have assumed that the countries of North America and Oceania will not import Soviet oil (Tables A10.3.2 and A10.3.3).

Allowing for the imports of Soviet oil, our next question concerns the imports originating in less developed regions. The relative shares of the various oil-producing countries will be determined by the economic and noneconomic factors referred to above. Although relative costs are of primary importance, traditional ties, ownership relations, political considerations, and other noneconomic factors considerably influence the outcome.

Production costs are the lowest in the Middle East and Libya, and higher in Venezuela, Indonesia, and Algeria. Cost considerations are likely to induce an increase in the share of the Middle East in the crude oil imports of North America, while Latin-American producers will enjoy almost the entire gain in the imports of petroleum products into this area.

On the other hand, despite the cost disadvantages of Algerian oil, political considerations and the endeavor to diversify the sources of supply are expected to contribute to a substantial expansion of oil exploration in Algeria. Algerian oil will be shipped almost exclusively to Europe, much of it to France. In the countries of Western Europe, petroleum imports from Libya and Nigeria will also assume importance, while Venezuelan producers may continue to account for one-tenth of Europe's crude oil imports. Much of the increase in European imports of petroleum products will also be supplied by Latin-American producers, notably the Netherlands Antilles. No imports from Asia have been projected.

The described pattern of trade does not take account of the fact that, as a result of the substitution of fuel oil for coal, a deficit in fuel oil and a surplus in light products may develop in Western Europe, while the opposite situation may prevail in North America. These imbalances promise an intensified exchange of petroleum products between the two areas. However, it is difficult to foresee the magnitudes involved, and since this trade would hardly affect the total exports of the various developing regions, it has not been taken into account in setting up the trade matrices.

Finally, the settling of the dispute between the Indonesian government and the oil companies will contribute to an increase in the share of Indonesian oil in the imports of Japan, Australia, and New Zealand, although, in absolute terms, Middle Eastern suppliers would still derive much of the gain from the rise of imports into these countries. The Middle East will also provide the increase in South African imports.

10.4 THE VALUE OF OIL IMPORTS

In estimating the export earnings developing countries derive from the sale of primary products, we have calculated with the f.o.b. value of exports. This procedure raises few problems with respect to most commodities. The situation is different in the case of petroleum, however, since the oil companies retain an amount often exceeding one-third of the f.o.b. price, and the actual exchange earnings of the host governments include only their share in oil profits and the disbursements of the oil companies related to their operations in the country in question.

Two procedures may be followed in regard to petroleum. We may include in the estimates of export earnings only that portion of the f.o.b. price which actually accrues to the countries where production takes place, or, alternatively, we may value exports at f.o.b. prices and consider the profit share of the oil companies as a service item in the balance of payments. Although the first procedure has the advantage of indicating the magnitude of actual earnings derived from petroleum exports, we have chosen to apply the second method in order to agree with international compilations of statistics and to assure a uniform treatment for all commodities. Therefore, prospective changes in f.o.b. prices are discussed in the present chapter, while the problem of royalties receives separate treatment.

The f.o.b. price of crude oil and petroleum products entering the free market (i.e., excluding shipments within integrated companies that are valued at the so-called posted price, which has been unchanged in recent years), has been declining since 1958. On the basis of the fragmentary information available, we may assume that in 1962 crude oil sold at prices 8–12 per cent lower than the price prevailing in 1960, while the fall in prices might have been somewhat greater in the case of fuel oil.

Opinions greatly differ as to the prospects of future price changes. One group of experts—of which Walter Levy is an eminent representative—argues that prices will have to rise again, since producer governments claim a larger share in profits, and costs of discovery and development are also on the increase [10]. On the other hand, Morris Adelman is of the opinion that the royalty paid by the oil companies is not an element of cost but represents a sharing of profits, and hence a raising of royalties would not affect prices. Adelman also suggests that the prospective oversupply of petroleum is bound to exert a downward pressure on prices.

One may object to Adelman's treatment of royalties on the basis that, under the present method of accounting, the royalty ceases to be a predetermined percentage of actual profits and, being calculated on the basis of posted prices, it becomes a cost item which varies with output. Given the trend toward concession agreements based on actual profits, this consideration is likely to lose its force in the future, however. At the same time, the marginal cost curve of oil production appears to be rather flat, and the possibilities of expansion are considerable at existing price and cost levels. Putting it differently, the main problem facing the oil producers today is that present prices and costs give incentive to expansion to an extent incompatible with the demand for oil. This circumstance has led to a fall in prices in recent years, and it continues to put pressure on prices.

In the absence of a system of international pro-rationing, prices may fall further and Adelman suggested that, in some distant future, an f.o.b. price of $7–$7.50 per ton for crude oil (as compared to Middle East posted prices of around $12.50) is not unthinkable [1]. It appears likely, however, that a price decline approaching this magnitude would lead to international agreements, and we have assumed here that the risk of further price cutting would induce producers to stabilize prices at a level not much below the present free-market price. It is difficult to rationalize an exact percentage, and it represents a measure of arbitrariness rather than a firm judgment that we have calculated with a 15 per cent decline from 1960 levels under the most likely income assumption, and 12 per cent for the case that the attainment of a higher growth rate in developed countries leads to larger consumption and imports of petroleum.

Additional difficulties arise in projecting the future prices of petroleum products. To begin with, the unit values calculated in trade statistics necessarily represent a weighted average of the lower prices of fuel oil and the higher prices of light products. Corresponingly, large differences are observed in unit values according to origin and destination. The imports of Australia and New Zealand, for example, that consist chiefly of gasoline, have a unit value about twice as high as imports of petroleum products into the United States. Future changes in the composition of imports will then lead to changes in unit values.

In the present study, it has been assumed that the composition of U.S. and Japanese imports of petroleum products will remain approximately unchanged, while the share of fuel oil in the imports of Western Europe, Oceania, and South Africa will rise. In view of this assumption, we have reduced the 1960 unit value of the imports of petroleum products by one-tenth in estimating the value of future imports into the latter areas.

As to changes in the prices of the individual petroleum products, the increased demand for fuel oil in Western Europe could lead to some firming of prices as compared to the level reached in 1962, while the expected oversupply in gasoline and other light derivatives might exert a downward pressure on the prices of the latter. Considering the relationship between the price of crude and that of the "mix" of products, we have assumed that, compared to 1960, the change in average product prices would approximately parallel projected changes in regard to crude oil.

These prices have been used in calculating the value of crude oil and oil products traded, irrespective of whether petroleum moves within integrated companies or in nonsheltered channels. This solution has been chosen, since the prices prevailing in the free market can be said to represent the "true" price of petroleum, while the price of crude oil moving within integrated companies is essentially an accounting matter. Accordingly, we have projected the value of crude petroleum imported by developed countries from underdeveloped areas to rise from $3.77 billion in 1960 to $6.48 billion by 1970 and $8.71 billion by 1975 under the most likely income assumption, and to $7.03 and $9.99 billion if the target rate of income growth is reached. The revelant figures for petroleum products are $1.30 billion in 1960, $1.59–1.74 billion in 1970, and $1.95–2.18 billion in 1975 (Table A10).

10.5 NATURAL GAS

Estimates on the consumption of natural gas in the developed countries, expressed in coal-equivalent, are shown in Table 10.2.1. In a number of developed countries, gas requirements are fully met by domestic supplies; others import part of their requirements, and several rely entirely on imports. But in 1960 only the United States imported natural gas from a developing country (Mexico).

Mexican natural gas is directed toward the southwestern United States and was valued at $6.7 million in 1960. However, Mexico also imported comparable amounts from the United States. We have assumed that the proportion of Mexican exports in U.S. consumption would be maintained throughout the period of projection.

Among other developed regions, Oceania is likely to remain self-sufficient during the period under consideration, but the countries of Western Europe and Japan will increasingly rely on imported gas. Although the Netherlands will emerge as a large producer of natural gas, and production in Germany, Austria, and Yugoslavia will also rise, the Common Market countries, the United Kingdom, and Spain are scheduled to import natural gas from Algeria. At the same time, the limited possibilities of expanding the production of natural gas in Japan will necessitate imports from the Middle East.

We have projected the production of natural gas in Western Europe to reach 27–28 million cubic meters in 1970 and 35–37 million cubic meters in 1975, as compared to 12 million cubic meters in 1960. Correspondingly, imports would amount to about 15 million cubic meters (20 million tons of coal-equivalent) in 1970 and approximately double this quantity in 1975. At the same time, Japanese imports originating in the Middle East may reach one million cubic meters by the early seventies. Imports would be somewhat higher if the target rate of income growth were reached.

Cost and price data on natural gas are few and far between. Under a 15-year contract the British Gas Council envisages purchasing natural gas at about 7.5 pence per therm [2]. If we assume that about two-thirds of this amount will be taken up by the cost of transporting natural gas in liquified form in refrigerated tankers, the f.o.b. price would be 2.5 pence per therm (about $9.00 per metric ton of coal-equivalent). According to the report of the European Communities, the price of natural gas for destinations on the Mediterranean coast of Western Europe would be about $14 per metric ton of coal-equivalent [6, p. 100]. About 60 per cent of this amount may be accounted for by the price at the place of production and the imputed transportation cost to the Algerian ports. With these figures in mind, we calculated with a price of $8.50 per metric ton of coal-equivalent and projected imports into Western Europe to amount to $170 million in 1970 and $337 million in 1970 under the most likely income assumption, and somewhat higher if the target rate of income growth is reached. The value of imports into Japan would not reach $20 million, however.

REFERENCES

[1.] ADELMAN, M. A. "Les prix pétroliers, 1963–1975," Revue de *l'Institut Francais du Pétrole* (forthcoming).

[2.] ADELMAN, M. A. "The Supply and Price of Natural Gas," *Journal of Industrial Economics,* Supplement, 1962.

[3.] COUNCIL OF EUROPE. *European Energy Problems,* Strasbourg, 1962.

[4.] EUROPEAN COAL AND STEEL COMMUNITY. *Eighth General Report of the High Authority.* Luxembourg, 1960.

[5.] EUROPEAN COAL AND STEEL COMMUNITY. *Outlook for Oil in the World and in the Community.* 3322/62. Luxembourg, May, 1962.

[6.] EUROPEAN COAL AND STEEL COMMUNITY, IN COLLABORATION WITH THE COMMISSION OF THE EUROPEAN ECONOMIC COMMUNITY, AND EURATOM. *Etude sur les perspectives énergétiques a long terme de la Communauté Européenne.* Luxembourg, 1962.

[7.] GRAYSON, LESLIE E. "Coordinated Energy Policy in the Common Market," *Social Research* (Autumn, 1961) , pp. 283–96.

[8.] JAPANESE ECONOMIC PLANNING AGENCY. *New Long-Range Economic Plan of Japan (1961–1970),* Tokyo: The Times of Japan, 1961.

[9.] LANDSBERG, HANS H., ET AL. *Resources in America's Future.* Baltimore: Johns Hopkins University Press, 1963.

[10.] LEVY, W. J. *Current and Prospective Developments in World Oil with General Reference to the German Federal Republic.* Koln: Bundesverband der Deutschen Industrie, 1961.

[11.] MASON, EDWARD S., ET AL. "Energy Requirements and Economic Growth," *Proceedings of the International Conference on the Peaceful Uses of Atomic Energy,* Vol. I. New York, United Nations, 1956, pp. 50–60.

[12.] ORGANIZATION FOR EUROPEAN ECONOMIC COOPERATION. *Europe's Growing Needs of Energy,* Paris, 1956.

[13.] ORGANIZATION FOR EUROPEAN ECONOMIC COOPERATION. *Toward a New Energy Pattern in Europe.* Paris, 1960.

[14.] PARETTI, V., AND BLOCH, G. *Energie et expansion économique en Europe.* Luxembourg, 1962 (mimeo).

[15.] ROBINSON, E. A. G., AND DANIEL, G. H. "The World's Need for a New Source of Energy," *Proceedings of the International Con-*

ference on the Peaceful Uses of Atomic Energy, Vol. I, New York,
United Nations, 1956, pp. 38–49.

[16.] SCHURR, SAM H., NETSCHERT, BRUCE C., ET AL. *Energy in the American Economy, 1850–1975.* Baltimore: John Hopkins Press, 1960.

[17.] UNITED KINGDOM, NATIONAL DEVELOPMENT COUNCIL. *Growth of the United Kingdom Economy to 1966,* London: Her Majesty's Stationery Office, 1963.

[18.] UNITED NATIONS *Economic Developments in the Middle East, 1959–1961.* New York, 1962.

[19.] UNITED NATIONS. *World Energy Supplies, 1957–1960.* Series J. New York, 1962.

[20.] U.S. SENATE INTERIOR COMMITTEE, NATIONAL FUELS AND ENERGY STUDY GROUP. *Report.* Washington, D.C., 1961.

CHAPTER 11

Trade Projections for Nonfuel Minerals and Metals

11.1 IRON ORE (SITC 281)

IRON is the second most abundant metallic element in the earth's crust and has found manifold applications from early times. In present-day industrial countries, iron is used almost exclusively in the form of steel in mining, manufacturing, construction, and transportation. These countries relied initially on domestically mined ore but, with the exhaustion of some of their deposits and the discovery of high grade ore in less developed areas, the latter have come to assume importance as suppliers of iron ore. By 1960, one-fourth of all iron ore consumed in the industrial economies originated in developing areas.

Next to France, Sweden, Canada, and the Soviet Union—the traditional exporters of iron ore—Venezuela has become a large exporter. In 1959–61, Venezuela provided approximately one-eighth of the iron ore entering world trade, while India, Malaya, Brazil, Chile, and Peru supplied about 3 per cent each. On the African continent, Algeria, Liberia, and Sierra Leone export increasing quantities. Among the larger producers, iron ore accounts for 6–7 per cent of the export earnings of Venezuela, Chile, and Algeria, but this proportion is the highest in Sierra Leone, where the sale of iron ore provides one-fifth of the total export income.

In order to estimate the future demand for iron ore, projections on the consumption of steel in the industrial countries need to be made. Two methods of estimation have been employed here. First, we have calculated time-series regressions for the period 1950–1960, with industrial production as the independent, and steel consumption as the dependent, variable for the European Common Market, the United Kingdom, Northern Europe, Southern Europe, and Japan, and have adjusted the resulting coefficients on the basis of information on prospective developments in steel-using industries. Second, a cross-section function has been fitted to observations relating to individual countries for the year 1957, with per capita GNP as the independent, and per capita steel utilization as the dependent, variable.[1] The final projections of steel consumption have then been derived from the results obtained by the use of the two methods.[2] A different procedure has been followed in the case of the United States, where the forecasts given in the Resources for the Future study, *Resources in America's Future* [4], have been adopted.[3] Subsequently, steel production in industrial areas has been estimated by allowing for net trade in steel.

In the next step, we have estimated the relative contribution of scrap and pig iron to the manufacture of steel and the iron ore requirements of pig iron production. In determining the quantity of scrap and pig iron used in the steelmaking process, available information on prospective changes in the application of steelmaking techniques and the supply and price of pig iron versus scrap have been utilized. Finally, estimates have been prepared on the relative shares of domestic production and imports in providing for future iron ore requirements.

North America

In the United States, the rate of increase of steel consumption fell behind the growth of industrial production in recent decades, and there has been little increase in per capita terms. These developments are related to interindustry shifts in production and to substitution among structural materials. Between 1940 and 1960, the decline in railroad investments led to an absolute fall in the use of steel in rail transportation while the shift toward light industrial products at the expense of structures retarded the growth of steel consumption in other sectors. At the same time, aluminum and plastics have encroached upon the market for steel in aircraft, consumer durables, and containers, and this loss has not been offset by the increased use of steel in residential construction. Note further that steel consumption was below the record 1955 level in

---

[1]Steel utilization is defined as steel consumption corrected for indirect trade in steel in the form of manufactured products [*9*, p. 12].

[2]In transforming projections of steel utilization into projections of steel consumption, we have made use of the relationship observed between steel consumption and utilization in individual countries.

[3]The medium projections of the Resources for the Future study have been accepted as "most likely" estimates for all metals, while the consumption levels corresponding to our higher income variant have been derived by utilizing the implicit elasticity calculated between the projected values of industrial production and metal consumption. Estimates for 1975 have been arrived at by interpolation.

1960—to a large extent because of the relatively low levels of automobile output and residential construction in the latter year.

Interindustry shifts and substitution among materials will also greatly affect the future demand for steel. According to the forecast of the Resources for the Future study, the largest gains would be made in sectors where steel consumption declined in absolute terms over the past two decades (rail, water, and air transportation), while substitution for steel would continue in the manufacturing of containers. The projections assume some increase in per capita steel consumption and a further decline in steel consumption in relation to industrial production [4, pp. 298–300]; in the period 1960–1975, a 1.0 per cent increase in industrial production is expected to be associated with a 0.8 per cent increase in steel consumption. Thus, the consumption of steel in the United States would reach 128 million tons in 1970 and 143 million tons in 1975, as compared to 90 million tons in 1960. On the other hand, with the expansion of the Canadian automobile industry, steel consumption may rise at approximately the same rate as industrial production in Canada (Table 11.1.1).

TABLE 11.1.1

STEEL CONSUMPTION IN INDUSTRIAL COUNTRIES
(million tons, crude steel equivalent)

	1950	1955	1960	1970I	1970II	1975I	1975II
United States	86.0	102.5	90.5	127.9	133.5	143.2	151.5
Canada	4.2	5.0	5.5	8.8	9.1	10.4	11.1
Common Market	23.6	42.7	58.1	92.8	99.3	114.1	122.8
United Kingdom	14.0	18.7	22.2	30.1	32.0	34.2	37.2
Northern Europe	5.1	7.9	10.9	16.8	18.0	19.7	21.8
Southern Europe	2.2	3.3	4.9	11.0	12.0	17.5	21.0
Japan	4.2	7.3	19.5	39.0	43.6	51.0	59.9
Industrial Countries, Total	139.3	187.4	211.6	326.4	347.5	390.1	425.3

Sources: United Nations, Statistical Yearbook, various issues.

Before 1950, the United States was a large exporter of steel products, while Canada imported a substantial proportion of her steel requirements. Since the early fifties, however, U.S. exports have been on the decline, and in 1960 the United States showed a small import balance. At the same time, imports into Canada have fallen to low levels. The Resources for the Future study forecasts an export balance of 0.9 million tons for the United States in 1970, but it appears questionable whether the improvement in the competitive position of the U.S. steel industry, necessary for an increase in exports, would in fact be forthcoming. In the present study, zero net trade has been assumed, so that steel production in North America would equal steel consumption in the period under consideration.

As to the use of pig iron in the steelmaking process, conflicting trends appear to be at work. The introduction of direct reduction techniques and the greater use of the oxygen process raises the proportion of pig iron in the metallic charge while the growth of electric steel making and the availability of cheap scrap act in the opposite direction. We have assumed that the latter influences will be stronger, and pig iron input as a ratio of steel output would decline from 66 to 63 per cent during the period of projection.[4] Finally, on the basis of historical experience, a one-to-one relationship between iron ore requirements and pig iron output has been assumed.

As regards the contribution of domestic production to iron ore requirements, different considerations apply to the United States and Canada. In the United States, the proportion of imported iron ore in home consumption rose from 8 per cent to 30 per cent during the fifties, while Canada exported increasing quantities. These partially interrelated trends are expected to continue in the future. On the one hand, in view of the availability of high grade ore abroad and the low iron content of domestic ore, it appears questionable whether the production of iron ore in the United States would exceed the level reached in 1960. On the other hand, increases in productive capacity in Quebec and the Carol Lake–Wabush Lake district give promise for the steady growth of Canadian iron ore exports in the period under consideration.

The assumed maintenance of 1960 levels of U.S. iron ore production conceals substantial shifts within the mining industry. Further expansion in the production of beneficiated ores is anticipated, while the output of underground mines producing ore for direct shipment to consumers will continue to decline. As a result of these developments, the iron content of domestically produced ore may rise from 53 per cent in 1960 to over 55 per cent in 1975. To meet domestic requirements, imports of iron ore into the United States would then have to increase from 21 million tons of iron-in-ore in 1960 to 33 million tons in 1970 and 41 million tons in 1975 under the most likely income assumption, and slightly higher if the target rate of income growth were reached (Table A11.1.1).

In 1960, one-fifth of U.S. iron ore imports originated in Canada, and shipments to the United States accounted for 60 per cent of

---

[4]In calculating this ratio, pig iron used in ferrous castings has also been taken into account. A slightly higher figure applies to Canada.

Canadian exports in this commodity. Canada is expected to further augment her share in U.S. imports but, with the rise of her exportable production, other destinations—chiefly the United Kingdom and Japan—will assume increasing importance as markets for Canadian ore (Table A11.1.2).

Western Europe

In the period 1950–1960, the consumption of steel rose at a rate exceeding the growth of industrial production in Western Europe, where the rapid expansion of the automobile industry and construction activity have contributed to the increase in the demand for steel (Table A11.1.3). Despite favorable expectations for the automobile, durable consumer goods, and electrical engineering industries, recent rates of growth in steel consumption are unlikely to be maintained, however, and, in the more developed countries of Europe, steel consumption is expected to rise at a rate somewhat lower than the growth of industrial production. On the other hand, rapid increases in the consumption of steel are foreseen in Southern Europe and in the less industrialized countries of Northern Europe.[5] Taken together steel consumption in Western Europe would surpass 150 million tons in 1970 and 185 million tons in 1975, as against 96 million tons in 1960.[6]

By comparison, the Dewhurst study expects steel consumption in Western Europe, excepting Turkey and Yugoslavia, to amount to 130 million tons in 1970 [*1*, pp. 609–10], while the estimate of the UN Economic Commission for Europe is 151.5 million tons for 1972 [*9*, p. 130]. Finally, the European Coal and Steel Community foresees steel consumption in the Common Market to approach 100 million tons in 1975 as against our estimates of 93–98 million tons [*2*, p. 338].

Steel exports from Western Europe have been rising during the last decade, reflecting the improvement in the competitive position of European—chiefly Common Market—industry. In 1960, net exports amounted to 12.7 million tons, accounting for 12 per cent of domestic production. However, with the increase of production capacity in the less developed countries—the main markets for European steel—some decline in exports is expected. In the present

---

[5]According to our projections, a 1.0 per cent increase in industrial production would be accompanied by a 0.95 per cent rise in steel consumption in the Common Market countries and the United Kingdom, 1.2 per cent in Northern Europe, and 1.3 per cent in Southern Europe.

[6]Under the higher income alternative, projected consumption levels are 161 and 205 million tons in 1970 and 1975, respectively.

study, we have assumed that, by 1975, steel exports from Western
Europe would not surpass 5 per cent of the domestic production of
steel, and would amount to about ten million tons a year.

The proportion of pig iron to crude steel was .72 in Western
Europe in 1960, exceeding the ratio observed in the United States
by a considerable margin. With the shift toward the oxygen process
in Western Europe, the observed disparity is likely to be maintained
during the period of projection, although the pig iron–steel ingot
ratio may fall to .70 in this area as a result of the increased use of
scrap in the furnace charge of the individual processes.

On the other hand, iron ore requirements per ton of pig iron are
lower in Western Europe than in the United States (850 kg per
ton). This discrepancy is explained by (1) the lesser quantities of
iron ore fed directly into the steel furnace, (2) the smaller amount
of ferrous metal required per ton of pig iron, and (3) the larger
quantity of calcined pyrites used in the ferrous metal load in
Western Europe. In conformity with the projection of the European
Coal and Steel Community [2, p. 369], no change in this ratio has
been envisaged. In this connection, note that actual and projected
differences in pig iron–steel and iron ore–pig iron ratios between the
United States and Western Europe approximately cancel out, so
that the quantity of iron-in-ore per ton of steel differs little in the
two areas.

The contribution of domestic ore to European iron ore requirements is difficult to assess. In most iron-producing areas, iron ore
is either high grade, direct shipping ore containing at least 50–55
per cent iron, or it is a lower grade ore which has been beneficiated
to attain an iron content of 65 per cent. In Western Europe, a 60
per cent shipping ore is produced in Sweden, 50 per cent in Southern Europe, but the largest European iron ore producer, France,
ships ores containing about 33 per cent iron. The future course of
European iron ore production will greatly depend on the prospects
for French ore.

According to the estimates of the UN Economic Commission for
Europe, 220 million tons of iron ore would be produced in Western
Europe around 1972, with an iron content of 81 million tons [*19,*
p. 159]. The ECE further assumes that French ore would fully share
in this increase. However, given the abundance of high grade ores
in Africa, South America, and Canada, it appears questionable that
French production would rise substantially. Rather, we have assumed a slowing down in the growth or iron ore production in
France and estimated mine output in Western Europe to reach 175

million tons in 1970 and 185 million tons in 1975, with an iron content of 65 and 70 million tons in the two years, respectively. Production would be somewhat larger under the high income variant, however.[7] Correspondingly, imports of iron-in-ore would double within a decade.

Japan

Steel consumption in Japan increased at a rate slightly exceeding the growth of industrial production during the fifties, and this relationship is expected to change little in the period of projection. The consumption of steel would thus reach 39 or 44 million tons in 1970 and 51 or 60 million tons in 1975, depending on the income assumption chosen. By comparison, the Ministry of International Trade and Industry projected steel consumption to amount to 44 millions tons in 1970 [*11*, p. 591]. At the same time, with the increased application of the oxygen process, the ratio of pig iron to steel may rise to a considerable extent. We have calculated with a ratio of 65 per cent in 1970 and 68 per cent in 1975 as against 55 per cent in 1960, while the above-quoted Japanese source foresees the possibility of an increase in this ratio to 70 per cent by 1970. Finally, the iron ore requirement per ton of pig iron has been projected to rise from 850 kg in 1960 to 900 kg in 1975.

Compared to requirements, domestic iron ore reserves are small in Japan, and the increase in the demand for iron ore will have to be satisfied almost exclusively by imports. As a result, imports of iron-in-ore may triple between 1960 and 1975.

Oceania and South Africa

Oceania will become a large exporter of iron ore, inasmuch as domestic steel production cannot conceivably absorb all of the ore under exploration in Australia. Australian shipments of iron-in-ore may reach 5 million tons in 1970 and 7 million tons in 1975, with Japan as the principal market. South Africa is also likely to remain a net exporter of iron ore.

The Price and Origin of Imports

With large deposits of high grade ores coming into exploitation in many parts of the world, and technological improvements under way in the beneficiation of iron ore [*3*], it appears unlikely that the price of iron ore would rise during the period under considera-

---

[7]For 1970, the Dewhurst study envisaged European ore production to amount to about 60 million tons of iron-in-ore [*1*, p. 615].

tion. At the same time, we have assumed that the mining companies will pursue a policy aimed at avoiding a decline in prices below the level experienced in 1960.

Changes in trade patterns are indicated by the exploitation of new deposits and the construction of facilities for the beneficiation of ore in Canada, South America, Africa, and Australia. A substantial part of this new capacity is being developed with the financial support or participation of steel-producing companies. Much of the new capacity in Africa involves European capital, for example, while steel companies in the United States are involved in the development of new facilities in Canada. In contrast, countries in Latin America discourage participation of mineral-consuming groups in the development of their resources.

During the period under consideration, the largest expansion in iron ore exports is expected to occur in North and West Africa, with Canada and Latin America following. The United States will increase its imports from Canada, and to a lesser extent, from Latin America. In turn, the countries of Western Europe are likely to obtain a major part of the increase in their import requirements from Liberia, Mauritania, and several other West Arican producers, although Latin America and Canada will also profit from the growth of European imports. Finally, Japan expects to rely heavily on Indian and Australian ore (Table A11.1.2).

According to our projections, the iron ore exports of developing countries, in terms of iron content, would increase by 75 to 100 per cent between 1960 and 1970 and 140 to 180 per cent between 1960 and 1975, depending on the rate of growth of incomes in the industrial countries. By 1975, developing countries may supply over 30 per cent of the iron ore requirements of industrial areas. Under the assumption of unchanged prices, export earnings will rise in the same proportion (Table A11).

11.2 MANGANESE ORE AND FERROMANGANESE
(SITC 283.7, 671.4)

Manganese is used chiefly as ferromanganese in steel manufacturing. Its importance in the steelmaking process is shown by the fact that, in addition to the properties of hardness and strength it provides when alloyed with iron, it also neutralizes the effects of sulphur and has deoxidizing characteristics. A smaller quantity of manganese (about 10 per cent of the manganese consumption in the industrial countries) is used as an oxidizing agent in chemicals and as a depolarizing agent in dry cell batteries.

The Soviet Union is the largest producer of manganese ore, accounting for about 45 per cent of world output, while among the major industrial countries only Japan supplies a substantial proportion of its own consumption. India, South Africa, and Brazil are also large producers and exporters, but export earnings derived from the sale of manganese exceed 5 per cent of total export receipts only in the case of Ghana and Morocco. With the exception of India, developing countries export manganese in the form of ore rather than as ferromanganese.

Since manganese finds its main uses in the steel industry, the future demand for manganese has been estimated by considering possible changes in the quantity of manganese per ton of steel, with further allowance made for manganese consumed in other industries. In general, it has been assumed that in industrial areas manganese consumption per ton of steel would converge toward the ratio observed in the United States (9 kg per ton).

North America

In the United States, the amount of manganese per ton of steel increased somewhat in the postwar period and reached 9 kg per ton in 1960. The Resources for the Future report expects this ratio to be maintained in the future, and this forecast has also been accepted in the present study. [4, p. 305]. A lower ratio pertains to the Canadian steel industry, however.

Canada does not produce manganese, while prices guaranteed by the federal government at levels more than double the world market price kept U.S. production at about 150 thousand tons of manganese-in-ore in the years 1955–1958. However, after the price support program had been discontinued in August, 1958, production fell to 46 thousand tons. Given the uneconomic production of low grade manganese ore in the United States, it can be expected that domestic ore will supply less than 5 per cent of home demand in the period of projection. Correspondingly, imports may rise from 1.0 million tons in 1960 to 1.3 million tons in 1970 and 1.5 million tons in 1975 (Table A11.2.1).

Western Europe

The amount of manganese used per ton of steel in Western Europe slightly exceeds the ratio observed in the United States, but the differences have been reduced in recent years and are expected to decrease further in the future. In 1960, home production supplied only about 5 per cent of domestic requirements, and given the smallness of economically exploitable reserves, this proportion is likely to fall rather than to increase in the future. Imports amounted to 1.3 million tons in 1960 and are projected to exceed 1.7 million tons in 1970 and 2.0 million tons in 1975.

Japan

In 1960, domestic production supplied about 60 per cent of the manganese requirements of the Japanese steel industry. However, resources of high grade ore do not appear to be sufficient to allow for an increase in production commensurate with the growth of steel production. Correspondingly, imports may reach 0.4 million tons in 1975 as against 0.1 million tons in 1960.

Oceania and South Africa

Australia is an exporter of manganese ore and, although reserves are modest in size, Oceania is expected to remain a net exporter during the period under consideration. At the same time, South Africa will continue to be one of the largest exporters of manganese.

The Price and Origin of Imports

The known reserves of high grade manganese ore in the world are adequate to satisfy expected needs for several decades, and there is little expectation for an upward movement of prices. On the other hand, should large quantities of manganese ore be brought on the world market by the Soviet Union and Mainland China, prices would tend to decline. We have calculated with constant prices in making projections, however, and have arbitrarily assumed that Russian and Chinese shipments taken together would about double between 1960 and 1975, the bulk of exports moving from the Soviet Union to Western Europe and a smaller quantity from China to Japan.

Aside from exports coming from the Sino-Soviet area, the present geographical pattern of trade in manganese is not likely to change substantially in the period under consideration. The United States will continue to rely chiefly on imports from Brazil, India, and Ghana, while South Africa, India, and Morocco are expected to provide a large proportion of the manganese needs of Western Europe. India will also remain the main supplier of Japan in manganese. Note, however, that new capacity is being developed in Gabon, Egypt, and British Guiana, and that some producers of manganese ore endeavor to ship manganese in the form of ferromanganese. Among developing countries, only India exported substantial quantities of ferromanganese in 1960.

Under the above assumptions, the exports of manganese (manganese-in-ore and ferromanganese) from developing countries would rise from 1.8 million tons in 1960 to about 2.4 million tons in 1970 and 2.8 million tons in 1975 under the most likely income assumption, and slightly higher if the target rate of income growth were reached. A larger increase will take place in the value of exports, however, by reason of the increase in the proportion of ferromanganese in these exports.

11.3 COPPER (SITC 283.1, 682.1)

Among nonferrous metals, separate projections have been prepared for copper, aluminum, lead, zinc, and tin. In regard to these metals, we have accepted the medium projection of the Resources for the Future study [4] on U.S. consumption as our "most likely" alternative, and have calculated with an implicit elasticity between metal consumption and industrial production to arrive at our high estimate. Available information on prospective trends as well as estimates prepared by the Royal Commission on Canada's Economic Prospects have been utilized in making projections for Canada.

In the case of the other industrial areas (European Common Market, United Kingdom, Northern Europe, Southern Europe, and Japan), we have fitted double- and semilogarithmic functions with industrial production as the independent, and metal consumption as the dependent, variable (Table A11.3.3). Preliminary projections have been made by the use of these functions; the double-logarithmic form has been employed in the case of aluminum, and the semilogarithmic form in regard to the other nonferrous metals. Subsequently, the estimates have been adjusted to take account of available information on future developments in metal-using sectors and on the use of secondary metal.[8]

In order to arrive at an estimate of gross metal requirements, separate projections have been prepared on the exports of metal from the main industrial areas. Finally, we have estimated the contribution of domestic ore production and imports of ores and metals to gross metal requirements.[9]

Among the main nonferrous metals, copper probably came ear-

---

[8]In contradistinction to the case of steel, a statistical relationship between the per capita utilization of metals and income per head could not be established in regard to nonferrous metals, chiefly because of the lack of information on the metal content of products traded.

[9]Although the imports of ores and metals have been separately estimated, only the consolidated matrices have been included in this study. The detailed projections are available on request.

liest into use, chiefly in ornaments and utensils. It is presently used in wires (electrical conductors), in alloyed form (brass and bronze), and as pure metal. In the United States, electrical applications predominate, followed by brass and bronze employed mainly in producers' durables, construction, and motor vehicles. In Western Europe, pure copper metal is used in sheets, plates, and tubes, while in several of these applications aluminum has replaced copper in the United States. Aluminum has been substituted for copper in high-tension transmission lines and some other electrical uses, too.

Copper ore deposits are concentrated in the western regions of the United States and Canada, the west coast of Latin America (Chile and Peru), a zone in Central Africa spanning the border areas of Northern Rhodesia and the Katanga province of the former Belgium Congo, and the Soviet Union. These areas, taken together, account for over four-fifths of world output, with the United States as the largest producer. Cooper-bearing ores contain, at most, 8 per cent metal; in the United States, less than 1 per cent. Hence, before smelting, the ore is concentrated to a copper content of about 33 per cent. But since the weight of concentrates still exceeds the weight of the smelted product three times, international trade takes place mainly in the form of unrefined (blister) and refined copper.

Exports of copper are of greatest importance for Chile and Rhodesia-Nyasaland. In 1959–61, the former derived 68 per cent of her export earnings from the sale of copper; the latter, 59 per cent. The corresponding ratios are 17 per cent for Peru, 30 per cent for the former Belgium Congo, and 32 per cent for Cyprus. By reason of the availability of cheap water transportation, Cyprus and the Philippines ship concentrates, while all other producers export almost exclusively blister and refined copper. Among industrial countries, Canada is a large copper exporter, while the United States and some European countries (e.g., Belgium) re-export copper in refined form.

In the United States, the consumption of refined copper (primary and secondary) fluctuated around 1.5 million tons during the fifties, with a drop to 1.4 million tons in 1960. Secondary copper accounted for about 0.4 million tons throughout the period. The shift to aluminum in high-voltage transmission lines and the decrease in the use of brass and bronze in producer and consumer durables and motor vehicles have been largely responsible for the observed stagnation of copper consumption.

For the next decade, the Resources for the Future study expects copper consumption to grow at rates approaching the rate of growth of industrial production, however, chiefly as a result of the expected rapid expansion in residential and communication construction that are large users of copper. But, with the increased availability of obsolete scrap, a slightly slower increase in the demand for primary copper is anticipated [*4*, p. 917]. The U.S. consumption of primary copper would thus rise by about one-half between 1960 and 1970 and two-thirds between 1960 and 1975. Similar changes are expected in Canada (Table 11.3.1).

Canada is a large exporter of refined copper and will further increase her exports during the period under consideration. On the other hand, due to the strong demand for copper in Western Europe coupled with the availability of unutilized refinery capacity in the United States, U.S. exports were unusually large in 1960, and

TABLE 11.3.1

CONSUMPTION OF PRIMARY COPPER IN INDUSTRIAL INDUSTRIES
(thousand tons)

	1950	1955	1960	1970I	1970II	1975I	1975II
United States	1073	1144	960	1400	1460	1580	1690
Canada	97	126	107	160	170	180	200
Common Market.	309	560	871	1320	1390	1560	1690
United Kingdom.	341	403	459	550	570	630	660
Northern Europe.	95	122	174	220	230	260	280
Southern Europe.	36	47	93	170	200	250	290
Japan	13	73	243	410	440	520	590
Industrial Countries, Total	1964	2475	2907	4230	4460	4980	5400

Source: Metallgesellschaft, Metal Statistics, various issues.

this performance is not likely to be repeated in the future. Rather, the construction of new refinery capacity in the developing countries will contribute to a fall in U.S. exports below the average of recent years.

With the projected decline in exports of refined copper, U.S. copper requirements would rise at a slower rate than domestic consumption. At the same time, a considerable degree of uncertainty surrounds the prospects for the U.S. production of copper ore, since the same companies own copper mines in the United States and abroad, and decisions on the exploitation of these mines depend not only on economic considerations but also on the political situation in the copper-producing countries.

In recent decades, increased mining activity has been accompanied by a decrease in the copper content of ores in the United States, and ore production, expressed in terms of copper content, has risen at a modest rate. Nevertheless, technological improvements have restrained increases in costs in the face of the lowering of the copper content of ore, and the announced expansion plans of mining companies indicate a continuation in the growth of output. In the present study, we have assumed that the relative contribution of domestic production and imports to U.S. copper requirements would remain approximately unchanged during the period of projection (Table A11.3.1).

Western Europe

Copper consumption in Western Europe expanded at a rate slightly exceeding the growth of industrial production during the fifties. By 1960, the per capita consumption of refined copper was 5.4 kg in Western Europe as compared to 6.8 kg in the United States. The U.S. consumption level has been surpassed in the United Kingdom (10.0 kg) and approached in the Common Market (5.8 kg) and Northern Europe (5.5 kg), while per capita consumption was below 1.0 kg in Southern Europe. Note, however, that the comparisons are distorted by reason of the fact that the United Kingdom and some of the Common Market countries (e.g., Belgium) export substantial quantities of manufactured products containing copper.

The expected expansion in the electrical engineering industries and in construction activity would promise a continuation of past trends in European copper consumption. Various influences will mitigate the rise of demand for primary copper, however. To begin with, the substitution of aluminum for copper in Western Europe has not progressed as far as in the United States. On the basis of a comparison of the experience of individual copper-using industries, a United Nations study has arrived at the conclusion that in the United States the annual rate of substitution for copper was double that in Europe during the fifties [*10*, pp. 38–39]. Possibilities for the substitution of aluminum for copper exist in the electrical industries, as well as in uses where pure copper metal is presently employed (sheets, plates, tubes, etc.). Further, we can expect that the proportion of secondary metal in European copper consumption will increase, thereby reducing the demand for primary metal.

As a result of the operation of these factors, the consumption of primary copper is likely to rise at a rate lower than the growth of industrial production in the more developed countries of Western Europe. Increases will be the smallest in the United Kingdom where per capita copper consumption is already at high levels. A rapid expansion is expected in Southern Europe, however, where copper consumption is much below the European average. In Western Europe taken as a whole, the consumption of primary copper is projected to rise from 1.6 million tons in 1960 to about 2.3 million tons in 1970 and 2.8 million tons in 1975, corresponding to an implicit elasticity of 0.8 in relation to industrial production.[10] At the same time, European exports of copper are bound to fall as refinery facilities are set up in the developing countries.

There are some copper ore deposits in the peripheral countries of Europe, but domestic ore supplied only 7 per cent of requirements in 1960. In the period under consideration, this ratio is likely to decline rather than increase, so that the rise in consumption will have to be supplied almost exclusively by imports. Within the increased imports, refined coper will gain at the expense of blister copper and copper concentrates.

Japan

Copper consumption in Japan grew at about the same rate as industrial production during the fifties. However, with substitution in favor of aluminum, a slowing down in the growth of consumption is foreseen. Japan presently covers about 35 per cent of her copper requirements by domestic production, as compared to 100 per cent in 1955. The degree of self-sufficiency is expected to decline further in the future, and by 1975, copper imports may amount to about 400 thousand tons as against 160 thousand tons in 1960.

Oceania and South Africa

Australia has an export surplus in copper and will continue to export to New Zealand and to industrial areas. South Africa is also a net exporter, but imports blister copper from Northern Rhodesia for refining. No change in these imports has been assumed.

The Price and Origin of Imports

The copper-mining areas of the world are known to have abundant reserves of copper-bearing ores that are mineable by today's standards. A survey by Parsons indicates an increase in the mining capacity of the noncommunist countries from 4.1 million tons in 1961 to 4.6 million tons in 1965 [5]. More recently, further developments have been announced in the United States and South Africa, so that we can follow Shea to assume that future copper require-

---

[10]By comparison, the Dewhurst study expects copper consumption to increase at a rate slightly exceeding that of industrial production [*1*, p. 629].

ments can be supplied at prices of about 30 cents per pound,[11] i.e., approximately 6 per cent below the price prevailing in 1960 [7].

In the noncommunist countries of the world, most copper mining is carried out by a few large companies, and the policy of these companies will largely determine the geographical composition of imports. On the basis of available information on developments in individual areas, we have assumed that, barring political disturbances, the present pattern of trade will be maintained throughout the period of projection. The major trade flows are directed from Chile and Canada to the United States, and from Northern Rhodesia and the Congo to Western Europe, although European imports from Canada, Chile, and Peru are also of importance. Finally, Latin-American producers will be the chief beneficiaries of the rise of imports into Japan (Table A11.3.2).

Under the most likely income assumption, we have projected the copper exports of developing areas to industrial countries to rise by two-thirds in the period 1960–1970, and to nearly double between 1960 and 1975. The value of exports will rise at a higher rate, however, by reason of the expected shift toward the exportation of copper in refined form. Among the major exporting areas, concentrates accounted for 5 per cent of the copper exports of Africa and Latin America in 1960, while the share of blister copper was one-third in the former area and one-half in the latter. With new refineries being set up in these regions, by 1975 the share of blister copper may fall to about one-fourth in the former and one-third in the latter. Correspondingly, export earnings on the relevant quantities will increase by the cost of refining copper, about $50 per ton. On the other hand, Cyprus and the Philippines may continue to export copper concentrates.

11.4 ALUMINUM (SITC 283.3, 513.6, 684.1)

Aluminum has come into widespread use only during this century but, with recent rapid expansion, it has replaced copper as the leading nonferrous metal. Aluminum has been substituted for steel in construction, transportation equipment, and electrical engineering; it has been substituted for copper as an electrical conductor, for lead in packaging, for tin in containers, for zinc in automobile parts, and it has also found application in newly established industries, such as electronics.

---

[11]Domestic price f.o.b. refinery New York, electrolic wirebars and ingots.

The increased use of aluminum is of considerable importance to the developing countries, since many of these have substantial reserves of aluminum-bearing ores. The earth's crust contains about 7 per cent aluminum, but commercially utilized deposits are concentrated in a few regions. The largest known deposits of bauxite, the main commercially utilized ore of aluminum, are in West Africa and in the Caribbean. In 1960, the major producers of bauxite were Jamaica, the Soviet Union, Surinam, British Guiana, and France. In Africa, Guinea and Ghana are large producers. A substantial proportion of world output enters international trade, and in 1960 the industrial countries imported about 70 per cent of their bauxite requirements.

In the production of aluminum metal, bauxite is first converted into alumina (aluminum oxide), and alumina is then smelted by an electrolytic process to produce aluminum. Both of these processes consume large amounts of energy, and hence alumina plants and aluminum smelting facilities are usually located at places where low cost electric power is available. Moreover, aluminum-producing facilities require capital investments of substantial magnitude, which fact has retarded their construction in developing countries.

The pattern of international trade had been characterized by the shipment of bauxite from less developed areas to industrial countries for transformation into alumina and subsequently aluminum, but more recently some of the less developed countries have come to export alumina. Larger quantities of alumina will be exported in the future as additional plants for converting bauxite into alumina are built in the major producing countries; several African producers are also establishing aluminum smelting facilities. Among the developing countries, only the Cameroons exported aluminum in 1960.

Bauxite provides a substantial proportion of the foreign exchange earnings of the main exporting countries. In 1959–61, Surinam derived 82 per cent of her export earnings from the sale of bauxite; British Guiana and Guinea (chiefly alumina), 25 per cent; and Jamaica, 22 per cent. At the same time, aluminum exports accounted for one-fifth of the export earnings of the Cameroons. The projected shift from the exportation of bauxite to alumina and to aluminum will increase the export earnings of the developing countries and will also reduce transportation costs, as over 2 tons of bauxite are needed to produce 1 ton of alumina, while the aluminum content of the latter is about 50 per cent.

North America

Aluminum consumption in the United States has been rising rapidly in recent decades, but it suffered a temporary setback in 1960. With the continuing growth of the U.S. economy, this upward trend is likely to continue. The Resources for the Future study projected aluminum consumption to double during the sixties (Table 11.4.1).[12] The largest increases in the use of aluminum are expected to take place in transportation equipment and in electrical engineering. The rate of growth of consumption will be even higher in Canada, where the per capita consumption of aluminum has not yet reached 6 kg.

TABLE 11.4.1

CONSUMPTION OF PRIMARY ALUMINUM IN INDUSTRIAL COUNTRIES
(thousand tons)

	1950	1955	1960	1970I	1970II	1975I	1975II
United States	823	1582	1539	3050	3400	3900	4400
Canada	59	83	104	230	260	330	380
Common Market	162	379	693	1450	1600	2100	2420
United Kingdom	184	291	360	560	620	720	820
Northern Europe.	46	120	150	300	330	400	480
Southern Europe.	7	22	61	220	270	400	520
Japan	19	50	151	430	500	680	840
Industrial Countries, Total	1300	2527	3058	6240	6980	8530	9860

Source: Metallgesellschaft, Metal Statistics, various issues.

Canada is the largest exporter of aluminum, accounting for about one-half of world exports. Shipments to her two principal markets, the United States and the United Kingdom, will continue to rise during the period under consideration, but sales to the European Common Market will be handicapped by reason of the 8 per cent preferential tariff. Still, Canada is likely to increase her share in the world market through the mid-sixties when the new African smelters come into operation. Yet, with the further extension of African production, Canada will increasingly turn toward the United States as a market for aluminum metal although the U.S. will also import aluminum from Africa.

Whereas the world demand for aluminum and the emergence of new competitors will determine the growth of the Canadian aluminum industry, U.S. exports of aluminum ingots are bound to fall

---

[12]Still, the RFF projection is considerably lower than some earlier estimates. It envisages primary aluminum consumption to reach 3.1 million tons in 1970, while, a few years earlier, Rosenzweig forecast consumption levels of 3.8 million tons by 1965 [6, pp. 8–80]. (The Rosenzweig estimate refers to the combined consumption of primary and secondary aluminum, but the latter is unlikely to exceed 6 per cent of the total.)

from the exceptionally high level experienced in 1960. In conjunction with these developments, the United States will increasingly rely on imports of bauxite, alumina, and aluminum to satisfy her domestic needs (Table A11.4.1).

Although improvements in technology may lead to the exploitation of low-yielding domestic ores, the increase in U.S. bauxite production will be small, if any, during the period of projection. At the same time, a consideration of relative production costs and plans for the future expansion of capacity indicate a rise in the share of aluminum in the combined imports of bauxite, alumina, and alumnium. Under the most likely income assumption, imports of aluminum may reach 0.4 million tons in 1970 and 0.7 million tons in 1975 as compared to 0.1 million tons in 1960, while the aluminum-equivalent of the imports of bauxite and alumina is estimated to rise from 2.0 million tons in 1960 to 2.2 and 2.7 million tons in 1970 and 1975, respectively. Substantially larger imports would be required, however, if the target rate of income growth were reached.

Canada does not produce bauxite and will continue to satisfy her requirements for domestic consumption and exports of aluminum importing bauxite and, increasingly, alumina.

Western Europe

European countries pioneered in the use of aluminum; in the years immediately preceding World War II, aluminum consumption in the United Kingdom and the present Common Market countries, taken together, was double that in the United States. With new applications found in the United States during and immediately following the war, this relationship was reversed by 1950. And, although aluminum consumption in Europe grew at a rapid rate during the fifties, in 1960 per capita consumption levels were still considerably below American standards, indicating possibilities for future expansion.[13]

Much of the increase in the use of aluminum is expected to take place in construction, transport equipment, and electrical engineering, although packaging uses will also expand at a high rate. In response to the availability of hydroelectricity, increases will be most rapid in the countries of Northern and Southern Europe, where aluminum consumption may rise at a rate double the rate

---

[13]In 1960, the per capita consumption of primary aluminum was 3.3 kg in Western Europe and 8.5 kg in the United States.

of growth of industrial production. The elasticity of demand for aluminum with respect to industrial production is likely to exceed 1.5 even in the United Kingdom, where per capita aluminum consumption is the highest in Europe (6.9 kg in 1960).

With account taken of prospective decreases in European exports of aluminum metal, aluminum requirements in Western Europe are projected to rise from 1.4 million tons in 1960 to 2.6 million tons in 1970 and 3.7 million tons in 1975 under the most likely income assumption, and to 2.9 and 4.3 million tons if the target rate of income growth is reached. This estimate is substantially higher than the 1.6 million ton figure given in the Dewhurst study for 1970 [*1*, p. 628], but recent events indicate that the latter greatly underestimated the possibilities for the growth of aluminum consumption in Europe.

In 1960, domestic production accounted for about two-thirds of European consumption of aluminum metal, and the remainder was imported chiefly from Canada and the United States (530 thousand tons in 1960). Among European producers, France, Greece, Yugoslavia, and to a lesser extent, Italy have relied on domestic ore, while other countries imported bauxite and alumina for further processing. Imports of bauxite and alumina (340 thousand tons of aluminum content in 1960) came from the Caribbean and, to a lesser extent, West Africa.

Domestic ore provided about 40 per cent of European aluminum requirements in 1960 and, during the sixties, the Common Market tariff on aluminum will give further impetus to the exploitation of bauxite reserves in this area. But, despite the availability of high grade reserves in France, Norway, Iceland, Yugoslavia, and Italy, the expansion of bauxite production in Western Europe is likely to slow down after 1970 when low cost aluminum will become available in larger quantities from Africa.

Taking account of available information on plans for the future expansion of capacity, we have projected aluminum production in Western Europe to rise from 0.9 million tons in 1960 to 1.6–1.7 and 1.9–2.1 million tons in 1970 and in 1975, respectively. To meet domestic requirements, the imports of aluminum metal would thus have to reach 1.0–1.2 million tons in 1970 and 1.8–2.1 million tons in 1975. In addition, Western Europe may import alumina and some bauxite, with an aluminum content of about 0.5 million tons.

Japan

Aluminum consumption in Japan increased eightfold during the fifties, but per capita consumption hardly surpassed 1.5 kg. Although past rates of growth cannot continue in the future, the possibilities for further substitution in favor of aluminum, and the expected expansion of the Japanese automobile and electrical engineering industries, give promise of further increases in aluminum consumption at a rate of about 10 per cent a year for the period of projection. Still, per capita consumption would not reach 7 kg by 1975.

Japan does not produce bauxite and satisfies her aluminum requirements chiefly with bauxite imported from Asia. Imports of aluminum metal (from Canada and the United States) are small and aluminum exports negligible. In the period under consideration, imports of aluminum metal are likely to shift to Oceania, but domestic aluminum requirements will still be largely supplied by home production based on imported ore.

Oceania and South Africa

Australia is presently a minor producer of aluminum, but recent discoveries of large bauxite deposits are being followed by the expansion of capacity of all three levels of fabrication (bauxite, alumina, and aluminum metal). Still, in view of the availability of hydroelectric energy in New Zealand, part of the Australian mine output is likely to be exported to New Zealand for further transformation. At the same time, the region as a whole will become a large exporter of aluminum.

South Africa does not produce bauxite but imports aluminum from industrial countries. We have assumed that this pattern of trade will continue during the period of projection.

The Price and Origin of Imports

We have noted above that during the period of projection the U.S. deficit in aluminum metal will be supplied chiefly by Canada, although African producers will get part of the U.S. market after 1970. There will be hardly any imports of aluminum metal from the Caribbean, however, while a partial shift from bauxite to alumina will take place.

At the same time, European imports of aluminum from the United States will largely disappear, while imports from Canada may reach 0.5 million tons by 1970 but will cease to increase afterwards. At the same time, if present plans are realized, African producers will get an increasing share of the European market, and European imports of aluminum from Africa may surpass one million tons by 1975. Small quantities of aluminum metal may be imported from the Soviet Union and the Caribbean, too, while the

Caribbean will remain Europe's chief supplier of bauxite and alumina. Finally, Japan will continue to rely on imports of bauxite and, to a lesser extent, alumina from Malaya and Sarawak, and she is expected to import some aluminum from the Soviet Union and Oceania.

These changes give expression to the shift from the exportation of bauxite to alumina and to aluminum in the developing countries. This shift will be most pronounced in Africa where the availability of cheap hydroelectric power provides possibilities for a rapid expansion in the production of aluminum. We have assumed that aluminum metal would account for three-fourths of African exports by 1975, while much of the remainder will be alumina.

In the absence of abundant hydroelectric power resources, the process of transformation will be slower in the Caribbean, with very little metal exported, although the share of alumina in exports may reach one-third as compared to 5 per cent in 1960. Finally, Asian producers are expected to export some alumina but no metal.

According to our projections, the bauxite, alumina, and aluminum exports of the developing countries, expressed in terms of metal content, would rise by over one-half between 1960 and 1970, and would double by 1975 (Table A11.4.2). But the value of these exports may increase about threefold during the sixties and fivefold between 1960 and 1975. These discrepancies are explained by reference to the shift from the exportation of bauxite to alumina and to aluminum, and by the high processing costs of aluminum as indicated by a comparison of unit values. In 1960, the average price of bauxite traded was $60–$70 per ton of aluminum content, compared to $130–$140 for alumina, and $480–$490 for aluminum. On the other hand, our calculations take account of a possible 6 to 8 per cent decline in aluminum prices.

The error possibilities associated with the projected pattern of trade should further be noted. Trade flows may undergo changes in response to modifications in the policies followed by the major aluminum companies, as witnessed by the cutback in the expansion plans of the Canadian aluminum industry in the late fifties. And although the projections of the export earnings of developing countries are little affected by the location of metal smelting in the industrial countries, the uncertainties related to the expansion of African metal output and the transformation from bauxite to alumina in the Caribbean influence the reliability of the results.

11.5 LEAD (CITC 283.4, 685.1)

Lead has found early uses in human history by reason of its resistance to corrosion and the ease with which it can be worked. Many of its modern applications are related to the automobile industry (storage batteries, soldering of radiators, and additives to gasoline), whereas the structural uses of lead include cable coverings as well as pipes, sheets, and other rolled products in construction. In many of these uses lead is recoverable and secondary lead is an important source of supply. In the United States, lead recovered from scrap accounts for about 40 per cent of consumption, while the corresponding proportion is 20–25 per cent in western Europe.

In the main industrial countries, the consumption of lead was rising at a slow pace during the interwar period. Larger increases were experienced in the Common Market countries and in Japan during the fifties, however, when the expansion of the automobile industry bolstered lead consumption. On the other hand, aside from a temporary fall in 1960, lead consumption in the United States has been stagnant over the last decade. This result is explained by the observed decline in structural uses and packaging where aluminum and plastics have encroached upon the market for lead, thereby offsetting the increases that have taken place in the automobile industry.

The Soviet Union and Australia are the leading producers of lead ore, followed by the United States, Mexico, and Canada. But the United States, as well as the countries of Western Europe and Japan, have come to rely increasingly on imports. In 1960, these countries imported about 60 per cent of their primary lead requirements, as compared to 50 per cent in 1950. About 60 per cent of the imports came from Australia, Canada, South Africa, and the Soviet Union, and 40 per cent from less developed areas.

Among developing countries, Mexico, Peru, Morocco, and Bolivia are large exporters of lead. Mexico exports chiefly lead metal; Peru exports metal as well as ore; while Morocco and Bolivia ship ores and concentrates. In 1959–61 Peru and Bolivia derived 7–8 per cent of their export earnings from the sale of lead, and the corresponding ratio was 4–5 per cent in Mexico and Morocco.

North America

In the United States, the consumption of lead (primary and secondary) averaged about 1.1 million tons during the fifties, of which lead recovered from scrap provided about 40 per cent. The Resources for the Future study expects further increases to take place in automobile uses, but foresees a decline in structural applications where substitution for lead will continue to take place. According to the RFF projections, lead consumption in 1970 would not exceed the level observed during the fifties, although some further increases may take place after 1970. But an increasing part of U.S. requirements will be satisfied by lead recovered from scrap, so that the demand for primary lead is not likely to reach the 1955 level even in 1975 (Table 11.5.1). Some increases in the consumption of primary lead may be forthcoming in Canada, however.

TABLE 11.5.1

CONSUMPTION OF PRIMARY LEAD IN INDUSTRIAL COUNTRIES
(thousand tons)

	1950	1955	1960	1970I	1970II	1975I	1975II
United States	803	735	528	620	640	680	720
Canada	50	54	41	50	50	60	70
Common Market......	290	453	545	620	640	690	730
United Kingdom	167	208	195	230	240	250	260
Northern Europe.......	83	95	126	160	170	180	190
Southern Europe.......	27	51	62	120	130	170	190
Japan	25	44	100	160	170	200	220
Industrial Countries, Total	1445	1640	1597	1960	2040	2230	2380

Source: Metallgesellschaft, Metal Statistics, various issues.

Domestic ore production nearly covered the lead requirements of the United States until World War II, but—with the exhaustion of some of the domestic deposits and the availability of low cost lead from abroad—domestic production subsequently declined while imports grew steadily. The period of falling prices after 1956 led to a further cutback in U.S. mine output, and only the imposition of quotas safeguarded production at a level of 220–230 thousand tons in terms of recoverable metal content. The quotas limited the annual commercial imports of unmanufactured lead—and zinc—into the United States to 80 per cent of the average yearly commercial imports during the period 1953–57. In the case of lead, 65 per cent of imports can enter in the form of metal, while the corresponding proportion is 26 per cent for zinc. Quotas are allocated to the major producing countries, and a residual amount is open to minor suppliers.

In the face of the unfavorable prospects for primary lead and the weak competitive position of the U.S. mining industry, the domestic production of lead ores can be maintained at present levels only under the umbrella of continued protection. We have assumed here that this protection would be forthcoming; thus imports would rise to the extent that the consumption of primary lead increased (Table A11.5.1). It has further been postulated that the relative shares of concentrates and metal in these imports would correspond to the proportions determined by quota regulations.

In distinction from the United States, Canada is a large exporter of lead. Canada ships lead concentrates to the United States and lead metal to the United States and the United Kingdom. A continuation of the expansion of Canadian lead output is foreseen and, given the expected small increase in domestic consumption, the increment in production will be largely exported.

Western Europe

The consumption of lead (primary and secondary) in Western Europe rose from 0.9 million tons in 1950 to 1.3 million tons in 1960. Despite the continuing expansion of the automobile industry, 1960. But, despite the continuing expansion of the automobile industry, a slowing down in the growth of lead consumption is anticipated by reason of the substitution of other materials for lead. Possibilities of substitution in favor of aluminum and plastic exist in cables, packaging, and in rolled products (sheets, pipes, tubes, etc.). In 1960, these uses accounted for over one-half of lead consumption in Western Europe, while the corresponding proportion was 15 per cent in the United States where the process of substitution has further advanced. Note also that, as far as available data on recovered lead permit the making of comparisons, the U.S. per capita consumption of lead appears to have been reached or approached in several highly industrialized European countries (United Kingdom, Germany, and Belgium).

On the basis of these considerations, and with account taken of the increased availability of secondary lead, we have projected the consumption of primary lead in Western Europe to reach 1.1 million tons in 1970 and 1.3 million tons in 1975, as compared to 0.9 million tons in 1960.[14] According to our projections, a 1 per cent increase in industrial production would be accompanied, on the average, by a 0.5 per cent rise in the consumption of primary lead. At the same time, in view of the continuing shipments of lead metal from Yugoslavia to the United States, European metal exports may be maintained approximately at present levels.

---

[14]The estimate of the Dewhurst study is 1.1 million tons for 1970 [*1*, p. 630].

In 1960, over 40 per cent of European lead requirements were supplied by domestic ore mined in Yugoslavia, Spain, Sweden, Germany, and Italy. Mine output will continue to increase, especially in Yugoslavia and Sweden, although probably at a slightly lower rate than consumption. Correspondingly, imports are projected to rise by over one-third between 1960 and 1970, and two-thirds between 1960 and 1975.

The countries of Western Europe imported 201 thousand tons of concentrates in 1960 as against 355 thousand tons of lead metal. Concentrates and metal had about equal shares in Common Market purchases, while the United Kingdom and other European countries imported chiefly lead metal. Among the main suppliers, Morocco and South Africa exported concentrates, whereas Australia, Mexico, Canada, and Peru shipped lead mainly in the form of metal. The approximate 6 per cent Common Market duty on metal, as against zero tariff on ores and concentrates, will protect the lead smelting industries of the Common Market countries, yet planned increases of refinery capacity in Morocco, Peru, and South Africa promise an increase in the share of metal in European imports. Imports of concentrates may also rise in absolute terms during the sixties and decline afterwards.

Japan

Lead consumption in Japan was growing at about the same rate as industrial production during the fifties, but it is expected to increase at a lower rate in the period of projection. Still, consumption may rise by about two-thirds between 1960 and 1970 and may double between 1960 and 1975.

Despite a threefold increase in domestic ore production, the degree of self-sufficiency in lead declined from 100 per cent in 1960 to 40 per cent in 1960 in Japan. Nevertheless, domestic reserves appear to be adequate to permit production to rise in proportion to the projected increase in consumption during the period 1960–1975, so that a slowing down in the rate of growth of imports is foreseen. The entire increment in imports is likely to take the form of metal.

Oceania and South Africa

Australia is the largest producer and exporter of lead. She provides for her own needs as well as for those of New Zealand. Exports from Southwest Africa (part of the customs territory of

South Africa) are also of importance. No change in the pattern of trade is envisaged during the period of projection.

The Price and Origin of Imports

Assuming present regulations to be maintained, the geographical composition of U.S. lead imports should change little in the period of projection. Some modifications in the pattern of European imports are expected, however. Continuing free access to the French market will contribute to the growth of Morocco's production, and the rise in South African exports may also be above average. Finally, much of the increase in Japanese imports will be supplied by Australia.

Our projections indicate that the lead exports of the developing countries, expressed in terms of lead content, would rise from 0.4 million tons in 1960 to 0.6 million tons in 1970 and 0.7 million tons in 1975 (Table A11.5.2). Within the increased imports, the share of metal may reach 70 per cent by 1975 as compared to 60 per cent in 1960, augmenting thereby the growth of the value of exports.

The fall in lead prices after 1956 was related to the decrease in U.S. consumption and stockpiling. Prices declined further after 1960, and the existence of large U.S. stockpiles will have a depressing influence on prices during much of the sixties. By 1970 the surplus in stockpiles may be removed, however, and assuming present U.S. import policies to continue, prices may return to approximately 1960 levels. On the other hand, Shea expects some rise in prices above the 1960 level [8] and an increase may in fact be forthcoming should U.S. import regulations be relaxed.

11.6 ZINC (SITC 283.5, 686.1)

Zinc finds its main uses in galvanized steel, diecastings, brass, and zinc oxides. The rate of increase of zinc consumption exceeded that of lead in recent decades, but the fall in the demand for brass products and diecastings on the part of the automobile industry, and the reduced use of zinc oxides in paints, led to a decline in U.S. zinc consumption after 1955. In most applications, zinc is not recoverable, and hence secondary zinc accounts for a relatively small part of consumption.

Lead and zinc deposits often occur in combination; thus, the major producers of lead ore also supply substantial quantities of zinc ore. In 1960, the United States, Canada, and the Soviet Union were the leading producers, followed by Australia and Mexico. Among developing countries, the mining of zinc ores is of importance also in Peru and the former Belgium Congo, but the smelting of zinc involves a more complex process than that of most non-ferrous metals, and hence developing countries export chiefly zinc concentrates rather than metal. Exports of zinc concentrates and metal account for about 3–4 per cent of the foreign exchange receipts of main exporting countries.

North America

The consumption of zinc declined in the United States during the second half of the fifties, but the projected expansion in construction activity and automobile production—the main uses of zinc—is expected to contribute to further increases during the period of projection; by 1970, the 1955 consumption level may again be surpassed. Increases in consumption are expected also in Canada (Table 11.6.1).

TABLE 11.6.1

CONSUMPTION OF PRIMARY ZINC IN INDUSTRIAL COUNTRIES
(thousand tons)

	1950	1955	1960	1970I	1970II	1975I	1975II
United States	1035	1123	870	1160	1200	1320	1400
Canada	49	53	49	60	60	70	80
Common Market.	360	548	687	890	930	1010	1090
United Kingdom	241	257	276	330	340	360	380
Northern Europe.	55	82	98	140	150	170	180
Southern Europe.	30	39	67	130	140	170	190
Japan	52	108	189	330	360	390	450
Industrial Countries, Total	1822	2210	2236	3040	3180	3490	3770

Source: Metallgesellschaft, Metal Statistics and U.S. Bureau of Mines, Mineral Yearbook.

The conclusions reached in regard to the production of lead ore in the United States pertain also to zinc, and we have assumed that domestic output would be stabilized at a level of 420 thousand tons. To meet increasing lead requirements, imports would then have to rise by about one-half between 1960 and 1970 and over three-fourths between 1960 and 1975 (Table A11.6.1). In view of the considerations noted in regard to lead, no change has been assumed in the composition of these imports, while we have assumed the disappearance of U.S. exports of zinc metal.

Canada produces zinc metal from domestic ore, chiefly for export. The United Kingdom and the United States are her largest markets, but exports to India and Japan are on the increase. In view of U.S. quota regulations, Canada also exports zinc concentrates to the United States. A continuing increase in exports is expected during the period of projection, with some slowing down after 1970.

Western Europe

Zinc consumption in Western Europe has been rising at about the same rate as industrial production in the last decade and, despite a possible retardation in the rate of growth of consumption, the outlook for zinc is better than for lead. Increases in the use of zinc are likely to be concentrated in the automobile industry and in steel galvanizing, while the prospects are less favorable for brass and bronze.

We have projected the consumption of primary zinc in Western Europe to reach 1.5 million tons in 1970 and 1.7 million tons in 1975 as compared to 1.1 million tons in 1960, corresponding to an implicit elasticity of 0.6 with respect to industrial production.[15] The smallest increase in consumption would take place in the United Kingdom, where U.S. consumption levels have been reached in 1960. At the same time, European exports of zinc metal to the United States may rise somewhat.

Italy, Germany, Spain, and Sweden are the main producers of zinc ore in Western Europe, and these countries have sufficient reserves to ensure an increase of production in proportion to the growth of consumption. Correspondingly, imports would rise from 0.6 million tons in 1960 to 0.9 million tons in 1970 and 1.1 million tons in 1975.

In 1960, about 60 per cent of European imports of zinc took the form of ores and concentrates—the remainder was metal. Zinc metal came chiefly from Canada, while ores and concentrates originated in Australia, Peru, Morocco, and the former Belgium Congo. With the setting up of smelters in Australia and some of the developing countries, the share of metal in European imports of zinc may reach one-half by 1970 and 60 per cent by 1975. In contrast, after a temporary increase during the sixties, the imports of concentrates may return to approximately the 1960 level.

Japan

The consumption of zinc increased nearly fourfold between 1950 and 1960 in Japan, while the degree of self-sufficiency declined from 100 to 73 per cent. With the expected slowing down in the growth of demand for zinc, however, production may keep up with the increase in consumption in the period of projection so that imports would rise at the same rate as consumption.

---

[15]The estimate of the Dewhurst study is 1.3–1.4 million tons for 1970 [*1*, p. 631].

Oceania and South Africa

Australia is a major producer of zinc, and exports chiefly zinc concentrates to Western Europe, the United States, and Japan. Exports will continue to rise during the period of projection and will increasingly take the form of metal. Australia will also provide for the zinc requirements of New Zealand.

While Southwest Africa exports zinc concentrates, South Africa imports zinc metal. We have assumed that the increase of South Africa's zinc requirements will be supplied from Southwest Africa.

The Price and Origin of Imports

Similar to the case of lead, no change has been assumed in the geographical composition of U.S. zinc imports. At the same time, the producers of the Belgium Congo, Algeria, and Morocco will have a preferential advantage in the EEC—or the French—market in zinc metal, and the share of Mexico and Peru in the imports of Western Europe may also rise, chiefly at the expense of the United States and Canada (Table A11.6.2). Nevertheless, by reason of the technical complexities of zinc smelting in the less developed countries, the shift from the exportation of concentrates to metal is likely to be slower in the case of zinc than in regard to lead.

In 1960, only 15 per cent of the zinc shipments of the developing countries were in the form of metal (chiefly from Mexico), and this proportion is not likely to surpass 35 per cent in 1975. Still, by reason of the high processing cost of zinc (in 1960, the average unit value of zinc metal entering world trade was $250 per ton, as compared to $130 for a ton of concentrates), the rise in the value of exports will substantially exceed the increase in trade volume.[16] Thus, the projected doubling in the volume of zinc exports from developing countries to industrial areas between 1960 and 1975 would be accompanied by approximately a 150 per cent increase in the value of exports.

11.7 TIN (SITC 283.6, 687.1)

Tin is used mainly in containers, solder, and bronze and brass goods. It is consumed in quantities considerably smaller than the other nonferrous metals discussed in the present chapter, but its high price makes the value of tin consumed in the industrial countries comparable to that of zinc or lead. And since industrial countries have to import practically all their tin requirements, tin oc-

---

[16]Similar to the case of lead, no change in unit values has been assumed.

cupies third place among nonferrous metals (behind copper and bauxite) in the export earnings of developing countries.

Much of the world's tin ore comes from a belt that runs from southern China through Thailand, Burma, and Malaya to Indonesia. Production in this area is derived from alluvial deposits where tin ores have been concentrated in the sand and gravel of river valleys and at the sea bottom. Another major producing area is the Andes in Bolivia and a third is located in Central Africa (chiefly Nigeria and the former Belgium Congo). The Soviet Union is also a producer of tin ore, while smaller quantities are mined in the United Kingdom, Portugal, and Japan.

Tin accounts for two-thirds of the export earnings of Boliva, one-sixth of the foreign exchange receipts of Malaya, and 5–6 per cent in the case of Indonesia, Thailand, and the former Belgium Congo. Bolivia, Nigeria, and the Congo ship tin in the form of concentrates. Malaya exports tin metal, and much of the tin ore produced in Indonesia and Thailand is also refined in Malaya for exportation in metal form. In contradistinction to the other major nonferrous metals, the ties between the producers and refiners of tin are rather loose, and the pattern of trade changes over time.

Tin comes under the International Tin Agreement—an international agreement between producing and consuming countries which was set up under the auspices of the United Nations "to insure adequate supplies of tin at reasonable prices and to prevent excessive fluctuations in the price of tin." The Agreement operates through purchases and sales of tin metal, should prices move outside prescribed limits.

North America

Substitution in favor of aluminum in containers, and the reduction of tin requirements per unit of output in tinplating, contributed to the decline of tin consumption in the United States during the last decade. In 1960, 75 thousand tons of tin metal were consumed, nearly one-third of which was secondary metal. A considerable degree of uncertainty surrounds the future prospects for tin. The Resources for the Future study projects some rise in consumption, but, with the increased availability of secondary metal, the demand for primary tin is expected to fall between 1960 and 1970, and to rise slightly afterwards. However, Canadian consumption may be maintained at present levels (Table 11.7.1).

The production of tin ore is practically nil in North America, and domestic requirements are supplied by imports of tin metal from Malaya and concentrates from Indonesia. With the continuing trend toward smelting in the producing countries, future requirments are likely to be met largely by imports of metal.

Western Europe

After some increases following the second world war, tin consumption (primary and secondary) in Western Europe stayed at a level of approximately 90 thousand tons. Consumption may rise somewhat during the period of projection, but part of the increase will take the form of secondary metal. Still, the consumption of primary tin may reach 75 thousand tons in 1970 and 80 thousand tons in 1975, as compared to 69 thousand tons in 1960.

The mine production of tin, expressed in terms of tin content, hardly surpassed 2 thousand tons in western Europe in 1960, and it is not expected to rise in the future. Imports come from Malaya and Mainland China (metal), as well as from Boliva, Nigeria, and the Congo (concentrates). The imported tin concentrates are refined in the United Kingdom, Belgium, and the Netherlands for domestic consumption and for export. This pattern of trade is expected to change, however, as developing countries increasingly turn toward the exportation of metal.

Japan

Japan is the only industrial country that has experienced a rapid expansion of tin consumption in recent years. By 1960, tin consumption in Japan reached 18 thousand tons, of which 85 per cent was primary metal. The demand for primary tin will increase at a slower rate during the period of projection, however, partly because the process of substitution for tin has hardly begun in Japan, and partly because secondary tin will supply an increasing part of Japanese tin requirements. On the other hand, the domestic production of tin will hardly change, so that imports will supply the entire increase in the consumption of primary tin.

Oceania and South Africa

Australia and New Zealand import tin metal from Malaya, while South Africa buys tin from the Congo. Some increases in imports have been assumed.

The Price and Origin of Imports

The price of tin fell to £800 per long ton in London in 1960, at which time there was substantial excess capacity. Prices fluctuated to a considerable extent in response to releases from U.S. stockpiles in 1961 and 1962, but greater stability is expected in later years when the London price may settle around the midpoint of the range of prices provided in the International Tin Agreement (£880). Correspondingly, in making projections, we have calculated with a 10 per cent increase in prices as compared to 1960. The same price assumption has been used with regard to concentrates.

Some changes in trade patterns are also expected. The United States is likely to buy tin from Latin America after the Bolivian smelter comes into operation, and Asian countries will also export more metal, thereby reducing shipments of concentrates to Europe for re-export in refined form. At the same time, mainland China is likely to turn increasingly to exporting tin in manufactured form; accordingly, we have assumed that Chinese shipments of tin would decline somewhat during the period of projection (Table A11.7.2).

All in all, the tin exports of developing countries are projected to rise from 117 thousand tons in 1960 to 134 thousand tons in 1970 and 143 thousand tons in 1975 under the most likely income assumption, and slightly higher if the target rate of income growth is reached. The share of tin metal in these exports may reach 80 per cent in 1975 as compared to 55 per cent in 1960. This shift will not greatly affect the value of exports, however, since the cost of smelting tin hardly exceeds 10 per cent of the price of concentrates, expressed in terms of tin content.

11.8 OTHER NONFERROUS METALS
(SITC 283.2, 8, 9, 285, 671.5)

Base Metals

Alloying metals such as nickel, chromium, tungsten, molybdenum, cobalt, and vanadium, as well as a number of special-purpose metals titanium, tantalum, zirconium), are included in this category. In finished form, these metals are traded chiefly among the industrial countries, although the United States purchases some ferroalloys world requirements in nickel. But nickel imports from New Caledonia are of importance for France, and in 1960 the United ing economies, shipped in the form of ores, concentrates, and metals, amounted to $213 million. Asia and the islands of Oceania had 40 per cent of this trade; Latin America and Africa, about 30 per cent each.

Several of the metals of this category are produced chiefly in the industrial countries. The United States is the major producer of molybdenum and vanadium, while Canada supplies most of the world requirements in nickel. But, nickel imports from New Caledonia are of importance for France, and in 1960 the United States imported substantial quantities of nickel oxide from Cuba. Although the United States is the largest producer of titanium minerals, she also imports some ore for re-export in metal form.

Chromite, the chief ore of chromium, is mined in South Africa, Southern Rhodesia, Turkey, the Philippines and, among the Soviet bloc countries, in the Soviet Union and Albania. Canada supplies some of the world's cobalt ore, but the largest reserves are in Northern Rhodesia and the former Belgium Congo. Finally, tungsten is exported from South Korea, Brazil, Boliva, and Australia, while Nigeria is a major producer of columbium and tantalum.

Among the importing areas, the countries of North America are self-sufficient in most of these metals, but derive their requirements of chromium, tungsten, and columbium from imports. The United States also buys nickel and titanium ore. In 1960, the value of these imports originating in less developed areas amounted to $55 million, of which zinc oxide imported from Cuba accounted for $20 million.

In Western Europe, tungsten is produced in Portugal and titanium in Norway, yet these countries meet only part of the requirements of European industry, and Western Europe is the major importer of alloying metals. Molybdenum and vanadium come from the United States, much of nickel from Canada, while chromium and the other metals of this group are supplied from a variety of sources. Imports from developing countries amount to $118 million in 1960. Finally, Japan is also a large importer of alloying metals, taking about one-fifth of the exports of developing countries.

The consumption of some of these metals, particularly those with specialized defense uses, has varied greatly from year to year. Treated as a group, however, we may presume that a relationship exists between their consumption and steel output, although titanium is a substitute for steel. Considering the increasing importance of alloyed steel and possible increases in the use of titanium, we have assumed that the demand for this group of metals will be rising at a rate somewhat higher than the output of steel. In making projections, further adjustments have been made for trade among industrial countries, and account has also been taken of the probable shift of U.S. nickel imports from Cuba to Canada, Puerto Rico, and Southeast Asia. Constant prices have been assumed in the projections.

Silver and Platinum Ores (285)

Ores and concentrates as well as waste and sweepings of silver, platinum, and platinum-type metals are included in this category. The value of the imports of these metals from developing countries amounted to $3 million in 1960, all of which came from Latin America. No definite trend has been shown in the last decade, and it has been assumed that this trade will remain at levels experienced in 1960 throughout the period of projection.

11.9 SCRAP METAL (SITC 282, 284)

Trade in scrap metal takes place chiefly among the industrial countries themselves. Western Europe and Japan are net importers of steel scrap, while the United States is the main source of these imports. The United States also ships nonferrous scrap to destinations in Europe and Japan. Imports of scrap metal from underdeveloped areas amounted to $89 million in 1960, of which $55 million was ferrous scrap.

In 1960, Japan imported $46 million worth of iron and steel scrap from developing countries, while the corresponding figure was $9 million for Western Europe. With the establishment of steel foundries in many underdeveloped countries, a decline in available scrap is indicated, however. Correspondingly, we have assumed that the imports of iron and steel scrap originating in the developing countries would fall during the period under consideration. Similar considerations apply to nonferrous scrap, although, given the relatively slow expansion of capacity for the processing of nonferrous metals in the less developed areas, the fall in their exports of nonferrous scrap is likely to be of smaller magnitude than in the case of steel scrap.

11.10 CRUDE FERTILIZERS AND OTHER
CRUDE MATERIALS (SITC 271, 272)

CRUDE FERTILIZERS (SITC 271)

This category includes natural fertilizers of animal and vegetable origin: sodium nitrates, phosphates, and crude potassic salts. Chile is the main exporter of sodium nitrates, phosphates originate chiefly in North Africa and the Netherlands Antilles, while European countries are the main exporters of potassic salts. In 1960, the exports of crude fertilizers from developing countries to developed economies were valued at $122 million, of which two-thirds went to Western Europe and the remainder was divided between the United States, Japan, and Oceania.

The United States is a net exporter of crude fertilizers. Imports account for a small portion of domestic consumption, and natural sodium nitrate—the main import—has declined in importance over the past decades. Domestic sources are judged to be adequate to meet future demand during the period of projection, and hence there is little expectation for a rise in imports from developing countries. Correspondingly, we have assumed that imports would remain at the level experienced in 1960, when $18 million worth of crude fertilizers were purchased from Latin America.

On the other hand, imports of crude fertilizers into Western Europe have shown an upward trend in recent years, although the share of developing countries in these imports declined. In 1960, imports from less developed countries were valued at $82 million, with phosphatic rock from Morocco and Tunisia accounting for about 90 per cent of the total. Smaller quantities of sodium nitrates originate in Chile, and there are some imports also from the Middle East and the Pacific Islands.

Natural rock phosphates are used in the manufacture of phosphatic fertilizers or are applied as ground rock phosphate. Since the imports of rock phosphates and the consumption of phosphatic fertilizers move parallel,[17] the imports of phosphatic rock have been projected by utilizing the relationship between agricultural output of vegetable origin and the consumption of phosphatic fertilizers. During the postwar period a 1.0 per cent increase in output appears to be associated with a 1.2 per cent rise in phosphatic fertilizer consumption. We have assumed agricultural output of vegetable origin to rise at an annual rate of 2 per cent per year, and projected the consumption of phosphatic fertilizers to increase by 27 per cent between 1960 and 1970, and 43 per cent between 1960 and 1975. The rise of imports from developing countries will be somewhat slower, however, since the share of these countries in total imports may continue to decline from the present 80 per cent level.

Japanese imports of crude fertilizers consist chiefly of rock phosphates. Imports from less developed countries ($8 million in 1960) account for about one-third of the total, and have fluctuated around 450 thousand tons during the last decade. With sizable additions to

---

[17]The domestic production of phosphatic rock in Western Europe is negligible. In 1960, production amounted to 50 thousand tons as compared to imports of 9.8 million tons.

fertilizer capacity under way, a rise in imports during the period 1960–1975 projected.

Finally, Australia and New Zealand import mainly rock phosphates from the Pacific Islands, with imports amounting to $13 million in 1960. The consumption of phosphate fertilizers increased at an annual rate of 5 per cent during the fifties, although the rate of increase did not exceed 3 per cent in the second half of the period. In making projections, we have calculated with an annual rate of growth of 2.5 per cent, and have assumed that imports of rock phosphates would rise in proportion to the consumption of phosphatic fertilizers. No change has been assumed in the prices and the geographical composition of imports.

OTHER CRUDE MINERALS (SITC 272)

This category includes numerous minerals classified in four subgroups: (1) stone, sand, and gravel; (2) sulphur and unroasted iron pyrite; (3) natural abrasives, including industrial diamonds; and (4) a variety of miscellaneous crude minerals. Imports from less developed countries come chiefly under the fourth group which includes natural asphalt and bitumen, clay and other refractory minerals, salt, crude asbestos, quartz, mica, fluorspar, as well as chalk and crude natural borates.

Imports of these minerals from developing countries were valued at $126 million in 1960, with nearly one-half going to Western Europe and over one-third to North America. Latin-American countries, chiefly Mexico, account for 35 per cent of this trade; and African exporters, for another one-fifth. Smaller quantities originate in the Middle East.

North American imports of crude minerals from less developed areas amounted to $47 million in 1960, with Mexico as the main supplier. Imports from developing countries have increased somewhat over the last decade, and some further increases have been projected.

European imports of crude materials originating in developing economies were valued at $59 million in 1960, with nearly one-half of the total coming from Africa, and the remainder divided between Latin America, the Middle East, and Asia. Although subject to large year-to-year fluctuations, an upward trend is indicated by the data, and we have projected imports from less developed countries to rise at an annual rate of 4 per cent, reaching $87 million in 1970 and $106 million in 1975. Some increases of imports into Japan ($12 million in 1960) and Oceania ($3 million) have also been projected, while prices have been assumed to remain at levels experienced in 1960.

REFERENCES

[1.] DEWHURST, J. FREDERIC, AND ASSOCIATES. *Europe's Need and Resources.* New York: Macmillan and Co., 1961.

[2.] EUROPEAN COAL AND STEEL COMMUNITY. *Tenth General Report.* Luxembourg, 1962.

[3.] HYDE, R. W.; LANE, B. M.; AND GLASER, W. W. "Iron Ore Resources of the World," *Engineering and Mining Journal* (December, 1962), pp. 84–88.

[4.] LANDSBERG, HANS H., ET AL. *Resources in America's Future.* Baltimore: Johns Hopkins Press, 1963.

[5.] PARSONS, A. B. "Copper Mining—What to Expect in the Year 2000 A.D.," *Mining World,* November, 1961.

[6.] ROSENZWEIG, J. E. *The Demand for Aluminum: A Case Study in Long-Range Forecasting.* Urbana, Illinois: Bureau of Economic and Business Research, College of Commerce and Business Administration of the University of Illinois, 1957.

[7.] SHEA, WILLIAM P. "The Price of Copper, 1960–75," *Engineering and Mining Journal* (August, 1959), pp. 91–94.

[8.] ————. "The Price of Lead, 1961–1975," *Engineering and Mining Journal* (September, 1961), pp. 98–102.

[9.] UNITED NATIONS ECONOMIC COMMISSION FOR EUROPE. *Long-Term Trends and Problems of the European Steel Industry.* Geneva, 1959.

[10.] UNITED NATIONS ECONOMIC AND SOCIAL COUNCIL. *Prospective Demand for Non-Agricultural Commodities.* Problems of Definition and Projection Methodology. New York, 1962.

[11.] U.S. BUREAU OF MINES. *Minerals Yearbook, 1960.* Washington, D.C.

CHAPTER 12

Trade Projections for Manufactured Goods

12.1 CHEMICALS (SITC 5)[1]

EXPORTS of chemical manufactures from underdeveloped areas to developed countries showed a moderate increase during the fifties and reached $119 million in 1960. North America and Western Europe share approximately equally in this trade, with 5 per cent of the total going to Japan and Oceania. Nearly two-thirds of the exports originate in Latin America, while the countries of Africa and Asia account for much of the remainder.

Essential oils and perfume materials constitute the largest single group in the chemical exports of less developed economies. India, Réunion, Taiwan, Morocco, Algeria, and the Malagasy Republic are the main exporters, and exports totaled $30 million in 1960. Since the final good (perfume) is a luxury item of consumption, trade in the intermediate product (essential oils and perfume materials) can be expected to increase more rapidly than the gross national product of the importing countries. An income elasticity of 1.6 has been assumed in the projections.

Organic chemicals form the second largest group in the chemical exports of the less developed countries, amounting to $22 million in 1960. In the same year, the exports of inorganic chemicals were valued at $13 million. Organic chemicals include, among other things, menthol exported by Brazil and Taiwan, ethyl alcohol from Peru and Brazil, and sundry items from Mexico; examples for inorganic chemicals are furfural from the Dominican Republic and iodine from Chile. Trade in these two groups of commodities has been increasing more or less steadily during the last decade and we have assumed that it will rise in proportion with the growth of GNP in the developed countries over the 1960–1975 period.

Dyeing and tanning extracts ($14 million in 1960) are a further item of some importance. Argentina is the main exporter; the United States, France, and Germany the principal importers. But

---

[1]Excluding alumina and nickel oxide.

329

Argentine exports compete with domestically produced substances in the developed countries and have failed to increase during the fifties. We have assumed that these exports will remain at the 1960 level throughout the period of projection.

Miscellaneous chemicals, exported chiefly by Argentina, medical and pharmaceutical products from Brazil, and a small quantity of manufactured fertilizers from Tunisia and Israel account for the remainder of the chemicals group. Trade in these commodities has been rising over the last decade but no definite trend is shown. We have assumed future increases to proceed *pari passu* with the growth of incomes in the developed countries.

Taken together, the exports of chemicals from the less developed areas to developed economies would rise by about one-half between 1960 and 1970, and 80 per cent between 1960 and 1975, under the most likely income assumption. Increases would be somewhat larger, however, if the target rate of income growth were reached.

12.2 LEATHER AND FOOTWEAR (SITC 61, 85)

In 1960, developed countries imported leather from developing economies in the value of $60 million, while footwear imports amounted to $21 million. With regard to leather, we will concentrate our attention on Western Europe, since this area takes about 90 per cent of the exports of developing countries. At the same time, much of the footwear exports of less developed areas are destined for the United States and the United Kingdom.

Exports and imports of leather approximately balance in Western Europe, but imports have been rising over time and accounted for 3 per cent of domestic consumption in 1960. India is the largest supplier of leather to Europe, with a trade value of $46 million in 1960. Much of this goes to the United Kingdom, where India enjoys an average preference of 9 per cent, while France and Germany import mainly leather made of goat and sheepskins that does not bear duty in the Common Market. France also imports leather from Morocco.

In conformity with our discussion of the export prospects for hides and skins (Chapter 9.1), leather imports into Western Europe have been assumed to rise by 20 per cent between 1960 and 1970 and 30 per cent between 1960 and 1975. Moroccan exports to France may expand at a higher rate, however, since Morocco does not have to pay the 12 per cent EEC duty in the French market. Imports into the United States and Oceania can also increase somewhat from their present low level, and the removal of restrictions is likely to be followed by a rapid expansion of imports into Japan.

Footwear exports of developing countries are small but have been growing rapidly in recent years. Exports doubled between 1953 and 1960 and were valued at $21 million in 1960, about four-fifths of which came from Hong Kong. Trade takes place chiefly in rubber footwear, with the United States and the United Kingdom each accounting for nearly one-half of the total. Hong Kong producers enjoy preferences of 20 per cent in Britain but pay duties of 15-20 per cent in the Common Market countries.

Exports to the United States and the United Kingdom may double within a decade, but in view of the high EEC tariff, sales to the Common Market countries are not likely to increase substantially. The prospects for exports to Japan are not favorable either, considering that Japan is a strong competitor in the world market.

Our projections indicate that the combined exports of leather and footwear from developing countries to developed economies would rise by about 50 per cent between 1960 and 1970 and 85 per cent between 1960 and 1975. Although exports from Latin America and Africa are expected to grow at the most rapid rate, the main benefit from the projected increase in trade would probably accrue to India and Hong Kong.

12.3 VENEER, PLYWOOD, WOOD AND CORK MANUFACTURES, AND PAPER (SITC 63, 64)

Plywood and veneer are of greatest importance within this category and will be given more detailed consideration here. Exports of plywood and veneer from underdeveloped areas to developed countries amounted to $35 million in 1960, as compared to exports of wood and cork manufactures of $7 million and paper and paper products of $8 million.

Plywood and veneer have assumed increasing importance in the timber consumption of developed countries since World War II. Their use has grown most rapidly in the United States and Canada, where the average consumption of plywood is $50m^3$ per 1000 capita. By comparison among European countries, the $10m^3$ level has been surpassed only in Finland, the United Kingdom, and Germany; and the European average does not exceed $8m^3$. Finally, consumption per 1000 capita is around $10m^3$ in Japan, Australia, and New Zealand, but it has not yet reached $1\ m^3$ in South Africa.[2]

---

[2]Reliable data on veneer are not available for most countries, but, at any rate, the bulk of veneer is used in plywood manufacturers.

Differences are observed in regard to trade patterns, too. Whereas imports of plywood and veneer of tropical origin have been rising rapidly in the United States, among the countries of Western Europe only the United Kingdom imports appreciable quantities of plywood from underdeveloped areas. Other European countries, as well as Japan, import hardwood logs for transformation by domestic wood processing industries. Japan is also a large exporter of plywood and accounted for over two-thirds of U.S. tropical plywood imports in 1960. Finally, Australia, New Zealand, and South Africa purchase small quantities of plywood.

As regards the future demand for plywood and veneer, note that past projections of U.S. consumption and imports have generally proved to be underestimates. For example, while the USDA Forest Service expected a doubling of consumption and a threefold rise in imports between 1952 and 1975, the level of consumption and imports envisaged for 1975 has been surpassed in 1961 [*3*, pp. 465–66, *4*, p. 34]. Domestic production provided for the increased consumption of softwood plywood, but the U.S. output of hardwood veneer logs hardly changed, so that the rise in the consumption of hardwood plywood and veneer had to be supplied by imports.

An important factor in the recent increase of U.S. hardwood plywood consumption has been the replacement of the traditional panel door by flush doors made largely of plywood. Between 1947 and 1958, the production of flush doors increased from a few hundred thousand to more than 15 million [*4*, p. 21]. Additional factors contributing to the rise of plywood consumption include its increased use in furniture making, containers, and mobile homes.

New uses for plywood are found almost daily, and it may not be unreasonable to assume that the approximately 50 per cent increase in the consumption of hardwood plywood experienced during the last decade would again take place during the sixties. With unchanged domestic production, this would necessitate a rise in imports by one and one-half times. Increases are likely to be smaller after 1970, however.

In 1960, the United States and Canada imported plywood and veneer of tropical origin in the value of $74 million, of which $54 million came after processing in Japan. During the period of projection, the Philippines and other producers in Southeast Asia are expected to get a larger share of the market, however, as these countries endeavor to ship more timber in processed form. On the basis of available information on the construction of wood processing facilities, we may expect imports from less developed areas to quadruple between 1960 and 1970, and to double between 1970 and 1975. Correspondingly, the share of the less developed countries in the imports of tropical plywood and veneer into North America would rise from 30 per cent in 1960 to nearly two-thirds in 1975.

Imports of tropical plywood and veneer into the United Kingdom amounted to $17 million in 1960, of which one-half came from Japan and the remainder chiefly from Nigeria and Israel. At the same time, the imports of the Continental countries hardly surpassed $5 million and originated largely in Gabon.

A comparison of U.S. and European consumption levels indicates that there are considerable possibilities for an increase in the consumption of plywood in Western Europe. However, it appears likely that—with the exception of plywood imported from Gabon—the countries of Continental Europe will continue to import hardwood logs and will effect the process of transformation domestically (cf. Chapter 93). Thus, although the United Kingdom will increase its purchases of plywood, imports are likely to remain comparatively small in absolute terms.

Japan does not import plywood but exports over one-fourth of her domestic output. On the other hand, Australia, New Zealand, and South Africa are importers, and about one-half of their imports come from tropical areas, chiefly Southeast Asia. Imports into Oceania and South Africa have been assumed to double within a decade.

Finally, developing countries exported wood and cork manufactures to developed economies in the value of $7 million in 1960, and Morocco and Tunisia also exported small quantities of paper to France ($7 million). While a rapid increase in the exports of wood and cork manufactures is foreseen, a rise in paper exports does not appear likely. Taken together, the exports of plywood, veneer, and other wood manufacturers from underdeveloped areas have been projected to increase about threefold between 1960 and 1970 and fivefold between 1960 and 1975. Among exporting areas, the countries of Southeast Asia are likely to make the largest gains.

12.4 YARN, COTTON FABRICS, AND CLOTHING
(SITC 651, 652, 941)

Within the category of manufactured goods, the less developed countries have shown the best export performance in cotton textiles and clothing (for short, cotton textiles). While in 1953 cotton textile exports to developed countries amounted to only $40 million, exports reached $316 million in 1960, accounting for nearly one-third of all manufactured exports of the developing countries. Most of this increase has taken place in cotton fabrics and in clothing, the exports of which were valued at $122 million and $167 million, respectively. In the same year, the exports of yarn and thread amounted to $27 million.

Among developing countries, India is the largest exporter of textile yarn (chiefly coir yarn), India and Hong Kong share much of the market in cotton textiles, and Hong Kong accounts for most of the trade in clothing. Taken together, over 90 per cent of cotton textiles exported by developing countries originate in Asia, while the remainder is divided among the countries of Latin America, Africa, and the Middle East.

Increases in textile imports have been concentrated in two markets: in the United States and the United Kingdom. In 1960, the former imported cotton textiles from less developed areas in the value of $134 million, and the latter, $113 million. Imports into other developed countries have been restricted by high tariffs and quotas, and so-called voluntary quotas made their appearance in the late fifties in the United States and the United Kingdom, too. As a result, the growth of British imports slowed down after 1959, while U.S. imports declined in 1961 and regained the 1960 level only in 1962. It appears, therefore, that the future prospects of the exports of cotton textiles from developing countries will be determined by changes in restrictive regulations rather than by the play of competitive forces.

The International Cotton Textiles Agreement signed in October, 1962 by 22 producing and consuming countries calls for a gradual expansion of trade in textiles over the next five years. The key clauses of the agreement state the obligation of the importing nations to increase their imports of textiles from low wage countries (less developed countries and Japan) during the period 1962–1967 at an annual rate of 5 per cent. The United Kingdom and Canada, however, attached reservations to the Agreement which exempted them from the application of the 5 per cent clause.[3] On the other hand, the Common Market countries accepted obligations for increases of 88 per cent over the 1962–1967 period, while the annual increase of imports would be 19 per cent in Austria and 15 per cent for Denmark, Norway, and Sweden [1].

Although the coverage of the Agreement does not exactly correspond to SITC groups 651, 652, and 842, trade in most of the

---

[3]Note further that the United States invoked the "market-disruption" clause of the Agreement and temporarily limited her imports to the 1961–62 level.

products included in these categories will be affected, and thus we have calculated with the rates of change specified in the Agreement in projecting the growth of imports of all cotton textiles. It has further been assumed that the Agreement will be extended until 1975, and that imports into all countries other than the United Kingdom and Canada will rise at an annual rate of 5 per cent in the years of 1967–1975. Finally, no change has been assumed in the origin of imports into individual areas.[4]

An increase in imports at the rates postulated does not appear to inflict a heavy burden on the importing nations, since textile products originating in developing countries would still account for only a small fraction of domestic consumption in 1975. Special considerations apply to the United Kingdom and Canada, however, where the share of these imports in domestic consumption is the largest.

Britain consumed 312 thousand tons of cotton textiles in 1960, one-third of which was imported [2]. In the same year, nearly one-half of British imports originated in developing countries. Should the 5 per cent annual rate specified in the Agreement be applied in the case of the United Kingdom, the rise in the imports of cotton textiles from developing countries would exceed the absolute increase of 50 thousand tons in the British consumption of cotton projected for the period 1960–1975 (Chapter 9.6). Such an outcome does not appear likely, however, and we have instead assumed that about one-half of the increment in consumption would be supplied by the developing countries, corresponding to a slightly over 2 per cent annual increase in imports. The same ratio has been applied in projecting imports into Canada.

According to our projections, the textile imports of the United States from developing countries would amount to $250 million in 1975 as compared to $134 million in 1960, while U.K. imports would rise from $113 million to $154 million; and the imports of Continental Europe, from $38 million to $178 million. Textile exports from developing countries to developed areas, taken together, would thus reach $658 million in 1975, representing an approximate threefold increase over the 1960 level.

12.5 JUTE MANUFACTURES (SITC 653.4 AND 656.1)

In 1960, developed countries imported jute manufactures from developing areas in the value of $175 million. Jute fabrics ac-

---

[4]An exception has been taken in the case of exports from Africa to the United States which fell temporarily during the base year.

counted for three-fourths of these imports, and jute sacks and bags for one-fourth. Sixty per cent of imports (almost exclusively jute fabrics) went to North America, and the remainder was approximately evenly divided between Western Europe (fabrics and jute bags) and Oceania (sacks and bags). India is the main supplier of jute manufactures to developed countries, but increasing quantities originate also in Pakistan.

According to the projections given in Chapter 9.4, future increases in the consumption of jute in North America would be supplied by imports of burlap, so that the imports of jute manufactures would rise by about 10 per cent between 1960 and 1970 and 17 per cent between 1960 and 1975. On the other hand, should existing restrictions be maintained, the share of jute manufactures in European imports would not rise substantially.

The Common Market levies a 23 per cent duty on jute fabrics, in addition to which quotas are also applied. These restrictions are often prohibitive; at the present, only Germany imports jute fabrics from India and Pakistan, and imports of sacks and bags, too, are small. A state monopoly limits the imports of jute manufactures also in the United Kingdom, which presently accounts for three-fourths of European imports. Nevertheless, some increases in the share of jute manufactures in European imports may be forthcoming, and we have assumed that, by 1975, 20 per cent of the jute consumption of Western Europe would be imported in the form of manufactures as against 15 per cent in 1960. Correspondingly, European imports of jute manufactures would rise by about 20 per cent between 1960 and 1970 and 40 per cent between 1960 and 1975. In view of our previous discussion (Chapter 9.4), increases will be smaller in Australia and New Zealand.

12.6 FLOOR COVERINGS AND OTHER TEXTILE PRODUCTS (SITC 653–657)[4]

The exports of developing countries included in this category amounted to $102 million in 1960. Floor coverings and tapestries formed the largest group ($60 million), followed by special textile products, such as ropes and cords ($25 million), and made-up textiles ($17 million).

Exports of floor coverings and tapestries from less developed areas expanded rapidly during the fifties and nearly tripled between 1953 and 1960. Iran, India, and Afghanistan are the largest sup-

[4]Excluding 653.4 and 656.1.

pliers, and Germany and Britain their main markets. India exports chiefly to the United Kingdom ($9 million in 1960) where she enjoys a Commonwealth preference, while the largest volume of trade occurs between Iran and Germany, ($20 million).

The Common Market countries purchase mainly high quality tapestry from developing economies, and the high EEC tariff will continue to serve as a barrier to imports of cheap carpets. Nevertheless, tapestries being a luxury good, a continuation of the rapid expansion of imports is expected, and it may not be unreasonable to assume that a 1 per cent increase in per capita incomes would be accompanied by a 2 per cent rise in imports per head. Smaller increases are likely to be forthcoming in imports into the United States and the United Kingdom which include low quality carpets. Taken together, the exports of floor coverings and tapestries originating in less developed areas may reach $140 million by 1975 as compared to $60 million in 1960.

Trade in cords and ropes takes place between Mexico and the United States. Exports rose rapidly during the fifties as Mexico shifted from the exportation of henequen fiber to shipping the final product. In view of the slow expansion of the demand for cordage, increases will be smaller in the future; we have projected exports to rise by 80 per cent between 1960 and 1975, while it took seven years to accomplish a comparable increase during the fifties. Finally, we have assumed that the growth of exports of made-up textiles will follow past trends.

According to our projections, the exports of carpets and other textiles included in this category would rise by 134–158 per cent between 1960 and 1975, depending on the income assumption chosen. Among exporting areas, the largest gain would be shown in the carpet-exporting countries of the Middle East and Asia.

12.7 SILVER, PRECIOUS STONES, PEARLS, AND JEWELRY (SITC 667, 681, 697)

This category includes precious stones and pearls, with exports of $55 million in 1960, as well as silver and platinum ($36 million) and jewerly ($3 million). Among developing countries, Israel is the largest exporter of precious stones and pearls, and accounted for over one-half of these exports in 1960. Exports rose rapidly during the fifties, increasing about fivefold between 1953 and 1960. The United States and Belgium are the principal importers.

Since precious stones and pearls are luxury goods, we can assume that imports will rise at a rate exceeding the growth of disposable income in the developed countries. In making projections, we have calculated with an income elasticity of import demand of 2. Correspondingly, the exports of developing countries to developed economies would approximately double between 1960 and 1970 and triple between 1960 and 1975.

A rapid increase is shown also in the imports of silver and platinum from developing countries, and the volume of trade rose sevenfold between 1953 and 1960. Mexico and Peru are the main suppliers, and Germany and Britain take much of the imports. More recently, imports into the United States have also increased as new uses for silver have been found, and it may not be unreasonable to assume that imports would double over the next decade. Similar considerations apply to jewelry.

12.8 MACHINERY AND METAL MANUFACTURES (SITC, 67, 68, 69, 7)[5]

At first glance, the exports of machinery and transport equipment from less developed countries seem to be unexpectedly large. The published data show less developed countries exporting $23 million worth of power generating machinery, $19 million worth of ships and boats, $11 million of electrical machinery, and even $7 million of aircraft to developed economies. Closer examination reveals, however, that most of these items are not genuine exports.

Almost all of trade reported in power generating machinery and aircraft consist of shipments to the United Kingdom for repair. The same holds for much of the electrical apparatus, while the exportation of ships and boats by Liberia and Panama can be properly classified as resale. We have therefore excluded these transactions in estimating actual trade, and regarded only shipments of electrical apparatus from Hong Kong as genuine exports ($6 million in 1960).

The metal manufactures exported by developing countries to developed economies consisted of $14 million worth of steel products, $18 million of worked copper, and $16 million of miscellaneous metal manufactures. Among steel products, Chile and Mexico export girders, bars, plates, and rods to the United States, while India and Egypt ship ingots, blooms, and slags to Italy, Britain, and Germany. Finally, India and Hong Kong sell miscellaneous metal manufactures to the United States and the United Kingdom, and much of worked copper imports originate in Chile.

Trade in these commodities has shown large fluctuations over the

---

[5]Excluding ferroalloys and unwrought metals.

last decade although an upward trend is evident. In the absence of information on changes in competitive conditions, it is hazardous to make a guess as to the future course of trade, and it is a measure of our ignorance rather than an expression of confidence that we have assumed a doubling of exports between 1960 and 1970 and a tripling between 1960 and 1975.

12.9 OTHER MANUFACTURED GOODS (SITC 62, 66, 8)[6]

Manufactured goods not classified elsewhere are included in this category, with exports of developing countries to developed areas amounting to $96 million in 1960. Of this total, $59 million comes under group 899 of the SITC which brings together a great variety of products (carving, basketwork, candles, umbrellas, wigs, etc.) Exports of the latter group of commodities originate chiefly in Hong Kong ($40 million in 1960) and are destined for the United States, the United Kingdom, Germany, and Canada. Trade in these products has been increasing rapidly in recent years, and, in the absence of specific indicators as to future developments, a doubling has been assumed for the next decade. A somewhat slower expansion is anticipated in regard to the other items included in this category, however, in the case of which smaller increases were experienced during the fifties.

REFERENCES

[1.] GENERAL AGREEMENT ON TARIFFS AND TRADE. *Long-Term Agreement Regarding International Trade in Cotton Textiles.* Geneva, 1963.

[2.] "Per Capita Fiber Consumption Levels." *Monthly Bulletin of Agricultural Economics and Statistics* (January, 1962), pp. 1–29.

[3.] RETTIE, J. C., AND HAIR, DWIGHT. "The Future Demand for Timber," *Timber Resources for America's Future.* Forest Resource Report No. 14. Washington, D.C., 1958.

[4.] U.S. DEPARTMENT OF AGRICULTURE, FOREST SERVICE AND AGRICULTURAL STABILIZATION AND CONSERVATION SERVICE. *The Demand and Price Situation for Forest Products.* September, 1962.

---

[6]Excluding 667, 841, 851, and 897.

APPENDIX TO CHAPTER 1

Methodological Problems in Forecasting International Trade

A1.1 OBJECTIVE AND SCOPE OF STUDY

This study aims at estimating the trade balance and, ultimately, the current account balance of less developed areas for 1970 and 1975. One possible method of estimation would be to build a foreign trade model that also included all trade among developed and among underdeveloped countries so as to encompass world trade in its entirety. We have not adopted this approach, however, since such a model would provide little additional information for the problem at hand, while it would greatly increase the difficulties of estimation.

To begin with, the time period for which data are available in the necessary breakdown is not long enough to enable us to deal with a large number of variables. Also, estimation of a world trade model would necessarily involve a high degree of aggregation, while structural changes reduce the applicability of aggregate relationships in making projections. Finally, the exchange of manufactured goods—the main products of the developed countries—is the most volatile part of international trade and even if we succeeded in establishing functional relationships with regard to trade in these commodities for past periods, these can hardly give indication of future developments.

Correspondingly, we have adopted a stepwise method of estimation in the present study. First, we have estimated future incomes in the developed countries and their imports from developing economies associated with projected income levels. Incomes in developed countries are regarded as exogenous in the model under the assumption that the feedback from their trade with developing economies is relatively small. But while we can assume a unidirectional relationship between incomes and import demand in the developed countries, prices and quantities are mutually interdependent. To take account of the interrelationship of prices and quantities, a method of successive approximations has been employed.[1]

Information given in national plans and estimates prepared by international organizations have been utilized in projecting the exports of developing countries to the Sino-Soviet area, while the future import requirements of less developed regions have been estimated with reference to expected changes in their gross domestic product and the relationship between GDP and imports. In contradistinction to the case of developed economies, in forecasting the national income of developing regions account has been taken of the effects of their export performance on economic growth. For this purpose, we have utilized the estimates on the future export earnings of developing countries contained in the earlier part of the study.

The availability of data permits the detailed estimation of the imports of developed countries from less developed areas, which account for 87 per cent of the export earnings of the latter. The methodological problems associated with these projections are discussed in this appendix, while the methods used in estimating trade with the Sino-Soviet area and the imports of developing regions are described in Chapter 4. Finally, in Chapter 5, problems arising from the estimation of service items are dealt with.

A1.2 THE CHOICE OF THE TIME PERIOD

In the present study, estimates have been provided for the years 1970 and 1975, and comparisons made with data for the year 1960. It is understood, however, that the forecasts should be interpreted as referring to the years centering around 1970 and around 1975 rather than to a particular year. International trade in any given year will be influenced by market conditions, crop failures and cyclical factors. Also, the rise in the GNP of industrial countries projected for 1970 may be attained in 1969 or 1971 instead of 1970.

At the time of preparation of the estimates, data on trade up to and including 1960 were available. This means that the period of projection extends over ten and fifteen years respectively. It is an often invoked rule of thumb that the period of projection should not be longer than the base period, the data of which are used in preparing the estimates. In the present instance, a decision had to be made as to the inclusion of interwar years in the period of ob-

---

[1]See section A1.5.

servation and the choice of years in the period following the Second World War.

In the postwar period, the use of data for the years 1950 to 1960 appeared to be the appropriate choice, although in the case of the United States the period of observation often includes the years 1947–1949. In the years before 1950, the postwar rationing, trade and payments restrictions, the reconstruction after the war, and the 1949 devaluation greatly influenced the course of international trade; thus, the experience of these years can be of little use in forecasting future developments. Finally, in a few cases when the Korean War greatly affected trade flows, only the period since 1953 has been considered.

A further problem relates to the inclusion of interwar years in the period of observation. Theoretically, the ideal solution would be to calculate regressions separately (1) for the interwar years, (2) for the period after World War II, and (3) for the entire period. If the differences between the coefficients, estimated from the three series of observations, are not statistically significant, (3) could be used as the best estimator [*10* p. 20]. For several reasons this approach has not been adopted in the present study, however.

Reference should first be made to the limitations of data on trade in the interwar years. Although some good compilations of trade statistics are available for this period, they are inferior in quality to postwar statistics, and differences in classification and inadequate breakdowns create further difficulties. Moreover, there is evidence of structural changes which had taken place during the forties as a result of the substitution of artificial for natural raw materials, the reduction of material input coefficients in a number of industries, and the observed tendency toward the lessening of income inequalities in several countries.

Some of the difficulties encountered in using time series encompassing several decades can be seen in estimates relating to the 1870–1938 period in the United Kingdom. It has been found that over this period economic variables (income and relative prices) explained less than 1 per cent of the variance in the consumption of tea and tobacco, while the corresponding figures for spirits and beer were 9 per cent and 17 per cent, respectively [27]. These results indicate that, over a period of several decades, changes in tastes or in income distribution will often overshadow the influence of economic variables. Although the observed consumption figures could still be "explained" by fitting sufficiently complicated functions of time to the data, this method has little usefulness for purposes of forecasting since it would amount to a simple extrapolation of time trends without reference to causal relationships between economic variables. Furthermore, in the present case, we do not even have a continuous series of observations, since data for the years 1940 to 1950 have to be excluded.

These considerations have induced us to exclude interwar data from the period of observation. In some instances, however, where the above objections carry less force, use has been made of results reached by other researchers on the basis of observations referring to the interwar period. The consumption of certain food items in the United States is an example.

The reader will note that some of the arguments invoked against the inclusion of interwar data in the period of observation also pertain to the question of whether observations for a period of ten years can serve as a basis for projections over a time span of fifteen years. Expressed differently, if systematic changes are expected to take place over long periods, it is questionable whether we can apply the experience of the fifties to 1975. These objections certainly possess validity, although one may note that while there is a ten year discontinuity between the usable series of interwar and post-World War II observations—during which time important structural changes have taken place—abrupt changes in the underlying relationships are less likely to occur during the period of projection, provided that peaceful conditions prevail. Thus, the experience of the late fifties may give a better indication of developments around 1975 than the experience of the late thirties for 1955. Nevertheless, time-series data for the period 1950–1960 need to be supplemented with information derived from other sources. As it will be seen below, intercountry comparisons and family budget studies assume importance in making projections in the case of commodities that are objects of final consumption, while in regard to intermediate goods information on prospective changes in the economic structure and a comparison of the experience of different areas can be of usefulness.

A further question relates to the choice of the time unit. Possible alternatives include the use of yearly and quarterly data. In the present study the choice has been made for relying on annual observations. Although quarterly data would promise a larger number of degrees of freedom, this is to a great extent illusory rather than real. To begin with, the degree of independence between consecutive quarterly observations may be small. On the other hand, although the year itself is an arbitrary unit, we can expect a greater degree of independence between observations relating to successive years. Furthermore, in using quarterly data we could not avoid the question of lags that are likely to be distributed over two or three periods and do not necessarily show constancy, while lagged relationships are less important in the case of yearly observations. Errors of observation due to the deficiencies of reporting trade and national income statistics, too, have a much greater impact on quarterly than on yearly data, and we would also have to adjust for seasonal variations in the former case.

Last but not least, although we may find evidence of association between, for example, changes in incomes and imports by using quarterly observations, for purposes of projection the length of the time period rather than the number of observations is relevant, since only the former can indicate whether the observed relationships are enduring. In other words, by increasing the number of observations for a period of given length we may reduce the standard error of the estimated coefficients, but this does not mean that the forecasting error is proportionately reduced. At any rate, in the present study, quarterly observations could have been used only in a limited number of cases, since for most European countries we do not possess quarterly data on gross national product and disposable income, although these would be necessary for fitting demand functions.

A1.3 METHODS OF PROJECTING IMPORTS

In choosing among alternative methods of projection, various criteria need to be taken into account. An efficient forecasting method should (1) employ a system of classification that best corresponds to the required breakdown of the estimates; (2) derive meaningful relationships between the variables considered; and (3) utilize available information on future developments. These criteria will be used in evaluating alternative forecasting methods below.

In projecting foreign trade, two methods have been generally applied: the projection of aggregate relationships [23, 24, 13, 32] and commodity-by-commodity forecast [28, 4, 33, 34, 9]. The first method involves fitting import demand functions for large aggregates of commodities and extrapolating these in the future; the second entails estimating the imports of individual commodities, either directly, or indirectly, as the difference between projected home demand and supply. These methods of projection will be denoted here as the "aggregate" and the "commodity" method.

Both methods have their advantages and disadvantages. With

regard to the second method, it has been argued that although better care can be taken of the specific needs of a national economy if a commodity-by-commodity estimate is prepared, "the benefits which the law of large numbers bestows on statistical analysis in aggregate terms are almost certainly lost by disaggregation reaching down closely to the commodity level" [24, p. 135]. In other words, compared to the results obtained by aggregation, separate estimates for individual commodities are likely to involve a larger unexplained variance.

Aggregate projections have deficiences of their own, however. Information with regard to technological change cannot be used in connection with the aggregate method, and the underlying assumption of unchanged composition within large commodity groups will seldom be warranted. Also, in the import demand function for temperate zone foods, the domestic food supply would have to be included among the explanatory variables, though substitutability should be considered between domestically produced and imported meat rather than between domestically produced and imported food in general. Finally, the application of the aggregate method gives rise to further difficulties if we aim at estimating the exports of individual areas, since in the latter case the commodity composition of the exports of each area will greatly influence the results.

Since the aggregate method does not provide sufficient information for making projections in the necessary breakdown, and it cannot handle information on technological change concerning individual commodities, the commodity method has appeared preferable for purposes of the present investigation. A further consideration has been that, while the advantages of the aggregate method following from the "law of large numbers" are of little relevance if compositional changes are expected to occur, the forecasting error is reduced if projections are prepared commodity-by-commodity and are subsequently aggregated.

As regards the choice between the direct and indirect method of estimating the future imports of individual commodities, note that the domestic demand function is a relatively stable relationship, while—especially in the case of agricultural commodities—supply can be subject to wide fluctuations. Also, supply is likely to respond to variables other than those determining consumption, and hence, the estimation of an import demand function can give rise to specification errors. Finally, the indirect estimation of imports enables us to take account of government policies that affect domestic production, while the error possibilities associated with this method can often be reduced if the degree of self-sufficiency rather than the absolute amount of home supply is estimated. Nevertheless, the direct method of estimation is preferable if imports are marginal or substitution possibilities between domestic and foreign supply are negligible.

In arriving at estimates of future demand, we have utilized information provided by time-series data, intercountry comparisons, and family budget surveys. In fitting demand functions we have generally used an income variable (gross national product, per capita disposable income, or industrial production) and a price variable (relative price), although in some instances we have also experimented with a time trend, a domestic supply variable, and the price of a competing product.

The restriction in the number of variables used follows from the shortness of the time series. Although the inclusion of more variables would generally reduce the unexplained variance, it also reduces the number of degrees of freedom and introduces additional disturbances due to inaccuracies in the data and other errors. Furthermore, the new variable often appeared to be intercorrelated with existing variables (e.g., time with industrial production and the price of substitutes with own price), thereby giving rise to large standard errors in the regression coefficients.

Intercountry comparisons are useful in the case of commodities where differences in tastes are relatively unimportant (sugar is an example, but not tea), and thus it can be assumed that countries reaching higher income levels will establish consumption patterns observed in present-day high income countries. In such cases, we have fitted cross-section and multicountry regressions. Cross-section functions are estimated from observations relating to a given year or an average of years in a number of countries, while multicountry functions combine time-series and cross-section data. Finally, the results of family budget studies have been utilized in forecasting demand for food and clothing.

The use of cross-section estimates has proved to be of especial importance in the present study, since time-series regressions for individual countries have often failed to give statistically significant results. And although intercountry differences in tastes and consumer habits give rise to errors in making projections for individual countries, forecasting errors will be reduced if the estimates refering to individual countries are subsequently aggregated.

Finally, while for several of the commodities projections have been prepared on a country-by-country basis, supply estimates refer to groups of countries. This solution has been chosen in order to avoid the difficulties associated with the estimation of trade within individual regions. In forecasting domestic supply, we have relied on available information regarding future trends and have also utilized estimates made by other researchers. After allowance made for trade among developed regions and with the Sino-Soviet area, the resulting estimates on future imports have been given in a matrix form, with North America, Western Europe, Japan, and Oceania and South Africa designated as importing areas, and Latin America, Africa, the Middle East, and Asia as exporters.

A1.4 THE CHOICE OF THE INCOME VARIABLE

Several variants of the income variable have been employed in the present study. These are: per capita disposable income, gross national product (total and per capita), industrial production, and —with respect to some raw materials—specific indicators regarding individual industries, which, in turn, are related to disposable income or gross national product.

Per capita disposable income can be used in estimating demand functions for commodities that are objects of final consumption, while in the case of raw materials the income variable should reflect the final and intermediate uses of these materials. Ideally, we should estimate the demand for materials by multiplying projected values of the various components of final demand by input coefficients derived from the inverse of an input-output matrix. For reasons to be mentioned below, we had to forego the use of this method in the present study, however.

An alternative method is to relate demand for particular materials to the activity of consuming industries. This procedure has proved to be useful in regard to some agricultural materials (e.g., apparel fibers) that are used mainly as inputs in consumer goods industries. In such instances, we have applied a direct and an indirect method of estimation. The first procedure involves relating demand for a raw material to disposable income or the gross national product, while the second consists in estimating the relationships between material consumption and the consuming activities as well as between these activities and disposable income (gross national product).

It has not proved practicable, however, to apply the end-use method in regard to nonfuel minerals and metals, which have a large variety of industrial uses. The main difficulties have arisen in connection with the estimation of input coefficients and the projection of activity levels in the relevant sectors. We have therefore resorted to an aggregate hypothesis and related demand for these materials to industrial production, with adjustments made on the basis of available information on expected changes in the main consuming industries. A similar method has been employed in regard to fuels, although in this case consumption has been expressed as a function of the gross national product.

Since per capita incomes, gross national product, and industrial production are used as explanatory variables in the estimates, it has been necessary to forecast gross national product, disposable income, population, and industrial production in the developing countries for 1970 and 1975. Income projections can be made in terms of large aggregates or by disaggregation, e.g., by setting up an input-out-put matrix for the target date and exploring the feasibility of providing for alternative combinations of final output.

It has not been feasible to make use of an input-output system in estimating GNP in the present study, since input-output tables are not available for the majority of countries under consideration, and, in cases where these are available, the input-coefficients are not applicable to the date of forecast. Thus, we had to have recourse to aggregate methods of projection, although in the case of the larger industrial countries separate estimates have been prepared for the three main sectors of the economy (agriculture, industry, and services).

Aggregate projections can proceed from the side of supply and that of demand. In the first case, the possibilities of expanding production are appraised on the basis of the availabilities of productive factors and their expected productivity in future periods; in the second, the components of final demand are estimated. But the second method also presupposes some assumptions with regard to the growth of supply.

In forecasting the future expansion of productive activity, one may attempt to fit a production function for the national economy, or for its main sectors, that would include labor, capital, and technological change as explanatory variables. For example, if an expanded form of the Cobb-Douglas function were used to incorporate a term for technological change, the following functional relationship could be employed:

(1) $$Y = bL^a K^\beta e^{rt}$$

Various efforts have been made to explain past growth in the United States in terms of an aggregate production function [*30,*

22, 29]. The framework of the production function has also been used by Knowles and Denison to prepare forecasts for the 1970's [20, 6]. This method has found little application for purposes of projection in Western Europe, however. Various problems related to the estimation of an aggregate production function are responsible for this situation. On the one hand, statistical information necessary for estimating the production function—especially data on the capital stock expressed in constant prices—are often not available; on the other, the length of the period of observation is restricted because structural changes impede the comparability of the interwar and postwar periods.

It has been suggested that, in projecting the national income of European countries, use should be made of the fragmentary information available on the coefficients of the aggregate production function. For the European Economic Community, for example, it has been proposed to accept values in the range of 0.5 to 2.0 per cent for the term representing technological change, with account taken of the results of past studies as well as the probable acceleration of growth resulting from the Common Market's establishment [25, p. 580]. On the other hand, in a more recent forecast for Belgium, it has been assumed that the establishment of the Common Market, coupled with growth-oriented government policies, would raise the rate of increase of technological improvements from its "historical trend" of 1.5 per cent to 2.25 per cent [15, p. 18].

But the above-mentioned difficulties of estimation do not permit us to establish a "historical trend" of technological change and the wide limits assumed in the Common Market study reduce the usefulness of this approach for purposes of projection. Further difficulties pertain to forecasting changes in the capital stock and to estimating production functions for individual sectors.

For these reasons, we have eschewed the use of aggregate production functions in our projections, and have come to rely on some necessarily crude substitutes for the above method. Two alternatives suggest themselves. Under the first, future levels of the gross national product are derived by extrapolating past trends in labor productivity, with the separate estimation of expected changes in the size and composition of the labor force and in hours worked. The second method involves estimating marginal capital-output ratios and saving ratios for the period of projection on the basis of past trends in these ratios. The rate of growth of GNP could then be derived by substituting the estimated values of marginal capital-output ratios and saving ratios into a function of the Harrod-Domar type.

The main deficiencies of these two methods are due to implicit *ceteris paribus* assumptions with regard to technological progress and capital-labor ratios. Yet, in several European countries, capital-labor ratios are expected to change as a result of the virtual constancy of the effective labor force, measured in terms of hours worked. Other things being equal, a forecast of gross national product based on the extrapolation of past productivity trends would lead to the underestimation of GNP in these countries, while an extrapolation of past trends in marginal capital-output ratios would result in its overestimation.

Forecasting by the use of marginal capital-output ratios has the further limitation that, in the absence of information on the sectoral distribution of new investment, the growth of output in individual sectors cannot be estimated. An additional consideration is that, by reason of the long gestation period of capital, labor productivity figures show greater constancy than do marginal capital-output ratios. For these reasons we have relied on labor productivity estimates in forecasting GNP, although in the case of countries where capital-labor ratios are expected to change significantly, we have checked the results by means of the second procedure.

But the application of the labor productivity method should not mean the simple extrapolation of past trends. In addition to variations in capital-labor ratios, labor productivity in Europe has been affected, for example, by postwar reconstruction, the process of catching up with technological developments elsewhere, and a rapid expansion of exports. These trends cannot be expected to continue unaltered, hence it has become necessary to consider possible changes in these variables as well as the impact of regional integration on economic growth. In addition, as noted above, in the case of the larger industrial countries separate estimates have been prepared for the main sectors of the economy (agriculture, industry, and services) in order to utilize information on sectoral productivity trends and to assess the contribution of the intersectoral movement of the labor force to economic growth.

Projections of labor inputs and productivity provide a forecast of aggregate supply. An alternative method of projection relies on estimating the final demand components: private and public consumption, investment, exports, and changes in stocks. We have attempted to use this method in regard to several larger countries and have seen our "supply" projections by and large confirmed.

But too much faith should not be put in the estimate of aggregate demand. For one thing, with the exception of defense expenditures and exports, the various components of final demand depend on the assumed growth rate. Also, in the absence of long term planning, the forecasting of public consumption would take the form of a simple extrapolation, and a considerable degree of uncertainty attaches to the rate of expansion of exports and the importation of manufactured goods, too. Last but not least, substitution among the various components of final demand can take place in response to price changes or modifications in economic policies: more butter and fewer guns, more housing and less luxury consumption.

A1.5. THE CHOICE OF THE PRICE VARIABLE

In the absence of money illusion, a doubling of all prices and money income will leave the quantity demanded unchanged. Thus, we can allow for the influence of changes in the general price level on consumption by deflating the money values of the explanatory variables by a general price index. This deflator can be a cost-of-living index or a wholesale price index depending on whether retail prices or wholesale prices (import prices) are used in the equation.

A further question relates to the choice of prices used in estimating the demand functions. Two considerations are relevant here. On the one hand, since demand equations depict behavioral relationships, we should include in the regressions the price which the users of a commodity respond to: retail prices in the case of foodstuffs, and wholesale prices in the case of raw materials. We could then calculate the elasticities at the retail level and at the wholesale level, respectively. On the other hand, the price paid to the supplier is relevant for the producer or exporter; hence, in appraising the future prospects of agricultural production or import trade, it would be necessary to calculate the elasticities at the farm or import level. The latter relationship could be derived from the users' demand functions if we included variables pertaining to the behavior of traders in the regression. In the case of imported foodstuffs, for example, if the quantity passing through the trading sector does not influence the marketing margin (the absolute difference between import price and retail price) and excise taxes are zero, we arrive at the derived demand equation as follows:

(2) $\qquad Q_c = a_1 + b_{11}P_r + b_{12}Y$

(3) $\qquad P_r = a_2 + b_{21}P_m + b_{22}R$

(4) $\qquad Q_c = a_3 + b_{31}P_m + b_{32}R + b_{33}Y$

when Q_c refers to the quantity consumed, P_r to retail prices, P_m to import prices, and R to the marketing margin.

Equation (4) can be used to estimate the elasticities at the import level, and this equation also provides an unbiased estimate of income elasticity at the retail level while typically underestimating the retail price elasticity. On the other hand, if the marketing margin depends on the quantity passing through the marketing sector, income and price elasticities at the retail level are generally underestimated [17, pp. 107–12]. An important exception is the case when the markup is fixed as a percentage of the import price. In the latter instance, equation (4) will estimate the true values of the elasticities at both the retail and import level.

The assumption of an unchanged percentage margin does not appear to be realistic, however, since the existence of a fixed cost of marketing (storage, transportation, etc.) as well as recent trends in marketing, indicate its flexibility. At the same time, in the absence of sufficient information on the behavioral equations applicable to the trading sector, the demand functions estimated on the import level cannot include variables pertaining to the latter.

The question arises whether, under such circumstances, estimation should be made at the retail or the import level. It is suggested here that the relationships among the variables in question are more stable at the retail level, since nonsystematic changes experienced during the period of observation in regard to the marketing margin (and excise taxes) would affect the measured values of the coefficients at the import level. Also, despite the error possibilities associated with retail price data, these are preferable to import prices since the latter are often calculated as unit values and are therefore affected by changes in quality and in the origin of imports. For these reasons, we have used retail prices in the demand functions for food and clothing. Retail prices converted by the use of purchasing-power parity ratios have been employed in fitting cross-section and multicountry regressions, too.

In estimating the demand for raw materials, we have experimented with wholesale as well as with import prices. The regression coefficients of price have not been statistically significant in any of these functions, however. This result can be explained by the fact that in short time series the effect of the income variable expressing a technological relationship between input and output swamps that of price, and, also, by the incorrect specification of the function.

Since the publication of Haavelmo's famous article in 1943 [16], much attention has been paid to the problem of correctly specifying the structural equations that give expression to the underlying relationships between economic variables. It has been emphasized that by employing the least-squares method for fitting demand functions to time-series data of prices and quantities, we do not arrive at the true demand function but the result will rather be a "mix" of demand and supply relations. This conclusion follows because market prices and quantities are determined jointly by functional relationships pertaining to demand and supply, while estimation by least squares requires that the demand function be independent of the manner in which the current values of the explanatory variables are determined. In other words, least-squares estimates will generally be biased if the equation contains current values of two or more endogenous variables, the latter being defined as one that is correlated with the unexplained residual. In order to estimate the unbiased values of the structural coefficients, we have then to specify the correct form of the functional relationships.

The least-squares estimation of demand functions does not involve specification errors due to the simultaneity of economic relations in the case of commodities whose import price is unaffected by variations in demand on the part of the country under consideration. In such instances, the explanatory variables in the regressions will be truly exogenous in the sense that they are not correlated with the unexplained residual. This situation pertains to cases where the quantity demanded by a given country is only a relatively small fraction of that bought on the world market. This will be generally true for the countries of Western Europe and Japan. On the other hand, despite recent developments that have reduced the sensitivity of world market prices to fluctuations in U.S. demand, for a number of commodities under review the import demand of the United States does not meet these conditions [37]. Still, the degree of specification error will be small in regard to commodities, such as coffee and cocoa, where the demand function is relatively stable while large fluctuations are observed with respect to supply.

But the demand for raw materials has not been stable over the last decade, and frequently parallel changes have taken place in the industrial countries. In such instances, price and demand moved in the same direction and we could not expect to estimate the "true" demand function from time-series observations. In other words, prices cannot be regarded as exogenous and least-squares estimation gives biased values of the structural coefficients (elasticities if a logarithmic function is used).

To derive unbiased estimates, it would be necessary to specify the underlying structural relationships—in the present case, the demand and supply functions on the world market. In the absence of sufficient information on the form of the supply functions, this has not been possible in the framework of the present study, and hence the effects of price changes on the consumption and imports of raw materials could not be indicated.

For purposes of projection, it is further necessary to forecast the prices of individual commodities for 1970 and 1975. Theoretically, the forecasting of future prices could proceed by estimating the demand functions of all users and the supply functions of all suppliers on the world market, or from a reduced form of these equations. Given the lack of information on supply functions, such a procedure could not find application here. Instead, a method of successive approximations has been employed.

Projections in regard to the prices of individual commodities have been made under the assumption that the prices of manufactured goods will remain unchanged throughout the period under consideration. In most instances, demand forecasts were first made assuming constant prices (average prices of the year 1960) for the commodity in question and the resulting estimates were compared with expected supply at that price. In the event of discrepancies, the estimates have been revised so as to arrive at an "equilibrium" price and quantity. Different procedures have been followed in regard to some agricultural raw materials (e.g., rubber) and for commodities that are subject to commodity agreements (e.g., coffee).[2] Assumed changes in prices are shown in Table A1.5.1.

A1.6 ESTIMATION FOR INDIVIDUAL COMMODITIES

Noncompeting Tropical Foods

Substitution relationships are of little importance for noncompeting tropical foods, hence the domestic demand equation for these products can be written as

$$(5) \qquad Q_c = a + bY + cP$$

when Q_c and Y refer to per capita consumption and disposable income per head, and P is the relative price of the commodity in question. Since these commodities are not produced domestically, the import demand function will be identical with the domestic demand function.

---

[2]See the discussion of individual commodities in the relevant chapters.

Time-series regressions have been estimated in individual countries for coffee for the postwar period, whereas for various reasons estimation has not appeared practicable for bananas, cocoa, tea, and spices. Consumption data are not available on a year-by-year basis for cocoa and spices; there is no information on banana prices in most countries, while noneconomic factors appear to overshadow economic variables in determining tea consumption.

Multicountry and cross-section regressions have also been fitted in the case of coffee, and intercountry comparisons have proved to be useful in regard to bananas and cocoa, too. Finally, consideration has been given to the results of budget studies with respect to all noncompeting tropical foods.

Temperate Zone and Competing Tropical Foods

The import demand function for a homogeneous commodity without close substitutes that is both imported and domestically produced (e.g., sugar) will take the form,

$$(6) \qquad M = (a + bY + cP) - S$$

The domestic supply of foodstuffs (S) depends mainly on last period's price and on weather conditions, and can be regarded as predetermined in the sense that it is independent of the unexplained residuals. Consequently, the coefficient of domestic supply in the import demand equation should be unity; if no relevant variables are omitted from the consumption function, a coefficient of domestic supply differing from unity would be due to errors of observation and other inaccuracies. We have therefore estimated the domestic demand function rather than the import demand function.

Different considerations apply to heterogeneous commodities, such as meat. By reason of the substitution between domestic and imported meat, an import demand function for meat ought to include a variable representing the possibility of substitution. Let us assume, for example, that beef is imported while pork is domestically produced. The demand for imported meat (beef) will then depend not only on the price of imported meat but also on the price of domestic meat (pork).

$$(7) \qquad M = a + bY + cP_f + dP_d$$

Due to the difficulties involved in estimating the prices of the home-produced and the imported varieties of the same commodity, and the intercorrelation between these variables, the application of this function has not given statistically significant results, however.

Neither could the results be improved upon by including a domestic supply variable in the regression, as in equation (8).

$$(8) \qquad M = e + fY + gP_t + hS$$

Correspondingly, we had to have recourse to separately projecting domestic demand and supply, with allowance made for possible changes in the composition of demand. Alternatively, imports have been estimated directly in cases where the domestic and the foreign varieties of the same commodity are not closely competitive or imports are marginal. In projecting consumption, account has also been taken of the results of intercountry comparisons and budget studies. In the majority of cases, consumption estimates have been prepared for individual countries, while supply estimates refer to country groupings.

Agricultural Raw Materials

The commodities of this group are used to a large extent in industries catering to consumer demand, although capital formation is an important form of final use in forest products, and some of these materials are also utilized in the production of intermediate goods.

Both the direct and the indirect method of estimation have been employed in regard to apparel fibers and rubber, and cross-section regressions have also found application here. Consumption has been projected for the apparel fibers, taken together, and for rubber, with the separate estimation of the breakdown of consumption among the main apparel fibers and between natural and synthetic rubber.

Prospective developments in the main end uses have been considered in regard to jute and other vegetable fibers, whereas in the case of hides and skins, and forest products, we have utilized the results of other studies and available information on expected future developments.

Several of the agricultural raw materials under review are not produced in the industrial countries. Rubber, tropical wood, and jute are examples. But while the domestic supply of natural fibers is negligible in Western Europe and Japan, the United States produces substantial quantities of cotton and wool. Similarly to the case of foodstuffs produced in developed countries, the supply of agricultural raw materials can be regarded as predetermined, hence the considerations made in connection with competing foodstuffs are relevant also here.

Fuels

Fuels have numerous final and intermediate uses, but the application of the end-use method has not appeared practicable in the present study. Rather, we have related energy consumption to the gross national product. Time-series regressions have been fitted to the data of individual countries for the 1950–1960 period and the resulting coefficients have been corrected on the basis of intercountry comparisons and information on prospective changes in the industrial structure.

The projected consumption of energy has been further broken down according to its main components: coal, oil, natural gas, and hydroelectricity. It is not expected that coal would be imported from less developed countries in appreciable quantities, hence only imports of oil—in the form of petroleum and petroleum products—and natural gas had to be estimated. But imports of oil are affected by policies followed with regard to coal in the developed countries. Further, in making projections, consideration had to be given to the quota restrictions imposed on imports of petroleum and petroleum products in the United States.

Nonfuel Minerals and Metals

While a large proportion of agricultural raw materials goes into the production of consumer goods, nonfuel minerals and metals find important uses in investment, government expenditure, and the production of intermediate goods. Given the variety of consuming activities, the application of the end-use method has not appeared practicable with respect to these commodities, and we have employed aggregate hypotheses—relating the demand for these materials to industrial production or the gross national product—instead. Adjustments have been made, however, to take account of prospective changes in the main metal-using sectors.

The import demand function will be identical with the domestic demand function in the case of minerals that are not produced in developed economies. On the other hand, if domestic production is of importance, the estimation of a domestic supply function would be in order since the production of minerals cannot be regarded as a predetermined variable. Domestic supply is likely to depend on the prices of the particular raw materials and on the prices of inputs that are used in their production. But, in the absence of adequate information on input prices, domestic supply functions for past periods have not be estimated.

Under these circumstances, a possible way to proceed would be to assume that the various influences which affect the imported quantities of particular minerals (the rate of expansion of domestic material production, changes in material-input coefficients, substitution between inputs, and changes in the composition of industrial production) are related to industrial production and relative prices or exhibit a time trend, so that an import demand function would include industrial production, relative prices, and time as independent variables. If these variables appeared to give a satisfactory explanation of past changes in imports, projections could be made under the assumption that the underlying relationships will continue during the period of forecast.

But functions of this form show the observed relationship between the variables included in the equations, without specifying the underlying structural relations. At the same time, these functions are based on the implicit assumption that domestic supply is related in some simple way to the independent variables of the regression.

The latter assumption has been made in some previous studies [1, 24], and has given good fits for raw materials taken as a group. These results can be explained if we consider that during the interwar period—the period of observation used in the above studies— the domestic production of raw materials in industrial countries expanded by and large proportionately with industrial output and, in cases when it did not, the imports of materials not produced domestically largely determined the outcome. On the other hand, postwar estimates of import demand functions for individual minerals did not yield acceptable results, chiefly because of nonsystematic changes that had taken place with respect to the domestic production—and stockpiling—of minerals.

Considering also prospective changes in the share of domestic supply in future consumption, it has been necessary to make use of the residual method of estimation in the present study: forecasting the consumption of particular minerals and estimating imports as the difference between future consumption and an extraneous estimate of domestic supply.

Manufactured Goods

The exports of manufactured goods from developing countries to developed economies is relatively small, and comprises chiefly commodities that can be produced from domestically available materials by the use of simple technological methods. In the case of several of these commodities, where the large share of labor costs in the cost of production gives an advantage to low-wage countries. imports into developed countries are regulated by quotas. In these instances, assumptions about future changes in quantitative restrictions had to be made in estimating future trade. In regard to other commodities, some simple relationship has been assumed between incomes and imports in the developing countries.

A1.7 THE CHOICE OF THE FUNCTION

Several functional forms have been used to estimate the income elasticity of demand for consumer goods from budget studies. In the interwar period Allen and Bowley [3] fitted linear regressions, but it was soon realized that the linear form is unsuited to the analysis of the consumption of most commodities because it is based on the assumption that the income elasticity of demand tends to unity as income increases. In a study of consumer expenditure in the United Kingdom, Stone [31] employed the logarithmic (doublelog) form; however, this has the disadvantage of yielding constant elasticity values although the income elasticities of demand for most foods have been shown to decline as income increases. In recent studies of budget data, the lognormal, Tőrnquist-type, semilogarithmic, and loginverse functions have been suggested as possible alternatives.

The lognormal function, a cumulative form of the lognormal curve of error, can represent the demand both for luxuries and necessities and it is capable of showing saturation levels of consumption. This functional form has been applied in British budget studies and it has given a very good fit [2]. However, its calculation involves an iterative procedure with the application of the maximum likelihood method, which is rather laborious.

The Tőrnquist system of functions belongs to the same family as the lognormal function and gave an excellent fit when applied to Finnish and Swedish family budget studies as well as in estimating multicountry demand functions [16, 27, p. 107ff.]. It shares, however, the problem of difficult computation with the lognormal function. In addition, objections can be raised against the use of different functional forms for necessities, semiluxuries, and luxuries, since luxury goods become necessities at higher income levels. Fisk has suggested that the triple system of curves be replaced by a modified form of the basic equation of the Tőrnquist system but has not been successful in easing the difficulty of its computation [8].

With the exception of satiety levels, the semilogarithmic function gives a similar shape as the Törnquist and the lognormal functions, and has an important advantage over them in the ease of calculation. The loginverse curve (the dependent variable expressed in logarithms and the inverse of the independent variable measured on the normal scale) shows satiety levels and gave, in some cases, nearly identical consumption levels over large ranges of observed incomes as the semilogarithmic function does. However, by testing for closeness and linearity of fit, Prais and Houthakker [26, pp. 95–96] have shown the semilogarithmic form to be superior to the loginverse function. The same authors found the semilogarithmic function applicable to foods while the logarithmic form yielded good results in the case of the nonfood items of consumption.

In budget studies, price does not appear as an explanatory variable and the amount spent on a commodity is usually taken as the dependent variable. In time-series analysis, however, we want to use income as well as prices as explanatory variables. The more complicated types of functions, such as lognormal or Törnquist-type equations, which have given good fits when applied to budget studies, have not been used in estimating regressions with two explanatory variables. The computational difficulties of such an application are likely to be forbidding and, at any rate, it would be difficult to justify the use of logistic forms for quantity-price relationships. Hence, our choice is restricted to the logarithmic, semilogarithmic, and loginverse functions.

Data over a period of ten years may not permit a definite choice among these functional forms since the logarithmic, semilogarithmic, and loginverse functions often give similar results over the range of observation in short time series. But the further one extrapolates beyond the range of observation, the greater the difference becomes. Hence we have to utilize available information on the underlying relationship in making such a choice. In the case of most foodstuffs, evidence on declining income elasticities rules out the use of the logarithmic function, while the loginverse function has the disadvantage that it shows price elasticities rising with an increase in incomes—a result contradicted by experience. By a process of elimination we would be left with the semilogarithmic function but this cannot be used for extrapolation over long periods since it does not show saturation levels.

To cope with these difficulties, we have adopted a two-step estimation procedure employed with good results by Wold and Juréen in forecasting the demand for foodstuffs in postwar Sweden [34, pp. 306–22]. In the first step, we estimated the income elasticities of demand for food in the individual countries for the year 1960 by utilizing the results of time-series regressions (a semilogarithmic function was used in most cases), intercountry comparisons, and family budget studies.[3] In the second step, future consumption levels were forecast by extrapolating along a Törnquist function, and further adjustments were made on the basis of an intercountry comparison of the resulting saturation levels.

Under this method, future levels of consumption and income elasticity are calculated by assuming that the values observed in the base year (in the present case, 1960) correspond to a point on the Törnquist function. For necessities the following relationships hold:

$$(9) \qquad Q_c = \alpha \ \frac{Y}{Y + \beta} \text{ and}$$

$$(10) \qquad \eta = \frac{\beta}{Y + \beta}$$

when α and β are constants and α expresses the satiety level. Since the values of Q_c, Y, and η are known for the period of observation, α and β can be calculated from equations (9) and (10) and future levels of consumption and income elasticity can be estimated by substituting assumed values of Y into these equations.

The Törnquist function can find application in making projections for high income countries where all foodstuffs can be classified as necessities. A semilogarithmic function has been used, however, in projecting the consumption of foodstuffs in low income countries (Yugoslavia, Greece, Turkey, etc.) in all instances when these foods are regarded as semiluxuries or luxuries.

In cases when prices are expected to change, price elasticities also need to be estimated. Elasticities calculated from data of the period of observation cannot be employed in forecasting the effect of price changes on consumption in 1970, since the price elasticities tend to decline with increases in incomes. Instead, two methods have been applied in the present study, depending on the substitutability of the commodities in question. In the case of commodities where substitution relationships are unimportant, price elasticities have been taken to be equal to income elasticities on the basis of relationships applicable to a demand function of the logarithmic form; in all other instances estimates have been made by utilizing information available on the relationship between price and income elasticities for past periods.

---

[3] The elasticities assumed for 1960 are shown in Table A1.7.1.

Demand for materials that are used as inputs in consumer goods reflects, in part, demand for the consumer goods themselves. Logarithmic forms of estimation have been employed here since these have given good fits for the nonfood items of consumption. Finally, logarithmic and semilogarithmic functions have been used in forecasting demand for raw materials that do not enter directly into the production of consumer goods.

A1.8. THE USE OF BUDGET ELASTICITIES IN PROJECTIONS

We have noted above that, in the present study, use has been made of income elasticities estimated from family budget data in forecasting demand. At this point, certain problems related to the use of budget estimates in projections will be discussed.

To begin with, in budget surveys demand elasticities are calculated, in most cases, with respect to total expenditure rather than income. For a single family, the conversion could be simply carried out by making use of the following relationship: the income elasticity of demand equals the elasticity of demand with respect to total expenditure multipled by the elasticity of total expenditure relative to income. This relationship has also been applied to cross-section data in several studies and an estimated average propensity to spend of 0.9 has been used as the conversion factor [*18, 26*]. Yet the propensity to save is expected to increase with income, and thus the described method is likely to lead to an overestimation of the income elasticity of demand.

Note also that budget estimates often give information only on expenditure for individual commodities rather than quantities bought. In cases when both elasticities have been calculated, the elasticity of the quantity bought has been shown to be uniformly lower than the elastictiy of expenditure at a given level of income, with the gap between the two elasticities increasing with the growth of income. In has been suggested that the difference between the two coefficients can be regarded as the quality elasticity (measured as the elasticity of the price paid in relation to income) since it reflected purchases of higher quality varieties of the same commodity at higher income levels [*26*, p. 109ff.]. In the United States, for example, the average price paid by the highest income group exceeded that paid by the group with the lowest income by 34 per cent in the case of beef and 28 per cent in the case of pork. These results led Fox [*11*, p. 80] to conclude that expenditure elasticities better represent the demand for agricultural products than do quantity elasticities, since a pound of meat bought by a high income family represents a greater demand upon agricultural resources than a pound of meat for a low income family. Similar arguments have been used in regard to fruits, cheese, and fish.

These considerations would imply that expenditure elasticities estimated from budget data should be used for purposes of projection in preference to quantity elasticities derived from budget data or from time series, since the latter cannot measure the shift in demand to the higher quality varieties of the same commodity. However, the higher price paid by the high income receiver reflects not only quality differences but also differences in packaging, processing, and marketing. In the United States, for example, the expenditure elasticity for cereals is positive while the quantity elasticity is negative, mainly because the cost of processing and packaging increases at higher income levels [12]. These reasons lead us to believe that expenditure elasticities are likely to overestimate, and quantity elasticities to underestimate, changes in demand on the farm level. It should also be added that budget elasticities often do not allow for the use of various foodstuffs (e.g., sugar, flour) in food preparations, although time-series data correctly include these in the observed quantities.

A further consideration relates to the much-discussed problem of aggregation [21, 36, 7]. Under the assumption of identical tastes, a family demand function can be derived from the budget data. On the other hand, aggregate consumption depends also on the joint distribution of families with regard to income, family size, and other variables. Thus in order to derive an aggregate demand function from the family demand function we need to know the joint distribution of these variables, or, failing this, we have to make certain assumptions as to how family incomes change as aggregate income rises. A sufficient but not necessary condition for aggregation is that the incomes of all families vary proportionately while family size remains unchanged.

Income distribution is changing, however, and this is reflected in the time-series estimates. It has often been pointed out, for example, that the tendency toward a more equitable income distribution in most European countries has contributed to the increase in per capita food consumption. In the United States, M. C. Burk [5] attributes 45 per cent of the increase in the market value of food per person since the interwar period to the change in income distribution. If we assume that changes in income distribution that accompanied the rise in incomes over the period of observation will continue over the period of forecast, income-elasticity coefficients derived from time-series data will be more appropriate for forecasting than budget elasticities. The application of the permanent income hypothesis to the problem at hand leads to similar conclusions. If consumption depends on permanent income, the budget elasticity will underestimate the true value of the income elasticity since the high and low income groups respectively include households with a large positive and a large negative transitory component of income [12].

Further problems arise in connection with changes in relative prices, the introduction of new goods, developments in marketing and processing, increases in the number of income earning housewives, changes in tastes and the urban-rural redistribution of the population. To give an example, while budget studies indicate that the income elasticity of demand for domestic servants is high, this does not mean that domestic service would rise over time.

These considerations demonstrate the difficulties associated with the use of budget elasticities in making projections. Still, given the shortness of the period of observation and the limitations of inter-country comparisons, we have utilized information derived from budget studies, with appropriate consideration given to possibilities of bias.

REFERENCES

[1.] ADLER, J. H.; SCHLESINGER, E. R.; AND WESTERBORG, EVELYN. *The Pattern of United States Import Trade Since 1923*. New York: Federal Reserve Bank of New York, 1952.

[2.] AITCHISON, J., AND BROWN, J. A. C. "A Synthesis of Engel Curve Theory," *Review of Economic Studies*, (1) 1954–55 pp. 35–46.

[3.] ALLEN, R. G. D., AND BOWLEY, A. L. *Family Expenditure*. London: Staples Press, 1935.

[4.] AUBREY, H. G. *United States Imports and World Trade*. Oxford: Clarendon Press, 1957.

[5.] BURK, M. C. "Some Analyses of Income-Food Relationships," *Journal of the American Statistical Association* (December, 1958), pp. 905–27.

[6.] DENISON, E. F. *The Sources of Economic Growth in the United States and the Alternatives Before Us*. New York: Committee for Economic Development, 1962.

[7.] FARRELL, J. M. "Some Aggregation Problems in Demand Analysis," *Review of Economic Studies*, (2), 1953–54, pp. 193–203.

[8.] FISK, P. R. "Maximum Likelihood Estimation of Törnquist Demand Equations," *Review of Economic Studies* (October, 1958), pp. 35–50.

[9.] FOOD AND ARGICULTURAL ORGANIZATION, *Agricultural Commodities —Projections for 1970.* Rome, 1962.

[10.] FOOTE, R. J. *Analytical Tools for Studying Demand and Price Structures.* Agricultural Handbook No. 146, U.S. Department of Agriculture, Washington, D.C., 1958.

[11.] FOX, K, A. "Factors Affecting Farm Income, Farm Prices, and Food Consumption," *Agricultural Economics Research* (July, 1951), pp. 65–82.

[12.] FRIEDMAN, MILTON. A *Theory of the Consumption Function.* Princeton: Princeton University Press, 1957.

[13.] GENERAL AGREEMENT ON TARIFFS AND TRADE. *International Trade, 1961.* Geneva, 1962.

[14.] GOREUX, L. M. "Income and Food Consumption," *Monthly Bulletin of Agricultural Economics and Statistics* (October, 1960), pp. 1–15.

[15.] LE GROUPE D'ETUDES DE LA COMPTABILITÉ NATIONALE. "L'eéconomie belge d'ici à 1975," *Europe's Future in Figures* (ed. R. C. GEARY), pp. 1–54. Amsterdam: North Holland Publishing Company, 1962.

[16.] HAAVELMO, TRYGVE. "The Statistical Implications of a System of Simultaneous Equations," *Econometrica* (January, 1943), pp. 1–12.

[17.] HILDETH, CLIFFORD, and JARRETT, F. G. A *Statistical Study of Livestock Production and Marketing.* Cowles Commission Monograph No. 15. New York: John Wiley & Sons, 1955.

[18.] HOUTHAKKER, H. S., AND TOBIN, J. "Estimates of the Free Demand for Rationed Foodstuffs," *Economic Journal.* (March, 1952), pp. 103–18.

[19.] JURÉEN, L. "Long-term Trends in Food Consumption: A Multi-Country Study," *Econometrica* (January, 1956), pp. 1–21.

[20.] KNOWLES, J. W. "The Potential Economic Growth in the United States," *Employment, Growth, and Price Levels.* Study Paper No. 20, U.S. Congress Joint Economic Committee, 1960.

[21.] MARSCHAK, JACOB. "Personal and Collective Budget Functions," *Review of Economics and Statistics* (November, 1939), pp. 161–70.

[22.] MASSELL, B. F. "Capital Formation and Technological Change in United States Manufacturing," *Review of Economics and Statistics* (May, 1960), pp. 182–86.

[23.] NEISSER, H., AND MODIGLIANI, F. *National Incomes and International Trade.* Urbana: University of Illinois Press, 1953.

[24.] NEISSER, H. "The United States Demand for Imports," *American Economic Review Papers and Proceedings* (May, 1957), pp. 134–47.

[25.] OFFICE STATISTIQUE DES COMMUNAUTÉS EUROPÉENNES. "Méthodes de prévision du développment économique à long terme," *Informations Statistiques.* No. 6. Rapport d'un groupe d'experts, 1960.

[26.] PRAIS, S. J., AND HOUTHAKKER, H. S. *The Analysis of Family Budgets.* Cambridge: Cambridge University Press, 1955.

[27.] PREST, F. W. "Some Experiments in Demand Analysis," *Review of Economics and Statistics* (February, 1949), pp. 33–49.

[28.] THE PRESIDENT'S MATERIAL POLICY COMMISSION. *Resources for Freedom.* Paley Commission Report. Washington, D.C.: U.S. Government Printing Office, 1952.

[29.] SOLOW, R. M. "Investment and Technological Progress," *Mathematical Methods in the Social Sciences.* Stanford: Stanford University Press, 1960.

[30.] SOLOW, R. M. "Technical Change and the Aggregate Production Function," *Review of Economics and Statistics* (August, 1957), pp. 312–20.

[31.] STONE, RICHARD. *The Measurement of Consumers' Expenditure and Behavior in the United Kingdom, 1920–1938,* Vol. I. Cambridge: Cambridge University Press, 1954.

[32.] UNITED NATIONS. *World Economic Survey,* Part I, New York, 1963.

[33.] UNITED NATIONS ECONOMIC COMMISSION FOR EUROPE. *Economic Survey of Europe in 1957.* Geneva, 1958.

[34.] UNITED NATIONS ECONOMIC COMMISSION FOR EUROPE. *Economic Survey of Europe in 1960.* Geneva, 1961.

[35.] WOLD, IN ASSOCIATION WITH JURÉEN, L. *Demand Analysis.* New York: John Wiley & Sons, 1953.

[36.] WOLFF, P. DE. "Income Elasticity of Demand, a Macro-economic and a Micro-economic Interpretation," *Economic Journal* (April, 1941), pp. 140–45.

[37.] ZASSENHAUS, H. K. "Direct Effects of a United States Recession on Imports: Expectations and Events," *Review of Economics and Statistics* (August, 1955), pp. 231–55.

APPENDIX TABLES

THE COMMODITY BREAKDOWN OF THE ESTIMATES OF EXPORT EARNINGS
FOR DEVELOPING COUNTRIES

Commodities	SITC[a] Numbers
Temperate Zone Foods	
1. Livestock, meat, fish, and eggs	00, 01, 03, 025
2. Cereals and feeding stuff	04, 08
3. Fruits other than bananas and vegetables	05 less 051.3
4. Beverages	11
Competing Tropical Foods	
1. Oilseeds, oils, and fats	02, 09, 4
2. Sugars, sugar products, and honey	06
3. Tobacco	12
Noncompeting Tropical Foods	
1. Bananas	051.3
2. Coffee	071
3. Cocoa	072, 073
4. Tea	074
5. Spices	075
Agricultural Raw Materials	
1. Hides and skins	21
2. Rubber	23
3. Forest products	24, 25
4. Textile fibers	26
5. Crude animal and vegetable matter	29
Fuels	
1. Coal	321
2. Crude petroleum	331
3. Petroleum products	332
4. Natural gas	341
Nonfuel Minerals and Metals	
1. Iron ore	281
2. Manganese ore and ferromanganese	283.7, 671.4
3. Copper ores, concentrates, and unwrought metal	283.1, 682.1
4. Aluminum ores, alumina, and unwrought metal	283.3, 513.6, 684.1
5. Lead ores, concentrates, and unwrought metal	283.4, 685.1
6. Zinc ores, concentrates, and unwrought metal	283.5, 686.1
7. Tin ores, concentrates, and unwrought metal	283.6, 687.1
8. Other nonferrous metals	283.2, 8, 9, 285, 671.5
9. Scrap metal	282, 284
10. Fertilizers and other crude minerals	271, 272
Manufactured Goods	
1. Chemicals	5 less 513.6
2. Leather and footwear	61, 85
3. Veneer, plywood, wood and cork manufactures, and paper	63, 64
4. Textile yarn, cotton fabrics, and clothing	651, 652, 841
5. Jute manufactures	653.4, 656.1
6. Floor coverings and other textile products	653-657 less 653.4 and 656.1
7. Silver, precious stones, pearls, and jewelry	667, 681, 897
8. Machinery and metal manufactures	67, 68, 69, 7[b]
9. Other manufactured goods	62, 66, 8 n.e.s.

Note: [a]United Nations Standard International Trade Classification.
[b]Excluding ferroalloys and unwrought metals.

TABLE A1.2.2

CONVERSION RATIOS FOR CALCULATING F.O.B. VALUES OF IMPORTS
(Freight and insurance as a percentage of c.i.f. prices)

Temperate Zone Foods			
Live animals	12	Roundwood	35
Meat	10	Sawnwood	30
Prepared and canned meat	6	Cork	20
Fish and fish preparations	12	Silk	3
Eggs	4	Wool	5
Cereals except rice	13	Cotton	5
Rice	7	Jute	10
Cereal preparations	7	Vegetable fibers	15
Feeding stuff for animals	15	Crude vegetable and animal	
Fresh fruits, except bananas	25	materials	15
Dried fruit	12		
Preserved fruit and fruit		Fuels	
preparations	10	Coal, coke	30
Vegetables	25	Crude petroleum	25
Alcoholic beverages	10	Petroleum products	15

Competing Tropical Foods		Nonfuel Minerals and Metals	
Oilseeds	15	Iron ore	40
Animal oils and fats	10	Iron and steel scrap	15
Vegetable and processed oils		Nonferrous ores and concen-	
and fats	8	trates, nonferrous scrap	12
Sugar	10	Silver and platinum	5
Sugar preparations	5	Copper	3
Tobacco	3	Aluminum	3
		Lead	5
Noncompeting Tropical Foods		Zinc	5
Bananas	40	Tin	2
Coffee	5	Other nonferrous metals	3
Cocoa and chocolate	5	Crude fertilizers	30
Tea	4	Other crude minerals	50
Spices	6		
		Manufactured Goods	8
Agricultural Raw Materials			
Hides and skins	10		
Crude rubber	4		

TABLE A1.5.1

ASSUMED CHANGES IN PRIMARY PRODUCT PRICES[a]
(index, 1960 = 100)

	1960	1970I	1970II	1975I	1975II
Oilseeds, oils, and fats	100	94	95	94	95
Coffee, arabica	100	100	100	100	100
robusta	100	105	105	105	105
Cocoa	100	90	91	90	91
Tea	100	93	94	93	94
Hides and skins	100	92	93	90	91
Rubber	100	60	62	60	62
Forest products	100	110	112	115	117
Wool	100	95	96	93	94
Cotton	100	95	96	93	94
Jute	100	85	86	85	86
Other vegetable fibers	100	93	94	93	94
Crude petroleum	100	85	88	85	88
Petroleum products	100	85	88	85	88
Copper	100	94	95	94	95
Aluminum	100	94	95	94	95
Tin	100	110	111	110	111

Note: [a]Changes in primary-product prices have been projected under the assumption that the prices
of manufactured goods will remain at 1960 levels. No price changes have been assumed in
regard to primary products not included in this table.

TABLE A1.7.1

ASSUMED INCOME ELASTICITIES FOR SELECTED FOODSTUFFS IN 1960

	Meat	Oranges	Sugar	Fats and Oils	Tobacco	Bananas	Coffee	Cocoa
United States	0.3	0	0	0	0	0	0.2[a]	0.35
Canada	0.3	0	0	0	0	0.2	0.56	0.35
Belgium-Lux	0.5	0.6	0.3	0	0.2	0.35	0.4	0.4
France	0.4[d]	0.6	0.3	0.2	0.4	0.35	0.5	0.6
Germany	0.55	0.6	0.3	0	0.3	0.35	0.8[b]	0.4
Italy	1.3	1.0	0.65	0.3	0.6	1.3	0.8[b]	1.0
Netherlands	0.65[d]	0.6	0.1	0	0.2	0.55	0.5	0.4
United Kingdom	0.4	0.7	0	0	0.2	0.5	1.0[b]	0.4
Austria	0.55[d]	0.8	0.1	0.2	0.3	0.65	0.8[b]	0.5
Denmark	0.4	0.8	0	0	0.3	0.5	0.2	0.5
Finland	0.7	0.8	0.1	0	0.3	--	0.2	1.0
Ireland	0.5	0.8	0.1	0	0.3	1.2	1.0[b]	0.7
Norway	0.6	0.6	0.1	0	0.3	0.5	0.2	0.4
Sweden	0.5	0.6	0.1	0	0.3	0.5	0.2	0.4
Switzerland	0.5	0.6	0.1	0	0.3	0.35	0.5	0.2
Greece	1.4	--	0.75	0.2	0.6	1.5	1.5	1.5
Portugal	1.4	--	0.65	0.3	0.6	1.5	1.5	1.5
Spain	1.4	--	0.65	0.2	0.6	0.65	1.5	0.8
Turkey	1.3	--	1.0	0.6	0.6	--	--	1.5
Yugoslavia	1.3	--	0.65	0.4	0.6	--	--	1.5
Japan	1.2[e]	1.1	0.7	1.1	0.4	--	--	--
Australia	--	--	--	--	0.3	--	1.0[c]	0.5
New Zealand	--	--	--	--	0.2	--	1.0[c]	0.5
South Africa	--	--	--	--	0.6	--	0.7	1.3

[a]See also text.
[b]Additional trend of 1 percent per year.
[c]Additional trend of 2 percent per year.
[d]Additional trend of 0.1 kg per year.
[e]Additional trend of 0.2 kg per year.

TABLE A2.2.1

TOTAL POPULATION OF DEVELOPED COUNTRIES
(thousands)

	1950	1955	1960	1970	1975
United States	151,683	165,270	180,670[a]	214,220[a]	235,600[a]
Canada	13,712	15,698	17,814	21,480	23,500
Belgium	8,640	8,869	9,153	9,630	9,880
France	41,736	43,279	45,542	49,600	51,560
Germany	46,904	49,185	53,373	57,340	58,660
Saar	943	992			
Italy	46,603	48,062	49,259	52,350	53,980
Luxemburg	296	304	315	343	355
Netherlands	10,114	10,751	11,486	12,792	13,490
West Berlin	2,139	2,195	2,200	2,200	2,200
United Kingdom	50,363	51,221	52,539	55,930	57,480
Austria	6,935	6,974	7,084	7,195	7,212
Denmark	4,269	4,439	4,581	4,861	5,015
Finland	4,009	4,241	4,456	4,889	5,135
Iceland	144	159	178	190	198
Ireland	2,969	2,921	2,834	2,837	2,846
Norway	3,265	3,429	3,589	3,900	4,078
Sweden	7,015	7,262	7,485	7,944	8,168
Switzerland	4,715	4,977	5,351	5,461	5,609
Greece	7,566	7,966	8,327	9,220	9,690
Portugal	3,441	8,765	9,125	9,428	9,641
Spain	27,868	28,976	30,128	32,965	34,374
Turkey	20,947	24,065	27,829	35,500	40,450
Yugoslavia	16,344	17,586	18,655	20,888	22,100
Japan	82,900	89,000	93,419	101,937	106,200
Australia	8,307	9,313	10,392	12,449	13,649
New Zealand	1,918	2,150	2,386	2,938	3,272
South Africa	13,970	15,651	17,594	22,600	25,800

Sources: OEEC, Twelfth Annual Economic Review, 1961 and Manpower Statistics, 1950-1960,
U.N. Demographic Yearbook, various issues.
Note: [a]--includes Alaska and Hawaii.

TABLE A2.2.2

POPULATION OVER 15 in DEVELOPED COUNTRIES
(thousands)

	1950	1955	1960	1970	1975
United States	110,920	116,472	124,589[a]	146,472[a]	159,600[a]
Canada	9,641	10,659	11,839	14,200	15,500
Belgium	6,834	6,935	7,003	7,450	7,650
France	32,239	30,687	33,387	37,460	38,950
Germany	35,852	38,610	41,951	44,160	45,930
Saar	721	779			
Italy	34,294	35,857	36,853	42,860	44,150
Luxembourg	280	247	254	276	286
Netherlands	7,150	7,536	8,042	9,511	10,145
West Berlin	1,758	1,857	1,920	1,920	1,920
United Kingdom	39,312	39,521	40,325	42,860	44,150
Austria	5,356	5,423	5,532	5,522	5,523
Denmark	3,147	3,261	3,426	3,697	3,776
Finland	2,806	2,938	3,095	3,505	3,753
Iceland	100	106	116	123	129
Ireland	2,116	2,041	1,970	1,999	2,010
Norway	2,467	2,548	2,668	2,932	3,046
Sweden	5,370	5,537	5,806	6,286	6,420
Switzerland	3,604	3,769	4,084	4,227	4,365
Greece	5,425	5,877	6,139	6,753	7,121
Portugal	5,953	6,253	6,488	6,935	7,137
Spain	20,530	21,428	22,527	23,908	24,837
Turkey	12,829	14,590	16,976	21,560	24,220
Yugoslavia	11,272	11,248	13,009	14,851	15,900
Japan	53,561	59,292	65,158	78,716	82,200
Australia	6,015	6,535	7,195	8,748	9,538
New Zealand	1,362	14,700	1,596	1,895	2,100
South Africa	8,656	9,779	10,828	13,951	15,926

Source: See Table A2.2.1.

Note: [a]Includes Alaska and Hawaii.

TABLE A2.3.1

UNITED STATES EMPLOYMENT AND PRODUCTIVITY IN THE MAIN SECTORS OF THE ECONOMY

	1947	1954	1957	1960	1970	1975	Percentage Change per Year					
							1947 to 1954	1947 to 1957	1954 to 1960	1947 to 1960	1960 to 1970	1970 to 1975
Annual Man-Hours, Billion												
Total private	122.9	123.7	129.4	129.4	148.7	157.8	0.1	0.4	0.8	0.4	1.4	1.2
Agriculture	22.3	16.3	14.8	13.5	10.2	9.0	-4.6	-4.4	-3.2	-3.9	-2.8	-2.6
Nonagricultural industries	100.6	107.4	114.7	116.0	138.5	148.8	0.9	1.3	1.3	1.1	1.8	1.4
Manufacturing	32.6	33.6	35.2	34.4	38.8	40.6	0.4	0.8	0.5	0.5	1.2	0.9
Nonmanufacturing	68.1	73.8	79.4	81.6	99.7	108.2	1.2	1.5	1.6	1.4	2.0	1.7
Private GNP per Man-Hour, 1954 Dollars												
Total private	2.11	2.67	2.90	3.13	4.06	4.59	3.4	3.2	2.7	3.1	2.6	2.5
Agriculture	0.76	1.24	1.40	1.61	2.43	2.96	7.2	6.3	4.5	5.9	4.2	4.0
Nonagricultural industries	2.41	2.89	3.09	3.31	4.18	4.69	2.6	2.5	2.3	2.5	2.4	2.4
Manufacturing	2.65	3.19	3.47	3.88	5.21	6.04	2.6	2.7	3.3	2.9	3.0	3.0
Nonmanufacturing	2.30	2.76	2.92	3.07	3.78	4.19	2.6	2.4	1.9	2.3	2.1	2.1

Sources: U.S. Department of Labor, Trends in Output per Man-hour in the Private Economy, 1909-1958, Bulletin No. 1249, Washington, 1959, p. A-19 and Economic Report of the President, 1962, p. 244.

UNITED STATES: GROSS NATIONAL PRODUCT, EMPLOYMENT AND PRODUCTIVITY, 1947-1975
(1960 Prices)

	1947	1954	1960	1970	1975	Percentage Change per Year				
						1947 to 1954	1954 to 1960	1947 to 1960	1960 to 1970	1970 to 1975
Gross National Product, billions	321.1	416.8	504.4	I 740.5 II 777.6	883.4 950.6	3.8	3.2	3.5	3.9 4.4	3.6 4.1
Labor Force, millions	61.8	67.8	73.1	85.7	93.4	1.3	1.3	1.3	1.6	1.7
Civilian Employment, millions	57.8	60.9	66.7	79.7	86.7	0.7	1.5	1.1	1.8	1.7
Average Annual Man-hours per Worker	2,182	2,070	2,019	1,939	1,891	-0.7	-0.4	-0.6	-0.4	-0.5
Man-hours, billions	126.1	126.2	134.7	154.6	163.9	0.0	1.1	0.5	1.4	1.2
GNP per man, dollars	5,555	6,844	7,562	I 9,291 II 9,759	10,189 10,964	3.0	1.7	2.4	2.1 2.6	1.9 2.4
GNP per man-hour, dollars	2.55	3.30	3.74	I 4.79 II 5.03	5.39 5.80	3.8	2.1	3.0	2.5 3.0	2.4 2.9

Sources: Economic Report of the President, 1962, pp. 133, 230, and Table A2.3.1.

We have assumed that during the period of projection the increase in GNP per man-hour will be 0.1 percentage point smaller than the rise in private output per man-hour.

TABLE A2.3.3

CANADA: GROSS NATIONAL PRODUCT, EMPLOYMENT AND PRODUCTIVITY, 1947-1975
(1957 Prices)

	1947	1954	1960	1970	1975	1947 to 1954	1954 to 1960	1947 to 1960	1960 to 1970	1970 to 1975
Gross National Product (Million Canadian $)	20,682	26,673	33,708	I 52,587 II 54,678	64,097 67,914	3.7	4.0	3.8	4.5 5.0	4.0 4.4
Employment (1,000)	4,832	5,243	5,955	7,547	8,370	1.2	2.2	1.6	2.4	2.1
Gross National Product per Man (Canadian $)	4,280	5,087	5,660	I 6,968 II 7,245	7,658 8,114	2.5	1.8	2.2	2.1 2.5	1.9 2.3

Sources: 1947: Dominion Bureau of Statistics, National Accounts, Income and Expenditure, 1926-56, and Canada Yearbook, 1957-58 and 1961.

1954-1960: OEEC, Manpower Statistics, 1950-1960, and U.N., Yearbook of National Accounts, 1961.

EUROPEAN ECONOMIC COMMUNITY: EMPLOYMENT AND PRODUCTIVITY IN THE MAIN ECONOMIC SECTORS

	1950	1955	1960	1970	1975	Percentage Change per Year				
						1950 to 1955	1955 to 1960	1950 to 1960	1960 to 1970	1970 to 1975
BELGIUM (1953 factor prices)										
Employment (1,000)										
All sectors	3,306	3,348	3,384	3,570	3,670	0.2	0.2	0.2	0.5	0.6
Agriculture	368	310	258	192	167	-3.3	-3.6	-3.4	-3.0	-2.8
Industry	1,550	1,587	1,574	1,680	1,725	0.5	-0.2	0.2	0.6	0.5
Services	1,388	1,451	1,552	1,698	1,778	0.9	1.4	1.1	0.8	0.9
Gross Domestic Product per Man (1,000 francs)										
All sectors	111	129	146	191	217	3.1	2.5	2.8	2.7	2.6
Agriculture	87	113	144	213	256	5.4	5.0	5.2	4.0	3.7
Industry	113	132	156	214	250	3.2	3.4	3.3	3.2	3.1
Services	114	128	136	166	182	2.3	1.2	1.8	2.0	1.9
FRANCE (1955 factor prices)										
Employment (1,000)										
All sectors	(18,077)	18,550	18,694	20,490	21,170	(0.7)	0.2	(0.4)	0.8	0.7
Agriculture		5,240	4,441	3,500	3,180		-3.3		-2.2	-2.1
Nonagriculture		13,310	14,253	16,990	17,990		1.4		1.5	1.2
Gross Domestic Product per Man (francs)										
All sectors	(6,857)	7,849	9,507	13,977	16,479	(3.5)	3.9	(3.7)	3.6	3.4
Agriculture		4,078	4,963	7,804	9,450		4.1		4.2	3.9
Nonagriculture		9,333	10,923	15,249	17,720		3.3		3.1	3.0
GERMANY (1954 factor prices)										
Employment (1,000)										
All sectors	20,030	22,827	a24,605 b25,005	25,700	26,430	2.7	1.5	2.1	0.3	0.6
Agriculture	5,020	4,285	a 3,585 b 3,595	2,670	2,300	-3.2	-3.4	-3.3	-3.0	-2.9
Industry	8,530	10,649	a11,975 b12,115	12,840	13,280	4.5	2.2	3.4	0.6	0.7
Services	6,480.	7,893	a 9,145 b 9,295	10,190	10,830	4.0	3.0	3.5	0.9	1.2

Gross Domestic Product per Man (1,000 marks)

All sectors	5.65	7.67 a, b	9.54 a / 9.55 b	13.51	15.94	6.3	4.2	5.3	3.5	3.4
Agriculture	2.34	3.16 a, b	4.39 a / 4.42 b	6.67	8.08	6.2	6.8	6.5	4.2	3.9
Industry	6.30	8.89 a, b	10.92 a / 10.90 b	15.83	18.98	7.1	4.2	5.7	3.8	3.7
Services	7.37	8.48 a, b	9.78 a / 9.77 b	12.39	13.90	2.9	2.9	2.9	2.4	2.3

ITALY (1954 factor prices)

Employment (1,000)

All sectors	(17,129)	18,020	19,836	21,310	21,950	(1.0)	1.9	(1.5)	0.7	0.6
Agriculture		6,884	6,225	5,100	4,630		-2.0		-2.0	-1.9
Industry		6,011	7,593	9,150	9,800		4.8		1.8	1.4
Services		5,125	6,018	7,060	7,520		3.3		1.7	1.4

Gross Domestic Product per Man (1,000 liras)

All sectors	(509)	657	790	1,132	1,340	(5.2)	3.6	(4.5)	3.7	3.5
Agriculture		411	492	728	873		3.7		4.0	3.7
Industry		807	961	1,395	1,675		3.6		3.8	3.7
Services		813	876	1,068	1,181		1.5		2.0	2.0

NETHERLANDS (1954 factor prices)

Employment (1,000)

All sectors	3,727	3,989	4,194	4,820	5,050	1.4	1.0	1.2	1.4	0.9
Agriculture	533	489	433	350	315	-1.7	-2.4	-2.1	-2.2	-2.0
Industry	1,543	1,676	1,766	2,020	2,100	1.7	1.1	1.4	1.4	0.1
Services	1,651	1,824	1,995	2,450	2,635	2.1	1.8	1.9	2.1	1.1

Gross Domestic Product per Man (guilders)

All sectors	5,248	6,380	7,381	9,688	11,003	4.0	3.0	3.5	2.8	2.6
Agriculture	4,859	6,155	7,589	11,233	13,470	4.8	4.3	4.5	4.0	3.7
Industry	5,094	6,331	7,367	10,093	11,728	4.4	3.1	3.8	3.2	3.1
Services	5,518	6,486	7,348	9,134	10,130	3.3	2.5	2.9	2.2	2.1

Sources: U.N., Yearbook of National Accounts, 1961; OEEC, General Statistics, July, 1961; and Manpower Statistics, 1950-1960.
Notes: a Excluding the Saar.
b Including the Saar.

EUROPEAN ECONOMIC COMMUNITY: GROSS NATIONAL PRODUCT, EMPLOYMENT, AND PRODUCTIVITY

	1950	1955	1960	1970	1975	Percentage Change per Year				
						1950 to 1955	1955 to 1960	1950 to 1960	1960 to 1970	1970 to 1975
BELGIUM (1953 prices)										
Gross National Product (billion francs)	400.3	470.7	531.1	I 731.9 / II 767.6	855.1 / 921.2	3.3	2.4	2.9	3.3 / 3.8	3.2 / 3.7
Employment (1,000)	3,306	3,348	3,384	I 3,570	3,670	0.2	0.2	0.2	0.5	0.6
Gross National Product per Man (1,000 francs)	121	141	157	I 205 / II 215	233 / 251	3.1	2.2	2.7	2.7 / 3.2	2.6 / 3.1
FRANCE (1956 prices)										
Gross National Product (billion francs)	144.4	179.3	220.4	I 343.0 / II 360.0	419.0 / 450.3	4.4	4.2	4.3	4.5 / 5.0	4.1 / 4.6
Employment (1,000)	18,077	18,583	18,750	I 20,490	21,170	0.5	0.2	0.3	0.8	0.7
Gross National Product per Man (new francs)	7,988	9,649	11,755	I 16,470 / II 17,570	19,790 / 21,270	3.9	4.0	4.0	3.6 / 4.1	3.4 / 3.9
GERMANY (1954 prices)										
Gross National Product (billion D. Marks)	113.1	174.4	a234.5 / b238.4	I 345.7 / II 362.6	420.2 / 451.7	9.1	6.1	7.6	3.8 / 4.3	4.0 / 4.5
Employment (1,000)	20,030	22,827	a24,605 / b25,005	25,700	26,430	2.7	1.5	2.1	0.3	0.6
Gross National Product per Man (Marks)	5,647	7,641	a9,530 / b9,534	I 13,450 / II 14,110	15,900 / 17,090	6.2	4.5	5.4	3.5 / 4.0	3.4 / 3.9
ITALY (1954 prices)										
Gross National Product (billion lires)	10,079	13,461	17,903	I 27,550 / II 28,910	33,850 / 36,390	6.0	5.9	5.9	4.4 / 4.9	4.2 / 4.7
Employment (1,000)	17,129	18,020	19,836	I 21,210 / II 21,950	21,950	1.0	1.9	1.5	0.7	0.7
Gross National Product per Man (1,000 lires)	588	747	903	I 1,299 / II 1,363	1,542 / 1,658	4.9	3.9	4.4	3.7 / 4.2	3.5 / 4.0

LUXEMBOURG (1954 prices)

Gross National Product (million francs)									
13,970	17,722	21,454	I 30,521	I 36,023	4.9	3.9	4.4	I 3.6	I 3.4
			II 32,044	II 38,761				II 4.1	II 3.9

Employment (1,000)									
136	140	145.5	157	163	0.6	0.8	0.7	0.8	0.8

Gross National Product per Man (1,000 francs)									
103	126	147	I 194	I 221	4.3	3.1	3.7	I 2.8	I 2.6
			II 204	II 238				II 3.3	II 3.1

NETHERLANDS (1958 prices)

Gross National Product (million guilders)									
25,950	33,830	40,870	I 61,890	I 70,730	5.4	3.9	4.6	I 4.2	I 3.6
			II 64,970	II 79,340				II 4.7	II 4.1

Employment (1,000)									
3,727	3,989	4,194	4,820	5,050	1.4	1.0	1.2	1.4	0.9

Gross National Product per Man (guilders)									
6,963	8,481	9,745	I 12,840	I 14,600	4.0	2.8	3.4	I 2.8	I 2.6
			II 13,480	II 15,710				II 3.3	II 3.1

Sources: Employment: OEEC, Manpower Statistics, 1950-1960, OEEC, General Statistics, May, 1950 and OEEC, Europe Today and in 1960, 8th Report, Vol. 2, 1957, p. 20.
Gross National Product: U.N. Yearbook of National Accounts, various issues. Also Tables A2.4.1-2.4.5.

Note: For Germany, data for 1950, 1955, and 1960a exclude the Saar, while 1960b, 1970, and 1975 include the Saar. 1960b was estimated from data published in Statistisches Bundesamt, Wirtschaft und Statistik, 1961.

TABLE A2.4.3

UNITED KINGDOM: EMPLOYMENT AND PRODUCTIVITY IN THE MAIN SECTORS OF THE ECONOMY
(1954 Factor Prices)

	1950	1955	1960	1970	1975	Percentage Change per Year				
						1950 to 1955	1955 to 1960	1950 to 1960	1960 to 1970	1970 to 1975
Employment (1,000)										
All Sectors	22,539	23,477	24,173	25,570	26,120	0.8	0.6	0.7	0.6	0.4
Agriculture	1,262	1,154	1,062	890	830	-1.8	-1.7	-1.7	-1.7	-1.7
Industry	11,400	12,189	12,454	13,200	13,450	1.3	0.4	0.9	0.5	0.4
Services	9,877	10,134	10,658	11,480	11,840	0.5	1.1	0.8	0.7	0.6
GDP per Man (pounds)										
All Sectors	632	692	763	952	1,059	1.8	2.0	1.9	2.3	2.2
Agriculture	565	665	832	1,118	1,277	3.3	4.6	4.0	3.0	2.7
Industry	577	638	716	934	1,062	2.1	2.4	2.2	2.7	2.6
Services	705	759	811	960	1,040	1.5	1.3	1.4	1.7	1.6

Sources: U.N., Yearbook of National Accounts, 1961; OEEC, Manpower Statistics, 1950-1960.

Notes: 1960 employment breakdown by sectors adjusted according to change resulting from new industrial classifications in 1959.

SOUTHERN EUROPE: GROSS NATIONAL PRODUCT, EMPLOYMENT, AND PRODUCTIVITY

	1950	1955	1960	1970	1975	1950 to 1955	1955 to 1960	1950 to 1960	1960 to 1970	1970 to 1975
GREECE (1954 prices)										
Gross National Product (million drachmas)	45,153	63,318	82,250	I 127,632 / II 140,492	159,886 / 184,605	7.0	5.4	6.2	4.5 / 5.5	4.6 / 5.6
Employment (1,000)	3,504	3,813	3,990	4,389	4,629	1.7	0.9	1.3	2.0	1.1
Gross National Product per Man (1,000 drachmas)	12.89	16.61	20.61	I 29.08 / II 39.88	34.54	5.2	4.4	4.8	3.5 / 4.5	3.5 / 4.5
PORTUGAL (1954 prices)										
Gross National Product (million escudos)	41,079	50,355	61,526	I 88,138 / II 97,042	106,232 / 122,674	4.2	4.1	4.1	3.6 / 4.7	3.8 / 4.8
Employment (1,000)	3,155	3,398	3,509	I 3,741	3,887	1.5	0.6	1.1	0.6	0.8
Gross National Product per Man (1,000 escudos)	13.02	14.82	17.53	I 23.56 / II 25.94	27.33 / 31.56	2.6	3.4	3.0	3.0 / 4.0	3.0 / 4.0
SPAIN (1955 prices)										
Gross National Product (million pesetas)	n.a.	n.a.	399.7	I 616.4 / II 678.4	758.6 / 875.7	n.a.	n.a.	n.a.	4.4 / 5.4	4.2 / 5.3
Employment (1,000)	n.a.	n.a.	11,085	I 12,115	12,550	n.a.	n.a.	n.a.	0.9	0.7
Gross National Product per Man (million pesetas)	n.a.	n.a.	36.06	I 50.88 / II 56.00	60.44 / 69.77	n.a.	n.a.	n.a.	3.5 / 4.5	3.5 / 4.5
TURKEY (1954 prices)										
Gross National Product (million lira)	13,570	18,424	25,222	I 45,211 / II 49,787	60,517 / 69,956	6.3	6.5	6.4	6.0 / 7.0	6.0 / 7.0
Employment (1,000)	9,708	10,854	12,429	I 16,579	19,145	2.3	2.7	2.5	2.9	2.9
Gross National Product per Man (lira)	1,398	1,697	2,029	I 2,727 / II 3,003	3,161 / 3,654	4.0	3.6	3.8	3.0 / 4.0	3.0 / 4.0
YUGOSLAVIA (1956 prices)										
Gross Domestic Product (billion dinar)	1,470	1,863	2,893	I 4,895 / II 5,380	6,246 / 7,199	4.9	9.2	7.0	5.4 / 6.4	5.0 / 6.0
Employment (1,000)	7,022	7,627	8,104	I 9,250	9,910	1.7	1.2	1.5	1.3	1.4
Gross Domestic Product per Man (1,000 dinar)	209	244	357	I 528 / II 582	631 / 728	3.1	7.9	5.5	4.0 / 5.0	3.6 / 4.6

Sources: Employment--In all cases except those noted below: OEEC, Manpower Statistics, 1950-1960, and OEEC, General Statistics, May, 1960.
Greece, 1960; Portugal 1955, 1960; Spain 1950, 1955, 1960; Turkey 1950, 1955, 1960; and Yugoslavia, 1950, 1955, 1960, estimated on the basis of OEEC, Demographic Trends, 1956-1976; ILO, Yearbook of Labor Statistics, and U.N., Demographic Yearbook, various issues.
Gross National Product--In all cases except those noted below: U.N., Yearbook of National Accounts, 1960 and 1961.
Turkey 1960, estimated on the basis of Gross Domestic Product figures given in above source; Yugoslavia 1950-1959 has been taken from U.N. Economic Commission for Europe, Economic Survey of Europe in 1961, Part II. Change between 1959 and 1960 estimated on the basis of U.N., National Accounts Statistics, 1961.

NORTHERN EUROPE: GROSS NATIONAL PRODUCT, EMPLOYMENT, AND PRODUCTIVITY, 1950-1975

		1950	1955	1960	1970	1975	Percentage Change per Year 1950 to 1955	1955 to 1960	1950 to 1960	1960 to 1970	1970 to 1975
AUSTRIA (1954 prices)											
Gross National Product (billion shillings)	I	70.3	97.1	125.2	167.9	192.7	6.6	5.2	5.9	3.0	2.8
	II				176.2	207.2				3.5	3.3
Employment (1,000)		3,198	3,406	3,560	3,551	3,552	1.3	0.9	1.1	0.0	0.0
Gross National Product per Man (shillings)	I	21,982	28,509	35,169	47,290	54,260	5.3	4.3	4.8	3.0	2.8
	II				49,610	58,350				3.5	3.3
DENMARK (1955 prices)											
Gross National Product (million kroner)	I	25,990	28,626	36,300	49,881	57,298	2.0	4.9	3.4	3.2	2.8
	II				52,358	61,614				3.7	3.3
Employment (1,000)		1,999	2,026	2,122	2,212	2,234	0.3	0.9	0.6	0.4	0.2
Gross National Product per Man (1,000 kroner)	I	13.00	14.13	17.11	22.55	25.64	1.7	3.9	2.8	2.8	2.6
	II				23.67	27.58				3.3	3.1
FINLAND (1958 factor costs)											
Gross National Product (1,000 million marks)	I	771.3	997.2	1,213.2	1,687.3	1,970.3	5.3	4.0	4.6	3.3	3.1
	II				1,771.3	2,119.4				3.8	3.6
Employment (1,000)		1,933	2,015	2,127	2,290	2,375	0.8	1.1	1.0	0.7	0.7
Gross National Product per Man-Year (1,000 marks)	I	399	495	570	737	830	4.4	2.9	3.6	2.6	2.4
	II				773	892				3.1	2.9
ICELAND (1954 prices)											
Gross National Product (million krona)	I	2,650	3,891	4,627	6,352	7,427	8.0	3.6	5.7	3.3	3.2
	II				6,734	8,106				3.9	3.8
Employment (1,000)		63	68	73	78	81	1.5	1.4	1.5	0.6	0.7
Gross National Product per Man-Year (1,000 krona)	I	42	57	63	81	92	6.5	2.2	4.1	2.6	2.4
	II				86	100				3.2	3.0
IRELAND (1958 prices)											
Gross National Product (million pounds)	I	545.6	613.7	646.0	832.5	919.2	2.4	1.0	1.7	2.6	2.0
	II				882.7	1,003.6				3.2	2.6
Employment (1,000)		1,228	1,172	1,097	1,139	1,139	-0.9	-1.4	-1.1	0.4	0
Gross National Product per Man (pounds)	I	444	523	588	731	807	3.3	2.4	2.8	2.2	2.0
	II				775	881				2.8	2.6

NORWAY (1958 prices)

Levels

Gross National Product (million kroner)	22,352	26,653	31,399	I 42,827 / II 44,951	50,070 / 53,842
Employment (1,000)	1,411	1,424	1,435	I 1,485	1,527
Gross National Product per Man (1,000 kroner)	15.84	18.72	21.88	I 28.84 / II 30.27	32.79 / 35.26

Rates

Gross National Product	3.6	3.3	3.4	3.2 / 3.7	3.2 / 3.7
Employment	0.2	0.1	0.1	0.3	0.5
Gross National Product per Man	3.4	3.2	3.3	2.8 / 3.3	2.6 / 3.1

SWEDEN (1954 prices)

Levels

Gross National Product (million krona)	37,250	43,482	51,324	I 69,425 / II 72,884	77,993 / 83,894
Employment (1,000)	3,015	3,060	3,210	I 3,425	3,451
Gross National Product per Man (1,000 krona)	12.35	14.21	15.99	I 20.27 / II 21.28	22.60 / 24.31

Rates

Gross National Product	3.1	3.4	3.2	3.1 / 3.6	2.3 / 2.9
Employment	0.3	1.0	.6	0.6	0.1
Gross National Product per Man	2.8	2.4	2.6	2.4 / 2.9	2.2 / 2.7

SWITZERLAND (1954 prices)

Levels

Gross National Product (1,000 million francs)	20.8	27.4	34.0	I 48.0 / II 50.3	56.0 / 60.2
Employment (1,000)	2,137	2,235	2,274	I 2,432	2,497
Gross National Product per Man (1,000 francs)	9.73	12.26	14.95	I 19.72 / II 20.68	22.41 / 24.09

Rates

Gross National Product	5.7	4.4	5.0	3.5 / 4.0	3.1 / 3.7
Employment	0.9	0.3	0.6	0.7	0.5
Gross National Product per Man	4.7	4.1	4.4	2.8 / 3.3	2.6 / 3.1

Sources: Employment--In all cases except those noted below: OEEC, Manpower Statistics, 1950-1960; OEEC, General Statistics, May, 1960, and OEEC, Europe Today and in 1960, 8th Report, Vol. 2, 1957, p. 20. Denmark 1960; Finland 1950, 1955, 1960; Iceland 1960; Sweden, 1950, 1955, 1960; Switzerland 1960 estimated on the basis of OEEC, Demographic Trends, 1955-1975, ILO, Yearbook of Labor Statistics, and U.N., Demographic Yearbook, various issues.

Gross National Product--In all cases except those noted below, U.N., Yearbook of National Accounts, various issues, and OEEC, General Statistics, July, 1961.

Iceland 1960; Ireland, 1950; and Switzerland 1960, estimated on the basis of OEEC, Twelfth Annual Economic Review, 1961, p. 146.

TABLE A2.5.1

JAPAN: EMPLOYMENT AND PRODUCTIVITY IN THE MAIN SECTORS OF THE ECONOMY
(1955 Prices)

	1950	1955	1960	1970	1975	1950 to 1955	1955 to 1960	1950 to 1960	1960 to 1970	1970 to 1975
Employment (1,000)										
All Sectors	35,720	40,880	44,720	48,690	50,800	2.7	1.8	2.3	0.9	0.9
Agriculture	18,430	17,400	15,540	11,540	9,910	-1.1	-2.2	-1.7	-2.9	-3.0
Industry	7,760	9,420	12,010	15,680	17,380	4.0	5.0	4.5	2.7	2.1
Services	9,530	14,060	17,170	21,470	23,510	8.1	4.1	6.1	2.3	1.8
NDP per Man (million Yen)										
All Sectors	132	161	232	360	.440	4.1	7.6	5.8	4.5	4.1
Agriculture	66	86	104	154	185	5.4	3.9	4.7	4.0	3.7
Industry	193	211	311	468	569	1.8	8.1	4.9	4.2	4.0
Services	208	219	292	392	452	1.0	5.9	3.4	3.0	2.9

Sources: U.N., Yearbook of National Accounts, 1961; Japan, Japan Statistical Yearbook and Japanese Economic Statistics.

Notes: Industry includes mining, manufacturing, and construction only. We have used the implicit GNP deflator for conversion of Net Domestic Product to constant prices.

TABLE A2.6.1

PURCHASING POWER PARITIES EXPRESSED IN TERMS OF 1955 UNITED STATES DOLLARS

	Disposable Income Conversion[a]	Gross National Product Conversion[b]		Disposable Income Conversion[a]	Gross National Product Conversion[b]
Canada (Dollars)	1.00	1.00	Iceland (Krona)	21.2	(21.2)
Belgium (Francs)	47.3	41.6	Ireland (Pounds)	.263	(.263)
France (Francs)	3.44	3.38	Norway (Kroner)	4.90	5.42
Germany (Marks)	2.91	2.95	Sweden (Krona)	4.48	(4.48)
Italy (Lires)	460	417	Switzerland (Francs)	4.06	(4.06)
Luxembourg (Francs)	43.0	(43.0)	Greece (Drachmas)	24.9	(24.9)
Netherlands (Guilders)	2.55	2.59	Portugal (Escudos)	17.25	(17.25)
United Kingdom (Pounds)	0.272	0.267	Turkey (Lira)	3.44	(3.44)
Austria (Shillings)	14.5	(14.5)	Yugoslavia (Dinar)	246.6	(246.6)
Denmark (Kroner)	5.31	5.11	Japan (Yen)	230	(230)
Finland (Marks)	232	(232)	Spain (Pesetas)	231	(23.1)

[a]Disposable Income Conversion: derived from Dewhurst, J. F. and Associates, Europe's Needs and Resources, Twentieth Century Fund, 1961, except as noted below:
Canada--assumed to be equal to 1955 exchange rate.
Turkey, Yugoslavia, Japan--derived from Wirtschaft und Statistik, January, 1957, April, 1960, and January, 1961.

[b]Gross National Product Conversion: Geometric average of parities calculated at U.S. and average European weights, derived from Gilbert, M. and Associates, Comparative Products and Price Levels, OEEC, 1958, with the exception of figures in parentheses in which case disposable income conversion is employed.

TABLE A2.6.2

INDUSTRIAL COUNTRIES: PER CAPITA GROSS NATIONAL PRODUCT
(1955 dollars)

	1950	1955	1960		1970	1975	1950 to 1955	1955 to 1960	1950 to 1960	1960 to 1970	1970 to 1975
United States	2,122	2,405	2,469	I	3,069	3,339	2.5	0.6	1.5	2.2	1.7
				II	3,223	3,593				2.7	2.2
Canada	1,600	1,720	1,770	I	2,290	2,552	1.5	0.6	1.0	2.6	2.2
				II	2,382	2,703				3.0	2.6
Belgium	1,142	1,307	1,430	I	1,878	2,132	2.8	1.8	2.3	2.7	2.6
				II	1,964	2,297				3.2	3.2
France	973	1,166	1,362	I	1,946	2,286	3.7	3.2	3.4	3.6	3.3
				II	2,042	2,457				4.1	3.8
Germany [1]	836	1,229	a.1,554	I	2,089	2,483	8.0	4.7	6.4	3.0	3.5
			b.1,548	II	2,192	2,669				3.5	4.0
Italy	532	689	894	I	1,294	1,542	5.3	5.3	5.3	3.8	3.6
				II	1,358	1,658				4.3	4.1
Luxembourg	1,142	1,141	1,651	I	2,156	2,459	4.3	3.2	3.7	2.7	2.7
				II	2,263	2,645				3.2	3.2
Netherlands	887	1,088	1,230	I	1,673	1,890	4.2	2.5	3.3	3.1	2.5
				II	1,756	2,034				3.6	3.0
United Kingdom	1,254	1,399	1,540	I	1,922	2,131	2.2	1.9	2.0	2.2	2.1
				II	2,018	2,291				2.7	2.6
Austria	723	993	1,261	I	1,664	1,905	6.5	5.0	5.7	2.8	2.7
				II	1,746	2,049				3.3	3.2
Denmark	1,191	1,262	1,551	I	2,008	2,235	1.2	4.2	2.7	2.7	2.1
				II	2,108	2,403				3.1	2.7
Finland	756	924	1,070	I	1,356	1,508	4.1	3.0	3.5	2.4	2.1
				II	1,424	1,622				2.9	2.6
Iceland	910	1,145	1,275	I	1,650	1,852	4.7	2.1	3.4	2.6	2.3
				II	1,748	2,020				3.2	2.9

Country		(1)	(2)	(3)	(4)	(5)	(6)	(7)	(8)	(9)	(10)
Ireland	I	616	704	763	983	1,083	2.7	1.7	2.2	2.5	1.9
	II				1,043	1,182				3.1	2.5
Norway	I	1,130	1,283	1,444	1,812	2,026	2.6	2.4	2.5	2.3	2.3
	II				1,899	2,178				2.8	2.8
Sweden	I	1,236	1,394	1,596	2,034	2,220	2.4	2.7	2.6	2.4	1.8
	II				2,134	2,390				2.9	2.4
Switzerland	I	1,097	1,371	1,583	2,189	2,485	4.6	2.9	3.7	3.3	2.6
	II				2,293	2,672				3.8	3.1
Greece	I	252	336	417	584	697	5.9	4.4	5.2	3.4	3.6
	II				643	804				4.4	4.6
Portugal	I	286	337	396	549	647	3.4	3.3	3.3	3.3	3.3
	II				604	747				4.3	4.3
Spain	I	n.a.	n.a.	574	809	955		0.5		3.6	3.3
	II				891	1,103				4.5	4.4
Turkey	I	215	254	301	423	497	3.4	3.4	3.4	3.5	3.3
	II				466	575				4.5	4.3
Yugoslavia	I	363	427	625	944	1,139	3.3	7.9	5.6	4.2	3.8
	II				1,038	1,313				5.2	4.8
Japan	I	(288)	400	595	922	1,129	(6.8)	8.3	(7.5)	4.5	4.1
	II				1,014	1,303				5.5	5.1

Sources: Gross National Product: Tables A2.3.1 – A2.5.1.
Population: Table A2.2.1.

Note: [1] 1950 to 1960a exclude the Saar.
1960b to 1975 exclude the Saar.

TABLE A2.6.3

INDUSTRIAL COUNTRIES: PER CAPITA DISPOSABLE INCOME IN NATIONAL CURRENCIES (1955 PRICES)

	1950	1955	1960	1970 I	1970 II	1975 I	1975 II
United States, dollars	1,525	1,660	1,762	2,190	2,300	2,383	2,564
Canada, dollars	1,058	1,175	1,296	1,675	1,742	1,867	1,981
Belgium, francs	38,764	44,131	49,439	64,750	67,880	73,690	79,370
France, francs	2,221	2,835	3,301	4,720	4,954	5,545	5,962
Germany, marks	1,569	2,422	3,136	4,234	4,441	5,031	5,407
Italy, 1,000 lira	169.1	200.1	241.0	348.7	365.2	416.3	446.7
Luxembourg, francs	31,798	41,119	47,604	62,200	65,300	70,960	76,330
Netherlands, guilders	1,414	1,901	2,172	2,955	3,101	3,338	3,590
United Kingdom, pounds	239.1	259.2	295.7	369.6	387.6	409.9	440.6
Austria, shillings	7,497	10,396	13,432	17,740	18,610	20,310	21,830
Denmark, kroner	4,948	4,842	5,827	7,549	7,924	8,402	9,035
Finland, 1,000 marks	112.5	146.1	153.2	194.4	204.0	216.1	232.4
Iceland, krona	12,442	16,401	16,775	21,690	22,990	24,350	26,560
Ireland, pounds	139.9	153.1	164.9	212.2	225.0	233.7	255.1
Norway, kroner	4,326	4,533	4,911	6,163	6,461	6,893	7,409
Sweden, krona	3,707	4,212	4,567	5,817	6,104	6,350	6,836
Switzerland, francs	3,198	3,929	4,380	6,066	6,355	6,886	7,404
Greece, drachmas	4,677	5,810	6,916	9,688	10,668	11,550	13,335
Portugal, escudos	3,823	4,647	4,768	6,612	7,340	7,793	8,998
Spain	n.a.	n.a.	9,685	13,780	15,022	16,111	18,598
Turkey, lira	548.6	742.0	857.2	1,205.3	1,326.4	1,415.4	1,635.8
Yugoslavia, dinar	39,111	46,685	69,763	105,470	116,090	127,700	147,460
Japan, yen	45,347	64,963	90,420	140,100	154,100	171,600	197,800

Sources:
Disposable income: in all cases except those noted below, U.N., Yearbook of National Accounts, 1957-1961.
Calculated from data in private consumption expenditures: Finland, 1950-1960, Italy, 1950-1960, Portugal, 1955, 1960 (from above source), Iceland, 1950, 1955, Luxembourg, 1950, 1955, Norway, 1950-1960, Switzerland, 1955, Turkey, 1950, 1955 (from OEEC, General Statistics, July, 1961). Private saving assumed to be the following percentage of private consumption expenditures: Iceland, Luxembourg, Switzerland, Turkey, 10 percent; Finland, 12 percent. Private saving assumed to be the following percentage of corporate plus private saving: Italy, 33 percent, Portugal, 50 percent, Norway, 40 percent.
Our estimates for: Iceland, 1960, Luxembourg, 1960, Switzerland, 1950, 1960, Turkey, 1960 and Yugoslavia, 1950, 1960.
All data deflated by Consumer Price Indices adjusted to a 1955 base. Source: In all cases except those noted below, OEEC, General Statistics, November, 1961. Japan and Finland, IMF, International Financial Statistics, December, 1961.

TABLE A2.7.1

OCEANIA AND SOUTH AFRICA: GROSS NATIONAL PRODUCT, EMPLOYMENT, AND PRODUCTIVITY[a]
(1955 Prices)

	1951	1955	1960	1970	1975	Percentage Change per Year 1951 to 1955	1955 to 1960	1951 to 1960	1960 to 1970	1970 to 1975
Australia										
Gross National Product (million pounds)	4,130	4,885	5,744	I 8,099 / II 8,591	9,563 / 10,446	4.3	3.3	3.7	3.5 / 4.1	3.4 / 4.0
Employment (1,000)	3,528	3,748	4,128	4,969	5,418	1.5	1.95	1.8	1.9	1.9
Gross National Product per Man (thousand pounds)	1,171	1,303	1,391	I 1,630 / II 1,729	1,765 / 1,928	2.7	1.3	1.9	1.6 / 2.2	1.6 / 2.2
New Zealand										
Gross National Product (million pounds)	845	978	1,129	I 1,572 / II 1,666	1,839 / 2,010	3.7	2.9	3.3	3.4 / 4.0	3.2 / 3.8
Employment (1,000)	746	807	891	1,090	1,196	2.0	2.0	2.0	2.0	1.9
Gross National Product per Man (thousand pounds)	1,133	1,212	1,267	I 1,442 / II 1,528	1,538 / 1,681	1.7	0.9	1.3	1.3 / 1.9	1.3 / 1.9
South Africa										
Gross National Product (million pounds)	3,124	3,795	4,955	I 7,483 / II 8,095	9,252 / 10,406	4.0	5.5	4.7	4.1 / 5.0	4.3 / 5.1
Employment (1,000)	5,107	5,670	6,278	7,729	8,660	2.1	2.0	2.1	2.2	2.3
Gross National Product per Man (thousand pounds)	661.7	669.3	789.3	I 953 / II 1,030	1,047 / 1,177	1.8	3.4	2.6	1.9 / 2.7	1.9 / 2.7

Sources: Employment--Estimated on the basis of national sources and the U.N. Yearbook.
Gross National Product--Australia: Estimates given in current prices in the U.N., National Accounts Statistics, 1961, deflated
by price index published in Economic Record, June, 1962.
New Zealand: Economic Record, December, 1958 and December, 1961.
South Africa: Estimates given in current prices in U.N., National Accounts Statistics, 1961, deflated
by wholesale price index.

Note: [a]For conversion into U.S. dollars, use can be made of purchasing power parities calculated by A. Maizels (U.S. $ per national currency unit): Australia--2.75, New Zealand--3.30, South Africa--3.35 (Industrial Growth and World Trade, Cambridge, Eng.: The University Press, 1963), p. 546.

TABLE A31.1

EXPORTS OF DEVELOPING COUNTRIES TO DEVELOPED ECONOMIES
($ million, current prices)

	1960					1970I					1970II					1975I					1975II				
	NA	WE	JA	OC	DC	NA	WE	JA	OC	DC	NA	WE	JA	OC	DC	NA	WE	JA	OC	DC	NA	WE	JA	OC	DC
Temperate Zone Foods																									
Meat and Eggs	94	283	3	5	385	162	247	9	6	424	176	267	13	7	463	200	261	13	6	480	226	301	16	6	549
Fish	86	30	2	–	118	142	33	1	1	177	142	33	2	–	177	191	35	2	–	228	191	35	2	–	228
Wheat and Rice	1	103	18	3	125	1	65	–	5	71	1	64	–	5	70	1	64	–	7	72	1	63	–	7	71
Coarse Grains	–	217	46	–	263	–	202	113	–	315	–	224	130	–	354	–	207	164	–	371	–	228	194	–	422
Feeding Stuff	12	262	7	–	281	28	342	26	–	396	31	351	28	–	410	40	379	38	–	457	48	399	45	–	492
Oranges	4	112	–	–	116	4	155	–	–	159	4	161	–	–	165	4	187	–	–	191	4	195	–	–	199
Fresh Fruit	86	69	2	4	161	102	88	4	5	199	102	90	5	5	202	112	97	6	6	221	112	100	7	6	225
Preserved Fruit	28	70	7	1	106	40	111	16	1	168	42	118	18	1	179	47	134	21	1	203	51	147	24	1	223
Vegetables	55	117	5	–	177	86	176	10	–	272	91	186	11	–	288	106	207	15	–	328	115	221	17	–	353
Beverages	4	257	–	–	261	5	144	–	–	149	5	144	–	–	149	6	156	–	–	162	6	156	–	–	162
Total	370	1,520	90	13	1,993	570	1,563	180	17	2,330	594	1,638	207	18	2,457	707	1,727	259	20	2,713	754	1,845	305	20	2,924
Competing Tropical Foods																									
Oilseeds	72	418	42	2	534	81	400	82	2	565	81	411	92	2	586	90	420	107	2	619	91	434	127	2	654
Vegetable Oils	54	257	3	9	323	60	244	5	12	321	60	252	5	13	330	67	259	5	15	346	67	273	6	15	361
Animal Fats	15	36	–	1	52	15	55	4	1	75	15	55	4	1	75	16	76	5	1	98	16	76	5	1	98
Sugar	584	297	98	3	982	456	262	131	4	853	456	272	143	4	875	469	272	153	4	898	470	284	166	4	924
Tobacco	39	187	–	10	236	43	248	–	8	299	43	255	–	8	306	51	264	–	8	323	51	276	–	8	335
Total	764	1,195	143	25	2,127	655	1,209	222	27	2,113	655	1,245	244	28	2,172	693	1,291	270	30	2,284	695	1,343	304	30	2,372
Noncompeting Tropical Foods																									
Bananas	100	140	4	2	246	123	176	23	4	326	123	180	25	4	332	135	195	33	4	367	135	200	36	4	375
Coffee	1,058	704	8	15	1,785	1,359	977	67	24	2,427	1,327	1,001	80	25	2,478	1,536	1,107	105	30	2,778	1,564	1,143	125	31	2,863
Cocoa	169	299	6	11	485	204	330	26	15	578	204	346	26	16	592	227	370	41	17	655	219	381	41	18	659
Tea	71	367	2	55	495	75	330	3	64	522	75	384	3	64	526	81	401	4	75	561	81	408	6	75	568
Spices	46	34	2	2	84	55	37	4	3	99	55	37	4	3	99	60	39	4	3	108	60	39	6	3	108
Total	1,444	1,544	22	85	3,095	1,814	1,908	123	110	2,895	1,829	1,948	138	112	4,027	2,039	2,112	189	129	4,469	2,059	2,171	212	131	4,573
Agricultural Raw Materials																									
Hides and Skins	64	149	5	1	219	63	149	9	1	222	63	151	12	1	227	65	154	16	1	236	65	158	19	1	243
Rubber	333	555	135	49	1,072	264	405	110	37	816	277	432	121	37	867	273	459	129	39	900	291	506	143	44	984
Forest Products	35	206	79	30	350	49	437	217	45	748	50	493	242	48	833	55	635	288	62	1,040	58	732	338	67	1,195
Wool and Silk	103	161	14	3	281	119	207	34	3	363	122	218	37	3	380	127	208	38	3	376	133	219	41	3	396
Cotton	33	499	189	6	727	35	581	258	12	886	36	604	269	13	922	38	585	285	13	921	39	630	296	14	979
Jute	9	113	11	6	139	8	104	15	8	135	8	107	16	9	140	8	107	19	9	143	8	111	21	9	149
Vegetable Fibres	41	104	21	11	177	46	132	27	17	222	46	137	28	18	229	46	151	33	21	251	46	157	35	23	261
Animal and Vegetable Matter	58	111	9	3	181	67	132	13	4	216	68	136	13	4	221	73	146	16	4	239	75	154	17	4	250
Total	676	1,898	463	109	3,146	651	2,147	683	127	3,608	670	2,278	738	133	3,819	685	2,445	824	152	4,106	715	2,667	910	165	4,457

Fuels

Coal	1,140	3	3																						8
Petroleum Crude	630	2,152	305	172	703	1,332	3,769	728	359	4,062	6,481	5	1,429	4,354	1,585	189	6,481	7,030	1,699	5,495	1,008	8,705	1,820	6,242	9,986
Petroleum Products	—	485	37	150	10	703	1,302	359	136	636	755	124	755	697	1,585	189	809	1,740	809	805	157	1,952	1,952	889	2,182
Natural Gas	8	—	—	—	—	8	8	—	—	170	11	11	11	179	189	—	12	201	12	337	16	365	13	365	394
Total	1,778	2,640	345	322	495	2,045	5,085	852	495	4,868	8,260	991	2,195	5,230	—	—	2,520	8,976	2,520	6,637	1,189	11,030	2,715	7,496	12,570

Nonfuel Minerals and Metals

Iron Ore	216	194	107		288	390	517	226		904	317	253		456	345	592	289	1,026	175	1,226	371	760	307	1,593	1,438
Manganese Ore	81	39	5	1	103	53	125	11		167	108	11		56	118	66	16	175	66	200	126	72	18	72	216
Copper	377	747	56	11	406	1,186	1,191	137	10	1,739	420	163	10	1,281	449	1,448	209	1,874	1,448	2,116	483	1,593	256	688	2,342
Bauxite and Aluminum	122	48	11	1	263	250	181	23	1	536	301	28	1	304	398	582	37	633	582	1,017	470	688	44	102	1,202
Lead	35	53	1	1	44	74	90	6	1	125	46	6	1	76	52	96	—	129	96	173	57	102	6	116	166
Zinc	27	36	3	4	46	71	70	5	4	126	48	5	4	77	58	101	10	134	101	173	62	116	10	187	192
Tin	103	115	23	7	115	164	248	37	8	324	118	39	8	169	124	180	39	334	180	352	129	187	41	256	366
Other Nonferrous Metal	57	119	39	1	67	196	216	90	1	354	72	105	1	211	82	236	115	389	236	434	87	256	140	15	484
Metal Scrap	1	29	59	—	—	25	89	40	—	65	—	40	—	—	—	15	25	65	15	40	—	40	25	15	40
Crude Fertilizer	65	142	25	16	74	190	248	31	21	316	68	31	21	190	80	219	36	310	219	358	80	224	36	224	363
Total	1,084	1,522	329	40	1,406	2,599	2,975	606	45	4,656	1,498	681	45	1,855	1,706	3,535	784	5,069	3,535	6,073	1,865	4,013	883	224	6,809

Manufactured Goods

Chemicals	54	59	5	1	81	87	119	10	1	176	84	11	1	93	96	106	15	189	106	218	103	116	15	109	235
Leather and Footwear	14	64	2	1	25	87	81	6	3	121	27	7	3	91	35	102	9	128	102	149	38	109	10	86	160
Veneer and Plywood	25	23	—	2	93	56	50	—	4	153	98	—	—	57	173	83	—	159	83	261	184	86	—	86	275
Cotton Textiles	145	151	—	20	219	269	316	1	35	523	219	4	35	269	281	332	1	523	332	658	281	332	—	332	658
Jute Manufactures	103	34	1	37	113	41	175	42	42	183	114	1	43	43	120	48	1	201	48	213	122	52	1	52	221
Other Textiles	39	59	1	3	65	110	102	3	5	183	67	3	5	120	77	146	4	195	146	234	81	166	4	166	258
Silver and Precious Metals	28	64	2	—	59	128	94	5	2	204	64	6	2	144	83	187	9	216	187	278	93	197	10	197	304
Machinery and Metal Manufactures	20	21	0	1	40	42	42	—	2	84	43	—	2	47	60	63	—	92	63	126	64	70	—	70	137
Other Manufactures	53	37	1	5	98	70	96	3	10	181	105	3	11	76	132	92	4	195	92	242	144	101	4	144	264
Total	481	512	12	70	790	890	1,075	28	104	1,812	821	31	106	940	1,057	1,154	42	1,898	1,154	2,379	1,110	1,229	44	1,229	2,512
GRAND TOTAL	6,597	10,831	1,404	664	7,931	15,184	19,496	2,694	925	26,734	8,262	3,030	1,002	16,124	9,407	18,901	3,557	28,418	18,901	33,054	9,913	20,764	4,180	1,360	36,217

Sources: Tables A6-12.

TABLE A3.1.2

EXPORTS OF DEVELOPING COUNTRIES BY REGION OF ORIGIN
($ million, current prices)

	1960	1970I	1970II	1975I	1975II
Temperate Zone Foods:					
Latin America	1,026	1,243	1,320	1,454	1,586
Africa	603	588	609	664	691
Middle East	102	129	135	146	154
Asia	262	370	393	449	493
Developing countries, total	1,993	2,330	2,457	2,713	2,924
Competing Tropical Foods:					
Latin America	894	783	797	845	862
Africa	637	696	723	743	786
Middle East	69	87	89	94	96
Asia	527	547	563	602	628
Developing countries, total	2,127	2,113	2,172	2,284	2,372
Noncompeting Tropical Products:					
Latin America	1,772	2,163	2,199	2,404	2,455
Africa	769	1,155	1,183	1,363	1,407
Middle East	4	6	6	6	6
Asia	550	631	639	696	705
Developing countries, total	3,095	3,955	4,027	4,469	4,573
Agriculture Raw Materials:					
Latin America	716	964	1,014	1,045	1,114
Africa	754	962	1,027	1,150	1,261
Middle East	113	131	131	132	139
Asia	1,563	1,551	1,647	1,779	1,943
Developing countries, total	3,146	3,608	3,819	4,106	4,457
Fuels:					
Latin America	1,982	2,416	2,638	3,060	3,363
Africa	176	1,355	1,451	2,354	2,531
Middle East	2,672	4,044	4,353	4,956	5,852
Asia	255	445	534	660	824
Developing countries, total	5,085	8,260	8,976	11,030	12,570
Minerals and Metals:					
Latin America	1,366	2,002	2,190	2,461	2,826
Africa	1,010	1,822	1,991	2,656	2,944
Middle East	40	55	58	70	70
Asia	559	777	830	886	969
Developing countries, total	2,975	4,656	5,069	6,073	6,809
Manufactured Goods:					
Latin America	175	301	321	393	424
Africa	89	169	179	237	251
Middle East	97	186	200	251	277
Asia	714	1,156	1,198	1,498	1,560
Developing countries, total	1,075	1,812	1,898	2,379	2,512
Total:					
Latin America	7,931	9,872	10,479	11,662	12,630
Africa	4,038	6,747	7,163	9,167	9,871
Middle East	3,097	4,638	4,972	5,655	6,594
Asia	4,430	5,477	5,804	6,570	7,122
Developing countries, total	19,496	26,734	28,418	33,054	36,217

Sources: Tables A6-A12.

($ million, current prices)

	1960					1970I					1970II					1975I					1975II				
	LA	AF	ME	AS	LDC	LA	AF	ME	AS	LDC	LA	AF	ME	AS	LDC	LA	AF	ME	AS	LDC	LA	AF	ME	AS	LDC
Foodstuffs (0,1)																									
LA	-	34	23	25	82	-	50	30	40	120	-	50	30	40	120	-	60	40	50	150	-	60	40	50	150
AF	12	-	36	44	92	20	-	50	60	130	20	-	50	60	140	20	-	60	80	160	20	-	60	90	170
ME	1	11	-	9	21	-	10	-	10	20	-	10	-	10	20	-	10	-	10	20	-	10	-	10	20
AS	12	62	104	-	178	20	80	140	-	240	20	80	150	-	260	20	100	160	-	280	20	110	180	-	310
LDC	25	107	163	78	373	40	140	220	110	510	40	140	230	120	540	40	170	260	140	610	40	180	280	150	650
Agr. Raw Materials (2,4 less 28)																									
LA	-	4	1	3	8	-	10	-	10	20	-	10	-	10	20	-	10	-	10	20	-	10	-	10	20
AF	10	-	28	108	146	10	-	40	120	170	10	-	40	120	170	10	-	50	130	190	10	-	60	130	200
ME	-	7	-	6	13	-	10	-	10	20	-	10	-	10	20	-	10	-	10	20	-	10	-	10	20
AS	75	16	16	-	107	90	20	30	-	140	100	20	30	-	150	110	20	40	-	170	120	20	50	-	190
LDC	85	27	45	117	274	100	40	70	140	350	110	40	70	140	360	120	40	90	150	400	130	40	110	150	430
Fuels (3)																									
LA	-	64	4	6	74	-	70	-	10	80	-	80	-	10	90	-	90	-	10	100	-	100	-	10	110
AF	4	-	-	-	4	-	-	-	-	-	-	-	-	-	-	-	-	-	-	-	-	-	-	-	-
ME	55	186	-	262	503	50	230	-	420	700	50	250	-	450	750	50	270	-	550	870	50	290	-	650	990
AS	4	-	4	-	8	-	-	-	-	-	-	-	-	-	-	-	-	-	-	-	-	-	-	-	-
LDC	63	250	8	268	589	50	300	-	430	780	50	330	-	460	840	50	360	-	560	970	50	390	-	660	1,100
Nonfuel Minerals and Metals (28,67,68)																									
LA	-	-	-	2	2	-	-	-	-	-	-	-	-	-	-	-	-	-	-	-	-	-	-	-	-
AF	11	-	-	29	40	10	-	-	40	50	10	-	-	40	50	10	-	-	50	60	10	-	-	60	70
ME	1	-	-	-	1	-	-	-	-	-	-	-	-	-	-	-	-	-	-	-	-	-	-	-	-
AS	7	-	1	-	8	10	-	-	-	10	10	-	-	-	10	10	-	-	-	10	10	-	-	-	10
LDC	19	-	1	31	51	20	-	-	40	60	20	-	-	40	60	20	-	-	50	70	20	-	-	60	80
Manufactured Goods (5-8 less 67,68)																									
LA	-	1	-	7	8	-	10	-	20	30	-	10	-	20	30	-	10	-	30	40	-	10	-	30	40
AF	16	-	24	5	45	20	-	40	10	70	20	-	50	10	70	30	-	60	20	110	40	-	70	30	140
ME	2	21	-	9	32	10	30	-	20	60	10	30	-	20	60	10	40	-	30	80	10	50	-	40	100
AS	70	122	46	-	238	80	140	70	-	290	80	140	80	-	300	90	150	90	-	330	90	150	100	-	340
LDC	88	144	70	21	323	110	180	110	50	450	110	180	130	50	470	130	200	150	80	560	140	210	170	100	620
Total Trade																									
LA	-	103	28	43	174	-	140	30	80	250	-	150	30	80	260	-	170	40	100	310	-	180	40	100	320
AF	53	-	88	186	327	60	-	130	230	420	60	-	140	240	440	70	-	170	280	520	80	-	190	310	580
ME	59	225	-	286	570	60	280	-	460	800	60	300	-	490	850	60	330	-	600	990	60	360	-	710	1,130
AS	168	200	171	-	539	210	240	240	-	680	210	250	260	-	720	230	270	290	-	790	240	280	330	-	850
LDC	280	528	287	515	1,610	330	660	400	770	2,150	330	700	430	810	2,270	360	770	500	980	2,610	380	820	560	1,120	2,880

Sources: U.N. Monthly Bulletin of Statistics, March and April, 1963, and national trade statistics.

TABLE A4.4.1

EXPORTS OF DEVELOPING COUNTRIES TO THE SINO-SOVIET AREA
($ million, current prices)

	1960					1970					1975				
	LA	AF	ME	AS	Total	LA	AF	ME	AS	Total	LA	AF	ME	AS	Total
Temperate Zone Foods	1	4	20	42	67	2	8	40	84	134	3	11	56	118	188
Competing Tropical Foods	163	7	1	11	182	393	14	2	20	429	400	20	3	28	451
Veg. Oil and Oilseeds	9	7	1	10	27	18	14	2	20	54	25	20	3	28	76
Sugar	154	–	–	–	154	375	–	–	–	375	375	–	–	–	375
Tobacco	–	–	–	1	1	–	–	–	–	–	–	–	–	–	–
Noncompeting Tropical Foods	49	48	1	29	127	175	102	1	52	330	252	169	1	71	493
Bananas	1	–	–	–	1	25	4	–	–	29	38	6	–	–	44
Coffee	35	2	1	4	42	130	25	1	16	172	188	70	1	27	286
Cocoa	13	46	–	–	59	20	73	–	–	93	26	93	–	–	119
Tea	–	–	–	19	19	–	–	–	28	28	–	–	–	35	35
Pepper	–	–	–	6	6	–	–	–	8	8	–	–	–	9	9
Agricultural Raw Materials	80	282	49	332	744	106	286	57	353	802	121	292	62	413	888
Rubber	–	–	–	275	275	8	–	–	291	291	7	–	–	344	344
Cotton	8	248	28	14	298	14	235	26	14	283	14	230	26	14	277
Wool	15	–	4	15	34	4	–	4	14	32	5	–	4	14	32
Jute	4	2	–	19	25	–	3	–	21	28	–	4	–	26	35
Other	53	32	18	9	112	80	48	27	13	168	95	58	32	15	200
Fuels	–	–	–	2	2	–	–	–	4	4	–	–	–	5	5
Nonfuel Minerals and Metals	9	16	–	23	48	18	32	–	42	92	25	45	–	57	127
Manufactured Goods	3	17	3	48	71	6	34	6	87	133	9	48	9	118	184
Textile yarns, fabrics	1	11	3	26	37	1	22	6	47	69	–	31	9	63	94
Other	3	6	3	22	34	6	12	–	40	64	9	17	–	55	90
Total	306	374	74	487	1,241	700	476	106	642	1,924	810	585	131	810	2,336

Sources: U.N., *Monthly Bulletin of Statistics*, March and April, 1963; FAO, *Trade Yearbook*, 1961; and national trade statistics.

TABLE A5.1.1

DEVELOPING COUNTRIES: RECEIPTS AND PAYMENTS ON ACCOUNT OF SERVICES, 1960[a]
($ billion)

	Latin America	Africa	Middle East	Asia	Developing Countries, Total
Freight and Insurance					
Receipts	0.13	0.10	0.02	0.11	0.36
Payments	0.79	0.53	0.25	0.64	2.21
Other Transportation					
Receipts	0.18	0.26	0.07	0.10	0.61
Payments	0.24	0.15	0.06	0.10	0.55
Travel					
Receipts	1.05	0.13	0.07	0.06	1.31
Payments	0.65	0.36	0.09	0.12	1.22
Investment Income					
Receipts	0.07	0.17	0.04	0.12	0.40
Payments	1.46	0.36	1.17	0.46	3.45
Government					
Receipts	0.24	1.19	0.27	0.65	2.35
Payments	0.17	0.18	0.12	0.17	0.64
Miscellaneous Services					
Receipts	0.48	0.21	0.07	0.22	0.98
Payments	0.62	0.27	0.06	0.30	1.25
Services, Total					
Receipts	2.15	2.06	0.54	1.26	6.01
Payments	3.93	1.85	1.75	1.79	9.32

Source: IMF, Balance of Payments Yearbook, Vols. 13 and 14, and national statistical publications.

Note: [a]For several smaller countries and territories, the figures include only estimated freight expenditures, spending by foreign governments, and investment income.

TABLE A5.1.2

OIL-COMPANY PROFITS IN DEVELOPING AREAS[a]
($ million, current prices)

	1960	1970I	1970II	1975I	1975II
Latin America ., ...	410	393	441	502	567
Africa.............................	56	335	364	541	589
Middle East	1,002	1,351	1,463	1,569	1,867
Asia..............................	56	83	104	117	152
Developing countries, total	1,524	2,162	2,372	2,729	3,175

Note: [a]Figures refer to company profits on crude oil and petroleum products exported to developed countries. In the case of the Middle East, profit on oil sold elsewhere has been separately estimated: $30 million in 1960, $40 million in 1970, $50 million in 1975.

Source: Quantities exported--Tables A10.3.2 and A10.3.3.
Value of exports--Table A10.

Unit costs:

	($ per ton) Crude Oil			Petroleum Products		
	1960	1970	1975	1960	1970	1975
Latin America	4.00	4.30	4.30	9.50	9.90	9.90
Africa....................	4.30	4.30	4.30	9.80	9.90	9.90
Middle East	1.40	1.50	1.50	5.90	6.10	6.10
Asia	6.20	6.20	6.20	11.70	11.80	11.80

Our estimate in part on the basis of information provided in United Nations, Economic Development in the Middle East, 1958-1961, New York, pp. 58-59.

Share of company profits in total profits:

	1960	1970	1975
Latin America	64	70	70
Africa....................	53	60	62
Middle East	53	60	62
Asia	53	60	62

Our estimate in part based on Symonds, E. Oil Advances in the Eastern Hemisphere, New York, First National City Bank, 1962. United Nations, Economic Development in the Middle East, 1959-1961, New York, 1962, and Petroleum Press Service, various issues. Profit shares for the year 1960 have been calculated with reference to oil prices indicated in international trade statistics.

TABLE A5.4.3

THE IMPACT OF CHANGES IN PRODUCTION AND TRADE POLICIES IN INDUS-
TRIAL COUNTRIES ON IMPORTS FROM DEVELOPING AREAS

	European Common Market			United Kingdom		
	1960	1970	1975	1960	1970	1975
TEMPERATE ZONE FOODS						
Beef and Veal						
Consumption, million tons[a]	3,447	4,648	5,200	1,135	1,303	1,413
index	100	135	151	100	115	124
Projected imports, $ million[b]	47	10	10	165	165	165
Hypothetical imports, $ million[c]	47	63	71	165	190	205
Hypothetical less projected imports, $ million	--	53	63	--	25	40
Wheat and Coarse Grains						
Consumption, million tons[d]	63.2	71.8	76.5	16.9	18.3	18.9
index	100	114	121	100	108	112
Projected imports, $ million[b]	221	155	155	40	39	40
Hypothetical imports, $ million	221	252	267	40	43	45
Projected less hypothetical imports	--	97	112		4	5

	Industrial Countries		
	1960	1970	1975
SUGAR			
Projected consumption, thousand tons[e]			
North America	9,670	11,482	12,623
Western Europe	10,644	12,598	13,958
Japan	1,336	1,937	2,273
Industrial countries, total	21,650	26,017	28,354
Estimated increase in consumption after the removal or tariffs and excise taxes, thousand tons[f]			
North America	348	413	454
Western Europe	856	869	963
Japan	445	542	568
Industrial countries, total	1,649	1,824	1,985
World market price of sugar, $ per ton	69	69	69
Estimated increase in consumption (imports), $ million	114	126	137

	Increase in 1970 imports of taxes and duties reduced by			
	50%	100%	50%	100%
	at 1957-59 prices[g]		at current prices[h]	
NONCOMPETITIVE TROPICAL FOODS				
EEC and EFTA, including Portugal				
Coffee	50.0	104.0	39	80
Cocoa	13.0	30.0	9	20
Tea	0.7	2.1	1	2
EEC, Bananas	2.5	5.2	2	5
	66.2	141.3	51	107

Notes: [a]Table 6.1.1.
[b]Table A6 and Ch. 6.1.
[c]Assuming imports to rise in proportion to domestic consumption.
[d]Our estimate.
[e]Table 7.2.1.
[f]Assuming average fiscal charges of 24 per cent in North America, 23 per cent in Western Europe, and 51 per cent in Japan. The corresponding arc-elasticities are -0.28, -0.5, and -1.0.
[g]"Tropical Fruit and Beverages: Duties and Taxes in Western Europe," *Monthly Bulletin of Agricultural Economics and Statistics*, December, 1962, p. 8.
[h]FAO, *Trade Yearbook*, various issues and Ch. 8.

TABLE A6.1.1

PER CAPITA MEAT CONSUMPTION IN INDUSTRIAL COUNTRIES
(kg, carcass weight)

	Prewar	1950	1955	1960	1970I	1970II	1975I	1975II
United States	64.7	75.6	81.5	84.0	89.1	90.2	91.0	92.5
Canada	61.7	69.8	81.4	79.9	86.8	87.7	89.1	90.3
Belgium-Lux.	47.2	45.6	52.1	59.3	67.3	68.6	71.0	73.1
France	55.2	56.0	68.2	73.3	83.3	84.6	87.5	89.2
Germany	52.8	35.0	47.1	56.0	66.3	67.8	72.1	75.3
Italy	20.1	16.0	19.5	28.1	41.6	43.3	48.1	50.7
Netherlands	37.5	30.8	43.8	46.5	57.1	58.6	61.4	63.9
United Kingdom	62.6	49.4	63.2	67.6	73.5	74.7	76.1	77.9
Austria	48.7	33.6	46.7	55.4	65.1	66.6	69.8	72.2
Denmark	74.6	60.5	59.4	67.5	74.3	75.5	76.9	78.7
Finland	33.0	28.0	34.0	32.0	37.5	38.8	40.2	42.0
Ireland	54.9	53.3	56.0	61.7	68.8	70.5	71.6	74.2
Norway	37.9	36.5	36.9	38.6	43.9	45.2	46.6	48.4
Sweden	49.0	51.0	50.4	49.8	55.8	57.0	57.9	59.7
Switzerland	53.2	45.5	50.3	57.2	66.4	67.7	69.9	71.9
Greece	19.5	11.5	17.8	23.1	33.4	36.5	39.0	43.6
Turkey	14.8	14.2	13.3	12.6	18.1	19.8	20.9	23.2
Portugal	15.0	16.1	18.5	18.8	27.0	29.2	30.9	34.6
Spain	.....	.....	14.1	17.9	26.7	28.8	30.6	34.2
Yugoslavia	.....	22.0	23.4	30.2	43.6	47.4	50.7	56.0
Japan	4.0	2.0	3.5	6.0	11.2	11.8	13.6	14.6

Sources: OECD countries and Yugoslavia--OECD, *Agricultural and Food Statistics*, 1959 and 1962. Finland and Japan--FAO, *Production Yearbook*, various issues.

TABLE A6.1.2

PER CAPITA FISH CONSUMPTION IN INDUSTRIAL COUNTRIES
(kg)

	Prewar	1950	1955	1960
United States[b]	4.9	5.2	4.7	4.8
Canada[a]	5.4	5.5	60.1	8.0
Belgium-Lux.[a]	9.5	11.0	11.6	9.3
France[a]	10.4	10.1	9.7	9.7
Germany[c]	6.8	7.3	7.3	6.8
Italy[a]	6.3	6.1	7.0	7.2
Netherlands[d]	9.4	9.7	7.7	6.5
United Kingdom[d]	11.9	11.0	9.9	9.7
Austria[a]	1.5	2.1	3.0	3.5
Denmark[c]	15.0	18.2	14.1	15.0
Finland[b]	6.0	8.0	11.0	11.0
Ireland[d]	3.0	2.4	4.1	4.7
Norway[d]	41.4	49.0	39.4	36.3
Sweden[c]	17.5	15.8	18.4	18.5
Switzerland[a]	1.4	2.2	2.7	3.3
Greece[a]	8.2	8.8	10.6	13.7
Portugal[a]	25.5	27.4	25.4	30.3
Spain[d]	.....	.....	20.4	25.2
Turkey[d]	0.6	1.5	3.4	3.0
Yugoslavia[d]	.....	2.0	1.4	1.1
Japan[b]	18.0	15.0	20.0	23.0

Sources: OECD Countries and Yugoslavia--OECD, *Agricultural and Food Statistics*, 1959 and 1962. Finland and Japan--FAO, *Production Yearbook*, various issues.
Notes: a) product weight, b) edible weight, c) fillet weight, d) landed weight.

TABLE A6.1.3

CROSS-SECTION, MULTICOUNTRY AND TIME-SERIES REGRESSIONS FOR MEAT[a]

	Double-log	R^2	Semi-log	R^2
Cross-Section[b]	log C = -0.63 + 0.79 log Y (0.09)	.82	C = -152.64 + 70.70 log Y (9.51)	.78
Multicountry[c]	log C = -0.85 + 0.87 log Y (0.03)	.81	C = -174.44 + 77.88 log Y (3.58)	.75

Individual Country[d]

Belgium-Lux.	log C = -1.05 + 0.94 log Y (0.14)	.841	C = -513.25 + 81.24 log Y (14.82)	.83
France	log C = +0.57 + 0.43 log Y (0.10)	.764	C = -126.01 + 66.54 log Y (15.02)	.77
Germany	log C = -0.04 + 0.59 log Y (0.02)	.990	C = -149.98 + 68.10 log Y (3.61)	.98
Italy	log C = -3.17 + 1.70 log Y (0.11)	.967	C = -200.24 + 83.76 log Y (5.78)	.96
Netherlands	log C = -1.04 + 0.93 log Y (0.06)	.964	C = -194.34 + 82.36 log Y (6.23)	.95
United Kingdom	log C = -2.54 + 1.45 log Y (0.29)	.756	C = -520.76 + 195.50 log Y (35.76)	.79
Austria	log C = +0.27 + 0.50 log Y (0.07)	.885	C = -113.52 + 56.77 log Y (9.14)	.87
Finland	log C = -0.27 + 0.64 log Y (0.07)	.709	C = - 95.67 + 46.20 log Y (11.41)	.70
Ireland	log C = -1.01 + 1.00 log Y (0.19)	.773	C = -305.14 + 131.16 log Y (24.92)	.78
Norway	log C = -1.31 + 0.97 log Y (0.17)	.793	C = -202.82 + 80.73 log Y (13.36)	.80
Switzerland	log C = -0.14 + 0.62 log Y (0.06)	.921	C = -166.72 + 73.44 log Y (7.73)	.91
Greece	log C = -2.52 + 1.58 log Y (0.22)	.894	C = -146.16 + 68.84 log Y (10.22)	.88
Yugoslavia	log C = +0.01 + 0.59 log Y (0.10)	.84	C = - 50.02 + 31.92 log Y (5.35)	.84

Notes:
a) Explanation of symbols: C = per capita meat consumption, dressed carcass weight; Y = per capita disposable income.
b) Observations refer to 1960 and include data for 18 industrial countries.
c) Observations refer to the years 1950-1960 and include data for 18 industrial countries.
d) Observations refer to 1950-1960.

TABLE A6.2.1

PER CAPITA HUMAN CONSUMPTION OF GRAINS IN INDUSTRIAL COUNTRIES
(kg; flour equivalent)

	Prewar	1950	1955	1960	1970I	1970II	1975I	1975II
United States[a]	89.8	73.6	66.2	63.7	61	60	59	57
Canada	90.7	76.3	72.8	66.0	64	63	62	60
Belgium-Lux.	112.1	103.8	101.9	89.1	75	73	70	68
France	121.3	118.5	111.7	103.2	87	84	80	76
Germany	110.5	106.4	95.4	81.4	71	69	67	64
Italy	152.3	148.1	139.2	132.4	115	112	102	97
Netherlands	100.8	94.2	88.6	79.7	70	63	65	62
United Kingdom	93.3	101.4	88.5	81.1	73	71	70	67
Austria	127.3	123.5	115.5	104.9	88	85	80	75
Denmark	91.7	101.8	89.0	76.4	69	68	67	65
Finland	128.0	135.0	118.0	113.0	97	94	89	84
Ireland[a]	130.4	130.1	128.6	110.5	99	96	92	87
Norway	117.3	115.6	96.9	78.9	74	72	70	67
Sweden	93.6	87.1	75.8	69.6	64	63	62	60
Switzerland	105.5	114.7	97.0	94.0	76	74	73	70
Greece[a]	158.5	153.4	160.4	158.2	143	139	134	128
Portugal[a]	96.7	119.0	102.5	111.3	101	98	94	89
Spain	......	......	107.7	108.2	100	97	93	88
Turkey	189.7	184.9	198.0	192.6	158	154	150	145
Yugoslavia[a]	......	174.0	183.4	183.5	149	145	140	135

Note: a) Data are given on a calendar year basis, (e.g., 1960 instead of 1960/61).
Source: OECD *Agricultural and Food Statistics*, 1959 and 1962. FAO, *Production Yearbook*.

TABLE A6.3.1

PER CAPITA CONSUMPTION OF FRESH FRUITS IN INDUSTRIAL COUNTRIES
(kg)

	Prewar	1950	1955	1960
United States	63.1	48.3	59.4	54.9
Canada	36.4	51.4	55.7	52.5
Belgium-Lux.	28.0	61.3	80.9	53.0
France	29.4	39.1	45.0	54.0
Germany	42.0	42.7'	65.6	86.8
Italy	33.7	53.5	65.0	76.4
Netherlands	38.3	47.6	51.0	58.6
United Kingdom	41.7	37.1	42.2	46.5
Austria.	41.6	48.2	52.0	86.8
Denmark	30.1	45.6	52.6	58.0
Ireland	19.5	28.0	29.7	27.8
Norway	31.0	27.5	39.7	57.7
Sweden	34.4	53.0	58.0	66.9
Switzerland	84.0	89.4	86.4	94.3
Greece	49.0	77.2	88.1	99.3
Portugal	40.5	56.8	59.4	70.4
Spain	.....	.....	62.9	83.0
Turkey	54.6	,59.1	65.8	94.3
Yugoslavia.	.....	.....	46.6'	56.9

Sources: OEEC, Agriculture and Food Statistics, 1959 and 1962.

TABLE A6.3.2

PER CAPITA ORANGE CONSUMPTION IN WESTERN EUROPE[a]

	Prewar	1950	1955	1960	1970I	1970II	1975I	1975II
Belgium-Lux.	8.5	10.7	12.3	12.7	14.8	15.2	15.8	16.4
Netherlands	8.4	6.0	11.3	16.0	18.4	18.8	19.4	19.9
Germany	4.9	4.4	9.0	12.8	15.2	15.5	16.5	17.1
France	6.1	9.0	15.0	13.5	16.5	16.9	17.8	18.4
Italy	6.7	9.6	11.5	12.9	17.3	18.0	19.8	21.4
United Kingdom	11.1	4.2	7.3	8.1	9.2	9.4	9.7	10.1
Austria	2.6	1.0	5.6	9.3	11.2	11.5	12.2	12.7
Denmark	2.7	4.2	6.6	7.5	8.9	9.2	9.5	10.0
Finland	1.9	1.5	5.4	5.3	6.4	6.6	6.9	7.3
Ireland	5.5	.....	5.1	5.3	6.5	6.7	6.9	7.4
Norway	7.9	4.9	14.8	13.8	14.8	15.2	15.7	16.3
Sweden	5.9	10.6	12.5	12.1	13.9	14.3	14.6	15.1
Switzerland	6.3	10.5	12.3	13.7	16.4	16.8	17.5	18.1
Greece	4.5	7.7·	18.4	18.4	20.5	20.7	21.2	21.5
Portugal	.....	.....	.....	12.8	14.0	14.5	15.5	16.5
Turkey	2.5	2.6	6.0	7.5	9.0	9.5	10.5	11.0
Yugoslavia	0.4	0.01	0.3	1.5	3.0	3.2	5.0	5.5

Source: FAO, Production Yearbook and Trade Yearbook, OECD, Foreign Trade Statistics.

Note: a) Censumption figures refer to apparent consumption, calculated from production and trade data. Estimates have not been provided for Spain.

TABLE A6.3.3

PER CAPITA CONSUMPTION OF FRESH VEGETABLES IN INDUSTRIAL
COUNTRIES (kg)

	Prewar	1950	1955	1960
United States	63.6	66.2	97.6	97.0
Canada	46.8	69.1	71.1	77.5
Belgium-Lux.	49.3	63.0	64.3	69.8
France	143.2	135.3	132.6	131.8
Germany	51.9	46.3	45.0	46.2
Italy	55.8	85.9	98.2	137.2
Netherlands	67.0	65.7	65.5	66.3
United Kingdom	54.5	58.6	57.7	59.6
Austria	57.8	60.8	62.7	67.4
Denmark	58.0	66.8	59.7	65.8
Ireland	53.2	58.9	61.2	62.8
Norway	19.3	23.9	32.2	34.2
Sweden	21.1	24.2	23.3	26.9
Switzerland	61.9	75.8	73.6	72.4
Greece	27.0	72.8	110.9	114.6
Portugal	109.7	108.4	112.2	104.4
Spain	......	......	102.7	122.5
Turkey	31.8	57.4	76.9	80.8
Yugoslavia	......	......	38.4	53.0

Sources: OEEC, Agricultural and Food Statistics, 1959 and 1962.

TABLE A6.4.1

WINE CONSUMPTION PER HEAD OF POPULATION OVER 15 IN INDUSTRIAL
COUNTRIES (kg)

	1934-38	1950	1955	1960
Belgium-Lux.	n.a.	n.a.	6.7	8.7
France	n.a.	152.6	149.4	182.4[a]
Germany	11.9	4.8	9.1	15.3
Italy	120.6	84.7	108.1	157.5
Netherlands	1.6	0.5	1.1	2.3[a]
Austria	22.2	14.2	14.8	25.0
Denmark	2.9	2.8	2.8	3.9
Ireland	n.a.	0.7	0.9	1.4
Norway	2.3	0.9	1.2	1.6
Sweden	1.4	1.2	2.7	4.1
Switzerland	57.2	34.8	33.6	48.4
Greece	59.6	36.9	46.8	51.3
Portugal	97.1	91.8	112.9	117.5
Yugoslavia	n.a.	......	18.8	35.6

Sources: OEEC, Agricultural and Food Statistics, 1959 and 1962, and population statistics.

Notes: a) 1959/60.

TABLE A6

TEMPERATE ZONE FOODS: VALUE OF IMPORTS
($ million at current prices)

	1960 NA	1960 WE	1960 JA	1960 OC	1960 DC	1970I NA	1970I WE	1970I JA	1970I OC	1970I DC	1970II NA	1970II WE	1970II JA	1970II OC	1970II DC	1975I NA	1975I WE	1975I JA	1975I OC	1975I DC	1975II NA	1975II WE	1975II JA	1975II OC	1975II DC
Meat & Eggs																									
LA	92	249	2	2	345	159	210	6	2	377	176	227	7	2	412	197	222	9	2	430	223	260	11	2	496
AF	—	21	—	2	23	—	21	—	3	24	—	24	—	3	27	—	17	—	3	24	—	22	—	3	25
ME	—	12	—	—	12	—	15	—	—	15	—	16	—	1	15	—	16	—	1	17	—	18	—	1	18
AS	2	1	1	1	5	3	1	3	1	8	—	—	6	2	8	3	1	4	2	9	3	1	5	1	10
LDC	94	283	3	5	385	162	247	9	6	424	176	267	13	7	463	200	261	13	7	480	226	301	16	6	549
Fish																									
LA	74	3	—	—	77	124	3	—	—	127	124	3	—	—	127	124	3	—	—	127	171	3	—	—	174
AF	5	27	—	—	32	7	30	—	—	37	7	30	—	—	37	7	30	—	—	37	7	32	—	—	39
ME	1	—	—	—	1	2	—	—	—	2	—	—	—	2	2	2	—	—	—	2	2	—	—	—	2
AS	6	—	2	—	8	9	—	2	—	11	9	—	2	—	11	9	—	2	—	11	11	—	2	—	13
LDC	86	30	2	—	118	142	33	2	—	177	142	33	2	—	177	142	35	2	—	228	191	35	2	—	228
Wheat & Rice																									
LA	1	52	—	—	53	1	26	—	—	27	1	25	—	—	27	1	24	—	—	26	1	23	—	—	24
AF	—	34	—	—	34	—	21	—	—	21	—	21	—	—	21	—	21	—	—	21	—	21	—	—	21
ME	—	—	—	—	—	—	—	—	—	—	—	—	—	—	—	—	—	—	—	—	—	—	—	—	—
AS	—	17	—	21	38	—	18	—	5	23	—	18	—	5	23	—	19	—	7	26	—	19	—	7	26
LDC	1	103	—	21	125	1	65	—	5	71	1	64	—	5	70	1	64	—	7	72	1	63	—	7	71
Coarse Grains																									
LA	—	199	23	—	222	—	184	45	—	229	—	202	52	—	254	—	189	65	—	254	—	208	75	—	283
AF	—	18	1	—	19	—	18	3	—	21	—	22	3	—	25	—	18	4	—	22	—	20	4	—	24
ME	—	—	—	—	—	—	—	—	—	—	—	—	—	—	—	—	—	—	—	—	—	—	—	—	—
AS	—	—	22	—	22	—	—	65	—	65	—	—	75	—	75	—	—	95	—	95	—	—	115	—	115
LDC	—	217	46	—	263	—	202	113	—	315	—	224	130	—	354	—	207	164	—	371	—	228	194	—	422
Feeding Stuff																									
LA	11	138	5	—	154	25	195	18	—	238	28	200	20	—	248	37	220	27	—	284	45	230	32	—	307
AF	1	58	1	—	60	2	70	3	—	75	2	72	3	—	77	2	75	—	—	77	2	80	5	—	87
ME	—	5	—	—	5	—	6	—	—	6	—	6	—	—	6	—	8	—	—	8	—	8	—	—	8
AS	1	61	—	—	62	1	71	5	—	77	1	73	5	—	79	1	76	7	—	84	1	81	8	—	90
LDC	12	262	7	—	281	28	342	26	—	396	31	351	28	—	410	40	379	38	—	457	48	399	45	—	492
Oranges																									
LA	2	9	—	—	11	2	13	—	—	15	2	13	—	—	15	2	14	—	—	16	2	15	—	—	17
AF	1	66	—	—	67	1	96	—	—	97	1	100	—	—	101	1	121	—	—	122	1	125	—	—	126
ME	1	37	—	—	38	1	46	—	—	47	1	48	—	—	49	1	52	—	—	53	1	55	—	—	56
AS	—	—	—	—	—	—	—	—	—	—	—	—	—	—	—	—	—	—	—	—	—	—	—	—	—
LDC	4	112	—	—	116	4	155	—	—	159	4	161	—	—	165	4	187	—	—	191	4	195	—	—	199

Other Fruit

	G1					G2					G3					G4					G5				
LA	34	34	–	1	69	40	44	1	–	85	45	44	1	–	90	48	44	2	–	94	50	44	2	–	96
AF	1	12	–	–	13	1	15	–	–	16	1	15	–	–	16	1	17	–	–	18	1	17	–	–	18
ME	3	15	–	–	18	4	19	–	–	23	4	16	–	–	20	4	21	–	–	25	4	22	–	–	26
AS	48	8	2	3	61	57	10	4	4	75	57	11	4	4	76	63	11	6	4	84	63	11	7	4	85
LDC	86	69	2	4	161	102	88	5	4	199	107	86	5	4	202	116	93	8	4	221	118	94	9	4	225

Preserved Fruit

	G1					G2					G3					G4					G5				
LA	10	14	–	–	24	15	24	–	1	40	24	16	1	–	41	29	17	–	1	47	32	17	1	1	51
AF	1	22	–	1	24	2	36	–	–	38	24	2	–	–	41	44	2	–	1	47	47	3	–	1	51
ME	4	17	–	–	21	4	22	–	–	27	21	4	–	1	27	25	4	–	–	29	27	4	–	–	31
AS	13	17	–	7	37	20	29	16	1	80	26	29	16	16	70	26	29	21	–	80	41	26	21	–	90
LDC	28	70	–	8	106	41	111	16	16	147	106	111?	21	21	179	134	111	21	21	203	147	100	24	24	223

Vegetables

	G1					G2					G3					G4					G5				
LA	45	11	–	–	56	71	16	–	–	87	71	16	–	–	92	85?	15	–	–	108	95	17	–	–	116
AF	–	86	–	–	86	–	129	–	–	129	129	–	–	–	135	150	–	–	–	150	160	–	–	–	160
ME	–	6	–	–	6	–	9	–	–	9	10	–	–	–	10	12	–	–	–	12	13	–	–	–	13
AS	10	14	5	–	29	15	22	10	–	47	15	22	18	20	51	25	58	15	20	58	27	58	15	20	64
LDC	55	117	5	–	177	86	176	10	–	272	176	207	18	20	288	207	328	15	115	328	221	115	15	115	353

Beverages

	G1					G2					G3					G4					G5				
LA	3	12	–	1	15	4	15	–	–	19	15	–	–	–	17	17	–	–	–	22	17	–	–	–	22
AF	1	244	–	–	128	1	128	–	–	129	128	–	–	–	139	139	–	–	–	140	139	–	–	–	140
ME	–	1	–	–	1	–	1	–	–	1	1	–	–	–	–	–	–	–	–	–	–	–	–	–	–
AS	–	–	–	–	–	–	–	–	–	–	–	–	–	–	–	–	–	–	–	–	–	–	–	–	–
LDC	4	257	–	–	144	5	144	–	–	149	144	–	–	–	156	156	–	–	–	162	156	–	–	–	162

Total

	G1					G2					G3					G4					G5				
LA	272	721	3	30	1026	441	730	69	3	1243	466	772	79	3	1320	563	786	101	4	1454	605	859	118	4	1586
AF	10	588	3	–	603	14	564	6	4	588	14	585	6	4	609	14	638	8	4	664	15	663	9	4	691
ME	9	93	–	–	102	11	118	–	–	129	11	124	–	–	135	11	135	–	–	146	11	143	–	–	154
AS	79	118	7	58	262	104	151	105	10	370	103	157	122	11	383	119	168	150	12	449	123	180	178	12	493
LDC	370	1520	13	90	1993	570	1563	180	17	2330	594	1638	207	18	2457	707	1727	259	20	2713	754	1845	305	20	2924

Source: U.N. *Commodity Trade Statistics*, 1960 and OECD *Trade by Commodities*, Foreign Trade Series C, 1960.

TABLE A7.1.1

CONSUMPTION OF OILS AND FATS IN THE UNITED STATES (kg)

	Food Products						Nonfood Products				
	Butter[a]	Lard	Marga-rine[a]	Short-ening	Cooking and Salad Oils[b]	All Food Products[c]	Soap	Drying Oil Products	Other Industrial Products	All Industrial Products	Total
1930	8.0	5.8	1.2	4.3	2.8	20.4	5.7	2.5	.7	8.9	29.3
1940	7.7	6.5	1.1	4.1	3.4	21.0	6.4	2.8	1.4	10.6	31.7
1950	4.9	5.7	2.8	5.0	3.9	20.8	5.4	3.6	3.5	12.5	33.3
1955	4.1	4.6	3.7	5.2	4.8	20.8	3.1	3.1	4.5	10.7	31.5
1956	3.9	4.4	3.7	4.9	4.9	20.5	2.9	2.9	5.0	10.9	31.4
1957	3.8	4.3	3.8	4.7	4.9	20.1	2.7	2.7	5.3	10.7	30.8
1958	3.8	4.4	4.1	5.1	4.8	20.5	2.4	2.4	5.7	10.6	31.1
1959	3.6	4.0	4.2	5.7	5.2	21.0	2.2	2.4	6.1	10.7	31.7
1960	3.4	3.5	4.3	5.7	5.2	20.6	2.2	2.1	6.6	10.8	31.4

Source: USDA Agriculture Marketing Service, The Fats and Oils Situation, various issues.

Notes: a) product weight; b) including other edible oils; c) fat content.

TABLE A7.1.2

PER CAPITA CONSUMPTION OF OILS AND FATS IN FOOD PRODUCTS IN WESTERN EUROPE
(kg, oil or fat content)

	Prewar a	Prewar b	Prewar c	1954 a	1954 b	1954 c	1957 a	1957 b	1957 c	1960 a	1960 b	1960 c	1970I a	1970I b	1970I c	1970II a	1970II b	1970II c	1975I a	1975I b	1975I c	1975II a	1975II b	1975II c
Belgium-Lux.	7.3	11.8	19.1	9.4	12.9	22.3	8.5	12.8	21.3	7.8	13.4	21.2	8.0	13.0	21.0	8.2	12.7	20.9	8.0	12.8	20.8	8.2	12.5	20.7
France	4.4	11.2	15.6	5.4	11.2	16.6	5.9	11.2	17.1	6.5	12.0	18.5	7.5	12.5	20.0	7.7	12.4	20.1	7.5	12.5	20.0	7.7	12.4	20.1
Germany	6.7	14.3	21.0	5.7	19.0	24.7	6.0	19.3	25.3	6.7	18.4	25.1	7.5	16.7	24.2	7.7	16.3	24.0	7.5	16.1	23.6	7.7	15.6	23.3
Italy	1.1	10.6	11.7	1.2	11.7	12.9	1.4	13.5	14.9	1.5	15.3	16.8	2.4	16.1	18.5	2.6	16.1	18.7	2.9	16.3	19.2	3.2	16.3	19.5
Netherlands	5.2	15.4	20.6	2.6	21.0	23.6	3.2	21.0	24.2	3.7	21.8	25.5	4.5	20.0	24.5	4.6	19.7	24.3	4.5	19.3	23.8	4.6	18.9	23.5
United Kingdom	9.2	12.1	21.3	5.3	16.6	21.9	6.6	15.9	22.5	6.9	15.6	22.5	7.3	15.0	22.3	7.5	14.7	22.2	7.3	14.8	22.1	7.5	14.5	22.0
Austria	3.0	14.3	17.3	3.4	13.3	16.7	3.5	14.8	18.3	3.6	14.4	18.0	4.2	14.3	18.5	4.3	14.3	18.6	4.2	14.5	18.7	4.3	14.5	18.8
Denmark	7.0	19.6	26.6	7.2	17.9	25.1	9.0	19.5	28.5	9.0	19.3	28.3	9.0	17.6	26.6	9.1	17.3	26.4	9.0	16.8	25.8	9.1	16.3	25.4
Ireland	10.6	2.9	13.5	14.1	5.2	19.3	15.3	5.0	20.3	15.1	6.3	21.4	13.5	7.7	21.2	13.8	7.4	21.2	13.5	7.7	21.2	13.8	7.4	21.2
Norway	6.3	18.6	24.9	3.3	23.1	26.4	3.1	22.9	26.0	3.1	20.5	23.6	3.5	19.1	22.6	3.6	18.8	22.4	3.5	18.5	22.0	3.6	18.2	21.8
Sweden	9.0	8.7	17.7	9.4	11.9	21.3	7.1	13.4	20.5	8.0	14.0	22.0	8.0	13.8	21.8	8.2	13.5	21.7	8.0	13.5	21.5	8.2	13.2	21.4
Switzerland	5.3	10.2	15.5	5.2	11.3	16.5	5.5	12.4	17.9	5.6	14.2	19.8	5.8	14.2	20.0	6.0	14.0	20.0	5.8	14.2	20.0	6.0	14.0	20.0
Greece	0.9	13.8	14.7	0.9	16.6	17.5	1.3	17.6	18.9	1.1	17.2	18.3	1.5	17.9	19.4	1.7	18.0	19.7	1.9	18.0	19.9	2.1	18.1	20.2
Portugal	0.4	13.9	14.3	0.6	13.0	13.6	0.6	15.9	16.5	0.5	14.9	15.4	1.0	15.9	16.9	1.2	16.1	17.3	1.4	16.2	17.6	1.6	16.5	18.1
Spain	...	...	...	0.2	15.5	15.7	0.2	16.7	16.9	0.2	19.2	19.4	0.3	20.3	20.6	0.3	20.6	20.9	0.4	20.7	21.1	0.4	20.9	21.5
Turkey	3.9	4.1	8.0	3.0	4.7	7.7	3.1	4.3	7.4	3.7	4.0	7.7	4.3	5.0	9.3	4.5	5.2	9.7	4.7	5.4	10.1	4.8	5.9	10.7
Yugoslavia	...	...	...	0.7	7.7	8.4	0.9	8.5	9.4	1.1	11.1	12.2	2.0	12.1	14.1	2.3	12.2	14.5	2.6	12.3	14.9	2.8	12.7	15.5

Notes: a) butter; b) oils and fats other than butter; c) oils and fats in human consumption.

Sources: OEEC, Agricultural and Food Statistics, 1959 and 1962.

TABLE A7.1.3

PER CAPITA CONSUMPTION OF OILS AND FATS (EXCLUDING BUTTER) IN WESTERN EUROPE
(kg, fat content)

	Prewar			1954			1957			1960			1970I			1970II			1975I			1975II		
	a	b	c	a	b	c	a	b	c	a	b	c	a	b	c	a	b	c	a	b	c	a	b	c
Common Market	12.2	5.2	17.4	14.5	3.8	18.3	15.2	4.7	19.9	15.8	5.6	21.4	15.4	6.7	22.1	15.2	7.0	22.2	15.2	7.5	22.9	15.0	8.0	23.0
United Kingdom	12.1	8.9	21.0	16.6	7.3	23.9	15.9	8.3	24.2	15.6	9.2	24.8	15.0	9.4	24.4	14.7	9.6	24.3	14.8	9.5	24.3	14.5	9.7	24.2
Northern Europe	12.3	6.9	19.2	13.6	5.7	19.3	14.8	6.2	21.0	15.0	5.9	20.9	14.7	6.5	21.2	14.4	6.7	21.2	14.5	7.0	21.5	14.2	7.3	21.5
Southern Europe	...	...	...	9.7	1.1	10.8	10.5	1.1	11.6	11.1	1.4	12.5	13.2	2.3	15.5	13.4	2.5	15.9	13.4	3.0	16.4	13.8	3.4	17.2

Sources: OECD, Agricultural Food Statistics, 1959 and 1962 and Food Balance Sheets, International Association of Seed Crushers, Proceedings, various issues.

Notes: Prewar estimates refer, in most cases, to the period 1934-1938.
   a) Oils and fats in food end-products, other than butter.
   b) Oils and fats in nonfood end-products.
   c) Oils and fats, other than butter, total.

TABLE A7.1.4

TIME-SERIES REGRESSIONS FOR BUTTER[a]

	Double-log	R^2	Semi-log	R^2
United States	$\log C_B = 3.79 - 0.98 \log Y - 0.33 \log \frac{P_B}{P_M}$ $(0.26)\quad(0.19)$	.79	$C_B = 28.32 - 7.50 \log Y - 2.48 \log \frac{P_B}{P_M}$ $(2.04)\quad(1.50)$	.79
Germany	$\log C_B = -0.48 + 0.48 \log Y - 0.30 \log \frac{P_B}{P_M}$ $(0.04)\quad(0.06)$	.95	$C_B = -11.33 + 6.66 \log Y - 4.31 \log \frac{P_B}{P_M}$ $(0.56)\quad(0.84)$	.95
Netherlands	$\log C_B = -2.69 + 1.17 \log Y - 0.40 \log \frac{P_B}{P_M}$ $(0.27)\quad(0.14)$	.80	$C_B = -19.00 + 8.27 \log Y - 3.43 \log \frac{P_B}{P_M}$ $(2.08)\quad(1.13)$	.79
United Kingdom	$\log C_B = -5.60 + 3.06 \log Y - 0.49 \log \frac{P_B}{P_M}$ $(0.52)\quad(0.26)$	.83	$C_B = -86.55 + 45.30 \log Y - 8.25 \log \frac{P_B}{P_M}$ $(7.24)\quad(3.59)$	.85
Sweden	$\log C_B = 5.41 - 1.47 \log Y - 0.48 \log \frac{P_B}{P_M}$ $(0.33)\quad(0.22)$	.75	$C_B = 97.59 - 29.28 \log Y - 8.50 \log \frac{P_B}{P_M}$ $(6.13)\quad(4.13)$	.77

Notes: a) Explanation of symbols: C_B = butter consumption in product weight equivalent per head of population; Y = per capita disposable income, P_B = deflated price of butter; P_M = deflated price margarine.

Observations refer to the period 1950-1960.

TABLE A7.2.1

PER CAPITA SUGAR CONSUMPTION IN INDUSTRIAL COUNTRIES
(raw equivalent, kg)

	Prewar	1950	1955	1960	1970I	1970II	1975I	1975II
United States	47.2	49.7	48.1	48.9	48.9	48.9	48.9	48.9
Canada	40.8	48.1	46.5	46.9	46.9	46.9	46.9	46.9
Belgium-Lux.	29.3	33.7	29.8	31.4	33.8	34.2	34.9	35.4
France	24.7	24.7	28.7	33.3	36.6	37.0	37.9	38.5
Germany	25.2	26.2	29.2	31.3	34.0	34.3	35.3	35.8
Italy	7.9	11.6	16.9	21.7	27.7	27.9	29.8	31.0
Netherlands[a]	27.9	38.5	41.3	46.0	47.2	47.4	47.7	47.9
United Kingdom.	49.0	39.2	53.6	55.2	55.2	55.2	55.2	55.2
Austria[a]	26.5	26.4	32.9	39.4	41.4	41.7	42.3	42.7
Denmark	55.3	48.4	50.1	59.3	59.3	59.3	59.3	59.3
Finland	28.1	30.6	41.5	43.4	44.3	44.5	44.7	44.9
Ireland	39.3	40.4	45.9	47.4	48.5	48.7	48.8	49.1
Norway	30.7	31.1	38.8	43.5	44.4	44.6	44.8	45.0
Sweden	49.3	54.5	45.7	46.1	47.1	47.3	47.4	47.7
Switzerland	41.0	43.6	44.2	47.8	49.2	49.3	49.6	49.8
Greece	11.1	9.9	11.9	13.8	17.6	18.7	19.7	21.6
Portugal	10.0	12.8	15.3	17.7	21.6	22.8	23.7	25.5
Spain	12.4[b]	8.5	13.4	17.5	21.7	22.8	23.6	25.4
Turkey	4.9	6.6	9.6	11.2	15.0	16.1	16.8	18.4
Yugoslavia.	5.5	8.5	11.7	17.0	21.8	24.1	22.9	25.8
Japan	12.3	4.8	12.2	14.3	19.0	20.1	21.4	23.0

Sources: United States--USDA, Consumption of Food in the United States,
and supplements per other countries--FAO, Trends and Forces of World Sugar
Consumption and direct communication from the FAO.

Notes: a) Adjusted for the sugar content of exports.
       b) 1931-35.

TABLE A7.3.1

TOBACCO CONSUMPTION PER HEAD OF POPULATION OVER 15 IN DEVELOPED
COUNTRIES (kg processed weight)

	Prewar	1950	1955	1960	1970I	1970II	1975I	1975II
United States	3.8	5.3	5.1	5.0	5.0	5.0	5.0	5.0
Canada	2.5	4.0	4.6	4.8	4.8	4.8	4.8	4.8
Belgium-Lux.	3.0	3.3	3.3	3.4	3.5	3.5	3.6	3.6
France	1.8	1.9	2.0	2.2	2.5	2.5	2.6	2.7
Germany	2.5	1.7	2.3	2.5	2.7	2.7	2.8	2.9
Italy	...	1.3	1.5	1.7	2.1	2.1	2.3	2.4
Netherlands.	4.2	3.4	4.0	4.3	4.3	4.3	4.3	4.3
United Kingdom	2.5	2.6	2.9	3.3	3.4	3.4	3.5	3.5
Northern Europe. . . .	...	2.2	2.3	2.4	2.6	2.6	2.7	2.7
Southern Europe. . . .	...	1.5	1.6	1.7	2.0	2.1	2.2	2.3
Japan	...	1.6	1.8	1.9	2.3	2.4	2.5	2.6
Australia.	1.9	2.1	3.0	3.3	3.5	3.5	3.6	3.6
New Zealand	2.4	3.2	3.0	3.5	3.6	3.6	3.7	3.7
South Africa.	...	2.3	2.3	2.1	...	...	...	...

Source: Tobacco Division, Foreign Agricultural Service, U.S. Department of
Agriculture and United Nations, Commodity Trade Statistics.

TABLE A7.2.2

MULTICOUNTRY AND TIME-SERIES REGRESSIONS FOR SUGAR[a]

	Double-log	R^2	Semi-log	R^2
Multicountry[b]	log C = -0.42 + 0.60 log Y - 0.37 log P (0.04) (0.05)	.82	C = -60.68 + 31.55 log Y - 24.04 log P (2.36) (3.51)	.77
Italy[c]	log C = -1.17 + 0.86 log Y - 0.40 log P (0.34) (0.26)	.97	C = -62.71 + 28.19 log Y - 13.78 log P (8.43) (6.42)	.98
Greece[c]	log C = -1.99 + 1.27 log Y - 0.20 log P (0.19) (0.38)	.85	C = -96.11 + 43.93 log Y - 9.87 log P (7.14) (14.00)	.83
Turkey[c]	log C = -1.91 + 1.20 log Y - 0.68 log P (0.16) (0.32)	.91	C = -51.22 + 25.18 log Y - 14.52 log P (3.87) (7.68)	.90
Yugoslavia[c]	log C = -1.12 + 0.88 log Y - 0.77 log P (0.13) (0.32)	.97	C = -53.16 + 27.16 log Y - 13.94 log P (3.66) (9.32)	.97
Portugal[c]	log C = -0.27 + 0.57 log Y - 0.07 log P (0.09) (0.07)	.84	C = -23.52 + 15.12 log Y - 1.57 log P (2.67) (1.86)	.82

Notes: a) Explanation of symbols. C = sugar consumption in raw sugar equivalent per head of population; Y = per capita disposable income; P = deflated sugar price.

b) Observations refer to the years 1950-1960 and include data for 17 industrial countries.

c) Observations refer to the years 1950-1960.

TABLE A7

COMPETING TROPICAL FOODS: VALUE OF IMPORTS
($ million at current prices)

	1960					1970I					1970II					1975I					1975II				
	NA	WE	JA	OC	DC	NA	WE	JA	OC	DC	NA	WE	JA	OC	DC	NA	WE	JA	OC	DC	NA	WE	JA	OC	DC
Oilseeds																									
LA	5	8	5	–	18	6	19	8	–	33	6	19	9	–	34	7	24	10	–	41	7	25	12	–	44
AF	2	258	11	1	272	2	263	17	1	283	2	273	19	1	295	3	282	22	1	308	3	294	27	1	325
ME	–	5	–	–	5	–	5	–	–	5	–	5	–	–	5	–	5	–	–	5	–	5	–	–	5
AS	65	147	26	1	239	73	113	57	1	244	73	114	64	1	252	80	109	75	1	265	81	110	88	1	280
LDC	72	418	42	2	534	81	400	82	2	565	81	411	92	2	586	90	420	107	2	619	91	434	127	2	654
Veg. Oils																									
LA	12	52	–	2	66	13	56	–	3	72	13	58	–	3	74	15	62	–	4	81	15	64	–	4	83
AF	14	152	–	2	168	16	149	–	3	168	16	154	–	3	173	17	156	–	4	177	17	165	–	4	186
ME	–	2	–	–	2	–	2	–	–	2	–	2	–	–	2	–	2	–	–	2	–	2	–	–	2
AS	28	51	3	5	87	31	37	5	6	79	31	38	5	7	81	35	39	5	7	86	35	42	6	7	90
LDC	54	257	3	9	323	60	244	5	12	321	60	252	5	13	330	67	259	5	15	346	67	273	6	15	361
Animal Fats																									
LA	14	32	–	1	47	14	51	–	1	66	14	51	–	1	66	15	71	–	1	87	15	71	–	1	87
AF	1	4	–	–	5	1	3	–	–	4	1	3	–	–	4	1	4	–	1	5	1	4	–	–	5
ME	–	–	–	–	–	–	–	–	–	–	–	–	–	–	–	–	–	–	–	–	–	–	–	–	–
AS	–	–	–	–	–	–	1	–	–	5	–	1	–	–	5	–	1	5	–	6	–	1	5	–	.6
LDC	15	36	–	1	52	15	55	4	1	75	15	55	4	1	75	16	76	5	1	98	16	76	5	1	98
Sugar																									
LA	451	213	42	1	707	315	172	66	1	554	315	177	72	1	565	313	180	77	1	571	313	185	84	1	583
AF	2	74	–	–	76	2	80	–	1	82	2	85	–	–	87	2	82	–	–	84	2	89	–	–	91
ME	–	–	–	–	–	–	–	–	–	–	–	–	–	–	–	–	–	–	–	–	–	–	–	–	–
AS	131	10	56	2	199	139	10	65	3	217	139	10	71	3	223	155	10	76	3	243	155	10	82	3	250
LDC	584	297	98	3	982	456	262	131	4	853	456	272	143	4	875	469	272	153	4	898	470	284	166	4	924
Tobacco																									
LA	33	23	–	–	56	30	28	–	–	58	30	28	–	–	58	36	29	–	–	65	36	29	–	–	65
AF	1	105	–	10	116	1	150	–	8	159	1	155	–	8	164	1	160	–	8	169	1	170	–	8	179
ME	3	59	–	–	62	10	70	–	–	80	10	72	–	–	82	12	75	–	–	87	12	77	–	–	89
AS	2	–	–	–	2	2	–	–	–	2	2	–	–	–	2	2	–	–	–	2	2	–	–	–	2
LDC	39	187	–	10	236	43	248	–	8	299	43	255	–	8	306	51	264	–	8	323	51	276	–	8	335
Total																									
LA	515	328	47	4	894	378	326	74	5	783	378	333	81	5	797	386	366	87	6	845	386	374	96	6	862
AF	20	593	11	13	637	22	645	17	12	696	22	670	19	12	723	24	684	22	13	743	24	722	27	13	786
ME	3	66	–	–	69	10	77	–	–	87	10	79	–	–	89	12	82	–	–	94	12	84	–	–	96
AS	226	208	85	8	527	245	161	131	10	547	245	163	144	11	563	271	159	161	11	602	273	163	181	11	628
LDC	764	1195	143	25	2127	655	1209	222	27	2113	655	1245	244	28	2172	693	1291	270	30	2284	695	1343	304	30	2372

Source: U.N. Commodity Trade Statistics, 1960 and OECD Trade by Commodities, Foreign Trade Series C, 1960.

TABLE A8.1.1

PER CAPITA BANANA CONSUMPTION IN INDUSTRIAL COUNTRIES
(kg)

	Prewar	1950	1955	1960	1970I	1970II	1975I	1975II
United States	10.5	8.7	8.9	10.8	10.8	10.8	10.8	10.8
Canada	4.5	4.8	8.5	9.6	10.1	10.1	10.2	10.3
Belgium-Lux.	2.7	4.3	5.5	7.0	7.5	7.6	7.8	8.0
France	2.4	4.8	6.3	7.7	8.6	8.7	9.0	9.1
Germany	1.8	1.7	4.3	8.1	8.7	8.8	9.1	9.3
Italy	0.4	0.2	0.9	1.8	3.5	3.7	4.5	4.7
Netherlands	3.6	2.1	3.1	5.2	6.0	6.1	6.3	6.5
United Kingdom	6.2	2.8	6.1	6.7	7.4	7.6	7.8	8.0
Austria	0.1	0.1	1.5	4.0	4.8	4.9	5.1	5.3
Denmark	0.9	0.	6.2	5.6	6.3	6.5	6.6	6.8
Finland	0.7	0.	1.8	1.7	3.0	3.2	3.8	4.0
Ireland	...	2.0	2.6	2.6	3.8	4.0	4.5	4.8
Norway	2.5	0.6	2.2	6.8	7.6	7.7	7.9	8.2
Sweden	1.6	4.3	6.6	5.2	5.8	5.9	6.0	6.2
Switzerland	1.6	2.6	4.0	8.4	9.3	9.4	9.6	9.8
Greece	...	...	...	0.6	1.0	1.1	1.2	1.3
Portugal	...	...	...	0.2	0.4	0.4	0.5	0.6
Spain	...	...	4.1	4.2	5.2	5.5	5.7	6.1
Turkey	...	...	...	...	...	...	...	...
Yugoslavia	...	...	...	0.1	0.8	0.9	1.2	1.4
Japan	1.7	0.1	0.3	0.4	2.5	2.7	3.4	3.8

Source: United States--USDA, Consumption of Food in the United States,
various issues. For all other countries--calculated from net import and population data.

TABLE A8.2.1

COFFEE CONSUMPTION PER HEAD OF POPULATION OVER 15 IN
DEVELOPED COUNTRIES (kg in green beans equivalent)

	Prewar	1950	1955	1960	1970I	1970II	1975I	1975II
United States	8.3	10.1	10.0	10.5	11.4	11.5	11.8	11.9
Canada	2.3	3.9	4.6	5.3	6.1	6.2	6.4	6.6
Belgium-Lux.	7.6	7.5	6.2	8.4	9.2	9.3	9.6	9.8
France	5.3	4.5	5.5	5.9	6.9	7.0	7.3	7.5
Germany	3.3	0.7	2.9	4.5	5.9	6.0	6.6	6.8
Italy	1.3	1.3	2.0	2.7	4.0	4.1	4.6	4.8
Netherlands	5.9	2.6	4.1	6.5	7.4	7.6	7.9	8.0
United Kingdom	0.4	1.0	0.8	1.3	1.7	1.7	1.8	2.0
Austria	1.2	0.9	1.1	2.2	3.0	3.1	3.4	3.5
Denmark	10.0	5.1	8.6	12.2	12.7	12.8	13.0	13.1
Finland	7.9	5.3	10.1	11.0	11.5	11.6	11.7	11.8
Ireland	0.1	0.2	0.2	0.3	0.4	0.4	0.5	0.5
Norway	8.2	6.0	8.3	11.0	11.4	11.5	11.6	11.8
Sweden	9.9	6.4	9.6	12.7	13.2	13.3	13.4	13.6
Switzerland	4.9	7.0	4.7	6.6	7.6	7.8	8.0	8.2
Greece	1.3	0.9	1.0	1.3	1.9	2.1	2.2	2.5
Portugal	1.0	1.1	1.6	1.7	2.6	2.8	3.0	3.4
Spain	...	0.3	0.4	0.7	1.1	1.3	1.4	1.5
Turkey	0.5	0.5	0.4	0.1	0.5	0.5	0.6	0.6
Yugoslavia	0.6	0.1	0.3	0.7	1.4	1.6	1.9	2.2
Japan	0.1	...	0.1	0.1	1.0	1.2	1.5	1.8
Australia	0.4	0.5	0.7	1.6	2.1	2.2	2.5	2.6
New Zealand	0.2	0.4	0.3	1.1	1.5	1.5	1.6	1.7
South Africa	2.2	2.0	1.1	1.1	1.3	1.3	1.4	1.4

Source: United States--USDA, Consumption of Food in the United States,
various issues. For all other countries--calculated from net import and population data.

TABLE A8.2.2

COFFEE CONSUMPTION IN THE UNITED STATES

	1	2	3	4	5
				Per Capita Coffee Consumption[a]	Cup-Yield
	Per Capita Disposable Income in 1955$	Retail Price of Coffee in 1955$	Green Bean Equivalent (kg)	Cups of Coffee per Day	Ratio[b] (Cups per Pound)
1947	1415	1.25	10.64	.....	.....
1948	1438	1.26	11.32	.....	.....
1949	1430	1.37	11.57	.....	45.9
1950	1525	1.95	10.08	2.60	52.6
1951	1521	1.97	10.43	2.69	52.3
1952	1534	1.93	10.73	.....	52.9
1953	1584	1.97	10.85	2.85	52.8
1954	1579	2.44	9.58	2.89	62.7
1955	1660	2.05	9.95	2.98	62.7
1956	1716	2.08	10.17	2.99	63.9
1957	1718	1.95	10.35	3.17	63.9
1958	1694	1.61	10.46	3.24	63.9
1959	1751	1.32	10.52	3.34	62.2
1960	1762	1.35	10.54	3.17	.....

Sources: 1. Economic Report of the President, 1961.
2. Bureau of Labor Statistics, Retail Prices by Cities, annual average, 1947-60.
3. USDA, Consumption of Food in the United States, 1909-1952, Agricultural Handbook No. 62 and Supplements.
4&5. U.S. Department of Commerce, Business and Defense Services Administration, Coffee Consumption in the United States, 1920-1965, Washington, 1961, pp. 23-24, and Pan-American Coffee Bureau, Annual Coffee Statistics, 1960, p. 34.

Notes: [a]Per head of population over 15. Cups of coffee per person recalculated from data relating to persons 10 years of age and over.
[b]Cup-yield ratio calculated for regular coffee only.

TABLE A8.4.1

TEA CONSUMPTION PER HEAD OF POPULATION OVER 15 IN DEVELOPED COUNTRIES (kg)

	Prewar	1950	1955	1960	1970I	1970II	1975I	1975II
United States	0.39	0.38	0.42	0.40	0.40	0.40	0.40	0.40
Canada	2.29	2.58	1.79	1.64	1.40	1.40	1.30	1.30
Belgium-Lux.	0.05	0.08	0.03	0.04	0.08	0.09	0.10	0.12
France	0.04	0.02	0.03	0.04	0.08	0.09	0.10	0.12
Germany	0.16	0.04	0.14	0.16	0.30	0.32	0.40	0.45
Italy	....	0.02	0.03	0.04	0.08	0.09	0.10	0.12
Netherlands	1.74	1.20	0.97	1.12	1.20	1.22	1.25	1.28
United Kingdom	5.39	4.10	5.35	5.61	5.60	5.60	5.60	5.60
Ireland	4.79	5.15	5.81	4.96	5.00	5.00	5.00	5.00
Austria	0.08	0.07	0.08	0.11	0.20	0.22	0.25	0.28
Denmark	0.20	0.50	0.28	0.37	0.40	0.41	0.43	0.44
Finland	0.04	0.25	0.11	0.14	0.18	0.19	0.20	0.21
Norway	0.09	0.24	0.10	0.16	0.20	0.21	0.22	0.23
Sweden	0.08	0.33	0.17	0.17	0.22	0.23	0.24	0.25
Switzerland	0.25	0.33	0.27	0.29	0.35	0.36	0.38	0.40
Greece	0.04	0.01	0.02	0.02	0.03	0.03	0.04	0.04
Portugal	0.03	0.01	0.01	0.02	0.04	0.04	0.05	0.05
Spain	....	....	0.02	....	0.02	0.02	0.02	0.02
Turkey	0.17	0.13	0.15	0.24	0.20	0.29	0.31	0.32
Yugoslavia	0.02	....	0.01	0.02	0.03	0.03	0.04	0.04
Australia	4.09	4.56	3.73	3.95	3.80	3.80	3.70	3.70
New Zealand	4.23	3.89	3.95	4.51	4.35	4.35	4.25	4.25
South Africa	0.95	1.90	1.10	1.30	1.40	1.40	1.50	1.50

Source: For all countries excepting the United States, calculated from net import and population data. For the United States, see USDA, Consumption of Food in the United States, and supplements.

Note: Excluding domestically produced teas.

TABLE A8.2.3

CROSS-SECTION, MULTICOUNTRY AND TIME-SERIES REGRESSIONS FOR COFFEE[a]

	Double-Log	R^2	Semi-Log	R^2
Cross-section[b]	$\log C = -0.04 - 5.30 \log P_c/P_t$ (1.08)	.67	$C = -10.54 - 271.55 \log P_c/P_t$ (80.49)	.49
Multicountry[c]	$\log C = -3.30 + 1.36 \log Y$ (0.17)	.42	$C = -37.40 + 14.75 \log Y$ (1.97)	.39
	$\log C = -1.23 + 0.78 \log Y - 0.74 \log P_c$ $(0.19) \quad (0.15)$	.55	$C = -17.80 + 9.29 \log Y - 6.95 \log P_c$ $(2.29) \quad (1.76)$	.49
	$\log C = -1.44 + 0.79 \log Y - 1.15 \log P_c$ $(0.18) \quad (0.18)$ $+0.54 \log P_t$ (0.16)	.61	$C = -20.32 + 9.43 \log Y - 11.94 \log P_c$ $(2.16) \quad (2.23)$ $+6.48 \log P_t$ (1.94)	.55
Individual Country[d]				
United States	$\log C = 1.73 - 0.21 \log Y - 0.13 \log P_c$ $(0.13) \quad (0.04)$	.59	$C = 28.39 - 5.35 \log Y - 3.24 \log P_c$ $(3.04) \quad (1.05)$	.59
France	$\log C = -0.72 + 0.52 \log Y - 0.18 \log P_c$ $(0.07) \quad (0.10)$	.93	$C = -11.34 + 6.06 \log Y - 2.43 \log P_c$ $(0.81) \quad (1.18)$	.93
Germany	$\log C = -6.45 + 2.40 \log Y - 0.15 \log P_c$ $(0.68) \quad (0.57)$	.95	$C = -29.67 + 11.53 \log Y - 1.15 \log P_c$ $(1.31) \quad (1.11)$	.99
Italy	$\log C = -4.30 + 1.88 \log Y - 0.59 \log P_c$ $(0.18) \quad (0.33)$	.93	$C = -18.34 + 8.13 \log Y - 1.80 \log P_c$ $(0.64) \quad (1.18)$	.95

[a]Explanation of symbols. C = coffee consumption in green beans equivalent per head of population over 15; Y = per capita disposable income; P_c = deflated coffee price; P_t = deflated tea price.

[b]Observations refer to 1960 and include data for the United States, Canada, Belgium, France, Germany, Italy, Netherlands, United Kingdom, Austria. In this equation C = ratio of coffee consumption to tea.

[c]Observations refer to the years 1953-60 and include data for the same countries as under (a), with the exception of the United Kingdom, Ireland, and Greece.

[d]Observations refer to 1950-1960.

TABLE A8.3.1

PER CAPITA COCOA CONSUMPTION IN DEVELOPED COUNTRIES
(kg)

	Prewar	1950–1952	1953–1955	1956–1958	1959	1960	1970I	1970II	1970I	1970II	1970I	1970II
United States	1.88	1.82	1.53	1.60	1.56	1.59	1.8	1.8	1.9	1.8	1.9	1.9
Canada	1.22	1.53	1.64	1.58	1.60	1.57	1.8	1.8	1.9	1.8	1.9	1.9
Belgium-Lux.	1.71	1.65	1.66	1.84	1.78	2.25	2.6	2.6	2.7	2.6	2.7	2.7
France	1.04	1.14	0.97	1.20	1.03	1.16	1.5	1.5	1.6	1.5	1.6	1.6
Germany	1.18	1.38	1.52	1.93	1.80	2.02	2.3	2.4	2.5	2.3	2.5	2.5
Italy	0.21	0.28	0.30	0.36	0.33	0.42	0.6	0.6	0.7	0.6	0.7	0.7
Netherlands	3.53	2.37	1.94	2.22	1.90	1.97	2.3	2.3	2.4	2.3	2.4	2.4
United Kingdom	1.72	2.14	2.14	1.90	1.62	1.81	2.0	2.1	2.0	2.1	2.0	2.0
Austria	0.96	0.82	0.99	1.43	1.61	1.73	2.1	2.1	2.2	2.1	2.2	2.2
Denmark	1.40	1.24	0.91	1.20	1.07	1.46	1.7	1.8	1.8	1.7	1.8	1.9
Finland	0.08	0.39	0.41	0.38	0.40	0.47	0.6	0.7	0.7	0.6	0.7	0.7
Ireland	0.79	0.95	0.60	0.58	1.00	0.83	1.0	1.0	1.0	1.0	1.0	1.0
Norway	1.17	1.38	1.10	1.11	1.12	1.30	1.5	1.8	1.6	1.6	1.7	1.6
Sweden	1.07	1.14	1.12	1.37	1.31	1.40	1.6	1.7	1.7	1.6	1.7	1.8
Switzerland	2.17	2.61	2.65	2.93	2.95	3.04	3.2	3.2	3.3	3.2	3.3	3.3
Greece	0.22	0.14	0.14	0.26	0.33	0.37	0.6	0.6	0.7	0.6	0.7	0.7
Portugal	0.07	0.08	0.09	0.09	0.11	0.13	0.2	0.2	0.3	0.2	0.3	0.3
Spain	0.44	0.31	0.48	0.62	0.67	0.69	0.9	1.0	1.0	0.9	1.0	1.1
Turkey	0.01	0.03	0.09	0.01	0.03	0.04	0.1	0.1	0.2	0.1	0.2	0.2
Yugoslavia	0.10	0.10	0.10	0.12	0.15	0.19	0.4	0.4	0.4	0.4	0.4	0.5
Japan	0.05	0.02	0.07	0.08	0.11	0.14	0.6	0.6	0.9	0.6	0.9	0.9
Australia	1.12	1.57	1.12	1.17	1.34	1.40	1.6	1.6	1.6	1.6	1.6	1.7
New Zealand	1.93	1.64	1.57	1.36	1.61	1.77	2.0	2.0	2.0	2.0	2.0	2.1
South Africa	0.25	0.24	0.30	0.30	0.21	0.27	0.3	0.4	0.4	0.3	0.4	0.4

Source: FAO, CCP Cocoa /61/7 and CCP Cocoa /62/4.

TABLE A8

NONCOMPETING TROPICAL PRODUCTS: VALUE OF IMPORTS
($ million at current prices)

	1960 NA	1960 WE	1960 JA	1960 OC	1960 DC	1970I NA	1970I WE	1970I JA	1970I OC	1970I DC	1970II NA	1970II WE	1970II JA	1970II OC	1970II DC	1975I NA	1975I WE	1975I JA	1975I OC	1975I DC	1975II NA	1975II WE	1975II JA	1975II OC	1975II DC
Bananas																									
LA	100	105	1	1	207	123	124	11	—	258	123	127	12	—	262	135	135	16	—	286	135	138	18	—	291
AF	—	35	—	—	35	—	51	—	2	53	—	52	—	2	54	—	59	—	2	61	—	61	—	2	63
ME	—	—	—	—	—	—	1	—	—	1	—	1	—	—	1	—	1	—	—	1	—	1	—	—	1
AS	—	—	3	1	4	—	—	12	2	14	—	—	13	2	15	—	—	17	2	19	—	—	18	2	20
LDC	100	140	4	2	246	123	176	23	4	326	123	180	25	4	332	135	195	33	4	367	135	200	36	4	375
Coffee																									
LA	925	477	5	4	1411	1090	625	46	7	1768	1096	641	55	7	1799	1180	704	74	9	1967	1191	726	86	9	2012
AF	130	203	2	9	344	257	308	13	14	592	263	315	15	15	608	336	352	19	17	724	352	365	24	18	759
ME	1	2	—	—	3	1	3	—	—	4	1	3	—	—	3	3	3	—	—	4	1	3	—	—	4
AS	2	22	1	2	27	11	41	8	3	63	12	42	10	3	67	19	48	12	4	83	20	49	15	4	88
LDC	1058	704	8	15	1785	1359	977	67	24	2427	1372	1001	80	25	2478	1536	1107	105	30	2778	1564	1143	125	31	2863
Cocoa																									
LA	89	52	2	—	143	80	38	7	—	125	80	39	7	—	126	88	41	9	—	138	88	42	9	—	139
AF	78	243	4	11	336	115	295	16	13	439	120	302	16	14	452	134	324	27	14	499	127	334	27	15	503
ME	—	—	—	—	—	—	—	—	—	—	—	—	—	—	—	—	—	—	—	—	—	—	—	—	—
AS	2	4	—	—	6	4	5	3	2	14	4	5	3	2	14	5	5	5	3	18	4	5	5	3	17
LDC	169	299	6	11	485	199	338	26	15	578	204	346	26	16	592	227	370	41	18	655	219	381	41	18	659
Tea																									
LA	—	1	—	—	1	—	1	—	—	1	—	1	—	—	1	—	1	—	—	1	—	1	—	—	1
AF	5	33	—	1	39	6	44	—	1	51	6	45	—	1	52	6	53	—	1	60	6	56	—	1	63
ME	—	—	—	—	—	—	—	—	—	—	—	—	—	—	—	—	—	—	—	—	—	—	—	—	—
AS	66	333	2	54	455	69	335	3	63	470	69	338	3	63	473	75	347	4	74	500	75	351	4	74	504
LDC	71	367	2	55	495	75	380	3	64	522	75	384	3	64	526	81	401	4	75	561	81	408	4	75	568
Spices																									
LA	7	3	—	—	10	8	3	—	—	11	8	3	—	—	11	9	3	—	—	12	9	3	—	—	12
AF	10	5	—	—	15	12	5	—	—	17	12	5	—	—	17	13	6	—	—	19	13	6	—	—	19
ME	1	—	—	—	1	1	—	—	—	1	1	—	—	—	1	1	—	—	—	1	1	—	—	—	1
AS	28	26	2	2	58	34	29	3	3	70	34	29	4	3	70	37	30	6	3	76	37	30	6	3	76
LDC	46	34	2	2	84	55	37	3	3	99	55	37	4	3	99	60	39	6	3	108	60	39	6	3	108
Total																									
LA	1121	638	8	5	1772	1301	791	64	7	2163	1307	811	74	7	2199	1412	884	99	9	2404	1423	910	113	9	2455
AF	223	519	6	21	769	393	703	29	30	1155	401	719	31	32	1183	489	794	46	34	1363	498	822	51	36	1407
ME	—	2	—	—	4	2	4	—	—	6	2	4	—	—	6	1	4	—	—	6	2	4	—	—	6
AS	98	385	8	59	550	118	410	30	73	631	119	414	33	73	639	136	430	44	86	696	136	435	48	86	705
LDC	1444	1544	22	85	3095	1814	1908	123	110	3955	1829	1948	138	112	4027	2039	2112	189	129	4469	2059	2171	212	131	4573

Source: U.N. Commodity Trade Statistics, 1960 and OECD, Trade by Commodities, Foreign Trade Series C, 1960.

TABLE A9.2.1

NEW RUBBER CONSUMPTION
(thousand tons)

	1950	1955	1960	1970I	1970II	1975I	1975II
North America	1349	1640	1676	2215	2312	2529	2691
United States	1279	1554	1583	2070	2160	2350	2500
Canada	70	86	93	145	152	179	191
Western Europe	562	824	1093	1707	1818	2095	2321
Belgium-Lux.[a]	13	27	27	39	42	46	51
France	112	156	221	364	385	449	489
Germany	95	176	254	408	434	511	575
Italy[a]	40	74	103	201	215	272	301
Netherlands	15	23	33	51	54	61	67
United Kingdom	226	273	296	389	409	436	468
Northern Europe[a]	46	67	99	139	147	160	175
Southern Europe[a]	15	29	59	116	132	160	195
Japan	61	93	230	429	476	544	630
Oceania and South Africa	40	94	105	147	156	172	187
Developed Countries, Total	2012	2651	3104	4498	4762	5340	5829

Notes: [a]Derived from trade statistics.
Source: International Rubber Study Group, Rubber Statistical Bulletin, various issues.

TABLE A9.2.2

CROSS-SECTION AND TIME-SERIES REGRESSIONS FOR RUBBER[a]

Cross-Section[b]		R^2
1955	$\log C = 0.58 + 1.18 \log I$	.91
	(0.09)	
1956	$\log C = 0.49 + 1.27 \log I$	.92
	(0.08)	
Individual Country[c]		
United States	$\log C = 1.54 + 0.80 \log I$	.82
	(0.12)	
Canada	$\log C = 3.17 + 0.85 \log I$	.87
	(0.10)	
Belgium.	$\log C = 0.44 + 1.90 \log I$	.78
	(0.33)	
France	$\log C = 3.01 + 1.05 \log I$	.99
	(0.04)	
Germany	$\log C = 2.68 + 1.20 \log I$	.98
	(0.05)	
Italy	$\log C = 2.93 + 0.91 \log I$	.88
	(0.11)	
Netherlands	$\log C = 1.41 + 1.41 \log I$	.98
	(0.07)	
United Kingdom.	$\log C = 3.64 + 0.86 \log I$	.78
	(0.15)	
Northern Europe. . . .	$\log C = 1.90 + 1.42 \log I$	.91
	(0.15)	
Southern Europe	$\log C = 2.32 + 0.89 \log I$	.82
	(0.14)	
Japan	$\log C = 3.00 + 0.97 \log I$	.96
	(0.06)	

Notes: [a]Explanation of symbols: C = rubber consumption, I = industrial
production.
[b]Observations include data for 20 developed countries.
[c]Observations refer to 1950-1960.

TABLE A9.4.1

PER CAPITA END-USE CONSUMPTION OF TEXTILE FIBERS IN THE UNITED STATES
(Kg., cotton equivalent)

Year	Clothing All Fibers	Clothing Cotton	Clothing Wool	Clothing Man-Made	Other Consumer Type Products All Fibers	Other Consumer Type Products Cotton	Other Consumer Type Products Wool	Other Consumer Type Products Man-Made	Home Furniture All Fibers	Home Furniture Cotton	Home Furniture Wool	Home Furniture Man-Made	Industrial Uses All Fibers	Industrial Uses Cotton	Industrial Uses Wool	Industrial Uses Man-Made	All Uses All Fibers	All Uses Cotton	All Uses Wool	All Uses Man-Made
1949	6.62	4.07	.59	1.96	1.92	1.22	.07	.63	2.96	2.31	.33	.32	4.17	2.71	.07	1.39	15.67	10.31	1.06	4.30
1950	7.20	4.36	.62	2.22	2.01	1.27	.07	.67	3.67	2.74	.39	.54	4.73	2.97	.11	1.65	17.61	11.34	1.19	5.08
1951	6.93	4.13	.51	2.29	1.79	1.13	.04	.62	3.33	2.56	.21	.56	5.07	3.14	.07	1.86	17.12	10.96	.83	5.33
1952	7.20	4.43	.56	2.21	1.81	1.18	.04	.59	3.45	2.59	.24	.62	4.71	2.42	.05	2.24	17.17	10.62	.89	5.66
1953	7.33	4.65	.56	2.12	1.80	1.20	.04	.56	3.77	2.76	.28	.73	4.58	2.11	.04	2.43	17.48	10.72	.92	5.84
1954	6.95	4.47	.52	1.96	1.78	1.20	.04	.54	3.66	2.68	.22	.76	3.96	1.95	.03	1.98	16.35	10.30	.81	5.24
1955	7.34	4.85	.55	1.94	1.89	1.23	.04	.62	4.01	2.75	.25	1.01	4.56	2.05	.03	2.48	17.80	10.88	.87	6.05
1956	7.40	4.92	.56	1.92	1.89	1.21	.04	.64	4.09	2.73	.26	1.10	4.09	1.88	.02	2.19	17.47	10.74	.88	5.85
1957	7.19	4.72	.53	1.94	1.81	1.13	.04	.64	3.99	2.56	.23	1.20	3.95	1.74	.02	2.19	16.94	10.15	.82	5.97
1958	7.08	4.67	.49	1.92	1.81	1.08	.04	.69	3.97	2.52	.21	1.24	3.65	1.57	.02	2.06	16.51	9.84	.76	5.91
1959	7.68	5.09	.53	2.06	1.94	1.11	.04	.79	4.37	2.69	.29	1.39	4.24	1.66	.02	2.56	18.23	10.55	.88	6.80
1960	7.49	4.95	.52	2.02	1.90	1.07	.04	.79	4.23	2.54	.27	1.42	3.86	1.53	.02	2.31	17.48	10.09	.85	6.54
1970I	8.20	5.00	.52	2.68	1.89	.95	.03	.91	5.09	2.35	.25	2.49	3.59	1.20	.01	2.38	18.77	9.50	.81	8.46
1970II	8.30	5.05	.53	2.72	1.89	.95	.03	.91	5.30	2.40	.26	2.64	3.59	1.20	.01	2.38	19.08	9.60	.83	8.65
1975I	8.40	5.00	.52	2.88	1.89	.90	.02	.97	5.50	2.30	.24	2.96	3.49	1.10	.01	2.38	19.28	9.30	.79	9.19
1975II	8.60	5.05	.53	3.02	1.89	.90	.02	.97	5.81	2.35	.25	3.21	3.49	1.10	.01	2.38	19.79	9.40	.81	9.58

Source: Textile Organon, November, 1961, and U.S. Department of Agriculture, Economic Research Service, Statistics on Cotton and Related Data Statistical Bulletin No. 99, Supplement, October, 1961. For the conversion ratios used, see p. 55.

TABLE A9.4.2

WOOL CONSUMPTION AND IMPORTS IN THE UNITED STATES
(thousand tons)

	1960	1970I	1970II	1975I	1975II
Apparel Wool					
Total Consumption (s)	157	186	191	205	210
Net Imports of Manufactures (s)	45	54	55	59	60
Mill Consumption (s)	112	132	136	146	150
Mill Consumption (c)	105	116	119	129	132
Domestic Production (c)	66	70	70	72	72
Estimated Gross Imports (c)	39	46	49	57	60
Changes in Stocks and					
Statistical Discrepancy (c)	-5	--	--	--	--
Actual Gross Imports (c)	34	46	49	57	60
Carpet Wool					
Total Consumption (s)	89	96	100	101	106
Net Imports of Manufactures (s)	13	16	17	17	18
Mill Consumption (s)	76	80	83	84	88
Mill Consumption (c)	71	80	83	84	88
Estimated Gross Imports (c)	71	80	83	84	88
Changes in Stock and					
Statistical Discrepancy (c)	-1	--	--	--	--
Actual Gross Imports (c)	70	80	83	84	88

Source: U.S. Department of Agriculture, <u>Wool Situation</u>, October, 1962, and March, 1963.

Notes: (a) Explanation of symbols: (s) scoured basis, (c) clean content.
(b) Inventory changes are reported to be -2.5 thousand tons in the case of apparel wool and -3.2 thousand tons in the case of carpet wool in 1960.

TABLE A9.4.3

PER CAPITA FIBER CONSUMPTION LEVELS IN WESTERN EUROPE AND JAPAN (Kg.)

	1953	1954	1955	1956	1957	1958	1959	1960	1970I	1970II	1975I	1975II
Common Market												
Cotton	4.3	4.7	4.4	4.7	5.3	4.8	4.8	5.2	5.7	5.8	6.0	6.2
Wool	1.5	1.5	1.4	1.6	1.8	1.4	1.6	1.6	1.7	1.8	1.7	1.8
Man-made	1.9	2.1	2.2	2.5	2.7	2.8	2.9	3.3	4.0	4.1	4.8	5.1
Total	7.7	8.3	8.0	8.8	9.8	9.0	9.3	10.1	11.4	11.7	12.5	13.1
United Kingdom												
Cotton	5.3	6.5	5.9	5.8	6.2	5.2	5.9	5.9	6.2	6.3	6.3	6.4
Wool	2.6	2.5	2.5	2.4	2.5	2.2	2.7	2.3	2.2	2.3	2.2	2.3
Man-made	3.0	3.2	3.2	3.5	3.8	3.1	3.7	4.4	4.7	4.8	4.8	5.0
Total	10.9	12.2	11.6	11.7	12.5	10.5	12.3	12.6	13.1	13.4	13.3	13.7
Northern Europe												
Cotton	4.3	4.7	4.6	4.6	5.1	4.6	4.8	5.1	5.6	5.7	5.9	6.1
Wool	1.9	1.8	1.9	2.0	2.1	1.8	2.0	2.0	1.9	2.0	1.9	2.0
Man-made	1.8	2.0	2.1	2.0	2.4	2.1	2.6	2.7	3.3	3.4	3.7	4.0
Total	8.0	8.5	8.6	8.6	9.6	8.5	9.4	9.8	10.8	11.1	11.5	12.1
Southern Europe												
Cotton	2.7	2.8	3.1	3.1	3.3	3.5	3.5	3.4	3.9	4.0	4.2	4.4
Wool	0.7	0.7	0.7	0.8	0.8	0.7	0.8	1.0	1.0	1.0	1.1	1.1
Man-made	0.6	0.7	0.9	1.0	1.0	1.0	0.9	0.9	1.5	1.8	1.8	2.3
Total	4.0	4.2	4.7	4.9	5.1	5.3	5.1	5.1	6.4	6.8	7.1	7.8
Japan												
Cotton	4.2	3.5	3.2	4.1	4.0	3.4	3.9	4.3	4.5	4.6	4.7	4.8
Wool	0.8	0.6	0.6	0.9	0.9	0.7	1.0	1.1	1.3	1.4	1.3	1.4
Man-made	2.0	2.3	2.3	2.5	3.0	2.0	2.9	3.7	4.8	5.0	5.4	5.9
Total	7.0	6.4	6.1	7.5	7.9	6.1	7.8	9.1	10.6	11.0	11.4	12.1

Source: Western Europe: FAO, Per Capita Fibre Consumption Levels, Commodity Bulletin Series No. 31; Rome, 1960, and "Per Capita Fibre Consumption Levels," Monthly Bulletin of Agricultural Economics & Statistics, January, 1962, pp. 1-28. Japan; Inter-national Cotton Advisory Committee, Prospective Trends in Consumption of Textile Fibres, Washington, 1962, p. 142.

TABLE A9.4.4

CONSUMPTION AND IMPORTS OF NATURAL FIBERS
IN WESTERN EUROPE AND JAPAN
(thousand tons)

	1960	1970I	1970II	1975I	1975II
Western Europe					
Cotton (lint)					
Domestic Consumption	1698	2047	2086	2180	2253
Net Exports of Cotton Goods	98	--	--	-50	-50
Mill Consumption	1796	2047	2086	2130	2203
Domestic Production	314	420	430	490	500
Exports of Cotton	42	42	42	42	42
Hypothetical Gross Imports	1524	1669	1698	1682	1745
Changes in Stocks & Stat. Discre.	98	--	--	--	--
Actual Gross Imports	1622	1669	1698	1682	1745
Wool (clean basis)					
Domestic Consumption	555	613	646	646	687
Net Exports of Cotton Goods	101	100	100	100	100
Mill Consumption	656	713	746	746	787
Domestic Production	128	148	150	160	163
Exports of Wool	16	15	15	15	15
Hypothetical Gross Imports	544	580	611	601	639
Changes in Stocks & Stat. Discre.	-41	--	--	--	--
Actual Gross Imports	503	580	611	601	639
Japan					
Cotton (lint)					
Domestic Consumption	404	460	470	500	510
Net Exports of Cotton Goods	226	300	310	340	350
Inventory Change in Cotton Goods	41	--	--	--	--
Mill Consumption	630	760	780	840	860
Domestic Production	--	--	--	--	--
Exports of Cotton	--	--	--	--	--
Hypothetical Gross Imports	671	760	780	840	860
Changes in Stocks & Stat. Discre.	30	--	--	--	--
Actual Gross Imports	701	760	780	840	860
Wool (clean basis)					
Domestic Consumption	100	132	143	138	149
Net Exports of Wool Goods	23	40	42	54	57
Mill Consumption	123	172	183	192	206
Domestic Production	2	3	3	3	3
Exports of Wool	2	3	3	3	3
Hypothetical Gross Imports	123	172	183	192	206
Changes in Stocks & Stat. Discre.	-8	--	--	--	--
Actual Gross Imports	115	172	183	192	206

Source: Western Europe: FAO, Monthly Bulletin of Agricultural Economics & Statistics, January, 1962; FAO, Production Yearbook and Trade Yearbook; U.N., Commodity Trade Statistics. Japan: International Cotton Advisory Committee, Prospective Trends in Consumption of Textile Fibres, 1962; FAO, Production Yearbook and Trade Yearbook.

TABLE A9.4.5

CROSS-SECTION AND TIME-SERIES REGRESSIONS FOR CLOTHING AND APPAREL FIBER[a]

	Double-Log	R^2	Semi-Log	R^2
Clothing Expenditure				
Cross-section[b]	log E = -0.14 + 0.72 log Y (0.11)	.78	E = -295.53 + 134.64 log Y (28.22)	.67
United States[c]	log E = 0.13 + 0.61 log Y (0.08)	.87	E = -735.01 + 287.14 log Y (36.43)	.86
Canada[d]	log E = 1.01 + 0.34 log Y (0.07)	.70	E = -156.27 + 87.45 log Y (18.84)	.70
EEC[d]	log E = -0.36 + 0.78 log Y (0.04)	.98	E = -288.75 + 126.93 log Y (7.10)	.97
United Kingdom[d]	log E = -2.19 + 1.21 log Y (0.04)	.92	E = -185.24 + 70.82 log Y (6.18)	.94
Other Europe[d]	log E = -0.59 + 0.81 log Y (0.08)	.92	E = -143.33 + 67.44 log Y (6.52)	.93
Fiber Consumption				
Cross-section[b]	log F = -0.62 + 0.55 log Y (0.06)	.80	F = -20.62 + 10.45 log Y (1.40)	.76
United States[c]	log Fc = -0.38 + 0.53 log Y (0.12)	.66	Fc = -59.42 + 24.96 log Y (0.75)	.65
EEC[e]	log F = -1.16 + 0.73 log Y (0.12)	.86	F = -33.80 + 14.82 log Y (2.57)	.85
United Kingdom[e]	log F = -1.33 + 0.77 log Y (0.10)	.90	F = -30.76 + 13.41 log Y (1.91)	.89
North Europe[e]	log F = -1.68 + 0.80 log Y (0.19)	.79	F = -44.75 + 18.33 log Y (3.92)	.79
South Europe[e]	log F = -1.23 + 0.78 log Y (0.20)	.72	F = -15.10 + 8.13 log Y (1.97)	.74

[a]Explanation of symbols: E = clothing expenditures per capita; F = per capita fiber consumption; Fc = per capita fiber consumption in clothing; Y = per capita disposable income.

[b]Observations include average data of the years 1959-1960 for 13 industrial countries in the case of clothing expenditure and 20 industrial countries in case of fiber consumption.

[c]Data are calculated per consuming unit and refer to the period 1949-1960.

[d]Data refer to the period 1949-1960.

[e]Data refer to the period 1953-1960.

TABLE A9

AGRICULTURE RAW MATERIALS: VALUE OF IMPORTS
(\$ million at current prices)

	1960 NA	WE	JA	OC	DC	1970I NA	WE	JA	OC	DC	1970II NA	WE	JA	OC	DC	1975I NA	WE	JA	OC	DC	1975II NA	WE	JA	OC	DC
Hides & Skins																									
LA	17	54	2	--	73	19	57	3	--	79	19	59	4	--	82	21	61	5	--	87	21	65	6	--	92
AF	10	52	0	--	62	9	49	--	--	58	9	49	--	--	58	9	49	--	--	58	9	49	--	--	58
ME	8	10	0	--	18	7	9	--	--	16	7	9	--	--	16	7	9	--	--	16	7	9	--	--	16
AS	29	33	3	1	66	28	34	6	1	69	28	34	8	1	71	28	35	11	1	75	28	35	13	1	77
LDC	64	149	5	1	219	63	149	9	1	222	63	151	12	1	227	65	154	16	1	236	65	158	19	1	243
Rubber																									
LA	3	3	0	--	6	2	2	--	--	4	3	2	--	--	5	3	2	--	--	5	3	3	--	--	6
AF	48	49	--	--	97	39	36	--	--	75	40	38	--	--	78	39	41	--	--	80	42	45	--	--	87
ME	--	--	--	--	--	--	--	--	--	--	--	--	--	--	--	--	--	--	--	--	--	--	--	--	--
AS	282	503	135	49	969	223	367	110	37	737	234	392	121	37	784	231	416	129	39	815	246	458	143	44	891
LDC	333	555	135	49	1072	264	405	110	37	816	277	432	121	37	867	273	459	129	39	900	291	506	143	44	984
Forest Products																									
LA	21	18	0	4	43	29	26	--	6	61	30	27	--	6	63	33	32	--	7	72	35	33	--	7	75
AF	5	140	0	5	150	8	311	--	11	330	8	353	--	12	373	8	465	--	18	491	8	539	--	21	568
ME	--	0	--	--	--	--	--	--	--	--	--	--	--	--	--	--	--	--	--	--	--	--	--	--	--
AS	9	48	79	21	157	12	100	217	28	357	12	113	242	30	397	14	138	288	37	477	15	160	338	39	552
LDC	35	206	79	30	350	49	437	217	45	748	50	493	242	48	833	55	635	288	62	1040	58	732	338	67	1195
Wool & Silk																									
LA	64	132	13	1	210	81	176	33	1	291	84	187	36	1	308	88	177	37	1	303	94	188	40	1	323
AF	1	5	--	0	6	1	7	--	1	8	1	7	--	1	8	1	7	--	1	8	1	7	--	1	8
ME	21	4	--	2	27	20	4	1	1	26	20	4	1	1	26	20	4	1	2	26	20	4	1	2	26
AS	17	20	1	0	38	17	20	1	--	38	17	20	1	--	38	18	20	1	--	39	18	20	1	--	39
LDC	103	161	14	3	281	119	207	34	3	363	122	218	37	3	380	127	208	38	3	376	133	219	41	3	396

Cotton / Jute / Vegetable Fibers / Animal & Veg. Matter / Total — commodity trade data

Category		1	2	3	4	5	6	7	8	9	10	11	12	13	14	15	16	17	18	19	20	21	22	23	24	25	26
Cotton	LA	16	176	124	4	320	17	219	181	8	425	17	230	192	9	448	18	223	205	9	455	18	244	216	10	488	16
	AF	13	261	26	1	301	13	285	29	2	329	14	298	29	2	343	15	288	28	2	333	16	306	28	2	352	13
	ME	0	48	4	1	53	1	63	5	–	71	1	62	5	–	70	1	60	5	–	68	1	66	5	2	74	0
	AS	4	14	35	–	53	4	14	43	–	61	4	14	43	–	61	4	14	47	–	65	4	14	47	–	65	4
	LDC	33	499	189	6	727	35	581	258	12	886	36	604	269	13	922	38	585	285	13	921	39	630	296	14	979	33
Jute	LA	–	–	–	–	–	–	–	–	–	–	–	–	–	–	–	–	–	–	–	–	–	–	–	–	–	–
	AF	–	–	–	–	–	–	–	–	–	–	–	–	–	–	–	–	–	–	–	–	–	–	–	–	–	–
	ME	–	–	–	–	–	–	–	–	–	–	–	–	–	–	–	–	–	–	–	–	–	–	–	–	–	–
	AS	9	113	11	6	139	8	104	15	8	135	8	107	16	9	140	8	107	19	9	143	8	111	21	9	149	9
	LDC	9	113	11	6	139	8	104	15	8	135	8	107	16	9	140	8	107	19	9	143	8	111	21	9	149	9
Vegetable Fibers	LA	17	15	0	0	32	20	35	4	2	61	20	38	4	2	64	20	47	5	3	75	20	50	6	3	79	17
	AF	8	60	4	6	78	9	69	9	9	96	9	71	10	10	100	9	76	14	11	110	9	79	15	13	116	8
	ME	–	–	–	–	–	–	–	–	–	–	–	–	–	–	–	–	–	–	–	–	–	–	–	–	–	–
	AS	16	29	17	5	67	17	28	14	6	65	17	28	14	6	65	17	28	14	7	66	17	28	14	7	66	16
	LDC	41	104	21	11	177	46	132	27	17	222	46	137	28	18	229	46	151	33	21	251	46	157	35	23	261	41
Animal & Veg. Matter	LA	16	16	0	0	32	19	22	2	–	43	20	22	2	–	44	21	25	2	–	48	22	27	2	–	51	16
	AF	12	46	1	1	60	14	49	2	1	66	14	50	2	1	67	15	52	2	1	70	15	54	2	1	72	12
	ME	4	11	0	0	15	4	14	–	1	18	4	15	–	1	19	5	17	–	1	22	5	18	–	1	23	4
	AS	26	38	8	2	74	30	47	9	3	89	30	49	9	3	91	32	52	12	3	99	33	55	13	3	104	26
	LDC	58	111	9	3	181	67	132	13	4	216	68	136	13	4	221	73	146	16	4	239	75	154	17	4	250	58
Total	LA	154	414	139	9	716	187	537	223	17	964	193	565	238	18	1014	204	567	254	20	1045	213	610	270	21	1114	154
	AF	97	613	31	13	754	93	806	40	23	962	95	866	41	25	1027	96	978	44	32	1150	100	1079	45	37	1261	97
	ME	33	73	3	3	113	32	90	5	4	131	32	90	4	4	131	33	90	5	5	132	33	97	5	4	139	33
	AS	392	798	289	84	1563	339	714	415	83	1551	350	757	454	86	1647	352	703	521	96	1779	369	881	590	103	1943	392
	LDC	676	1898	463	109	3146	651	2147	683	127	3208	670	2278	738	133	3819	685	2445	824	152	4106	715	2667	910	165	4457	676

Source: U.N., Commodity Trade Statistics, 1960 and OECD Trade by Commodities, Foreign Trade Series C, 1960.

TABLE A10.1.1

CONVERSION RATIOS USED IN EXPRESSING ENERGY SOURCES
IN COAL EQUIVALENTS

	Coal Equivalent (metric tons)
Coal, anthracite and bituminous (metric tons)	1.0
Coal briquettes (metric tons)......................	1.0
Coke of anthracite or bituminous coal (metric tons).......	0.9
Coke of brown coal or lignite (metric tons)	0.67
Pitch coal (metric tons)	0.67
Lignite briquettes (metric tons)....................	0.67
Lignite (metric tons) France, Austria, Greece, Italy, Portugal, Yugoslavia...	0.5
Other countries	0.3
Peat (metric tons)	0.5
Crude petroleum (metric tons).....................	1.3
Petroleum products (metric tons)...................	1.5
Liquified petroleum and refinery gases (metric tons)......	1.67
Natural gas (1,000 cubic meters)	1.33
Manufactured and coke oven gases (1,000 cubic meters)....	0.6
Electricity (1,000 kwh)........................	0.125

Note: For the years 1950-1954, the U.N. used the coefficient 0.6 for electricity.
Data were adjusted so as to reflect the 0.125 coefficient for all years
1950-1960.

Source: United Nations, <u>World Energy Supplies</u>, 1957-1960, New York, 1962.

TABLE A10.1.2

TIME-SERIES REGRESSION FOR ENERGY CONSUMPTION

	Double-Log	R^2
United States	$\log C = 0.93 + 0.84 \log Y$ (0.05)	.97
Canada	$\log C = 0.46 + 1.00 \log Y$ (0.09)	.94
Belgium-Lux.	$\log C = 0.08 + 0.55 \log Y$ (0.19)	.49
France	$\log C = 0.18 + 0.80 \log Y$ (0.11)	.87
Germany	$\log C = 0.86 + 0.60 \log Y$ (0.05)	.93
Italy	$\log C = -0.57 + 1.87 \log Y$ (0.09)	.98
Netherlands	$\log C = -0.13 + 1.02 \log Y$ (0.06)	.97
United Kingdom	$\log C = 1.84 + 0.43 \log Y$ (0.11)	.65
Austria	$\log C = -0.85 + 0.98 \log Y$ (0.07)	.96
Denmark	$\log C = -0.51 + 1.04 \log Y$ (0.16)	.82
Finland	$\log C = -5.19 + 1.97 \log Y$ (0.14)	.96
Ireland	$\log C = -1.78 + 0.90 \log Y$ (0.56)	.22
Norway	$\log C = -1.22 + 1.47 \log Y$ (0.12)	.94
Sweden	$\log C = -1.14 + 1.48 \log Y$ (0.18)	.88
Switzerland	$\log C = -0.94 + 1.27 \log Y$ (0.12)	.92
Greece	$\log C = -1.91 + 1.29 \log Y$ (0.16)	.87
Portugal	$\log C = -1.87 + 1.34 \log Y$ (0.05)	.99
Turkey	$\log C = -0.06 + 1.04 \log Y$ (0.14)	.86
Yugoslavia	$\log C = -3.92 + 1.53 \log Y$ (0.19)	.88
Japan	$\log C = -0.83 + 0.92 \log Y$ (0.05)	.97

Notes: Explanation of symbols: C = energy consumption in coal equivalent
Y = Gross National Product

TABLE A10.3.1

CONSUMPTION, PRODUCTION, AND TRADE IN CRUDE OIL AND PETROLEUM
PRODUCTS
(million tons of coal equivalent)

	NA	WE	1960 JA	OC	DC
Consumption	642.8	252.7	37.9	20.5	953.9
Production	507.1	20.0	0.7	0.0	527.8
Hypothetical net imports	135.7	232.7	37.2	20.5	426.1
Exports	18.3	27.2	6.0	4.3	55.8
Hypothetical gross imports	154.0	259.9	43.2	24.8	481.9
Changes in stocks and statistical discrepancy	-2.7	-3.8	+0.6	-0.3	-6.2
Actual gross imports	151.3	263.7	43.8	24.5	483.3
Crude oil	89.5	217.1	35.1	16.7	358.4
Petroleum products	61.8	46.6	8.7	7.8	124.9

			1970I					1970II		
	NA	WE	JA	OC	Total	NA	WE	JA	OC	Total
Consumption	856	545	103	42	1544	872	582	120	47	1621
Production	665	48	2	1	716	679	49	2	1	731
Net Imports	189	497	105	41	832	193	533	118	46	890
Exports	20	45	15	8	88	21	47	16	9	93
Gross Imports	209	542	120	49	920	214	580	134	53	981
Crude oil	126	472	100	40	738	129	505	112	43	789
Petroleum products	83	70	20	3	182	85	75	22	10	192

			1975I					1975II		
	NA	WE	JA	OC	Total	NA	WE	JA	OC	Total
Consumption	983	717	150	60	1910	1017	796	187	72	2072
Production	751	59	3	2	815	775	61	3	2	841
Net Imports	232	658	147	58	1095	242	735	184	70	1231
Exports	24	60	20	10	114	25	64	23	11	123
Gross Imports	256	718	167	68	1209	267	799	209	81	1356
Crude oil	161	628	139	56	974	168	701	173	67	1109
Petroleum products	95	90	28	12	225	99	98	36	14	247

Sources: Consumption and production--United Nations, World Energy
Supplies 1958-1961, Series J. Trade--United Nations, Commodity Trade Statistics and U.S. Bureau of Mines, International Petroleum Trade.

Note: Trade figures do not include movement into entrepot and subsequent re-exports.

TABLE A10.3.2

CRUDE PETROLEUM IMPORTS INTO DEVELOPED AREAS
(million tons)

	1960 NA	WE	JA	OC	DC	1970I NA	WE	JA	OC	DC	1970II NA	WE	JA	OC	DC	1975I NA	WE	JA	OC	DC	1975II NA	WE	JA	OC	DC
SB	--	6.6	1.0	--	7.6	--	27	5	--	32	--	31	6	--	37	--	38	8	--	46	--	50	10	--	60
NA	--	0.2	0.5	--	.7	--	--	--	--	--	--	--	--	--	--	--	--	--	--	--	--	--	--	--	--
LA	41.7	16.9	--	0.1	58.7	52	35	--	--	87	54	38	--	--	92	67	48	--	--	115	69	54	--	--	123
AF	0.2	9.5	--	--	9.7	4	77	--	--	81	4	80	--	--	84	7	131	--	--	138	7	136	--	--	143
ME	23.2	133.1	21.3	8.9	186.5	35	224	62	19	340	37	229	68	20	354	43	265	82	25	415	46	299	101	31	477
AS	3.8	0.6	4.2	3.9	12.5	6	--	10	12	28	6	--	13	13	32	7	--	17	18	42	7	--	22	21	50
Total	68.9	166.9	27.0	12.9	275.7	97	363	77	31	568	101	378	87	33	599	124	482	107	43	756	129	539	133	52	853

Source: United Nations, Commodity Trade Statistics and U.S. Bureau of Mines, International Petroleum Trade.

TABLE A10.3.3

PETROLEUM PRODUCT IMPORTS INTO DEVELOPED COUNTRIES
(million tons)

	1960 NA	WE	JA	OC	DC	1970I NA	WE	JA	OC	DC	1970II NA	WE	JA	OC	DC	1975I NA	WE	JA	OC	DC	1975II NA	WE	JA	OC	DC
SB	--	7.5	0.2	--	7.7	--	10	1	--	11	--	11	2	--	13	--	13	3	--	16	--	15	4	--	19
NA	--	2.6	2.9	0.3	5.8	--	3	3	--	6	--	3	3	--	6	--	4	3	--	7	--	4	4	--	8
LA	39.6	12.5	--	0.2	52.3	52	23	--	--	75	54	25	--	--	79	59	30	--	--	89	62	32	--	--	94
AF	--	0.1	--	--	0.1	--	--	--	--	--	--	--	--	--	--	--	--	--	--	--	--	--	--	--	--
ME	1.2	6.4	2.1	3.3	13.0	3	11	6	4	24	3	11	7	4	25	4	13	9	5	31	4	14	11	5	34
AS	--	1.8	0.6	1.3	3.7	--	--	3	2	5	--	--	3	3	6	--	--	4	3	7	--	--	5	4	9
Total	41.2[a]	31.1[b]	5.8	5.3[c]	83.4	55	47	13	6	121	57	50	15	7	129	63	60	19	8	150	66	65	24	9	164

Source: United Nations, Commodity Trade Statistics and U.S. Bureau of Mines, International Petroleum Trade.

Notes: [a] Including 0.4 million tons imported from Japan.
[b] Including 0.2 million tons imported from Australia.
[c] Including 0.2 million tons imported from Western Europe.

TABLE A10

FUELS: VALUE OF IMPORTS
($ million at current prices)

	1960 NA	1960 WE	1960 JA	1960 OC	1960 DC	1970I NA	1970I WE	1970I JA	1970I OC	1970I DC	1970II NA	1970II WE	1970II JA	1970II OC	1970II DC	1975I NA	1975I WE	1975I JA	1975I OC	1975I DC	1975II NA	1975II WE	1975II JA	1975II OC	1975II DC
Coal																									
LA	—	—	—	—	—	—	—	—	—	—	—	—	—	—	—	—	—	—	—	—	—	—	—	—	—
AF	0	3	—	—	3	—	—	—	—	—	—	—	—	—	—	—	—	—	—	—	—	—	—	—	—
ME	—	—	—	—	—	—	—	—	—	—	—	—	—	—	—	—	—	—	—	—	—	—	—	—	—
AS	—	—	3	—	3	—	—	5	—	5	—	—	5	—	5	—	—	8	—	8	—	—	8	—	8
LDC	—	3	3	—	6	—	—	5	—	5	—	—	5	—	5	—	—	8	—	8	—	—	8	—	8
Crude Petroleum																									
LA	752	270	—	1	1023	799	475	—	—	1274	854	535	—	—	1389	1029	652	—	—	1681	1092	760	—	—	1852
AF	2	167	—	—	169	34	1151	—	—	1185	35	1237	—	—	1272	60	1957	—	—	2017	62	2104	—	—	2166
ME	333	1706	247	110	2396	428	2436	611	199	3674	466	2582	693	217	3958	527	2886	808	263	4484	580	3378	1030	337	5325
AS	53	9	58	61	181	71	—	117	160	348	74	—	158	179	411	83	—	200	240	523	86	—	268	289	643
LDC	1140	2152	305	172	3769	1332	4062	728	359	6481	1429	4354	851	396	7030	1699	5495	1008	503	8705	1820	6242	1298	626	9986
Petroleum Products																									
LA	621	316	—	14	951	686	446	—	—	1132	737	501	—	—	1238	786	581	—	—	1367	858	640	—	—	1498
AF	1	3	—	0	4	—	—	—	—	—	—	—	—	—	—	—	—	—	—	—	—	—	—	—	—
ME	8	144	26	98	276	17	190	63	91	361	18	196	76	94	384	23	224	95	114	456	24	249	120	118	511
AS	—	22	11	38	71	—	—	47	45	92	—	—	48	70	118	—	—	62	67	129	—	—	80	93	173
LDC	630	485	37	150	1302	703	636	110	136	1585	755	697	124	164	1740	809	805	157	181	1952	882	889	200	211	2182
Natural Gas																									
LA	8	—	—	—	8	10	—	—	—	10	11	—	—	—	11	12	—	—	—	12	13	—	—	—	13
AF	—	—	—	—	—	—	170	—	—	170	—	179	—	—	179	—	337	—	—	337	—	365	—	—	365
ME	—	—	—	—	—	—	—	9	—	9	—	—	11	—	11	—	—	16	—	16	—	—	16	—	16
AS	—	—	—	—	—	—	—	—	—	—	—	—	—	—	—	—	—	—	—	—	—	—	—	—	—
LDC	8	—	—	—	8	10	170	9	—	189	11	179	11	—	201	12	337	16	—	365	13	365	16	—	394
Total																									
LA	1381	586	—	15	1982	1495	921	—	—	2416	1602	1036	—	—	2638	1827	1233	—	—	3060	1963	1400	—	—	3363
AF	3	173	—	—	176	34	1321	—	—	1355	35	1416	—	—	1451	60	2294	—	—	2354	62	2469	—	—	2531
ME	341	1850	273	208	2672	445	2626	683	290	4044	484	2778	780	311	4353	550	3110	919	377	4956	604	3627	1166	455	5852
AS	53	31	72	99	255	71	—	169	205	445	74	—	211	249	534	83	—	270	307	660	86	—	356	382	824
LDC	1778	2640	345	322	5085	2045	4868	852	495	8260	2195	5230	991	560	8976	2520	6637	1189	684	11030	2715	7496	1522	837	12570

Source: U.N., *Commodity Trade Statistics, 1960* and OECD, *Trade by Commodities, Foreign Trade Series, C,* 1960.

TABLE A11.1.1

CONSUMPTION, PRODUCTION AND TRADE IN STEEL, PIG IRON AND IRON ORE
(million tons, steel or iron content)

	1960				
	US	CA	WE	JA	IC
Crude Steel Consumption	90.5	5.5	96.1	19.5	211.6
Net Steel Exports	-0.4	-0.2	12.7	2.6	14.7
Crude Steel Production	90.1	5.3	108.8	22.1	226.3
Pig Iron Production	60.5	4.0	78.9	12.3	155.7
Iron Ore Requirement	60.5	3.5	67.1	10.5	141.1
Iron Ore Production	47.9	10.8	53.3	1.6	113.5
Hypothetical Iron Ore Imports.	12.6	-7.3	13.8	8.9	28.0
Actual Iron Ore Imports.	20.9	-9.3	16.0	8.3	35.9
Changes in Stocks and Statistical Discrepancy	8.3[a]	-2.0[b]	2.2[c]	-0.6	7.9

	1970I					1970II				
	US	CA	WE	JA	IC	US	CA	WE	JA	IC
Crude Steel Consumption	127.9	8.8	150.7	39.0	326.4	133.5	9.1	161.3	43.6	347.5
Net Steel Exports	--	--	10.0	1.5	11.5	--	--	10.0	1.5	11.5
Steel Ingot Production	127.9	8.8	160.7	40.5	337.9	133.5	9.1	171.3	45.1	359.0
Pig Iron Production.	80.6	6.2	112.5	26.3	225.6	84.1	6.4	119.9	29.2	239.6
Iron Ore Requirement	80.6	5.6	95.6	23.7	205.5	84.1	5.8	101.9	26.3	218.1
Iron Ore Production	50.0	23.7	65.0	3.0	141.7	50.5	25.8	66.0	3.0	145.3
Iron Ore Imports[d]	32.6	-20.1	31.6	20.7	64.8	35.6	-22.1	36.9	23.3	73.8

	1975I					1975II				
	US	CA	WE	JA	IC	US	CA	WE	JA	IC
Crude Steel Consumption	143.2	10.4	185.5	51.0	390.1	151.5	11.1	204.8	59.9	427.3
Net Steel Exports . . . . , .	--	--	10.0	1.5	11.5	--	--	10.0	1.5	11.5
Steel Ingot Production	143.2	10.4	195.5	52.5	401.6	151.5	11.1	214.8	61.4	438.8
Pig Iron Production.	90.2	7.3	136.9	34.1	268.5	95.5	7.8	150.4	39.9	293.6
Iron Ore Requirement	90.2	6.6	115.6	30.7	243.1	95.5	7.0	127.9	35.9	266.3
Iron Ore Production	51.0	29.5	70.0	4.0	154.5	52.0	32.5	72.0	4.0	160.5
Iron Ore Imports[d].	41.2	-24.9	46.6	26.7	89.6	45.5	-27.5	56.9	31.9	106.8

Sources: Steel consumption, production, and trade, pig iron production, iron ore production--U.N., *Statistical Yearbook, 1961,* and U.S. Bureau of Mines, *Minerals Yearbook, 1960.* Iron ore imports--Table A 11.1.2.

Notes: [a]Increases in commercial stocks in the United States were reported to amount to 5.1 million tons in the *Minerals Yearbook, 1960* (p. 578) and 6.2 million tons in *Resources in America's Future* (p. 876). At the same time, exports of iron ore (chiefly to Canada) amounted to 2.8 million tons.

[b]Includes imports of 2.4 million tons.

[c]Includes exports of 1.8 million tons.

[d]Allowing for U.S. exports of 2 million tons to Canada and European exports of 1.0 million tons to varied destinations.

TABLE A11.1.2

IRON ORE IMPORTS INTO INDUSTRIAL COUNTRIES
(million tons, iron content)

	1960				1970I				1970II				1975I				1975II			
	US	WE	JA	IC	US	WE	JA	IC	US	WE	JA	IC	US	WE	JA	IC	US	WE	JA	IC
LA	14.4	5.3	0.8	20.5	18.1	9.5	4.2	31.8	20.1	12.4	5.0	37.5	20.2	13.5	6.0	39.7	22.0	19.0	8.0	49.0
AF	0.6	6.0	--	6.6	2.0	14.5	1.5	18.0	2.0	16.0	1.5	19.5	4.0	24.0	2.5	30.5	4.0	27.4	2.5	33.9
ME	--	--	--	--	--	--	--	--	--	--	--	--	--	--	--	--	--	--	--	--
AS	0	1.8	6.3	8.1	--	2.5	9.5	12.0	--	2.5	10.5	13.0	--	3.0	11.0	14.0	--	3.0	12.4	15.4
LDC	15.0	13.1	7.1	35.2	20.1	26.5	15.2	61.8	22.1	30.9	17.0	70.0	24.2	40.5	19.5	84.2	26.0	49.4	22.9	98.3
CA	5.9	2.9	1.0a	9.8	11.5	5.1	1.5	18.1	12.5	6.0	1.5	20.0	15.0	6.1	1.8	22.9	16.0	7.5	2.0	25.5
OC	--	--	0.2	0.2	1.0	--	4.0	5.0	1.0	--	4.8	5.8	2.0	--	5.4	7.4	3.5	--	7.0	10.5
Total	20.9	16.0	8.3a	45.2a	32.6	31.6	20.7	84.9	35.6	36.9	23.3	95.8	41.2	46.6	26.7	114.5	45.5	56.9	31.9	134.3

Source: United Nations, Commodity Trade Statistics and U.S. Bureau of Mines, Minerals Yearbook, 1960.
Note: aIncludes some U.S. ore.

TABLE A11.1.3

TIME-SERIES AND CROSS-SECTION REGRESSIONS FOR STEEL[a]

	Double-Log	R^2	Semi-Log	R^2
Cross-Section[b]				
Utilization (1957)	log u = -2.06 + 1.45 log y (0.14)	.85	u = -1419.2 + 558.2 log y (62.1)	.83
Consumption (1957)	log c = -2.57 + 1.61 log y (0.19)	.80	c = 1409.5 + 551.3 log y (60.1)	.82
Consumption (1960)	log c = -2.32 + 1.52 log y (0.17)	.82	c = -1458.8 + 567.7 log y (79.8)	.74
Individual Countries				
Common Market	log C = 1.27 + 1.12 log I (0.08)	.95	C = -16250.8 + 9754.6 log I (664.2)	.96
United Kingdom	log C = 1.00 + 1.10 log I (0.23)	.71	C = -7254.3 + 4414.9 log I (933.3)	.71
Northern Europe	log C = 0.92 + 1.40 log I (0.12)	.94	C = 36290.4 + 20762.3 log I (1995.0)	.92
Southern Europe	log C = 1.33 + 0.92 log I (0.07)	.95	C = -6598.6 + 4025.4 log I (427.9)	.91
Japan	log C = 0.71 + 1.05 log I (0.06)	.97	C = -3833.8 + 2278.0 log I (264.1)	.89

Notes: [a]Explanation of symbols: C = steel consumption, u = steel utilization
I = industrial production, c = per capita steel consumption, u = per capita steel utilization, y = per capita GNP.
[b]18 countries of Western Europe.

TABLE A11.2.1.

MANGANESE IMPORTS INTO INDUSTRIAL COUNTRIES[a]
(thousand tons, manganese content)

	1960				1970I				1970II				1975I				1975II			
	NA	WE	JA	IC	NA	WE	JA	IC	NA	WE	JA	IC	NA	WE	JA	IC	NA	WE	JA	IC
LA	399	20	--	419	500	30	10	540	520	30	10	560	560	40	10	610	590	50	10	650
AF	301	481	2	784	370	640	10	1020	380	670	10	1060	410	780	20	1210	430	850	30	1310
ME	--	--	--	--	--	--	--	--	--	--	--	--	--	--	--	--	--	--	--	--
AS	232	238	109	579	290	310	230	830	300	330	250	880	330	360	330	1020	350	390	360	1100
LDC	932	739	111	1782	1160	980	250	2390	1200	1030	270	2500	1300	1180	360	2840	1370	1290	400	3060
SB	--	245	6	251	--	350	20	370	--	380	30	410	--	440	50	490	--	500	70	570
OC	98	289	--	387	140	380	--	520	150	400	--	550	170	450	--	620	180	480	--	660
Total	1030	1273	117	2420	1300	1710	270	3280	1350	1810	300	3460	1470	2070	410	3950	1550	2270	470	4290

Sources: OECD, Trade by Commodities, Foreign Trade, Series C, 1960 and national trade statistics.

Note: [a]Excluding trade in ferromanganese among industrial countries.

TABLE A11.3.1

CONSUMPTION, PRODUCTION AND TRADE IN COPPER
(thousand tons, copper content)

	1960				
	US	CA	WE	JA	IC
Consumption of Copper Metal	960	107	1597	243	2907
Copper Metal Exports	394	252	110	1	757
Gross Copper Requirement[a]	1394	370	1758	251	3773
Copper Content of Ore Production	980	398	126	89	1593
Hypothetical Copper Content of Imports	414	-28	1632	162	2180
Changes in Stocks and Statistical Discrepancy	95[b]	28	13	--	136
Actual Copper Content of Imports	509	--	1645	162[c]	2316

	1970I					1970II				
	US	CA	WE	JA	IC	US	CA	WE	JA	IC
Consumption of Copper Metal	1400	160	2260	410	4230	1460	170	2390	440	4460
Copper Metal Exports	200	310	100	--	610	200	330	100	--	630
Gross Copper Requirement[a]	1650	480	2430	420	4980	1710	520	2570	450	5250
Copper Content of Ore Production	1080	480	150	130	1840	1120	520	150	130	1920
Copper Content of Imports	570	--	2280	290	3140	590	--	2420	320	3330

	1975I					1975II				
	US	CA	WE	JA	IC	US	CA	WE	JA	IC
Consumption of Copper Metal	1580	180	2700	520	4980	1690	200	2920	590	5400
Copper Metal Exports	170	350	80	--	600	170	380	80	--	630
Gross Copper Requirement[a]	1800	550	2860	540	5750	1920	600	3090	610	6220
Copper Content of Ore Production	1180	550	160	150	2040	1260	600	160	150	2170
Copper Content of Imports	620	--	2700	390	3710	660	--	2930	460	4050

Source: Consumption and production--Metallgesellschaft, Metal Statistics, various issues. Exports of metal--OECD, Trade by Commodities, Foreign Trade, Series C, 1960 and national trade statistics. Imports--Table A10.3.2.

Notes: [a]Consumption and imports of copper metal augmented by 3 percent to account for smelting losses.
[b]The Resources for the Future study reports increases in stocks of 110 thousand tons in 1960 (p. 906).

TABLE A11.3.2

COPPER IMPORTS INTO INDUSTRIAL COUNTRIES
(thousand tons, copper content)

	1960				1970I				1970II				1975I				1975II			
	NA	WE	JA	IC	NA	WE	JA	IC	NA	WE	JA	IC	NA	WE	JA	IC	NA	WE	JA	IC
LA	313	405	16	734	340	680	80	1100	350	730	100	1180	360	820	130	1310	390	890	160	1440
AF	17	729	32	778	30	1230	60	1320	30	1310	70	1410	40	1490	90	1620	40	1630	110	1780
ME	2	25	--	27	--	40	--	40	--	40	--	40	--	50	--	50	--	50	--	50
AS	17	--	32	49	20	--	50	70	20	--	50	70	20	--	60	80	20	--	70	90
LDC	349	1159	80	1598	390	1950	190	2530	400	2080	220	2700	420	2360	280	3060	450	2570	340	3360
NA	128[b]	439	47[c]	614	140	270	50	460	150	280	50	480	160	270	50	480	170	290	50	510
OC	32	47	35	104	40	60	50	150	40	60	50	150	40	70	60	170	40	70	70	180
Total	509	1645	162	2316	570	2280	290	3140	590	2420	320	3330	620	2700	390	3710	660	2930	460	4050

Sources: OECD, Trade by Commodities, Foreign Trade, Series C, 1960 and national trade statistics.
Notes: [a] Copper ores and concentrates, unrefined and refined copper.
[b] Includes 20 thousand tons imported from Western Europe.
[c] Includes 6 thousand tons imported from Western Europe.

TABLE A11.3.3

TIME-SERIES REGRESSIONS FOR NON-FERROUS METALS

	Double-Log	R^2	Semi-Log	R^2
Copper				
Common Market	log C = 0.29 + 1.22 log I (0.10)	.94	C = -3232.4 + 1896.6 log I (147.5)	.95
United Kingdom	log C = 0.28 + 1.17 log I (0.30)	.63	C = -2035.8 + 1229.1 log I (285.3)	.67
Northern Europe	log C = -0.33 + 1.17 log I (0.14)	.89	C = - 542.8 + 322.1 log I (39.5)	.88
Southern Europe	log C = -0.84 + 1.07 log I (0.20)	.76	C = - 113.1 + 66.8 log I (12.1)	.77
Japan	log C = 0.06 + 0.97 log I (0.08)	.95	C = - 539.8 + 324.7 log I (38.5)	.84
Aluminum				
Common Market	log C = 1.10 + 1.75 log I (0.08)	.98	C = 2605.9 + 1437.3 log I (124.8)	.94
United Kingdom	log C = 1.06 + 1.69 log I (0.35)	.72	C = 1770.9 + 989.8 log I (210.6)	.71
Northern Europe	log C = 2.57 + 2.15 log I (0.27)	.88	C = - 604.0 + 329.0 log I (26.9)	.94
Southern Europe	log C = 5.68 + 3.13 log I (0.20)	.97	C = 145.4 + 74.8 log I (9.3)	.88
Japan	log C = -1.04 + 1.33 log I (0.03)	.99	C = - 328.6 + 187.6 log I (21.4)	.90
Lead				
Common Market	log C = 1.06 + 0.75 log I (0.07)	.93	C = -1067.0 + 721.0 log I (62.3)	.94
United Kingdom	log C = 0.78 + 0.79 log I (0.20)	.65	C = - 659.6 + 446.3 log I (108.7)	.65
Northern Europe	log C = 0.14 + 0.87 log I (0.10)	.90	C = - 269.1 + 173.2 log I (18.5)	.91
Southern Europe	log C = -1.93 + 1.53 log I (0.22)	.84	C = - 119.6 + 67.0 log I (6.4)	.92
Japan	log C = -0.61 + 1.10 log I (0.14)	.87	C = - 224.9 + 134.4 log I (17.0)	.87
Zinc				
Common Market	log C = 0.80 + 0.92 log I (0.07)	.96	C = -1661.2 + 1048.7 log I (67.9)	.96
United Kingdom	log C = 0.32 + 1.00 log I (0.29)	.57	C = - 810.8 + 510.7 log I (143.6)	.58
Northern Europe	log C = -0.99 + 1.38 log I (0.23)	.79	C = - 310.1 + 178.7 log I (29.8)	.80
Southern Europe	log C = -1.69 + 1.29 log I (0.32)	.65	C = 74.7 + 41.2 log I (9.9)	.66
Japan	log C = 0.20 + 0.86 log I (0.05)	.98	C = - 322.9 + 206.7 log I (12.1)	.91
Tin				
Western Europe	log C = 0.66 + 0.53 log I (0.09)	.81	C = - 87.77 + 70.53 log I (10.9)	.82
Japan	log C = -0.92 + 0.85 log I (0.07)	.94	C = - 24.3 + 15.3 log I (1.7)	.90

Explanation of symbols: C = metal consumption, 1,000 tons.
I = industrial production.

TABLE A11.4.1

CONSUMPTION, PRODUCTION AND TRADE IN ALUMINUM
(thousand tons, aluminum content)

	1960				
	US	CA	WE	JA	Total
Consumption of Primary Aluminum	1539	104	1264	151	3058
Aluminum Metal Exports	259	501	94c	--	854
Gross Aluminum Requirement	1798	605	1358	151	3912
Aluminum Content of Ore Production[a]	450	--	561	--	1011
Hypothetical Aluminum Content of Imports	1348	605	797	151	2901
Changes in Stocks and Statistical Discrepancy	732b	19	75	27	853
Aluminum Content of Actual Imports[a]	2080	624	872	178	3754

	1970I					1970II				
	US	CA	WE	JA	Total	US	CA	WE	JA	Total
Consumption of Primary Aluminum	3050	230	2530	430	6240	3400	260	2820	500	6980
Aluminum Metal Exports	50	850	50	--	950	100	1000	50	--	1150
Gross Aluminum Requirement	3100	1080	2580	430	7190	3500	1260	2870	500	8130
Aluminum Content of Ore Production	500	--	1100	--	1600	500	--	1160	--	1660
Aluminum Content of Imports	2600	1080	1480	430	5590	3000	1260	1710	500	6470

	1975I					1975II				
	US	CA	WE	JA	Total	US	CA	WE	JA	Total
Consumption of Primary Aluminum	3900	330	3620	680	8530	4400	380	4240	840	9860
Aluminum Metal Exports	50	1000	50	--	1100	50	1200	50	--	1300
Gross Aluminum Requirement	3950	1330	3670	680	9630	4450	1580	4290	840	11160
Aluminum Content of Ore Production	550	--	1400	--	1950	550	--	1550	--	2100
Aluminum Content of Imports	3400	1330	2270	680	7680	3900	1580	2740	840	9060

Sources: Consumption and production--Metallgesellschaft, *Metal Statistics*, various issues. Exports of metal--OECD, *Trade by Commodities*, Foreign Trade, Series C, 1960 and national trade statistics. Imports-- Table A10.4.2.

Notes: [a]The aluminum content of the production of and trade in bauxite has been estimated on the basis of available information of the metal content of bauxite ore in the producing countries.
[b]The *Resources for the Future* study reports an increase of 135 thousand tons in stocks of unwrought aluminum while according to information provided in the 1960 *Mineral Yearbook* 460 thousand tons of aluminum-in-ore was added to commercial stocks and the strategic stockpile in 1960.
[c]Includes 15 thousand tons of exports of aluminum.

TABLE A11.4.2

ALUMINUM IMPORTS INTO INDUSTRIAL COUNTRIES[a]

(thousand tons, aluminum content)

	1960				1970I				1970II				1975I				1975II			
	NA	WE	JA	IC	NA	WE	JA	IC	NA	WE	JA	IC	NA	WE	JA	IC	NA	WE	JA	IC
LA	2452	219	7	2678	3030	380	30	3440	3510	440	30	3980	3650	380	50	4080	4200	500	50	4750
AF	107	155	3	265	300	550	--	850	350	650	--	1000	530	1240	--	1770	630	1430	--	2060
ME	--	--	--	--	--	--	--	--	--	--	--	--	--	--	--	--	--	--	--	--
AS	--	10	140	150	--	--	300	300	--	--	370	370	--	--	450	450	--	--	550	550
LDC	2559	384	150	3093	3330	930	330	4590	3860	1090	400	5350	4180	1620	500	6300	4830	1930	600	7360
NA	141	479	23	643	300	500	--	800	350	550	--	900	450	500	--	950	550	600	--	1150
SB	--	9	--	9	--	50	20	70	--	70	20	90	--	100	40	140	--	160	60	220
OC	--	--	5	5	50	--	80	130	50	--	80	130	100	50	140	290	100	50	180	330
Total	2700	872	178	3750	3680	1480	430	5590	4260	1710	500	6410	4730	7270	680	7680	5480	2740	840	9060

Sources: OECD, Trade by Commodities, Foreign Trade Series C, 1960 and national trade statistics.

Note: [a]Bauxite, alumina, and aluminum.

Trade Prospects for Developing Countries

TABLE A11.5.1

CONSUMPTION, PRODUCTION AND TRADE IN LEAD
(thousand tons, lead content)

	1960				
	US	CA	WE	JA	Total
Consumption of Primary Lead	528	41	928	100	1597
Lead Metal Exports	2	134[a]	67	--	203
Gross Lead Requirement	530	175	995	100	1800
Lead Content of Ore Production	224	187	356	40	807
Hypothetical Lead Content of Imports	306	-12	639	60	993
Changes in Stocks and Statistical Discrepancy	6	13[a]	-83	-13	-77
Lead Content of Actual Imports	312	1	556	47	916

	1970I					1970II				
	US	CA	WE	JA	Total	US	CA	WE	JA	Total
Consumption of Primary Lead	620	50	1130	160	1960	640	50	1180	170	2040
Lead Metal Exports	--	200[b]	60	--	260	--	220	60	--	280
Gross Lead Requirement	620	250	1190	160	2220	640	270	1240	170	2320
Lead Content of Ore Production	230	250	400	70	950	230	270	410	70	980
Lead Content of Imports	390	--	790	90	1270	410	--	830	100	1340

	1975I					1975II				
	US	CA	WE	JA	Total	US	CA	WE	JA	Total
Consumption of Primary Lead	680	60	1290	200	2230	720	70	1370	220	2380
Lead Metal Exports	--	230[b]	60	--	290	--	260[b]	60	--	320
Gross Lead Requirement	680	290	1350	200	2520	720	330	1430	220	2700
Lead Content of Ore Production	230	290	420	80	1020	230	330	430	90	1080
Lead Content of Imports	450	--	930	120	1500	490	--	1000	130	1620

Sources: Consumption and production--Metallgesallschaft, *Metal Statistics*, various issues. Exports of metal--OECD, *Trade by Commodities*, Foreign Trade, Series C, 1960 and national trade statistics. Imports--Table A10.5.2.

Notes: [a]Includes exports of 47 thousand tons of lead-in-ore.
[b]Includes exports of 30 thousand tons of lead-in-ore.

TABLE A11.5.2

LEAD IMPORTS INTO INDUSTRIAL COUNTRIES[a]
(thousand tons, lead content)

	1960				1970I				1970II				1975I				1975II			
	NA	WE	JA	IC	NA	WE	JA	IC	NA	WE	JA	IC	NA	WE	JA	IC	NA	WE	JA	IC
LA	137	136	13	286	170	180	30	380	180	190	30	400	200	220	40	460	220	240	40	500
AF	5	137	--	143	10	200	--	210	10	200	--	210	10	260	--	270	10	270	--	280
ME	1	--	--	--	--	--	--	--	--	--	--	--	--	--	--	--	--	--	--	--
AS	--	3	--	3	--	--	--	--	--	--	--	--	--	--	--	--	--	--	--	--
LDC	143	276	13	432	180	380	30	590	190	390	30	610	210	480	20	730	230	510	40	780
SB	--	30	--	30	--	50	10	60	--	50	10	60	--	50	10	60	--	60	10	70
CA	49	71	8	128	70	90	10	170	80	100	10	190	80	100	10	190	80	110	10	200
WE	33	--	--	33	40	--	--	40	40	--	--	40	40	--	--	40	50	--	--	50
OC	87	179	26	292	100	270	40	410	100	290	50	440	120	300	60	480	130	320	70	520
Total	312	556	47	915	390	790	90	1270	410	830	100	1340	450	930	120	1500	490	1000	130	1620

Sources: OECD, Non Ferrous Metals, 1960 and national trade statistics.
Note: [a]Lead ores, concentrates, and unwrought metal.

TABLE A11.6.1

CONSUMPTION, PRODUCTION AND TRADE IN ZINC
(thousand tons, recoverable zinc content)

| | 1960 | | | | |
	US	CA	WE	JA	Total
Consumption of Primary Zinc	870	49	1128	189	2236
Zinc Metal Exports	69	341[a]	45	5	460
Gross Zinc Requirements	939	390	1173	194	2696
Zinc Content of Ore Production	395	390	490	138	1413
Hypothetical Zinc Content of Imports	544	--	683	56	1283
Changes in Stocks and Statistical Discrepancy	-21	--	-82	25	-78
Zinc Content of Actual Imports	523	--	601	81	1205

| | 1970I | | | | | 1970II | | | | |
	US	CA	WE	JA	IC	US	CA	WE	JA	IC
Consumption of Primary Zinc	1160	60	1490	330	3040	1200	60	1560	360	3180
Zinc Metal Exports	--	520[b]	60	10	590	--	540	60	10	610
Gross Zinc Requirement	1160	580	1550	340	3630	1200	600	1620	370	3790
Zinc Content of Ore Production	420	580	650	240	1890	420	600	670	250	1940
Zinc Content of Imports	740	--	900	100	1740	780	--	950	120	1850

| | 1975I | | | | | 1975II | | | | |
	US	CA	WE	JA	IC	US	CA	WE	JA	IC
Consumption of Primary Zinc	1320	70	1710	390	3490	1400	80	1840	450	3770
Zinc Metal Exports	--	600[c]	60	10	670	--	650	60	10	720
Gross Zinc Requirement	1320	670	1770	400	4160	1400	730	1900	460	4490
Zinc Content of Ore Production	420	670	720	280	2090	420	730	750	300	2200
Zinc Content of Imports	900	--	1050	120	2070	980	--	1150	160	2290

Sources: Consumption and production, Metallgesellschaft, Metal Statistics and U.S. Bureau of Mines, Minerals Yearbook. Exports of metal--OECD, Trade by Commodities, Foreign Trade, Series C, 1960 and national trade statistics. Imports--Table A10.6.2.

Note: [a]Includes exports of 154 thousand tons of zinc-in-ore.

TABLE A11.6.2

ZINC IMPORTS INTO INDUSTRIAL COUNTRIES[a]
(thousand tons, recoverable zinc content)

	1960				1970I				1970II				1975I				1975II			
	NA	WE	JA	IC	NA	WE	JA	IC	NA	WE	JA	IC	NA	WE	JA	IC	NA	WE	JA	IC
LA	261	107	20	388	360	150	30	540	380	170	30	580	440	180	40	660	480	210	50	740
AF	8	127	--	135	20	260	--	280	20	260	--	280	30	320	--	350	30	350	--	380
ME	--	10	--	10	--	20	--	20	--	20	--	20	--	20	--	20	--	20	--	20
AS	--	12	1	13	--	20	10	30	--	20	10	30	--	20	10	30	--	20	10	30
LDC	269	256	21	546	280	450	40	870	400	470	40	910	470	540	50	1060	510	600	60	1170
SB	--	66	--	66	--	60	--	60	--	60	--	60	--	70	--	70	--	70	--	70
CA	188	159[b]	16	363	270	180	20	470	290	190	20	500	330	190	20	540	360	200	30	590
WE	34	--	7	41	50	--	--	50	50	--	--	50	50	--	--	50	60	--	--	60
OC	32	120	37	189	40	210	40	290	40	230	60	330	50	250	50	350	50	280	70	400
Total	523	601	81	1205	740	900	100	1740	780	950	120	1850	900	1050	120	2070	980	1150	160	2290

Sources: OECD, Non Ferrous Metals, 1960 and national trade statistics.

Notes: [a] Zinc ores, concentrates, and unwrought metal.
[b] Includes imports of 37 thousand tons from the United States.
[c] Includes imports of 37 thousand tons from the United States.

TABLE A11.7.1

CONSUMPTION, PRODUCTION AND TRADE IN TIN
(thousand tons, tin content)

	1960			
	NA	WE	JA	IC
Consumption of Tin Metal	56	69	15	140
Tin Metal Exports	1	9	--	10
Gross Tin Requirement	57	78	15	150
Tin Content of Domestic Ore Production	--	2	1	3
Hypothetical Tin Content of Imports	57	76	14	147
Stockpiling, Inventory Changes, and Statistical Discrepancy	--	-6	-2	-8
Tin Content of Actual Imports	57	70	12	139

	1970I				1970II			
	NA	WE	JA	IC	NA	WE	JA	IC
Consumption of Tin Metal	53	75	18	146	54	77	19	150
Tin Metal Exports	--	5	--	5	--	5	--	5
Gross Tin Requirement	53	80	18	151	54	82	19	155
Tin Content of Domestic Ore Production	--	2	1	3	--	2	1	3
Tin Content of Imports	53	78	17	148	54	80	18	152

	1975I				1975II			
	NA	WE	JA	IC	NA	WE	JA	IC
Consumption of Tin Metal	56	80	20	156	58	83	21	162
Tin Metal Exports	--	5	--	5	--	5	--	5
Gross Tin Requirement	56	85	20	161	58	88	21	167
Tin Content of Domestic Ore Production	--	2	1	3	--	2	1	3
Tin Content of Imports	56	83	19	158	58	86	20	164

Sources: Consumption and production--Metallgesellschaft, Metal Statistics, various issues. Exports of metal--OECD, Trade by Commodities, Foreign Trade Series C, 1960 and national trade statistics. Imports--Table A10.7.2.

TABLE A11.7.2

TIN IMPORTS INTO INDUSTRIAL COUNTRIES[a]
(thousand tons, tin content)

	1960				1970I				1970II				1975I				1975II			
	NA	WE	JA	IC	NA	WE	JA	IC	NA	WE	JA	IC	NA	WE	JA	IC	NA	WE	JA	IC
LA	1	17	--	18	3	20	--	23	3	20	--	23	4	21	--	25	5	22	--	27
AF	--	18	--	18	--	19	--	19	--	19	--	19	--	20	--	20	--	20	--	20
ME	--	--	--	--	--	--	--	--	--	--	--	--	--	--	--	--	--	--	--	--
AS	47	23	11	81	45	32	15	92	46	34	16	96	47	35	16	98	48	37	17	102
LDC	48	58	11	117	48	71	15	134	49	73	16	138	51	76	16	143	53	79	17	149
WE	9	--	--	9	5	--	--	5	5	--	--	5	5	--	--	5	5	--	--	5
OC	--	2	--	2	--	2	--	2	--	2	--	2	--	2	--	2	--	2	--	2
SB	--	10	1	11	--	5	2	7	--	5	2	7	--	5	3	8	--	5	3	8
Total	57	70	12	139	53	78	17	148	54	80	18	152	56	83	19	158	58	86	20	164

Sources: OECD, Trade by Commodities, Foreign Trade Series C, 1960 and national trade statistics.
Note: [a]Tin ores, concentrates, and unwrought metal.

TABLE A11

NONFUEL MINERALS AND METALS : VALUE OF IMPORTS
($ million at current prices)

	1960					1970I					1970II					1975I					1975II				
	NA	WE	JA	OC	DC	NA	WE	JA	OC	DC	NA	WE	JA	OC	DC	NA	WE	JA	OC	DC	NA	WE	JA	OC	DC
Iron Ore																									
LA	208	83	12	--	303	261	149	63	--	473	290	194	75	--	559	292	211	90	--	593	318	298	120	--	736
AF	8	84	--	--	92	27	203	20	--	250	27	224	20	--	271	53	336	33	--	422	53	417	--	--	470
ME	--	--	--	--	--	--	--	--	--	--	--	--	--	--	--	--	--	--	--	--	--	--	--	--	--
AS	--	27	95	--	122	--	38	143	--	181	--	38	158	--	196	--	45	166	--	211	--	45	187	--	232
LDC	216	194	107	--	517	288	390	226	--	904	317	456	253	--	1026	345	592	289	--	1226	371	760	307	--	1438
Manganese Ore																									
LA	33	1	1	--	34	42	2	--	--	44	44	2	2	--	46	48	3	--	--	51	51	4	--	--	55
AF	27	27	0	--	54	34	37	--	--	71	35	39	0	--	74	38	46	1	--	85	41	50	1	--	92
ME	--	--	--	--	--	--	--	--	--	--	--	--	--	--	--	--	--	--	--	--	--	--	--	--	--
AS	21	11	5	--	37	27	14	11	--	52	29	15	11	--	55	32	17	15	--	64	34	18	17	--	69
LDC	81	39	5	--	125	103	53	11	--	167	108	56	11	--	175	118	66	16	--	200	126	72	18	--	216
Copper																									
LA	334	264	15	--	613	344	420	71	--	835	358	457	90	--	905	368	513	117	--	998	403	562	145	--	1110
AF	30	470	21	11	532	50	748	37	10	845	50	806	44	10	910	68	912	56	10	1046	68	1008	69	10	1155
ME	2	12	--	--	14	--	18	--	--	18	--	18	--	--	18	--	23	--	--	23	--	--	--	--	23
AS	11	1	20	--	32	12	--	29	--	41	12	--	29	--	41	13	--	36	--	49	12	--	42	--	54
LDC	377	747	56	11	1191	406	1186	137	10	1739	420	1281	163	10	1874	449	1448	209	10	2116	483	1593	256	10	2342
Bauxite and Aluminum																									
LA	118	18	1	--	137	219	54	3	--	276	253	60	3	--	316	295	74	5	--	374	346	95	5	--	446
AF	4	29	--	--	33	44	196	--	--	240	48	244	--	--	292	103	508	--	--	611	124	593	--	--	717
ME	--	--	--	--	--	--	--	--	--	--	--	--	--	--	--	--	--	--	--	--	--	--	--	--	--
AS	--	1	10	--	11	--	--	20	--	20	--	--	25	--	25	--	--	32	--	32	--	--	39	--	39
LDC	122	48	11	--	181	263	250	23	--	536	301	304	28	--	633	398	582	37	--	1017	470	688	44	--	1202
Lead																									
LA	33	29	1	--	63	41	36	6	--	83	43	38	6	--	87	49	46	8	--	103	54	50	6	--	110
AF	2	23	--	1	26	3	38	--	1	42	3	38	--	1	42	3	50	--	1	54	3	52	--	1	56
ME	--	--	--	--	--	--	--	--	--	--	--	--	--	--	--	--	--	--	--	--	--	--	--	--	--
AS	--	1	--	--	1	--	--	--	--	--	--	--	--	--	--	--	--	--	--	--	--	--	--	--	--
LDC	35	53	1	1	90	44	74	6	1	125	46	76	6	1	129	52	96	8	1	157	57	102	6	1	166
Zinc																									
LA	25	16	2	--	43	41	27	5	--	73	43	30	5	--	78	50	37	7	--	94	54	43	10	--	107
AF	2	17	--	4	23	5	41	--	4	50	5	41	--	4	50	8	61	--	4	73	8	67	--	4	79
ME	--	1	1	--	1	--	--	--	--	--	--	--	--	--	--	--	3	--	--	3	--	3	--	--	3
AS	--	2	1	--	3	--	3	--	--	3	--	3	--	--	3	--	3	--	--	3	--	3	--	--	3
LDC	27	36	3	4	70	46	71	5	4	126	48	77	5	4	134	58	101	10	4	173	62	116	10	4	192

Category																				
Tin																				
LA	2	29	–	1	31	7	45	–	–	53	1	7	45	–	50	10	53	1	–	50
AF	1	36	–	1	38	–	43	–	–	43	–	–	43	–	46	–	43	–	–	46
ME	–	–	–	–	–	–	–	–	–	–	–	–	–	–	–	–	–	–	–	–
AS	100	50	23	6	179	108	76	7	37	228	7	111	81	39	84	114	238	7	39	84
LDC	103	115	23	7	248	115	164	8	37	324	8	118	169	39	180	124	334	8	39	180
Other Non-Ferrous																				
LA	30	24	8	–	62	17	41	–	20	78	–	17	46	25	51	22	88	–	25	51
AF	11	54	3	–	68	15	85	–	5	105	–	15	90	5	100	20	110	–	10	100
ME	0	2	3	–	5	–	5	–	5	10	–	–	5	5	5	–	10	–	10	5
AS	16	39	25	1	81	35	65	1	60	161	1	40	70	70	80	40	181	1	70	80
LDC	57	119	39	1	216	67	196	1	90	354	1	72	211	105	236	82	389	1	115	236
Scrap Metal																				
LA	1	5	4	–	10	–	5	–	–	5	–	–	5	–	10	–	5	–	–	10
AF	0	19	10	–	29	–	15	–	10	25	–	–	15	10	5	–	25	–	5	5
ME	0	3	1	–	4	–	5	–	–	5	–	–	5	–	–	–	5	–	–	–
AS	0	2	44	–	46	–	–	–	30	30	–	–	–	30	15	–	30	–	20	15
LDC	1	29	59	–	89	–	25	–	40	65	–	–	25	40	–	–	65	–	25	–
Crude Minerals																				
LA	51	15	15	2	70	57	20	3	2	82	3	28	20	2	24	61	53	3	2	24
AF	8	99	7	1	115	10	131	1	9	151	1	33	131	9	150	11	174	–	11	150
ME	0	15	1	–	16	–	21	–	1	22	–	–	21	1	23	–	22	–	1	23
AS	6	13	15	13	47	7	18	17	19	61	17	7	18	19	22	8	61	17	22	22
LDC	65	142	25	16	248	74	190	21	31	316	21	68	190	31	219	80	310	21	36	219
Total																				
LA	835	484	45	2	1366	1029	799	4	170	2002	4	1083	897	206	1009	1195	2190	4	254	1009
AF	93	858	41	18	1010	188	1537	16	81	1822	16	216	1671	88	2219	304	1991	16	116	2219
ME	2	33	5	–	40	–	49	–	6	55	–	–	52	6	59	–	58	–	11	59
AS	154	147	238	20	559	189	214	25	349	777	25	199	225	381	248	207	830	25	403	248
LDC	1084	1522	329	40	2975	1406	2599	45	606	4656	45	1498	2845	681	3535	1706	5069	45	784	3535

Source: U.N., Commodity Trade Statistics, 1960 and OECD, Trade by Commodities, Foreign Trade Series C, 1960.

MANUFACTURED GOODS : VALUE OF IMPORTS
($ million at current prices)

	1960 NA	WE	JA	OC	DC	1970I NA	WE	JA	OC	DC	1970II NA	WE	JA	OC	DC	1975I NA	WE	JA	OC	DC	1975II NA	WE	JA	OC	DC
Chemicals																									
LA	44	30	2	–	76	63	42	3	–	108	67	44	4	–	115	77	50	5	–	132	82	54	5	–	141
AF	2	17	0	1	20	3	26	1	1	31	4	28	1	1	34	4	32	2	1	39	5	35	2	1	43
ME	0	4	0	0	4	–	7	–	–	7	–	7	–	–	7	–	9	–	–	9	–	10	–	–	10
AS	8	8	3	0	19	12	12	6	–	30	13	14	6	–	33	15	15	8	–	38	16	17	8	–	41
LDC	54	59	5	1	119	78	87	10	1	176	84	93	11	1	189	96	106	15	1	218	103	116	15	1	235
Leather & Footwear																									
LA	5	–	–	–	5	8	–	–	–	8	8	–	–	–	8	11	–	–	–	11	11	–	–	–	11
AF	–	4	–	–	4	–	7	–	–	7	–	7	–	–	7	–	9	–	–	9	–	9	–	–	9
ME	–	–	–	–	–	–	–	–	–	–	–	–	–	–	–	–	–	–	–	–	–	–	–	–	–
AS	9	60	2	1	72	17	80	6	3	106	19	84	7	3	113	24	93	9	3	129	27	100	10	3	140
LDC	14	64	2	1	81	25	87	6	3	121	27	91	7	3	128	35	102	9	.3	149	38	109	10	3	160
Veneer & Plywood																									
LA	4	–	–	–	4	10	–	–	–	10	11	–	–	–	11	15	–	–	–	15	16	–	–	–	16
AF	4	19	–	–	23	8	42	–	–	50	8	43	–	–	51	12	63	–	–	75	12	65	–	–	77
ME	–	4	–	–	4	–	9	–	–	9	–	9	–	–	9	–	13	–	–	13	–	14	–	–	14
AS	17	–	–	2	19	75	5	–	4	84	79	5	–	4	88	146	7	–	5	158	156	7	–	5	168
LDC	25	23	–	2	50	93	56	–	4	153	98	57	–	4	159	173	83	–	5	261	184	86	–	5	275
Cotton Textiles																									
LA	5	1	–	–	6	11	4	–	–	15	11	4	–	–	15	14	4	–	–	18	14	4	–	–	18
AF	9	8	–	–	17	6	20	–	–	26	6	20	–	–	26	9	27	–	–	36	9	27	–	–	36
ME	2	4	–	–	6	3	9	–	–	12	3	9	–	–	12	4	11	–	–	15	4	11	–	–	15
AS	129	138	–	20	287	199	236	–	35	470	199	236	–	35	470	254	290	–	45	589	254	290	–	45	589
LDC	145	151	–	20	316	219	269	–	35	523	219	269	–	35	523	281	332	–	45	658	281	332	–	45	658
Jute Manufactures																									
LA	–	–	–	–	–	–	–	–	–	–	–	–	–	–	–	–	–	–	–	–	–	–	–	–	–
AF	–	–	–	–	–	–	–	–	–	–	–	–	–	–	–	–	–	–	–	–	–	–	–	–	–
ME	–	–	–	–	–	–	–	–	–	–	–	–	–	–	–	–	–	–	–	–	–	–	–	–	–
AS	103	34	1	37	175	113	41	1	42	197	114	43	1	43	201	120	48	1	44	213	122	52	1	46	221
LDC	103	34	1	37	175	113	41	1	42	197	114	43	1	43	201	120	48	1	44	213	122	52	1	46	221

Carpets & Other Textiles

LA	23	—	1	—	2	—	26	38	3	—	43	3	38	—	44	44	3	—	4	51	45	4	—	53
AF	—	—	—	—	—	—	2	2	—	—	6	—	2	—	6	3	—	—	6	8	3	6	—	9
ME	4	—	33	—	—	—	37	6	—	—	66	—	6	—	71	7	—	—	89	86	7	89	—	96
AS	12	1	23	1	1	3	37	19	2	3	68	2	21	—	74	23	3	3	67	89	26	67	4	100
LDC	39	1	59	3	3	3	102	65	5	3	183	5	67	2	195	77	7	4	166	234	81	166	7	258

Silver & Precious Metals

LA	3	1	29	1	—	1	33	7	—	3	70	8	67	3	78	10	—	—	99	101	11	99	5	115
AF	1	—	13	—	—	—	14	3	—	—	28	3	29	—	32	5	—	—	41	41	5	41	—	46
ME	20	—	12	—	—	—	32	41	—	—	65	44	26	—	71	57	—	—	36	91	64	36	—	102
AS	4	1	10	—	—	—	15	8	2	2	31	9	22	1	35	11	—	—	21	45	13	21	5	41
LDC	28	2	64	1	—	2	94	59	5	2	204	64	144	2	216	83	—	—	197	278	93	197	10	304

Machinery

LA	9	—	3	—	—	—	12	18	—	—	24	19	6	—	25	27	—	—	10	36	29	10	—	39
AF	0	—	0	—	—	—	6	—	—	—	12	—	14	—	14	—	—	—	20	18	—	20	—	20
ME	0	—	4	—	—	—	4	—	—	—	8	—	9	—	9	—	—	—	13	12	—	13	—	13
AS	11	0	8	1	—	2	20	22	8	2	40	24	18	—	44	33	—	—	27	60	35	27	3	65
LDC	20	0	21	1	—	2	42	40	16	2	84	43	47	—	92	60	—	—	70	126	64	70	3	137

Other Manufacturing

LA	13	—	1	—	—	—	13	21	—	—	23	23	2	—	25	27	—	—	2	29	29	2	—	31
AF	1	—	2	—	—	—	3	3	5	—	9	9	5	—	9	4	—	—	6	11	4	6	—	11
ME	3	—	7	—	—	—	10	6	13	—	19	73	15	—	21	8	—	—	19	25	8	19	—	27
AS	36	1	28	1	5	3	70	68	50	9	130	105	54	—	140	93	3	3	74	177	103	74	4	195
LDC	53	1	37	1	5	3	96	98	70	10	181	105	75	3	195	132	3	4	101	242	144	101	15	264

Total

LA	106	3	64	2	2	6	175	176	116	3	301	185	126	7	321	225	3	—	173	393	237	173	10	424
AF	17	—	71	1	1	1	89	25	141	2	169	26	150	1	179	37	2	2	209	237	38	209	2	251
ME	29	—	68	—	—	—	97	56	129	1	186	59	140	—	200	76	1	—	192	251	83	192	2	277
AS	329	9	309	67	5	21	714	533	504	98	1156	551	524	23	1198	719	100	118	655	1498	752	655	32	1560
LDC	481	12	512	70	5	28	1075	790	890	104	1812	821	940	31	1898	1057	106	126	1229	2379	1110	1229	44	2512

Source: U.N., Commodity Trade Statistics, 1960 and OECD, Trade by Commodities, Foreign Trade Series C, 1229.

General Index

This book has been set on the Linotype in 9 and 10 point Baskerville Light, leaded 2 points. Part and chapter numbers and chapter titles are in 18 point Radiant Medium; part titles are in 24 point Radiant Medium. The size of the type page is 25 by 43 picas.